From the Protestant Reformation to the Twentieth Century

VOLUME III   REVISED EDITION

A History of

CHRISTIAN

THOUGHT

From the Protestant Reformation to the Twentieth Century

JUSTO L. GONZÁLEZ

Abingdon Press
NASHVILLE

A HISTORY OF CHRISTIAN THOUGHT, REVISED EDITION
VOL. III

Copyright © 1975 by Abingdon Press

Chapter 16, Appendix, Preface to the Second English Edition, footnotes, and editorial revisions
copyright © 1987 by Abingdon Press

This book is printed on acid-free recycled paper.

Library of Congress Cataloging-in-Publication Data

González, Justo L.
A history of Christian thought.
Includes bibliographical references.
CONTENTS—v. 1. From the beginnings to the Council of Chalcedon.—v. 2. From Augustine to the
eve of the Reformation.—v. 3. From the Protestant Reformation to the twentieth century. 1.
Theology. Doctrinal—History. I. Title. BT21.2.G6   230'.09   74-109679

ISBN 0-687-17184-9 (v. III)
ISBN 0-687-17185-7 (the set)

Quotations from Luther's Works (noted LW), vol. 34, are used by permission of Fortress Press.

Quotations from The Latin Works of Huldreich Zwingli, ed. S. M. Jackson, et al., and published by the
Heidelberg Press in 1912-29, are used by permission of the United Church Press.

Quotations from Calvin: Institutes of the Christian Religion, Volume XX and Volume XXI, The Library
of Christian Classics, edited by John T. McNeill and translated by Ford Lewis Battles. Published in the
U.S.A. by The Westminster Press. Copyright © MCMLX, by W. L. Jenkins. Used by permission.

98 99 00 01 02 03 — 25 24 23 22 21 20

MANUFACTURED IN THE UNITED STATES OF AMERICA

Preface to the Second English Edition

It has now been more than ten years and ten printings since the first publication of *A History of Christian Thought*—the first volume was published in English in 1970, and the third in 1975. I have been extremely pleased by its widespread use in universities and seminaries. I am also grateful to colleagues who, both in published reviews and in personal correspondence, have suggested ways in which that first edition could be improved. In the preparation of this revised edition, I have endeavored to take account of their criticism and suggestions.

It is still my purpose to produce a book that can serve as an introduction to the subject for readers with little or no theological training, giving them both the basic knowledge needed for further theological and historical studies and a vision of the rich variety of Christian thought through the ages. Therefore, I have sought to avoid sweeping generalizations or purely personal views, which might make the book more interesting to my colleagues, but less useful to my intended readers.

The changes in this new edition are many. Most of them are bibliographical matters, updating references and taking into account more recent research. Where such research has led me to correct my views on a particular subject, this is reflected in changes in the text. Some chapters have been radically reorganized—in particular, the chapter on nineteenth-century Protestant theology. At the suggestion of numerous reviewers, I have also added a chapter on contemporary theology.

Since the first edition was published, I have also become aware of two factors deeply affecting the history of Christian theology, and seldom sufficiently recognized. The first is the liturgical and communal setting in which theology develops. A fuller understanding of medieval theology, for instance, would require a parallel consideration of theological treatises and discussions on the one hand and of the monastic liturgy of the hours on the other. While connections between liturgy and theology appear repeatedly throughout these three volumes, I feel that there is much more work to be done in this area, and I confess that I have not done enough of it to weave the two into a single fabric throughout the entire history of Christianity.

The second factor in the history of Christian theology of which I have become more profoundly aware is the social and economic context and content of theology. This is a field to which I have been devoting much interest in recent years. My studies along these lines have enriched my appreciation for many of the theologians discussed in these three volumes, and deepened my understanding of a number of seemingly abstract theological issues. I have referred to economic matters at a few points in this revised edition. However, given the purpose of this book, to serve as an introduction to students who do not necessarily know the more traditional intepretations, I have refrained from rewriting the entire history from the perspective of this particular insight. I hope to do this in two separate works now in preparation—one on the history of Christian views on economics, and another on how the different types of theology that can be discerned in the history of Christianity relate to these and other issues.

To a large degree, history is autobiography—or perhaps one should say that it is the prolegomena to one's biography. In any case, our view of who we are, both as individuals and as a community of faith, depends in large measure on what we understand our history to be. As this revised edition goes to press, it is my prayer that its readers will gain new understandings from it, and thus be aided in what is after all the primary task of the Christian community: being faithful and obedient in the world in which we have been placed.

J. L. G.
Decatur, Georgia
September 19, 1986

Preface to the First English Edition

This third volume of *A History of Christian Thought* has posed for its author problems of a somewhat different nature than did the previous two. The main source of these difficulties has been the fact that it was precisely at the beginning of the period covered here—the sixteenth century—that some of the most painful and enduring breaks in the Christian church took place. In consequence, it is precisely in the centuries discussed in this volume that it is most difficult to be ecumenical in scope. Most previous histories written by Protestants suffer not only from a Protestant bias, but also from a North Atlantic one. Roman Catholicism was usually seen from this perspective, and therefore the Catholic Reformation was reduced almost entirely to anti-Protestant polemics and to some mention of the Jesuits—without proper background in Salmantine theology and the system of Suárez. The Eastern tradition was usually ignored or declared to be—as in the case of Harnack—a gross misrepresentation of Christianity. Protestants discussed the philosophical background of theology in terms of British empiricism and German idealism, with little attention given to the significance of French Cartesianism. French and Mediterranean Catholics often took the opposite tack. In brief, as most histories of theology were written decades ago, the nineteenth century was taken as normative—and this was precisely the century in which Roman Catholic and Protestant theology were most out of contact with each other.

In this volume, I have attempted to overcome some of the narrowness of this perspective, making use of my own personal background as one who grew up a Protestant in the midst of a predominantly Catholic culture—and who still claims much of both traditions. It will be obvious to the reader that I am writing from a Protestant standpoint. It should be equally obvious that I have attempted to be ecumenical in scope. I am certain that new weaknesses and errors will soon be found in this attempt. But I trust that my efforts will contribute in some measure to the growing sense of unity among Christians of all persuasions.

Readers may miss a more detailed discussion of twentieth century theology than that which appears at the end of the present volume. As I have explained in that last chapter, such a discussion, in order to be of any value, would have to involve a scope and methodology different from those employed in the rest of the book. On the other hand, I trust that the very brief outline of issues discussed there will enable students of contemporary theology to tie their studies with the developments that have preceded them.

At another point I have found it necessary to limit the scope of this third volume more than the previous two. This is in the extent of bibliographical notes. The bibliography concerning this period is so enormous that I have had to limit references to those books and articles which would in turn yield other references to readers interested in pursuing the matter more fully. Otherwise the bibliographical references would have become inordinately cumbersome.

Once again, I owe a debt of gratitude to many who have made this work possible. My secretary, Mrs. Mirella Revuelta de Ribas, put in long extra hours in the difficult process of preparing for the press a manuscript that often bore the marks of my own lack of discipline. My wife, Dr. Catherine Gunsalus González, has provided much more than her support and encouragement, for her insights into Calvinism, the nineteenth century, and other theological matters—she is Associate Professor of Church History at Columbia Theological Seminary—have been exceedingly helpful. For them, as symbols of many others, I wish to record a word of gratitude.

Finally, even at the risk of sounding pious, I wish to acknowledge that in the very process of research and reflection required by this entire project, I have become increasingly aware of the grace and love of the God to whom the theology of all ages has sought to witness.

J. L. G.
San José, Costa Rica
August 11, 1974

Contents

List of Abbreviations

ARG	*Archiv für Reformationsgeschichte*
ATGran	*Archivo Teológico Granadino*
BAC	*Biblioteca de Autores Cristianos*
BLittEcc	*Bulletin de Littérature Ecclésiastique*
BRAH	*Biblioteca de la Real Academia de la Historia*
BullPhMed	*Bulletin de Philosophie Médiévale*
CienTom	*Ciencia Tomista*
CR	*Corpus Reformatorum*
CTJ	*Calvin Theological Journal*
Denzinger	*Enchiridion Symbolorum Definitionum et Declara tionum* (ed. Denzinger and Rahner), 31st edition, 1957
DicLit	*Diccionario Literario*
DTC	*Dictionnaire de Théologie Catholique*
DTT	*Dansk Teologisk Tidsskrift*
EncCatt	*Enciclopedia Cattolica*
EstEcl	*Estudios Eclesiásticos*
HumChr	*Humanitas Christianitas*
LCC	*Library of Christian Classics*
LuthOut	*Lutheran Outlook*
LW	*Luther's Works* (St. Louis and Philadelphia)

McCQ	*McCormick Quarterly*
Mansi	*Sacrorum Conciliorum Nova et Amplissima Collectio* (ed. Mansi)
ModSch	*Modern Schoolman*
MQR	*The Mennonite Quarterly Review*
NCatEnc	*New Catholic Encyclopedia*
NSch	*The New Scholasticism*
QFRgesch	*Quellen für Reformationsgeschichte*
RGG	*Die Religion in Geschichte und Gegenwart. Dritte Auflage*
RHE	*Revue d'Histoire Ecclésiastique*
RHPhRel	*Revue d'Histoire et de Philosophie Religieuse*
RivStIt	*Rivista Storica Italiana*
RThPh	*Revue de Théologie et Philosophie*
SchArchVk	*Schweizerisches Archiv für Volkskunde*
SJT	*Scottish Journal of Theology*
ThLZ	*Theologische Literaturzeitung*
ThZschr	*Theologische Zeitschrift*
VoxEv	*Vox Evangelii*
WZMLU	*Wissenschaftliche Zeitschrift der Martin-Luther Universität*
ZschrKgesch	*Zeitschrift für Kirchengeschichte*
ZSTh	*Zeitschrift für systematische Theologie*

I

The End of an Era

There are moments in the history of humankind that seem to be pregnant with future possibilities—although not so much by virtue of the clear promise that they offer, as because the old ways have run their course and it is necessary to venture in new directions. Such was the case at the end of the fifteenth century and the beginning of the sixteenth. In a way, the epic of Columbus is symbolic of the period, for when the traditional trading routes to the East were closed he set out in search of new pathways, and discovered instead a new land. In similar fashion, the great religious upheavals of the sixteenth century, and the new theological lands discovered through them, resulted from the need to search for new routes as it became increasingly evident that the medieval synthesis was no longer tenable or capable of resurrection.

The factors that contributed to the dissolution of that synthesis are so interrelated that it is impossible to disentangle them from one another. However, for the sake of an orderly exposition, one could say that the most significant of these factors were the birth of the modern European nations, skepticism regarding the hierarchy of the church, the alternative offered by mysticism, the impact of nominalism on scholastic theology, and the humanism of the Renaissance. These we shall now treat in that order.

The Growth of National Sentiment

Perhaps the most significant political phenomenon of the early sixteenth century was the birth of the modern nations. Indeed, that time marks the transition from medieval feudalism to the centralized monarchies of the modern age.

Although later Spanish historians portrayed the period from 711 to 1492 as a constant and glorious struggle against the infidel, the truth is that during that entire period Christian Spain was deeply divided within itself as various rulers sought after their own interests, even if this implied an occasional alliance with the Moor against a Christian neighbor. It was only in the last quarter of the fifteenth century, when Isabella of Castile married Ferdinand of Aragon, that the definite step was taken for the birth of a united Spain. Relatively soon thereafter, this unity seemed to have been achieved, for in 1492 the Moors were expelled from their last stronghold in Granada, and Ferdinand conquered Portugal and Navarre in 1512.

As a result of the wars against the Moors, Spain closely identified her nationhood with her Catholic faith, and the spirit of her efforts to regain the entire peninsula—as well as the spirit of the conquest of the New World—was that of a great and constant crusade against the infidel.

And yet, Spain was Catholic in her own way. She had never been effectually a part of the Holy Roman Empire—which could be seen in the negative reaction of many Spaniards when their king Charles I was elected Holy Roman Emperor. When she now joined—and soon led—the ranks of Catholic Christendom, she did so on her own terms. The ecclesiastical hierarchy was subject to the crown—de facto in Spain itself, and de iure in the New World—through the granting by Alexander VI of the patronato real, which practically made the sovereigns of Spain and Portugal the rulers of the church in their possessions overseas. The Inquisition, a staunch defender of orthodoxy, was effectively controlled by the crown, and its function became both the preservation of the Catholic faith and the purification of Spanish blood and culture—through frequent trials of supposed crypto-Jews and crypto-Moslems. Finally, many popes of the period were effective, although sometimes unwilling, tools of Spanish policy.

France entered the sixteenth century as the most centralized monarchy in Western Europe. In Spain and England, there were a number of limitations on the authority of kings; but most of these limitations did not exist in France. The Hundred Years' War with

England played a role in France similar to that played in Spain by the crusade against the Moors: it was the rallying point of French national sentiment. There was a time when France seemed to have become the new center of Christendom, for even the papacy itself had come to reside under her shadow, at Avignon. When the papacy returned to Rome, it could not wrestle from the king of France the control which he had gained over the church in his domains.

England emerged from the fifteenth century as a recently consolidated nation. It was precisely at the turn of the century that Henry VII finally overcame the last significant Yorkist opposition. Thereafter, his conciliatory policy, implemented in his marriage to Elizabeth of York, was generally successful. When he died, in 1509, he was succeeded by his son Henry VIII, heir to the claims of both Lancaster and York. This political unification was preceded and accompanied by a growth of national sentiment. As the Hundred Years' War was the predominant feature in English foreign policy during the fourteenth and fifteenth centuries, and as the papacy in Avignon was closely allied to French interests, the growth of nationalism in England was coupled with the awareness that the interests of the papacy were often contrary to those of England. As a result, laws were enacted to prevent English funds from reaching the coffers of the papacy. Thus, the Acts of Annates, Appeals, and Supremacy, which severed ties with Rome and made the Church of England independent, were the culmination of a long series of attempts to curb the influence of the pope in the affairs of the kingdom.

At the beginning of the sixteenth century—and well after its end—Germany was a motley patchwork of practically sovereign states. Although the Holy Roman Emperor was supposed to rule over them, in fact his powers were greatly limited by the often conflicting interests of powerful nobles. Furthermore, the emperors of the house of Habsburg, being at once hereditary rulers of parts of Germany and elected rulers of the entire nation, quite often placed their hereditary interests above those of the whole and thus hindered the process of national unification. But in spite of its political division, Germany was permeated by nationalism in two ways. The first of these was the growth of nationalistic feeling even beyond and in spite of feudal borders. The second was the founding of

independent nations—Switzerland, the Netherlands, Bohemia—
which withdrew from what had traditionally been called Germany.
In either case, nationalism was a growing feature among a people
who had previously thought of themselves as the very heart of the
Holy Roman Empire.

In summary, at the beginning of the sixteenth century Western
Europe no longer thought of itself as a single empire, where there
was a sole emperor wielding the temporal sword, with a religious
counterpart in Rome holding the spiritual sword. On the contrary, a
host of new nations were claiming to be sovereign states; and these
claims often conflicted, not only with those of the emperor, but also
with those of the pope. Thus modern nationalism was a significant
factor in the dissolution of the medieval synthesis, and opened the
way for the religious cleavage that would come about with the
Protestant Reformation.

An added factor leading to change was the development of
commerce and a monetary economy. This was closely connected with
the growth of cities, whose economic and political power was rapidly
surpassing that of the landed nobility. Capital became a commodity
handled and administered by cities and by large banking houses.
The ranks of the poor nobility increased to the point that they
became a distinct social class. The poverty of the peasantry was
accentuated by the concentration of wealth in the cities and by the
fact that such wealth was now derived from commerce rather than
agriculture. The sixteenth century also saw an unprecedented rate
of inflation,[1] probably accelerated by the influx of precious metals
from the New World. Since wages did not keep pace with the price of
food and other necessities, the lot of the peasants and of the urban
poor became considerably worse. The growth of commerce and the
beginnings of agricultural capitalism undercut the old feudal system
in most of Western Europe. New methods of warfare made the
knights and other lesser nobility, who lived by war, increasingly
impoverished and obsolete. Under these new conditions, pope and
emperor, prelates and lords, found it difficult to retain the control

---

[1]See J. D. Gould, *The Great Debasement: Currency and the Economy in Mid-Tudor England* (Oxford:
Clarendon, 1970); Peter H. Ramsey, ed., *The Price Revolution in Sixteenth Century England* (London:
Methuen, 1971); Peter Burke, ed., *Economy and Society in Early Modern Europe* (New York: Harper &
Row, 1972).

that they had formerly enjoyed. The entire system of ecclesiastical administration had been developed to serve in a feudal society. The power of the city and of capital was not sufficiently recognized in civil and ecclesiastical structures. The unhappy peasants provided a fertile field for revolution. The disempowered nobles sought new causes to espouse in order to reassert their leadership. In short, Europe was ripe for change; and this was so precisely at a time when the traditional ecclesiastical hierarchy was losing a great deal of its prestige and power.

The Declining Authority of the Hierarchy

Even apart from the growth of nationalism, the ecclesiastical hierarchy had been losing power and prestige. This decline began immediately after the peak of papal power in Innocent III. But the process was greatly accelerated during the fourteenth and fifteenth centuries, when three consecutive events led the papacy from one low point to another. These three events were the move to Avignon, the Great Western Schism, and the capture of the papacy by the spirit of the Italian Renaissance.[2] Each of these stages in the decline of the papacy was accompanied by heavy financial needs. The papal court at Avignon required vast sums of money in order to cover the expenses of its luxurious living. The popes and antipopes of the Great Schism made every possible effort to secure funds with which to strengthen their rival claims to be the legitimate successors of St. Peter. The popes of the Renaissance felt compelled to bring together as much of the monetary resources of Europe as possible, in order to finance their patronage of the arts and their frequent wars and intrigues.

In consequence, while the papacy needed more and more funds, and devised ingenious methods of collecting them, that same papacy was losing the prestige that it had once had throughout Europe. Therefore, ecclesiastical taxation became both more onerous and less easily justifiable; and this in turn strengthened the wave of nationalism that was sweeping Europe.

---

[2] See vol. 2 of this *History*, pp. 305-6.

Very often the interests of taxation conflicted with the best interests of the church, and in such cases abuses became common. For instance, John XXII—noted for his elaborate means of ecclesiastical taxation—began collecting the income of vacant posts throughout Western Europe. As long as a post remained vacant, its income was to be sent to the Holy See; thus, the insatiable papal budget profited from unfilled vacancies. The result was a multiplication of vacant posts and a practical situation very similar to the absenteeism that many of the best popes had so strenuously opposed. The practice of creating new posts and selling them—the very simony that earlier reformers had decried—became common under Alexander VI and Leo X. Finally, the sale of indulgences, which became such a *cause célèbre* during the early stages of the Lutheran reformation, was given new impetus and carried to greater excesses because funds were needed to complete the magnificent art of St. Peter's in Rome.

As was to be expected, corruption and greed were present also at the lower levels of the hierarchy. Various prelates developed systems of taxation that were similar to that of John XXII, although on a smaller scale. At the local parish level, simony and absenteeism once again became common.

This is not to say that the entire hierarchy of the church was corrupt. On the contrary, there were many able and upright leaders who upheld the high moral standards that their positions were expected to require. One such leader was the Spanish Cardinal Francisco Ximenes de Cisneros, who combined outstanding intellectual achievements with strict asceticism. But in spite of the many efforts of Ximenes and others like him, corruption was widespread.

The net result of this state of affairs in the practical life of the average believer usually was not so much doubt regarding the efficacy of ecclesiastical ministrations—about such a thing there could be no doubt, for the efficacy of the sacraments was *ex opere operato*—as a tendency to divorce such ministrations from the ethical requirements of daily life. But then, some of the more enlightened, aware of the ethical demands of the gospel, must have asked whether there was not another way of being Christian. That other way which some found was the route of mysticism.

Mysticism as an Alternative

As has been said before,[3] the fourteenth and fifteenth centuries witnessed a widespread revival of mystical piety. Usually, this mysticism did not attack the church openly, nor was it characterized by the intense emotional exaltation that is usually called mysticism. On the contrary, most of these mystics of the late Middle Ages were quiet and scholarly persons who devoted themselves to study, meditation, and contemplation, but who did not set out to convert the entire church to their understanding of the Christian life. Nevertheless, their mere existence and their exemplary lives, coupled with the fact that many of them made little of the ecclesiastical hierarchy, made many wonder whether this was not an alternative way of being Christian.

Perhaps the most significant result of the mystical movement—although there were other important mystical schools in Spain, Italy, and England—was the founding of the Brethren of the Common Life. The Brethren led lives of intense devotion; but instead of spending their time in seclusion or occupying ecclesiastical posts, they made learning and teaching their own form of ministry. Instead of following the stern ascetic practices of some of the older orders, the Brethren of the Common Life spent their time in study, meditation, and manual labor. Two of their most significant contributions were the mass production of manuscripts and the creation of schools where the best learning of the time was made available to youth. Erasmus of Rotterdam was educated in one of these schools, and his classical learning, meticulous scholarship, irenic spirit, and profound devotion bore the mark of the Brethren of the Common Life.[4] Through this movement—and others like it—the laity was given greater participation and insight into the nature of Christianity. Therefore, its contribtion to the events of the sixteenth century was by no means small.

The Impact of Nominalism

Perhaps the popularity of so-called nominalism in the late Middle Ages[5] is the best indication of the process of dissolution through

---

[3] *Ibid.,* pp. 324-26.
[4] See A. Hyma, *The Brethren of the Common Life* (Grand Rapids: Eerdmans, 1950).
[5] See pp. 317-24.

which the medieval synthesis was going. The imposing unity of the Middle Ages at their peak was possible only under the premise that there is an ultimate unity of all things, and that this unity is somehow discernible from the human perspective. Universals were real; they were there, with a givenness even greater than one's own personal existence. They could be known with a certainty and permanence far greater than any knowledge of individual beings. Beginning from them, the entire universe was a logical hierarchy of which the ecclesiastical and civil hierarchies were reflections. It was under this premise—more Neoplatonic than Christian in its origin—that the early Middle Ages operated and developed. But by the end of the thirteenth century it was increasingly apparent that this understanding of reality was becoming less and less viable. One could trace the beginning of the process to the reintroduction of Aristotle into the West; and one could say therefore that Thomism, which was the high point of the medieval synthesis, also introduced into that synthesis the seed of its destruction. This is so because the emphasis on the particular, which was reintroduced with Aristotle, was ultimately subversive of the Neoplatonic notions described above. In any case, the dissolution of the synthesis is more easily discernible in John Duns Scotus, and quite apparent by the time of Ockham.

The nominalists of the fifteenth century did not deny the existence of universals. What they denied was that through the universals the human mind has a definite perception of the ultimate nature of reality. In a way, this latter denial was more subversive than the former, for in its extreme form it implied that reality is not subject to human logic, and that therefore no theological synthesis is possible—witness the distinction between God's absolute and ordered powers, the insistence on will above reason, and the claim that God could just as logically have become incarnate in an ass. Nominalism subverted the medieval synthesis in less obvious but deeper ways than its support of conciliarism. Nominalism undercut the very premises on which that synthesis was built.

But, while destroying the very foundations of the medieval synthesis, nominalism had little to offer in its place. While many of its leaders were deeply religious, a relatively facile joining of piety and constructive theology was no longer possible for them. This does not mean that they were intent on destroying medieval theology or that they rejected orthodox Catholic doctrine. On the contrary, they were strictly orthodox and questioned only those points of doctrine which had not yet been declared dogma of the church. What they actually did was simply to declare that some of the premises of the medieval synthesis were untenable, and to attempt to build a new system of theology on the basis of new premises. They did create impressive systems. But none of these could withstand the method of theological critique that they themselves had applied to earlier theologians. As a result, theological debate became increasingly complex and entangled with fine points of logic. The competing systems, though impressive as intellectual efforts, and in spite of often being grounded on profound piety, were difficult to apply to the life of the church. Thus, a general distrust of theologians developed that was not apparent in earlier centuries. This distrust received its most articulate expression in the works of Erasmus and his fellow humanists.

Erasmus and the Humanists

One of the most remarkable and significant developments of the fifteenth and the sixteenth centuries was the humanistic movement, which began in Italy but soon spread throughout Western Europe. During the Middle Ages there had always been those who cherished the Latin classics and used them as sources for their reflection and writing. But in the fifteenth century, as part of the great Renaissance of interest in classical antiquity that became manifest in architecture, painting, and sculpture, there was also a revival of studies in classical literature. This revival was aided by the fall of Constantinople, for the numerous Byzantine scholars who sought refuge in Italy brought with them their knowledge of the Greek language and literature. Soon Greek became the common possession of educated people throughout Europe, and thus a wide new avenue was opened into the treasures of antiquity.

The invention of printing with movable type gave new impetus to the humanistic movement. Heretofore it had been necessary to rely entirely on manuscripts, whose fidelity to the original was rendered doubtful through a long process of copying and recopying. Although the possibility of attempting to reconstruct the original texts through careful collation of various manuscripts had occurred to some during the Middle Ages, such a project had never been undertaken on a significant scale. Indeed, it would have been pointless to spend long hours trying to reconstruct the best possible text, only to have to entrust that text to a process of successive copying similar to that which had corrupted the originals in the first place. But this situation changed when a means was invented whereby a large number of identical copies of a text could be produced at relatively little cost. Thus, many of the leading humanists gave themselves to the arduous task of collating manuscripts and producing critical editions of the writings of antiquity as well as of the Fathers of the Church and the biblical text. The most significant of these enterprises was the Greek New Testament, published by Erasmus in 1516. Four years later, a group of scholars at the university of Alcalá de Henares, in Spain, under the direction of Cardinal Francisco Ximenes de Cisneros, published the Complutensian Polyglot Bible, which included texts in Hebrew, Greek, Aramaic, and Latin. In Italy, Lorenzo Valla, a secretary to the pope, applied the new methods of textual criticism to the so-called Donation of Constantine, on which stood the papal claims to temporal power, and declared it to be spurious. All over Europe the ready availability of texts that had formerly been scarce and difficult to obtain fired the imagination of those who were attempting to return to the original sources of their faith and their civilization.[6]

This return to the sources took different forms. In Italy, Marsiglio Ficino and Pico della Mirandola attempted to develop a vast system of truth that combined Christianity with Neoplatonism and even the mysteries of the Jewish cabala. At its source, they claimed, all truth must be one, and therefore they sought to bring together all these ancient sources in order to achieve real understanding. Many others in Italy went much further than this, and attempted to substitute ancient pagan practices and beliefs for the Christian tradition, which they regarded as standing between them and classical antiquity.[7] Although he was by no means a humanist, Luther himself may be

---

[6] The work and significance of Erasmus, Ximenes, and Valla, particularly for the interpretation of Scripture, are studied by J. H. Bentley, *Humanists and Holy Writ: New Testament Scholarship in the Renaissance* (Princeton: Princeton University Press, 1983). See also H. Holeczek, *Humanistische Bibelphilologie als Reformproblem bei Erasmus von Rotterdam* (Leiden: Brill, 1975).

[7] On these and other Italian humanists, the best study is C. Trinkaus, *"In Our Image and Likeness": Humanity and Divinity in Italian Humanistic Thought*, 2 vols. (Chicago: University of Chicago Press, 1970).

said to have shared in this urge to return to the sources when he insisted on the authority of the Bible over tradition.[8] But the most common attitude of the humanists, at least before the outbreak of the Protestant Reformation, was that of Erasmus, who advocated a return to the sources of Christianity. Yet he felt that this in itself required a spirit of moderation and charity, which he later saw neither in the defenders of traditional Christianity nor in the proponents of the Protestant faith.

As the most representative and influential of the humanists, Erasmus deserves special attention in this context. His work indeed does show that an era was coming to an end. But it also shows something of the continuity between the previous age and the one that was now beginning. Erasmus cannot be properly understood if he is interpreted merely as a moderate reformer who lacked the courage to follow his views to their ultimate consequences.[9] He did not become Protestant, not because he lacked courage, but because his sincere convictions did not lead him in that direction. He remained a Catholic because he felt that, in spite of all the corruption in the Catholic Church, which he constantly decried, it was within that church that he could best be a Christian, and it was from that church that he expected the true reformation of Christianity to come.

The reformation that Erasmus advocated was in the field of ethics rather than dogmatics. This was so, not because he believed the church and its late medieval theologians to be right on every point, but rather because he felt that correct theological affirmations were of secondary importance when compared with the actual practice of the Christian life. He found very little to admire in the theology of scholasticism, and he felt compelled to condemn and ridicule it for its hairsplitting; but he did not propose, as did the Protestant reformers, to substitute a new theology for the old. He was content

---

[8] L. W. Spitz, *The Protestant Reformation: 1517-1559* (New York: Harper & Row, 1985), p. 82, lists several instances of the influence of the humanists on Luther during his early years. See also M. Grossmann, *Humanism in Wittenberg: 1485-1517* (Nieuwkoop: B. de Graaf, 1963); R. P. Becker, ed., *German Humanism and Reformation* (New York: Continuum, 1982).

[9] There is an excellent summary of the history of the interpretation of Erasmus in M. Hoffmann, *Erkenntnis und Verwirklichung der wahren Theologie nach Erasmus von Rotterdam* (Tübingen: J. C. B. Mohr, 1972), pp. 10-27. As this includes an extensive bibliography, I am content to refer the reader to it. A very readable introduction to the life and work of Erasmus is R. H. Bainton, *Erasmus of Christendom* (New York: Scribner's, 1969). See also R. L. DeMolen, ed., *Erasmus of Rotterdam: A Quincentennial Symposium* (New York: Twayne, 1971).

with returning to what he regarded as the simple teachings of Jesus. These teachings he interpreted—as many had done before him—through Stoic and Platonic eyes. To him, what was essential was the "philosophy of Christ," which was basically a rational, moderate, and orderly way of living.

This does not mean, however, that Erasmus reduced Christianity to a series of moral principles. He did believe all the traditional doctrines of the church, and especially the doctrine of the incarnation. He did not claim that what one believes makes no difference. What he did claim was that true Christian doctrine was a relatively uncomplicated thing, and that scholasticism had theologized it almost beyond recognition. And, while these theological calisthenics were taking place, the practice of Christian living had suffered. In his *Colloquia*, Erasmus repeatedly satirized monks and their practices. The grounds for his animadversion toward monasticism were both the hypocrisy that he saw in actual monastic life and a deeper feeling that what Christ demands is not what is commanded in monastic rules. Erasmus could accept and respect asceticism. In fact, he himself was something of an ascetic after a Stoic fashion, and the ancient Christian writer whom he most admired was the extremely ascetic Jerome. But he had little use for the notion that one could best serve God by withdrawing from the world and devoting one's time to religious exercises. Asceticism is a sort of discipline, like that of a soldier, and must be directed to the end of Christian living. On the other hand, he had no respect for those who abandoned this discipline and gave themselves to their own passions, as can be seen in his mordant mockery of Pope Julius II, whose worldly penchant he criticized in the treatise *Julius Excluded from Heaven*.

The "philosophy of Christ," as Erasmus sees it, starts from the fact that truth is one, and that therefore God is active wherever true wisdom is found. Here he turns to the doctrine of the Logos and draws from it conclusions similar to those drawn earlier by Justin, Clement, Augustine, and Bonaventure. The Logos who was incarnate in Christ is the same that spoke in the philosophers, and thus Erasmus can go so far as to request "St. Socrates" to pray for him.

This in turn means that the ethical commandments of Christ,

which are at the very heart of the Christian life, are very close to the ethical counsel of the Stoics and the Platonists. When Paul speaks of the enmity between "spirit" and "flesh," he means essentially the same as the Stoics when they speak of "reason" and "passions." Basically, the human task in this world is to dominate passions through the exercise of reason. "This, then, is the sole way to happiness: first, know yourself; second, do not submit anything to the passions, but all things to the judgment of the reason."[10]

In order to do this, we have the joint resources of prayer and knowledge, the two weapons of the Christian soldier. "Pure prayer directed to heaven subdues passion, for it is a citadel inaccessible to the enemy. Knowledge furnishes the intellect with salutary opinions so that nothing else may be lacking."[11] Typically, Erasmus insists that prayer must be sincere, and that what is important is not its length or its form. As to knowledge, its main source is the study of Scripture, for "there is . . . no temptation so formidable, that an eager study of the Scripture will not easily beat it off."[12] When searching other interpreters for wisdom in understanding the Scriptures, Erasmus recommends those "especially who depart as much as possible from the literal sense,"[13] among them Paul, Origen, Ambrose, Jerome, and Augustine. Although Erasmus himself never went as far as Origen in his allegorization of Scripture, his freedom to depart from the literal meaning of the text was one of the main reasons for the popularity of his *Paraphrases*, or commentaries on the New Testament.

Erasmus thus stands in a long tradition of Christian thinkers and scholars, and the tension that he experienced with the rest of the established church was very similar to that experienced by others within that tradition. Clement spoke of himself and those who were able to understand his teachings as "Christian gnostics"; Origen had serious difficulties with the ecclesiastical authorities of his time; Augustine's theology was rejected by several of his most influential contemporaries. Likewise, Erasmus saw himself as both within and without the bounds of the established church. He saw himself within

---

[10] *Enchiridion* (LCC, 14:315).
[11] *Ibid.* (LCC, 14:302).
[12] *Ibid.* (LCC, 14:303).
[13] *Ibid.* (LCC, 14:305).

it because he was always its faithful son, he believed its doctrines, and he never rebelled against its authorities. On the other hand, he felt compelled to measure that church by the standards of what he believed to be the gospel, and thus as it were to stand over against it in a critical attitude that was not always welcome.

Taking all this into consideration, one can understand the attitude of Erasmus toward the Protestant reformation. He himself was a reformer. Long before Luther's name was ever heard outside Germany, Erasmus was being discussed throughout Western Europe as the champion of a much needed reformation. He carried on an extensive correspondence, and a great deal of this was devoted to furthering the cause of church reform throughout Europe. He had admirers and followers in the main courts of Europe, and there were among them several crowned heads. An increasing number of bishops, cardinals, and other ecclesiastical leaders were coming to agree with him on the need for a deeper, simpler, more sincere form of Christianity. For a while it seemed likely that the church in Spain would be the first to be reformed along Erasmian lines. England was not far behind. France and Navarre would probably follow. And then, unexpectedly, a mighty wind arose out of Germany that changed the entire situation. As the Lutheran movement progressed, and as Catholic leaders attempted to prevent its growth, it became increasingly necessary for everyone to take a stance vis-à-vis that movement. In Spain, where the churches seemed to have been about to undergo a profound reformation, talk of reform became tantamount to treason against Charles I, who at Worms, under the name of Charles V, had been affronted by Luther. In France, Germany, and elsewhere, the lines were being drawn that would eventually lead to religious wars. Moderation had become impossible. Erasmus was, by temperament as well as by conviction, a moderate, and therefore his position became increasingly difficult.

Protestants felt that, if Erasmus was to be true to what he had been advocating for years, he must join forces with them. This was not a proper reading of what Erasmus had been saying, for he had never advocated schism, and he felt that the Protestants themselves were too immersed in their own theological debates to be able to comprehend the simple teachings of the gospel. Furthermore, he and Luther were diametrically opposed in their approach to reformation. Erasmus' irenic spirit found much to dislike in Luther's bellicosity. For some time, Erasmus had refrained from an open attack on Luther, arguing that perhaps the success of Protestantism was a sign that God had judged the corruption of the church to be such that a drastic surgeon was needed.[14] Events, however, forced him to change his tactics. He was being accused of being a Lutheran at heart, and Protestants were using his writings and his fame to further their cause. Henry VIII of England, Pope Adrian VI, and a host of friends and foes urged him to clarify his position. He finally decided to attack Luther, and chose to do so by composing the treatise *On Free Will*, for here was an issue on which he clearly and sincerely disagreed with Luther. The latter responded with a vitriolic attack in *The Bondage of the Will*, where he showed once again that tendency toward exaggeration which Erasmus himself had deplored in him. After that incident, Erasmus moved further and further away from the Protestants, to the point that toward the end of his life he was accepting many things in the Catholic Church that he had formerly condemned. Although Protestants of humanistic inclinations, such as Philip Melanchthon, continued to hold him in great esteem, the general opinion among Protestants was that Erasmus was simply a weak and cowardly man who did not have the courage to stand up to his own convictions. This estimation, however, is not a fair evaluation of his motives, and is based on an incorrect interpretation of his views.

Erasmus did not fare much better within the Catholic camp, for here also there was little place for his spirit of moderation. Although he was able to live out his remaining years in relative peace in the midst of a world in turmoil, many of his followers—especially in Spain and Italy—did not fare as well. He himself was condemned by the Sorbonne, which took upon itself the task of safeguarding the newly defined Catholic orthodoxy. Twenty-three years after his death, when the first index of forbidden books was drawn up by Paul IV, his works were included in it.

This is why Erasmus represents the end of an age. After his time, and for almost four centuries, it would be very difficult to hold the

---

[14] Quoted in J. Huizinga, *Erasmus and the Age of Reformation* (Torchbooks; New York: Harper, 1957), p. 161.

moderate and conciliatory position between Protestantism and Catholicism that he took. In a sense, he was the last of a long series of moderate, non-schismatic reformers that is a persistent feature of medieval western Christianity.

But Erasmus was also the beginning of a new age. It was the age of the printing press, of books, and of scholarship. His critical editions of the New Testament and of early Christian writers were the beginning of a vast enterprise that continues to this day. This enterprise has resulted in numerous reinterpretations of historical facts, and these in turn have had a profound influence on the further development of Christian thought. Significantly enough, it was he who inaugurated modern biblical research by editing the Greek text of the New Testament; and when, four centuries later, Protestants and Catholics began to speak to each other in what could be described as an Erasmian spirit of toleration, their first steps in their newly established dialogue took place around the biblical scholarship to which Erasmus made such a great contribution.

II

The Theology of Martin Luther

Martin Luther is without any doubt the most significant Christian theologian of the sixteenth century, and therefore it is proper to begin our discussion of sixteenth-century Christian thought, as has been customary, with a summary of Luther's theology. However, a word of caution is necessary at this point. Although Luther is indeed of paramount significance, and although most Christian theology during the sixteenth century—Catholic as well as Protestant—was a commentary and a debate on Luther, it is nevertheless true that significant theological work was taking place in the Catholic and Eastern camps, quite apart from any discussion of Luther's claims. Therefore, readers must be warned that, if they are to gain a total picture of sixteenth-century theology, they must not allow the vital issues being debated in connection with the Protestant movement to eclipse the important theological work being done in other contexts. They will find a discussion of such work in the chapters that I have devoted to Catholic and Eastern theology in the sixteenth century, which have been placed after the entire discusson of early Protestant thought for reasons of logical clarity, not of chronology.

With that word of caution, we may now turn to the theology of Martin Luther.

Martin Luther is, like Augustine, one of those thinkers whose theology is so closely bound up with his life that one cannot understand one apart from the other. Therefore, that being the best possible entrance into his theology, we shall begin this chapter with a brief summary of the spiritual pilgrimage that eventually led him to break with Rome, in order then to study the most significant features of his more mature theology.

The Spiritual Pilgrimage

The young Luther seems to have been very much like most young men of his time, except for two things. The first was that he was given to acute changes in mood, leading to periods of depression; the second was that he was perhaps more religiously inclined than the average youth around him.[1] When he entered the monastery in 1505, he did so because of a vow made to St. Anne during a thunderstorm; yet later developments would seem to indicate that what he feared most during that thunderstorm was not death itself, but the prospect of dying without being prepared for it. He thus entered the monastery to prepare for death—to make himself agreeable in the sight of God.

Having embraced the monastic way of life, Luther gave himself to it completely. He was twenty-one years old at the time, and he was not a man to take his new vocation frivolously. After a year as a novice he took permanent vows, and his superiors were sufficiently satisfied with him to decide that he should be ordained to the priesthood. During this entire period one finds no indication that Luther was an unwilling monk or that he found his vows burdensome. On the contrary, according to his own words, he did everything within his power to be an exemplary monk. He had abandoned the world and entered the monastery in order to assure himself of his salvation, and he would not now succumb to the temptation of becoming a comfortable, self-satisfied monk. He would proceed with the business that had brought him to the monastery and lead as ascetic a life as he could possibly endure. This asceticism he carried to such an extent that in later years he believed that his continuous fasting and mortification had done his body permanent harm.

But this strenuous spiritual exercise seemed to do his soul little

---

[1] An excellent and very readable biography of Luther is R. H. Bainton, *Here I Stand: A Life of Martin Luther* (New York and Nashville: Abingdon-Cokesbury Press, 1950). See also M. Brecht, *Martin Luther: His Road to Reformation* (Philadelphia: Fortress, 1985); H. G. Haile, *Luther: An Experiment in Biography* (Garden City, N.Y.: Doubleday, 1980); R. Marius, *Luther* (Philadelphia: Lippincott, 1974). A debatable, but very imaginative, study is that of E. H. Erikson, *Young Man Luther: A Study in Psychoanalysis and History* (New York: W. W. Norton, 1958). On this debate, see R. A. Johnson, ed., *Psychohistory and Religion: The Case of Young Man Luther* (Philadelphia: Fortress, 1977).

good. He was awed by the holiness and justice of God. How could he be certain that he had done enough? This should have been no problem, for the church had a treasury of merits, earned by Christ and his saints, that could be applied to sinners whose works were insufficient to merit salvation. Yet even this confidence was shattered when, on a pilgrimage to Rome, Luther saw the abuse into which relics and other means of attaining merit had fallen. He had arrived at Rome full of hope and faith; he left with a painful doubt that the means of salvation offered by the church were indeed valid—and this is the first indication that we have that he allowed himself to doubt the established doctrine of his time.

He was then transferred to Wittenberg, in a move that was to have enormous consequences for the rest of his life, as well as for the history of the church. It was there that he met his fellow Augustinian and superior Johann von Staupitz. Staupitz was an understanding and learned man, who was able to listen to Luther's fears and anxieties without feeling compelled to condemn him. When Luther confided in him his doubts regarding his own salvation, Staupitz lent him a sympathetic ear. But then Luther began having misgivings about confession. These misgivings were not due to disbelief. He still believed that through confession and penance sins could be forgiven. His problem stemmed from the fact that he discovered that it was impossible to confess all his sins. No matter how hard he tried, some sins remained unconfessed and unforgiven, for sin was such a deep and permeating thing that it was impossible to pull it out to its very roots. Staupitz then introduced him to the German mystics. Here was an alternate way of salvation, one which relied not on the forgiveness of individual sins, but simply on completely entrusting oneself to God. All that one had to do was to leave aside one's own self-interest and pride, and trust only in God. Here Luther found a measure of rest, and one can hear an echo of the teachings of the mystics in his later insistence on salvation by faith. But this again was insufficient. The very efforts to destroy one's ego are in themselves acts of pride. Furthermore, the mystics claimed that the road to salvation lay simply in giving oneself to the love of God, and Luther found that his deepest reaction before the most holy, who required of him a holiness that he could not attain, was not one of love, but of hate.

It was at this juncture that Staupitz decided that Luther was to study, become a doctor, and teach at the university of Wittenberg. Furthermore, he was to be given pastoral responsibilities. It is impossible to know the reasons behind Staupitz's decision. Perhaps he was following the example of Jerome, who had decided to study Hebrew and translate the Bible when he found that his unholy dreams had followed him to his monastic retreat at Bethlehem. Perhaps he felt that if Luther was compelled to focus his attention on the doubts and needs of others, his own doubts and needs would recede into the background. In any case, the net effect of this decision was to direct Luther to the study of Scripture, where he would eventually find an answer to his doubts.

Following Staupitz's indications, Luther gave himself fully to the study of the Bible. He began lecturing on the Psalms in 1513, and by 1517 had also lectured on Romans and on Galatians.

By that time, although his break with the established church was just about to begin, his theology had taken its basic permanent shape. From then on, his further theological developments would be further clarifications and applications of what he had discovered during those early years of biblical research. Therefore, we must pause and attempt to draw the main lines of his newly discovered understanding of God and of God's relationships with humanity.

Briefly stated, Luther's problem was one of sin and grace, or of justice and love. How could God, the most holy, the most righteous, be appeased by a man like Luther, who knew himself to be an unrighteous and unholy sinner? His study of the Psalms gave Luther the first glimmers of hope that an answer could be found.[2] Like almost all exegetes of his time, he interpreted the Psalms christologically. In them Christ spoke and made himself manifest. Thus, when he came to the twenty-second Psalm, which Christ himself had begun to recite from the cross, "My God, my God, why hast thou forsaken me," Luther discovered that Christ himself had been subject to the agonies of desolation which he suffered. Christ himself had been as forsaken as the most abject sinner. This he had

---

[2] This obviously refers to his formal study of Psalms, for the purpose of his lectures. As a monk, Luther followed the ancient tradition of reciting the Psalms regularly, and therefore he knew most of them by heart.

done for Luther's sake. He was not only the righteous judge; he had also been willing to sit with the accused. Somehow the righteous God whom Luther felt compelled to hate was also the loving God who in Christ had been utterly forsaken for Luther's sake. In some mysterious way, justice and love are interconnected. This was the beginning of Lutheran theology.

The great discovery, however, came some time later, when Luther was studying the epistle to the Romans. Years later, he would recount his experience as follows:

> I had indeed been captivated with an extraordinary ardor for understanding Paul in the Epistle to the Romans. But up till then it was not the cold blood about the heart, but a single word in Chapter 1, "In it the righteousness of God is revealed," that stood in my way. For I hated that word "righteousness of God," which, according to the use and custom of all the teachers, I had been taught to understand philosophically regarding the formal or active righteousness, as they called it, with which God is righteous and punishes the unrighteous sinner.
>
> Though I lived as a monk without reproach, I felt that I was a sinner before God with an extremely disturbed conscience. I could not believe that he was placated by my satisfaction. I did not love, yes, I hated the righteous God who punishes sinners, and secretly, if not blasphemously, certainly murmuring greatly, I was angry with God. . . .
>
> At last, by the mercy of God, meditating day and night, I gave heed to the context of the words, namely, "In it the righteousness of God is revealed, as it is written, 'He who through faith is righteous shall live,' " There I began to understand that the righteousness of God is that by which the righteous lives by a gift of God, namely by faith. And this is the meaning: the righteousness of God is revealed by the gospel, namely, the passive righteousness with which merciful God justifies us by faith. . . . Here I felt I was altogether born again and had entered paradise itself through open gates. There a totally new face of the entire Scripture showed itself to me.[3]

---

[3] *Preface to the Latin Writings* (*LW*, 34:336-37). It should be noted that, although this passage is often quoted as a description of what was taking place in Luther's mind in those early years, Luther himself places it at a later date. See Spitz, *The Protestant* . . . , p. 65.

Luther was not one to keep this discovery to himself. Its significance was too great, and he must not hide it under a bushel. Soon he had convinced most of his colleagues at Wittenberg. But his discovery must be broadcast farther afield. To this end, Luther wrote ninety-seven theses, ostensibly to be defended by a student at Wittenberg in one of the exercises usually required of candidates for the bachelor's degree; but he also had them printed, and he offered to defend them himself against any opponent. In these theses, Luther put forth his deep sense of the far-reaching effects of human sinfulness. "Man, being a bad tree, can only will to do evil."[4] "One must concede that the will is not free to strive toward whatever is declared good."[5] This is closely connected with Luther's own experience of not allowing God to liberate him from his bondage: "Man is by nature unable to want God to be God. Indeed, he himself wants to be God, and does not want God to be God."[6] This in turn leads to the primacy of grace: "On the part of man, however, nothing precedes grace except ill will and even rebellion against grace."[7] One cannot even remove the obstacles that stand in the way of grace, and moral virtue is of no account in this respect, for "there is no moral virtue without either pride or sorrow, that is, without sin."[8] The reason for this is that "every deed of the law without the grace of God appears good outwardly, but inwardly it is sin."[9] In summary, "we do not become righteous by doing righteous deeds but, having been made righteous, we do righteous deeds."[10]

Although at this time Luther conceived of himself as a good Catholic and a true son of the organized church,[11] he did hope to create a debate that would draw attention to his discovery. In this, however, he failed. "It may have been the most carefully planned act of public defiance in Luther's career, and it seems completely to have misfired. Here, surely, might have been the opening broadside of a great controversy. . . . But nothing happened. . . . Not for the first,

---

[4] *Disputation against Scholastic Theology*, thesis 4 (*LW*, 31:9).
[5] *Ibid.*, 10 (*LW*, 31:10).
[6] *Ibid.*, 7.
[7] *Ibid.*, 30 (*LW*, 31:11).
[8] *Ibid.*, 38.
[9] *Ibid.*, 76 (*LW*, 31:14).
[10] *Ibid.*, 40 (*LW*, 31:12).
[11] Indeed, at the conclusion of his theses (*LW* 31:16) he says, "We believe we have said nothing that is not in agreement with the Catholic Church and the teachers of the church."

or the last, time did Luther find his best plans came to nothing, while immense and unintended consequences came when least expected."[12]

These "immense and unintended consequences" came in connection with the issue of indulgences. Luther's pilgrimage to Rome, and his later theological development, had convinced him that trust in the merits and relics of the saints was in vain. He had found such trust a hindrance rather than a help in his spiritual pilgrimage. In Wittenberg, Frederick the Wise had collected a vast number of relics, and these were supposed to grant release from purgatory to those who saw them and made the proper contributions. Long before the outbreak of the Reformation, Luther had preached against these practices, and had incurred the displeasure of Frederick, who counted on the income derived from the contributions of the faithful. Actually, since part of that income was used for the university, Luther himself indirectly received part of the benefits. Frederick, however, would not silence Luther simply because the monk had displeased him or hurt his income. Thus, Luther continued his pastoral functions in spite of his disagreement with his prince on this subject. This was the state of affairs when the issue of indulgences was brought to the foreground by a proclamation of Leo X, granting Albert of Brandenburg the right to sell a new indulgence in his territories. Luther did not know it at the time, but several persons in high positions had been involved in the negotiations leading to this proclamation, and the sums involved were considerable. Ostensibly, however, the purpose of this new sale of indulgences was the need to complete the basilica of St. Peter in Rome, where work had been stopped for some time for lack of funds. Frederick the Wise did not allow the vendors to enter his territories, for they would compete with the indulgence that was available at the Wittenberg church. But some of Luther's parishioners went across the border to purchase the new indulgence, and upon returning reported to Luther that the vendors were making outrageous claims regarding the efficacy of their merchandise.

It was then that Luther composed his famous ninety-five theses, whose real title is *Disputation on the Power and Efficacy of Indulgences.*

---

[12] G. Rupp, *Luther's Progress to the Diet of Worms,* reprint (New York: Harper, 1964), pp. 46-47.

He composed them in Latin, for what he was seeking was not a commotion but rather a scholarly dispute with intellectuals, in which he hoped to prove that his theses were correct. This was nothing new. Luther himself had earlier proposed other theses that he hoped would cause a furore, and nothing had happened. Now, when he expected nothing to happen, he did create a furore.

The theses, having been written with a single problem in mind, were not as thorough an exposition of Luther's main tenets as the *Disputation against Scholastic Theology* summarized above. In general, the attack is directed not against the pope, but rather against the preachers of indulgences. The claims of these preachers are detrimental to the pope, for they make the laity ask such questions as why the pope, if he has power over purgatory, does not simply release all the souls therein out of love, rather than waiting until he has been given "miserable money with which to build a church."[13] In a similar fashion, putting his words in the mouth of "the laity," Luther voices the feelings of those who felt that once again Germany was being fleeced by Rome. Thus he claims that "the laity" may ask, "Why does not the pope, whose wealth is today greater than the wealth of the richest Crassus, build this one basilica of St. Peter with his own money rather than with the money of poor believers?"[14] But in spite of this, Luther felt that his previous unheeded attack on scholastic theology went much deeper and should have created a greater stir than these theses on the subject of indulgences.

What Luther did not realize when he posted his theses was that he was stepping on some powerful toes, and that he was stirring grievances that had long been waiting to be expressed. Without his knowledge, the ninety-five theses, originally written in Latin as the academic document they were, were translated into German, printed, and widely distributed throughout the country. Pope Leo X, one of the most unworthy men ever to occupy the see of Peter, was unable to understand the deep spiritual issues involved in the controversy; nor did he care to understand them. He simply saw the German monk as an obstacle to his plans, and commissioned the general of the Augustinians to silence him. In this, however, he did

---

[13] Thesis 82 (*LW*, 31:32).
[14] Thesis 86 (*LW*, 31:33).

not succeed, for the German chapter apparently did not take action against Luther. Rather it was decided that a debate would take place at Heidelberg between Luther and the conservative theologian Leonard Baier, and that Luther would complete the *Explanations of the Ninety-five Theses,* on which he had been working. We shall have occasion to refer to the Heidelberg Disputation when we consider Luther's understanding of the task of the theologian. Let it suffice to say here that, although Luther was unable to convince his opponents, a number of younger theologians were won to his side through this debate. In his *Explanations,* however, Luther shows the inner struggle through which he is going, trying to hold fast to the traditional doctrine on papal authority and the power of the keys, and yet finding that the papacy as it exists is hardly reconcilable with the gospel.

> I cannot deny that everything which the pope does must be endured, but it grieves me that I cannot prove that what he does is best. Although, if I were to discuss the intention of the pope without becoming involved with his mercenary hirelings, I would say, briefly and with confidence, that one must assume the best about him. The church needs a reformation which is not the work of one man, namely, the pope, or of many men, namely the cardinals, both of which the most recent council has demonstrated, but it is the work of the whole world, indeed it is the work of God alone. However, only God who has created time knows the time for this reformation. In the meantime we cannot deny such manifest wrongs. The power of the keys is abused and enslaved to greed and ambition.[15]

Luther hoped that his *Explanations,* sent to the pope with a humble apology, would be the end of the matter. He did not know that by that time Leo and his curia had decided to condemn and excommunicate him. This action, however, was delayed on account of political circumstances. It was necessary to elect an emperor to succeed Maximilian. The most likely candidate was King Charles I of Spain—who later took the name of Charles V—but his election would be disastrous for Leo's policies, for Charles would then hold

---

[15] *LW,* 31:250.

him in a vise formed by Spain and Germany to the west and north, and Naples and Sicily to the south. Frederick the Wise was one of the imperial electors, and was even a likely compromise candidate for the purple. Therefore the pope felt compelled to grant some consideration to Luther, for whom Frederick demanded a fair trial. A series of negotiations followed, with the distinguished scholar Cardinal Cajetan—whom we shall discuss in another chapter—as the pope's main representative. But these negotiations came to naught as the participants on both sides became increasingly aware that what stood between them, more than the concrete issue of indulgences, was two very different conceptions of the Christian faith.

As the years went by, and as he unfolded the implications of his basic theological stance, Luther burnt more and more bridges behind him. In 1519, in a debate at Leipzig with John Eck von Ingolstadt, he was driven by the artful Eck to declare that the authority of the Bible is superior to that of popes and councils, and that the latter had erred. Eck accused him of being a Hussite. Although surprised at the time, Luther soon came to acknowledge that on many points he agreed with John Hus. In 1520, he wrote three significant treatises: *The Freedom of a Christian, Address to the German Nobility*, and *The Babylonian Captivity of the Church*. The first he addressed to the pope, together with a conciliatory letter in which he claimed that Leo was like "a lamb among wolves," or "Daniel among lions." In an irenic spirit, and under the heading of Christian freedom, he expounded his basic understanding of the Christian life. The other two treatises, however, led him even farther from the Roman Church. The *Address to the German Nobility* denied the authority of the pope over secular rulers and over Scripture, and claimed that it was the secular power, and not the pope, who must now call a council for the reformation of the church. He made it very clear, however, that he was not appealing to armed power, for the needed reformation would not come through such means. But what made the treatise significant was that in it Luther spelled out many of the German grievances against Rome, and thus the reform movement became entwined with German nationalistic feeling. In *The Babylonian Captivity,* he attacked the sacramental system of the church. According to this treatise, there are only three sacraments; baptism, the eucharist, and penance. He denied transubstantiation and the sacrifice of the mass. He also insisted on the priesthood of all believers, which he had already defended in the *Address to the German Nobility*. With this attack on the sacramental system, it became apparent even to the most dispassionate—Erasmus among them—that the breach was irreparable. But that was of little consequence, for just as Luther was preparing to publish his treatise John Eck arrived with the papal bull of excommunication.

"Arise, O Lord, and judge your own cause . . . for foxes have arisen seeking to destroy the vineyard."[16] Thus began the bull by which, after calling on the Lord, Peter, Paul, and the entire church, Leo recounted the errors of Martin Luther, condemned them, and excommunicated their author and his followers. The bull ended with an appeal to Luther, promising that, should he recant, he would be received with "fatherly love." The official proclamation of the bull was accompanied in Rome with the burning of Luther's books, and similar ceremonies took place in various parts of Germany and the Netherlands as the bull was proclaimed in each new city. To this Luther responded by assembling his students outside the city gates at Wittenberg, and burning copies of the canon law, the decretals, and several works of scholastic theology. To these he then added a copy of the bull itself. Technically, he was not yet an obdurate heretic, for the bull had not been proclaimed in Saxony; but for all practical purposes, and as far as the ecclesiastical authorities were concerned, the die was cast. Luther was a heretic, and those who chose to follow him chose the route of excommunication and possible physical danger.

There now remained the action of the state. This took place at the Diet of Worms in 1521. Charles—by now Holy Roman Emperor—had hesitated about inviting Luther to the Diet, but Frederick the Wise and others had insisted that Luther must be given a fair hearing. Luther himself went to Worms convinced that he was going to what could well be his death, and that he would escape that end only if God decided to spare him. The events at Worms are well known. With memorable and dramatic words, Luther refused to recant. After some hesitation, the Diet decided to ban Luther and to

---

[16] Bull *Exsurge Domine*, in C. J. Barry, ed., *Readings in Church History*, (Westminster, Md.: Newman Press, 1965), 2:28.

forbid anyone to offer him shelter. From that moment, from the point of view of the state as well as from that of the church, Luther and his followers were no longer part of the one true church, but a band of heretics struggling for their life and attempting to bring others into their fold.

The ensuing events did little to shape Luther's theology.[17] The basic perspective of that theology had been determined while he was still a virtually unknown university professor. That perspective had unfolded into full-blown opposition to traditional theology in the years between 1517 and 1521. By 1521, Luther's theology was fully developed. The treatises that followed formed part of his mature theology, and therefore it is not necessary for our purpose here to recount the rest of his life. Rather, we must now turn to some of the most significant features of his theology.

The Task of the Theologian

As early as 1518, in the *Heidelberg Disputation*, Luther set forth what amounted to an entire program for an approach to theology. This he proposed by opposing two forms of theology: a "theology of glory" and a "theology of the cross." These two differ in their subject matter, for one is concerned primarily with God in glory, whereas the other sees God as hidden in suffering.

> A theology of glory calls evil good and good evil. A theology of the the cross calls the thing what it actually is.
>
> This is clear: He who does not know Christ does not know God hidden in suffering. Therefore he prefers works to suffering, glory to the cross, strength to weakness, wisdom to folly, and, in general, good to evil. These are the people whom the apostle calls "enemies of the cross of Christ" [Phil. 3:18], for they hate the cross and suffering and love works and the glory of works. Thus they call the good of the cross evil and the evil of a deed good. God can be

---

[17] This is not to say, however, that Luther did not discover further implications of his earlier theological discoveries. A significant example of such development is his attitude toward marriage. His understanding of justification by faith led him to reject the distinction between commandments and counsels of perfection on which the monastic life was based. This in turn led him to renounce the principle of monastic and clerical celibacy. After he himself was married, he gained further insights into the value of marriage and the traditional negative views on women. See J. D. Douglass, "Women in the Continental Reformation," in R. R. Reuther, ed., *Religion and Sexism* (New York: Simon and Schuster, 1974), pp. 292-318.

found only in suffering and the cross, as has already been said. Therefore the friends of the cross say that the cross is good and works are evil, for through the cross works are dethroned and the old Adam, who is especially edified by works, is crucified. It is impossible for a person not to be puffed up by his good works unless he has first been deflated and destroyed by suffering and evil until he knows that he is worthless and that his works are not his but God's.[18]

These paragraphs—and their general context in the *Heidelberg Disputation*—are of great import, for in them Luther is responding to the questions that are of central and primary importance in every theology, namely: What is theology? What is the proper task of the theologian? What are the data with which the theologian works? It is evident that upon the answer particular theologians give to these questions depends much of what their theology will be.

In these paragraphs, Luther is arguing that there is a theology of glory and a theology of the cross.[19] A theology of glory attempts to see God as manifested in works. A theology of the cross believes that God can be rightfully spoken of and rightfully worshiped only as seen in suffering and the cross. A theology of glory is blind and puffed up, for it claims that we in our actual sinful state can see God's works as such, and God in them. It is the theology to which Paul refers in Romans: "claiming to be wise, they became fools." Over against this type of theology stands the theology of the cross, which is the only true theology. It does not claim to discover God's own self, but rather is content with knowing God in revelation, that is in suffering and in the cross.

This does not mean that there is no natural knowledge of God. On the contrary:

There is a twofold knowledge of God: the general and the particular. All men have the general knowledge, namely, that God is, that He has created heaven and earth, that He is just, that He punishes the wicked, etc. But what God thinks of us, what He wants to give and to do to deliver us from sin and death and to save

---

[18] *Heidelberg Disputation*, thesis 21 (*LW*, 31:53).
[19] W. v. Loewenich, *Luthers Theologia Crucis* (Munich: Kaiser Verlag, 1954); H. Sasse, "Luther's Theologia Crucis," *LuthOut*, 16 (1951): 263-66; 305-8.

us—which is the particular and the true knowledge of God—this men do not know. Thus it can happen that someone's face may be familiar to me but I do not really know him, because I do not know what he has in his mind. So it is that men know naturally that there is a God, but they do not know what He wants and what He does not want.[20]

The general or natural knowledge of God is the reason that all races have their gods. They knew that there was divinity above them, but they knew not what this divinity was. Similarly, the philosophers have this natural knowledge of God, but it takes them not one bit closer to understanding the true nature of God. The same may be said of the ethical standards that are inscribed in all hearts; they show that there is a God, but not who God is or what God wills for us.

In a different context, while commenting on the Gospel of John, Luther calls these two types of knowledge of God "legal" and "evangelical" knowledge. This is closely connected with the law-gospel theme, to which we shall return shortly. In any case, here again Luther asserts that there are two kinds of knowledge of God. Reason can offer a "legal knowledge" of God. The philosophers had this knowledge, and so does everyone, for it is inscribed in our hearts. The other kind of knowledge, "evangelical knowledge," "does not grow up in our garden, and nature knows nothing at all about it."[21] Changing the metaphors, Luther claims that there is a "right-handed" and a "left-handed" knowledge of God. The latter we can gain through the abilities that God has given us. The former, which is the proper knowledge of God, must come from above.

This is the first reason that Luther rejects the theology of glory: it deals with the "general" or "left-handed" knowledge of God; it does not recognize the great difference between this and the proper knowledge of God; it attempts to attain to the proper knowledge of God by the same methods of one who uses a ladder to reach a pigeon loft.

The second reason Luther feels compelled to reject the theology of glory is that it attempts to see God face to face, forgetting that "no man shall see God and live." "The people of Israel did not have a God

---

[20] *Lectures on Galatians,* 1535 (*LW,* 26:399-400).
[21] *Sermons on the Gospel of St. John* (*LW,* 22:152-53).

who was viewed 'absolutely,' to use the expression, the way the inexperienced monks rise into heaven with their speculations and think about God as He is in Himself. From this absolute God everyone should flee who does not want to perish, because human nature and the absolute God—for the sake of teaching we use this familiar term—are the bitterest of enemies. Human weakness cannot help being crushed by such majesty, as Scripture reminds us over and over."[22]

The God of the Bible is always revealed in hiddenness;[23] the absolute one is known by us only in the concrete, which God has chosen as a means for revelation. In several contexts, Luther affirms that the difference between the Christian God and that of the Turks is that the latter are forced to speak of God in vague terms, for they do not know God in hiddenness, which is the true revelation. "But those who want to reach God apart from these coverings exert themselves to ascend to heaven without ladders (that is, without the Word)."[24]

This is why the text in the *Heidelberg Disputation* quoted above makes so much of "God hidden in suffering." Only there can God be truly known—that is, known with an "evangelical knowledge."

What Luther rejects in denying the title of true theology to the "theology of glory" is both moralism and rationalism. Walther von Loewenich, in commenting on this text, shows that there is a certain ambiguity in it, and argues that such ambiguity is not altogether unintentional. What are the "works" by which God is not properly known? In most of this text, they seem to be the entire creation, but then in some instances they may be works by which humans attempt to please God. Luther rejects "works" in both of these senses, and von Loewenich claims that there is in this double rejection the overcoming of the ambiguity, and in the ambiguity a profound meaning, for in the two poles of the ambiguity Luther is rejecting one and the same thing in its two parallel manifestations or products. In rejecting human works as valid for salvation, Luther rejects

---

[22] *Commentary on Psalm 51:1 (LW, 12:312).*

[23] J. Dillenberger, *God Hidden and Revealed: The Interpretation of Luther's "Deus absconditus" and Its Significance for Religious Thought* (Philadelphia: Muhlenberg Press, 1953); E. Grislis, "Martin Luther's View of the Hidden God." *McCQ*, 21 (1967): 81-94.

[24] *Lectures on Genesis*, 1:2 (LW, 1:14).

moralism. In rejecting God's works as a means to know the Divine, he rejects rationalism. Ethics and theory of knowledge do not simply stand side by side, with no relationship whatsoever, but they belong together with that longing for direct communion with the absolute God which constitutes theology of glory. In a similar ambiguity, which is the counterpart to the former, Luther uses the term "cross" to refer both to the cross of Christ and to that to the Christian, and this in turn shows that the theology of the cross has to do not only with the content of that theology, but also with the manner and the standpoint from which it is done.

As a result of this understanding of the task and method of theology, Luther's views on the relationship between theology and philosophy were very different from those of the scholastics.[25] He could not accept the Thomistic view according to which faith adds to the natural knowledge of God certain things that reason by itself could never have discovered. This view does not give sufficient weight to the fact that all natural knowledge of God is "law," and therefore does not overlap with the knowledge of God as revealed in the gospel. In order to refute these views, Luther on occasion used the critique that later scholasticism had applied to them. But even the view of the later scholastics he could not accept, for what they were in fact doing was simply eroding the Thomistic principle without completely rejecting it. Luther, on the other hand, saw a radical opposition between the theology of glory—which included both Thomism and nominalism—and the theology of the cross. Philosophy as an introduction to theology was to be rejected, not simply because reason was weak, but because it was searching after the "absolute" or "naked" God, who is very different from the "hidden" God of Scripture.

As there is a twofold knowledge of God, there is also a twofold use of reason. Luther can refer to it as a "whore," and then again as a "very useful tool." This seeming contradiction is easily resolved if one keeps in mind that for Luther reason, as well as every other human endowment, bears the mark of the fall, and can only serve its

---

[25] W. Link, *Das Ringen Luthers um die Freiheit der Theologie von der Philosophie* (Munich: Kaiser Verlag, 1940); B. Hägglund, *Theologie und Philosophie bei Luther und in der occamistischen Tradition: Luthers Stellung zur Theorie von der doppelten Wahrheit* (Lund: C. W. K. Gleerup, 1955); L. Grane, *Contra Gabrielem: Luthers Auseinandersetzung mit Gabriel Biel in der Disputatio Contra Scholasticam Theologiam 1517* (Copenhagen; Gyldendal, 1962).

proper function when redeemed. Reason is able to help us in our horizontal life; it can help us order society; it can lead to useful inventions such as the printing press; it is one of our means of finding sustenance in the world. "And it is certainly true that reason is the most important and the highest in rank among all things and, in comparison with other things of this life, the best and something divine. It is the inventor and mentor of all the arts, medicines, laws, and of whatever wisdom, power, virtue, and glory men possess in this life. By virtue of this fact it ought to be named the essential difference by which man is distinguished from the animals and other things."[26]

Even after sin, reason is to be respected as "that most beautiful and most excellent of all creatures." And yet, this does not free it from the curse of all things fallen, for it "remains under the power of the devil."[27] When it comes to the "proper" and "evangelical" knowledge of God, reason takes the side of flesh against spirit, of works against faith, of law against gospel. "It is up to God alone to give faith contrary to nature, and ability to believe contrary to reason."[28]

Although the knowledge of God that reason by itself can attain is "legal knowledge," and reason is thus closely connected with the law, this does not mean that reason by itself can take the place of the law. This is so because natural reason, belonging to the flesh, is always seeking to excuse itself, and thus cannot hear the word of condemnation that God speaks in the law. By ourselves, we do not know the evil that exists even in our virtues. Reason can never tell this, for it is part of us and caters to our desires.

> Therefore, it is only the law which shows that these [virtues] are evil—not, to be sure, in themselves, for they are the gifts of God, but because of that deeply hidden root of sin which is the cause of men being pleased with, relying, and glorying in these things which are not felt to be evil. . . .
>
> In the midst of so much wisdom, goodness, righteousness, and religiousness, they do not will to be evil, nor can they recognize that they are, because they do not listen. You see therefore, how incomparably the law transcends natural reason, and how bottomless is the sin of which it gives us knowledge.[29]

---

[26] *The Disputation Concerning Man*, theses 4-6 (*LW*, 34:137).
[27] *Ibid.*, thesis 24 (*LW*, 34:138-39).
[28] *Disputation Concerning Justification*, arg. 5 (*LW*, 34:160).
[29] *Against Latomus*, 3 (*LW*, 32:226).

This is why Luther has little use for philosophy within the realm of theology. "Indeed, no one can become a theologian unless he becomes one without Aristotle."[30] Philosophical truth is to theological truth as law is to gospel, or as human righteousness is to divine righteousness. In outward things the law and reason rule. But the judgment that is true for us is not true for God, for God judges differently. The subject of both theology and philosophy is the same, and this means that for Luther there is a relationship between these two disciplines. But that relationship is not one of simple continuity. Rather, it is the relationship that exists between the general or legal knowledge, and the proper or evangelical knowledge of God. Both deal with God; but they see differently, and the one cannot simply lead into the other.

Luther's evaluation of mysticism is also illuminating. During his spiritual pilgrimage the German mystics had provided him with a measure of temporary relief, and he had experienced some of the joys that they described. He always felt great respect for them. But he was also acutely aware of what he took to be the shortcomings of mysticism.[31] In some instances, his critique of mysticism is such that he fails to do justice to it. Luther agreed with the mystics that humility was the only possible attitude before the Godhead. His reason for humility, however, is not simply the enormous contrast between the divine and the human, between the Creator and his creature, but rather the self-denial of God in Christ. Luther's humility before God is not simply that of a lesser being before the Most High, but that of a sinner before the loving holy one. Although he had more sympathy for the German mystics than for scholastic theology, Luther felt that the "negative theology" of the mystic was still a form of "theology of glory," and not a "theology of the cross." It has a notion of suffering and of humility; but it draws these, not from the Crucified, but from its own concept of the absolute God. The mystics' emphasis on experience gained a sympathetic hearing from Luther, who insisted that what is important is not to know God, but that God is "pro me." Yet, even this emphasis he could not wholly accept, for the mystic

---

[30] *Disputation against Scholastic Theology*, thesis 44 (*LW*, 31:12).

[31] An excellent summary of Luther's stand vis-à-vis the German mystics may be found in Link, *Das Ringen Luthers*, pp. 341-50. This section follows the main lines of his argument. See also R. Seeberg, *Die religiösen Grundgedanken des jungen Luther und ihr Verhältnis zu dem Ockamismus und der deutschen Mystik* (Berlin: Walter de Gruyter, 1931).

concept of experience was not directly related to God as hidden in the cross. The starting point of theology is neither reason nor experience, but God's own action and Word.

The Word of God

The Word of God is the starting point for theology. By Word of God Luther means the Scriptures, but he also means a great deal more. The Word is the eternal second Person of the Trinity, which existed in God from all eternity; the Word is God's power as manifested in the creation of all things; the Word is the incarnate Lord; the Word is the Scriptures, which witness to it; the Word is the proclamation through which the Word in Scripture is actually heard by the believers. Although the term "Word" is obviously used here in various senses, there is a close and important relationship between these different forms of the Word of God.

Let us turn first of all to the eternal Word, the second Person of the Trinity. In a passage that is reminiscent of some of the early Greek theologians, Luther speaks of this unuttered Word of God. After showing how we think words within ourselves before we express them, Luther says:

> This same picture may be applied to God. God, too, in his majesty and nature, is pregnant with a Word or a conversation in which He engages with Himself in His divine essence and which reflects the thoughts of His heart. This is as complete and excellent and perfect as God Himself. No one but God alone sees, hears, or comprehends this conversation. It is an invisible and incomprehensible conversation. His Word existed before all angels and all creatures existed, for subsequently He brought all creatures into being by means of this Word and conversation.[32]

But God has spoken; the Word has been uttered. This is the power through which all things were made out of nothing, for God's Word is not just an act of self-disclosure, but is also the action and power of God. Commenting on Genesis 1:3, "God said: Let there be light," Luther writes: "This expression is indeed remarkable and unknown

---

[32] *Sermons on the Gospel of John*, 1 (*LW*, 22:10).

to the writers of all other languages, that through his speaking God
makes something out of nothing. And so here for the first time
Moses mentions the means and the instrument God used in doing
His work, namely, the Word."[33]

Thus, Luther is perfectly orthodox when it comes to the doctrine
of the Trinity.[34] He had very strong words for those who denied it,
whom he called the "new Arians." But this doctrine, which in the
order of logic precedes the incarnation, in the actual order of our
knowledge is possible only through the event of Jesus Christ.[35] That
event is the supreme Word of God through which every other word
is to be heard and understood.

The value of Scripture then is not to add to the Word of God in
Christ, "for this much is beyond question, that all the Scriptures
point to Christ alone."[36] This is Luther's point of departure in the
interpretation of Scripture as well as in dealing with its authority. Let
us turn first to the question of the authority of Scripture.

As is well known, Luther claimed that tradition—especially the
most recent tradition of the Middle Ages—must be rejected in favor
of Scripture. His reasons for so claiming had nothing to do with a
desire to innovate. On the contrary, throughout his career Luther
found that his most bitter opponents were not only some staunch
Roman Catholics, but also those in the Protestant camp who wished
to do away with the entire tradition of the church. His own practice
was to reject only those traditional views and practices which
contradicted "the clear sense of Scripture." His reason for this was
that he believed that tradition had erred, and that it had to be
brought back to the true meaning of the gospel through the
authority of Scripture, which is above tradition, the church, the
theologians, and Luther himself. Commenting on Galatians 1:9, he
says: "Here Paul subordinates himself, an angel from heaven,
teachers on earth, and any other masters at all to Sacred Scripture.

---

[33] *Lectures on Genesis*, 1:3 (*LW*, 1:16). Cf. *Commentary on Psalm 20:* "When God speaks a word, the thing expressed by the word immediately leaps into existence."

[34] See J. Koopmans, *Das altkirchliche Dogma in der Reformation* (Munich: Kaiser Verlag, 1955), pp. 60-64.

[35] J. Pelikan, *Luther the Expositor,* companion volume to *LW* (St. Louis: Concordia, 1959), p. 53: "From the Word of God in Jesus Christ one could know the Word of God as the Second Person of the Trinity, but not vice versa."

[36] *Avoiding the Doctrines of Men,* 1 (*LW*, 35:132).

This queen must rule, and everyone must obey, and be subject to, her. The pope, Luther, Augustine, Paul, an angel from heaven— these should not be masters, judges, or arbiters but only witnesses, disciples, and confessors of Scripture."[37]

Against this it was argued by the Roman Catholics that the church had created Scripture and had established its canon, and that this showed that the church had authority over Scripture. Luther's response to this argument was that, although it is true that the church established the canon, the gospel established the church, and what he is arguing for is not strictly the primacy of Scripture but the primacy of the gospel to which Scripture attests.[38] As a matter of fact, the proper form of the gospel is its live, oral proclamation. Christ commanded the apostles not to write, but to proclaim. This was what they did at first, and they put the gospel down in writing only at a later stage, as a means to guard it from distortion—such distortion as tradition has now introduced. Therefore, the claim that the church established the canon is true; but the gospel established the church, and the authority of Scripture is not in the canon, but in the gospel.

This is why Luther felt free to take certain liberties with the canon of Scripture, while still insisting on the primacy of Scripture over tradition. The most commonly known case is that of the Epistle of James, which always caused him difficulties through its insistence on works over against faith. In his preface to that epistle, Luther starts by pointing out that the ancient church did not accept it as apostolic. He himself is willing to admit that it is a good book and a good statement of the law of God. But he rejects its apostolicity.

> In the first place it is flatly against St. Paul and all the rest of Scripture in ascribing justification to works. . . .
> In the second place its purpose is to teach Christians, but in all this long teaching it does not once mention the Passion, the resurrection, or the Spirit of Christ. He names Christ several times; however he teaches nothing about him, but only speaks of general

---

[37] *Lectures on Galatians, 1535 (LW*, 26:57-58).

[38] *Theses concerning Faith and Law*, thesis 41 (*LW*, 34:112): "The Scriptures must be understood in favor of Christ, not against him. For that reason they must either refer to him or must not be held to be true Scriptures." Cf. Pelikan, *Luther the Expositor*, p. 67: "The Scriptures were the 'Word of God' in a derivative sense for Luther—derivative from the historical sense of Word as deed and from the basic sense of the Word as proclamation." Cf. N. Nøjgaard, "Luthers Ord- og Bibelsyn," *DTT*, 7 (1944): 129-54, 193-214.

faith in God. Now it is the office of a true apostle to preach of the
Passion and resurrection and office of Christ, and to lay the
foundation for faith in him. . . . Again, whatever preaches Christ
would be apostolic, even if Judas, Annas, Pilate, and Herod were
doing it.[39]

Although in this text, written for believers at large, Luther insisted
on the value of the Epistle as a book of law, within the university
setting and among his friends and students, he felt free to confess
that he was inclined to toss it out of the canon.[40] His attitude toward
the book of Revelation was similar. Therefore, Luther was no
biblicist. His primary authority was not the canon of the Bible, but
the gospel that he found in that Bible and that was the touchstone for
its interpretation.

The proper way to interpret any given text is to place it under the
light of its context, in order to discover what the author's intention is.
The same is true of Scripture, where every text must be interpreted
in the light of the total message of the Bible, and of its author, the
Holy Spirit. When Luther says that the Bible must be its own
interpreter, he does not mean simply that the exegete is to compare
texts. He means also that the central message of the Bible, the gospel,
is the only key to biblical interpretation. But the gospel can be
understood and received only through the intervention of the Spirit,
and therefore Scripture must be interpreted with the guidance of the
Spirit.[41] There is an outward and an inward Word. The former is the
Word in Scripture; the latter is the Holy Spirit. The outward Word
by itself can be heard by the ear but not by the heart. It requires the
work of the Holy Spirit to become audible by the heart. Here Luther
is fighting against adversaries on both sides. On the one hand, stand
the Roman Catholics, who insist that Scripture can be properly
interpreted only by means of the authority of tradition. On the other

---

[39] LW, 35:396.

[40] The Licentiate Examination of Heinrich Schmedenstede, 19 (LW, 34:317): "That epistle of James gives us
much trouble, for the papists embrace it alone and leave out all the rest. Up to this point I have been
accustomed just to deal with and interpret it according to the sense of the rest of Scriptures. For you will
judge that none of it must be set forth contrary to manifest Holy Scripture. Accordingly, if they will not
admit my interpretations, then I shall make rubble also of it. I almost feel like throwing Jimmy into the
stove, as the priest in Kalenberg did." The reference here is to a priest who used the wooden statues of
the apostles as firewood to heat a room. Luther himself did not approve of such excesses.

[41] See R. Prenter, Spiritus Creator (Philadelphia: Muhlenberg Press, 1953), pp. 101-30; G. Ebeling,
Luther: An Introduction to His Thought (London: Collins, 1970), pp. 93-109.

hand are the radical reformers whom Luther calls "enthusiasts," who claim that the revelation of the Spirit goes beyond that found in Scripture. Against both of these, Luther claims that Scripture must be interpreted by the Spirit, but that the Spirit, being its author, does not teach us other things than the gospel, which is in Scripture. This is what he means when he insists that the meaning of the Bible is clear, but that we are unable to understand it through our own powers.

> To put it briefly, there are two kinds of clarity in Scripture, just as there are also two kinds of obscurity: one external and pertaining to the ministry of the Word, the other located in the understanding of the heart. If you speak of the internal clarity, no man perceives one iota of what is in the Scriptures unless he has the Spirit of God. . . . For the Spirit is required for the understanding of Scripture, both as a whole and in any part of it. If, on the other hand, you speak of the external clarity, nothing at all is left obscure or ambiguous, but everything there is in the Scriptures has been brought out by the Word into the most definite light, and published to all the world.[42]

The question of the clarity of Scripture, and the freedom that everyone has to interpret it, became crucial when some of the "enthusiasts," taking literally the commandments of the Old Testament, began disrupting the social order. Luther now felt compelled to explicate in what sense the Old Testament is authoritative for Christians and in what sense it is not. This he did in a series of works of which the clearest and most succinct is the sermon *How Christians Should Regard Moses*.[43] Here Luther states very clearly that the law of Moses, which was intended as the civil law of the Jews, is not binding on Christians. "In the first place I dismiss the commandments given to the people of Israel. They neither urge nor compel me."[44] The law of Moses was indeed God's Word; but it was God's Word to the Jews, and Christians are not Jews. This is true not

---

[42] *The Bondage to the Will* (*LW*, 33:29).
[43] *LW*, 35:161-74. See also P. Althaus, *The Theology of Martin Luther* (Philadelphia: Fortress Press, 1966), pp. 86-102; H. Gerdes, *Luthers Streit mit den Schwärmern um das rechte Verständnis des Gesetzes Moses* (Göttingen: Vandenhock & Ruprecht, 1955).
[44] *LW*, 35:166.

only of the so-called ceremonial law, but of the entire law of Moses, including the Ten Commandments. Moses is God's lawgiver for the Jews, but not for us. If there are in Moses laws that we ought to accept, we are to regard them as applicable to us not on the authority of Moses, but on the authority of natural law. Indeed, much that is contained in the law of Moses, such as the prohibition of stealing, adultery, and murder, is known by all persons because it is engraved in their hearts. Therefore, Christians must obey these laws on the authority not of Moses, but of nature.[45] Then there are some laws, such as the tithe and the year of jubilee, which may seem good to us, and one could wish that they were applied in the Empire. But again the value of these laws is not in the fact that Moses gave them, but rather in their intrinsic rational value. Also the "examples of faith, love, and of the cross,"[46] as well as of the opposite and their consequences, which are found in Moses, are to be cherished and heeded by Christians. Yet all of this should not be used to compel Christians to obey particular Jewish commandments simply because they are to be found in the Old Testament. "Now if anyone confronts you with Moses and his commandments, and wants to compel you to keep them, simply answer, 'Go to the Jews with your Moses; I am no Jew.'"[47]

On the other hand, there is a great deal of value for the Christian in Moses and in the Old Testament in general, for "I find something in Moses that I do not have from nature: the promises and pledges of God about Christ."[48] Interpreted christologically, as pointing toward Christ, the Old Testament is of great importance for Christians. Indeed, it is of such importance that the New Testament adds nothing but the fulfillment of what had already been promised and the revelation of the full meaning of the promise.[49]

---

[45] Cf. R. Nürnberger, "Die lex naturae als Problem der vita christiana bei Luther," ARG, 37 (1940):1-12.

[46] LW, 35:173.

[47] Ibid., p. 166. Such utterances and other much stronger ones, have earned Luther the accusation of anti-Semitism. Typical is the work by P. F. Wiener, Martin Luther: Hitler's Spiritual Ancestor (London: Hutchinson, 1945). There is no doubt that Luther accepted uncritically much of the prejudice of his time, and that his authority gave such prejudice added status. See H. A. Oberman, The Roots of Anti-Semitism in the Age of Renaissance and Reformation (Philadelphia: Fortress, 1984).

[48] Ibid., p. 168.

[49] Althaus, The Theology of Martin Luther, pp. 86-87.

Law and Gospel

The main contrast that Luther sees within Scripture is not that between the two testaments, but that which exists between law and gospel.[50] Although there is more law than gospel in the Old Testament, and more gospel than law in the New, the Old Testament is not to be simply equated with law, nor the New with gospel. On the contrary, the gospel is also present in the Old Testament, and the law can still be heard in the New. In fact, the difference between law and gospel has to do with two functions that the Word of God plays in the heart of the believer, and thus the same Word may be law or gospel, according to the manner in which it speaks to the believer. In order to clarify this, it will be necessary to discuss what Luther means by these two terms.

The law is the will of God, and it is known in the natural law, which is known by all, in the civil institutions—such as the state and the family—that express that natural law, and in the positive utterance of God's will in revelation. Law has two primary functions:[51] as civil law, it restrains the wicked and provides the order necessary both for social life and for the proclamation of the gospel; as "theological" law, it bares before us the enormity of our sin.[52]

It is in this theological function that the law is significant for an understanding of Luther's theology. Law is the will of God; but when that will is contrasted with human reality it becomes a word of condemnation and awakens the wrath of God. In itself, the law is good and sweet; but after the fall humanity has become incapable of fulfilling God's will, and thus the law has become for us a word of judgment and wrath. "So the law reveals a twofold evil, one inward and the other outward. The first, which we inflict on ourselves, is sin

---

[50] T.M. McDonough, *The Law and the Gospel in Luther: A Study of Martin Luther's Confessional Writings* (London: Oxford University Press, 1963); Althaus, *The Theology of Martin Luther*, pp. 251-73; Ebeling, *Luther: An Introduction*, pp. 110-24; G. Heintze, *Luthers Predigt von Gesetz und Evangelium* (Munich: Kaiser Verlag, 1958).

[51] *Lectures on Galatians, 1535* (*LW*, 26:274-75). See Ebeling, *Luther: An Introduction*, pp. 125-40.

[52] Although he never uses that particular phrase, Luther did believe that there was a "third use of the Law" (*tertius usus legis*), as we shall see when we discuss his understanding of the Christian life. See W. Joest, *Gesetz und Freiheit: Das Problem des tertius usus legis bei Luther und die neutestamentliche Paraenese* (Göttingen: Vandenhoeck & Ruprecht, 1961); G. Ebeling, "Zur Lehre vom triplex usus legis in der reformations Theologie," *ThLZ*, 75 (1950):235-46; F. Borchers, "Ley y evangelio y el 'tercer uso de la ley' en Lutero," *VoxEv*, 5 (1964): 51-81.

and the corruption of nature; the second, which God inflicts, is wrath, death, and being accursed."[53]

Otherwise stated, the law is the divine "no," pronounced upon us and all human enterprise. Although its origin is divine, it can be used both by God, leading us to the gospel, and by the Devil, leading us to despair and hatred of God. This is true not only of the Old Testament, but also of the New, and even of the words of Christ; for if we do not receive the gospel, Christ's words stand simply as more stringent claims upon our tortured conscience. By itself, the law leaves us in despair, and therefore playthings of the Devil.[54]

But the law is also God's means to lead us to Christ, for when we hear God's "no" upon ourselves and upon all our efforts we are ready to listen to God's loving "yes," which is the gospel. The gospel is not a new law, simply clarifying God's demands upon us; it is not a new way in which we can placate the wrath of God; it is the undeserved "yes," which in Christ God has pronounced upon us. The gospel liberates us from the law, not by enabling us to fulfill the law, but by declaring it fulfilled for us. "The gospel proclaims nothing else but salvation by grace, given to man without any works and merits whatsoever."[55]

And yet, even within the gospel and after having heard and accepted God's word of grace, law is not entirely left behind. Although justified, we are still sinners, and the word of God still shows us our condition. The difference is that now we need not despair, for we know that, in spite of our wretchedness, God accepts us. We can then truly repent of our sins without attempting to cover them up, either by denying them or by trusting in our own nature.[56] To this we shall return as we consider Luther's doctrine of justification. Let it suffice to say here that this law-gospel dialectic is the focal point of Luther's theology, apart from which his views on

---

[53] *Against Latomus*, 3 (*LW*, 32:224).

[54] *Lectures on Galatians, 1535* (*LW*, 26:10): "In affliction and in the conflict of conscience it is the devil's habit to frighten us with the Law and to set against us the consciousness of sin, our wicked past, the wrath and judgment of God, hell and eternal death, so that thus he may drive us into despair, subject us to himself, and pluck us from Christ."

[55] *Sermon*, October 19, 1522 (*LW*, 51:112).

[56] *Lectures on Galatians, 1535* (*LW*, 26:158): "But blessed is the man who knows this amid a conflict of conscience, who, when sin attacks him and the Law accuses and terrifies him, can say: 'Law, what is it to me if you make me guilty and convict me of having committed many sins? In fact, I am still committing many sins every day. This does not affect me; I am deaf and do not hear you.'"

such things as justification, predestination, and ethics cannot be understood.

The Human Condition

The first thing to be said about us in our present state is that we are sinners. This does not mean simply that we have sinned or even that we still sin, but rather that our entire nature is informed by sin. Commenting on the fifty-first psalm, Luther writes: "Hence it is great wisdom to know that we are nothing but sin, so that we do not think of sin as lightly as do the pope's theologians, who define sin as 'anything said, done, or thought against the Law of God.' Define sin, rather, on the basis of this psalm, as all that is born of father and mother, before a man is old enough to say, do, or think anything. From such a root nothing good before God can come forth."[57]

Our sin is so deep that we cannot discover it by ourselves. We can compare our deeds with what natural law requires of us and thus learn that we have broken that law. We can be aware of our sins against the civil order. All this can trouble our conscience. But still we will not know what it means to be a sinner. We will not know the extent of our own evil and corruption, for our very nature, sinful as it is, will hide our sinfulness from us. Sin is a pervasive human reality.

> Furthermore, one must note, particularly at this point, the statement that no one can know all his sins. This becomes especially obvious when one takes a look at the magnitude of original sin. . . .
>
> Truly, therefore sin is as stupendous a thing as He is stupendous who is offended by it. But Him Heaven and earth cannot contain.
>
> Rightly, therefore, Moses calls sin a secret thing, the true magnitude of which the mind cannot encompass. Even as God's wrath, even as death, is infinite, so sin also is infinite.[58]

Our sinfulness is called "flesh" in Scripture. It is significant that Luther, unlike most earlier exegetes, points out a fact on which most modern scholarship agrees, namely, that "flesh" and "spirit," as used by Paul to refer to the human condition, are not the same as the

---

[57] *Commentary on Psalms 51* (*LW*, 12:307).
[58] *Commentary on Psalms 90:8* (*LW*, 13:117).

bodily and the incorporeal in us. While accepting the biblical division of human nature into body, soul, and spirit, he does not equate this with the Pauline warfare between flesh and spirit. Flesh is not the base lusts of the body—although these are indeed related to it—but is the whole person craving after self-justification.[59] Our predicament is not that we are tempted by flesh, but that we are flesh.

This was what caused Luther's virulent attack on Erasmus when the latter came out in defense of free will.[60] From Luther's perspective, Erasmus had no notion of the nature of the gospel, as was seen in the fact that he regarded the issue at hand as peripheral, and when he then proceeded to list what he thought was important, he produced "such a list as any Jew or Gentile totally ignorant of Christ could certainly draw up with ease."[61] Indeed, for Erasmus the notion of free will was simply something that was required by his understanding of the Christian life as one of virtue and rectitude. Luther, on the other hand, believed that the affirmation of free will, as if we were capable of choosing to do good on our own, was a denial of human sinfulness, and proof that one had heard the Word of God in neither law nor gospel. The bondage of the will to evil was for Luther a clear fact, intimately connected with the dialectic between law and gospel, and with the pervasiveness of human sin.

We can only will evil. Our best virtues, admirable though they are from the point of view of civil law, in no way bring us any closer to God. This is not because our will is constrained, but because it is so imbued with sin that it freely chooses evil. There is nothing left in us by which we can actively please God or even move toward the Divine. Our will—in the oft quoted image—is like a beast standing between two riders, namely, God and the Devil. In our present state, the Devil has become the rider, and there is nothing that we can do to unhorse him.

---

[59] *Commentary on Galatians*, 3:3 (*LW*, 26:216): "Here Paul is opposing the Spirit and the flesh. By 'flesh' he does not mean sexual lust, animal passions, or the sensual appetite. . . . No, he is discussing the forgiveness of sins, the justification of the conscience, the attainment of righteousness in the sight of God, and liberation from the Law, sin, and death. And yet he says here that after they have forsaken the Spirit, they are now being ended with the flesh. Thus 'flesh' is the very righteousness and wisdom of the flesh and the judgment of reason, which wants to be justified through the Law. Therefore, whatever is best and most outstanding in man Paul calls 'flesh,' namely, the highest wisdom of reason and the very righteousness of the Law." Cf. *LW*, 33:275.

[60] Cf. W. v. Loewenich, "Gott und Mensch in humanistischer und reformatorischer Schau: Eine Einführung in Luthers Schrift 'De servo arbitrio'," *HumChr*, 3 (1948): 65-101.

[61] *The Bondage of the Will*, 1 (*LW*, 33:29).

Nothing is left to us of which we can boast. All that we still have is the capacity to be turned in the right direction—a capacity that is absolutely passive and that we therefore cannot turn into actuality. But for God this suffices. It is this passive capacity of the will that God addresses in the Word, turning our will toward God, so that once again, even in the midst of our sinful condition, we may have communion with God. This is the gospel of redemption in Jesus Christ.

The New Creation

Luther's understanding of the work of Christ includes all the themes that had become traditional in his time, and need not detain us here.[62] What is significant is that in Jesus Christ we hear the word that liberates us from the bondage to sin, death, and the Devil.

This is the word of justification. Justification is not something that we achieve or merit. It is not even something that God grants us on the basis of our future achievements.[63] Justification is, first of all, the decree of absolution that God pronounces upon us, declaring us justified in spite of our sinfulness. This is the typical Lutheran doctrine of "imputed justice." Justification is not God's response to our righteousness, but the loving, forgiving declaration by God that we, in spite of our sin, are now absolved, declared to be righteous. Commenting on the text in Acts where God declares to Peter that certain unclean animals were clean, Luther says that "as he pronounced those animals clean, which according to his own law were still unclean, so he pronounces the Gentiles and all of us righteous, although as a matter of fact we are sinners just as those animals were unclean."[64] Thus, what happens to a person who is justified is not that some supposed merits are acknowledged and accepted, but that "he is considered fully and perfectly righteous by God who pardons and is merciful."[65] This may seem to be a harsh

---

[62] Althaus, *The Theology of Martin Luther*, pp. 201-23, rightly criticizes G. Aulén's claim that Luther typifies what he calls the "dramatic" view of atonement (*Christus Victor* [London: S.P.C.K., 1931]), pp. 119-38. See also the article by Althaus, "Das Kreuz und das Böse," *ZSTh*, 15 (1938): 1768-80; C. Stange, "Das Heilswerk Christi nach Luther," *ZSTh*, 21 (1950): 112-27.

[63] Cf. H. Bornkamm, "Justitia dei in der Scholastik und bei Luther," *ARG*, 39 (1942): 30-62; B. Hägglund, *The Background of Luther's Doctrine of Justification in Late Medieval Theology* (Philadelphia: Fortress Press, 1971).

[64] *The Disputation Concerning Justification* (*LW*, 34:168).

[65] *Ibid.* (*LW*, 34:152-53).

doctrine. Indeed, all who still live at the level of the "natural man" will consider it to be so, because "human nature, corrupt and blinded by the blemish of original sin, is not able to imagine or conceive of any justification above and beyond works."[66] But still it is to be accepted if one is not to deny the very nature of the gospel, for this is so basic to a true understanding of the Christian faith, that it "even by itself creates true theologians."[67]

"Justification by faith" is the name commonly given to Luther's understanding of justification. This is proper, for Luther does indeed assert that justification comes by faith alone. What actually happens is that God imputes to us the righteousness of Christ, who acts "like an umbrella against the heat of God's wrath." But, as we have no other way of comprehending Christ and his righteousness than by faith, it is faith that places us under the protection of this umbrella. "Therefore, faith alone justifies without our works."[68] All that one can do by the grace of God is believe, and thus appropriate unto oneself the righteousness of Christ.

On the other hand, the phrase "justification by faith" can be easily misinterpreted, as if Luther were simply saying that the only work necessary for salvation is faith. But for Luther faith is not a work. It is not an effort on the part of the intellect to believe, nor is it an effort on the part of the will to trust. Rather, it is the work of the Holy Spirit in us. If one wishes to speak of faith as a work, one may do so; but faith is a work of God, and not a human work. Here again, this can be properly understood only in the light of Luther's dialectic between law and gospel. Works—that is, all human efforts—belong under the heading of law, whereas faith and justification—divine works, and not human—belong under the heading of gospel.

> Faith is not properly referred to as our work according to the Scriptures, but now and then as a kind of work of God. There are two teachings, law and promise; and law and work are correlatives, just as promise and faith are. Therefore, we ought not to call faith works, but faith the faith of promise not a faith of law. Conversely, work is a work of the law, not a work of faith. Accordingly, faith

---

[66] *Ibid.* (*LW*, 34:151).
[67] *Ibid.* (*LW*, 34:157).
[68] *Ibid.* (*LW*, 34:153).

does not look to the law, nor is it a work. For that is properly called a work which belongs to the law. Faith, then, is not a work, since it looks only toward the promise.[69]

The notion of imputed justification results in the assertion that a Christian is at once justified and a sinner—*simul justus et peccator*.[70] If justification does not depend on our own righteousness, but on God's loving imputation, it follows that "whoever is justified is still a sinner."[71] Justification does not mean that we are made perfect or that we cease to sin. This Luther takes to be Paul's experience, as described in Romans 7.[72] Throughout earthly life, the Christian will continue to be a sinner; but a sinner justified and thus liberated from the curse of the law.

On the other hand, this does not mean—as has often been claimed in caricatures of Luther's thought—that justification means nothing for the actual life of the Christian. On the contrary, justification is also the work by which God, besides declaring us to be righteous, also makes us conform to this decree, by leading us into righteousness. Therefore, "a man who is justified is not yet a righteous man, but is in the very movement or journey toward righteousness."[73] And "the start of a new creature accompanies this faith."[74] "For he first purifies by imputation, then he gives the Holy Spirit, through whom he purifies even in substance. Faith cleanses through the remission of sins, the Holy Spirit cleanses through the effect."[75]

This is the Christian life: a pilgrimage from righteousness to righteousness; from the initial imputation of righteousness by God, to the time when we will actually be made righteous by God. In this pilgrimage, works play an important role, although not as a means to achieve salvation, but as a sign that true faith has indeed been received. The author of the Epistle of James—although not always a felicitous writer—is right in that faith without works is dead. This is

---

[69] *Ibid.* (*LW*, 34:160).

[70] Besides the various introductions already cited, see I. Felter, "Simul justus et peccator," *DTT*, 12 (1950): 19-39.

[71] *The Disputation Concerning Justification* (*LW*, 34:152).

[72] *Against Latomus*, 3 (*LW*, 32:237).

[73] *The Disputation Concerning Justification* (*LW*, 34:152).

[74] *Ibid.* (*LW*, 34:153).

[75] *Ibid.* (*LW*, 34:168).

so, not because works give life to faith, but because only a dead and nonexistent faith can fail to produce works. "We should confirm our possession of faith and the forgiveness of sin by showing our works."[76] "We should not be a part of the church in number only, as the hypocrites, but also by our works, so that our heavenly Father may be glorified."[77]

It is at this point that the law—especially the Decalog and the commandments in the New Testament—plays a new role for the believer. Its civil function, as necessary for the order of society, still continues. Its "theological" function, that of showing us our sin, is still necessary, for the justified person is still a sinner. But the Christian now relates differently to this aspect of the law. "But now I discover that the Law is precious and good, that it was given to me for my life; and now it is pleasing to me. Formerly it told me what to do; now I am beginning to conform to its requests, so that now I praise, laud, and serve God. This I do through Christ, because I believe in Him. The Holy Spirit comes into my heart and engenders a spirit in me that delights in His words and works even when he chastises me and subjects me to cross and temptation."[78]

Thus the law now has a different function, for it at once chastises the sinners that Christians still are, and shows them the path to follow in their desire to do what is pleasing to God. The reason that Luther felt it was necessary to insist on this use of the law was the claim made by some of the enthusiasts, that, because they had the Spirit, they were no longer subject to the commands of the law. Luther saw the chaotic consequences that would follow from such an assertion, and therefore corrected it by saying that, while the Christian is no longer subject to the curse of the law, the law is still a true and proper expression of God's will. Obviously, this does not refer to the entire law of the Old Testament, for, as has already been pointed out, that was given to the Jews, and expressed God's will to them at that point. It refers rather to the moral laws expressed in both testaments, which conform to the natural law and the principle of love, which is paramount in the New Testament.

---

[76] *The Sermon on the Mount, Matt. 6:14-15* (*LW*, 21:149-50).
[77] *The Disputation Concerning Justification* (*LW*, 34:162).
[78] *Sermons on the Gospel of John* (*LW*, 22:144).

The Church

As a result of his rebellion against the established church, and of his insistence on the authority of a single Christian with the support of Scripture, Luther has often been depicted as a prophet of individualism and as a proponent of direct and personal communion with God apart from the church. Nothing could be farther from the truth. Luther was a churchman, and throughout his life he insisted on the fundamental role that the church plays in the life of the believer. He can speak of "Mother Church," and affirm that "she is a true housemother and the bride of Christ. Through the Gospel she magnificently adorns Christ's home with many children."[79] He can be grateful that "by the grace of God we here in Wittenberg have acquired the form of a Christian church."[80] While dedicating a church at Torgau, he said that "God very wisely arranged and appointed things, and instituted the holy sacrament to be administered to the congregation at a place where we can come together, pray, and give thanks to God."[81] And "when we have heard God's Word we also lift up to God our common, united incense, that is, that we call upon him and pray to him together."[82] Furthermore, he can insist, as Cyprian had done centuries earlier, that there is no salvation outside the church.[83] It can even be affirmed that Luther discovered new depths in the traditional affirmation of belief in "the communion of saints."[84]

Therefore, Luther differed from the church of his time, not on the importance of the church, but on the very definition of the nature of the church and its authority. As is well known, he came to reject the authority of the pope, and claimed that "the keys of the pope are not keys but husks and shells of the keys."[85] This again was something that many had claimed before him, especially during the papacy in Avignon and the Great Schism. But Luther went further, and asserted that the supreme authority in the church is the Word of God. It is the preaching and hearing of the Word, and not apostolic

---

[79] *Commentary on Psalm* 68 (*LW*, 13:14).
[80] *Lectures on Galatians, 1535* (*LW*, 26:45).
[81] *Sermon, October 5, 1544* (*LW*, 51:337).
[82] *Ibid.* (*LW*, 51:343).
[83] *Confession Concerning Christ's Supper*, 1528 (*LW*, 37:368).
[84] So Althaus, *The Theology of Martin Luther*, pp. 294-313.
[85] *The Keys* (*LW*, 40:349).

succession, that characterizes the true church, for the church is born of the Word, is nourished by it, and dies without it. This in turn means that any ecclesiastical authority that hinders the activity of that Word is to be replaced.[86]

On the other hand, Luther had a sense of history and tradition, which made him aware of the fact that it was the papal church that preserved the Word of God throughout the ages. This he was willing to acknowledge, especially when he found himself confronted by more radical Protestants who rejected tradition altogether and attempted to return directly to the Bible.

> The whole thing is nonsense. . . . We on our part confess that there is much that is Christian and good under the papacy; indeed everything that is Christian and good is to be found there and has come to us from this source. For instance we confess that in the papal church there are the true holy Scriptures, true baptism, the true sacrament of the altar, the true keys for the forgiveness of sins, the true office of the ministry, the true catechism in the form of the Lord's Prayer, the Ten Commandments, and the articles of the creed. . . . I contend that in the papacy there is true Christianity, even the right kind of Christianity, and many great and devoted saints.[87]

Thus, Luther was neither an individualist who had no vision of the corporate nature of Christianity, nor a radical innovator who had no sympathy for its tradition. Although he had been led by what he believed to be the authority of the Word to reject much of what tradition had bequeathed him, he still realized that he was part of that tradition. As one of his interpreters has said, "this 'no' to tradition is not a basic and universal 'no,' but is always spoken in a

---

[86] Concerning the Ministry (LW, 40:37): "For since the church owes its birth to the Word, is nourished, aided and strengthened by it, it is obvious that it cannot be without the Word. If it is without the Word it ceases to be a church . . . and if papal bishops are unwilling to bestow the ministry of the Word except on such as destroy the Word of God and ruin the church, then it but remains either to let the church perish without the Word or to let those who come together cast their ballots and elect one or as many as are needed of those who are capable."

[87] Concerning Rebaptism (LW, 40:231-32). This text, however, is not to be interpreted as an ecumenical gesture, for in the next paragraph Luther goes on to assert that the pope is the Antichrist. It is quoted here simply to show that Luther was aware of the fact that he stood in a tradition through which he had received much of his faith, and that if he now rebelled against that tradition he had to do so as its son and product.

specific situation."[88] There are numerous indications that it was always with profound regret that he pronounced such words of rejection.

The most significant feature of Luther's ecclesiology, and the one that seems to determine much of the rest, is the universal priesthood of believers.[89] Here again Luther has been misrepresented, as if he were claiming simply that every Christian is his or her own priest. This is true,[90] but what is most important is that every Christian is a priest to others, "for as priests we are worthy to appear before God to pray for others and to teach one another divine things."[91] This common priesthood of all in behalf of all binds the church together, for no Christian may claim to be such without accepting the honor and responsibility of priesthood.

Obviously, this understanding of the priesthood, which Luther derives from his exegesis, undercuts the hierarchical vision of the church that the Roman Catholics defended. Luther was well aware of this, and pointed it out as early as 1520, in *The Babylonian Captivity of the Church*.[92] Thus, the universal priesthood of believers is the force that at once binds Luther's church together and liberates it from subjection to hierarchical authority.

On the other hand, Luther did not wish to leave the door open to "those who qualify themselves and preach whatever they please."[93] The public preaching of the gospel is an awesome responsibility[94] and should not simply be entrusted to anyone. Among the universal priesthood, God calls some to this ministry. This call has to be attested by the community, for "today, He calls all of us into the ministry of the Word by a mediated call, that is, one that comes

---

[88] Althaus, *The Theology of Martin Luther*, p. 335.

[89] *Treatise on the New Testament* (*LW*, 35:101): "Therefore all Christian men are priests, all women priestesses, be they young or old, master or servant, mistress or maid, learned or unlearned. Here there is no difference."

[90] *The Misuse of the Mass* (*LW*, 36:139): "Thus every Christian on his own may pray and have access to God."

[91] *The Freedom of a Christian* (*LW*, 31:355).

[92] (*LW*, 36:112): "If they were forced to grant that all of us who have been baptized are equally priests, as indeed we are, and that only the ministry was committed to them . . . they would then know that they have no right to rule over us except insofar as we freely concede it."

[93] *Sermon*, August 27, 1531 (*LW*, 51:224).

[94] Just how awesome Luther felt it to be, may be seen in the following text, from the sermon quoted above (*LW*, 51:222): "If I could come down with good conscience, I would rather be stretched upon a wheel or carry stones than preach one sermon. For anyone who is in this office will always be plagued; and therefore I have often said that the damned devil and not a good man should be a preacher."

through means, namely, through man."[95] This usually means a call through a prince, magistrate, or congregation. The "sectarians," who claim that they have been called to preach their doctrines from place to place, and this call has come directly to them from the Spirit, are "liars and impostors."

The Sacraments

The Word of God comes to us first of all in Jesus Christ. But, in a derivative sense, it comes also through Scripture, through the preaching of the gospel, and through the sacraments. The sacraments are physical acts that God has chosen to be signs of the promise. They are intimately connected with faith and with the Word, for their function is precisely to be another form in which the Word is heard in faith. In order to qualify as a sacrament, an act must have been instituted by Christ and must be bound with the promise of the gospel. Therefore, there are only two sacraments: baptism and the eucharist.

Baptism is the sign of justification. "Baptism, then, signifies two things—death and resurrection, that is, full and complete justification."[96] In it, the Word of God comes to us, and therefore it is no more and no less than the gospel itself. However, as there is a tension in justification between the imputation of justice and the fact that righteousness is an eschatological promise, so is there a tension in baptism. Baptism is the beginning of the Christian life, but it is also the sign under which that entire life takes place. The person who is at once justified and a sinner must constantly die and be resurrected.

Baptism is indissolubly bound with faith. There can be no true sacrament without faith. This does not mean, however, that faith must precede baptism. What happens, rather, is that in baptism, as in faith, the initiative is God's, who bestows faith. "True, one should add faith to baptism. But we are not to base baptism on faith. There is quite a difference between having faith, on the one hand, and depending on one's faith and making baptism depend on faith, on the other. Whoever allows himself to be baptized on the strength of

---

[95] *Lectures on Galatians*, 1:1 (*LW*, 26:17).
[96] *The Babylonian Captivity of the Church* (*LW*, 36:67).

his faith, is not only uncertain, but also an idolator who denies Christ. For he trusts and builds on something of his own."[97]

This was the main reason that Luther insisted on infant baptism:[98] to deny baptism to infants, on the ground that they have no faith, would imply that the power of baptism—and therefore of the gospel—depends on our ability to receive it. This would simply be a new form of justification by works.

It was on the question of the eucharist, however, that Luther found himself involved in the most bitter and prolonged controversies, not only with Roman Catholics, but also with the more extreme reformers, and even with the relatively moderate Swiss reformers.[99]

Luther's main objections to the Roman doctrine and practice of the Lord's Supper may be found in *The Babylonian Captivity of the Church,* where he claims that this sacrament is held by the church in a threefold captivity. The first is the withholding of the cup from the laity; the second is the doctrine of transubstantiation, which makes the sacrament a captive of Aristotelian metaphysics; the third is the doctrine that the mass is "a good work and a sacrifice." Later, Luther rejected other Roman Catholic practices, such as the saying of private masses. But in general his opposition to Roman Catholicism in this regard had been clearly defined by the time he wrote this treatise.[100] As these views were condemned by the Roman church, and as other issues became more important, this particular aspect of the polemics receded into the background, although Luther continued holding the views expressed in *The Babylonian Captivity.*

A more lengthy and involved controversy developed when some in the Protestant camp began suggesting that Luther had not gone far enough, and that the bodily presence of Christ in the sacrament was to be denied.[101] Again, this is not the place to narrate that controversy. Later on, in discussing the Swiss reformers and the Anabaptists, their

---

[97] *Concerning Rebaptism (LW,* 40:252).

[98] See P. Althaus, "M. Luther über die Kindertaufe," *ThLZ,* 73 (1948): 702-14.

[99] The fact that in general he had to contend first with the Roman Catholics, and later with the Protestants, shaped the development of his thought. There is a brief but excellent summary of that development in Althaus, *The Theology of Martin Luther,* pp. 375-91.

[100] On the question of how much Luther retained of traditional eucharistic doctrine, see: H. Hilgenfeld, *Mittelalterlich-traditionelle Elemente in Luthers Abendmahlsschriften* (Zurich: Theologischer Verlag, 1971).

[101] W. Köhler, *Zwingli und Luther: Ihr Streit über das Abendmahl nach seinen politischen und religiösen Beziehungen,* 2 vols. (Gütersloh: C. Bertelsman, 1948, 1953).

views will be expounded in more detail. Let it suffice to say here that in general Luther's opponents claimed that Christ's presence in the Lord's Supper was "symbolic" or "spiritual" rather than bodily, and that the act of communion was essentially one of remembrance of the Lord's passion.

These views Luther could not accept. His reasons for this were not that they were too radical—he had shown his willingness to be radical when the situation demanded it—but that they contradicted what he took to be the clear sense of Scripture,[102] and that they were grounded on views that differed from the teaching of Scripture. The text of the Bible said clearly and unambiguously "This is my body." Therefore, that was exactly what Christ meant. In this respect, Luther was convinced that the Romans were closer to the true meaning of Scripture than his Protestant opponents. Therefore, he declared, he would rather eat the body of Christ with the papists than eat bread with the enthusiasts.

Two basic objections were made by his opponents; but these were two objections that Luther could not accept, for they contradicted his basic understanding of the biblical message.

The first objection was that the body of Christ was in heaven, at the right hand of God, and could not therefore be on the altar.[103] To this Luther responded that the body of Christ was not in heaven like a bird in its nest. The "right hand of God" is everywhere, and therefore Christ's body is present everywhere—in other words, it is ubiquitous. This is very closely connected with Luther's understanding of the incarnation. His doctrine of the two natures tends to be unitive rather than divisive, with a strong emphasis on the *communicatio idiomatum*. Through the incarnation, the body of Christ

---

[102] *The Sacrament of the Body and Blood of Christ* (LW, 36:335-36) : "For we have before us the clear text and the plain words of Christ: 'Take, eat; this is my body, which is given for you. Drink of it, all of you, this is my blood, which is poured out for you. Do this in remembrance of me.' These are the words on which we take our stand. They are so simply and clearly stated that even they, our adversaries, must confess that it is difficult to interpret them otherwise. Yet they pass these clear words by and follow their own thoughts, making darkness for themselves in the midst of the bright light."

[103] *Ibid.* (LW, 36:342): "They also say that he sits at the right hand of God, but what it means that Christ ascends to heaven and sits there, they do not know. It is not the same as when you climb up a ladder into the house. It means rather that he is above all creatures and in all and beyond all creatures. That he was taken up bodily, however, occurred as a sign of this. . . . They speculate thus, that he must ascend and descend from the heavens through the air, and that he lets himself be drawn down into the bread when we eat his body. Such thoughts come from no other source than from foolish reason and the flesh."

has not ceased to be a physical body; but it has been endowed with the predicates of the divine nature. Therefore, the body of Christ has the power to be everywhere at the same time. But in this case, as in the more general case of God's revelation, everywhere would mean nowhere unless God had chosen a particular locus and said "This is my body."[104] What we have here is a situation parallel to that of the theology of glory and the theology of the cross. The theologian of glory, seeking the absolute God, the one who is present in all the works of creation, does not find God. The theologian of the cross seeks and finds God as hidden in the sacrament of the altar.

The second objection has to do with the relationship between the physical and the spiritual.[105] Briefly stated, that objection was as follows: faith is a spiritual matter; the spirit has nothing to do with the flesh; therefore, the bodily presence of Christ would have nothing to do with faith. Luther saw clearly that this was the sort of thought that moved most of the opponents of the bodily presence. And he also saw that this contradicted his understanding of "flesh" and "spirit" as they are used in the New Testament. The opposite of spirit is not body, but flesh, and this is not our physical aspect, but our self-reliance and our rebelliousness. The spiritual comes to us in the physical. It comes to us in the body of Christ hanging on the cross. And it comes also in the body of Christ present in the elements.

When asked how the bodily presence took place, Luther simply responded that he did not know and that it was not his place to ask. He rejected transubstantiation, first of all, because it made the sacrament a captive of Aristotle, and second, because it denied the permanence of the bread and the wine. His own teaching was that the bread and the wine, while remaining such, also became vehicles in which the body and blood of Christ were present. Later theologians called this view "consubstantiation," to indicate that the substances of the elements remained and that the body and blood were added to them. The body of Christ is in the bread; the bread is still bread; the rest is a mystery and is best left as such.

---

[104] *Ibid.*: "Although he is present in all creatures, and I might find him in stone, in fire, in water, or even in rope, for he certainly is there, yet he does not wish that I seek him there apart from the Word, and cast myself into the fire or the water, or hang myself on the rope. He is present everywhere, but he does not wish that you grope for him everywhere. Grope rather where the Word is, and there you will lay hold of him in the right way."

[105] Pelikan, *Luther the Expositor*, pp. 145-51.

As we shall see later on, these were views that other reformers could not accept and that therefore became one of the main points of contention, first between Luther and the Swiss reformers, and later between the Lutheran and the Reformed confessions.

The Two Kingdoms

Luther's understanding of the relationship between church and state is usually stated as the doctrine of the two kingdoms, or the two realms.[106] This is correct, although it must be clarified. The doctrine of the two kingdoms does not mean what is understood today by separation of church and state. Rather, it is a doctrine that is closely related to Luther's distinction between law and gospel, and that cannot be understood apart from that distinction.

Basically, what Luther has to say regarding church and state is that God has established two kingdoms. Both are God's creation, and both stand under God's rule. But one is under the law—in its first, or "civil" function—and the other is under the gospel. The civil order has been established by God to restrain the wicked and curb the most extreme consequences of their sin. Its ruler does not have to be a Christian, for the basic law by which one is to govern can be discerned by natural reason. Furthermore, most rulers are not Christians, and the existence of a Christian ruler should be more cause of surprise than the opposite case. The believers, however, belong to a different kingdom. It is the kingdom of the gospel, where one is no longer subject to the law. In this kingdom civil rulers have no authority, just as believers, as such, have no authority in the civil rule. But here one must remember that in this life every believer is at once justified and still a sinner. Therefore, as sinners, we are all subject to the civil rule.

This distinction between the two kingdoms has certain practical consequences. Of these, the most important are that Christians should not presume on the support of the state or of physical force for true religion, and that rulers should not make the church a mere tool of their civil government. Luther himself, when warned that a certain duke was wishing him ill, affirmed that he had a protection that was much stronger than any princely sword, and that he would

---

106 There is a good summary of recent discussion on this subject in H. Bornkamm, *Luther's Doctrine of the Two Kingdoms in the Context of His Theology* (Philadelphia: Fortress Press, 1966), pp. 1-4.

not fear if for nine days dukes nine times more ferocious than the particular duke in question would rain upon him. He insisted that the state should not use its power to persecute heretics, for matters of faith could not be decided by the sword. When John of Saxony considered giving up his civil functions because his Christian conscience was disturbing him, Luther admonished him to remain in the position where God had placed him. When, on the other hand, some of the enthusiasts began attempting to establish theocracies, Luther condemned their efforts.

In any case, the doctrine of the two kingdoms is not a way of delimiting God's action in the world. Both kingdoms are ruled by God. And they are not simply coextensive with the church and the state. Rather, the doctrine of the two kingdoms is the law-gospel principle as applied to our daily life within our historical situation. Therefore, as the borders between law and gospel are at once very important and not clearly set in a fixed way, so the boundaries between the two kingdoms, though very important, cannot simply be identified with the distinction between church and state or between two different types of activity, one religious and the other secular.[107]

Luther died at Eisleben, the place of his birth, on February 18, 1546. By that time the reformation that he unleashed had spread throughout Europe, and it was clear that it would not be a fire easily quenched. Also by that time the followers of that reformation had become divided by petty nationalisms as well as by theological differences. Some of these he saw as less Christian than the Roman Church, which he had so bitterly attacked. Many came to view him as practically a papist. But very few, be they Roman Catholics, Lutherans, or Anabaptists, were not greatly influenced by this man and his work. How that influence endured will be seen in the following chapters.

---

[107] *Ibid.*, p. 8: "These 'kingdoms' are not rigidly fixed provinces into which the Christian's existence is divided. He cannot live only in one or the other. He must live in both, and whether he will or not, he must continually act in both." See W. D. J. Cargill Thompson, *The Political Thought of Martin Luther* (Brighton, Sussex: Harvester, 1984).

III

Ulrich Zwingli and the Beginning of the Reformed Tradition

The reform movement begun by Luther soon counted adherents and sympathizers in various parts of Europe. The entire continent was ripe for reformation, and in various places that reformation took the Protestant direction. In varying degrees, the entire movement was influenced by Luther. But the forces unleashed by Luther could not be controlled by any one person—certainly not by Luther himself. Thus arose various diverging views that agreed with Luther on some points but strongly disagreed on others. At first there seemed to be no pattern to these various views, for the possible points of divergence were many, and therefore an exhaustive description of Protestant theology in the sixteenth century would require separate discussions of at least two dozen significant theologians. Fortunately, however, it is possible to classify Protestant theology in the sixteenth century into four basic groups or traditions: the Lutheran, the Reformed, the Anabaptist, and the Anglican. This classification does not seem to be too much of an oversimplification, and thus will be used here for reasons of clarity. As in the previous chapter we discussed the beginning of the Lutheran tradition, we must now turn to Ulrich Zwingli, in whom the Reformed tradition has its earliest theologian. In later chapters we shall discuss the Anabaptist and Anglican traditions, as well as the further development of Lutheranism with Melanchthon and his contemporaries, and the high point of Reformed theology with John Calvin.

Ulrich Zwingli and Luther differed in many ways. The most noticeable of these is the manner in which each of them came to his basic convictions: whereas Luther followed an anguished spiritual pilgrimage dealing with the basic issue of his relationship with God, Zwingli was led by patriotic and intellectual considerations.[1]

Zwingli's patriotism was aroused by the practice of mercenary service, which was one of the main sources of income for many Swiss towns and villages. For generations, the Swiss had enjoyed the reputation of being brave and solid soldiers, and had capitalized on that reputation by selling their services to foreign princes. In Zwingli's time this had become accepted practice and hardly a voice was heard against it, although many acknowledged that the life of mercenary soldiers, having to supplement their income by looting, was not conducive to the highest moral standards. Zwingli himself supported the practice of mercenary service, and profited economically from it. But after the battle of Marignano (1515), where large numbers of Swiss soldiers died for an unworthy cause not their own, and when others simply sold themselves to Francis I for a higher price, Zwingli began attacking the practice of mercenary service. These attacks were not well received by some of his parishioners in the town of Glarus, and he felt compelled to leave that parish. As the years went by, these patriotic concerns became closely connected with the reformation of the church, and therefore Zwingli's reform movement always had nationalistic and political overtones. This can be seen in his insistence that the law of the gospel is not only for individual Christians but that states also are expected to obey it. Thus, it was both fitting and symbolic that Zwingli, whose first frictions with the established church were the result of his concern for the honor of his country and the lives of its soldiers, should die at

---

[1] The best biography is that of O. Farner, *Huldrych Zwingli*, 4 vols. (Zurich: Zwingli Verlag, 1943-60). See also: J. Courvoisier, *Zwingli* (Geneva: Labor et Fides, 1947); J. Rilliet, *Zwingli: Third Man of the Reformation* (London: Lutterworth Press, 1964); M. Haas, *Huldrych Zwingli und seine Zeit: Leben und Werk des Zürcher Reformators* (Zurich: Theologischer Verlag, 1982); U. Glaber, *Huldrych Zwingli: Eine Einfürung in sein Leben und sein Werk* (München: Beck, 1983); E. J. Furcha and H. W. Pipkin, eds., *Prophet, Pastor, Protestant: The Work of Huldrych Zwingli After Five Hundred Years* (Allison Park, Pa.: Pickwick Publications, 1984); W. P. Stephens, *The Theology of Huldrych Zwingli* (Oxford: Clarendon, 1985). A good introduction to a number of subjects is the collection of essays in G. W. Locher, *Zwingli's Thought: New Perspectives* (Leiden: Brill, 1981). Further resources in H. W. Pipin, ed., *A Zwingli Bibliography* (Pittsburgh: Pittsburgh Theological Seminary, 1972).

the battle of Cappel, where he had accompanied the troops of Zurich as their chaplain.[2]

Zwingli's intellectual interests ran along the lines of Erasmian humanism. His father and other relatives had made it possible for him to receive an excellent education. His studies took him to the universities of Vienna and Basel. At Basel he met a number of fellow students who later would be his companions in the task of reformation. He also studied there under Thomas Wyttenbach, who attacked indulgences even before Luther, and whom Zwingli later credited with having taught him the sufficiency of Christ for salvation.[3] But it was especially Erasmus himself who captivated the mind of the young scholar.

Zwingli had visited Erasmus at Basel in 1515. The famous humanist had made a profound impression on the young Swiss. But the influence of Erasmus on Zwingli took place mostly through the written word. In his early years, concerned about mercenary service as he was, Zwingli found support in the pacifism of Erasmus.[4] As events unfolded, and Zwingli became involved in the political and military considerations connected with the defense of the reformation in the Protestant cantons, he abandoned the pacifist position. In 1523 Ulrich von Hutten took refuge in Zurich, and from there wrote a treatise attacking Erasmus. As Erasmus blamed Zwingli for the protection that Zurich gave Hutten, this incident was the end of their friendship. But in spite of this, Zwingli continued admiring the Dutch scholar and holding his works and his methods of inquiry in high regard. Therefore, even after the end of their friendship, Erasmus was one of the main influences shaping Zwingli's thought.[5]

The Sources and Task of Theology

Luther came to the conviction of the priority of Scripture above tradition through a long struggle in which he discovered the tension

---

[2] W. Schaufelberger, "Kappel (1531): Die Hintergründe einer militärischen Katastrophe," *SchArchVk,* 51 (1955): 34-61.

[3] J. Rilliet, *Zwingli: Third Man of the Reformation,* pp. 27-28.

[4] J. Rogge, *Zwingli und Erasmus: Die Friedensgedanken des jungen Zwingli* (Stuttgart: Calwer Verlag, 1962).

[5] A. Rich, *Die Anfänge der Theologie Huldrych Zwinglis* (Zurich; Zwingli Verlag, 1949), p. 9-72, 151-64.

between the two; Zwingli's case was different.[6] He approached the Scriptures as a Christian humanist. His return to the Bible was part of the general return to the sources that characterized the humanist movement. As a humanist, he believed that the way to rediscover the true nature of Christianity was to discover the message of Scripture and apply it to the renewal of Christianity. Even apart from its inspiration, the Bible had historical priority, and thus was a better witness than later tradition. But the Bible is also inspired, and therefore the priority of Scripture is not only a historical, humanistic assertion, but also one that one makes on the basis of faith. In fifteen theses for debate that Zwingli published early in 1523, he clearly states that it is impossible to understand Scripture apart from divine guidance. He does not simply study it as a humanist would study any other text. But he does apply to the interpretation of Scripture the principles that he had learned from his humanistic studies, and therefore his exegesis tends to be less allegorical than had become customary.

As in the case of Luther, Zwingli understands by "Word of God" not only the Scriptures, but also the creative action of God. It is of this active Word that he says that "the whole course of nature must be altered rather than that the Word of God should not remain and be fulfilled."[7] However, as the Scriptures are an expression of that Word, they are also infallible and certain to be fulfilled. "In his Word we can never go astray. We can never be deluded or confounded or destroyed in his Word. If you think there can be no assurance or certainty for the soul, listen to the certainty of the Word of God. The soul can be instructed and enlightened . . . so that it perceives that its whole salvation and righteousness, or justification, is enclosed in Jesus Christ."[8]

This does not mean, however, that the only way in which we can know God is through Holy Scriptures. On the contrary, the existence of God can be known by human reason. "*What* God is is perhaps

---

[6] A. Rich, "Zwinglis Weg zur Reformation," *Zwingliana*, 8 (1948): 511-35.

[7] *Of the Clarity and Certainty or Power of the Word of God* (*LCC*, 24:70).

[8] *Ibid.* (*LCC*, 24:84).

above human understanding, but not *that* God is."[9] All the heathen have known God in some fashion or another, although some have gone so far as to divide him into several different deities, while others have known that there is only one God. The reason for this is not that humans possess a "natural" knowledge of God, for "the knowledge of God which we credit to some natural agency is really from God."[10]

On the other hand, the true knowledge of God—the knowledge of *what* God is—can come to us only through divine revelation, in Scripture. Our knowledge of God is so far removed from God's reality that in comparison a beetle knows more about us than we know about God. The reason for this is the wide chasm separating the creature from the Creator—a chasm of which Zwingli is acutely and constantly aware.

This in turn means that, although the philosophers did know some things about God and we may well find them coinciding with the teachings of Scripture, we are not to take them as sources for our theology.

> All, therefore, is sham and false religion that the theologians have adduced from philosophy as to what God is. If certain men have uttered certain truths on this subject, it has been from the mouth of God, who has scattered even among the heathen some seeds of the knowledge of Himself, though sparingly and darkly; otherwise they would not be true. But we, to whom God Himself has spoken through His Son and through the Holy Spirit, are to seek these things not from those who were puffed up with human wisdom, and consequently corrupted what they received pure, but from the divine oracles. For when men began to disregard these, they fell into all that is fleshly, *i.e.,* into the inventions of philosophy. . . . Such is the arrogance of the flesh that gave itself out as theology. We wish to learn out of His mouth what God is, lest we become corrupt and do abominable works.[11]

Thus, in theory at least, Zwingli wishes to draw his entire theology

---

[9] *On True and False Religion*, in *The Latin Works of Huldreich Zwingli*, ed. S. M. Jackson, *et al.*, 3 vols. (Philadelphia: Heidelberg Press, 1912–29), 3:58. Hereafter this edition will be referred to as *Lat. Zwingli.*

[10] *Ibid.*, p. 59.

[11] *Ibid.*, p. 62.

out of Scripture.[12] And yet, when, immediately after these words, he goes on to discuss the nature of God, most of his argument seems to be taken from the philosophers rather than from Scripture. This illustrates the manner in which humanism works in Zwingli's theology: the need to return to the sources points in the direction of the sole authority of Scripture, but the humanistic appreciation for antiquity makes him see a great deal of agreement between Scripture and the best of antiquity. This will be seen again as we discuss the relationship between divine providence and predestination.

Providence and Predestination

Zwingli's notion of God is closely connected with the notion of the absolute. His arguments for monotheism are based not so much on Scripture as on the claim that the existence of more than one absolute being is a logical impossibility.[13] Therefore, the biblical assertion that all things are in God is to be taken very literally, meaning "that nothing is hidden from Him, nothing unknown to Him, nothing beyond His reach, nothing disobedient to Him." The mosquito's sting has been foreknown and foreordained by God, and to ask why God made this and other seemingly evil things is "a vain and useless feminine [!] curiosity."[14] All that we can do about God's creation, with its seeming contradictions, is to accept it and believe that all these things are done on the basis of a plan that God's infinite wisdom has not wished to reveal to us. Thus the doctrine of providence as here expounded is not merely the affirmation that we can trust God for our sustenance and well-being, but also the assertion that the relationship between God and the world is such that everything takes place through the will of God.[15]

It is from this perspective that Zwingli approaches the doctrine of predestination, "for the whole business of predestination, free will,

---

[12] *Ibid.* (*Lat.Zwingli*, 3:98): "It is, therefore, madness and utter impiety to put the enactments and decrees of certain men or certain councils upon an equality with the word of God. For if their dicta are like God's word, it is the word that must be embraced, not the authority of men; if they are unlike it, they are to be rejected and shunned."

[13] *An Exposition of the Faith* (*LCC*, 24:246).

[14] *On True and False Religion* (*Lat. Zwingli*, (3:67).

[15] *Sermon, August 10, 1530* (*Lat. Zwingli*, 2:136): "Providence is the enduring and unchangeable rule over and direction of all things in the universe."

and merit rests upon this matter of providence."[16] God not only knows all things, but also does all things, for "secondary causes are not properly called causes," and God alone is the primary cause of all things.[17] To deny this, would be to deny the very nature of God, as even the pagan philosophers knew.[18] Anything less than absolute predeterminism would impinge on the sovereignty and wisdom of God.

On creating humankind and the angels, God knew that some among them would fall—knew and ordained it. God's purpose in doing this was that all could better understand the nature of righteousness by contrasting it with unrighteousness. The fall of Satan and of Adam and Eve did not happen against the will of God. "God wrought both of these things. . . . Yet He is not Himself unrighteous, nor is what He did unrighteousness as far as he is concerned, for He is not under the law."[19] Furthermore, this should not lead to the conclusion that God is wicked or does not love creation, for it was actually out of love that God did these things, so that we all might know the true nature of faithfulness and righteousness.

On the basis of this doctrine of predestination,[20] Zwingli can easily refute every attempt to base salvation on works. Salvation is the result of divine election and not of any effort on our part. What then of the many texts in Scripture that seem to connect salvation with works? They are easily explained if only one keeps in mind that human works—as well as everything else that happens in creation—are the result of God's predestination. In those who are elected, God produces good works, and therefore good works are necessary to salvation, not in the sense that they produce it, but in the sense that election is also election to good works.[21] On the other hand, the opposite is also true of the reprobate, in whom God works evil; and yet this evil is imputed to them who are under the law, and not to God, who is above it.

---

[16] *On True and False Religion* (*Lat. Zwingli*, 3:70).
[17] *Sermon, August 20, 1530* (*Lat. Zwingli*, 2:138).
[18] *Ibid.*, p. 153.
[19] *Ibid.*, p. 176.
[20] Cf. G. W. Locher, "Die Prädestinationslehre Huldrych Zwinglis," *ThZschr*, 12 (1956) : 526-48.
[21] *Sermon, August 20, 1530* (*Lat. Zwingli*, 2:189).

Election and reprobation thus manifest themselves in outward signs, so that one can have a fairly accurate measure of who the elect are, and especially of one's own election. Those who claim election, but abandon God in moments of adversity, are not really among the elect.[22] Those who live in evil are probably among the reprobate, although they may also be among those predestined to salvation whose election has not been manifested yet. As to the pagans of antiquity, and any others who have not had the opportunity to hear the gospel, they may well be among the elect, for they will be judged on a different basis—and here Zwingli affirms that he would choose the lot of Seneca or of Socrates rather than that of the Pope.[23]

One of the most interesting traits in Zwingli's theology is his insistence on God's desire to communicate. The entire process of creation is a communication of God.[24] And as the crown of that creation God made us, who can communicate with the Divine.

In our fallen state, it is impossible for us to know ourselves. We are as difficult to catch as squid, for we too are apt to hide by obscuring the waters when someone is about to catch us. "He has such recklessness in lying, such readiness in pretending and concealing, that when you think you have caught him somewhere, you find he has long since slipped away elsewhere."[25] Thus, just as we need divine revelation in order to know God, we also need it in order to know ourselves.[26] The reason for this is the fall, which consisted in Adam's disobedience to the law of God for reason of self-love. Self-love is the root of all sin, for Adam broke the law by seeking to be like God. This original sin of Adam is not strictly transmitted to his progeny; what is transmitted is the result of that sin, which Zwingli prefers to call "a disease"[27] This in no way mitigates the consequences of original sin, for Zwingli asserts that the reason the "theologians and hypocrites of animal appetite" insist on freedom of choice is that they do not know

---

[22] *Ibid.*, pp. 199-200.
[23] *Ibid.*, p. 201.
[24] *On True and False Religion* (*Lat. Zwingli*, 3:70-71).
[25] *Ibid.*, pp. 76-76.
[26] *Ibid.*, p. 76: "The knowledge of God is denied to our understanding because of its feebleness and His glory and splendor, but the knowledge of man, because of his boldness and readiness in lying and dissembling." 3:119: "It is a result brought by the Divine Spirit alone that man knows himself."
[27] *An Account of the Faith* (*Lat. Zwingli*, 2:40-41).

the depth of the consequences of original sin[28]—an assertion that is not entirely consistent with his other claim that the very nature of God precludes free will.

In summary, predestination and the denial of freedom of choice follow from the nature of God as well as from our present state.

Law and Gospel

As a result of his different approach to theology, Zwingli's understanding of law and gospel is not the same as Luther's. His answer to the question of the manner in which the law has been abolished, and the manner in which it is still valid, is much simpler than Luther's and therefore lacks the depth of the views of the German reformer. Zwingli sets out by distinguishing between three laws: the eternal law of God, as expressed in the moral commandments, the ceremonial laws, and the civil laws. The last two are of no consequence for this question, for they have to do with the outer person, and the matter of sin and righteousness has to do with the inner. Therefore, only the moral laws of the Old Testament are to be considered here, and these have by no means been abolished. The civil laws have to do with particular human situations. The ceremonial laws were given for the time before Christ. But the moral law expresses the eternal will of God and therefore cannot be abolished. What has happened in the New Testament is rather that the moral law has been summarized in the commandment of love. The gospel and the law are in essence the same. Therefore those who serve Christ are bound to the law of love, which is the same as the moral law of the Old Testament and the natural law inscribed in all hearts.[29] Thus, the first point at which Zwingli differs from Luther in this respect is his assertion that the law abides and that the gospel in no way contradicts it.

The second point of divergence between the two reformers with reference to the law has to do with their evaluation of it. Zwingli has not undergone the experience of feeling damned by the law, which has been formative for Luther. Therefore, he cannot accept Luther's assertion that the law is terrible and that its function is to speak God's

---

[28] *On True and False Religion* (Lat. *Zwingli,* 3:83).
[29] *Ibid.,* pp. 137-38.

word of judgment upon us. The reference to Luther is clear when Zwingli says that "at our time some persons of the first importance, as they think, have spoken without sufficient circumspection about the law in saying that the law is only to terrify, damn, and deliver over to torments. In reality, the law does not do that at all, but, on the contrary, sets forth the will and nature of the Deity."[30]

From this follows Zwingli's understanding of the gospel, which is in many ways similar and in many ways different from Luther's. Like Luther, Zwingli believes that the gospel is the good news that sins are remitted in the name of Christ. Like the German reformer, he asserts that this forgiveness can be received only when one is conscious of one's own wretchedness—although he assigns this function to the Spirit rather than to the law.[31] But he insists much more than Luther on the objective result of the gospel, making us whole and able to obey the law. "It would have been laughable if He to whom everything that is ever to be is seen as present had determined to deliver man at so great a cost, and yet had intended to allow him immediately after his deliverance to wallow in his old sins. He proclaims, therefore, at the start, that our lives and characters must be changed."[32]

Therefore, in the final analysis law and gospel are practically the same.[33] This follows logically from Zwingli's understanding of divine providence and predestination. The will of God is always the same, and it has been revealed in the law. The function of the gospel, then, is to liberate us from the consequences of our having broken the law and to enable us to obey it.

The Church and the State

Zwingli's doctrine of the church is closely related to his doctrine of predestination.[34] In the strict sense, the church is the company of the elect. Since these will not be clearly manifested until the last day, this church is invisible to human eyes. But the confession of the name of

---

[30] *Sermon, August 20, 1530 (Lat. Zwingli, 2:166).*
[31] *On True and False Religion (Lat. Zwingli, 3:119).*
[32] *Ibid., 3:120.*
[33] *CR, 89:79.*
[34] A brief but illuminating discussion of his development may be found in J. Courvoisier, *Zwingli: A Reformed Theologian* (London: Epworth Press, 1963), pp. 51-56.

Christ and a life according to his commandments are reasonable signs of election, and therefore the company of those who have these signs is also called the church. The former is the "bride of Christ," and is the one that can properly be called "spotless." This is the church that cannot err, for it is predestined to be obedient to Christ. The latter—that is, the company of those who show signs of election—may err, but nevertheless is a necessary although provisional sign of the true church. Thus the contrast between the visible and the invisible church is an attempt not to lessen the importance of the earthly community, but to show how the church can be at once the number of the elect and a community living at a time when election has not been clearly manifested.

> We also believe that there is only one holy, catholic, that is, universal Church, and that this Church is either visible or invisible. According to the teaching of Paul, the invisible Church is that which came down from heaven, that is to say, the Church which knows and embraces God by the enlightenment of the Holy Spirit. To this Church belong all who believe the whole world over. It is not called invisible because believers are invisible, but because it is concealed from the eyes of men who they are: for believers are known only to God and to themselves.
>
> And the visible Church is not the Roman pontiff and others who bear the mitre, but all who make profession of faith in Christ the whole world over. In this number there are those who are called Christians falsely, seeing they have no inward faith. Within the visible church, therefore, there are some who are not members of the Church elect and invisible.[35]

As the visible church is to be a sign of the invisible, and as its task is the proclamation of the gospel, it has the obligation and the authority to discipline its ranks. Furthermore, as this church exists in local communities, that task is entrusted to the local congregations. "And so it is the office of these churches . . . to reject one who is shamelessly delinquent," and to decide on the orthodoxy of their pastors.[36] Although no single person can excommunicate another, the

---

[35] *An Exposition of the Faith* (LCC, 24:265-66). Cf. *Reply to Emser* (*Lat. Zwingli*, 3:366-82).
[36] *Reply to Emser* (*Lat. Zwingli*, 3:375).

congregation as a whole may do so in the case of an "open sinner."[37] This, however, in no way affects the sinner's relationship with God, for that is only a matter of election; it is rather a sign that the person in question seems to be a reprobate. If at a later time the sinner gives signs of election, he or she is to be readmitted into the congregation. In a similar fashion, the congregation must appoint those who are to be its ministers and will nurture it in the faith, but at the same time must judge them according to the Word of God, to see whether they are in truth ministers of that Word.

When it comes to the question of the relationship between church and state, Zwingli established between them a closer connection than did Luther.[38] This again has to do with his understanding of the function of the divine law. Although the Christian law is higher than civil law, they both express the one divine will, and there is no break between them. Thus, even those who are not among the elect, and who therefore do not follow the evangelical law, are subject to the law of God as it is manifested in the rulers and the civil law. Furthermore, owing to the historical circumstances in Zurich, Zwingli often speaks as if church and state were coextensive, or rather as if there were only one body called "church" with two offices or functions: government and ministry. "In the Church of Christ government and prophecy are both necessary, although the latter takes precedence. For just as man is necessarily constituted of both body and soul, the body being the lesser and humbler part, so there can be no Church without government, although government supervises and controls those more mundane circumstances which are far removed from the things of the Spirit."[39]

Thus, Zwingli seems to be speaking in terms that are closely parallel to the conceptions that justified the activities of Innocent III centuries earlier, although his Christendom has been greatly reduced in size. As he played an important role within the council that constituted the government in Zurich, the actual practice of government came very close to being a theocracy.

---

[37] *Sixty-seven Theses*, 31-32 (*CR*, 89:276-77).

[38] A. Farner, *Die Lehre von Kirche und Staat bei Zwingli* (Tübingen: J. C. B. Mohr, 1930); H. Schmid, *Zwinglis Lehre von der göttlichen und menschlichen Gerechtigkeit* (Zurich: Zwingli Verlag, 1959), pp. 221-58; R. C. Walton, *Zwingli's Theocracy* (Toronto: University Press, 1963).

[39] *An Exposition of the Faith* (*LCC*, 24:267-68).

The Sacraments

Zwingli's theory of sacraments was developed in opposition to
three other views: the Lutheran, the Catholic, and the Anabaptist.
This is clear in the treatise *On True and False Religion,* where Zwingli
offers his most succinct discussion of the general theory of
sacraments and outlines his discussion of the subject by describing
the views of these three groups and then proceeding to respond to
them. Against the Catholics, he argues from the original meaning of
the word "sacramentum" as an act of initiation or a pledge, and thus
denies that the sacraments "have any power to free the conscience."[40]
Against Luther—whom he does not mention by name—Zwingli
argues that the sacraments cannot be said to be outward signs of such
a nature that when they are performed an inward event takes place,
"for in this way the liberty of the Spirit . . . would be bound."[41]
Finally, against the Anabaptists, Zwingli objects that, if the
sacraments are simply signs of something that has already taken
place, they are useless. Against all these positions, he then proposes
one that places the community of believers at the center: "The
sacraments are, then, signs or ceremonials . . . by which a man proves
to the church that he either aims to be, or is, a soldier of Christ, and
which inform the whole church rather than yourself of your faith.
For if your faith is not so perfect as not to need a ceremonial sign to
confirm it, it is not faith. . . . For faith is that by which we rely on the
mercy of God unwaveringly, firmly, and singleheartedly."[42]

These sacraments are two in number: baptism, by which
Christians are initiated, and the Lord's Supper, which shows that
Christians keep in mind Christ's passion and victory and are
members of his church.[43]

Given this understanding of the sacraments, baptism cannot be
said to wash away the sins of the baptized. This would seem to lead
Zwingli into the camp of the Anabaptists, who insisted that children
should not be baptized. For this reason he felt compelled to write
extensively, showing how his position was compatible with infant

---

[40] *Lat. Zwingli,* 3:181.
[41] *Ibid.,* p. 183.
[42] *Ibid.,* p. 184.
[43] *Ibid.*

baptism. His argument is based on the analogy between circumcision and baptism as signs of the covenant.[44] Just as the ancients signaled their incorporation into Israel by the act of circumcision, so do Christians now signal incorporation into the church by the act of baptism. The fact that infants cannot believe is of minor consequence, for in any case what baptism signifies is not salvation through human achievement, but salvation through the grace of God. Thus the baptism of an infant is a reminder to the church of the grounds for its own salvation.

It was the Lord's Supper, however, that gave rise to the long controversy between Zwingli and Luther first, and later between their followers. For Zwingli, as for Luther, this was no small matter, "for I fear that if there is anywhere pernicious error in the adoration and worship of the one true God, it is in the abuse of the Eucharist."[45] The reason that the common errors with regard to the Lord's Supper must be avoided is that they are the beginning of all the various forms of idolatry that have crept into the church through the centuries. The truth is that the eucharist is no more than what its very name says: "the thanksgiving and common rejoicing of those who declare the death of Christ."[46] The sixth chapter of John, where Christ speaks of our eating his flesh, must be understood within its context, which has to do with believing in him, for "he is a means of salvation to us not by being eaten but by being slain."[47] As to the words of institution, the verb "is" must be understood in the sense of "signifies," as in so many other cases in which Christ says that he is a door, a shepherd, or a way.

For two basic reasons Zwingli was compelled to insist that Christ was not bodily present in the eucharist. The first was his understanding of the relationship between the material and the spiritual; the second was his view of the incarnation. Since in both of these he differed from Luther, the latter was right when he said, "We are not of the same spirit."

The first reason for rejecting the bodily presence may be seen

---

[44] J. W. Cottrell, *Covenant and Baptism in the Theology of Huldreich Zwingli* (Ann Arbor: University of Michigan Microfilms, 1971).

[45] *On True and False Religion* (*Lat. Zwingli*, 3:198-99).

[46] *Ibid.*, p. 200.

[47] *Ibid.*, p. 205.

when Zwingli says that "for the gaining of salvation I attribute no power to any elements of this world, that is, to things of sense."[48] "For body and spirit are such essentially different things that whichever one you take it cannot be the other."[49] Thus Zwingli's rejection of the bodily presence stems, in part at least, from the presupposition that the sacrament, in order to be spiritually profitable, must be purely spiritual. To assert the opposite would be dangerously close to idolatry.

The second reason for Zwingli's rejection of Luther's views is his understanding of the incarnation. If Luther's Christology is of the unitive type that in the patristic period was associated with the city of Alexandria, Zwingli's is of the divisive type that was characteristic of Antioch. He cannot accept the notion that the incarnation is such that through the *communicatio idiomatum* the human nature has become ubiquitous.[50] If Christ ascended to heaven and sits at the right hand of God, his body cannot be elsewhere.

Given their divergent presuppositions, it is not surprising that Luther and Zwingli, in spite of their common zeal for the reformation of the church, and in spite also of their earnest desire to reach an agreement at Marburg—although this is not the picture drawn by many historians—were unable to reach such an agreement.

In summary, Zwingli was in some ways a more radical reformer than Luther, and in other ways more conservative. He went much further than Luther in rejecting the traditional practices of the medieval church. One could almost say that, whereas Luther rejected only those elements in tradition which could be proven to contradict the clear text of Scripture, Zwingli took an opposite tack, rejecting everything except that which could be proven by Scripture. His task was the restoration of ancient Christianity. Zwingli's Zurich did away with the organ in the cathedral, in spite of the fact that Zwingli himself was an accomplished musician. In his views on the

---

[48] *Ibid.*, p. 211.

[49] *Ibid.*, p. 214.

[50] This is the function of Zwingli's doctrine of "alloeosis," which he draws from ancient rhetoric and which serves to explain the fact that Scripture speaks as if there were a real communication of properties *(communicatio idiomatum)* between the two natures of Christ. See G. W. Locher, *Die Theologie Huldrych Zwinglis im Lichte seiner Christologie* (Zurich: Zwingli Verlag, 1952), pp. 128-32.

sacraments, Zwingli went much further than Luther. And yet, something of the radical nature of Luther's experience has been lost in Zwingli's theology. No longer does one find here the dialectic of rebellion and redemption, of law and gospel, which was so fundamental for Luther. Nor do we hear the Word of God in radical judgment of every human word. Salvation by grace is now something that can almost be deduced from the divine omnipotence. The law has once again become our friend. Thus it would be inexact to say that Zwingli is a more radical reformer than Luther—in fact he mitigated a number of Luther's discoveries. But it would be even more inexact to say that he was more moderate than his German counterpart, for in many things he went far beyond Luther. Perhaps a proper assessment is that in Zwingli the Swiss reformation took its own shape, profoundly molded by Luther as well as by humanism, but also the product of the unique political and social circumstances that obtained in Switzerland. It is also fair to say that, through Calvin and later the entire Puritan tradition, the influence of Zwingli and the Swiss reformation was at least as significant as Luther's.

IV

Anabaptism and the Radical Reformation

The reformation advocated by Luther and Zwingli questioned
many of the teachings and practices of the traditional church, but it
accepted without too many misgivings a great many of the traditional
views regarding the state and its authority. Although their views on
the relationship between church and state differed considerably,
Luther and Zwingli agreed on the positive value and authority of the
state. Both taught that—within certain limits—Christians must obey
the state, and that they are called to serve in their different functions
within that state. It was unavoidable, however, that as the search for
original and purely scriptural Christianity was carried further some
would claim that the tension between the church and the Roman
Empire in the first centuries of Christianity was somehow normative,
that the church is not to be allied with government, that a true church
is always inviting persecution, and that the conversion of Constantine was therefore the great apostasy that marked the end of pure
Christianity.

This was one of the most common characteristics of a wide variety
of movements that developed immediately after the Lutheran
reformation.[1] This was not a new phenomenon, but one that had a
long tradition in the Middle Ages. The Waldensians, the early
Franciscans, the Fraticelli, and a host of other such movements had
embodied the dissatisfaction of many with the accepted state of

---

[1] A good general study of the entire movement is G. H. Williams, *The Radical Reformation*
(Philadelphia: Westminster Press, 1962).

affairs, especially in that which had to do with the relationship between Christian life and the existing powers. Therefore one should not be surprised that during the sixteenth century, and especially in Protestant territories, where so many of the traditional patterns of authority were being questioned and abolished, such movements proliferated. During the early stages of the Reformation, Luther and his followers had to contend with the extremism of Andreas Bodenstein von Carlstadt,[2] one of Luther's colleagues at Wittenberg, who felt that brother Martin had not gone far enough and who therefore took advantage of Luther's exile in the Wartburg to radicalize the reformation in Wittenberg. At Zwickau a movement developed whose "prophets" claimed that the Bible was not necessary, since they had the Spirit. Although Luther managed to eradicate such views from Wittenberg, they continued expanding in other parts of Germany. In 1524 the peasants revolted. This again was, in a way, the continuation of a long tradition of peasant rebellions. On this occasion the movement led to general insurrection and to bloody repression. It had as one of its prophets a man who had been profoundly influenced by Luther's views, Thomas Müntzer. Although Luther had repudiated Müntzer, many still linked Luther with the rebellion. Luther encouraged the princes to stamp it out by violence, and later called on them to show mercy on the vanquished peasants.[3] This episode, and others like it, convinced many of the more radical that Luther's reformation had not gone far enough, while the more conservative were reinforced in their opinion that Luther and his followers had opened a Pandora's box that they could not control.

Yet, not all the radical reformers were political revolutionaries. This was a picture drawn by Catholics, Lutherans, and Reformed in order to discredit a movement that all branches of established Christianity found embarrassing and even dangerous. To draw this picture, they pointed to the few real extremists among the radical reformers and presented them as typical of the entire movement.

---

[2] G. Fuchs, "Karlstadts radikal-reformatorisches Wirken und seine Stellung zwischen Müntzer und Luther," *WZMLU*, 3 (1954) : 523-51. C. A. Pater, *Karlstadt as the Father of the Baptist Movements* (Toronto: University of Toronto Press, 1984).

[3] See H. Kirchner, *Luther and the Peasants' War* (Philadelphia: Fortress, 1972); R. C. Crossley, *Luther and the Peasants' War* (New York: Exposition, 1974).

Therefore, in order to correct that picture, we must distinguish between the early leaders of the movement—most of whom were pacifists; the extremist wing, which developed under the pressure of persecution; and the final shape of the movement as it eventually survived. Furthermore, we must also distinguish between those whose final authority was the Bible, and others whose claims were based on the Spirit or on reason. From this follows the outline of the present chapter, which will discuss Anabaptism under three headings—"early," "revolutionary," and "later"—and will then turn to the spiritual and rationalist reformers.

The Early Anabaptist Movement

Although its opponents tried to connect the Anabaptist movement with the Zwickau prophets and Thomas Müntzer,[4] the truth seems to be that the actual Anabaptist movement began in Zurich, among some who thought that Zwingli was too moderate and cautious in his theology and policies.[5] Some of these were native Zurichers, and others were exiles who had come to that city because the Reformation was making headway in it. For some time they had been arguing that the New Testament required Christians to go much further than Zwingli was willing to go. They believed that the Reformation must purify not only theology but also the actual lives of Christians, especially in what had to do with social and political relationships. Therefore, the church should not be supported by the state, neither by tithes and taxes, nor by the use of the sword. Christianity was a matter of individual conviction, which could not be forced on anyone, but rather required a personal decision for it. It then follows that infants should not be baptized, for they cannot make such a decision. At first, these "Brethren"—as they called themselves—simply questioned infant baptism but did not rebaptize those who had been baptized as children.

---

[4] Cf. H. S. Bender, "Die Zwickauer Propheten, Thomas Müntzer und die Täufer," *ThZschr*, 8 (1952): 262-78; English version in *MQR*, 27 (1953): 3-16. Significant light on Müntzer as a mystic is shed by H. J. Goertz, *Innere und äussere Ordnung in der Theologie Thomas Müntzers* (Leiden: E. J. Brill, 1967). On his writings, see: G. Franz, "Bibliographie der Schriften Thomas Müntzers," in *Zeitschrift f. Thür. Gesch.*, new series, 34 (1940): 161-73.

[5] E. B. Bax, *Rise and Fall of the Anabaptists*, reprint (New York: American Scholar Publications, 1966), pp. 1-27; C. P. Clasen, *Anabaptism: A Social History, 1525–1618* (Ithaca: Cornell University Press, 1972), pp. 1-14; U. Gastaldi, *Storia dell'anabattismo: Dalle originia Münster (1525-1535)* (Torino: Claudiana, 1972); W. R. Estep, *Anabaptist Beginnings (1523-1533): A Source Book* (Nieuwkoop, B. de Graaf, 1976); E. Arnold, *The Early Anabaptists* (Rifton, N.Y.: Plough, 1984).

The momentous step was taken on January 21, 1525, when the exiled priest George Blaurock asked another of the Brethren, Conrad Grebel, to baptize him. This Grebel did, and immediately Blaurock began baptizing other members of the community. As all these people, being born in Christian homes, had been baptized, the opponents of the movement called them "Anabaptists," which means "rebaptizers." This name was not altogether exact, for the Anabaptists did not believe that they were rebaptizing anyone, but considered that they were rather administering the only valid form of baptism. Furthermore, the name is inexact in that the Anabaptists held a number of tenets that were at least as important to them as adult baptism, and therefore the name given them tends to focus attention on what is really the result, and not the basic reason, of their disagreement with other Christians. In any case, the decision to rebaptize themselves and others was a fateful one, for the ancient laws of Theodosius and Justinian had decreed the death penalty for any who practiced rebaptism. Those laws had been instituted against the Donatists, who were being punished for their civil rebelliousness more than for their heresy; but in spite of that they were now applied to the Anabaptists, and hundreds were killed.

On the other hand, although the most influential Anabaptist movement did begin in Zurich, there does not seem to be any connection between the Zurich group and at least two other places where similar views seem to have developed independently: Augsburg, and the Po Valley. The leader of the Augsburg conventicle was Hans Denck, who seems to have been influenced by Luther as well as by the Rhineland mystics. Although his best known disciple, Hans Hut, had earlier been a follower of Thomas Müntzer, the teachings of the prophet of revolution do not seem to have influenced him beyond a deep concern for social justice. In the Po Valley and its surroundings, a similar group arose under the leadership of Camilo Renato. This group—indirectly influenced by Michael Servetus—denied not only infant baptism, but also the traditional doctrines of the Trinity and the immortality of the soul.

As we cannot here follow all the strains of Anabaptism as they converge and diverge,[6] we must focus our attention on the leaders

---

[6] A good summary of the literature on the entire movement may be seen in W. Köhler, "Das Täufertum in der neueren kirchenhistorischen Literatur," *ARG*, 37 (1940) : 93-107; 38 (1941) : 349-65; 40 (1943) : 246-71; 41 (1944) : 164-87. On primary sources see *Quellen zur Geschichte der Täufer*, in several numbers of *QFRgesch*.

who seem to be most representative of the entire movement. Two of these are Conrad Grebel and Hans Denck. Therefore, they will serve as the basis for our exposition of early Anabaptist theology.

The goal after which Conrad Grebel (*ca.* 1498–1526)[7] and the other Anabaptist leaders were striving was the total restoration of New Testament Christianity. This had to be done not only in basic issues of theology, but also in matters of liturgy and church government. Thus, when Grebel and his Zurich associates learned that Thomas Müntzer was repudiating infant baptism—although not rebaptizing—and that he had translated the liturgy and had composed a number of hymns in German, they wrote congratulating him on his stance concerning baptism, but also arguing that singing in church had no basis in the New Testament and therefore was to be rejected.[8] It was this urge to restore primitive Christianity that led them to their views regarding the church and its relationship with the state.

It is clear that the nature of the church in the New Testament was very different from the traditional practice—both Catholic and Protestant—of making the church coextensive with the civil community. In the New Testament, the church is a community gathered from the world at large, very different from it, and consisting only of those who have personally decided to be incorporated into the body of Christ. At one point, Grebel and his friends suggested to Zwingli that such a church be formed at Zurich.[9] Denck and others preferred the terms "community" and "congregation" rather than "church."[10] All that we have to do to join this church is to repent of our sins and die to them, hold fast to Christ, and lead a new life.[11] Once we do this and express to the community our desire to join, we are to be received as brothers and sisters in Christ.

---

[7] H. S. Bender, *Conrad Grebel, c. 1498–1526: The Founder of the Swiss Brethren Sometimes Called Anabaptists* (Goshen, Ind.: The Mennonite Historical Society, 1950). See especially the bibliography on pp. 301-11. J. C. Wenger, *Conrad Grebel's Programatic Letters of 1524* (Scottdale, Pa.: Herald, 1985); L. Harder, ed., *The Sources of Swiss Anabaptism: The Grebel Letters and Related Documents* (Scottdale, Pa.: Herald, 1985).

[8] *Letter to Thomas Müntzer*, September 5, 1524 (*LCC*, 25:75): "We understand and have seen that thou hast translated the Mass into German and hast introduced new German hymns. That cannot be for the good, since we find nothing taught in the New Testament about singing, no example of it."

[9] Cf. *CR*, 91:33.

[10] Cf. *QFRgesch*, 24:41, 84, 109; F. H. Littell, *The Anabaptist View of the Church: An Introduction to Sectarian Protestantism* (Hartford: American Society of Church History, 1952).

[11] *CR*, 91:369.

This community is to receive no support from the world and its powers. Its ministers are chosen by it—not by the state—and supported through the voluntary giving of the members.[12] The state is not to be absolutely rejected. It has a function, and Christians do well in obeying its laws as long as they do not impinge upon the conscience. But the state deals with outer, "worldly" matters, and must not be allowed to attempt to rule over spiritual matters.[13] The sword must not be drawn to defend the faith.[14] On the contrary, the fellowship of believers must be ready to be a suffering community; indeed, it will be a suffering community, for the world does not understand its ways, but despises them. Although some Anabaptists disagreed, Grebel thought that Christians might attempt to elect fellow believers to positions of authority, in the hope that they would rule according to the will of God. But Christians are not to overthrow evil rulers, nor are they to defend themselves against them in any way other than by being ready to face persecution. Not even against a foreign enemy, nor against the Turks, may true believers arm themselves. As will be clearly seen, these views were regarded as subversive by authorities in a Christendom threatened by the Turks, and in Swiss cantons, such as Zurich, menaced by the Catholic cantons. This was one of the main reasons that the Anabaptists were persecuted.

What leads a person—man or woman, for most Anabaptists were egalitarian in this respect—into the true faith is not predestination. The doctrine of predestination, especially as taught by Zwingli, is an abomination and a way to excuse us and blame God for our sin. In no way can God be said to be the cause of evil, for God is good.[15] It is our will, in our rebellion against God, that creates evil. Sin consists in seeking oneself, in not yielding to God (*ungelassenheit*). "Yielding" (*gelassenheit*) is typical of the will of God. It is because God yields to the human will, and does not violate it, that we are allowed to continue as we are.[16] In Christ and in his suffering we have the clear manifestation of the divine willingness to yield. We in turn must yield to God if we are to become true Christians. Before God, what we do is

---

[12] *Ibid.*, 91:405.

[13] *Ibid.*, 93:33; *QFRgesch*, 24:85.

[14] Grebel in *Letter to Thomas Müntzer* (*LCC*, 25:80). Cf. H. S. Bender, *The Anabaptists and Religious Liberty in the Sixteenth Century* (Philadelphia: Fortress Press, 1970).

[15] *QFRgesch*, 24:28.

[16] *Ibid.*, p. 33.

nothing; and only what we do not do, our yielding and allowing God to take over, is something.[17]

The beginning of faith is in the hearing of the Word.[18] But upon this must follow conversion, whereby we turn away from our sin and self-will and yield to God. In conversion, through the blood of Christ, all sins are washed away and the convert enters into a new and holy life. This does not mean that we are free from sin, but that we now have power to resist it. If, on the other hand, we claim conversion and yet lack this power, our faith is not true. Such a person is a hypocrite, and must be banned from the fellowship of believers.[19] This, and the life of sin and perdition that goes with it, is to be feared more than death at the hands of the persecutors. The latter, rather than being feared, should be welcomed, for it is a sign that one stands in the tradition of the prophets, apostles, and early Christians.

All religious ceremonies must be simple and without excessive ritual.[20] They must adhere strictly to the practice of the New Testament. As has been said above, there is to be no liturgical singing. The central act of worship is the reading of the Word and its exposition. Baptism and the Lord's Supper are symbols of inner realities. Baptism is a symbol of conversion and of the washing away of sin,[21] and therefore is to be administered only to adult believers. Most of the early Anabaptists—it should be pointed out—baptized by pouring rather than by immersion. It was later that, in their efforts to approach the New Testament as much as possible, Anabaptists began baptizing by immersion. The Lord's Supper was usually administered in small groups, and its symbolism was connected with the fellowship that binds Christians among themselves and with Christ. The unworthy were not allowed to participate, for this would break down the symbolism of union.

In summary, early Anabaptism was an attempt to be consistent with the Protestant claim of a return to the authority of the New Testament. If this was to be taken seriously—so they claimed—it was

---

[17] *Ibid.*

[18] As in the case of Luther, the meaning of "Word" is multiple. But here the two most common meanings are the "inner Word" in everyone and the written Word in Scripture. Cf. *ibid.*, p. 38; 43-44. W. Wiswedel, "Zum 'Problem inneres und äusseres Wort' bei den Täufern des 16. Jahrhundert," *ARG*, 46 (1955): 1-20.

[19] *LCC*, 25:79-80.

[20] *QFRgesch*, 24:108-9.

[21] *LCC*, 25:80-81. Here Grebel argues that the sacrifice of Christ has freed children from the curse of original sin and that they are "saved without faith."

necessary to abandon all practices that had crept into the life of the church through the centuries. Above all, one must take the Sermon on the Mount quite literally and live by it, paying no attention to the many objections that unfaith raises about such a course of action.

The Revolutionary Anabaptists

The teachings of the early Anabaptists were not well received by either Catholics or most Protestant leaders. The ancient laws condemning to death all who practiced rebaptism were soon revived, and the history of Anabaptism became a long list of martyrs and exiles. At first the Protestants were reluctant to persecute the Anabaptists, for they knew what it was to be under the ban of the Empire. Therefore, a series of debates took place in which neither party succeeded in convincing its opponents. Finally, the persecution extended to all but a few Protestant lands, whose lords still felt uneasy about using the power of the state to punish heretics. In a few years, most of the early leaders of the movement were dead. Grebel escaped a martyr's end by dying of the plague. Dr. Balthasar Hübmaier (1485–1528), the reformer of Waldshut, and one of the most outstanding converts to Anabaptism, died gallantly at the stake.[22] Countless others followed a similar fate. But in spite of persecution—and partly because of it—the movement grew and spread. Many who left their homes fleeing persecution disseminated Anabaptist teachings in other parts of Europe. Large numbers of Anabaptists emigrated to places in Central Europe where there was greater tolerance.

Another consequence of persecution was further division within the movement, which had never been united, and the development of more radical positions. From the very beginning there were some in the movement who believed that they should possess all things in common, while others held opposite views. As so often happens under the pressure of persecution, eschatological expectation became very vivid and imminent for some, who became convinced that they were living in the latter days. The more moderate Swiss leaders were dead, and there was no one to check the proliferation of

---

[22] A dramatic, although dated, biography is H. C. Vedder, *Balthasar Hübmaier: The Leader of the Anabaptists*, reprint (New York: AMS Press, 1971). A very thorough study, with excellent bibliographical references is T. Bergsten, *Balthasar Hübmaier: Seine Stellung zu Reformation und Täufertum* (Kassel: J. G. Oncken, 1961).

extremism. Others among the more moderate had fled to Moravia, where there was some security. The more radical elements came rapidly to the foreground.

The bridge between the older and the radical Anabaptists may be seen in the person of Melchior Hoffman (ca. 1500–1543), a skinner by trade, who first became a Lutheran, then a Zwinglian, and finally an Anabaptist.[23] It was probably in Strasbourg, where there was a measure of tolerance, that he was rebaptized. Partly through his influence, Strasbourg became the center of an Anabaptist movement that spread along the Rhine Valley and well into the Netherlands. His orthodoxy was questioned even more than that of other Anabaptists, since he held Christ's flesh to have come down from heaven.[24] His preaching became increasingly apocalyptic, and he began claiming revelations of an impending end, when Christ would return and establish his kingdom in a New Jerusalem. As the movement was gaining strength in Strasbourg, many were convinced that this city would be the New Jerusalem. Hoffman's fanatical followers flocked to Strasbourg. In response, the opposition of the authorities became harsher. Hoffman predicted that he would be imprisoned for six months and that then the end would come. When he was in fact incarcerated the fanaticism of his followers rose to new heights. However, as the second part of his prophecy did not come true, his followers began reinterpreting what he had said. Hoffman had rejected the absolute pacifism of the earlier Anabaptists, claiming that when the Lord came he would require his followers to take the sword in order to establish his kingdom and destroy his enemies. What had been a future expectation with Hoffman now became a present call to arms with many of his followers. The Lord was calling his faithful to take up arms and establish godliness upon the earth.

Such was the radical preaching of John Matthys, a baker from Haarlem in the Netherlands, and of his most famous disciple, John of Leiden. As the situation in Strasbourg grew more difficult for the radical Anabaptists, their eyes began turning toward Münster, the principal city of Westphalia, where an uneasy truce between Catholics and Protestants created a situation of greater tolerance

---

[23] P. Kawerau, *Melchior Hoffman als religiöser Denker* (Haarlem: F. Bohn, 1954).
[24] *Ibid.*, pp. 46-50.

than elsewhere.[25] Radical Anabaptists began flocking to the city and eventually—after long and complicated political and even armed maneuvering—gained power in it. They then elected a new government from among themselves and proclaimed that the end was at hand. John Matthys and John of Leiden were in the city by this time, and their preaching contributed to the inflaming of the masses. Every event was taken to be a sign from on high, while many had visions and received other forms of revelations. A state of general tension ensued. The bishop, outside the city, was eagerly killing as many Anabaptists as he could. The Anabaptists, on their part, began by burning and otherwise destroying all the manuscripts, works of art, and other reminders of the traditional faith, and then went on to expel from the city all the "godless"—meaning Catholics and moderate Protestants. After Matthys died in a sortie against the besieging troops of the bishop, John of Leiden became the leader of the movement, which grew even more radical than before. Increasingly, the "saints" in Münster turned to the Old Testament for guidance. A woman, claiming that she had been called to be a new Judith, entered the bishop's camp hoping to kill him, but her plans were discovered and she was tortured and killed. By now the female population of the town far outnumbered the male, and so John of Leiden, appealing to the authority of the patriarchs in the Old Testament, decreed that polygamy was to be practiced, and that every woman in town was to be joined to man. Shortly thereafter John and his followers overcame a conspiracy to surrender the town to the bishop. When, by what seemed to be a miracle, they defeated the bishop's forces in open combat, John had himself proclaimed King of the New Zion. But the new Israel was not destined to last long. Although the bishop was running out of economic resources to continue his siege, the city had been reduced to abject hunger and was taken through the treachery of a small band of deserters. The atrocities that followed matched those committed earlier by the self-styled prophets. The "king" was placed in a cage, exhibited throughout the nearby region, and finally tortured and executed.

Later Developments Within the Anabaptist Movement

The fall of the New Jerusalem was a death blow for the revolutionary Anabaptists. While Münster held, it was a symbol and a

---

[25] Bax, *Rise and Fall of the Anabaptists*, pp. 117-331.

hope for many throughout Germany and the Netherlands who hoped that the day of the Lord would come, when the high would be put down and the lowly would be exalted. But after the fall of that stronghold and the humiliating end of its "king," the more moderate Anabaptists came to the fore once again. The pacifist groups, which had never disappeared, now regained strength. The Münster episode was never forgotten, and the opponents of Anabaptism constantly pointed to it as a sign of the consequences to which Anabaptism could lead. But in spite of this the movement, having now returned to its original pacifism, managed to survive.

Typical among the new leaders of the movement, and certainly the most influential of them, was Menno Simons (1496–1561),[26] a Dutch Catholic priest who early in 1536 decided to join the Anabaptists. At first he hesitated between the followers of Melchior Hoffman and those of Obbe Philips, but soon he decided to join the Obbenites. When Obbe Philips left the movement, Menno became its natural leader.

Menno Simons had no use for the violence advocated and practiced by the Münster movement, which seemed to him to pervert the very heart of Christianity. "How can it be harmonized with the Word of God that one who boasts of being a Christian could lay aside the spiritual weapons and take up the carnal ones?"[27] Thus, Mennonite pacifism is not simply a peripheral characteristic of the movement, but rather belongs to the very essence of Menno's understanding of the gospel. This is one of the reasons that it has been a constant characteristic of all Mennonite bodies through the centuries.

Menno's main task was to draw a clear distinction between the radical Anabaptists of Münster and the more moderate wing of the movement. Thus, in the *Foundation of Christian Doctrine,* a work that in tone and purpose is very similar to some of the early apologies and that has become his most widely read book, Menno states that the purpose of his writing is to show the distinction. "Seeing then that Satan can transform himself into an angel of light, and sow tares among the Lord's wheat, such as the sword, polygamy, an external

---

[26] F. H. Littell, *A Tribute to Menno Simons: A Discussion of the Theology of Menno Simons and Its Significance for Today* (Scottdale, Pa.: Herald Press, 1971). H. S. Bender, *Menno Simons' Life and Writings* (Herald Press, 1936). See also the entire series of the *MQR.* His works: *The Complete Writings of Menno Simons,* ed. J. C. Wenger (Herald Press, 1966).
[27] *The Complete Writings of Menno Simons,* p. 46.

kingdom and king, and other like errors on account of which the innocent have to suffer much, therefore we are forced to publish this our faith and doctrine."[28]

The basic tenor of Menno's theology is one of separation from the world, whose "spirit, doctrine, sacrament, worship, and conduct are quite diverse from Christ's Spirit, Word, sacrament, worship, and example, and are alas nothing but a new Sodom, Egypt, and Babylon."[29] The basis for this separation is, as in the case of the earlier Anabaptist, personal conversion and repentance, which is symbolized and proclaimed by baptism. The true church thus becomes once again the fellowship of the faithful. Those who in that fellowship show that they are not true believers are to be banned from the church, and the entire congregation is to shun them—although Menno made it very clear that this shunning was not to be vindictive, but rather a loving call to repentance.[30]

On two points Menno was accused of departing from the basic doctrines of the early councils: on the Trinity and on the incarnation. With reference to the former, it is true that he avoided using the term "Trinity," but his reasons for this were not his supposed rejection of Trinitarian doctrine, but his intense desire to use only scriptural language. Indeed his Confession of the Triune God[31] clearly affirms traditional Trinitarian doctrine. On the matter of the incarnation, it is true that Menno departed from orthodox doctrine by asserting that the flesh of Christ descended from heaven and that Mary contributed no more than the nourishment of that flesh.[32] This was a view that caused lengthy debates, and the Mennonites eventually abandoned it.

In summary, Menno—and other late Anabaptist leaders with him—returned to the original pacifist stance of the early Anabaptists. Although some of them added their own peculiar theories—like Menno's on the incarnation[33]—to the original theology of the Swiss Brethren, the general consensus soon brought the vast majority of Anabaptists to more conservative tenets. This does not mean,

---

[28] Ibid., p. 107.

[29] Ibid., p. 181.

[30] LCC, 25:263-71. Cf. F. C. Peters, "The 'Ban' in the Writings of Menno Simons," MQR, 29 (1955) : 16-33.

[31] The Complete Writings, pp. 489-98.

[32] Ibid., p. 794.

[33] Which he probably derived from Melchior Hoffman.

however, that they reached an agreement on all theological issues, for the history of the Anabaptist movement for the next four hundred years was one of repeated divisions on doctrinal grounds, and the numerous confessional formulas that were proposed never succeeded in gaining the support of the majority.

The Spiritualists and Rationalists

The description of the Anabaptist movement and the classification of its various groups and leaders are difficult enough, but even more so is such a discussion of those whom we have called "spiritualists" and "rationalists." Most of these persons had strong mystical tendencies, and they therefore tended to be more concerned with the spiritual life of the individual than with the reformation of the church at large. Many of them felt that the inspiration of the Spirit was above Scripture, and some even claimed that the written Word was to be set aside in favor of the Word that God speaks directly to the human spirit. Others insisted on applying human reason to the message of Scripture, and thus proposed interpretations of the gospel that often denied the Trinity or the incarnation. To these thinkers we must now turn, realizing that there were great differences among them, and that they have been included under a common heading for reasons of clarity and convenience and not because they formed a cohesive movement in any sense of the word.

Caspar Schwenckfeld (1489–1561) proposed what he thought was a middle way between Catholicism and Lutheranism. But it was in reality an alternative that neither Catholics nor Protestants could accept. This suggested *via media* started from a dichotomy between the "inner" and the "outer," or between the spiritual and the material. This means that the Holy Spirit is free to act, and is bound neither by the church nor by Scriptures. Therefore, although the Bible is infallible because it expresses the action of the Spirit in the prophets and the apostles, what is important is not to study Scripture, but to receive the inspiration of the Spirit. Without such inspiration, Scripture cannot be properly understood—and one receives the impression that with it Scripture is barely needed. There is also an "inner" and an "outer" church; the two do not coincide in any way, and participation in the outer church does not warrant salvation. All that the best ministers—after the time of the apostles—can do is point to Christ, in the hope that their hearers will also hear the inner word. The sacraments are also interpreted in the light of the basic dichotomy. The elements in the sacraments, being material, cannot in any way mediate the spiritual. The most they can do is to direct the outer person to Christ. But here again there is a spiritual dimension. "There is a twofold bread: an earthly which comes from the earth and a heavenly which comes down from heaven. If the bread is twofold, there is necessarily also a twofold breaking, namely, for the external and internal man. The earthly and outer bread is broken in representation for the outer man; the heavenly bread, that is, the incarnate Word of God, is broken in reality for the inner and reborn man."[34]

Obviously, the problem with this sort of interpretation is that the connection between the material and the spiritual in the Supper is not spelled out. If the Spirit remains absolutely free to act, can one still claim that there is any such connection? Would it not be best to abstain from material communion, which seems to mislead so many, and participate only in the spiritual feast? This was actually what Schwenckfeld recommended, although only as a temporary measure until people could be properly educated.

When dealing with the incarnation, Schwenckfeld took a position that was similar to those held by Melchior Hoffman and by Menno Simons. He did not say that the flesh of Christ came from Heaven, but he insisted that it was not created. This led him into involved theological arguments and distinctions that were never accepted by his opponents, who accused him of Monophysism and a number of similar heresies. Although Schwenckfeld always affirmed his basic agreement with the Chalcedonian definition, his Christology was at best unclear.

Sebastian Franck (*ca.* 1499–*ca.* 1542), another spiritualist reformer, was profoundly influenced by Erasmus.[35] He basically agreed with Schwenckfeld, but carried the latter's views to their logical conclusion.[36] The written word of the Bible now became a mysterious

---

[34] Quoted by P. I. Maier, *Caspar Schwenckfeld on the Person and Work of Christ* (Assen: Van Gorcum, 1959), p. 20.

[35] R. Kommoss, *Sebastian Franck und Erasmus von Rotterdam*, reprint (Nedeln/Liechtenstein: Kraus, 1967). On Franck, see also H. Weigelt, *Sebastian Franck und die lutherische Reformation* (Gütersloh: Gerd Mohn, 1972); J. Lindeboom, *Een Franc-tireur der Reformatie: Sebastian Frank* (Arnheim: Van Loghum Slaterus, 1952).

[36] R. M. Jones, *Spiritual Reformers of the 16th and 17th Centuries*, reprint (Boston: Beacon Press, 1959), pp. 46-63. The above does not mean that he was a disciple of Schwenckfeld, although the two did know each other.

and unclear manifestation of the eternal word, so that one could only understand its true meaning if one had the revelation of that eternal word. This word he called "Christ," but he did not identify it with Jesus. On the contrary, God is constantly revealed. In each of us there is a spark of the divine, and it is to this that spiritual reality addresses itself. All externals are unnecessary. The early church needed the sacraments because it was spiritually immature. A mature spirituality requires no external means.

The Spaniard Juan de Valdés (ca. 1500–1541) followed a different line.[37] His religiosity was a combination of the intellectual refinement of Erasmus with the mysticism of the "alumbrados"[38]—an ill-defined group that was repeatedly condemned by the Spanish inquisition. He sought communion with God through meditation and gathered around himself, in Naples, a sizable and distinguished group of disciples. As his main concern was for inner piety, his conflicts with the established hierarchical authorities were always relatively mild. But precisely this emphasis on the inner life made him be suspected by Catholics as well as by Protestants.[39] With his disciple Bernardino Ochino (1487–1563), his teachings took an anti-Trinitarian turn. Ochino, who had been an outstanding Capuchin preacher, joined the Protestants of Geneva for a while, but eventually was forced into a long series of exiles that led him as far as Poland, and finally, Moravia.[40]

In the following century, spiritualistic tendencies were evinced by George Fox (1624–1691), the founder of the Quaker movement.[41] The son of a weaver, and never formally trained in theology, Fox spent a number of years in an earnest spiritual quest, until in 1646 he discovered what he thereafter called the "inner light," which is Christ living in the believer. His trust in this inner light led him to reject

---

[37] B. B. Wiffen, *Life and Writings of Juan de Valdés, Otherwise Valdesso, Spanish Reformer in the Sixteenth Century* (London: B. Quaritch, 1865). D. Ricart, *Juan de Valdés y el pensamiento religioso europeo en los siglos XVI y XVII* (Mexico City: El Colegio de México, 1958).

[38] On the alumbrados, see M. Menéndez Pelayo, *Historia de los heterodoxos españoles*, 2 vols., reprint (Madrid: Biblioteca de Autores Católicos), 2: 169-206; M. Asín Palacios, "Sadilíes y alumbrados," *Al-Andalus*, 9-16 (1944–51).

[39] Theodore Beza, Calvin's successor in Geneva, said that the three worst monsters of his time were Valdés, Servetus, and Loyola. Ricart, *Juan de Valdés*, p. 14.

[40] R. H. Bainton, *Bernardino Ochino, esule e riformatore senese del cinquecento, 1487–1563* (Fierenze: G. C. Sansoni, 1941).

[41] R. M. Jones, *George Fox: Seeker and Friend* (London: George Allen & Unwin, 1930); W. V. Noble, *The Man in Leather Breeches: The Life and Times of George Fox* (New York: Philosophical Library, 1953); H. E. Wildes, *Voice of the Lord: A Biography of George Fox* (Philadelphia: University of Pennsylvania Press, 1965).

what had traditionally been considered to be exterior means of grace, such as the church and the sacraments. To him, the spiritual eating and drinking of the body and blood of Christ were of far greater significance than the actual eating and drinking of bread and wine in communion—which in fact could become an obstacle in the way of true communion. Fox, however, did not allow his emphasis on the inner light to lead him or his followers away from the need for Christian fellowship, or away from the obligation to seek social justice. The former concern was the reason for the founding of the Society of Friends of the Truth—also known, after 1650, as the "Quakers." The latter interest has been manifest in Quaker involvement in social issues—usually from a pacifist standpoint— and finds its roots in the following words of Fox himself:

> How are you in the pure Religion, to visit the sick, the fatherless, and the widows, when both blind, and sick, and halt and lame lie up and down, cry up and down almost in every corner of the city, and men and women are so decked with gold and silver in their delicate state, that they cannot tell how to go. Surely, surely you know not that you are one mould and blood, that dwell upon the face of the earth. Would not a little out of your abundance and superfluity maintain these poor children, halt, lame, and blind, or set them at work that can work and they that cannot, find a place of relief for them; would not that be a grace to you?[42]

With Michael Servetus (1511–1553) and Faustus Socinus (1539–1604) anti-Trinitarianism came to the foreground. Servetus was a man of profound religious conviction who, however, felt that the doctrine of the Trinity was unsound.[43] In his native Spain, that doctrine had been a stumbling block to Jews and Moslems for centuries. He therefore took up the late medieval doubts regarding the rationality of the doctrine of the Trinity,[44] coupled them with sixteenth-century humanistic and Protestant endeavors to return to the sources of Christianity in the New Testament, and rejected the

---

[42] *Doctrinals to Magistrates*, quoted in H. van Etten, *George Fox and the Quakers* (New York: Harper, 1959, p. 66.

[43] R. H. Bainton, *Hunted Heretic: The Life and Death of Michael Servetus, 1511–1553* (Boston: Beacon Press, 1953).

[44] R. H. Bainton, "Michael Servetus and the Trinitarian Speculation of the Middle Ages," in B. Becker, ed., *Autour de Michel Servet et de Sebastien Castellion* (Haarlem: H. D. Tjeenk Willink & Zoon, 1953), pp. 29-46.

Trinity and the eternal generation of the Son as rationally untenable and as not to be found in Scripture. As is well known, he fled from the Catholic inquisition only to be burned as a heretic in Calvin's Geneva. His views, however, did not die. They found sympathetic ears among some Anabaptists who had been questioning the doctrine of the Trinity. They also found an echo in Laelius Socinus and, more significantly, in his nephew Faustus. Faustus Socinus became one of the most influential anti-Trinitarian theologians in Poland,[45] where his disciples multiplied. In 1605, the year after his death, these followers set down his teachings in the Racovian Catechism. In the seventeenth century the introduction of Socinian writings and ideas into England was one of several formative influences in the birth of Unitarian theology.

Thus the Reformation set in motion by Luther had come to its final consequences. Luther and his followers looked upon these extreme reformers with horror. The same was true of the Reformed theologians of Switzerland and Strasbourg. They felt that these extreme views denied many things that had long been considered to be central to the Christian faith. Catholic polemists pointed out that once the dams of ecclesiastical authority were broken there was no way to prevent the flood of extreme positions, and that the proliferation of sects was therefore a logical consequence of the Reformation. This was partly true. And yet, one must point out that the mood of sixteenth-century Europe was such that the traditional patterns of authority were breaking down, and that the Reformation was then both a cause and a consequence of that breakdown. Luther's success was possible because the old systems of authority were losing their hold on Europe. On the other hand, traditional authority finally collapsed in much of Europe because Luther was successful.

What now remained to be done on the part of the more traditional reformers—Lutheran and Reformed—was to establish their theology on more systematic grounds than had been possible during the early years of struggle. It is to these developments that we must now turn.

---

[45] O. Fock, *Der Sozinianismus*, reprint (Aalen: Scientia Verlag, 1970); S. Kot, *Socinianism in Poland: The Social and Political Ideas of the Polish Antitrinitarians in the Sixteenth and Seventeenth Centuries* (Boston: Starr King Press, 1957).

V

Lutheran Theology to the Formula of Concord

The founders of the two great Protestant traditions, Luther and Zwingli, were followed by others who at once systematized and mitigated those traditions. As we shall see in the next chapter, Calvin became the heir to Zwingli's reformation, and the two may be said to be the founders of the Reformed tradition; but the general trend of Calvin's theology was a movement away from Zwingli and toward Luther. The same may be said about the man who played a similar role in the Lutheran tradition, Philip Melanchthon, for the development of his theology can be seen as a movement away from Luther and toward Bucer and Calvin. This, and the fact that Melanchthon mollified Luther's theology on a number of other points, gave rise to several controversies within the Lutheran churches. Other controversies arose, quite independently of the differences between Melanchthon and Luther, when lesser lights proposed views that seemed to threaten the core of Protestantism—as, for instance, in the case of Osiander. These various controversies finally led to the *Formula of Concord* (1577), around which most of the Lutheran churches rallied. Thus, the present chapter will be divided into two sections: first we shall discuss Melanchthon's theology; then we shall summarize the most significant controversies that divided Lutherans during the sixteenth century, and we shall see how the *Formula of Concord* responded to these controversies.

The Theology of Philip Melanchthon

Melanchthon joined the faculty at the University of Wittenberg in 1518, just as the Lutheran reformation was beginning to take shape.[1] His field of teaching was Greek and his scholarly interests were philological, but he soon fell under the spell of Luther and turned to biblical and theological studies. In contrast to Luther, Melanchthon came from a background of humanistic studies, and even after the bitter debate on free will between Luther and Erasmus he never ceased being an admirer of the great Dutch humanist.[2] Indeed, one could argue that most of the differences between Luther's theology and that of Melanchthon stem from the influence of the humanistic spirit in the younger of the two.

Luther was well aware of the difference between him and his favorite disciple, especially in temperament and gifts. In an oft quoted reference to such differences, he said: "I am rough, boisterous, stormy, and altogether warlike. . . . I must remove stumps and stones, cut away thistles and thorns, and clear the wild forests, and Master Philippus comes along softly and gently, sowing and watering with joy, according to the gifts which God has abundantly bestowed upon him."[3] This was the reason that, when the need arose to write a confession of faith to present to the Diet of Augsburg (1530), and it became clear that what was needed was a conciliatory statement that most Protestants[4] could sign and that would not alienate possible sources of support, Melanchthon was chosen for the task.

Melanchthon's particular gifts made him the great systematizer of Lutheran theology. They also were the reason he progressively developed views that many considered a betrayal of original Lutheranism. Melanchthon's gifts as a systematic thinker came to the forefront in 1521, when he published the *Loci communes rerum*

---

[1] An excellent biography is C. L. Manschreck, *Melanchthon: The Quiet Reformer* (Nashville: Abingdon Press, 1958). See also the references in P. Fraenkel, *Zwanzig Jahre Melanchthonstudium* (Geneva: Droz, 1967); L. C. Green and C. D. Froelich, eds., *Melanchthon in English* (St. Louis: Center for Reformation Research, 1982).

[2] Cf. W. Maurer, *Der junge Melanchthon zwischen Humanismus und Reformation*, 2 vols. (Göttingen: Vandenhoeck & Ruprecht, 1969).

[3] Quoted by H. H. Lentz, *Reformation Crossroads: A Comparison of the Theology of Luther and Melanchthon* (Minneapolis: Augsburg, 1958), p. 2. See also V. Vajta, *Luther and Melanchthon in the History of the Reformation* (Philadelphia: Muhlenberg, 1961).

[4] Throughout this volume, the followers of the Reformation in its various modalities are called "Protestants" for reasons of clarity, although in truth that name did not appear until the Diet of Speier in 1529.

theologicarum—Basic Theological Themes—which was in fact the first systematization of the main Protestant tenets. This book had enormous success, and soon went through several printings, translations, and revisions—the latter by Melanchthon himself.

In each new edition of the *Loci*, Melanchthon showed how he was departing from original Lutheranism and being increasingly influenced by humanism and by the Reformed tradition. Therefore, these several editions of the same work are invaluable for the historian who seeks to follow the chronological development of Melanchthon's theology. Obviously, it is impossible to follow the details of that development within the brief compass of this chapter.[5] However, given the importance of Melanchthon's changing views for the course of Lutheran theology in the sixteenth century, I shall indicate, as I expound Melanchthon's theology, those points at which the differences between his earlier and his later views are most significant.

The first edition of the *Loci* differed very little from Luther's views. In fact, the latter was so enthused by it that, in one of his typically hyperbolic statements, he said that it should be included in the canon. But later editions began showing a different spirit, to the point that the Lutheran churches were divided—especially after the death of both theologians—between "Lutherans" and "Philippists."

The *Loci* of 1521 expressed at the very outset the principles of Luther's theology of the cross—although in less dialectical terms than Luther.

> We do better to adore the mysteries of Deity than to investigate them. What is more, these matters cannot be probed without great danger, and even holy men have often experienced this. The Lord God Almighty clothed his Son with flesh that he might draw us from contemplating his own majesty to a consideration of the flesh, and especially of our weakness. . . . Therefore, there is no reason why we should labor so much on those exalted topics such as "God," "The Unity and Trinity of God," "The Mystery of Creation," and "The Manner of the Incarnation." What, I ask you,

---

[5] Three excellent studies of this nature are E. Bizer, *Theologie der Verheissung: Studien zur theologischen Entwicklung des jungen Melanchthons* (Neunkirchen: Neunkirchen Verlag des Erziehungsvereins, 1964); W. H. Neuser, *Die Abendmahlslehre Melanchthons in ihrer geschichtlichen Entwicklung* (Neunkirchener Verlag des Erziehungvereins, 1968); C. E. Maxey, *Bona Opera: A Study in the Development of the Doctrine in Philip Melanchthon* (Nieuwkoop: B. de Graaf, 1980).

did the Scholastics accomplish during the many ages they were examining only these points?[6]

Theology then must have a practical purpose, and must deal with issues such as sin and its power, grace, the law, and justification, for "to know Christ means to know his benefits, and not as *they* [i.e., the Scholastics] teach, to reflect upon his natures and the modes of his incarnation."[7]

The reason that Christian theologians at various times have taught the doctrine of free will is that they let themselves be influenced by philosophy. On this point, however, the teachings of the philosophers and those of Scripture are diametrically opposed, for whereas the former affirm free will, Scripture denies it. And this is not a matter of small consequence, for the doctrine of free will obscures the benefits of Christ. This is only one of the many instances in which the clear teachings of Scripture have been abandoned in favor of philosophy. The result is that "apart from the canonical Scriptures, there is no reliable literature in the church. In general, whatever has been handed down in the commentaries reeks with philosophy."[8]

The same negative view of human powers may be seen in the manner in which Melanchthon deals with the virtues of the pagans. He concedes that there are many things that, from a purely human perspective, one must admire in Socrates, Zeno, and Cato. "Nevertheless, because these characteristics were in impure minds, and further, because these simulated virtues arose from love of self and love of praise, they ought not to be considered real virtues but vices."[9] Natural law, although given by God, is no trustworthy guide, for human reason has been so blinded and perverted by sin that it can no longer speak accurately of natural law.[10] Thus, the general impression one receives when reading this first edition of the *Loci* is that Melanchthon is profoundly convinced of the radical discontinuity between reason and revelation, between the fallen human creature and God's purposes, and between creation as it now exists and redemption.

---

[6] *LCC*, 19:21.
[7] *Ibid.*, pp. 21-22.
[8] *Ibid.*, p. 23.
[9] *Ibid.*, p. 34.
[10] *Ibid.*, p. 50.

If we now compare this with the *Loci* of 1555, we shall see that the changes are very significant. To begin with, this edition of the *Loci* opens with lengthy expositions on God, the Trinity, and Creation—precisely three of the topics that in the earlier edition he had dismissed, not as untrue, but as impenetrable to the human mind and as not directly related to the "benefits of Christ." When dealing with the knowledge of God that the wise among the pagans had, he now does not deny it, but rather agrees that Xenophon, Plato, Aristotle, and Cicero knew that there is an almighty, wise, just, and good God. Their knowledge of God although true, was insufficient, for they knew of the existence and nature of God but did not know of God's intentions toward them or of the gospel.[11] This still does not go beyond Luther's distinction between the "general" and the "proper" knowledge of God. But it is significant that Melanchthon saw fit to substitute this generally positive word for the negative one in the earlier edition. Furthermore, when discussing the Trinity, and in general throughout the entire work, he is now willing to grant a great deal of authority—although an authority that is always derived from Scripture—to the "Fathers" and commentators whom he so acrimoniously rejected in 1521.

The point at which the different spirit of the newer *Loci* becomes most apparent is in the discussion of sin, our fallen state, and free will. Whereas the emphasis of the section on sin in the first edition had been the corruption of humanity, the emphasis now lies in seeking to show that God is not the creator of sin. In the discussion of original sin, this poses no great problem, for Melanchthon can claim, together with most Christian tradition, that God did not will or cause sin. It was the devil and humans, without any coercion from God, that fell into sin out of their own free wills.[12] It is when discussing the will in fallen humanity that Melanchthon shows, not so much that he has departed from original Lutheran doctrine, as that his concerns are very different from Luther's. Here he distinguishes between two realms in which one can speak of free will. The first is the ability to decide what one's outer members will do, that is, to decide one's actions. This will still remains in fallen humanity. The second realm

---

[11] C. L. Manschreck, ed., *Melanchthon on Christian Doctrine: Loci communes (1555)* (New York: Oxford University Press, 1965), pp. 5-6.

[12] *Ibid.*, p. 45.

is that which has to do with our relationship with God and the corruption of our own nature. Here we have no free will, "for we cannot in and of ourselves ignite in our hearts a firm belief in God."[13] Therefore, although we cannot of ourselves attain the faith that justifies, we can—and must—govern our various deeds according to the strength of the will that still remains in us. Furthermore, even in matters having to do with justification, Melanchthon seeks to avoid the most extreme consequences of Luther's teachings, and makes it clear that the human will plays a part. "We should not think that a man is a piece of wood or a stone, but as we hear the word of God, in which punishment and comfort are put forth, we should neither despise nor resist it."[14] And, quoting Chrysostom's words to the effect that God draws us to salvation, Melanchthon comments "however, he draws the one who is willing, not the one who resists."[15] Thus, Melanchthon would say that in conversion there are three concurrent causes: the Word, the Spirit, and the human will. This is what his opponents—and the opponents of the *Leipzig Interim,* which will be discussed further on—called "synergism," meaning that in salvation God and the human creature work jointly.

Another point at which Melanchthon was accused of abandoning his earlier, and more Lutheran, position was the doctrine of the eucharist. In the 1521 edition of the *Loci,* there is only a brief reference to the Lord's Table, and there the emphasis is not on the presence of Christ—which was not then at issue—but on the denial of the power of the sacrament to justify, and of the repeated sacrifice of Christ. In the *Augsburg Confession* of 1530, which was written by Melanchthon, the real presence of the body and blood of Christ in the bread and wine is starkly affirmed, and the opposite view is rejected.[16] However, at that time Melanchthon's main concern was the purely spiritualistic doctrines of Zwingli and the Anabaptists. As a number of moderate reformers—such as Bucer and Calvin—began offering views of the real presence that Melanchthon found acceptable, his own views moved closer to theirs, to the point that in the end he was accused of being a crypto-Calvinist. In fairness to Melanchthon, however, one must note, first, that he was never totally

---

[13] *Ibid.,* pp. 57-58.
[14] *Ibid.,* p. 60.
[15] *Ibid.*
[16] *CR,* 26:278.

in accord with Luther's views on the Lord's Supper[17] and, second, that the same conciliatory spirit that Luther praised in him compelled him to seek an understanding with the Reformed. Unfortunately, however, his attempts at conciliation with other Protestant groups led him to change the text of the *Augsburg Confession,* deleting from its article on the Supper the phrase "truly present," and omitting also the rejection of opposite views. Likewise, he modified the original text of the *Confession* in places where it seemed that human capabilities had been dealt with too harshly. The resulting texts of the *Confession* are what is usually called the *Variata* editions. Although his motives in doing this may have been commendable, it was a very unwise thing to do. It was true that he was the author of the *Confession.* But by now it was an official document of the Lutheran churches, and therefore the *Variata* editions, instead of producing a rapprochement with the Reformed churches, simply resulted in bitter controversies within the Lutheran camp, and in a further hardening of the Lutheran position over against the Calvinist interpretation of the Supper.

This was further complicated by the fact that Melanchthon's leadership in the Lutheran churches had been seriously weakened by his acceptance of the *Leipzig Interim.* Charles V had defeated the Protestants in the field of battle, and in 1548 imposed on them a document written by two Roman Catholics and the Lutheran John Agricola. This document, known as the *Augsburg Interim,* was supposed to bring Catholics and Protestants together on a temporary basis until a council could decide the issues in dispute. Owing to particular circumstances and to the opposition of Melanchthon and others, the *Augsburg Interim* was mollified in Saxony, and the resulting document was the *Leipzig Interim,* which Melanchthon accepted. As has happened in many parallel cases in the history of the church, this "creed by decree" was not successful, for the opposition of the masses was too great. But while the *Interims* of Augsburg and Leipzig were in force, many Protestant leaders had to suffer for their refusal to accept them. The result was that confidence in Luther's old companion faltered, and that Lutheran theologians began pointing out the distance that separated Melanchthon from Luther. Melanchthon claimed that what he had

---

[17] Neuser, *Die Abendmahlslehre Melanchthons,* pp. 354-63.

accepted in the *Interim* were *adiaphora,* that is, things that one was free to accept or reject without being unfaithful to Scripture. This gave rise to the adiaphoristic controversy (see the next section of this chapter) and served only to weaken further the authority of Melanchthon among Lutherans.

We shall have occasion to refer further to Melanchthon as we turn to the controversies that divided the Lutheran churches in the sixteenth century, and thus it is not necessary to discuss here every aspect of his theology. A general word, however, seems to be in order. There is no doubt that Melanchthon's spirit was very different from Luther's, for the latter emphasized correct doctrine above unity, and the general tenor of Melanchthon's efforts was in the direction of emphasizing unity above total agreement in doctrine. Furthermore, Melanchthon introduced into Lutheran theology a humanistic spirit that was not Luther's. In many ways, this made it impossible for him to remain faithful to all of Luther's tenets—and those who claimed that he was subtly twisting Luther's theology were partially right. But it also allowed him to bring the reform movement in Germany into closer contact with the humanistic tradition. It was not in vain that he received the title of *Praeceptor Germaniae,* for he was indeed the great teacher of Germany, and the long tradition of German theological scholarship has in him its first outstanding exponent. On the other hand, perhaps the differences between Luther and Melanchthon have been overemphasized as a result of controversies that took place after their time. Those who insist on Luther's staunch stands against doctrinal deviation tend to forget that at the Colloquy of Marburg Luther seemed ready to accept intercommunion with Zwingli and the Swiss until Melanchthon pointed out that this might create irreconcilable difficulties with the Emperor and the Catholics. But it is still true that Melanchthon's flexibility was such that in his later years, instead of contributing to the unity of the Lutheran confession, it became a cause for further divisions. It is significant that in the controversies that we shall now study, Melanchthon's voice, whenever he was involved, was seldom a determining factor in the outcome. Thus, through his flexibility— especially with reference to the *Interim*—Melanchthon lost his position of leadership and thereby left the Lutheran churches at the mercy of bitter controversies that divided and weakened them until a measure of agreement was reached in the *Formula of Concord* of 1577.

Controversies Within the Lutheran Camp

The controversies that took place within the Lutheran tradition around the middle of the sixteenth century have been classified in various ways. None of these classifications is entirely satisfactory, for these various controversies are so interrelated that it is difficult to determine where one ends and the other begins. Therefore, for the sake of simplicity, we shall classify these controversies according to a very simple principle: first we shall discuss the controversies that took place before the sharp distinction between Lutherans and Philippists—or Melanchthonians—and then we shall turn to those other disputes which arose as a result of the differences between the theology of Luther and that of Melanchthon. The first category includes the antinomian and the Osiandrian controversies, to which we now turn.

The antinomian controversy—from *anti* and *nomos,* "against law"—took place in three stages. The first two revolved around John Agricola and involved both Luther and Melanchthon. The last stage may be said to have begun in 1556, at a synod in Eisenach.

John Agricola (1494–1566) was one of Luther's early companions in the University of Wittenberg. He was born at Eisleben, Luther's birthplace.[18] In 1519 he was with Luther at the Leipzig debate. He was also present at most of the diets that marked the main stages of the Reformation—Speier in 1526 and 1529, Augsburg in 1530 and 1547–48, and Regensburg in 1541. When Luther had him sent to Eisleben, Agricola blamed Melanchthon for his removal from the university. It is possible that his later invectives, first against Melanchthon and later against Luther, may have been connected with his wounded pride. In 1548 he lost all claim to a position of leadership among the Protestants by being one of the authors of the *Augsburg Interim.*

The first stage of the controversy broke out when Agricola attacked Melanchthon's *Instructions for Visitors.*[19] Melanchthon had written these instructions at Luther's request, and in them he maintained that it was necessary to help believers understand better what was expected of them as far as moral life was concerned, and he

---

[18] J. Rogge, *Johann Agricolas Lutherverständnis, unter besonderer Berücksichtigung des Antinomismus* (Berlin: Evangelische Verlagsanstalt, 1961).

[19] *CR,* 26:7-28.

therefore recommended that the law—and especially the Decalog—
was to be preached often, not only to bring sinners to repentance, but
also so that believers could gain a better idea of the will of God, and
seek to obey it. Agricola objected to such instructions, which seemed
to him a concession to the Roman Catholics. It is possible that his
objection was colored by jealousy, as he had had to leave the
university and Melanchthon was one of its most outstanding
professors. In any case, Luther brought them together at Torgau
(1528) and managed a reconciliation. In this first stage of the
controversy, the question was mostly whether repentance follows
faith, or vice versa. Agricola held the first opinion, and Melanchthon
the second. As a result of the Torgau meeting, further editions of the
Instructions included the following paragraph:

> But some hold that nothing should be taught to precede faith and
> that repentance follows from and after faith, in order that our
> opponents [i.e., the Catholics] might not be able to say that we have
> recanted our teaching. One ought to remember that repentance
> and law belong to the common faith. For one must of course first
> believe that God is the one who threatens, commands, and
> frightens, etc. So it is best for the unschooled, common people that
> such phases of the faith retain the name of repentance,
> commandment, law, fear, etc., so that they may the better
> distinguish and understand the faith in Christ which the apostles
> call justifying faith, i.e., which makes righteous and takes away sin.
> This the faith which stems from commandment and repentance
> does not do, yet it causes the common man to have doubts
> concerning the meaning of faith and to raise pointless questions in
> his mind.[20]

Thus the first stage of the controversy ended in a compromise.
This, however, was not to be the end of the matter, for nine years
later, in 1537, Agricola once again went to Wittenberg, and there he
published a series of theses in which he attacked both Melanchthon
and Luther. His position now became an explicit antinomianism.
According to him, the law had no function in the preaching of the
gospel, and therefore its proper place was in the courthouse rather
than in the pulpit. Moses should be sent to the gallows, and anyone
who preaches his teachings has not begun to understand what the

---

[20] *LW*, 40:275. Also in *CR*, 26:51-52. Cf. Melanchthon's letter to Justus Jonas in *CR*, 1:914:18.

gospel is all about. The preaching of the law cannot bring about repentance, for true repentance requires faith, and faith can only come from the hearing of the gospel. Nor is the law useful for the moral guidance of Christians, for they do the will of God, not out of an exterior commandment, but out of an inner impulse. In a way, his position was a one-sided exaggeration of Luther's early strictures against the law. But precisely for that reason it was necessary for Luther to refute him, so as to avoid misunderstandings regarding his own views. Thus, Melanchthon, Agricola's original target, sat on the sidelines while Luther refuted Agricola in a series of theses debated publicly. Agricola took the matter to the Elector, and as a result had to leave for Brandenburg. He finally recanted, but when he attempted to visit Luther again in Wittenberg Luther would not receive him.

The third stage of the antinomian controversy evolved out of the debate over the teachings of George Major, which we shall discuss further on in this chapter. In that controversy, Nicholas von Amsdorf (1483–1565), one of the staunchest defenders of Luther's theology against its many innovators, had affirmed that good works were in no way necessary for salvation. This was taken up by Andrew Poach (1516–1585), who added that the function of the law in the Christian life is only to accuse the sinner and show him his sinfulness. Poach and his followers carried the Lutheran principle of Christian freedom to its extreme, claiming that Christians are not subject to any obedience, and returning to Agricola's contention that only the gospel, and not the law, was to be preached. In other words, they absolutely rejected the "third use of the law" as a guide for the Christian.

The antinomian position was finally rejected in 1577 by the *Formula of Concord*. As we shall see later, the main purpose of that *Formula* was to put an end to the division between the strict Lutherans and the Philippists—by that time both Luther and Melanchthon were dead. But it also attempted to settle other disputes that had weakened the Lutheran confession. One of these was the antinomian controversy. Since on this point the strict Lutherans agreed with the Philippists, article six of the *Formula* affirms the third use of the law for believers "after they are reborn, and although the flesh still inheres in them, to give them on that account a definite rule according to which they should pattern and regulate their entire life."[21] After a series of positive affirmations, there follows the condemnation of antinomianism: "Accordingly we condemn as dangerous and subversive of Christian discipline and true piety the erroneous teaching that the law is not to be urged, in the manner and measure above described, upon Christians and genuine believers, but only upon unbelievers, non-Christians, and the impenitent."[22]

Although the views of the antinomians were rejected and excluded by the *Formula of Concord,* such opinions appeared again, with some variations, in other contexts. Calvin had to contend with the "libertines," who were in reality antinomians. In seventeenth century England, "antinomianism" was one of the convenient tags that the more conservative theologians applied to the numerous sects that arose at that time. A similar question appeared also in New England in the case of Anne Hutchinson.[23] Thus, although orthodox Lutheranism excluded antinomianism through the *Formula of Concord,* the issue has been posed repeatedly throughout the course of Protestant theology.

The Osiandrian controversy revolved around the teaching of Andrew Osiander (1498–1552), about whom R. Seeberg has said that "among the men of second rank in the Reformation period, he was perhaps the greatest."[24] The leader of the reformation in Nuremberg, he attended the Colloquy of Marburg in 1529, and the Diet of Augsburg in 1530. At the time of the *Augsburg Interim* he had to leave Nuremberg, and became a professor at the University of Königsberg. It was almost at the end of his life, in 1550, that he published the *Disputation on Justification,* which was to be the cause of the controversy. This was followed, among others, by another treatise *On the Sole Mediator Jesus Christ and Justification by Faith.*

---

[21] T. G. Tappert, ed., *The Book of Concord: The Confessions of the Evangelical Lutheran Church* (Philadelphia: Muhlenberg Press, 1959), pp. 479 80. Used by permission of Fortress Press.

[22] *Ibid.,* p. 481.

[23] W. K. Stoever, *A Faire and Easie Way to Heaven: Covenant Theology and Antinomianism in Early Massachusetts* (Middletown, Conn.: Wesleyan University, 1978); S. R. Williams, *Divine Rebel: The Life of Anne Marbury Hutchinson* (New York: Holt, Reinhart and Winston, 1981).

[24] R. Seeberg, *Text-Book of the History of Doctrines* (Grand Rapids: Baker Book House, 1958), vol. 2, p. 372, n. 2. See E. Hirsch, *Die Theologie des Andreas Osiander und ihre geschichtlichen Voraussetzungen* (Göttingen: Vandenhoeck & Ruprecht, 1919). See also G. Seebass, *Bibliographia Osiandrica: Bibliographie der gedruckten Schriften Andrea Osiander d. A. (1496-1552)* (Nieuwkoop: B. de Graaf, 1971).

Although the main issue at stake in this controversy was the doctrine of justification, Osiander did not propose his view on this matter in isolation from the entire system of theology. On the contrary, his understanding of justification was part and parcel of a total theological outlook that differed in many points from that of the other reformers. Briefly stated, Osiander was a mystic, and his theology was, generally speaking, one of mystical union with Christ the eternal Word of God. This most of the other reformers feared, for it tended to obscure the distance between God and us and to focus attention on the eternal Word rather than on the historical revelation of God.

His mysticism of the Word may be seen in the manner in which Osiander deals with Adam and the image of God in him. The image of God is not something to be found in Adam as a creature. The image is the Son himself—a common theme in early Christian theology. Adam is said to have been made after the image of God, because before the foundation of the world God had decided that the Son was to become incarnate. Thus the incarnation was God's eternal purpose, and not a response to sin. Even if Adam had not fallen, Christ would have become incarnate. But, even before the incarnation, humankind was created so that the image of God—that is, the Son—could dwell in it. This was the case of Adam before the fall, for the Son dwelt in him and made him righteous. It was this that he lost when he sinned.

This means that what we now need for our justification is the renewed indwelling of the Son. Because of the fall, the incarnation took on an additional purpose: the redemption and justification of humankind. The redeeming work of Christ means both that he was innocently subjected to the wrath of God, and thus earned the forgiveness of sins for all humankind, and that he fulfilled the law in our name, so that its strict obedience is no longer required of us in order for us to be declared righteous. In order for this righteousness to be true of an individual, however, one must be justified. This Christ does by dwelling in that person. Thus, justification is not, as for Luther, imputed by God out of loving grace, but is rather something that God finds in us because Christ is in us. The righteousness of the believer is the indwelling God. In language reminiscent of the Cappadocians' treatment of the union of divine and human in Christ, Osiander affirms that what actually happens when Christ comes to dwell in the believer is that the ocean of his divine righteousness engulfs the small drop of our sinfulness, and that God then looks at that vast ocean of purity rather than at the small drop of sinfulness and declares us to be righteous.

This justifying indwelling of Christ in us takes place through the "outer word" of Scripture and proclamation; but it is the "inner word," the Word as the Second Person of the Trinity, that is important in this context. The humanity of Christ, and the words that he spoke as a man, are the vehicle for his divinity. But in the last analysis it is the divinity of Christ that justifies us and can properly be called the Mediator.

These views drew attacks from several quarters. As we shall see in the next chapter, Calvin repeatedly refuted the theories of Osiander. There were already reasons for tension between Melanchthon and Osiander, for the latter had refused to accept the *Interim* and was exiled in Königsberg, while the Wittenberg professor claimed that he could accept the Leipzig version of the *Interim* without surrendering any of the essentials of the gospel, and chose to remain at Wittenberg. Thus one should not be surprised that Melanchthon took this opportunity to show that his rival was not as orthodox as he claimed to be. In a series of treatises, and in the so-called *Saxon Confession* of 1551—actually another variation of the *Augsburg Confession*—Melanchthon declared that Osiander had departed from the clear teaching of the gospel, and that by claiming that God justifies us by virtue of the righteousness of Christ in the sinner the professor at Königsberg was abandoning the doctrine of imputed righteousness and coming dangerously close to Roman Catholicism.[25] The Italian theologian Francesco Stancaro went so far in attempting to refute Osiander that he claimed that Christ is mediator only according to his human nature and not according to his divinity—a position held earlier by Peter Lombard and others.[26] But perhaps the most cogent refutation of Osiander was that of Matthias Flacius.

Matthias Flacius (1520–1575) has been hailed as the best Lutheran theologian of the second generation. He certainly was one of the staunchest defenders of strict Lutheranism against the "innovations"

---

[25] Cf. Manschreck, ed., *Loci*, p. 179.
[26] O. Ritschl, *Dogmengeschichte des Protestantismus*, 4 vols. (Göttingen: Vandenhoeck & Ruprecht, 1908–1927), 4:475.

of Melanchthon and others. He knew Luther only a few years, for he came to Wittenberg about five years before the reformer's death. But in spite of this he became a devout admirer of Luther and a convinced follower of his teachings. A professor of Hebrew at Wittenberg when the *Interim* was proclaimed, he decided to go into exile rather than submit to it. He then became one of the most famous professors at the University of Jena, founded precisely to defend strict Lutheranism from the Philippists who had taken possession of Wittenberg.[27] We shall see him involved in a number of other controversies, always defending the strict Lutheran position. Against Osiander, he claims—besides the obvious point that Osiander's doctrine of justification is no longer imputed justice— that the Königsberg professor divorces Christ's satisfaction from the justification of the believer, and thus obscures the centrality of that satisfaction. Osiander had said that redemption and justification cannot be the same; for the former took place fifteen hundred years ago, whereas the latter is still taking place in individual Christians. Against such an argument, Flacius retorts that the connection between redemption and justification is much closer than Osiander admits. The function of redemption is not simply to make justification possible. The act of redemption is the same as the act of justification, for when we are justified God simply counts us as righteous by virtue of redemption. This distinction is important, for Osiander's position tends to place the emphasis on the eternal Word of God, by virtue of whose presence God justifies the sinner. If this is the case, it is difficult to see what is the function of the sacrificial act of the incarnate Word. According to Flacius, God justifies us, not because of the eternal Word in us, but on account of Christ's obedience. Finally, Osiander's claim that the incarnation was foreordained as the climax of creation, even apart from the fall, again obscures the connection between the historic obedience of Christ and the justification of the sinner. Therefore, Osiander's views pervert more than an aspect of the doctrine of justification; they undercut the very heart of the gospel.[28]

---

[27] The classical study is W. Preger, *Matthias Flacius Illyricus und seine Zeit, 2 vols.* (Erlangen: T. Bläsing, 1859-61). See also L. Haikola, *Gesetz und Evangelium bei Matthias Flacius Illyricus* (Lund: CWK, 1952).

[28] See Haikola, *Gesetz und Evangelium*, pp. 85-95 and 254-57. He underscores the difference between Flacius and Luther in their respective understandings of justification (pp. 85-96). On this last point, Flacius ignores a long line of theologians, dating as far back as Irenaeus, who saw the incarnation as the climax of creation, without thereby undercutting the relationship between incarnation and redemption.

As in the case of the other controversies discussed in this section, the *Formula of Concord* responded to the issues raised. In order to do this, it focused its attention on the question of whether Christ justifies according to his divine nature (Osiander) or according to his humanity (Stancaro).

> A question has arisen, According to which nature is Christ our righteousness? Two false and mutually contradictory teachings have invaded some churches.
>
> One party has held that Christ is our righteousness only according to his Godhead. When he dwells in us by faith, over against this indwelling Godhead, the sins of all men are esteemed like a drop of water over against an immense ocean. Others, however, held that Christ is our righteousness before God only according to his human nature.
>
> In opposition to these errors just recounted, we believe, teach, and confess unanimously that Christ is our righteousness neither according to the divine nature alone nor according to the human nature alone. On the contrary, the entire Christ according to both natures is our righteousness solely in his obedience which as God and man he rendered to his heavenly Father into death itself.[29]

In further explanation, the *Formula* affirms that God forgives our sins "purely by his grace, without any preceding, present, or subsequent work, merit, or worthiness."[30] Finally, among the views condemned is that which holds "that faith does not look alone to Christ's obedience, but also to his divine nature (in so far as it dwells and works within us), and that by such indwelling our sins are covered up."[31]

The two controversies that we have just discussed—the Osiandrian and the antinomian—never divided the principal leaders of Lutheranism. Strict Lutherans as well as Philippists agreed in rejecting the views of Osiander and of the antinomians. The controversies to which we shall now turn produced deeper divisions. In all of them, in one way or another, the issue is one between strict adherence to Luther's principles on the one side, and the Philippist mitigation of those principles on the other. In some cases,

---

[29] Tappert, ed., *The Book of Concord*, pp. 472-73.
[30] *Ibid.*, p. 473.
[31] *Ibid.*, p. 475.

Melanchthon himself stood at the center of the dispute; in other cases, other Philippists were the ones who opposed strict Lutheranism. On the other hand, the so-called strict Lutherans were not always faithful to the original reformer's spirit. The point at which this was most noticeable was in their efforts to clarify every single point of doctrine, and to see the true faith threatened at every turn. This was not Luther's spirit, for—although he was seriously concerned about correct faith, and although he was always firm in his theological stance—he allowed greater doctrinal latitude than did his later followers.

In a sense, then, the controversies that we shall now recount are a single great controversy, and the issue at stake is—paradoxically enough—whether Luther's discovery of the freedom of justification by grace is binding or not. Obviously, the issue is one that cannot be resolved, for no matter which way one turns one is denying a fundamental aspect of Luther's great discovery. Thus, these controversies can be compared to those that followed Origen and Augustine, and are the aftermath of genius followed by lesser spirits.

The first great controversy that we shall discuss had to do with the *Interim,* and is also known as the adiaphoristic controversy. Although we have already made brief reference to that controversy, we must now examine it more fully, for it illustrates the nature of the conflict between the Philippists and the strict Lutherans. When Charles and the Diet of Augsburg (1548) proclaimed the *Augsburg Interim,* most Protestants refused to accept it. Although the Lutheran theologian Agricola had participated in its composition, the *Interim* was in fact a Roman Catholic document in which all the traditional doctrines and practices were restored. The only significant concessions to the Protestants were marriage of the clergy, communion in both kinds, and justification by faith. But even the latter was couched in such terms that it amounted to justification by works. Since many Protestants refused to accept the *Augsburg Interim,* hundreds were killed and many pastors went into exile. In electoral Saxony, however, the situation was complicated by the fact that Duke Maurice had obtained his rule over the area by treachery againt the legitimate ruler, John Frederick. Actually, it was Duke Maurice's treason that had both given him the electorate and made Charles V undisputed master of the Empire. But Maurice realized that he could not rule the electorate against the opposition of its staunchly

Protestant population. Therefore, he invited Melanchthon to return to Wittenberg and reopen the university. This Melanchthon and his followers would not do as long as the *Augsburg Interim* was in force. Maurice was placed in a delicate position, caught between the Emperor and the Protestants. He attempted repeatedly to persuade the Lutheran professors to return to the university. Melanchthon insisted that the *Interim* was against the Word of God and that therefore he could not subscribe to it.[32] His colleagues supported him. But, on the other hand, their situation was not easy, for they saw that ultimately the decision would have to be made between remaining firm and allowing the Protestant churches to be destroyed on the one hand, and reaching some sort of compromise on the other. After a long series of negotiations and disputes, Melanchthon and most of the Wittenberg theologians felt that they could in good conscience accept a modified version of the *Augsburg Interim,* which came to be called the *Leipzig Interim.* This salvaged the doctrine of justification by faith, but in most other matters returned to pre-Reformation practices. The only other significant concession was that the mass was no longer considered a meritorious sacrifice. On this basis, Melanchthon, Bugenhagen, and other Wittenberg theologians accepted the *Interim* as the lesser of two evils and set about the task of making sure that the preaching of justification by faith, which they considered to be the core of the gospel, was continued throughout Saxony. Their theological justification for this compromise lay in the distinction between the essential and the nonessential—the adiaphora.[33] In essential matters—especially the doctrine of justification by faith, which is the core of the gospel—one must not compromise. But compromise on the adiaphora is often required for the peace of the church. To confuse the essential with the adiaphora, and insist in every detail of the latter, is to deny Christian freedom, and may lead back into justification by works.

But in all this they had not taken into account the Protestants in other parts of Germany, who were suffering for their refusal to accept the *Augsburg Interim.* The Leipzig arrangement seemed like treason to them. The rightful elector of Saxony was in prison. His sons were in exile, hoping to organize a new center for Protestant theology in the University of Jena. How could the Wittenberg

---

[32] *CR*, 6:853-57.
[33] *Ibid.,* 7:332.

theologians claim they were being faithful to the gospel simply because they had salvaged one or two items from the *Interim?* Were they justified in asserting that they had retained the essential, and yielded only in matters that were adiaphoristic?

The leader of the strict Lutherans was Matthias Flacius, whom we encountered when dealing with the Osiandrian controversy. He refused to see any significant difference between the *Augsburg Interim* and the revised version adopted at Leipzig. Indeed, his treatise *Against the Interim,* published in 1549 after the Leipzig compromise, was directed against the edict of Augsburg, and he simply claimed that all he said in it could be applied to the situation in Saxony. It is also claimed that, in order to show Melanchthon in a bad light, he published supposed letters of the Wittenberg professor that had been changed and otherwise misinterpreted.[34] It is certainly true that charity and moderation were not his most outstanding characteristics during the entire affair.

The main argument of Flacius and others who took his stance—Nicholas von Amsdorf, John Aurifaber the Younger, and others—was that at a time when a clear confession of faith is necessary nothing is adiaphoristic. Many of the things accepted in the *Interim,* although in themselves unimportant, become crucial when they are taken as symbols for a denial of the gospel. Furthermore, the simple folk who do not understand the difference between the essential and the adiaphora are given an occasion for scandal by all the ceremonies and observances, which they will necessarily interpret as meaning that the old religion had been restored.

Melanchthon replied by insisting on the distinction between the essential and the adiaphora. What Flacius and his party are doing is simply proposing a new form of popery in which all things will be regulated, there will be no "freedom of the Christian man," and emphasis will once again fall on externals rather than on justifying faith. If one understands correctly the doctrine of justification by faith, one will surely realize how unimportant the concessions made at Leipzig really are.[35]

---

[34] Manschreck, ed., *Melanchthon,* pp. 290-91.
[35] *CR,* 7:382-86.

The *Interim* did not last long, for it proved to be a total failure. Charles V abdicated in favor of Ferdinand, and in 1555 the Peace of Augsburg put an end to the period of the *Interim*. But the abrogation of the *Interim* did not end the controversy between Flacius and his supporters—whom Melanchthon called "God's chancery"—and the Wittenberg theologians. This rivalry, even after Melanchthon's death, was the background for most of the controversies discussed in the rest of this chapter.

Once again, this controversy was settled by the *Formula of Concord*, which granted Melanchthon's distinction between the essentials and the adiaphora, but agreed with Flacius that there are circumstances in which the adiaphora cease to be such. The issue at stake is clearly and succinctly stated:

> There has also been a division among theologians of the Augsburg Confession concerning those ceremonies or church usages which are neither commanded nor forbidden in the Word of God but have been introduced into the church in the interest of good order and the general welfare.
>
> The chief question has been, In times of persecution, when a confession is called for, and when the enemies of the Gospel have not come to an agreement with us in doctrine, may we with an inviolate conscience yield to their pressure and demands, reintroduce some ceremonies that have fallen into disuse and that in themselves are indifferent things and are neither commanded nor forbidden by God, and thus come to an understanding with them in such ceremonies and indifferent things? One party said Yes to this, the other party said No.[36]

The affirmative section agrees that ceremonies and other practices that are neither commanded nor forbidden in Scripture are matters that each church can decide for itself, as long as the weak in the faith are not scandalized. But—and this was Flacius' point—"in time of persecution, when a clearcut confession is demanded of us, we dare not yield to the enemies in such indifferent things . . . . In such a case it is no longer a question of indifferent things, but a matter which has to do with the truth of the Gospel, Christian liberty, and the sanctioning of public idolatry, as well as preventing offense to the

---

[36] Tappert, ed., *The Book of Concord*, pp. 492-93.

weak in faith."[37] Finally, the churches of the *Augsburg Confession* condemn the view that asserts that yielding in the adiaphora is permissible in times of persecution, as well as those who attempt to impose or to abolish the adiaphora by force.

The Majoristic controversy may be seen as a further episode in the adiaphoristic dispute. George Major (1502–1574), rector of the University of Wittenberg, had followed Melanchthon's lead in the affair of the *Interim*. As part of his defense of the position taken by the Wittenberg theologians, Major asserted that good works are necessary for salvation, as well as for retaining it. In this he was not going any further than Melanchthon, although the latter used more guarded language by avoiding the juxtaposition, in the same phrase, of works and salvation. Thus, he would say that works are necessary as an outcome of faith, and that faith is necessary for salvation; but he would not bring these two propositions together, for fear they might be interpreted in the sense of justification by works.[38] Major's unguarded assertion drew the attacks of Flacius and Amsdorf, the two main leaders of the strict Lutheran party. Flacius limited his attack to a restatement of Luther's main proposition of justification by faith, and pointed out that Major's words were injurious to that doctrine. Amsdorf went further, and raised Luther's hyperbolic attacks on works to the level of dogmatic statements, claiming that good works destroy salvation.

On this issue, the *Formula of Concord* took an intermediate position, reaffirming the doctrine of salvation by faith, pointing out that the *Augsburg Confession* did however speak of the necessity of good works, and rejecting the extreme statements of the two parties in dispute. "Accordingly we reject and condemn spoken and written formulations which teach that good works are necessary to salvation; likewise, that no one has ever been saved without good works . . . . We also reject and condemn as offensive and as subversive of Christian discipline that bald statement that good works are detrimental to salvation."[39]

The synergistic controversy was another episode of the running debate between the Philippists and the strict Lutherans. The *Leipzig Interim* proposed that the human will collaborates with God in the

---

[37] *Ibid.*, p. 193.
[38] *CR*, 9:498-99.
[39] Tappert, ed., *The Book of Concord*, p. 477.

process of salvation. As we have already seen, as the years went by Melanchthon came to an increasing emphasis on the freedom of the will, which, he said, distinguished a human being from a piece of wood or a stone.[40] In 1555, the Philippist theologian John Pfeffinger published a series of *Propositions on Free Will* in which he repeated Melanchthon's tripartite formula of concurring causes in conversion, namely, the Word, the Spirit, and the will. Furthermore, he suggested that the fact that some assent to the call of faith, and others do not, is due to the freedom of the will. Victorin Strigel held a series of similar theses in 1560, in a public disputation with Flacius. In this case, as in most of the other controversies of the period, the leaders of the strict Lutherans were Amsdorf and Flacius.

In this particular controversy, however, Flacius, the staunch defender of strict Lutheranism, allowed himself to be carried beyond the bounds of traditional Christian orthodoxy. This was the cause of his downfall, for when he refused to recant he had to go into exile. He finally died, a broken man, in a Catholic convent where he had taken refuge. The issue being debated, which cost him his position as the mouthpiece of the strict Lutherans, was original sin. The synergistic controversy had moved quite naturally from the matter of the participation of the will in conversion to the question of original sin, for if the will is somehow bound this is a result of original sin. In the controversy with Strigel, and later in his publications dealing with the freedom of the will, Flacius put forth the view that original sin is not an accident, but the substance of fallen human existence. When Adam was created, he was able to bear the image of God because he still had his original righteousness. He thus had a will that could collaborate with God. But the fall changed things radically, for as its consequence Adam lost his original righteousness, his free will—not in external matters, but in his ability to turn toward God—and even the image of God. What we have is no longer the image of God, but the image of Satan. Otherwise stated, the "substance of Adam before the fall"—or at least its "most important part"—was his original righteousness. Our substance now is sin. When we are converted, what takes place is a war between the image of Satan and the image of God—or between the substance of the old creation, and the substance of the new. This position soon drew fire

---

[40] *CR*, 9:766.

from several quarters as being at once a denial of Luther's *simul iustus et peccator,* and bordering on Manichaeism. On this point, even the strict Lutherans felt that they could no longer support their erstwhile champion, who as has already been said, remained firm in his position, and as a result was forced into exile and eventually an obscure death.

Still, however, the issue of synergism, or of whether or not the will collaborates with God in conversion, was not solved, and remained a subject of disagreement between the Philippists and the strict Lutherans. In its first two articles, the *Formula of Concord* addressed itself to this and other related questions. The question of original sin was posed at the very opening of the *Formula:*

> The principal question in this controversy is if, strictly and without any distinction, original sin is man's corrupted nature, substance, and essence, or indeed the principal and best part of his being (that is, his rational soul in its highest form and powers). Or if there is distinction, even after the Fall, between man's substance, nature, essence, body, and soul on the one hand, and original sin on the other hand, so that man's nature is one thing and original sin, which inheres in the corrupted nature and corrupts it, is something else.[41]

In response to this controversy, the *Formula* asserts that there is a distinction between human nature and original sin, not only in the original state of creation, but also at present. The fallen human creature is still a creature of God, and God does not create evil substances. Therefore, the *Formula* condemns "as a Manichaean error the teaching that original sin is strictly and without any distinction corrupted man's substance, nature, and essence, so that no distinction should be made, even in the mind."[42] On the other hand, it guards against the opposite error—that of considering sin a slight corruption of human nature—which would lead to Pelagianism. Thus, it asserts that "this damage is so unspeakable that it may not be recognized by a rational process, but only from God's Word," and that "no one except God alone can separate the corruption of our nature from the nature itself."[43]

---

[41] Tappert, ed., *The Book of Concord,* p. 466.
[42] *Ibid.,* p. 468.
[43] *Ibid.,* p. 467.

The second article of the *Formula,* which deals with free will, responds to the question of synergism: "The question is, What powers does man posses in spiritual matters after the fall of our first parents and before his regeneration? Can man by his own powers, before he is reborn through the Holy Spirit, dispose and prepare himself for the grace of God? Can or can he not accept the grace of God offered in the Word and the holy sacraments?"[44]

The answer to all these questions is that there are no such powers, for fallen human will "is not only turned away from God, but has also become an enemy of God, so that he desires and wills only that which is evil and opposed to God."[45] We cannot convert ourselves to God, nor can we make a beginning toward our own conversion, nor are we able to obey God's law after conversion. On the other hand, God does not force the will, but rather the Holy Spirit guides the will and opens the heart to enable one to hear the gospel. Thus, there are only two efficient causes of conversion: the Holy Spirit and the Word of God, and the will cannot be said to be a third concurring cause. As to external matters, however, such as the movement of our members, we have freedom, and determinism is rejected.

The next three controversies that we shall discuss were different from the preceding ones in that they were essentially born out of the encounter, not between strict Lutherans and Philippists, but rather between Lutheranism and Calvinism. This is not to say that they were always debates between Lutherans and Calvinists, for true Calvinists had very little participation in the first two of them. They were rather controversies, mainly among Lutherans, having to do with the issue of how much Calvinistic influence could be tolerated in Lutheranism. In those controversies, those who were influenced by Calvin—or by similar but independent views—were called crypto-Calvinists by the strict Lutherans.

The eucharistic controversy had as its background the disagreement between Luther and Zwingli regarding the presence of Christ in the Lord's Supper. As is well known, this was the point around which their differences crystalized at the Colloquy of Marburg in 1529. Not all the Protestants, however, subscribed to the views of one of these two reformers. On the contrary, in the Rhine basin and in

---

[44] *Ibid.,* p. 469.
[45] *Ibid.,* p. 470.

southern Germany there were many who sought an intermediate position between symbolic remembrance and bodily presence. At first, these sentiments found their clearest expression in Martin Bucer, the reformer of Strasbourg. In 1536, Bucer reached an agreement with Luther and his party. The hope was that this *Wittenberg Concord* would be accepted by the southern German cities and by at least some of the Swiss. This, however, never happened. In 1549, Calvin, Bucer, and a number of Swiss and southern German leaders came together in the *Zurich Consensus*. This again was a mediating document between Zwinglian and Lutheran views. But the Lutherans—Luther himself had died three years earlier—never accepted it.

Thus matters stood when Joachim Westphal, a strict Lutheran pastor at Hamburg, published a book pointing out the differences between Calvin and Luther, especially regarding the Lord's Supper.[46] Until that time (1552) such differences had hardly been noticed. Westphal's attack made very little impact among the Calvinists, and Calvin himself responded in a slightly contemptuous manner.[47] But within the Luthern camp the reaction was very different, for many Lutherans who did not entirely agree with Luther on this matter were now forced to take a stand. From the point of view of the strict Lutheran party, the difference between Zwingli and Calvin—if there was any—was immaterial, for both denied the ubiquity of the glorified body of Christ, its physical presence in the Supper, and the partaking of that body by unbelievers.

Melanchthon refused to take an open stand.[48] He clearly felt that further controversies would only disrupt the peace of the church. He himself was a friend of Calvin, whom he had met in Frankfurt in 1539. He also had as a precedent the fact that Luther, who knew Calvin's *Institutes* and other writings, had always expressed favorable feelings toward the Swiss leader. But Melanchthon's reticence, coupled with the fact that a number of Philippists came out in support of Calvinistic or similar views, earned him and his party the title of "crypto-Calvinists." Disputes flared throughout Germany.[49] In Heidelberg, the strict Lutheran Tilmann Hesshusen had a

[46] Ritschl, *Dogmengeschichte*, 4:10-13.
[47] *CR*, 37:1-252. See also below, p. 156.
[48] *Ibid.*, 8:736; 9:960.
[49] Ritschl, *Dogmengeschichte*, 4:10-13.

controversy with Wilhelm Klebitz, who claimed to have received his
eucharistic doctrine from an Englishman, but whose views agreed
with those of Calvin. A similar debate took place in Bremen between
Albert Hardenberg and John Timann. Although Hardenberg—following Melanchthon's lead—tried to avoid the issue, Timann forced
him to define his position, and the net result was that the city of
Bremen went over to the Calvinist camp. The outcome of the
controversy at Heidelberg was eventually the same, for when the
elector Frederick III tried to settle the dispute by asking for
Melanchthon's advice, the latter simply responded that the answer to
the dispute was not difficult to find, although to give it would be
dangerous. The elector understood this as an endorsement of
Calvinism and, as his own convictions also inclined him in that
direction, the entire Palatinate became Calvinist, not only in its
eucharistic doctrine, but also in its worship and other matters. This
was expressed in the *Heidelberg Catechism* of 1563, written by the
Reformed theologians Zacharias Ursinus and Caspar Olevianus. In
Saxony itself the struggle was bitter. Once again the strict Lutherans
took to the battlefield against the Philippists. Joachim Curaeus, one
of the Philippists, published an anonymous treatise in which he
declared that unbelievers do not truly partake of Christ in
communion, and that the *communicatio idiomatum* was not to be
understood—as Luther had proposed—in such a way that the
glorified body of Christ could be said to be ubiquitous. This open
attack on Luther's doctrine gave the strict Lutherans the opportunity
to gain a condemnation of Calvinism in 1574. As Melanchthon was
dead by then, his doctrine was declared to have been the same as
Luther's. As a corollary of these debates, the theory of the ubiquity of
the risen body of Christ was also widely discussed. Some, while
attempting to cling to Luther's understanding of the eucharist,
rejected the theory of ubiquity. Others claimed that Luther's
doctrine was so closely connected with that theory that it stood or fell
with it.

Once again, the *Formula of Concord* attempted to settle these issues,
to which it devoted its seventh article. "The question is, In the Holy
Communion are the true body and blood of our Lord Jesus Christ
truly and essentially present, if they are distributed with the bread
and wine, and if they are received orally by all those who use the
sacrament, be they worthy or unworthy, godly or godless, believers

or unbelievers, the believers for life and salvation, the unbelievers for judgment? The Sacramentarians say No; we say Yes."[50]

As the earlier strict Lutherans, the *Formula of Concord* refuses to grant any significance to the differences between Zwingli and Calvin. The followers of Zwingli it calls "crass Sacramentarians," whereas the Calvinists are "subtle Sacramentarians, the most harmful kind." The latter "in part talk our language very plausibly and claim to believe a true presence of the true, essential, and living body and blood of Christ in the Holy Supper but assert that this takes place spiritually by faith. But under this plausible terminology they really retain the former crass opinion that in the Holy Supper nothing but bread and wine are present and received with the mouth."[51]

Against these two sorts of "Sacramentarians," it is affirmed that the body and blood of Christ are truly present, distributed, and received, in the bread and the wine, and that this is for unbelievers as well as for believers—although those who are not converted and do not repent eat to their own judgment and condemnation.

The eucharistic controversy necessarily led to the question of the hypostatic union, for the disagreement between Luther and the Reformed theologians was closely connected with their different views regarding the union of two natures in the person of Christ. The Lutheran position, requiring the ubiquity of the body of Christ, was based on the opinion that the union of the two natures was such that the properties of the divinity were transferred to the humanity—the *communicatio idiomatum*—in a literal fashion, and that therefore the risen body of Christ had received from his divinity its ability to be in various places at the same time. The Reformed position, on the other hand, underlined the distinction between the two natures and had a more restricted view of the *communicatio idiomatum,* and therefore insisted on the impossibility of the body of Christ being present in heaven and in a multitude of churches at the same time. Thus the "crypto-Calvinists" either limited or rejected the *communicatio idomatum,* whereas the strict Lutherans emphasized it. Although many were involved in this controversy, the most significant contribution was that of Martin Chemnitz (1522–1586), who in 1571 published a treatise *On the Two Natures of Christ.* Here he

---

[50] Tappert, ed., *The Book of Concord,* pp. 481-82.

[51] *Ibid.,* p. 482.

proposed an understanding of the hypostatic union according to which when the divinity was united to the humanity the latter received the attributes of the divinity in the fullest measure in which humanity is capable of such attributes. This did not take place at the resurrection, but in the incarnation itself. The limitations that we see in the historic life of Jesus are real, but only because the divine nature restrains itself. Thus they are limitations imposed not by the nature, but by the will. In consequence, the body of Christ can be present wherever he chooses to be present. It is not that his body is omnipresent, as if this were part of its nature, but rather that it can be present wherever he chooses. Therefore, a better term than ubiquity is "multivolipresence"—the ability to be in several places, as he wills. The inclusion of the volitional element is important, for this means that the body of Christ is not indiscriminately present everywhere, but only present where he chooses—namely, in the sacrament of communion. Chemnitz also clarified the meaning of the *communicatio idiomatum,* showing that this means, first, the communication of the properties of the two natures to the one Person; second, the communication between the two natures, so that the actions of one can be predicated of the other; and third, the empowerment of the human nature by the divine, so that it may be able to do what is necessary for the salvation of humankind. This would later be taken up by Lutheran scholasticism.[52]

In response to this controversy, the *Formula of Concord* affirmed that the *communicatio idiomatum* takes place "in deed and in truth" so that "God is man and man is God," and Mary is the "mother of God." Following Chemnitz, it is affirmed that, by reason of the personal union, Christ always possessed "the omnipotent majesty and power of God," but that he dispensed with it "in the state of humiliation." These christological affirmations are then related to the question of the eucharistic presence, which was the original cause of the debate. "Therefore he is able and it is easy for him to impart to us his true body and blood which are present in the Holy Supper."[53]

Finally, brief mention must be made of the controversy regarding predestination, which took place not among Lutheran theologians but rather between the Lutheran and the Reformed. It never

---

[52] Ritschl, *Dogmengeschichte,* 4:70-106.
[53] Tappert, ed., *The Book of Concord,* pp. 487-89.

developed into a widespread public debate, and was amicably settled in Strasbourg in 1563. In spite of that settlement, however, the writers of the *Formula of Concord* realized that the doctrine of predestination could be approached in two different ways, and that these different approaches could lead to serious controversies—as did indeed happen among Lutherans in the United States three centuries later. The *Formula* therefore devoted its eleventh article to predestination. Here it is claimed that the doctrine of election is to be approached, not through reason nor through the law, but through the knowledge the believer has that salvation rests in Christ. This distinction is important, for a doctrine of predestination that is not based on the gospel will lead to doubt and despair, whereas a correct understanding of election is a most comforting assurance. In other words, predestination must not be viewed a priori, as if it were derived from the natural knowledge of God, but rather a posteriori, through the knowledge of the love of God revealed in Christ. Therefore, although every Christian must declare that salvation is the result of divine and unmerited election, we must refrain from developing a doctrine of double predestination, attempting to explain the lot of the reprobate.

These were the main issues debated within the Lutheran tradition in the formative period after the first great surge of the Reformation, and especially after Luther's death. As we have repeatedly seen, the *Formula of Concord* sought—and in great measure succeeded—to put an end to these controversies. The process by which it was composed was complicated and need not detain us here, except to point out that its main architects—among many others of lesser importance—were Jacob Andreae and Martin Chemnitz.[54] As to its general tone, it would be fair to say that it was an attempt to bring together a divided church, in a Melanchthonian spirit of concord and around Lutheran orthodoxy. Therefore, wherever the two great reformers clearly disagreed, the *Formula* opted for Luther's position, but there is still a great deal of Melanchthon's spirit in it.

As to its result, the *Formula of Concord* succeeded in establishing a clear line of demarcation between Lutheranism and Calvinism, and

---

[54] T. R. Jungkuntz, *Formulators of the Formula of Concord: Four Architects of Lutheran Unity* (St. Louis: Concordia, 1977).

in bringing together most of the Lutheran bodies. The former was a necessary price to pay for the latter, and the *Formula* can be credited for putting an end to a period when "the passion displayed and the worship of formulas reminded of the worst periods of the dogmatic struggles upon Byzantine territory."[55] Practically completed in 1577—some minor revisions were made during the next three years, especially in the Preface—the *Formula* was officially published in 1580. It was soon signed by 8,188 theologians and ministers, as well as by 51 princes and lesser lords, and 35 cities. Published together with the Apostles', Nicene, and Athanasian creeds, and with the *Augsburg Confession* and a number of other basic Lutheran documents, it became known as *The Book of Concord,* and for four centuries has been one of the principal unifying elements within the Lutheran confession.

---

[55] Seeberg, *Text-Book,* 2:378.

VI

The Reformed Theology of John Calvin

The conflict between Luther and Zwingli on the interpretation of the Lord's Supper was symbolic of two different approaches to theology. Generally speaking, Luther's influence was stronger in the northern sections of Germany, while Zwingli's was most noticeable in Switzerland and southern Germany. Along the Rhine basin, and especially in Strasbourg with its reformer Martin Bucer (1491–1551),[1] there was an attempt to develop a mediating position that would bring together the two branches of Protestantism. These attempts failed in the political sense, for the *Wittenberg Concord* of 1536, which joined northern Lutherans with Bucer and his party, and which had been drafted in the hope that it would be accepted by the Swiss and southern Germans, was not successful.[2] In 1549 a *Zurich Consensus*[3] was reached by several of the southern German and Swiss leaders, among them Henry Bullinger (1504–1575),[4] who had succeeded Zwingli in Zurich, and John Calvin, who was by now the acknowledged leader of the reformation in Geneva. Bucer agreed with this latter document, for Calvin's views, which had been

---

[1] Bucer's mediating spirit is well documented in J. V. Pollet, *Martin Bucer: Etude sur la correspondance*, 2 vols. (Paris: Presses Universitaires de France, 1958, 1964). His Latin and German works are being published jointly by the Presses Universitaires de France and Gerd Mohn (Gütersloh).

[2] *CR*, 3:375-84.

[3] *Ibid.*, 35:735-44.

[4] A good introduction to Bullinger is A. Bourvier, *Henri Bullinger: Réformateur et conseiller oecuménique* (Neuchâtel: Delachaux & Niestlé, 1940). His *Of the Holy Catholic Church* is translated in *LCC*, 24:288-325. See also the bibliography in *LCC*, 24:356-57.

influential in the shaping of the *Consensus,* bore Bucer's imprint. The Lutherans never accepted this new agreement, and the result was that Switzerland and vast sections of Germany followed the reformed theology of Calvin, which—partly through Bucer's influence—was in reality a mediating position between Zwinglianism and Lutheranism. Thus, although Bucer failed in his attempts to bring Lutheranism and Zwinglianism together, he did succeed indirectly by contributing to the final, more moderate, shape of Reformed theology. To complete the irony of practical failure and theological success, Bucer was forced to abandon Strasbourg in 1549, owing to the advances of the Catholic reaction; but he then went to Cambridge, where he made a significant contribution to the final shape of the Anglican reformation.

It was left to John Calvin (1509–1564) to give Reformed theology its characteristic shape.[5] Although the outward course of Calvin's early years can be ascertained with some detail,[6] the data regarding his intellectual and religious development are very scarce.[7] Calvin himself—in contrast to Luther—was not inclined to be very communicative in this respect. He must have come in contact with humanism from an early age, for in his youth he was a friend of the king's physician, William Cop, who in turn was in close contact with Erasmus and Budé. It is significant, however, that when two of his law professors, Pierre de l'Estoile and Andrea Alciati, became involved in a bitter controversy, Calvin took the side of the conservative de l'Estoile against the humanist Alciati.[8] As a matter of fact, his first published work was the preface that he wrote to his friend Duchemin's *Antapologia* against Alciati. But this did not mean

---

[5] The bibliography on Calvin being too extensive to cite here, I refer the reader to the following bibliographies: A. Erichson, *Bibliographia Calviniana,* reprint (Nieukaap: B. de Graff, 1960); W. Niesel, *Calvin-Bibliographie: 1901-59* (Munich: Kaiser Verlag, 1961); D. Kempff, *A Bibliography of Calviniana, 1959-1974* (Potcherfstroom: Institut vir Bevorderins van Calvinisme, 1975). Other bibliographies appear periodically in *CTJ*. Having pointed out these bibliographies, which in turn will lead the reader to others, I have refrained from other bibliographical references in the present chapter, except in the section on Calvin's early life.

[6] J. Pannier, *L'enfance et la jeunesse de Jean Calvin* (Toulouse: Société d'éditions, 1909).

[7] J. Pannier, "Recherches sur la formation intellectuelle de Calvin," *RHPhRel,* 10 (1930): 145-76, 264-85, 410-47; F. Callandra, "Appunti sullo svilluppo spirituale della giovanezza di Calvino," *RivStlt,* ser. 5, 5 (1939): 175-225; F. Wendel, *Calvin: Sources et évolution de sa pensée religieuse* (Paris: Presses Universitaires de France, 1950), pp. 3-26; W. F. Dankbaar, *Calvin: Sein Weg und sein Werk* (Neunkirchen: Erziehungsverein, 1959), pp. 1-28.

[8] There are a number of articles and books on Calvin's studies, as may be seen in the bibliographies mentioned above. However, the controversy between Alciati and de l'Estoile has not been sufficiently studied with reference to the development of Calvin's thought.

that he had rejected humanism,[9] for the circle in which he moved was formed entirely by humanists—Duchemin among them—and shortly after writing the preface to the *Antapologia* he began work on his commentary on Seneca's *De Clementia,* which he hoped would gain him the admiration of humanist circles.

As a publication, the commentary on Seneca was a failure, for it did not attract the attention that the young humanist had hoped.[10] But it is very valuable as a source for the study of the development of Calvin's convictions.[11] Although some have claimed that the commentary was intended as a veiled defense of the persecuted Protestants, such an interpretation is hardly tenable. In spite of this, the commentary is significant on two counts. The first and most important is its witness to the profound influence of humanism on Calvin as late as 1532. Although Calvin would later reject what he took to be the pride and the faintheartedness of the humanists, he always had great regard for humanism itself. This may be seen in his attitude toward tradition and the need to return to the sources, and in the fact that it was always easy for him to communicate with others of similar background, such as Melanchthon and Bucer. Second, one can already see in the commentary on Seneca some indications of Calvin's later strictures regarding the natural virtues of the pagans.[12]

It is impossible to establish the exact date of Calvin's conversion. It seems certain that sometime between 1533 and 1534 he experienced that "sudden conversion" by which he abandoned "the superstitions of the Papacy."[13] Almost immediately thereafter, he completed the *Psychopannchia,*[14] which attempted to refute the doctrines of some Anabaptists that the souls of Christians sleep after death, awaiting the final resurrection. Unfortunately this treatise, which would otherwise be a very significant source for the study of Calvin's theological development, exists only in editions of 1542 and later. As Calvin frequently corrected his writings for new editions, it is

---

[9] On Calvin and humanism, see Q. Breen, *John Calvin: a Study in French Humanism* (Grand Rapids: Eerdmans, 1931); D. Lerch, "Calvin und der Humanismus," *ThZschr,* 7 (1951): 284-99; B. Hall, *John Calvin: Humanist and Theologian* (London: Philip, 1956).

[10] Breen, *John Calvin,* p. 90.

[11] *Ibid.,* pp. 86-99.

[12] *CR,* 33:39, 112, 154.

[13] *Comm. in lib. Psalmorum,* preface (*CR,* 59:22).

[14] *CR,* 29:1-252. There is an English translation by H. Beveridge in *Tracts and Treatises in Defense of the Reformed Faith by John Calvin* (Grand Rapids: Eerdmans, 1958), 3:413-90.

difficult to know how much of the text now available was already in the edition of 1532.

In any case, by 1535 Calvin was already writing the preface to the first edition of the *Institutes of the Christian Religion,* which would be published in Basel—where he was now exiled—in 1536.[15] Although that first edition of the *Institutes* was hardly more than the skeleton of the final product of 1559—the 1536 edition had six chapters, whereas the 1559 edition had eighty—it was already a significant work that immediately drew the attention of several leaders of the Reformation. One of them was Guillaume Farel (1489–1565), the leader of the reformation in Geneva. Calvin saw himself as primarily a scholar, and wanted to devote his time to study and writing. But these plans were changed when war forced him to make a detour in a trip from France to Strasbourg. That detour took him to Geneva, where Farel demanded that he remain and take the reins of the reformation. As Calvin would not hear his plea, Farel warned him of eternal damnation. Calvin decided to stay, and thus began his career as a leader of the Reformation. It was in that capacity, prompted by new problems and issues, that he continued to develop the *Institutes* until they reached their final form in 1559.[16] It is possible to follow Calvin's theological development, and the issues that were posed by various controversies, by simply following the growth of the *Institutes*—in structure as well as in size and content—as they went through successive editions. The 1536 edition was little more than a catechism addressed as an apology to the king of France. It showed little originality, and relied heavily on Luther. The second edition (1539) revealed the growing influence of Bucer and other Reformed theologians, and also reflected a greater involvement in the life of the church, as well as a concern to refute the doctrines of Servetus regarding the Trinity and of the Anabaptists on infant baptism and the nature of the church. By 1559, the *Institutes* had developed into a systematic exposition of Reformed theology, in clear disagreement not only with Roman Catholics, but also with Lutherans, Anabaptists, and anti-Trinitarians. This systematic exposition of the Protestant

---

[15] *CR,* 29:1-252.

[16] There is also a French edition of 1560, translated from the Latin text of 1559, probably by Calvin himself. See Wendel, *Calvin,* pp. 85-86; J. Cadier, in his preface to the French edition (Geneva: Labor et Fides, 1955), pp. x-xiii.

faith became one of the basic documents of the Reformed tradition, and will be the main source for our study of Calvin's theology.

The Knowledge of God

Calvin opens his *Institutes* by asserting that nearly all that humans can know consists of two parts: the knowledge of God and the knowledge of self.[17] The true knowledge of self, where we discover our own misery and insufficiency, also makes us realize that we need to seek after the knowledge of God. But, since in our present condition we are too prone to deceive ourselves, claiming that we are what we are not, and obscuring our infirmities,[18] the proper place for true wisdom to begin is with the knowledge of God. Calvin agrees with Luther on the insufficiency of the mere knowledge of the existence of God, although when he discusses the "proper" knowledge of God the emphasis falls not so much on God's attitude toward us, but rather on our proper attitude toward God. "Now, the knowledge of God, as I understand it, is that by which we not only conceive that there is a God but also grasp what befits us and is proper to his glory, in fine, what is to our advantage to know of him."[19]

There is in every person a natural awareness of divinity, as even the practice of idolatry testifies.[20] But this awareness is only sufficient to make one inexcusable, for it is only a "seed of religion" planted in us through God's mysterious inspiration, which only a few nurture and none succeed in bringing to fruition.[21] In general terms, the same is true of the knowledge of God through creation and through the order of the world, where God's power is manifested.[22]

Once again, this divine imprint in the world and its order suffices to render one inexcusable,[23] but—owing to the evil in the human heart—does not produce true knowledge of God.[24]

Thus, we cannot know God because we are so enslaved by sin that such knowledge is impossible. But there is another limitation

---

[17] *Inst.*, 1. 1. 1.
[18] *CR*, 43-346.
[19] *Inst.*, 1. 2. 1 (*LCC*, 20:39).
[20] *Ibid.*, 1. 3. 1.
[21] *Ibid.*, 1. 4. 1; *CR*, 58:477; 89:58.
[22] *Inst.*, 1. 5. 1-3; *CR*, 54:204, 281; 62:297; 63:452.
[23] *Inst.*, 1. 5. 4, 13.
[24] *Ibid.*, 1. 5. 12, 14; *CR*, 71:346.

imposed on our knowledge of God, and that has to do with the great distance between Creator and creature. We cannot know God, not only because we are sinners, but also because we are finite creatures and God is infinite. This in turn means that we must not seek to know God in highest glory, but only as revealed, mainly through Scripture.

> Let us use great caution that neither our thoughts nor our speech go beyond the limits to which the Word of God itself extends. For how can the human mind measure off the measureless essence of God according to its own little measure, a mind as yet unable to establish for certain the nature of the sun's body, though man's eyes daily gaze upon it? Indeed, how can the mind by its own leading come to search out God's essence when it cannot even get to its own? Let us then willingly leave to God the knowledge of himself . . . . But we shall be "leaving it to him" if we conceive him to be as he reveals himself to us, without inquiring about him elsewhere than from his Word.[25]

Thus, God's revelation does not make the divine essence known to us, for this we can neither grasp nor endure. In revelation, God is "accommodated" to our limited perception.[26] This is the function of the Scripture, and indeed of all revelation, whose "anthropomorphisms" are due, not to the divine essence itself or to an imperfection in revelation, but to our limited capacity, to which God has adapted all communications to us.[27]

Although, strictly speaking, the Word of God is the second Person of the Trinity,[28] Scripture can also be called the Word of God,[29] for it is God's witness to us,[30] and its content is Jesus Christ himself.[31] Scripture does not derive its authority from the church.[32] On the contrary, the church is built on the foundation of the prophets and apostles, and that foundation is now to be found in Scripture.[33] Although there are reasonable grounds for believing the Scriptures

---

[25] *Inst.*, 1. 13. 21 (*LCC*, 20:146).
[26] *CR*, 54-387; 57:356. Note the similarity between this and Luther's "hidden God."
[27] *Ibid.*, 56:567, 676, 694; 57:70.
[28] *Inst.*, 1. 13. 8.
[29] *Inst.*, 1. 7. 1; *CR*, 64:302.
[30] *CR*, 56:617.
[31] *Inst.*, 4. 8. 5; *CR*, 37:825; 75:125.
[32] *Inst.*, 1. 7. 1.
[33] *Ibid.*, 1. 7. 2.

to be authoritative,[34] these are not sufficient to prove that they are the Word of God. This can be known only through the inner witness of the Spirit.[35] On the other hand, this does not mean that the so-called revelations of the Holy Spirit are to be preferred to the clear testimony of the written text.[36] Any supposedly divine spirit that does not lead to Scripture, and through it to Christ, must be rejected. When Paul says that "the letter kills," he means not the written text of Scripture, but the literal understanding of the law, which does not see Christ in it; likewise, the spiritual interpretation of Scripture is that which sees Christ in it.

The Bible clearly condemns all idolatry and "Papist superstition," such as the use of images.[37] Here Calvin transfers to the Catholic use of images all the strictures of the Old Testament against the idols of the pagans. To attempt to represent God or the divine through an image is to diminish the divine glory. Although it is true that God did at times use material signs—the cloud, or the pillar of fire—these signs were temporary, and in the very act of passing away were intended to show that God cannot be properly represented by material signs. As to St. Gregory's argument—that images are the books in which the ignorant learn the Christian faith—one should note that all that can be learned through images is at best frivolous. The traditional distinction between *dulia* and *latria* is mere words, and does not excuse those who venerate images from the charge of idolatry. Although Calvin rejected the use of images because he considered it unscriptural, he did not go as far as Zwingli, who agreed with the Anabaptists in rejecting everything that did not have clear scriptural warrant. Thus, while Calvin and many Calvinists in later times used much of the traditional worship of the Church, other Calvinists greatly influenced by Zwingli reduced the use of music in worship to that which could be clearly found in Scripture, namely, the singing of psalms. Given these different orientations, the Reformed tradition has been much poorer than the Lutheran or the Catholic in the production of Christian art, pictorial as well as musical.

---

[34] *Ibid.*, 1. 8.
[35] *Ibid.*, 1. 7. 4-5; *CR*, 76:401.
[36] *Inst.*, 1.9.
[37] *Ibid.*, 1. 10-12; *CR*, 54:157; 56-316; 88:577.

The God revealed in Scripture is triune.[38] At this point, Calvin's theology does not depart from what was generally held to be orthodox.[39] He does acknowledge that the terminology used in the doctrine of the Trinity is nowhere to be found in Scripture. But he argues that it must be kept because it is the only way to express clearly the doctrine of Scripture in the face of such heretics as Servetus. It was indeed the affair of Servetus—and some other minor affairs of a similar nature—that prompted Calvin to devote his attention to this doctrine. Whereas the first edition of the *Institutes* simply mentioned and affirmed the Trinity, each subsequent edition gave more space to it, until the last one devoted to it an entire lengthy chapter.[40] In any case, Calvin's understanding of the Trinity is entirely orthodox and traditional, and is mentioned here only to show that although Calvin insists on the sole authority of Scripture he is willing to interpret that Scripture in the light of the early ecumenical councils. The same can be said regarding ancient Christian writers, whom he quotes often and usually with approval.

God, the World, and Humanity

The true God has been revealed as Creator so that we may distinguish God from the idols.[41] This is the reason why Moses put down the narration of the six days of creation: to stop idle speculation about the nature of God, and show the difference between God and all the idols that were being made by humans. The end and culmination of creation was Adam, although he is not the highest of all creatures, for the angels are above him. If Moses does not mention them, that is because he wanted to present the story of Genesis as simply as possible and it was not necessary to deal with the subject of angels in order to accomplish his purpose. But angels do exist. They are the spiritual servants of God. Those who have fallen have become demons. Angels, although higher beings than humans, are not to be worshiped. In any case, Calvin avoids the complicated speculations about angelic hierarchies that had become traditional during the Middle Ages, following Pseudo-Dionysius, for "the

---

[38] *Inst.*, 1. 13. Cf. *Defensio doct. de trin. contra Serv.* (*CR*, 36:453-644); *Actes du procès de Servet* (*CR*, 36:721-872).

[39] Koopmans, *Das altkirchliche Dogma*, pp. 66-75.

[40] Wendel, *Calvin*, pp. 122-23.

[41] *Inst.*, 1. 14. 1-2.

theologian's task is not to divert the ears with chatter, but to strengthen consciences by teaching things true, sure, and profitable."[42] Furthermore, the only way in which angels communicate with us is through the intercession of Christ,[43] and therefore one ought to be more concerned about the knowledge of Christ than about the knowledge of angels.

Given the length of his discussion of them,[44] Calvin seems to be more interested in the demons than in the angels. The reason for this is twofold: the knowledge of demons and their ways of acting is important for the Christian life; and the question of the Devil and his cohort, and of their relationship to the will of God, is intimately connected with the issues of the divine will and predestination. Demons are evil not by nature, but by their own sinful corruption, for—as Augustine had said—no nature is in itself evil. They are personal beings, and those who say that they are simply our own evil inclinations had better be more careful lest they fall to their wiles.

What is important to know about the creation is not all the details of its origin or of its present functioning, but the fact that it has all been made with us in mind. This is why Adam was created last. The human creature is composed of body and soul. The soul, which Calvin calls "the best part," is immortal, although created.[45] This last point Calvin underscores against Servetus, who claimed that when God breathed upon Adam, a portion of the divine substance had been given to him, and that this was the soul. Such a view Calvin flatly rejects. The soul was created by God out of nothing[46] and does not participate in the divine essence.[47]

The image of God in Adam was not so much in the body as in the soul. In a derivative and almost allegorical sense, one can attribute the *imago Dei* also to the body; but properly it belongs to the soul.[48] As to the—by now almost traditional—distinction between the "image" and the "likeness," Calvin rejects it, affirming that what we have here is simply another instance of the Hebrew custom of using parallel expressions to refer to a single thing. Basically then, the image of

---

[42] *Ibid.*, 1. 14. 4 (*LCC*, 20:164).
[43] *Ibid.*, 1. 14. 12.Cf. *CR*, 70:128.
[44] *Inst.*, 1. 14. 13-19. Cf. *CR*, 64:448; 73:361.
[45] *Inst.*, 1. 15. 2.
[46] *CR*, 72:401.
[47] *Ibid.*, 62:455.
[48] *Inst.*, 1. 15. 3. Cf. *CR*, 60:620.

God in Adam resided in his soul and had to do with the authority that
God gave him to rule over the rest of creation. All this, however, has
to do with Adam before the fall, for after the sin of Adam what
remains of the divine image is no longer recognizable. "There is no
doubt that Adam, when he fell from his state, was by this defection
alienated from God. Therefore, even though we grant that God's
image was not totally annihilated and destroyed in him, yet it was so
corrupted that whatever remains is frightful deformity."[49]

The fall is then the sign under which we all live, and therefore a
great deal that could be said about Adam as he was created cannot be
said of us as we actually exist. This is important for Calvin, for it is on
the basis of the fall that he can hold at once the depravity of human
nature and the loving goodness of God. To this, however, we shall
return when discussing our present plight.

In spite of the fall, God continues being the ruler of the entire
creation. Here one hears the echo of Zwingli, for the doctrine of
providence is closely tied with predestination. All things take place
under the rule and action of God. This does not mean simply that
God is the primary cause of all things, but also that God intervenes in
all particular instances.[50] This includes the order of nature, as well as
the general lives of all persons, and the lives of believers, although
each of these God rules in a different way.[51] Furthermore,
providence is not mere foreknowledge, but the actual production of
the events in question.[52] And, if one accuses Calvin of advocating the
fatalism of the Stoics, he retorts that it is not so, for he believes not in
an inner necessity in things, but in a universal divine rule.[53]

This is a very useful doctrine—so Calvin asserts—for it shows that
we are to thank God for all good things, and that in times of adversity
we are to be patient and trusting. It should be no cause to despise
those whom we would otherwise consider our benefactors, for now
we see that it is God who has chosen them to do this service. And it
ought to be no reason for acting irresponsibly, for those who really
understand this doctrine are willing to subject themselves to the
sovereignty of God and should not find it burdensome, while those

---

[49] *Inst.*, 1. 15. 4 (*LCC*, 20:189).
[50] *Ibid.*, 1. 16. 3.
[51] Cf. *Contre la secte phantastique des libertins* (*CR*, 35:145-252).
[52] *Inst.*, 1. 16. 4.
[53] *Ibid.*, 1. 16. 8.

who reject it are robbing God of glory and are thereby showing their own rebelliousness.

Therefore, let all the glory be to God. God's is the glory, not only in the elect, but also in the reprobate, who are also fulfilling the divine will. For even the evil and reprobate are doing the *hidden* will of God. Their evil is in resisting God's *revealed* will, and for this they will be punished.[54] But they are still in the hands of God, who uses their evil for justice and for the divine glory. Finally, if any attempt to make this doctrine more palatable by distinguishing between an active and a permissive will of God, and then claiming that God actively wills good, but only permits evil, let them know that this is another attempt to diminish the glory of God, and to make God subject to our own judgment.[55]

Although it is clear from the foregoing that there is a direct relationship between providence and predestination, it is significant that Calvin's more detailed discussion of predestination comes later, under the discussion of Christ's work of salvation. In other editions of the *Institutes* this is even clearer. The importance of this is that for Calvin predestination is not a doctrine to be studied as if it followed from the divine omnipotence and omniscience, but is rather a doctrine that can be understood properly only from the perspective of grateful faith that knows its own salvation in spite of its shortcomings. The doctrine of predestination is a way by which the elect render to God all the glory for their salvation.

The Human Condition

If, as Calvin says at the beginning of the *Institutes*, almost all human wisdom consists in the knowledge of God and of ourselves, it follows that a significant portion of Christian theology must be devoted to anthropology. It is to this subject that Calvin turns in the second book of his *Institutes*, where he states clearly, however, that the knowledge he is now seeking is not the same that the philosophers spoke of when they said "know thyself." The difference is that the philosophers did not know of the fall and therefore when they sought after the knowledge of human nature they were seeking after worth and virtue, when in fact they ought to have been looking at unworthiness

---

[54] *Ibid.*, 1. 17. 5.
[55] *Ibid.*, 1. 18. 1.

and depravity. For us who know of the fall, knowledge of ourselves implies, first of all, the original integrity with which we were created. This is important, for in affirming such integrity one is also affirming the wisdom and goodness of the Creator. But the notion of the fall is also important, for it allows us to see ourselves as we really are, in all our need and misery, and yet insist on the goodness of God.

> God's truth, therefore, agrees with the common judgment of all mortals, that the second part of wisdom consists in the knowledge of ourselves; yet there is much disagreement as to how we acquire that knowledge. According to carnal judgment, man seems to know himself very well, when, confident in his understanding and uprightness, he becomes bold and urges himself to the duties of virtue and, declaring war on vices, endeavors to exert himself with all his ardor toward the excellent and the honorable. But he who scrutinizes and examines himself according to the standard of divine judgment finds nothing to lift his heart to self-confidence. And the more deeply he examines himself, the more dejected he becomes, until, utterly deprived of all such assurance, he leaves nothing to himself with which to direct his life aright.[56]

The reason we find ourselves in this condition is the sin of Adam, which is inherited by all his descendants. Adam's great sin was not simply disobeying God, but was first of all the sin of incredulity, for he disbelieved what God had told him and lent his ear to the serpent. This in turn led to ambition, pride, and ingratitude, as a result of which Adam lost the original integrity that had been granted to him for safekeeping, not only for himself, but also for his posterity. Original sin, then, is not simply something that we learn by imitation. Nor is it a corruption of the body, transmitted from parents to children as one transmits a physical trait. It is rather "a hereditary depravity and corruption of our nature, diffused into all parts of the soul, which first makes us liable to God's wrath, then also brings forth in us those works which Scripture calls 'works of the flesh.' "[57] This means, therefore, that although original sin is hereditary and exists already in the womb,[58] the reason for its transmission is not in the sensuality in which a person is conceived, but simply in the fact of

---

[56] *Ibid.*, 2. 1. 3 (*LCC*, 20:243-44).
[57] *Ibid.*, 2. 1. 8. (*LCC*, 20:251).
[58] *CR*, 61:654.

being a child of Adam. Furthermore, it is not just the guilt of Adam that is transmitted, but also the sin, which in turn engenders more sin in us.[59]

This is the doctrine of natural human depravity, on which Calvin insists.[60] This depravity, however, is not "natural" in the sense that it follows from human nature as it was created. On the contrary, human nature in itself is good. What is evil is the corruption that has been brought into human nature by sin. What has actually happened in the fall is that the supernatural gifts that Adam originally had are now lost, while the natural gifts are now corrupted.[61] The supernatural gifts that are now lost were the faith and the integrity necessary to eternal beatitude. The natural gifts, on the other hand, were the intellect and the will; and both of these have been corrupted by the fall.

The corruption of the human intellect is not such that it has been entirely destroyed.[62] In fact, the fallen human intellect still conserves a natural desire for truth, and this is a reminder of its original condition. But even this search for truth leads us into pride and vanity. Among earthly things, we have a natural knowledge of the need for social order, although we must of necessity pervert that order. We can also understand something of the functioning of things around us, even though we use that understanding for evil. Thus, even after the fall, God's grace has continued blessing us, for all these things are gifts of the Holy Spirit.

It is when we come to the knowledge of "heavenly things" that the corruption of the intellect becomes most obvious, for in this respect the keenest minds are blinder than the most blind. If one finds "here and there" in the writings of the philosophers bits of truth about God, the reason for this is not their perspicacity, but rather that God "gave them a slight taste of his divinity that they might not hide their impiety under a cloak of ignorance."[63] The only manner in which we can hear or know anything about God is through ears and a mind that only the Spirit can give. It is true, on the other hand, that we do have a certain natural knowledge of the will of God, through that

---

[59] *Inst.*, 2. 1. 8.
[60] *CR*, 74:375, 673; 78:322-24; 79:251.
[61] *Inst.*, 2. 2. 12. Cf. *CR*, 78:257.
[62] *Inst.*, 2. 2. 12-25.
[62] *Inst.*, 2. 2. 12-25.
[63] *Ibid.*, 2. 2. 18 (*LCC*, 20:277).

which is commonly called "natural law." Paul himself affirms the existence of such law. But the function of that law, in our present condition, is not to let us know the will of God, but to render us inexcusable. Without the revealed law of God, the natural law is not sufficient to know the good.

The will has also been corrupted.[64] We still have a natural tendency to seek what is good for us, but this is hardly more than the "natural appetite" that can be found in all animals. Our will is now tied to sin, and therefore there is not a single one of us who truly seeks God. What we call "virtues" in the pagans were no more than splendid vices; and what true virtue they had they owed not to their nature, but to the grace of God. We are incapable of moving toward the good by our own volition. "Because of the bondage of sin by which the will is held bound, it cannot move toward good, much less apply itself thereto; for a movement of this sort is the beginning of conversion to God, which in Scripture is ascribed entirely to God's grace."[65] The will is like a horse led by its rider; and in our fallen state the rider is the Devil.[66] We do what the Devil wants us to do, and yet we do it voluntarily. We gladly acquiesce to the promptings of the Devil, because our will coincides with such promptings. And even in this God is being served and glorified, for God uses Satan as well as fallen humanity in order to fulfill the divine will.[67] Once again, nothing takes place without God actively willing it.

The Function of the Law

When Calvin speaks of "law" he usually means by that term something different from what Luther meant. By law he normally does not mean the counterpart of the gospel, but rather the revelation of God to ancient Israel, in the "books of Moses" as well as throughout the Old Testament.[68] Thus, the relationship between law and gospel, rather than being dialectical, becomes almost continuous.[69] As we shall see, there are differences between the two testaments, but essentially their content is the same: Jesus Christ. This is of fundamental importance, for the knowledge of God's will

---

[64] Ibid., 2. 2. 26-3. 2.
[65] Ibid., 2. 3. 5. (LCC, 20:294).
[66] Ibid., 2. 4. 1.
[67] Ibid., 2. 4. 5.
[68] CR, 77:525.
[69] Ibid., 56:564.

would be useless without the grace of Christ. The ceremonial law had Christ as its content and end, for without him all ceremonies are void.[70] The only reason why the sacrifices of the ancient priests were acceptable unto God was the promised redemption in Jesus Christ. In themselves, given our corruption, any sacrifices that we might offer to God must be unacceptable.[71]

But it is in the moral law that one can see most clearly the continuity between the old and the new. In fact, the moral law has a threefold purpose.

The first purpose of the law—and here Calvin agrees with Luther—is to show us our sin, misery, and depravity. When we see in the law what God demands of us, we are brought face to face with our own shortcomings. This does not enable us to do God's will, but it does force us to stop trusting in ourselves and to seek the help and grace of God.[72]

The second purpose of the law is to restrain the wicked.[73] Although this does not lead to regeneration, it is nevertheless necessary for social order. As many obey the law out of fear, the threats that are included in the law serve to strengthen this function. Under this heading, the law also serves those who, while being predestined to salvation, have not yet been converted. In forcing them to heed the will of God, it prepares them for the grace to which they have been predestined. Thus, many who have come to know the grace of God testify that before their conversion they felt compelled by fear to obey the law.

Finally, the third use of the law—*tertium usus legis*—is to reveal the will of God to those who believe.[74] This is an emphasis that was to become typical of the Reformed tradition and that gave it a great deal of its austerity in matters of ethics. Calvin himself, on the basis of this third use of the law, is compelled to devote a large section of his *Institutes* to expound the moral law. Calvin's basic contention is that Christ has abolished the curse of the law but not its validity. Where antinomianism errs is in claiming that, because God in Christ has abolished the curse of the law, Christians are no longer bound by the

---

[70] *Ibid.*, 78:603.
[71] *Inst.*, 2. 7. 1.
[72] *Ibid.*, 2. 7. 6-9; *CR*, 51:701; 54:398; 73:610; 76:151.
[73] *Inst.*, 2. 7. 10-11. Cf. *CR*, 65:265.
[74] *Inst.*, 2. 7. 12; *CR*, 56:115, 627; 57:111; 76:165.

law. In truth, the law cannot be abolished, for it expresses the will of
God, which never changes. What has been abolished, besides the
curse of the moral law, is the ceremonial law. The reason for this is
clear: the purpose of the ancient ceremonies was to point to Christ,
and such pointing is no longer necessary once the full reality has
been revealed.

The "third use of the law" means that Christians must study the
law with care, not only as a word of damnation that constantly throws
them back upon the grace of God, but also as the basis on which to
determine what their actions are to be. In this study and
interpretation of the law, three fundamental principles must be kept
in mind. The first is that God is spirit, and that for this reason God's
commandments have to do both with outward actions and with
sentiments within the heart. This is true of the entire law, and
therefore what Christ does in the Sermon on the Mount is simply to
make explicit what was already implicit, and not to promulgate a new
law. The law of Christ is none other than the law of Moses.[75] The
second is that every precept is at once positive and negative, for every
prohibition implies a command, and vice versa.[76] Therefore, nothing
is left out of the law of God. Third, the fact that the Decalog was
written in two tables shows that religion and justice must go hand in
hand.[77] The first table deals with duties toward God; the second has
to do with relations with our neighbors. The basis of justice is thus the
service of God, and the latter is impossible without just dealings with
others.

Thus, there is a fundamental continuity between the Old
Testament and the New.[78] Basically, this continuity has to do with the
fact that the will of God revealed in the Old Testament remains
eternally the same, and with the further fact that the core of the Old
Testament was the promise of Christ, of whom the New speaks as an
accomplished fact. Nevertheless, there are also some significant
differences between the two testaments. These differences are five.[79]
First, the New Testament speaks clearly of the future life, whereas
the Old only promises it by means of earthly signs. Second, the Old

---

[75] *Inst.*, 2. 8. 6-7; *CR*, 73:174.
[76] *Inst.*, 2. 8. 8-10.
[77] *Ibid.*, 2. 8. 11.
[78] *Ibid.*, 2. 10; 3. 17.
[79] *Ibid.*, 2. 11.

Testament offered only the shadow of what is substantially present in the New, namely, Christ. Third, the Old was temporary, while the New is eternal. Fourth, the essence of the Old Testament is law, and therefore servitude, whereas the essence of the New is the gospel of freedom. Here we must note, however, that whatever in the Old Testament is promised is not law, but gospel. Finally, the Old Testament was directed to a single people, whereas the message of the New is universal. But in spite of these differences, the basic thrust of Calvin's discussions of law and gospel is one of continuity, and the difference between the two is one of promise and fulfillment. In this, Calvin differed substantially from Luther. And this was in part what allowed Calvinism to develop more detailed ethical programs than did the Lutherans.

Jesus Christ

As in the case of the Trinity, Calvin follows traditional orthodoxy when he discusses the person of Christ and his work.[80] In Christ there are two natures in a single person, so that "he who was the Son of God became the Son of man—not by confusion of substances, but by unity of person."[81] Although councils may err—and in fact have erred—the first ecumenical councils correctly represented the biblical testimony regarding the person of Christ. Therefore, the main lines of Calvin's Christology need not detain us here.

There are, however, three points at which a study of Calvin's Christology may prove significant. The first concerns his attempts to defend the traditional dogma against its detractors. This is significant, both because it forced Calvin to spell out his own Christology and because it serves to illustrate some of the unorthodox ideas held by rationalists and others. Second, Calvin's description of the work of Christ in terms of the triple office of king, prophet, and priest—usually called the *triplex munus*—became common in Reformed theology. Third, his understanding of the hypostatic union is closely connected with his position on the presence of Christ in the Lord's Supper.

The first point at which contemporary controversies forced Calvin

---

[80] Koopmans, *Das altkirchiche Dogma*, pp. 86-97.
[81] *Inst.*, 2. 14. 1 (*LCC*, 20:482).

to develop his theology was the reason for the incarnation.[82] His main opponent here was Osiander,[83] although Servetus was also envisioned.[84] Osiander claimed that, even if Adam had not fallen, Christ would still have become incarnate. His main argument for this was that Adam's creation according to the image of God, who is Christ, already promised that Christ would take humanity upon himself. Therefore, the purpose of the incarnation is not the redemption of humankind but the fulfillment of creation. It is the fall that has given the incarnation its present purpose, which therefore is contingent. This was no innovation, for it had been held by most Franciscan theologians during the Middle Ages. But Calvin rejected it as vain speculation. What we know of Christ according to the biblical witness is that he became incarnate for our redemption. There is no indication, apart from the "tickling curiosity" of Osiander, that the incarnation had any other purpose than our redemption. This controversy is significant, for it tended to ground Calvin's Christology on soteriology.

Another point at which the controversies of his time helped Calvin develop his Christology had to do with the human nature of Christ. As we have already seen, Menno Simons and some other Anabaptists held that Christ did not have an earthly flesh, but that his body had come down from heaven and had taken form in the Virgin's womb. Some also tried to exempt Jesus from the lineage of Adam. These "new Marcionites," as Calvin called them, forced him to insist on the humanity of Christ, and on his physical descent from Adam.[85]

Calvin's doctrine of the hypostatic union, which we shall discuss shortly, was developed in opposition to Servetus.[86] In rejecting the Trinity, which had been the background on which traditional Christology had been developed, Servetus was led to reject also a great deal of that Christology. The main point at issue here was whether Christ could be called the Son of God before the

---

[82] *Ibid.*, 2.12.

[83] Osiander, or Hosemann (1498–1552), was a pastor at Nuremberg and Königsberg whose views on the *imago Dei*, the incarnation, and justification Calvin as well as Melanchthon and other Protestant leaders felt compelled to reject. On the issue at hand, see his *An filius Dei fuerit incarnatus*. See also above, pp. 104-6.

[84] In his *Christianismi restitutio* Servetus had held the same views as Osiander regarding the necessity of the incarnation.

[85] *Inst.*, 2. 13.

[86] *Ibid.*, 2. 14. In this debate, Calvin also had in mind the Italian Giorgio Blandrata. Cf. his *Ad quaestiones Blandratae responsum* (*CR*, 37:321 32).

incarnation, or not. Servetus claimed that the title "Son of God" meant that Jesus had been begotten in Mary's womb by the Holy Spirit. Before the incarnation he was to be called "Word," and only after the incarnation was he properly a "Son." Furthermore, Servetus differed from Calvin in still another way: whereas Calvin frequently insisted on the distance that separates God and humanity, Servetus felt that this was exaggerated. Something of the Spirit of God is in every human being. Therefore, for him the problem is not the union of two opposite natures, but how this particular man can be called Son of God in a special sense that is not applicable to other creatures. In order to solve this problem, Servetus emphasized the unity within Christ to a point that Calvin could not accept. Calvin therefore accused him of reviving the ancient heresy of the monophysites. How he did that is not particularly significant, for he simply made use of the traditional arguments that had become common by this time. What is significant is that in this discussion Calvin developed a Christology that, while remaining orthodox, tended to emphasize the distinction between the two natures in Christ rather than the unity of the person and the *communicatio idiomatum*. This is fully consistent with Calvin's opinions regarding the value of humanity before God as well as with his theory of the presence of Christ in the Lord's Supper—as we shall see in a later section of this chapter.

Finally, another opponent who helped shape Calvin's Christology was Franceso Stancaro, who held that Christ is our mediator only through his human nature.[87] It is likely that he came to this conclusion trying to refute Osiander, who claimed that Christ was mediator only according to his divinity. Against both, Calvin asserted that, because the work of redemption took place through the hypostatic union, everything in Christ that has to do with redemption is to be ascribed to the unity of the person, and not to one nature or another. The significance of this is that toward the end of his life Calvin came to emphasize the *communicatio idiomatum* to a greater degree than he had before—although he had never denied it.

---

[87] As this matter came to Calvin's attention in 1560, after the *Institutes* had received their final shape, its influence cannot be found in that work. See Calvin's *Responsum ad Polonos contra Stancarum* (*CR*, 37:333-42) and *Responsio ad Polonos de controversia mediatoris* (*CR*, 37:345-58).

Calvin discusses the work of Christ in terms of three offices—*triplex munus*. Christ is at once prophet, king, and priest. The very title "Christ" signifies this triple office, for it means "anointed," and in the Old Testament kings, prophets, and priests were anointed.[88] Christ is the prophet par excellence, because in him all prophecies are fulfilled. The prophecies of the Old Testament had no other content that Christ himself. This prophetic office of Christ is extended not only to his mouth, so that his words are prophetic, but also to his entire body, so that in each of his actions, as well as in the present preaching of the gospel, the power of the Holy Spirit can be seen. Christ is king of the church as well as of individual believers. As such, he rules over us. But his rule is such that he shares with his subjects all that he has received. The kings of the Old Testament, like the prophets, point to this supreme and unique king. As a priest, Christ has come before God to present himself in sacrifice. In so doing, he fulfilled all the ancient sacrifices, which had no validity other than in him. And he has also made his followers priests, for he has now enabled them to present themselves before God as a living sacrifice.

Finally, the third main characteristic of Calvin's Christology is his constant concern to avoid any confusion of humanity and divinity in Christ. In this he tended to agree with Zwingli against Luther, who emphasized the unity of the person above the distinction of the two natures. This was significant because Calvin—like Zwingli—could not accept Luther's use of the *communicatio idiomatum* as an argument for the ubiquity of the resurrected body of Christ, and therefore for the possibility of its presence on the altar. Like Zwingli, Calvin argued that the ubiquity of the divine had not been communicated to the body of Christ, and that he could not therefore be present in heaven and on several altars at the same time. Within this context, he pointed out that, although the divinity of the Second Person was fully present in Jesus, it was not circumscribed by his humanity. His wondrous descent was such that he was still in heaven while he was also in Jesus; and when he was being born from the Virgin's womb he was still filling the entire universe.[89] This is what later theologians came to call the *extra calvinisticum*, and it became a characteristic emphasis of Reformed Christology.

---

[88] *Inst.*, 2. 15.
[89] *Ibid.*, 2. 13. 4.

If one were to attempt to characterize Calvin's Christology in a few sentences, one could say that, while strictly orthodox, that Christology leans more toward the ancient Antiochenes than toward the Alexandrians, and also that it has a very strong soteriological rather than metaphysical emphasis.

Redemption and Justification

Calvin understands the work of Christ in terms of satisfaction.[90] Through his obedience unto death, Christ has merited for us the forgiveness of sins. In this manner, God's justice and love have been satisfied.

But the fact that Christ died and thus merited salvation for humankind does not make that salvation effective for all. What makes Christ and all his benefits available to the believer is the inner and secret operation of the Holy Spirit.[91] This is the reason that Paul calls the third person of the Trinity "the spirit of adoption," and also "the guarantee and seal" of our inheritance. The Holy Spirit leads to Christ. The main work of the Spirit is none other than faith in Christ.[92]

As this is basic to an understanding of Calvin's view of the Christian life, we must pause to discuss the nature of faith as Calvin defines it. "Now we shall possess a right definition of faith if we call it a firm and certain knowledge of God's benevolence toward us, founded upon the truth of the freely given promise in Christ, both revealed to our minds and sealed upon our hearts through the Holy Spirit."[93]

This means that faith has a cognitive element. It is not just an attitude of trust. But neither is it something that the mind discovers through its natural means. It is a gift of God, not a human achievement. Not everything, however, that passes under the name of faith really deserves that name. Faith has a definite content. It is faith in Christ. Every other use of the term "faith" is inexact and may lead to serious error. Thus, for instance, the notion of "implicit faith" proposed by Catholic theologians uses the term incorrectly, for its

---

[90] *Ibid.*, 2. 17.
[91] *Ibid.*, 3. 1. 1.
[92] *Ibid.*, 3. 1. 4.
[93] *Ibid.*, 3. 2. 7 (*LCC*, 20:551). Cf. *CR*, 78:447-85.

object is the church and not Jesus Christ.[94] There is, indeed, a sense in which our faith is always imperfect while we live on earth; but its perfection lies not in the church, but in the final consummation. The fact that faith implies "a firm and certain knowledge" does not exclude the battle of the spirit against the flesh, or the doubt that goes with it. But when one has true faith there is, even in the midst of that battle, an underlying assurance of God's love. This assurance is grounded on God's promise, which is none other than Christ himself, and is imprinted in the heart of the believer by the Holy Spirit. Thus, faith is something that only the true believers—the elect—can have. It is more than knowledge of God and the divine will. The Devil has such knowledge, but does not have faith, for he does not participate in the promise.[95]

Given this understanding of faith, Calvin insists on the Protestant doctrine of justification by faith. This is essentially, as in the case of Luther, not a justification based on something that God finds in the believer and in view of which one is declared just. To say that God justifies does not mean primarily that a sinner is made objectively just. What it means is that God declares the sinner to be just. The justice of Christ is like a robe that a sinner puts on by faith, and clothed in it is declared to be just. Herein lies the difference between justification by works and justification by faith. Justification by works is that which attempts to affirm its own righteousness, and thus to satisfy God's demand for righteousness. "On the contrary, justified by faith is he who, excluded from the righteousness of works, grasps the righteousness of Christ through faith, and clothed in it, appears in God's sight not as a sinner but as a righteous man. Therefore, we explain justification simply as the acceptance with which God receives us into his favor as righteous men. And we say that it consists in the remission of sins and the imputation of Christ's righteousness."[96]

This is the true and sole function of faith. Faith is not the trust by which we accept that which we cannot prove by reason but authority tells us. There are indeed things that are believed on the basis of the authority of Scripture, but belief in such things is not faith. The role

---

[94] *Ibid.,* 3. 2. 2-3.
[95] Calvin rejects the scholastic distinction between faith that is "formed"—that is, has received the "form" by charity, and "unformed" faith. What the scholastics call "unformed faith" is not true faith.
[96] *Inst.,* 3. 11. 2 (*LCC,* 20:726-27).

of faith is to join the believer with Christ in such a way that the justice of Christ is imputed to the believer, in spite of sin.

As in the case of his Christology, Calvin felt the need to make the doctrine of justification by faith more explicit when it was attacked or misinterpreted. During his early years, his opponents in this respect were the Roman Catholics; but when Osiander, himself a Protestant, proposed an understanding of justification that Calvin could not accept, that polemic also contributed to the clarification of Calvin's views. Osiander was led by his mystical tendencies and by his desire to show that the imputation of justice was not an arbitrary decree, to suggest that what actually happens in justification is that the essence of Christ is present in the believer, and that this essence is so joined with the human soul that one is "essentially justified." What this then means is that righteousness is not "imputed," as in Luther, but that God actually sees divine righteousness in us. This was closely related with what has been said above, that Osiander taught that Christ was mediator according only to his divinity. Justification is the presence of divinity in us. By virtue of this divinity, God at once declares and makes us just. These views Calvin could not accept for two main reasons. In the first place, they tend to obliterate the distance between God and us. Calvin was willing to affirm that justification takes place through union with Christ. But he would not accept an interpretation, such as Osiander's, that implied what Calvin called a "mixture of substances" between God and the believer. In the second place, Osiander's doctrine of justification was unacceptable to Calvin because it did away with the necessity of the incarnation and sufferings of Christ. If God justifies us because of Christ's divinity—which after all is the same as the Father's and the Spirit's—what need is there for the cross of Christ? "For even though Christ if he had not been God could not cleanse our souls by his blood, nor appease his Father by his sacrifice . . . because the power of the flesh is unequal to so great a burden, yet it is certain that he carried out all these acts according to his human nature."[97]

The importance of the doctrine of justification by faith is such that without it there is no true religion.[98] The reason for this claim, as in the case of Luther, is that any other understanding of justification

---

[97] *Ibid.*, 3. 11. 9 (*LCC*, 20:735). Cf. *ibid.*, 3. 11. 12.
[98] *CR*, 74:23.

leads to pride, and only in an attitude of humility can one receive the mercy of God.[99] This insistence on humility before God, on the distance that separates the divine nature from the human, and on the need to trust God rather than oneself, runs throughout Calvin's theology and is one of its main characteristics.

Justification by faith, however, does not mean that the Christian is to be content with the imputation of righteousness, and to continue wallowing in sin. It is true that the justified Christian is still a sinner, and will continue to be throughout this earthly life. But it is also true that the justified Christian seeks to show the fruits of justification. This is the main thesis of a section in the *Institutes* usually called *Treatise on the Christian Life*,[100] which was repeatedly published separately from the larger work.[101] The fact that this treatise was very popular set its imprint on later Calvinism, and especially on the Puritan tradition. The thesis of this treatise is succinctly expressed in its first paragraph: "The object of regeneration . . . is to manifest in the life of believers a harmony and agreement between God's righteousness and their obedience, and thus to confirm the adoption that they have received as sons."[102]

Although the justified sinner does not cease being a sinner, the divine act of justification is also one of regeneration. In the elect God creates the love of righteousness by the example of the divine holiness and through their communion with Christ. The work of regeneration is God's work in the believer, progressively[103] creating anew the divine image that had been deformed through sin.[104] The result is the Christian life, which abounds in good works. These works, however, do not justify. They are the result and sign of justification.[105]

The basic rule of the Christian life is that Christians belong not to themselves, but to the Lord.[106] This in turn leads to self-denial, both in relation to others and in relation to God. In relation to others, Christians deny themselves by forgiving and being humble, as well as

---

99 *Inst.*, 3. 12. 7.
100 *Ibid.*, 3. 6-10.
101 First in French (1545); *Traité très excellent de la vie chrétienne*. Shortly thereafter in English (1549): *The Life or Conversation of a Christian Man*. Frequent reprints.
102 *Inst.*, 3. 6. I (*LCC*, 20:684).
103 *CR*, 77:312.
104 *Ibid.*, 79:208.
105 *Inst.*, 3. 18.
106 Note the influence of Luther's very popular treatise *On the Freedom of the Christian Man*.

by serving others in love. In relation to God, self-denial means subjecting oneself to God's judgments, seeking to do nothing but God's will, and carrying the cross. The carrying of the cross is not something that happens to some unfortunate Christians, but is a necessary sign of the Christian life. The Christian attitude toward one's cross, however, is very different from the Stoic attitude. The Stoic seeks self-control and fortitude; the Christian simply trusts in God and admits to weakness. Thus, the Stoic's trials simply add to pride and sin, whereas the Christian's cross leads away from self and toward trust in God.[107]

Although an important part of the Christian life is being able to meditate on the life to come as a remedy against excessive love of this life and fear of death,[108] the Christian must still learn how to use the present life and its goods.[109] This dilemma cannot be solved through an easy recourse to either austerity or intemperance, for neither of these is what God wants of the Christian. Intemperance makes one live for the present life, forget that one is a pilgrim on earth, and disobey God's law. Austerity, as preached by the ascetics, is also wrong, for it adds to the divine commandment rules that are not in God's law. Between these two extremes, the basic principle that the Christian is to follow is that everything is to be used for the purpose for which it was created. This in turn implies four basic rules to be applied in the use of things in this world: First, we must see the Creator in all things used, and be grateful. Second, we are to use this world as if not needing it, being ready to withstand poverty and to be moderate in times of abundance. Third, all that we have is to be seen as a trust from God, on which an accounting will be demanded. Finally, we are to take into account our own calling, that is, the function in which God has placed us in life, for the proper use of things depends on our function.[110]

Thus we see once again, now in the context of the doctrines of justification and regeneration, how Calvin's understanding of law and gospel, being different from Luther's, produces in him a greater emphasis than Luther's on the kind of life that a Christian must lead.

---

[107] *Inst.*, 3. 8. 9.

[108] *Ibid.*, 3. 9.

[109] *Ibid.*, 3. 10.

[110] In passing, one should note the conservatism implied in this last rule, which in fact says that station in life is a divine calling, and that one should do nothing to change it. Likewise, in this context, Calvin denies that any private citizen has the right to rise against a tyrant. Inst., 3. 10. 6.

This difference between the two reformers, which does not seem great when one compares them, would eventually produce a marked difference between the Lutheran tradition and the Reformed.

Predestination

Calvin is well known for his doctrine of predestination, which many scholars have declared to be the center of his theology.[111] But such an understanding of Calvin's theology is the result of a distortion of perspective produced by later controversies. Calvin did affirm the doctrine of double predestination, and as the years went by he progressively expanded the section that the *Institutes* devoted to it. But the inconspicuous place that the four chapters on the subject occupy in the *Institutes*[112] should be a warning that the doctrine of predestination, important as it may be, is not the clue that opens the door to the rest of Calvin's theology. Nor is his doctrine of predestination, as in the case of Zwingli, a corollary of divine providence. It is significant that Calvin discusses providence in the first book of the *Institutes* and then postpones the question of predestination to the end of the third book, where he is dealing with the Christian life, and just before he moves on to ecclesiology. The reason for this is that predestination is for Calvin above all a practical doctrine, one that reinforces justification by faith and at the same time provides the foundation for ecclesiology.[113]

Furthermore, the separation of predestination from the general providence of God shows that Calvin will not attempt to prove predestination out of divine omnipotence and omniscience. To do so would be to try to penetrate the secret counsels of God and would be the height of pride and impiety.[114] "Let this, therefore, first of all be before our eyes: to seek any other knowledge of predestination than what the Word of God discloses is not less insane than if one should purpose to walk in a pathless waste, or to see in darkness."[115] Predestination is indeed a difficult and perilous doctrine. But it is scriptural, and therefore it ought to be taught and preached.

[111] See Wendel, *Calvin*, pp. 199-200, nn. 99 and 100.
[112] *Inst.*, 3. 21-24.
[113] Wendel, *Calvin*, p. 204.
[114] *CR*, 76:314; 82:57.
[115] *Inst.*, 3. 21. 2 (*LCC*, 21:923).

Furthermore, the peril implied in the doctrine is not such for the true believer, but only for the unbeliever who is seeking for ways to mock true Christian doctrine, and such a person will mock the faith whether Christians teach predestination or not.[116]

"We call predestination God's eternal decree, by which he determined with himself what he willed to become of each man."[117] Thus Calvin defined predestination. The rest of his four chapters on the subject is mere explanation of this definition, response to objections, and adducing of scriptural material to support it.

The doctrine of election runs throughout the Old Testament, where Israel is constantly depicted as God's chosen people—owing not to some action or decision on Israel's part, but to the sovereign decree of God. Furthermore, not all of Abraham's lineage are elected, but only some among them. Finally, some are chosen individually, as is clearly affirmed in numerous New Testament texts—especially in Romans and Galatians.[118]

God's decree of election does not depend on divine foreknowledge.[119] Predestination is not simply God's decision to deal with a person according to what God foreknows regarding that person's future actions and attitudes. On the contrary, the fact that election is a sovereign decree means that it does not depend on any human action, past, present, or future. It is an independent decision on God's part.

The same is true of the reprobate. God actively decides not to grant them the hearing of the Word, or to make them hear it in such a way that their hearts are hardened by it.[120] In a mysterious manner, which none can fathom, they are justly condemned, and in their damnation the glory of God is served.[121]

The elect, on the other hand, can be certain of their salvation. This does not mean that one is to trust one's own faith, and to claim that it will assure one's salvation. It does mean that a person who has true faith looks at Scripture, and at Christ in it, and in him finds assurance of salvation.[122] This is why those who attempt to penetrate the divine

---

[116] *Ibid.*, 3. 21. 3-4.
[117] *Ibid.*, 3. 21. 5. (*LCC*, 21:926).
[118] *Ibid.*, 3. 21. 5-7.
[119] *Ibid.*, 3. 22. 1-7.
[120] *Ibid.*, 3. 24. 12-13.
[121] *Ibid.*, 3. 24. 14.
[122] *Ibid.*, 3. 24. 4-5.

counsels without Scripture lose themselves in an abyss of despair, while those who approach Scripture with true faith find consolation and assurance in the doctrine of election. Those who have true faith trust not in themselves, but in Christ, and thus have an assurance that is also humble. This does not make them sinless. They are still lost sheep.[123] But their assurance keeps them in that trust in Christ which is the only way to salvation.

Several objections can be raised against this doctrine.[124] The first is that, although God does indeed elect some for salvation, God does not predestine others to damnation. Such a possibility Calvin dismisses as a childish notion. Election means nothing unless there is reprobation. Furthermore, all divine decrees are active, and although it is true that those who perish are damned for their sin, God actively decides to reprobate them. Second, some could object that this doctrine shows God to be unjust, in condemning some for sins that they have not yet committed. To this Calvin answers that God's will is the criterion of justice, that it is its own law, and that therefore God's decrees are necessarily just, no matter what we might think of them. Third, it would seem that God first foreordains that we should sin and then punishes us for our sin. To this there is no answer but to affirm that God's will is incomprehensible and mysterious, whereas we know through revelation that God is just, that we have sinned, and that the reprobate will be condemned for their sins. How all this can be true at the same time, we cannot fathom.

Thus, in summary, Calvin's doctrine of predestination is based—or at least claims to be—not on speculations regarding God's omnipotence and omniscience, but on the witness of Scripture. Predestination as a logical conclusion drawn from what reason claims to know of the nature of God he rejects as one more instance of human pride attempting to outreach itself. Scriptural predestination is double—that is, there is predestination for election as well as for reprobation—and does not depend on God's foreknowledge of future human actions. Although this is a great mystery, such double predestination in no way detracts from God's justice and love. As for Christian theology, the doctrine of predestination serves a double

---

[123] *Ibid.*, 3. 24. 11.
[124] *Ibid.*, 3. 23.

function, being at once a stark affirmation of salvation by the sole grace of God, and the foundation for ecclesiology. To the latter we must now turn.

The Church

Calvin establishes a clear distinction between the visible and the invisible church. Strictly speaking, only the latter, which is formed by all the elect, living, and dead, is the true, universal church. Only it is the body of Christ, for only the elect are members of his body, and in the visible church there are many who are not elect. However, Calvin does not carry this distinction to the point of opposing the two churches. On the contrary, the visible church is a necessary and useful expression of the invisible church, and as long as we remain in this life the visible church must be our church.

> For we have said that Holy Scripture speaks of the church in two ways. Sometimes by the term "church" it means that which is actually in God's presence, into which no persons are received but those who are children of God by grace of adoption and true members of Christ by sanctification of the Holy Spirit. Then, indeed, the church includes not only the saints presently living on earth, but all the elect from the beginning of the world. Often, however, the name "church" designates the whole multitude of men spread over the earth who profess to worship one God and Christ. . . . In this church are mingled many hypocrites who have nothing of Christ but the name and outward appearance . . . . Just as we believe, therefore, that the former church, invisible to us, is visible to the eyes of God alone, so we are commanded to revere and keep communion with the latter, which is called "church" in respect to men.[125]

Thus, the relationship between the invisible and the visible church is not one of opposition, but one in which the visible church, the only church that it is given to us in this earthly life to know, is a sign of the invisible communion of the elect. Christians are not to abandon the visible church under guise of being members of an invisible body. God has placed the visible church in the world to be the "exterior means" for the proclamation of the Word and for the believer's

---

[125] *Ibid.,* 4. 1. 7 (*LCC,* 21:1021-22).

sanctification. God's freedom is not impaired by having chosen to bind us to earthly means such as the visible church, and therefore those who claim that the church must be only spiritual, because God is spirit, belittle God.[126] The visible church has been ordained by God to be the mother of the faithful, and only those can have eternal life who have the church as their mother.[127]

Therefore, it is with the visible church that Calvin's ecclesiology is concerned. The invisible church is always in the background, for the visible is only a sign and servant of the invisible. But when Calvin says "church," except in the few cases where he explicitly says that he is referring to the company of the elect, he means the visible company on earth, in which the wheat and the tares are mixed.[128] It is with this church, a visible, earthly, fallible community, that the rest of this section is concerned.

Although only God knows who the elect are, there are signs indicating who are to be accounted as such. These are those who confess God and Christ, participate in the sacraments, and lead a good life. Therefore, the two marks of the church are the preaching of the Word and the administration of the sacraments. "Wherever we see the Word of God purely preached and heard, and the sacraments administered according to God's institution, there, it is not to be doubted, a church of God exists."[129] These two marks make it possible to judge whether a church is true or not. The personal holiness of its members is not a proper mark of the true church, as the Anabaptists claim, for the members of the true church are not all elect and even those who are elect continue being sinners. The holiness of the church is not in the moral purity of its members, but in the holiness of its head and in the promise that the elect have received. On the other hand, the Roman Church is not a true church, for it has departed from the true preaching of the Word. Where the Word of God is not honored, there is no church. Against this, the appeal to apostolic succession is of no avail, for true apostolicity is derived not from the laying on of hands, but from the preaching of

---

[126] *Ibid.*, 4. 1.5.
[127] *Ibid.*, 4. 1. 4.
[128] In the *Institutes* (4. 1. 4) he clearly states that his intention is to deal with the visible church. In this emphasis on the visible church he was influenced by Bucer. Cf. Wendel. *Calvin*, pp. 223-25.
[129] *Inst.*, 4. 1. 9. (*LCC*, 21:1023).

the doctrine of the apostles.[130] Yet, there are certain "traces" of the church in the Roman Church—notably baptism—and therefore, although the pope is the main leader of the reign of Antichrist, there may still be true churches in the Roman communion.[131]

Calvin paid much more attention to the organization of the church than did Luther. In general, he believed—together with the other Reformed leaders, such as Zwingli and Bucer—that the restoration of Christianity required a return to the primitive organization of the church. In this he disagreed with Luther, who considered such things to be of secondary importance as long as the gospel was properly proclaimed. As a result, churches in the Lutheran tradition follow a wide spectrum of organizational patterns, whereas most Reformed churches are governed according to the basic principles proposed by Calvin. This difference is not peripheral, but has to do with the fundamental difference between Luther and the Reformed theologians regarding the goals of the Reformation. While Luther believed that it was necessary to leave aside only those elements in the tradition of the church which contradicted Scripture, Calvin and the Reformed theologians felt that the reformation that was needed must go further and restore primitive Christianity after the pattern of the New Testament. Thus, church order was for Luther something that must always depend on temporal circumstances, whereas for Calvin and the Reformed tradition it was part of the very nature of the church. On the other hand, however, it must be said that Calvin never understood his own instructions regarding church order as literal restoration of the practices of the New Testament period, but rather as an effort to take what the New Testament says about the church and embody it in a pattern of church order. It was the later Reformed tradition that tended to claim that the model offered by Calvin was the one that had scriptural sanction above any other.

Although we cannot enter here into the details of church order as proposed by Calvin, two points are significant because they illustrate Calvin's ecclesiology. These two points are the election of pastors and the administration of discipline.

The election of pastors is to be made jointly by the church (by

---

[130] *Ibid.*, 4. 2. 1-4.
[131] *Ibid.*, 4. 2. 11-12.

which he means the local church that they are to serve) and the pastors (by which he means other pastors from other churches).[132] The significance of this is that for Calvin the local church is *the* church. The church is not a superstructure embracing the entire world. But, on the other hand, each local church must be measured by the criteria of the preaching of the Word and the administration of the sacraments. Thus, the local church elects its own pastors, who must be people whom it judges to be exemplary both in doctrine and in life. But the other pastors who must coincide in this judgment are there to guarantee that local churches do not go astray from the teaching of Scripture. This is the fundamental ecclesiological consideration behind the "presbyterian" form of government, which has become typical of Reformed churches.

Second, the administration of discipline follows a similar pattern. Discipline is necessary in the church, not to insure its holiness—which is in Christ—but to seek to preserve the honor of Christ, whose name is trampled by open violation of his will. The church can discipline its members by private and public admonitions, and, in extreme cases of obdurate misbehavior, by excommunication.[133] The purpose of discipline is threefold: to avoid the profanation of the body of Christ and of the Lord's Supper, to prevent the corruption of others in the church, and to call the sinner to repentance.[134] Against Roman Catholic practice, Calvin affirms that discipline is to be administered jointly by the pastors and the church.[135] Against what he claims is the practice of the Anabaptists, it is to be administered in a spirit of love, recognizing that those who administer it are not themselves pure.[136] Thus, the basic traits of Calvin's ecclesiology can be seen once again in his directions for the administration of discipline.

The Sacraments

With characteristic clarity and directness, Calvin begins his lengthy discussion on the sacraments in the *Institutes* by offering two definitions of what he understands a sacrament to be.

---

[132] *Ibid.*, 4. 3. 3.
[133] *Ibid.*, 4. 12. 2.
[134] *Ibid.*, 4. 12. 5.
[135] *Ibid.*, 4. 12. 7.
[136] *Ibid.*, 4. 12. 12-13.

First, we must consider what a sacrament is. It seems to me that a simple and proper definition would be to say that it is an outward sign by which the Lord seals on our consciences the promises of his good will toward us in order to sustain the weakness of our faith; and we in turn attest our piety toward him in the presence of the Lord and of his angels and before men. Here is another briefer definition: one may call it a testimony of divine grace toward us, confirmed by an outward sign, with mutual attestation of our piety toward him.[137]

In developing his view of sacraments, Calvin is seeking to avoid the Roman Catholic and Lutheran positions on the one hand, and the Zwinglian and Anabaptist theories on the other.

Against Zwingli and the Anabaptists, Calvin argues that the sacraments are indeed efficacious. To deny such efficacy on the grounds that they can be received by unbelievers as well as by the faithful would make as much sense as to deny the power of the Word because some hear it and do not heed it. As to the argument that faith is the gift of the Spirit, and that the sacraments therefore do not strengthen or augment it, those who so argue must realize that it is precisely the Spirit that makes the sacraments efficacious. Furthermore, here again one can draw a parallel between the sacraments and the Word, for the latter is not efficacious except through the action of the Spirit.[138] Those who claim that the sacraments are mere symbols regard as primary what is in fact secondary; for, whereas it is true that one of the purposes of the sacraments is to serve as testimonials before the world, it is also true that this is only a secondary function, and that their primary purpose is to serve and fortify the faith of the partaker.

On the other hand, those who claim that the sacraments have the power to justify and to bestow grace are also mistaken. Their mistake consists in confusing the "figure" of the sacrament with the "truth" in it. "For the distinction signifies not only that the figure and the truth are contained in the sacrament, but that they are not so linked that they cannot be separated; and that even in the union itself the matter must always be distinguished from the sign, that we may not transfer to the one what belongs to the other."[139] Such confusion leads to

---

[137] Ibid., 4. 14. 1. (LCC, 21:1277).
[138] Ibid., 4. 14. 7, 9-10.
[139] Ibid., 4. 14. 15 (LCC, 21:1290).

superstition, which consists in placing one's faith in what is not God. This perverts the very nature of the sacrament, whose purpose is precisely to exclude any other claim to justification, and to focus faith in Jesus Christ. In fact, Christ himself is the true substance of all sacraments, for he is the source of their strength, and they promise and grant nothing but him.[140] The sacraments therefore have no other purpose than the purpose of the Word, which is to offer and present Jesus Christ.[141]

In summary, if one follows Calvin's views on the sacraments, "nothing is given to them which should not be given, and conversely nothing taken away which belongs to them."[142]

One finds sacraments in the Old Testament, such as circumcision, purifications, and sacrifices. These were no different from the sacraments in the New Testament, for their substance and meaning was also Jesus Christ. The difference is that whereas the sacraments of the Old Testament announced his future coming, the sacraments of the New show him as he has been given and manifested. Their efficacy, however, is the same, for their content is the same.[143]

The sacraments of the New Testament are only two: baptism and the Lord's Supper. The other rites that usually receive the title of sacrament are not really such, for nowhere in the New Testament is there any indication that God instituted them as signs of his grace, and the ancient writers of the church do not give them that title.[144]

The purpose of baptism—as of every sacrament—is twofold: it serves faith, and it is a confession before others. Those who leave aside the first of these—by which he means Zwingli and the Anabaptists—are missing the primary function of baptism. As an aid to faith, baptism is a true sign of the remission of sins, of the death and resurrection of the believer with Christ, and of union with him. The remission of sins connected with baptism has to do not only with original sin and other past sins, but also with future sins. The washing that takes place in baptism is not such that it avails only for the past. That would be the case if the believer were washed of sins by water. But it is the blood of Christ that washes away sin, and the blood avails for the entire life of the believer. Thus, the question of

---

[140] *Ibid.,* 4. 14. 16.
[141] *Ibid.,* 4. 14. 17.
[142] *Ibid.* (*LCC,* 21:1293).
[143] *Ibid,* 4. 14. 18-26.
[144] *Ibid.,* 4. 19. 1-3.

post-baptismal sins, which was an important issue in the Patristic period and eventually developed into the penitential system, was no problem for Calvin. His answer was simply that baptism was valid throughout life, and not only at the moment of its celebration. Obviously, this idea is closely connected with the doctrine of imputed righteousness, for what happens at baptism is not that one is actually made clean and sinless, but that the justice of Christ is declared to be the believer's. As this justice is of permanent value, baptism is for life and cleanses all sins, past and future. In consequence, baptism does not restore one to Adam's state before the fall. Its function is strictly Christocentric, and its power lies in the union with Christ, which it signifies.[145]

Against the Anabaptists, Calvin affirms that children are to be baptized, and that the rite is valid regardless of the person who administers it. The latter point did not detain him long, for all he had to do was insist that the power of baptism does not come from the minister, that none is truly worthy of administering so holy a rite, and that therefore one is to trust in the power of God acting in baptism rather than in the authority of the person administering it. The other point—that infants are to be baptized—caused him greater difficulties. His insistence on finding scriptural authority for this practice, which is neither attested nor denied in the New Testament, forced him to offer several arguments in favor of infant baptism none of which is eminently successful. But in any case, infant baptism is practiced as a sign of justification by grace and of God's loving care, not only for us, but also for our posterity.[146]

As to the manner in which baptism is to be administered, Calvin feels that immersion and sprinkling are both acceptable, and that the choice between these two forms is a matter of no consequence. What is important is that Christians limit themselves to the simple practice of the New Testament, and reject all the pomp that has been added to the ceremony through the centuries.[147] As a part of the public ministry of the church, it is to be administered only by the pastors, and not by midwives or other private persons.[148]

The Lord's Supper is the other sacrament of the New Testa-

---

[145] *Ibid.*, 4. 15. 1-12.
[146] *Ibid.*, 4. 16. Cf. J. D. Benoit, "Calvin et le baptême des enfants," *RHPhRel*, 1 (1937):457-73.
[147] *Ibid.*, 4. 15. 19.
[148] *Ibid.*, 4. 15. 20.

ment.[149] Calvin feels that this sacrament has been given by God to nourish the faithful, but that Satan has obscured it, both by the "superstitions" of traditional eucharistic doctrine and by the debates among Protestants.[150] Therefore, he divides his discussion of the sacrament into two sections: first, a positive one, in which the need and benefits of the Supper are shown, and then a negative one, in which he addresses himself to the excesses and debates that Satan has introduced into eucharistic theology.[151] This shows that his main concern here is the teaching of the faithful, and that he feels that the attempt to clarify fine points of doctrine is an obligation imposed upon him by circumstances. Thus, Calvin's eucharistic theology did not develop, as his opponents often claimed, out of a curious rationalism that sought to clarify every point of doctrine. However, given the purpose of this study, we shall abandon Calvin's distinction between two levels of theological discourse, and simply expound the most salient features of his understanding of the Supper.

Calvin's doctrine of the Supper is summarized in the following text from the *Institutes,* on which most of the rest is no more than a commentary and clarification:

> First, the signs are bread and wine, which represent for us the invisible food that we receive from the flesh and blood of Christ. For as in baptism, God, regenerating us, engrafts us into the society of his church and makes us his own by adoption, so we have said, that he discharges the function of a provident householder in continually supplying to us the food to sustain and preserve us in that life into which he has begotten us by his Word.
>
> Now Christ is the only food of our soul, and therefore our Heavenly Father invites us to Christ, that, refreshed by partaking of him, we may repeatedly gather strength until we shall have reached heavenly immortality.
>
> Since, however, this mystery of Christ's secret union with the devout is by nature incomprehensible, he shows its figure and image in visible signs best adapted to our small capacity. Indeed, by giving guarantees and tokens he makes it as certain for us as if we had seen it with our own eyes. For this very familiar comparison

---

[149] Besides the pertinent sections in the various editions of the *Institutes,* the most significant material in Calvin's writings is to be found in *CR,* 37.

[150] *Inst.,* 4. 17.1.

[151] The first section is *Inst.,* 4. 17. 1-11. The second, 4. 17. 12-37. Then follow other sections, mostly on the administration of the Supper.

penetrates into even the dullest minds: just as bread and wine sustain physical life, so are souls fed by Christ. We now understand the purpose of this mystical blessing, namely, to confirm for us the fact that the Lord's body was once for all so sacrificed for us that we may now feed upon it, and by feeding feel in ourselves the working of that unique sacrifice; and that his blood was once so shed for us in order to be our perpetual drink.[152]

Thus, the first thing to be said about communion is that it is a visible sign of the union with Christ, which is itself invisible. Communion does not bring about that union. Rather, union with Christ is the result of faith and therefore of the work of the Spirit. The notion that communion somehow effectuates that union must be excluded as magical. Furthermore, the "signs" are to be distinguished from the "substance." Here Calvin uses the term "substance," not in the metaphysical sense, but rather in the sense of "meaning" or "significance."[153] Thus, when he distinguishes between the signs and the substance, what he is saying is that one must not confuse the bread and the wine with the body and blood of Christ, or the acts of eating and drinking with spiritual union with that body and blood.

On the other hand, however, Calvin does not reduce the Supper to a mere service of remembrance, or the function of the elements to spiritual symbolism. The term translated above by "represent" implies presence of the represented—perhaps a better translation would be "show." It is not merely that the bread and the wine stand for the body and blood of Christ, but rather that they show the participant that the body and blood of Christ are available through the action of the Spirit. "Now here we ought to guard against two faults. First, we should not, by too little regard for the signs, divorce them from their mysteries, to which they are so to speak attached. Secondly, we should not, by extolling them immoderately, seem to obscure somewhat the mysteries themselves."[154] It is at this point that he must part company with the Spiritualists, who claim that when

---

152 *Inst.*, 4. 17. 1 (*LCC*, 21:1360-61).

153 H. Gollwitzer, *Coena Domini: Die altlutherische Abendmahlslehre in ihrer Auseinandersetzung mit dem Calvinismus* (Munich: Kaiser Verlag, 1937), pp. 120 ff., shows that Calvin uses the term "substance" in three different ways when discussing the Lord's Supper. He then argues that a great deal of the opposition to Calvin's views had to do with this careless use of so basic a term.

154 *Inst.*, 4. 17. 5 (*LCC*, 21:1364-65).

Jesus says that his flesh must be eaten he means simply that one must believe in him. This interpretation in turn implies that the physical sacraments are unnecessary, and even a hindrance to true faith. Calvin retorts that it is true and that there is no other way to eat the Lord's flesh than through faith, but that faith leads to the physical eating of the elements. "Or, if you want it said more clearly, for them eating is faith; for me it seems rather to follow from faith."[155]

After one distinguishes in the Supper between the visible signs and the spiritual reality, there are still three things to be considered in that reality: the signification, the matter, and the effect. The signification is in the promises, of which the physical signs speak. The matter of the sacrament is Christ himself, for what the believer receives is the spiritual participation in his body and blood. The effect is in the believer, who receives redemption, justice, sanctification, and life eternal.[156] Thus, the center of the sacrament, its contents, is Christ himself, who in it continues his priestly office; and therefore it is correct to say that in participating in the sacrament one becomes a partaker in Christ's body and blood. This is important, for to limit the presence of Christ to his spirit would be tantamount to Docetism.[157] It is the body and blood of Christ that have bought our redemption, and it is of them that we partake in communion. This does not mean, however, that the body of Christ is locally present. The body of Christ is in heaven, and it is through the power—"virtue"—of the Spirit that the believer is joined to that body and receives its benefits.[158] This is what is usually called Calvin's "virtualism."

It is thus clear that Calvin rejects the Zwinglian and Anabaptist as well as the Catholic and the Lutheran views on the eucharistic presence of Christ. However, he devotes most of his time to refuting Catholic and Lutheran views. The Catholic doctrine of transubstantiation, and its understanding of the words of consecration and their effect, he declares to be close to "magic incantation."[159] He also rejects the adoration of the sacrament,[160] and the keeping of the cup from the laity.[161] But to him the crucial issue is the substantial and local

---

[155] *Ibid.* (*LCC*, 21:1365).
[156] *Ibid.*, 4. 17. 11.
[157] *Ibid.*, 4. 17. 7.
[158] *Ibid.*, 4. 17. 10.
[159] *Ibid.*, 4. 17. 15.
[160] *Ibid.*, 4. 17. 35-37.
[161] *Ibid.*, 4. 17. 47-50.

presence of the body of Christ, a belief held by both Catholics and Lutherans, which he rejected. As in the case of Zwingli, Calvin's opposition to the Lutheran and Catholic positions stems from his Christology. In order to say that the body of Christ is physically present in the Supper, it is necessary to say also that the glorified body of Christ now shares in the divine nature in such a way that it is ubiquitous. Calvin takes the ascension of Christ quite literally, and seems to think that his body is now in a heaven somewhere beyond the visible sky—although he also says, like Luther, that "the right hand of God" is a way of saying that Christ now sits in a position of supreme authority over the entire creation. His Christology, as has already been said, is of the "divisive" type usually associated with Antioch. He holds that the unity of the person must not be such that it destroys the distinction between the two natures. This is precisely what he saw the Lutherans doing when they claimed that the glorified body of Christ is ubiquitous. Such a claim injures the humanity of Christ, and Calvin therefore cannot accept it.[162] As a result, he insists on the point that the body of Christ remains in heaven. However, he avoids a purely symbolic understanding of the presence of Christ by adding that although his body does not descend to us, the Spirit raises us to it, so that we are joined to it and partake of its benefits.[163] And, if anyone asks exactly how this is possible, all that Calvin wishes to venture is that this mystery is too great to be comprehended by the human mind or expressed in human words.[164]

Finally, it is important to point out that, although Calvin was often accused by his adversaries of being too rationalistic in his understanding of the Supper and of not holding it in high regard, the truth is that he was always awed by the mystery of the action of God in the sacrament. "For, whenever this matter is discussed, when I have tried to say all, I feel that I have as yet said little in proportion to its worth. And although my mind can think beyond what my tongue can utter, yet even my mind is conquered and overwhelmed by the greatness of the thing. Therefore, nothing remains but to break forth in wonder at this mystery, which plainly neither the mind is able to conceive nor the tongue to express."[165]

---

[162] *Ibid.*, 4. 17. 30.
[163] *Ibid.*, 4. 17. 31.
[164] *Ibid.*, 4. 17. 32.
[165] *Ibid.*, 4. 17. 7 (*LCC*, 21:1367).

The historical importance of Calvin's doctrine of the eucharist, and of the controversies in which he was involved with the Lutherans as a result of that doctrine, is that they marked the definitive break between the reformed and the Lutheran traditions. The *Zurich Consensus* of 1549 had joined the Zwinglian and Calvinistic elements in Switzerland and southern Germany. Calvin's systematic and literary abilities were making his views popular in other parts of Germany. When Joachim Westphal published five volumes showing the differences between Luther and Calvin, especially on communion, many became convinced that there was a movement to supplant Lutheranism throughout Germany. Melanchthon held views that were suspected as being Calvinistic. As a result, the controversies among Lutherans that we discussed in the preceding chapter developed into an attempt to purge Lutheranism of every trace of Calvinism. The lines between the two confessions became increasingly rigid, and the constant polemic tended to seek out hidden points of disagreement and bring them to the forefront. In all this, however, Calvin played only a minor role, and he seems never to have been interested, as the more extreme Lutherans claimed, in infiltrating Germany with Calvinism.[166]

Church and State

The last chapter of the *Institutes,* almost as an afterthought, poses the question of civil government. This was a very live issue for Calvin himself, for throughout his career in Geneva he had been struggling to gain more independence for the ecclesiastical authorities vis-à-vis the civil government. Geneva had received her reformation from Bern and had been organized according to the pattern of that other city, where the triumphant bourgeoisie had retained control of all affairs, religious as well as political. In 1538, both Calvin and Farel decided to go into exile rather than accept the law promulgated by the council that communion was to be offered to all. Upon Calvin's return, he insisted on certain ordinances that guaranteed a measure of independence to the ecclesiastical authorities—the origin of the "consistory" was a compromise between Calvin and the Council in this respect. If, toward the end of his life, he found himself

---

[166] As a matter of fact, his three responses to Westphal were relatively brief, and he seems to have paid relatively little attention to the entire matter. See his *Defensio doctrinae de sacramentis* (*CR*, 37:1-40); *Secunda defensio contra Westphalum* (*CR*, 37:41-120); *Ultima admonitio ad Westphalum* (*CR*, 37:137-252).

practically as master of the city, it was not because he believed that ecclesiastical authorities should be above the civil ones, but because that was the practical outcome of his struggle.

In theory at least, Calvin's view was that there is a difference of jurisdictions between church and state.

> Therefore, in order that none of us may stumble on that stone, let us first consider that there is a twofold government in man: one aspect is spiritual, whereby the conscience is instructed in piety and in reverencing God; the second is political, whereby man is educated for the duties of humanity and citizenship that must be maintained among men. These are usually called the "spiritual" and the "temporal" jurisdiction (not improper terms) by which is meant that the former sort of government pertains to the life of the soul, while the latter has to do with the concerns of the present life—not only with food and clothing but with laying down laws whereby a man may live his life among other men holily, honorably, and temperately. For the former resides in the inner mind, while the latter regulates only outward behavior. The one we may call the spiritual kingdom, the other, the political kingdom. Now these two, as we have divided them, must always be examined separately; and while one is being considered, we must call away and turn aside the mind from thinking about the other. There are in man, so to speak, two worlds, over which different kings and different laws have authority.[167]

In the *Institutes*, therefore, he is not interested in developing an independent theory of the state, one which as to be accepted by Christians as well as non-Christians. His concern is rather the question of how Christians must view the state and relate to it. He therefore rejects the view of the Anabaptists that the state is unclean and that Christians must abstain from any contact with it. On the contrary, the state is created by God, who has called its magistrates to their function, which is to serve divine justice. As a result, the state has the legitimate right to impose the penalty of death, to raise taxes, and to wage just and necessary wars. The same divine authority is the basis of civil laws, which are expressions of the natural law that all know. Therefore, it is legitimate for Christians to be magistrates, as

---

[167] *Inst.*, 3. 19. 15 (*LCC*, 20:847).

well as to appeal to the civil authorities and to bring suit against another—although always avoiding a spirit of hate and vengeance.[168]

All three basic forms of government—monarchy, aristocracy, and democracy—are easily corrupted.[169] More often than not, magistrates stray from the right path. Many become tyrants. But in spite of this, they still have their authority from God and must be obeyed. If one reads the Old Testament accounts of the many tyrants who ruled over Israel, it becomes apparent, first, that God gave them their power in order to chastise Israel, and second, that God always found a way to destroy them when their time had come. Therefore, private Christians must not resist the authority of their rulers, even if they be weak or evil.[170] At two points, however, there is an exception to this general rule—and both of these points would prove significant for later events in which Calvinists resisted what they considered to be tyranny. The first exception is that lower magistrates, whose duty it is to defend the interests of the people, would be shirking their responsibility if they did not call the tyrant to task.[171] The second exception, based on the continuing kingship of Christ, is that we must always obey God before human rulers, so that a Christian must refuse to obey any civil law or demand that is contrary to God's law.[172] As these two exceptions can be applied to many different conditions, according to what one understands to be God's commandments, and who the lower magistrates are, a substantial segment of Calvinism was later able to take very revolutionary stands, in spite of the basically conservative stance of Calvin himself.

The Significance of Calvin's Theology

The foregoing may have given the impression that, in systematizing the theology of the Protestant Reformation, Calvin has lost some of the freshness and vitality that was to be found in Luther and the early reformers. This is true to an extent, for any reader of the *Institutes* will readily see the difference between the orderly, almost punctilious style of Calvin, and the dramatic and vibrant paradoxes of Luther. As the years went by, and new controversies and

---

[168] *Ibid.*, 4. 20. 1-21.
[169] *Ibid.*, 4. 20. 8.
[170] *Ibid.*, 4. 20. 22-30.
[171] *Ibid.*, 4. 20. 31.
[172] *Ibid.*, 4. 20. 32.

opponents arose, Calvin added new chapters and sections to his *Institutes,* as if it were necessary to tackle in them every question being debated at the time. This obviously meant that what was originally a small handbook on the Christian faith eventually became a voluminous and comprehensive systematization of Christian doctrine.

But this process of systematization should not be seen as a negative development. The very fact that Calvin included in his *Institutes* extensive sections having to do with issues being debated at the time shows his pastoral concern. He intended his *Institutes* to be, not a perennial systematization of Christian doctrine, but a practical handbook for those who were attempting to live as Christians in those difficult days—and this was his intention even when he wrote the bulky last edition of his work. Furthermore, the very nature of the *Institutes* themselves, where it is easy to find Calvin's treatment of any particular subject, has drawn attention away from his other works—especially his biblical commentaries—which would serve to give us a more complete picture of Calvin as a person and as a pastor.

Then also, Calvin did make a significant contribution to Protestant theology by drawing its attention to questions other than those of soteriology. Due to Luther's overwhelming experience of his inability to attain salvation, and of the resulting need for the grace of God, a great deal of Protestant theology—especially in the case of Luther himself—had dealt almost exclusively with the question of salvation. Theology was approached through soteriology. This was necessary at a time when one of the principal factors obscuring the nature of the gospel was precisely the excessive and bulky systematization of scholastic theology. But if carried to an extreme it could have resulted in a neglect of other fundamental aspects of the Christian faith. Calvin himself points this out when he says—although criticizing at this point the Catholic Sadolet rather than Luther—that "it is not very sound theology to confine a man's thoughts so much to himself, and not to set before him as the prime motive of his existence zeal to show for the glory of God. For we are born first of all for God, and not for ourselves. . . . It certainly is the duty of a Christian man to ascend higher than merely to seek and secure the salvation of his own soul."[173]

---

[173] *Reply to Sadolet (LCC,* 22:228). This is also pointed out, although with some partisan exaggeration, by Charles Miller in John H. Bratt, ed., *The Rise and Development of Calvinism* (Grand Rapids: Eerdmans,

In many ways, Calvin stands between Luther and the later Calvinists, and we should take care not to read him in the exclusive light of the manner in which others developed his theology at a later date. For one must always remember that, in spite of all the controversies between Lutheran and Reformed, and in spite of the fact that on a number of points Calvin felt constrained to disagree with Luther, the truth is that Calvin always saw himself as a faithful exponent of the basic tenets of the Lutheran reformation. Had it not been for the development of Lutheran and Calvinistic orthodoxies, later theologians in both camps would have found that Calvin's claim to such a title was not altogether unfounded. This may be seen, for instance, in the manner in which Calvin approaches the authority of Scripture, as compared with the later Calvinists. For him, Scripture is not the starting point, to be interpreted as a lawyer interprets a book of law. On the contrary, the reason that Scripture is authoritative for him is the experience of grace. His starting point, rather than Scripture, is the providence and love of God. His goal is not so much correct doctrine as the glory of God—although obviously, this is a matter of emphasis and of the structure of this theology, and he would never separate the two.

This can also be seen in matters having to do with church order. At a later date many came to equate Calvinism with the presbyterian form of government. There is no doubt that what Calvin outlines in his *Institutes,* and what he advocated for Geneva, was the matrix of later presbyterian polity. But he did not take this form of government to be essential to the nature of the church. His polity was grounded in his studies of the New Testament. But any church where the Word of God is correctly proclaimed, and the sacraments duly administered, is to be taken for a true church. Here again he stands between Luther and the later Calvinists, for Luther had paid much less attention than Calvin to the actual polity of the church, whereas many of the later Calvinists elevated Calvin's views on church order almost to the level of the essential marks of the church.

Calvin, then, is not to be dissmised easily. Such easy dismissal takes place both when he is accused of having destroyed the Protestant

---

1959), p. 33: "The Lutheran movement, which began with a righteous cry against a grossly abused but peripheral doctrine of the Church, the granting of Indulgences, tended to seize upon single issues. Luther himself was so obsessed by the doctrine of Salvation by Faith that many other phases of Christian life suffered total neglect."

Reformation by making it too rigid and systematic, and when he is interpreted only in the light of the next few generations that claimed him as their theological mentor. He must be read anew, in the light of his profound pastoral concerns and of the historical moment in which it was his lot to live—at the very end of the formative period of Protestant theology. From this perspective he emerges as one of the most significant Christian theologians of all time.

VII

The Reformation in Great Britain

The fourth major tradition arising from the Protestant Reformation—besides the Lutheran, Reformed, and Anabaptist—is the Anglican, which took shape in England through a complicated process.[1] This process began during the reign of Henry VIII and reached its culmination under Elizabeth. Two features in that development will determine our methodology in the early part of this chapter. The first is that the history of the Reformation in England is dominated by political events and by the varying attitudes of monarchs. This is not to say, as is commonly assumed, that Henry VIII or any other monarch produced the Reformation *ex nihilo*. On the contrary, there was a vast reform movement, dating back to the days of John Wycliffe, whose propaganda was very influential in the final direction that the Anglican Church took. But it is still true that the leading figures in the English struggle were not the reformers themselves, but the monarchs whom they either served or defied—sometimes unto death. The other feature of the English Reformation is that it was not dominated by one or two outstanding figures. None of its chief exponents attained the theological

---

[1] The bibliography on the English Reformation is too extensive to cite here. As general introductions, and guides for further bibliography, see F. Heal and R. O'Day, *Church and Society in England: Henry VIII to James I* (Hamden, Conn.: Archon Books, 1977); P. Milward, *Religious Controversies of the Elizabethan Age: A Survey of Printed Sources* (London: Scholar Press, 1978); P. Collison, *The Religion of Protestants: The Church in English Society, 1555-1625* (Oxford: Clarendon, 1982); D. L. Edwards, *Christian England: From the Reformation to the Eighteenth Century* (Grand Rapids: Eerdmans, 1983).

prominence of Luther or Calvin, although theologians such as Cranmer, Jewel, Latimer, Ridley, Hooper, and others each made significant contributions. Given these two characteristics of the English Reformation, it seems best, when attempting to give a general introduction to its theology, to begin with a brief narration of the process by which the Elizabethan settlement was reached, and then to discuss the theology of the main reformers—although thematically rather than individually.

The Anglican Reformation

As was said above,[2] the reform movement of John Wycliffe did not die. All indications are that at the beginning of the sixteenth century there were substantial remnants of Lollardism in various regions of England. Also seeking the reformation of the church, but in a different way and with goals similar to those of Erasmus, were the humanists, led by John Colet (*ca.* 1467–1519). A member of this humanist circle was Thomas More (1478–1535), who would later die as a martyr when he refused to accept the breach with Rome. Finally, there was the influence of Continental Protestantism. The writings of Luther were widely read in England before the condemnation of 1521, and, judging from the reports of attempts to destroy such writings, they were still readily available after that condemnation. From his exile on the Continent, William Tyndale (*ca.* 1494–1536) translated the New Testament into English, and had it smuggled back into his homeland. He was strangled as a heretic in the Netherlands. Other early advocates of reform along Protestant lines were John Frith, Robert Barnes, and George Joye.[3]

But all these efforts would probably have come to naught had not Henry VIII been compelled by political circumstances to break with Rome. The break came over the request that his marriage with Catherine of Aragon be annulled. Henry had always had doubts about the validity of his marriage, for Catherine was the widow of his older brother Arthur. When Arthur died, Ferdinand of Spain insisted that Catherine return to her homeland with her dowry. As Henry VII could ill afford the loss of either the dowry or the good will of Spain, he proposed that Catherine be wedded to his younger

---

[2] Vol. 2 of this *History*, pp. 327-32.
[3] W. A. Clebsch, *England's Earliest Protestants: 1520–1535* (New Haven: Yale University Press, 1964).

son Henry, who was now the heir to the throne. There was a great deal of doubt as to whether such a marriage was permissible, but eventually the two kings prevailed on the pope to grant a dispensation. In spite of this, Henry was always uneasy about the validity of his marriage to Catherine. His doubts seemed to be confirmed when all their children, except Mary, died at an early age. The very succession to the throne was endangered—and England had just come out of a long period of civil strife precisely over the issue of succession. This was the reason Henry asked that his marriage be annulled. That he was unfaithful to his wife, there is no question. But for that he did not need to set her aside. The problem was that he must secure the succession to the throne by having a legitimate son. For a time the proposal was that his bastard son, the Duke of Richmond, be declared to be legitimate. But that was not possible, and Cardinal Campeggio even suggested that the Duke of Richmond marry his half-sister Mary. Finally Henry requested from the pope that his marriage be annulled. This the pope could hardly grant, for Catherine was the aunt of Charles V, and Charles practically controlled Rome.

Henry appealed to the major universities in Europe—Protestant as well as Catholic—and their verdict was that the pope did not have the authority to grant a dispensation against the commandments of Scripture, and that therefore Henry's marriage to his brother's widow had never been legitimate. However, the universities could issue an opinion, but the actual declaration of annulment had to come from the pope. The latter suggested that Henry take a second wife secretly—the same advice that Luther gave to Philip of Hesse in somewhat similar circumstances. Henry then decided to take matters into his own hands. In a series of measures he progressively took control of the church. He revived ancient laws forbidding appeals to Rome, and cut the funds being sent to the pope. When the see of Canterbury became vacant, he had Thomas Cranmer (1489–1556) appointed to it. Cranmer was a moderate reformer who had been influenced by Luther. But the reason for Henry's choice was that Cranmer felt that the judgment of the universities regarding Henry's marriage was sufficient to annul it. By then, Henry had gone ahead and privately married Anne Boleyn, for she was now pregnant and Henry wanted to make her child legitimate. Ironically, the child turned out to be another girl, who later would reign as Queen

Elizabeth. The pope ordered Henry to leave Anne and reinstate Catherine within ten days, or be excommunicated. Henry then took a bold course, and in a series of acts of Parliament in 1534 the King was declared to be the supreme head of the church in his domains, his marriage with Catherine was pronounced void, Anne was accepted as Queen of England, and her daughter Elizabeth was made the legitimate heir to the throne, unless Henry were to have a male child.

Henry was not interested in changing the practices and doctrines of the newly constituted Church of England. On the contrary, he felt that the denial of papal authority would not cause him too many difficulties with his subjects as long as the life of the parishes remained substantially unchanged. But there were other factors at play that led him in the opposite direction. He wanted the Protestant theologians in Germany to declare that he had been right in setting Catherine aside. They said that the marriage should never have taken place, but that once married to her, Henry had no right to dismiss her. Hoping to entice them, Henry began negotiations for a political religious alliance that he had no intention of signing. This in turn forced him to appear less strict against the Protestants in England than he would have liked to be. Using these circumstances, Cranmer pressed for reforms. The result was that some minor changes were made in the life of the church, but that its theology and practices were far from being Protestant.

The Ten Articles of 1536 asserted the authority of the Bible, the ancient creeds, and the first four ecumenical councils—thus tacitly denying the authority of later tradition. Three sacraments are mentioned: baptism, the eucharist, and penance. In the eucharist, Christ is really and physically present. Salvation is by faith *and* good works. Images, prayers for the dead, purgatory, clerical vestments, the invocation of saints, and other such traditional practices were retained, and it was forbidden to deny them. Slightly later, mostly through Cranmer's influence, parish priests were ordered to place a large English Bible in a convenient place in church where the laity would be able to read it. Another significant change that Cranmer achieved during Henry's reign was the singing of the litany in English. Although there was significant opposition to this among the laity, the new custom soon began gaining adherents.

Perhaps the most important step that Henry took in religious matters after the Act of Supremacy was the dissolution of monasteries. This was done through a series of measures, aimed first at smaller houses, and then at the entire monastic movement. Henry's reasons for doing this seem to have been his desire to gain possession of the treasures that some monasteries had gathered through the centuries, and the fact that monastic houses were a focus of resistance to his proclaimed independence from Rome. Those who opposed his measures were crushed; some were even put to death. Thus Henry became master of vast amounts of wealth to lavish on his supporters. These in turn became staunch defenders of the independent church, for their own wealth depended on it.

By 1539, Henry felt that he no longer needed the support of the Protestants on the Continent, and he therefore proceeded to give his church the strongly orthodox flavor that he preferred, and that he hoped would prevent the divisions that were taking place among Protestants. This was done in the Six Articles, passed by Parliament against Cranmer's protest but under the direction of the King. Here it was declared that to deny transubstantiation, or to advocate communion in both kinds, was heresy, punishable by death and confiscation of property. The same was said of clerical celibacy, and priests who had married must now set their wives aside. In order to show that he was yielding neither to the pope nor to the Protestants, Henry made sure that a token group of Catholics and Lutherans were executed for their ideas.

Such was the state of affairs when Henry died in 1547, leaving his throne to his only male heir, Edward VI, the son of his third wife. Edward was a sickly child of nine years whose reign would last slightly over six years. During that time the kingdom was ruled first by the Duke of Somerset, and later by the Duke of Northumberland. Both regents—although probably for different reasons—supported the cause of reformation along Protestant lines. Cranmer gained great ascendancy at this time and used his influence to move the Church of England toward Protestantism. The many measures taken during the new regime included the reading of the Bible in English during the service, the publication of Twelve Homilies— three of them by Cranmer—to insure that preaching throughout the nation conformed to right doctrine, the abolition of the Six Articles, the order that communion was to be administered to the laity in both kinds, permission for the clergy to marry, and many others. But the most significant achievement of the reign of Edward VI, in the religious field, was the composition and publication of the *Book of Common Prayer*. This was prepared by several theologians, under the leadership of Cranmer. Its first edition, introduced into the churches in 1549, was ambiguously conservative, except for the fact that the entire liturgy was now in English. The second edition, published in 1552, was much more radical. Cranmer himself had now come to deny both transubstantiation and consubstantiation, and adhered to views similar to those of Calvin. As this was precisely the time when Charles V had defeated the Protestants in Germany, many German Protestants found refuge in England—notably Martin Bucer, the reformer of Strasbourg—and further increased the influence of Protestant ideas. Many English who had been exiled on the Continent now returned, bringing with them ideas that were closer to Zwingli than to Luther. These leaders, such as John Hooper (*ca.* 1495–1555) and Nicholas Ridley (*ca.* 1503–1555), had an increasing influence on the shape that the reform movement was taking. As a result, the *Book of Common Prayer* of 1552 is clearly Protestant in its inspiration. That communion is no longer considered a sacrifice may be seen in the fact that this book speaks no longer of an "altar," but of a "table." The ambiguities remained, for all the leaders of the Reformation were aware that England was not ready for a radical change; but whereas in the earlier ambiguous documents of the Church of England the most obvious interpretation had been along the lines of traditional Catholicism, now this second *Book of Common Prayer*, although still ambiguous, seemed to lean in the direction of a Protestant—and even Zwinglian—understanding of communion. The main leaders of the reform movement during this time were—besides Thomas Cranmer—Nicholas Ridley, John Hooper, and Hugh Latimer (*ca.* 1485–1555).

The death of King Edward in 1553 changed matters radically. Although steps had been taken to prevent precisely such an occurrence, Mary succeeded to the throne. She immediately had Parliament declare that her mother's marriage with Henry VIII had been valid, and that all the religious laws of Edward VI were henceforth annulled. After a series of complicated negotiations, relations with Rome were restored. Her marriage with Philip of Spain strengthened the Catholic hand. Then followed the long list of martyrs, which merited her the name of "Bloody Mary." Cranmer, by now an old man, was forced to sign a retraction. When he was then led to the pyre, he held out to be burnt first his right hand, which had signed the recantation. Such an act made him a popular hero. Others were cheered as they marched to death. When Mary began returning to the church some of its ancient monastic possessions, opposition to her rule rose to new levels. At one point, however, did she stay her hand: she did not heed the repeated admonitions from her father-in-law, Charles V, that her half-sister Elizabeth be executed.

Thus, when Mary died in 1558, after having reigned for five years and a few months, she was succeeded by Elizabeth. The new queen proceeded cautiously but firmly along the path to a national church that could embrace as many of her subjects as possible. She allowed some freedom of expression, but insisted on uniformity of worship by restoring the *Book of Common Prayer*—the second edition, with some further revisions. When the bishops appointed by Mary refused to accept Elizabeth's supremacy over the church, they were deposed and replaced by the exiled bishops of the time of Edward VI, or by new bishops. Although in general she avoided bloodshed, she knew how to be firm when the occasion demanded strong action. Of her many executions—about as many as those of her half-sister Mary, although during a reign almost ten times as long—the most famous one was that of Mary Stuart, Queen of Scots, who had taken refuge in England when Presbyterianism—under the leadership of John Knox—and her own unwise policies, had cost her her throne. When Elizabeth learned of intrigues to have her replaced by her cousin Mary, and to restore Roman Catholicism in England, she reluctantly ordered Mary's execution.

What gave definitive shape to Anglicanism during the reign of Elizabeth was the promulgation of the Thirty-nine Articles of Religion. These were basically a revision of the Forty-two Articles of Edward VI, which had been drawn up by Cranmer in the hope that they would strike a balance between Lutheranism and Calvinism, while excluding Roman Catholicism and Anabaptism. In 1563 the Convocation revived and revised the articles of Edward VI and, after a series of delays that had to do mostly with political expediency, their final form was established and promulgated in 1571. As these articles are the crystallization of the theology of the English reformers, we shall discuss their content as we expound that theology.

As throughout Europe, the basis of the Reformation in England was the authority of Scripture. In England itself, the tradition of Wycliffe and the Lollards was a significant influence in this direction. Tyndale's work of Bible translation was based on that principle, which was the main bond connecting him with the Continental Reformation—indeed, his tendency to legalism was very different from the core of Luther's theology.[4] In his *Preface to the Bible,* in 1540, Cranmer wrote:

> If any thing be necessary to be learned, of the Holy Scripture we may learn it. If falsehood shall be reproved, thereof we may gather wherewithal. If any thing be to be corrected and amended, if there need any exhortation or consolation, of the Scripture we may well learn. In the Scriptures be the fat pastures of the soul; therein is no venomous meat, no unwholesome thing; they be the very dainty and pure feeding. He that is ignorant shall find here what he should learn. He that is a perverse sinner shall there find his damnation, to make him to tremble for fear. He that laboureth to serve God shall find there his glory, and the promissions of eternal life, exhorting him more diligently to labour.[5]

John Jewel (1522–1571), one of the leading theologians of the Elizabethan period, wrote an *Apology of the Church of England,* in which he attempted to show that both Scripture and the ancient tradition of the church support the views of the Anglican Church. He therefore referred frequently to tradition and the early Christian writers. But when it comes to the question of where final authority lies, it is clear that such authority belongs only to Scripture.

> Wherefore, if we be heretics, and they (as they would fain be called) be catholics, why do they not as they see the fathers, which were catholic men, have always done? Why do they not convince and master us by the divine Scriptures? Why do they not call us again to be tried by them? . . . If we be heretics, which refer all our controversies unto the Holy Scriptures and report us to the selfsame words which we know were sealed by God himself, and in comparison of them set little by all other things . . . how is it meet to

---

[4] *Ibid.,* pp. 168-74.
[5] In G. E. Duffield, ed., *The Work of Thomas Cranmer* (Appleford, Berkshire: The Sutton Courtenay Press, 1964), p. 37.

call them, which fear the judgment of the Holy Scriptures, that is to say, the judgment of God himself, and do prefer before them their own dreams and full cold inventions?[6]

This sentiment that what they were doing and teaching found its source in the Scriptures was one of the pillars of the Anglican Reformation. This was the reason that Tyndale and Cranmer—in the tradition of Wycliffe—made every possible effort to see that the Bible, in the vernacular, was available to everyone in England.[7] This may be seen in the Thirty-nine Articles, of which the sixth reads: "Holy Scripture containeth all things necessary to salvation: so that whatsoever is not read therein, nor may be proved thereby, is not to be required of any man, that it should be believed as an article of the Faith, or be thought requisite or necessary to salvation."

Likewise, the reason that the Nicene, Athanasian, and Apostles' creeds are to be received as authoritative is that "they may be proved by most certain warrants of holy Scripture" (article 8). And, although the church has the right to estabish liturgical practices and even to decide on controversies rearing questions of faith, "yet it is not lawful for the Church to ordain any thing that is contrary to God's Word written, neither may it so expound one place of Scripture, that it be repugnant to another. Wherefore, although the Church be a witness and a keeper of holy Writ, yet, as it ought not to decree any thing against the same, so besides the same ought it not to enforce any thing to be believed for necessity of salvation" (article 20).

This means that apostolic churches—Jerusalem, Alexandria, Antioch, and Rome—can err and have in fact erred (article 19); and the same is true of general councils (article 21).

On the other hand, the English reformers—or at least the majority of them—felt that there was a positive value in tradition and that, although the traditional church had erred in a number of things, its order and practices ought to be retained, except in those cases in which they conflicted with the authority of Scripture. This allowed the English Reformation to proceed at first with less turmoil than the Continental Reformation. The *Book of Common Prayer,* for instance, included some radical changes. It instituted the celebration of holy

---

6 J. Jewel, *An Apology of the Church of England,* ed. J. E. Booty (Ithaca: Cornell University Press, 1963), p. 20.
7 P. E. Hughes, *Theology of the English Reformers* (London: Hodder & Stoughton, 1965), pp. 13-24.

offices in the vernacular. Where matters of doctrine were at stake, it changed the wording of the traditional ceremonies. But it retained as much of the traditional service as possible. The same was done regarding church order. Therefore, the laity was able to move into the new conditions without unnecessary disturbance. This policy was due in part to Elizabeth's goal of attaining a compromise that the vast majority of her subjects could accept. But it was also due to the attitude of most of the Anglican reformers, who felt that matters of liturgy and church order were adiaphoristic, and that, this being the case, there was no need to insist on changing every detail of the liturgy so that it would conform to scriptural practices. Jewel was expressing the sentiments of the Church of England when he wrote:

> Nevertheless we keep still and esteem, not only those ceremonies which we are sure were delivered us from the apostles, but some others too besides which we thought might be suffered without hurt to the church of God . . . ; but, as for all those things which we saw were either very superstitious, or unprofitable, or noisome, or mockeries, or contrary to the Holy Scriptures, or else unseemly for sober and discreet people . . . these, I say, we have utterly refused without all manner exception, because we would not have the right worshiping of God any longer defiled with such follies.[8]

In this he was following the lead of Cranmer, who had taught that ceremonies—even those found in the New Testament—are not necessarily binding on the church of all ages. By extending to the New Testament the traditional distinction—usually applied only to the Old—between moral and ceremonial commandments, Cranmer was able to say that the particular liturgical prescriptions of Paul, or the decisions of the council of Jerusalem, had only a passing authority, and are not to be required of all in modern times.[9]

This found expression in the thirty-fourth of the Thirty-nine Articles, which deals with "the Traditions of the Church":

> It is not necessary that Traditions and Ceremonies be in all places one, or utterly like; for at all times they have been divers, and may be changed according to the diversities of countries, times,

---

[8] Jewel, *An Apology*, p. 37.
[9] G. W. Bromiley, *Thomas Cranmer Theologian* (New York: Oxford University Press, 1956), pp. 20-22.

and men's manners, so that nothing be ordained against God's Word. Whosoever, through his private judgment, willingly and purposely, doth openly break the traditions and ceremonies of the Church, which be not repugnant to the Word of God, and be ordained and approved by common authority, ought to be rebuked openly, (that others may fear to do the like), as he that offendeth against the common order of the Church, and hurteth the authority of the Magistrate, and woundeth the consciences of the weak brethren.

Every particular or national Church hath authority to ordain, change, and abolish, ceremonies or rites of the Church ordained only by man's authority, so that all things be done to edifying.

At this point, however, this article has gone beyond the teachings of Cranmer. What is here affirmed is that, because particular liturgical practices are not commanded or forbidden in Scripture, the authority to establish such practices belongs to the church, and that no individual has the right to change them. Thus, although liturgical practice is said to be a matter in which Scripture allows great latitude, that latitude is limited to the ecclesiastical—and, in practice, the civil—authorities. This was important for Elizabeth's policy of creating a national church with as little dissent as possible, for uniformity in worship was bound to create a measure of uniformity in belief, and experience on the Continent showed that if total freedom were allowed there would soon be a proliferation of sects. This was something that Elizabeth could not tolerate, for it was contrary to her plans for the aggrandizement of England. But her solution to the problem of divisions within the churches of the Reformation, as seen in this article, was one that many of her subjects could not accept. This was especially true of those who had been influenced by the reformed theology of Zwingli and Calvin, and who therefore believed that the liturgical traditions of the medieval church were in themselves perversions of scriptural simplicity and should be abolished. Thus was born the Puritan movement, which in the following century would shake England to its very foundations.

Justification by faith was the other great pillar of the Protestant Reformation. It was also a constant feature in the theology of the English reformers. In his prologue to Romans, Tyndale affirms that "the sum and whole cause of the writing of this epistle is to prove that a man is justified by faith only."[10] John Frith also felt that this was the core of the gospel, although he held that it was more exact to say, not that God imputes righteousness to the believer, but that God decides not to impute sin.[11] In a similar vein Cranmer wrote that "our faith doth come freely by the mere mercy of God . . . without any of our desert or deserving."[12] Although the Six Articles of Henry VIII attempted to mollify the reformers by asserting that justification took place through faith and works, the reformers saw clearly that this was tantamount to a denial of the doctrine of justification by faith, and opposed any such understanding of that doctrine. Accordingly, the eleventh of the Thirty-nine Articles asserts that "we are accounted righteous before God, only for the merit of our Lord and Saviour Jesus Christ by Faith, and not for our own works or deservings." Then the twelfth article reasserts the value of good works, although in a strictly Protestant sense. "Albeit that Good Works, which are the fruits of Faith, and follow after Justification, cannot put away our sins, and endure the severity of God's Judgement; yet they are pleasing and acceptable to God in Christ, and do spring out necessarily of a true and lively Faith; insomuch that by them a lively Faith may be evidently known as a tree discerned by the fruit."

Works done before justification "are not pleasant to God, forasmuch as they spring not of faith in Jesus Christ, neither do they make men meet to receive grace" (article 13). Likewise, the notion of works of supererogation "cannot be taught without arrogance and impiety" (article 14).

As in the case of the Continental Reformation, the affirmation of justification by faith was intimately connected with the rejection of the penitential system of the church, for the two were mutually contradictory. This included the rejection of purgatory, for which there was no place once it was decided that one's eternal destiny had to do not with having done more or fewer works or with having committed more or fewer sins, but with an entirely gratuitous gift of God. In one of his fiery sermons, Latimer could list all the various indulgences, and then refer to "that our old ancient purgatory

---

[10] Quoted in Hughes, *Theology of the English Reformers,* p. 48.
[11] Clebsch, *England's Earliest Protestants,* p. 134.
[12] Quoted in Hughes, *Theology of the English Reformers,* p. 54.

pickpurse"[13] and "the abuse of this monster purgatory."[14] Decades later, Jewel insisted: "And as for their brags they are wont to make of their purgatory, though we know it is not a thing so very late risen amongst them, yet is it no better than a blockish and an old wives' device."[15] Finally, the twenty-second of the Articles rejects, along with purgatory, indulgences and a number of other Roman Catholic practices. "The Romish Doctrine concerning Purgatory, Pardons, Worshipping and Adoration, as well of Images as of Reliques, and also invocation of Saints, is a fond thing vainly invented, and grounded upon no warranty of Scripture, but rather repugnant to the Word of God."

We have already shown how the Thirty-nine Articles granted the national church the right to make all decisions regarding liturgy, church order, and other such matters that are neither commanded nor prohibited by Scripture. But we must now attempt to discern something of the ecclesiology of the English reformers.

The English reformers referred frequently to the traditional distinction between the visible and the invisible church. Usually, however, this distinction was used not in order to disparage the visible church,[16] but in order to explain how it can claim to be the company of the redeemed and yet be so full of sin and sinners. In this sense, Ridely refers to Augustine's notion of a "mixed church" in which the wheat and the tares cannot be separated from each other. In this visible mixed church the invisible church of the true believers exists, although for the present it is mingled with many who are not among the redeemed. For this reason the visible church can err—and has in fact erred.[17] But on the other hand, this is the only form that the invisible church takes on earth, and therefore one is not authorized simply to withdraw from the mixed church in order to belong to a supposedly invisible community with no earthly shape. As the Elizabethan settlement became a reality, the emphasis moved

13 A. G. Chester, ed., *Selected Sermons of Hugh Latimer* (Charlottesville: The University Press of Virginia, 1968), p. 19.

14 *Ibid.*, p. 20.

15 Jewel, *An Apology*, p. 36.

16 The most notable exception is John Foxe, *To the True and Faithful Congregation of Christ's Universal Church* (LCC, 26:77-78): "Who, beholding the Church of Rome to be so visible and glorious in the eyes of the world, so shining in outward beauty, to bear such a port, to carry such a train and multitude, and to stand in such high authority, supposed the same to be the only right Catholic mother. The other, because it was not so visibly known in the world, they thought therefore it could not be the true Church of Christ. Wherein they were far deceived."

17 Hughes, *Theology of the English Reformers*, pp. 228-29.

away from the distinction, and toward an affirmation that the Church of England was indeed the church of Christ in England. That this does not exactly correspond with the invisible church is still true; but the visible church, in spite of its "mingled" state, is the spiritual home of believers. Of this visible church, the Church of England is the proper expression in this particular kingdom, although it does not claim to be the entire catholic body of Christ.

> We believe that there is one church of God, and that the same is not shut up (as in times past among the Jews) into some one corner or kingdom, but that it is catholic and universal and dispersed throughout the whole world. So that there is now no nation which can truly complain that they be shut forth and may not be one of the church and people of God. And that this church is the kingdom, the body, and the spouse of Christ; and that Christ alone is the prince of this kingdom; that Christ alone is the head of this body; and that Christ alone is the bridegroom of this spouse.[18]

On this point the Thirty-nine Articles show the influence of reformed theology, and especially of Calvin, which had become strong during the reign of Edward VI, and had increased when many English reformers who were forced by Mary Tudor to take refuge on the Continent returned to their homeland during the reign of Elizabeth. As with Calvin, the two identifying marks of the true church have become the preaching of the Word and the administration of the sacraments. The first half of article nineteen reads: "The visible Church of Christ is a congregation of faithful men, in the which the pure Word of God is preached, and the Sacraments be duly administered according to Christ's ordinance in all those things that of necessity are requisite to the same."

By this time, Calvinistic influence is also clearly discernible in the doctrine of the sacraments. In his early years as a reformer, Cranmer held to the doctrine of the physical presence of the body of Christ on the sacrificial altar. He later came to the conclusion that the sacrifice of Christ is not repeated in communion, and orders went out that tables should be substituted for altars.[19] In 1550 he wrote a series of comparisons between his views and those of the Roman Church—

---

[18] Jewel, *An Apology*, p. 24.
[19] Duffield, *The Work of Thomas Cranmer*, pp. 234-37.

which he turned into caricatures in order to make them appear in the worst possible light. In these comparisons his Calvinistic leanings are evident. Although these comparisons are too lengthy to quote in full, a selection from them suffices to show their general direction.

> For they teach, that Christ is in the bread and wine: but we say, according to the truth, that he is in them that worthily eat and drink the bread and wine.
>
> They say, that Christ is received in the mouth, and entereth in with the bread and wine: we say, that he is received in the heart, and entereth by faith.
>
> They say, that every man, good and evil, eateth the body of Christ: we say, that both do eat the sacramental bread and drink the wine, but none do eat the body of Christ and drink his blood, but only they that be lively members of his body.
>
> They say, that Christ is corporally in many places at one time, affirming that his body is corporally and really present in as many places as there be hosts consecrated: we say, that as the sun corporally is ever in heaven, and no where else . . . so likewise our Saviour Christ bodily and corporally is in heaven, sitting at the right hand of his Father, although spiritually he hath promised to be present with us upon earth unto the world's end.[20]

It is clear that, in rejecting Roman Catholic doctrine on this point, Cranmer has also rejected Luther's views and adopted Calvin's position. The sacrament is not merely a symbol of what takes place in the heart, but neither is it the physical eating of the body of Christ. This must be so, because the body of Christ is in heaven and therefore our participation in it can only be spiritual. Only the believers are true partakers of the body and blood of Christ, for the unbelievers eat and drink no more than bread and wine—and condemnation upon themselves, for the profanation of the Lord's Table. These views are reflected in the Thirty-nine articles, of which the twenty-eighth says that "the Body of Christ is given, taken, and eaten, in the Supper, only after an heavenly and spiritual manner." The next article says of the wicked that "in no wise are they partakers of Christ," although "to their condemnation [they] do eat and drink the sign or Sacrament of so great a thing."

---

[20] *Ibid.*, pp. 124-26.

This marked Calvinistic influence would prove very significant for the history of Christianity in England during the seventeenth century, for the events that then took place were in part due to the unavoidable conflicts between the moderate Calvinism of the established church, and the more radical views of those who felt that the Calvinistic reformation had been betrayed by the Elizabethan settlement.

The theory of ministry and the actual practice in the Elizabethan settlement provide an example of this conflict. In their controversy with Roman Catholicism, the English reformers had often argued against apostolic succession as the criterion of apostolic authority. In 1550, John Hooper wrote: "As concerning the ministers of the Church, I believe that the Church is bound to no sort of people or any ordinary succession of bishops, cardinals, or such like, but unto the only Word of God."[21] Likewise, even after the Elizabethan settlement, Jewel responded to Catholic arguments: "Succession, you say, is the chief way for any Christian man to avoid anti-christ. I grant you, if you mean succession of doctrine!"[22] But this line of argument, which served to refute the claims to authority on the part of the Roman Church, would be subversive to discipline if applied indiscriminately in England. The notion of a state church would be unworkable if that church did not somehow control the rite of ordination, by which some become its leaders. For this reason Jewel, the same who argued that authority comes from the succession of doctrine, said that "no man hath power to wrest himself into the holy ministry at his own pleasure and list."[23] If the Church of England did not somehow reserve for herself the sole right to ordain ministers and to regulate worship, Elizabeth and her counselors feared, Anabaptist chaos would engulf the realm. Therefore, article thirty-six of the Thirty-nine Articles endorsed the ordinal of Edward VI affirming that it "doth contain all things necessary to such Consecration and Ordering: neither hath it anything, that of itself is superstitious or ungodly." Those ordained according to the rites and regulations of that book were declared to be "rightly, orderly, and lawfully consecrated and ordered."

---

[21] Quoted by Hughes, *Theology of the English Reformers,* p. 179.
[22] *Ibid.*
[23] Jewel, *An Apology,* p. 26.

The best exponent of the theology behind the Elizabethan settlement is Richard Hooker (1554–1600), whose eight books *Of the Laws of Ecclesiastical Polity* set out to provide a foundation for this settlement. Since only the first five books were published during his lifetime, there is some question as to whether the text of the others has been altered to fit later controversies. In any case, there is no doubt that Hooker saw the "State Ecclesiastical" as coextensive with the "Civil State." The church and the state are the same, composed of the same people, and distinguishable only because their roles are different. For the government of the church, three criteria are to be employed: Scripture, Tradition, and Reason. On those matters about which it speaks clearly, the Bible is the final authority, and ought not to be doubted. But there are many matters—including the form of government of the church—on which there is no clear Scriptural teaching. Those things which tradition supports, and are not contradicted by the Bible, should be kept, as long as they are not contrary to reason. But even in these things, while tradition offers guidelines, they are not absolute. Thus, on the very controverted matter of the episcopacy, while Hooker was its ardent supporter, he did not consider its lack to be sufficient reason to reject the validity of the Reformed churches.[24]

The Beginnings of Dissent

The fact that the articles denied that the ordinal of Edward VI had in it anything "superstitious or ungodly" indicates that there were some who held that it did. This was to be expected, for the many exiles who had left England during the time of Mary, and had then come under the direct influence of the Continental Reformation, felt that the Church of England was not going far enough in the restoration of the true worship of God. The notion that ceremonies, vestments, and the like were adiaphora, which were to be regulated by the church in each nation, did not appeal to those who in their exile in Holland, Frankfurt, and Geneva had come to believe that the simplicity of Reformed worship was required by the New Testament. Because these radical Calvinists demanded that the Church be

---

[24] See E. Grislis and W. S. Hill, eds., *Richard Hooker: A Selected Bibliography* (Pittsburgh: Pittsburgh Theological Seminary, 1971); R. K. Faulkner, *Richard Hooker and the Politics of a Christian England* (Berkeley: University of California Press, 1981); S. Archer, *Richard Hooker* (Boston: Twayne, 1983).

purified according to the doctrines and practices of the New Testament, they were called Puritans. As is well known, their impact on the history of England was great. But, as they represent a development within the Reformed tradition which is best understood under that heading, we shall discuss their theology in the chapter devoted to later developments within Calvinism.

Another event of significance that took place in Great Britain while Elizabeth was reigning in England was the Reformation in Scotland under the leadership of John Knox. Politically this resulted in the exile and eventual execution of Mary Stuart. Theologically, it represented the development of Calvinism into Presbyterianism in its classical form. This too, however, is to be discussed in the chapter on later Calvinism.

The Elizabethan settlement may then be seen as an attempt to develop a middle way between Roman Catholicism and the shape that the Protestant Reformation was taking on the Continent. As a result, it had to struggle with the more radical elements within it—and this struggle did result in political upheavals. But in the long run, the Anglican via media would survive as the most characteristic form of Christianity in England, while other forms—from Roman Catholic to extreme Protestant—would continue existing alongside it.

VIII

Theology in the Catholic Reformation

During the sixteenth and early seventeenth centuries, a powerful movement for inner reformation swept through the Roman Catholic Church. As this movement was in part a response to the Protestant Reformation, it is usually called the Counterreformation. There is some justification for that name, for a great deal of the theology of the period was influenced by the Protestant movement, attempting either to refute it, or to make certain that the accusations that Protestants leveled against the Catholic Church would henceforth be unwarranted. But, on the other hand, to attempt to describe this vast movement simply in terms of response to the Protestant threat is an error in perspective, introduced by historians for whom the whole world seems to have been contained in the events that took place in Germany, Switzerland, and England. From the Catholic—and specially the Spanish—perspective, matters seemed quite different. Spain, which was one of the main centers of Catholic theological activity during the sixteenth century, was only peripherally affected by the Protestant Reformation. It is true that her soldiers found themselves fighting wars in Germany and Flanders. But even at the time of such wars the campaigns that caught the imagination of most Spaniards were those which were taking place in the "Indies." Thus, Spanish theological activity during the sixteenth century, although aware of the existence of Protestantism and intent on its refutation, was concerned also with many other problems that gave rise to theological reflection. Such was the case, for instance, of Francisco de

196

Vitoria, whom we shall study further on in this chapter, and one of whose concerns was the theological justification and implications of the conquest of the New World. Even the question of grace and its relationship to human capabilities, which was posed partly as a result of Protestant challenges, was discussed as vehemently among Catholics themselves as in controversies between Protestants and Catholics. The Jesuits, usually interpreted in terms of a reaction against Protestantism, were much more than that, and they soon had missionaries around the entire globe, quite independent of any Protestant challenge. In the thought of Francisco Suárez, the great theologian of the Jesuit order, the concern with refuting Protestantism played only a minor role. Therefore, from the point of view of Catholics involved in the movement that we now call the Counterreformation, that movement was not simply—or primarily—an attempt to respond to Protestantism.

The second reason that it is inexact to refer to the Catholic reformation of the sixteenth century as the Counterreformation is that it had already begun when the Protestant Reformation appeared on the scene. We have already shown how Erasmus was laboring for a reformation of the church—and had in fact become a symbol of it—before Luther protested against the sale of indulgences. Erasmus had a vast network of correspondents, many of whom were committed to the same ends. In Spain, the reformation of the church had begun with Cardinal Ximenes de Cisneros. This was intended to be a thorough reformation. Its base would be a return to the biblical sources of the Christian faith, and to this end Ximenes had the Complutensian Polyglot Bible compiled (1517) and published (1522).[1] Such a return, as well as other tasks within the proposed reformation, required well-educated leaders, and such education was the purpose behind the founding of the University of Alcalá. Finally, the entire Spanish nation must be brought into the renewed church, and this led to the expulsion of the Jews (1492), to

---

[1] The following words, said by Cardinal Ximenes upon receiving the last volume of this Bible, show something of the nature of the reformation for which he hoped. "If up to this point I have done many difficult things for the public cause, I beg you, my friends, not to congratulate me for any of these as much as you should congratulate me for this edition of the Bible which, in these critical times, opens the sacred sources of our religion, from which will flow a theology much purer than any derived from less direct sources." Quoted by Conde de Cedillo, *El Cardenal Cisneros, Gobernador del Reino*, 3 vols. (Madrid: Real Academia de la Historia, 1921–28), 1:195.

the development of the Inquisition, and—later—to the expulsion of the Moors. This program of reformation on two fronts—sound theological scholarship and firm repression of dissidents—was to characterize the entire period of the Catholic reformation. Although eventually applied to the struggle against Protestantism, it was already present at the beginning of the sixteenth century, in the policies of Ximenes de Cisneros.

For these reasons, we must avoid the error of most Protestant historians of theology, for whom Catholic theology in the sixteenth century is scarcely more than the refutation of Protestantism. On the contrary, we must pay equal attention to other movements and concerns that were occupying the efforts of Catholic theologians, quite independent—or at least relatively independent—of Protestantism. For reasons of clarity and logical sequence in our discussion, we shall depart slightly from the strict chronological order of events and theologians, and attempt to organize the period under discussion in more readily understandable units. Admittedly, this systematization of the period is somewhat artificial—every systematization is—and we shall find ourselves having to refer to some theologians, such as Báñez and Suárez, in more than one context. But the reader will be able to follow us through the complicated theological developments of this period by keeping in mind the following outline.

First we shall summarize the anti-Protestant polemics of the sixteenth century. This is probably the least interesting development of the period, for most of it is mere repetition of arguments used earlier against others whom the church condemned as heretics. Then we shall turn to the Dominican school, which includes such theologians as Cardinal Cajetan, Francisco de Vitoria, and Domingo Báñez. Each of these made significant contributions to Catholic theology. Third, we shall study the development of the Jesuit school, culminating in the vast system of Francisco Suárez. We shall then summarize the controversies that took place within the Catholic Church regarding the doctrine of grace. Although this will take us beyond the sixteenth century, we shall include in these controversies the theories of Molinism and Jansenism. Finally, we shall return to the middle of the sixteenth century to study the Council of Trent and to show how it summarizes and symbolizes the theological developments that took place both before and after it.

Let us, then, turn to the anti-Protestant polemics of the sixteenth century.

Anti-Protestant Polemics

The foremost opponent of the Protestant Reformation during its early years was John Eck (1486–1543),[2] a professor at Ingolstadt. He was already a well-known theologian when the controversy broke out, for he had published in 1514 a treatise on predestination and grace in which he argued for a conditional form of predestination, based on the teachings of Bonaventure. He also had proposed that loans on interest—up to 5 percent—be allowed, and for this reason his opponents called him "the Fuggers' theologian"—the Fuggers were one of the principal banking houses of Germany, and were involved in the transactions connected with the indulgences against which Luther protested in his ninety-five theses.

Eck responded to Luther's theses with a short treatise, which in turn drew a brief response from Luther. He then debated, first with Carlstadt, and then with Luther, at the Leipzig Disputation. His report on that debate he published in 1502 in a treatise, *On the Primacy of Peter against Luther*. Against Melanchthon's *Loci communes*, he published in 1525 his *Enchiridion locorum communium*, which was his most significant work. He then moved against the Swiss reformers and wrote against Zwingli *On the Sacrifice of the Mass* (1527), and a *Rejection of Zwingli's Articles* three years later. At the same time he published a *Refutation of the Augsburg Confession*. Finally, he turned to the refutation of Martin Bucer, against whom his last works—notably his *Apology for Catholic Principles*—were directed.

Thus, Eck had occasion during his career to refute both the Lutherans and the Reformed. Although Protestants usually depict him as a champion of obscurantism and as a man who was intent on using force to repress views with which he disagreed, this portrait is not quite just. It is true that Eck was one of three men charged with publishing in Germany the bull *Exsurge*, and that in that capacity he often had recourse to political force. It is also true that he rejected all attempts at conciliation short of a total retraction on the part of the

---

[2] J. Grering, *Johann Eck als jungen Gelehrter* (Münster: Aschendorff, 1906); K. Rischar, *Johann Eck auf dem Reichstag zu Augsburg, 1530* (Münster: Aschendorffsche Verlagsbuchhandlung, 1968); W. Klaiber, *Ecclesia militans: Studien zu den Festtagspredikten des Johannes Eck* (Münster: Aschendorff, 1982).

Protestants. But he was an able scholar and a good pastor of his flock. It is significant that he undertook a translation of the Bible into German, which he published in 1537. He also left records of his work as a parish priest that show his profound concern for the spiritual nurture of his parishioners. Although not in the same terms as Luther, he too protested against the abuses that took place in the sale of indulgences, and demanded from the curia a thorough reformation of the church. His theology, however, was not original, and was limited mostly to a repetition of the arguments that had been proposed before him. As was to be expected, given the issues being debated, he concentrated his attention on questions of authority, grace and predestination, and the sacraments.[3]

Much more obscurantist was the attitude of James Hochstraten (1460–1527).[4] Even before the beginning of the Protestant Reformation, he had been involved in a bitter controversy with an Italian jurist who claimed that it was a mortal sin for the German princes to leave exposed the bodies of executed criminals. Hochstraten came out in defense of the princes, and the controversy became involved and prolonged. He then became prior of Cologne, which also made him inquisitor of that and two other ecclesiastical provinces. As such, he became entangled in the Reuchlin affair. Supporting Pfefferkorn, he said that all Jewish books except the Bible should be confiscated and destroyed. Reuchlin argued that there was much to be learned from the books which Hochstraten and Pfefferkorn proposed to destroy. Hochstraten then brought to bear his authority as inquisitor, accusing Reuchlin of heresy. But Reuchlin appealed, and the affair dragged on for years. All these events earned Hochstraten the scorn of humanist circles in and beyond Germany. In fact, he was one of the targets of the *Epistolae obscurorum virorum,* which began appearing in 1515 as a satire against people such as Hochstraten.

Hochstraten's position was rather precarious at the outbreak of the Reformation. He had been relieved as prior of Cologne, the humanists had made him the object of their mockery, and Rome seemed inclined to dismiss him as an overzealous fanatic. Then

---

[3] E. Iserloh, *Die Eucharistie in der Darstellung des Johannes Eck: Ein Beitrag zur vortridentinischen Kontroverstheologie über das Messopfer* (Münster: Aschendorffsche Verlagsbuchhandlung, 1950).

[4] R. Coulon, "Hochstraten, ou mieux, Hoogstraten, Jacob," *DTC,* 7:11-17.

Luther's protest changed the entire situation. When the University of Louvain asked its counterpart at Cologne to examine the writings of Luther, Hochstraten became the leader of the anti-Lutheran party.[5] His main writing in the new controversy was a dialogue in which Augustine refuted the theses that Luther had held at Leipzig. From then on, he published a series of polemical writings against Luther, mostly on the question of justification by faith.

John (Dobneck) Cochlaeus (1489–1552)[6] was the outstanding orator among the adversaries of Protestantism. He concentrated his attacks on Luther, who is the target of most of his 190 works. Among other writings, the most significant is his biography of Luther, a highly biased account that for centuries was one of the main sources of Catholic studies on Luther's life, and thus greatly hindered the dialogue between the Catholic and Protestant traditions. His method of argumentation was daring and often bizarre. For instance, in order to show the dangers of the free examination of Scripture, he tried to prove on the basis of scattered texts that Satan ought to be obeyed, that Jesus Christ is not God, and that Mary lost her virginity. Although he did not believe these things, but rather used them as a *reductio ad absurdum* of Protestant claims on the interpretation of Scripture, those writings in which he attempted such exegetical legerdemain were later placed in the *Index* of forbidden books. Thus, while Protestants often considered him one of their worst enemies, Catholics found that his defense of their positions could be as dangerous as the heresies that he attempted to refute.

Peter Canisius (1521–1597),[7] the first German Jesuit, is often called "the apostle to Germany." His task was indeed one of counterreformation in the strict sense, for he was deeply disturbed by the state of the church in the Catholic territories in which he worked, and therefore insisted on the need for a "true" reformation in order to give at least a partial response to the "false" reformation of the Protestants. As ignorance was one of the greater evils that he found in his travels, he devoted a great deal of attention to the reform of universities and the founding of seminaries. His program of university reform combined firmness against Protestantism with

---

[5] Erasmus, *Opera* (1703), 3:1361.

[6] A standard study is M. Spahn, *Johannes Cochlaeus: Ein Lebensbild, aus der Zeit der Kirchenspaltung* (Berlin: Felix L. Dames, 1898; reprint Nieuwkoop: B. de Graaf, 1964).

[7] J. Brodrick, *Saint Peter Canisius* (London: Geoffrey Chapman, 1963).

interest in erudition, for he made sound doctrine and solid scholarship two of the main criteria for appointment to university faculties. He also followed the lead of Protestantism—and of many of the Catholic reformers during the Middle Ages—by making preaching one of his main occupations and, when he became Provincial of the Order for Germany, Austria, and Bohemia, by instructing his subordinates to do likewise. His program of reformation included participation in political events, so as to direct them for the good of the church, and he therefore was present at several diets of the Empire. At Trent, he was one of the opponents of any concessions to Protestantism, although he also argued for a thorough reformation within the Catholic Church.

Canisius was a prolific writer, but two of his works merit special attention: his trilogy of catechisms, and his refutation of the "Centuriators" of Magdeburg. His three catechisms, addressed as they were to three different audiences—children, youth, and intellectuals—made a significant impact throughout Germany. The refutation of the "Centuriators," however, is much more interesting. At Magdeburg a group of Lutheran theologians, under the leadership of Flacius, had undertaken the writing of the history of the church from a Protestant point of view. As this was divided into centuries, one for each volume of the work (it never got beyond the thirteenth), the whole was called the "Centuries of Magdeburg."[8] Canisius undertook to refute this work, although—interestingly enough—not by an appeal to history, but by attempting to show that the practices that the Protestants decried as innovations had their origin in Scripture. Thus an ironic situation developed in which Protestants were attempting to prove through tradition that the Roman Catholic Church had departed from the authority of Scripture, and the Catholic Canisius was trying to show on the basis of Scripture that the Protestant reconstruction of tradition was wrong. The theological method of Canisius in this vast project— which he never completed—is singular, for he planned to write five books, each on one of the main personalities that the New Testament

---

[8] See J. Massner, *Kirchliche Überlieferung und Autorität im Flaciuskreis: Studien zu den Magdeburger Zenturien* (Berlin: Lutherisches Verlagshaus, 1964); H. Scheibe, *Die Entstehung der Magdeburger Zenturien: Ein Beitrag zur Geschichte der Historiographischen Methode* (Gütersloh: G. Mohn, 1966). On the Catholic response, see J. L. Orella, *Respuestas católicas a las Centurias de Magdeburgo (1559-1588)* (Madrid: Fundación Universitaria Española Seminario Suárez, 1976).

places around Jesus—except that the fifth book would include both John and James—and to relate to each of them a number of the Catholic doctrines and practices that the Magdeburg historians claimed were later perversions of the original faith. Thus, the first book, dealing with John the Baptist, attaches to him the Catholic doctrines of penance and justification, while the second relates to the Blessed Virgin such issues as celibacy, virginity, and the veneration of saints. The remaining three books were never written.

While Hochstraten was the champion of the anti-Lutheran forces at Cologne, James Latomus (1475–1544)[9] was his counterpart at the University of Louvain, where he was rector. Unfortunately for him, he tended to confuse Protestantism with humanism, and thus drew the fire of both parties. Typical of his attitude is the dialogue that he published in 1519 on the relationship between philological and theological studies. His conclusion was that a theologian has sufficient basis for understanding Scripture in the tradition of the Church, about which one can read in Latin, and that knowledge of Greek and Hebrew is therefore superfluous. Also, a fair knowledge of Latin suffices for the theologian, who does not need the polished style that has recently become fashionable. As was to be expected, this drew a staggering volley from Erasmus and his fellow humanists, who correctly understood it to be an attack on them and their endeavors. The following year, in a treatise giving the reasons for Luther's condemnation by the faculty at Louvain, Latomus began a controversy with Luther that lasted several years. Luther always considered Latomus one of his least impressive adversaries, and the responses that he wrote against the Louvain theologian show that he did not deign to devote too much time or attention to his arguments.[10] Latomus then widened his sphere of action and wrote treatises against such diverse theologians as Oecolampadius, William Tyndale, and Melanchthon. Evaluating his work, a Catholic scholar has said that it is "entirely representative of his time. Shaggy in its form, insufficiently documented in a positive way, carrying on a weight of assertions which have not been verified."[11] And yet, that same scholar goes on to point out that the work of Latomus set the

---

[9] E. Amann, "Latomus, Jacques," *DTC*, 8:2226-28.

[10] *LW*, 32:135-260.

[11] Amann, "Latomus," 8:2627-28; J. Étienne, *Spiritualisme érasmien et théologiens louvanistes* (Louvain: Publications universitaires, 1956).

stage for the later work of such theologians as Cardinal Bellarmine.

The approach of William Van der Linden (1525–1588)[12] was very different. He did attack the Protestants on many points. His *Panoplia* insisted on the doctrine of a written and an oral Word of God. The first is Scripture, the second is tradition; and both coincide when properly interpreted. He also defended Catholic doctrine on many other issues, such as vows of celibacy, the primacy of Peter, the mass, and so forth. But he always manifested a conciliatory spirit—especially toward the Lutherans, in distinction to the Reformed. As late as 1568, he tried to show that it was still possible for Lutherans and Catholics to be reunited on a mutually agreed basis. At the same time, he was urging the Catholic bishops to reform their churches, for without such reformation he thought unity would remain impossible.

Albert Pigge (1490–1542)[13]—also known as Pighius—was an ardent defender of papal authority, as may be seen in his *Affirmation of the Ecclesiastical Hierarchy*, published in 1538. He there asserted that no pope had ever erred, and attempted to show that such cases as those of Liberius, Honorius, and others, were the result of historical misrepresentations and of the interpolation of ancient texts. These views, which were still held by many as late as the nineteenth century, were instrumental in the developments that led to the promulgation of papal infallibility by the First Vatican Council. However, in other matters he proved to be distant from Catholic orthodoxy. He is considered to have been one of the forerunners of Molinism, to be discussed further on. Also, in his attempts to bring about a rapprochement with the Protestants at the Diet of Worms of 1540, he developed the theory of a "double justification"—one justification being inherent in the just; the other being the imputed righteousness of Christ. This view did not satisfy the parties involved in the controversy, and was later condemned by the Council of Trent. He also conflicted with Catholic theology in his view of sin, which he declared to be "imputed." His writings on these subjects were placed in the *Index* of forbidden books in 1624. Nevertheless, his work did have a lasting influence, especially since many of his views on the history of the church were taken up by

---

[12] E. Amann, "Lindanus (Van der Linden), Guillaume Damase," *DTC*, 9:772-76.

[13] R. Bacmer, "Pigge, Albert (Pighius)," *NCatEnc*, 11:358-59; H. Jedin, *Studien über die Schriftstellertätigkeit Albert Pigges* (Münster: Aschendorff, 1931).

Cardinals Bellarmine and Baronius and through them came to form part of the accepted historiographical tradition of the Catholic Church.

The great anti-Protestant theologians, however, were members of a later generation, who could draw on the work of their predecessors, and had also had more time to see the manner in which the teachings of the reformers worked out in actual practice. Although there were many anti-Protestant polemists in the second half of the sixteenth century and the beginning of the seventeenth, two names stand out as symbolizing the best in the attempt to refute the Protestants. These two are Bellarmine and Baronius.[14]

Robert Bellarmine (1542–1621),[15] who was declared to be a saint of the Catholic Church in 1930, was without any doubt one of the foremost church leaders of his time. Although theological work was by no means his only activity, his claim to fame in the field of theology came when it was decided to found at Rome a chair of "controversy," designed especially for the benefit of those students who would have to return to places such as Germany and England where Protestantism was a strong force. Bellarmine was called to occupy the new chair in 1576, and he retained this post until 1588, when he was appointed to other duties—he became a cardinal in 1599. As professor of controversy, Bellarmine had occasion to compile and organize arguments against the various Protestant doctrines. These were published under the title of *Disputationes de controversiis christianae fidei adversus hujus temporis haereticos*, beginning in 1586 and ending in 1593. In spite of the fact that this work is mostly a compilation of previous arguments, its clarity and systematization are such that it became the main weapon of anti-Protestant polemics

---

14 Francis de Sales (1567-1622) is often mentioned in this context. He concentrated his efforts on the refutation of Calvinism, beginning in 1603, when he was appointed to the region of Chablais, in Savoy, where Calvinistic influence was great. With the support of the Duke of Savoy, he braved the opposition of the populace, and did so with such firmness and undaunted courage that many were won to the Catholic faith. In this work, he combined a great deal of personal courage and a spirit of forgiveness with the force that the Duke could bring to bear upon his subjects. As a result of his efforts, he was consecrated bishop of Geneva, although he was never able to take possession of his see, for Geneva was then firmly in the hands of the Reformed. Twice he visited his see, and on one of those occasions he held—at the pope's request—an interview with Beza, hoping to convert him. A man of undoubted sanctity, Francis wrote a number of treatises on mystical theology, which became the source of Salesian spirituality. In the field of systematic theology, however, his contribution was not outstanding—and the same is true of his brief refutations of Protestantism.

15 X. Le Bachelet, "Bellarmin," *DTC*, 2:560-99; R. Kirste, *Das Zeugnis des Geistes und das Zeugnis der Schrift: Das testimonium spiritus sancti internum als hermeneut.-polem. Zentralbegriff bei Johann Gerhard in der Auseinandersetztung mit Robert Bellarmin* (Göttingen: Vandenhoeck und Ruprecht, 1976).

for several centuries. It includes practically all the points at issue between Catholics and Protestants, beginning with the doctrine of the Word of God, and then going on to such questions as the authority of the pope, monasticism, purgatory, sacraments, indulgences, etc. In general, Bellarmine abstained from the complicated arguments and subtle distinctions of scholastic theology. On the contrary, his arguments are usually clear-cut appeals to authority—first of all that of Scripture, which the Protestants would acknowledge, but also that of the early Christian writers, the councils, and even the general consensus of theologians.

However, Bellarmine's controversies were not only against the Protestants. In 1590 Sixtus V was about to add Bellarmine's writings to the *Index* when death prevented him from doing so. The reason for this was Bellarmine's view—shared, as we shall see, by many distinguished theologians of his time—that the pope did not have direct temporal power over the entire world. When in 1609 the treatise *De potestate papae* by William Barclay was published in London, Bellarmine responded with a refutation in which he argued that the pope did have indirect temporal authority over the Christian world, and that he could therefore depose heretical princes. This view was the result of an earlier controversy that he had with James I of England and his theologians. Bellarmine also took part in the controversies on the subject of grace, where he tended to favor Molina's notion of a *scientia media* (that issue will be discussed in another section of this chapter). Finally, as a member of the Holy Office, he was involved in the trial of Galileo, which ended in 1616 with the declaration that the notion that the earth revolves around the sun is heretical. However, Bellarmine's participation in these procedures was not as high-handed as popular history has made it seem, for he always showed respect and admiration for Galileo's learning.

What Bellarmine did in the field of systematic polemics, Cardinal Cesar Baronius (1538–1607) did in the field of history.[16] This he did through the publication, beginning in 1588 and ending with his death in 1607, of the *Ecclesiastical Annals*. The twelve volumes that he was able to publish discussed the history of the church up to the year

---

[16] J Wahl, "Baronius, Cesar, Ven.," *NCatEnc*, 2:105-6; G. de Libero, "Baronio, Cesare," *EncCatt*, 2:885-89; G. Franceschini, "Anales eclesiásticos," *DicLit*, 2:218.

1198. Their purpose was to refute the *Centuries* of the Magdeburg theologians, which tried to show that the Catholic Church had departed from the primitive doctrines and practice of early Christianity. Although his work had the inevitable errors that such an undertaking necessarily involves, it has been hailed as the beginning of modern ecclesiastical historiography. It is true that its polemical purpose detracts for its objectivity; but in spite of this, Baronius on the Catholic side, and the Magdeburg "Centuriators" on the Protestant, forced the attention of Christianity upon its own history. As the debate continued, both sides were obliged to develop scientific methods of research that could not be easily refuted by the opponents, and thus modern critical historiography took its first steps.

Dominican Theology

During the sixteenth century, the Dominican school of theology showed a great deal more vitality than did its Franciscan counterpart. Within the Franciscan tradition, it was a period in which the number of separate branches multiplied, but little was done in the way of original theological work. Most members of the vast Franciscan family considered Scotus as the greatest theologian in the Order. Others—notably the Capuchins—came to regard Bonaventure as their theological mentor. Their interest in Bonaventure led Sixtus V to place his name among the recognized doctors of the church in 1588. Some attempted to combine Bonaventure and Scotus in various ways. But in general, Franciscan theology during the sixteenth century did not show the vitality that it had manifested in the three preceding centuries.

Roman Catholic theology was therefore dominated by the Dominicans during the earlier part of the sixteenth century, until they had to share that hegemony with the theologians of the recently founded Society of Jesus.

This Dominican dominance was related to the process whereby the *Summa Theologica* of Thomas supplanted the *Sentences* of Peter Lombard as the main text to be commented on in the schools.[17] Thomas thus attained increasing influence, culminating in 1567,

---

[17] P. Mandonnet, "Frères Prêcheurs (La théologie dans l'ordre des)," *DTC*, 6:906-8; R. Guelluy, "L'évolution des méthodes théologiques à Louvain, d'Erasme à Jansénius," *RHE*, 37 (1941); 31-144.

when Pius V declared him to be a doctor of the church. The immediate result of this was that, whereas most of the great theological works from the thirteenth to the fifteenth centuries were commentaries on the *Sentences,* most of the great theological works in the sixteenth were commentaries on the *Summa.* The two first to publish such commentaries were Conrad Köllin and Thomas de Vio Cajetan. Cajetan's commentary, however, was considered so much better that Köllin's was completely eclipsed. Apart from Cajetan's work, Dominican theology found its ablest exponents among a series of outstanding scholars who occupied the main chair of theology in the University of Salamanca—Vitoria, Cano,. Soto, Medina, and Báñez. Therefore, after discussing Cajetan's theology, we shall follow the development of Thomism in Salamanca.

Thomas de Vio Cajetan (1468–1534)[18] was an active church leader who was connected with several of the most significant developments of his time. When political circumstances threatened the church with schism, he suggested to the pope that a general council be called, in order to deal with the issues at hand as well as with the reformation of the church. When the council came together in 1512, he appeared before it and set as its agenda the reformation of the church, the restoration of morality, the conversion of unbelievers, and the task of winning heretics (mainly the Averroists of Padua) back to the fold of the church. In 1517 he was named papal legate to Germany, and as such he was called to deal with the two very important and difficult questions of the election of the new emperor and of Luther's protest. He met with Luther at Augsburg, and showed far more patience than the majority of the defenders of traditional Christianity. He later was a legate to Hungary, and eventually a cardinal.

Cajetan's literary production was enormous, especially for one who was so involved in the practical affairs of church government. Realizing that the Protestant challenge would require better biblical foundations for the defense of Roman Catholicism, he undertook a series of biblical commentaries. When he died in 1534, he had done the entire New Testament—except the book of Revelation, which he said he could not understand—and the Old Testament to the beginning of Isaiah. His exegetical method in these commentaries is

---

[18] P. Mandonnet, "Cajétan (Thomas de Vio, dit)," *DTC,* 2:1313-29; B. Hallensleben, *Communicatio: Anthropologie und Gnadenlehre bei Thomas de Vio Cajetan* (Münster: Aschendorff, 1985).

significant, for he usually avoids the allegories that had been so popular throughout the centuries, and affirms the literal sense of the text, except when the result is clearly contrary to the rest of Scripture or to the teaching of the church. He also wrote a number of philosophical commentaries, and many theological works of minor importance. But his greatest fame is due to his *Commentaries on the Summa,* which were published from 1507 to 1522. These commentaries attained such a degree of influence that when Leo XIII gave orders in 1879 that the works of Thomas Aquinas be edited and published—in what is usually called the Leonine edition, still in progress—he also directed that Cajetan's commentaries should be published with the *Summa* itself. This position of authority, however, was not reached without a struggle, for in 1544 the Sorbonne—which had become the bulwark of orthodoxy during the struggles connected with the Reformation—condemned Cajetan's commentaries, and in 1570 Pius V had them expurgated of what he and his counselors considered to be errors—such as, for instance, that unbaptized infants could be saved.

Cajetan was clearly a person standing in two ages at the same time. He realized that the scholastic theology of the past three centuries must be given a new form in a new age. Yet, his own style is typically scholastic, with hardly a trace of influence from the new elegance of the humanists. Although it is clearly impossible to review here the totality of his theology—most of which in any case is the same as Thomas'—it is possible to point out some of the points at which his work was most influential or debated in later years. His attempts to defend Thomas' theory of analogy against the univocity of being put forth by Scotus led him to distinguish between three realities: the essence of a thing, its subsistence, and its existence.[19] This in turn meant that essence was prior to existence, which—as Báñez would later point out—was a distortion of the views of Thomas, for whom the act of existing is the fundamental act of being.[20] Cajetan's interpretation, however, won the day, and through the influence of Suárez and others became the traditional understanding of Thomas' metaphysics.

---

[19] M. McCanles, "Univocalism in Cajetan's Doctrine of Analogy," *NSch,* 42 (1968): 18-47.
[20] But cf. J. P. Reilly, "Cajetan: Essentialist or Existentialist?" *NSch,* 41 (1967): 191-222; N. J. Wells, "On Last Looking into Cajetan's Metaphysics," *NSch,* 42 (1968): 112-17.

Another point at which Cajetan departed from Aquinas was in his view of the power and limits of reason. This became clear in the debate with the Averroists of Padua,[21] in which he remained firm on the conviction that the individual soul is immortal, but came to the conclusion that this could not be proved by reason but was rather to be believed on the basis of revelation. For this reason, when the Lateran Council condemnd the new Averroistic tendencies, Cajetan agreed with its decision; but when it went further and ordered all professors of philosophy to teach the individual immortality of the soul he voted against such a step, for he believed that philosophy could not prove a doctrine that the church held solely on the basis of revelation. Another point at which Cajetan differed from accepted tradition was in denying that the words of institution in communion, "this is my body," proved the real presence of Christ's body on the altar. Again, he did believe in such presence, but claimed that this was to be accepted on the basis of the authority of the church, for the text of Scripture was not absolutely clear.

Cajetan's views—especially his exegetical methods—drew the opposition of Ambrose Catharinus (1487–1553) and John Chrysostom Javelli (ca. 1470–ca. 1538). In the course of their attacks on Cajetan and on Luther, these theologians developed theories on the question of grace and predestination that were some of the first steps in the great controversy on that issue that involved many of the most distinguished Roman Catholic theologians of the sixteenth century.

In spite of the significance of Cajetan's work, the great center of Dominican theology during the sixteenth century was the University of Salamanca, in Spain, whose main chair of theology was occupied almost without interruption by a succession of outstanding scholars.[22] This tradition began in 1526, when Francisco de Vitoria (1492–1546) won the main chair of theology at Salamanca. Vitoria had spent some years at Paris, and had come to appreciate the work of the

---

21 See vol. 2 of this History, pp. 290-91.
22 C. Pozo, "Teología español postridentina del siglo XVI. Estado actual de la investigación de fuentes para su estudio," ATGran, 29 (1966): 87-124; A. Ibáñez-Ibarra, La doctrina sobre la tradición en la escuela salmantina, siglo XVI (Vitoria: ESET, 1967); F. Ehrle, "Los manuscritos vaticanos de los teólogos salmantinos del siglo XVI," EstEcl, 8 (1929): 98-147; L. Martínez Fernández, Fuentes para la historia del método teológico en la Escuela de Salamanca (Grenada: 1973). On the course and context of Spanish theology in the sixteenth century, I know of no better work than the monumental study by M. Andrés, La teología española en el siglo XVI, 2 vols. (Madrid: Editorial Católica, 1976-77). On the School of Salamanca, see his bibliography on vol. II, p 382.

humanists.[23] Therefore, he brought with him to the prestigious chair both elegance of style and a keen interest in the ancient patristic sources. He was also convinced that the theology of Thomas provided the best answers to the problems of the new times, and therefore—even though he had to use a subterfuge to evade the clear mandate of the statutes of the University—he introduced to Salamanca the custom, by then established in Paris, of commenting on Thomas instead of the Lombard. He thus gave birth to a type of Thomism with humanistic elegance and a concern for problems of actuality. To a greater or lesser extent, this will be characteristic of all his disciples and followers—and, in one way or another, all the great Spanish Dominican theologians of the sixteenth century were his followers.

Vitoria had a broad conception of his work as a theologian. "The task of a theologian is so wide that no argument, no debate, no subject, seems to be alien to the profession of the theologian."[24] He therefore lectured on a variety of subjects, usually commenting on Thomas and, to a lesser degree, on the *Sentences*. Of the many issues that he discussed, however, none illustrates his interest in problems of actuality better than the question of the conquest of the New World and the right that the Spanish had to launch such an enterprise. His work in this field had very little influence on the actual practice of the conquest, but it was of enormous importance as the beginning of the theory of international law.[25]

In his lectures *On the Indes* and *On the Right of War*, Vitoria set out by destroying seven traditional arguments that could be adduced in favor of the conquest of America. The first of these false arguments was the claim that the emperor was master of the whole world. This was a view commonly held at the high point of the Middle Ages, but it had never been put into full practice, even in western Europe. Vitoria therefore rejected it, with the further comment that, even if

---

[23] V. Beltrán de Heredia, "Orientación humanística en la teología vitoriana," *CienTom*, 72 (1947): 7-27.

[24] *De pot. civ.* (*BAC*, 198:149).

[25] A. Naszályi, *Doctrina Francisci de Vitoria de statu* (Rome: Scuola Salesiana del Libro, 1937); J. W. Scott, *The Spanish Origin of International Law: Francisco de Vitoria and His Law of Nations* (Oxford: Clarendon Press, 1934); B. Hamilton, *Political Thought in Sixteenth-century Spain: A Study of the Political Ideas of Vitoria, De Soto, Suárez, and Molina* (Clarendon Press, 1963); D. Ramos et al., *La ética en la conquista de América: Francisco de Vitoria y la Escuela de Salamanca* (Madrid: Consejo Superior de Investigaciones Científicas, 1984). On Vitoria's sources, see M. Beuchot, "El primer planteamiento teológico-jurídico sobre la conquista de América: John Mair," *CienTom*, 103 (1970), 213-30.

the emperor did have such lordship over the entire world, his authority would never be such that he could depose legitimate lords in the Indies, just as the emperor could not depose a legitimate king in Europe. The second possible argument for the conquest of America was that the pope had universal authority and had granted these lands to the kings of Spain. This view had many proponents, for many interpreted the bulls of Alexander VI, in which he granted the lands of the New World to the Spanish Crown, as an actual donation from the pope to the king. Vitoria was the first to reject such an argument, as well as the presuppositions on which it stood. According to Vitoria, the pope had no civil dominion over the entire world, and if he had it he could not simply grant it to another sovereign. Furthermore, as the pope had no authority over unbelievers, the refusal on the part of the Indians to accept his authority was not a just cause to declare war on them or to dispossess them of their lands. The influence of Vitoria on this score was great, and by the end of the century most theologians shared the view that the pope had no direct temporal power over the entire world. This was the reason that Sixtus V was making ready to add Vitoria's name to the *Index*—together with Bellarmine's—when his death prevented him from doing so (1590).

The right of discovery, also adduced as a just reason for the conquest, was equally rejected by Vitoria. The reason for this was simple: the lands that the Spanish claimed to have discovered were not in fact abandoned. They had their rightful owners, and could not be said to have been "discovered" in the strict sense.

The fourth fallacious reason for the conquest was that, in rejecting the Christian faith, the Indians had given the Spanish reason to punish them for their unbelief, and to force them to accept the true faith. Vitoria rejected this argument by pointing out that before they had the opportunity to hear the gospel—and to hear it with sufficient grounds for belief—the Indians did not sin by not believing it. The Indians would be guilty of unbelief only after the faith had been preached to them with sufficient signs—of love and of miracles—to make it credible. But even after they had heard such preaching, and by rejecting the faith had been made guilty of unbelief, the Indians were still the legitimate rulers of their domains, and their lack of faith was no reason to attempt to force them into believing.

The fifth argument that Vitoria rejected was the claim that

Christian rulers had the right to impose morality on the "barbarians" when the latter disobeyed the mandates of natural law. Such a claim would turn every war against unbelievers into a just war, for all unbelievers are idolatrous, and among all people sins against nature have been known to take place.

The sixth argument was that the Spanish were the legitimate rulers of lands granted to them by the Indians. To this Vitoria responded that this would only be true if such cession had taken place without any show of force or deceit, and with both the rulers and the subjects of the ceded lands agreeing to the transfer with full understanding of its implications.

Finally, the Spanish would have the right to conquer the New World if God had granted them those lands, as God gave Israel the promised land. Such claims Vitoria rejected by affirming that the ancient dispensation of Israel is now past, and that the prophetic gifts that could guarantee such a grant are no longer given.

Vitoria then offered a number of legitimate reasons for the conquest of America. It is not necessary to enumerate them here. In general, they are based on natural law, and the main argument is that the Spanish have the right and the obligation to make war on the Indians if they make their subjects suffer such things as human sacrifices, or if they attack an ally of the Spanish, or if they persecute the Christians within their domains, and so on.

The significance of these views for the development of international law was great. Here for the first time Christian theologians were speaking in terms of a community of nations, each with its legitimate rulers, embracing Christians as well as unbelievers. Thus it was obvious that the relations between such nations had to be regulated by principles other than Christian laws and traditions. Although Vitoria was certainly a Spaniard, and as such was willing to justify the Spanish enterprise in ways that may not seem legitimate today, it is significant that he made an impact on the conscience of Spain, and that Charles V for a time considered total withdrawal from the New World. Vitoria also influenced and inspired the Dominican Bartolomé de Las Casas, the great defender of the Indians in Spanish America.[26]

---

[26] V. D. Carro, "The Spanish Theological-Juridical Renaissance and the Ideology of Bartolomé de Las Casas," in J. Friede and B. Keen, ed., *Bartolomé de Las Casas in History: Toward an Understanding of the*

Melchior Cano (1509–1560),[27] who succeeded Vitoria in the main chair of theology at the University of Salamanca, followed along the same lines as his predecessor. He also was an elegant humanist in his style, and a convinced Thomist in his theology. Although he attacked the mysticism of the *alumbrados* when he became convinced that it was heterodox and akin to Protestantism, he himself wrote a spiritual treatise *On Victory over the Self*. His most important work, however, was his *De locis theologicis* [On theological themes] in which he set forth a systematic discussion of theological method and the sources of Christian truth. These sources are ten: Scripture, oral tradition, the universal church, councils, the Roman Church, the "Fathers," the scholastics, natural reason, the philosophers, and history. After discussing the relative value of each, and the manner in which they are to be understood and interpreted, Cano goes on to elaborate some principles for the use of these sources, first in polemics and then in the exposition of Scripture. The importance of this treatise is that it is the epitome of theological methodology in this "second scholasticism," showing at once its agreement with the former scholastics, and its new spirit, deeply influenced by humanism— especially in the elegance of its style. Furthermore, the fact that Cano recognizes all these sources in such a systematic fashion means that theology becomes much more a matter of citing authorities and showing their agreement than of the use of natural reason and logic. Thus a new method was proposed that was very different from what had developed in the medieval schools.

Domingo de Soto (1494–1560),[28] who had been Vitoria's and Cano's colleague at the University of Salamanca, succeeded to their chair when Cano became a bishop. He was one of the main opponents of Catharinus' views on grace, to which he opposed the teachings of Thomas. He also continued Vitoria's tradition of investigation into the foundations of international law.

Man and His Work (DeKalb: Northern Illinois University Press, 1971), pp. 237-77. See also: V. D. Carro, "Bartolomé de Las Casas y las controversias teológico-jurídicas de Indias," *BRAH,* 132:231-68; P. I. André-Vincent, *Bartolomé de Las Casas, prophète du Nouveau Monde* (Paris: J. Tallandier, 1980). In his zeal to defend the Indians, Las Casas suggested that blacks be brought from Africa as slaves.

[27] B. de Heredia, "Melchor Cano en la Universidad de Salamanca," *CienTom* 43 (1933): 178-208; F. Marín Sola, "Melchor Cano et la conclusion théologique," *RevThom* (1920), 121-41.

[28] P. Eyt, "Histoire et controverse antiluthérienne: Dominique Soto," *BLittEcc,* 68 (1967): 81-106; P. Eyt, "Un témoin catholique de la primauté de l'Ecriture au XVIe siècle," *BLittEcc,* 68 (1967): 161-79; V. Beltrán de Heredia, *Domingo de Soto: Estudio biográfico documentado* (Madrid: Cultura Hispánica, 1961); J. C. Martín de la Hoz, "Las relecciones inéditas de Domingo de Soto," *BullPhMed,* 25 (1983), 143-144.

Bartolomé Medina (1528–1580)[29] followed the interest of the Dominicans at Salamanca on moral theology. In his commentaries on the *Summa*, which he published in 1577 and 1578, he proposed the theory of "probabilism," which later was widely discussed. The basis of this theory is simply that, since it is lawful to hold a probable opinion, it is also proper to follow a course of moral action that is probably correct. A probable opinion is not simply one that one could hold, for in that case all opinions would be probable and even heresy would be acceptable, for some people do hold such views. What Medina means by "probable" is a view supported by reason and by wise counsel, but not by a final and undeniable authority. An unreasonable opinion is not probable. But in the case of probable opinions the level of certitude is such that, while one is justified in following that opinion, it is still possible that another view might be shown to be more probable. Does this then mean that a person always has to follow the most probable opinion? Certainly not, for as long as the probable remains such it is lawful to follow another course of action than that dictated by it.[30] As to how far Medina would have carried these views, interpreters are in disagreement. Some hold that what Medina meant by "probable" was the certitude that one can have in contingent matters, whereas others claim that he meant simply opinions that are somewhat doubtful. If what he held was the latter, then he may be said to be the founder of "probabilism." In its final form—one certainly not held by Medina—probabilism claims that if there is doubt as to whether an action is sinful or not one may act as if it were not sinful, even if the greater probability is on the side of its sinfulness. This view, held by some Jesuit casuists, was later attacked by the Jansenists, who held that in such a case one should take the more rigorous course of action. Probabilism was eventually condemned by Alexander VII (1667) and by Innocent XI (1679); but in various modified forms it continued being the accepted teaching among Jesuit theologians.

The last great author of the Dominican school of Salamanca was Domingo Báñez (1528–1604),[31] whose style and approach to theology are more scholastic and less humanistic than those of his predecessors. As a great deal of his significance lies in his

---

[29] M. M. Gorce, "Medina (Barthélemy de)," *DTC*, 10:481-85.
[30] Medina, Comm. ad I^a II^{ae}, q. 19, a. 6.
[31] P. Mandonnet, "Báñez, Dominique," *DTC*, 2:140-45.

participation in the controversy regarding grace, predestination, and free will, we must postpone a discussion of that aspect of his theology until we come to that debate. However, Báñez is significant in other ways. For instance, in order to refute the views of Protestantism, he made one of the starkest affirmations of the authority of the church and its tradition above the written text of Scripture. According to him, it is absolutely necessary "to assert that Sacred Scripture is in the church of Christ: Sacred Scripture is first of all in the heart of the church, and secondarily in the books and editions."[32] Although such blunt affirmations were never made official doctrine of the Catholic Church, they did serve to shape the thought of many theologians throughout the eighteenth and nineteenth centuries.

Another point at which Báñez' doctrines merit discussion is his insistence on the primacy of the act of existence over eternal essences. Here he differed from Cajetan in his interpretation of Thomas, for Cajetan's essentialism appeared to him as a misreading of the Angelic Doctor.[33] *Esse,* the act of being, is neither substance nor accident, but prior to them. These metaphysical views created difficulties for Báñez from two sources. The first was the Jesuits, whose understanding of Thomist metaphysics was different, and who felt that metaphysical differences were at the heart of their disagreement with Báñez and the Dominicans on the questions of grace, predestination, and free will. Thus, Jesuit philosophers have repeatedly tried to show that Báñez does not interpret Thomas correctly.[34] The other source of difficulties that Báñez had to face was the Inquisition, for his doctrine of the primacy of existence, when applied to the eucharist, resulted in the conclusion that there remains in the consecrated host the original existence of the bread. These views were brought to the attention of the Inquisition by the famous poet and—not so famous—theologian Fr. Luis de León, and later by Luis de Molina, the main adversary of the Dominicans in the

---

[32] *Scholastica commentaria in Primam Partem S. Theologicae,* q. 1, a. 8 (ed. L. Urbano [Madrid: I.E.V.A., 1934], p. 71).

[33] *The Primacy of Existence in Thomas Aquinas,* trans. B. J. Llamzon (Chicago: Regnery, 1966). This is a translation of Báñez' commentary to the *Summa,* I^a, q. 64. In his introduction Llamzon summarizes Báñez' views as follows: "He insists on Aquinas' teaching that esse is the *first act by which* anything is real at all. Esse, he says, is not substance, nor is it an accident. It is not an essential constituent, nor in any way to be understood as a classification among the predicaments. Esse transcends all these: it is the act by which any of these causes *are* causes. . . . Essence relates to esse only as a limit, and the very reality of that limit is from esse." (P. 12.)

[34] W. J. Hill, "Báñez and Bañezianism," *NCatEnc,* 2:48-50.

controversy on grace and predestination. Their contention was that Báñez was proposing a theory on the eucharist that was akin to the Lutheran theory of "consubstantiation," which by then had been condemned by the Council of Trent. Báñez responded by making it clear that he believed that the substance of the bread was no longer present in the consecrated element, but that God did not create a new existence in the act of consecration. He thus affirmed the doctrine of transubstantiation, but pointed out that the act of existence of the bread remains the same.[35] These explanations, however, did not satisfy his opponents—especially among the Jesuits—who repeatedly called the attention of the Inquisition to Báñez' eucharistic doctrine.

Jesuit Theology

Of the many events that shook the Christian church during the sixteenth century, the quiet founding of the Society of Jesus is without any doubt one of the most significant, both for the history of the Catholic Church as an institution and for the history of its theology. Its founder, Ignatius of Loyola (1491–1556),[36] was the youngest son of a wealthy Basque who traced his lineage to the time before the invasion of the Moors. His early years were spent in military pursuits—or rather, in the pursuit of glory through military deeds. These dreams came to an abrupt end when, while heroically defending the city of Pamplona against the French, one of his legs was broken. In spite of the fact that he had the bone broken anew twice, to have it reset, his leg never healed properly, and the resulting limp guaranteed that he would never be able to make a glorious name for himself in the field of battle. This great disappointment made him turn to readings of a spiritual nature, seeking to find comfort in his misery. There he read of the great army of saints and martyrs who had served Our Lady through privations, heroic valor, and apostolic zeal. His mind wavered between these two ideals, the military and the religious, until he had a vision that he later narrated in the third person:

> Being awake one night, he clearly saw an image of Our Lady with the Holy Infant Jesus, and that vision consoled him vastly for a

---

[35] *Schol. Comm. in I^{am}*, q. 4, a. 2 (ed. Urbano, pp. 173-74).

[36] See the excellent bibliographies in I. Iparraguirre and C. de Dalmases, ed., *Obras Completas de San Ignacio de Loyola (BAC,* 86), pp. lxix-lxxx, 20-22, 143-49, 366-67.

long time, and afterwards he felt such revulsion towards his past life, and especially things of the flesh, that it seemed like all the notions which had been imprinted on his soul were now erased. Thus, from that moment until this August of '53, when these words are being written, he never consented to the things of the flesh; and this zeal shows that the whole matter was from God, although he himself would not then affirm such a thing, and dared say only what had happened.[37]

He then went in pilgrimage to the hermitage of Montserrat, a hill of holy fame in Aragon, and there he devoted himself to his Lady in rites reminiscent of the watching of arms in traditional chivalry. From there he went on to Manresa to live as a beggar in extreme asceticism. Yet the early stages of his life as a monk were very similar to Luther's. He had confessed his sins at Montserrat, but still it seemed to him that he had not confessed them all. He sought out those who were supposed to be the best spiritual leaders in the region, but to no avail. Finally a "very spiritual man," whom Ignatius seems to have admired, told him to write down all his sins. Ignatius followed his advice to the letter, and yet it would not quiet his conscience. He wished he could be freed from the need to look back and discover every one of his sins, and he was tempted to request this from his confessor when the latter suggested that he confess only those past sins which were very clear. But to Ignatius all his past sins were very clear, and therefore this relaxation of the strict discipline of the confessional was no help to him. Seeking help directly from God, he would spend seven hours a day praying in his cell. He would cry out aloud in his prayers: "Help me, Lord, for I find no cure in men, nor in any creature. If I knew where to look, no effort would be too great. Show me, Lord, where to seek, and I shall do whatever may be necessary, even if I have to let myself be led by a dog."[38]

While in these prayers his despair took him to the very edge of blasphemy; he repeatedly considered suicide as a solution to his anguish, and was held from jumping through his window only by the thought that it would be a great sin. He then thought that perhaps God was demanding a great sacrifice before granting him forgiveness. He therefore determined to fast until God answered

---

[37] *Autobiography*, 1. 10 (*BAC*, 86:35).
[38] *Ibid.*, 3. 23 (*BAC*, 86:46).

him, or until he would be so near death that to continue fasting would be suicide. For a whole week he did not eat a thing, but when he told his confessor what he was doing he was commanded to break his fast. Thereafter he enjoyed two days of peace, but on the third day his doubts assailed him again. He was once again praying and confessing his sins to God, one by one, all over again, and at the same time considering the possibility of abandoning the whole enterprise, when he suddenly received the realization that God did not require such minute confession of every past sin, "and from that day on he was free of those anxieties, for he was certain that in his mercy our Lord had wished to free him."[39]

The result of his newly found freedom was that his enormous vitality was now liberated to lead him to great enterprises. He went to Palestine, hoping to settle there as a missionary to the Turks. But the Franciscans who were in charge of the shrines of the Latin church would not allow him to remain in the Holy Land. They were probably afraid that this overzealous, mystical, and relatively unlearned Basque would be more of a hindrance than a help. Ignatius then decided that he must return to school, for his lack of theological learning would always hinder his work. He probably could have hastened matters and have been ordained in a few years. But he was convinced of his need for solid learning, and therefore—although he was already a mature man—returned to the classroom, filled with students many years his juniors, and devoted twelve years to study. He went first to Barcelona, and then to Alcalá—the famous university that Ximenes had founded as a center for the reformation of the church. By this time he had gathered a small number of followers, mostly among his fellow students, and the Inquisition began eyeing him with suspicion. After having been imprisoned, tried, and acquitted by the Holy Office, he and a number of his companions left for the famous University of Salamanca. But there again they had troubles with the Inquisition, and this time with whole band was imprisoned and tried. Although they were found innocent of heresy, Ignatius was ordered to refrain from teaching until his studies had been completed.

His difficulties with the Inquisition in Spain encouraged Ignatius to leave for Paris, where the Sorbonne had become the center of

---

[39] *Ibid.*, 3. 25 (*BAC*, 86:47).

Roman Catholic orthodoxy. He went as a student and as a beggar, but soon another band of followers had formed around this man of extraordinary charisma. This small group of nine—among them Francis Xavier and Diego Laínez—would be the core of the Society of Jesus. In August of 1534, Ignatius took his group of followers to Montmartre, and there they swore poverty, chastity, and obedience to the pope. They also vowed to make a pilgrimage to Jerusalem and to work for the conversion of the Turks, unless the pope would absolve them of such vows and set them to another task. Finally, in 1539, the small group decided to form a permanent organization, with a superior elected among themselves to whom they would vow obedience. In 1540 Paul III approved the new order, and Ignatius was elected to be its first general. Almost immediately the Society of Jesus became a powerful instrument in the hands of the popes of that time, who were very seriously devoted to the task of reforming the Catholic Church and refuting the Protestants. Francis Xavier, one of Ignatius' original companions when the Society was first formed, became a missionary to the Orient, and there established churches and Jesuits in a number of countries. We have already seen the work of Peter Canisius and of Bellarmine, attempting to stem the tide of Protestantism. When Ignatius died in 1556, there were over a thousand Jesuits, distributed throughout Europe as well as Brazil, India, Congo, and Ethiopia.

Although at first Ignatius did not conceive of the Society as a teaching order, he did have high regard for study and was convinced that members of the Society must have the best training available. To this end he spelled out in the *Constitutions* of the Society the program of spiritual training and academic education that prospective members of the Society must follow. These *Constitutions* show a great concern for uniformity and list the books that are to serve as the main study source and as textbooks to be discussed in class. In the field of philosophy, Aristotle was to be preferred; and "in theology the Old and the New Testaments will be read, and the scholastic doctrine of Saint Thomas."[40] Thus Thomas became the official doctor of the new order. But this was not a final and exclusive decision, for Ignatius added that the *Sentences* should also be read, and that if in the future another theological system should appear, which would not be

---

[40] *Const.*, 4. 14 (*BAC*, 86:474).

contrary to Thomas but would be "better adapted to our time," it could also be included among the books to be read, although with great care and after the considered approval of the Society. Ignatius seems even to have hoped that the Society could develop such a theology, for he asked Diego Laínez to write a manual of theology that could serve for the education of the Jesuits. Laínez undertook this task, but his many other occupations did not permit him to complete it, and all that he left were notes on the sources that he presumably would have used. Furthermore, some of the earlier Jesuits were Scotists rather than Thomists. Such was the case of the Coimbra professor Pedro de Fonseca (1528–1599), whose main interests were metaphysical rather than theological, and whose significance for the history of Jesuit theology lies in that he applied to the question of predestination the theory of the *scientia media,* which we shall have occasion to discuss when we come to the controversies on grace and presdestination. Another point at which Jesuit theology soon developed characteristics of its own was in its concentration on "positive theology," drawn mainly from the "Fathers" and Scripture, rather than using only the scholastic method. This could already be seen in the notes that Laínez left, and it became apparent in the work of Francisco de Toledo (1532–1596).

Among the Jesuit theologians of the sixteenth century, we have already discussed Bellarmine and Canisius, whose main work was the refutation of Protestantism. Luis de Molina we shall discuss in the next section of this chapter, for his name is intimately connected with the controversies on grace and predestination. Therefore, we now turn to the most distinguished Jesuit theologian of the sixteenth and early seventeenth centuries—Francisco Suárez (1548–1617).

Suárez was born in Granada and studied at Salamanca, where he came into contact with the long and prestigious tradition of Dominican theology. Having joined the Society of Jesus while still in his teens, he devoted to it his entire life. This he spent teaching in several cities in Spain—Avila, Segovia, Valladolid, Alcalá, and Salamanca—as well as in Rome and, for the last twenty years of his life, at Coimbra, in Portugal. A scholar at heart, he avoided excessive involvement in the politics of his time; and even in theological and philosophical issues he avoided unnecessary controversy. However, as was inevitable, he was drawn into several debates, as will be seen in our exposition of his thought.

Although there is indeed a Suarezian system, he never composed a systematic theology. In the field of metaphysics, his *Disputationes metaphysicae* do give a systematic account of his views. But his theological treatises, while dealing with almost every aspect of Christian theology, do so as independent monographs. The editors of his works, however, have attempted to systematize his theology by placing the various treatises in the same order in which their subject matter is discussed in the *Summa* of Thomas. Thus, although the chronological order has been violated, the twenty-seven volumes of the works of Suárez form a veritable summa.

The *Disputationes metaphysicae* are a treatise on systematic metaphysics. Up to that time, the teaching and writing of metaphysics had taken the shape of commentaries on Aristotle, with the author agreeing or disagreeing at various points. But Suárez reorganized the entire subject matter of metaphysics, discussing various questions in the order that seemed best to him rather than in that prescribed by the *Metaphysics* of Aristotle—which, after all, is really a juxtaposition of independent treatises. Also, under each heading, Suárez compiled opinions that show an incredibly vast erudition, and thus brought philosophers from vastly different backgrounds— Greeks, Jews, Moslems, Scholastics, Renaissance scholars—into dialogue with one another. He then offered his own opinions, always taking into consideration the multitude of options that were open to him.[41]

This is hardly the place to attempt to summarize the content of the fifty-four *Disputationes metaphysicae*. In general, let it suffice to say that Suárez was a Thomist who had been influenced by Scotus.[42] Although there are diverging interpretations of Suárez, especially at the point of his agreement or disagreement with Thomas, there are a number of characteristics of Suárez' metaphysics that should be pointed out as illustrations of the manner in which he differed from Thomas. Probably the most characteristic divergence between

---

[41] Two general studies are F. Copleston, *A History of Philosophy*, vol. 3, part 2 (London: Burns, Oates & Washbourne, 1953), pp. 353-405; H. Seigfried, *Wahrheit und Metaphysik bei Suarez* (Bonn: Bouvier, 1967). On more specialized, but important, issues see W. M. Neidle, *Der Realitätsbegriff des Franz Suarez nach den Disputationes Metaphysicae* (Munich: Heuber, 1966); J. P. Doyle, "Suarez and the Reality of the Possibles," ModSch, 45 (1967-68):29-8; K. Werner, *Franz Suarez und die Scholastik der letzen Jahrhunderte* (New York: B. Franklin, 1963); P. Dumont, *Liberté humaine et concours divin d'après Suárez* (Paris: G. Beauchesne et fils, 1936).

[42] E. Elorduy, "Duns Scoti influxus in Francisci Suarez doctrinam," in *De doctrina Ioannis Duns Scoti: Acta Congressus Scotistici . . . 1966 celebrati* (Rome: Pontificia Universitas Gregoriana, 1968), 4:307-37.

Thomas and Suárez—certainly the most debated by later scholars—was the manner in which they regarded the relationship between essence and existence. Thomas had said that there is a real distinction in creatures between essence and existence. Suárez, on the contrary, denied such a real distinction, and argued that it is in the mind rather than in the creatures themselves, although it has an objective basis. The exact meaning of this "objective basis"—*cum fundamento in re*—is the point debated among later interpreters, for the interpretation of that phrase determines Suárez' closeness to or distance from Aquinas. But in any case, it is true that one does not find in Suárez the clear affirmation of the primacy of the act of existence that, as Báñez had pointed out, is a fundamental part of Thomas' metaphysics. Other divergences can be found between the two philosophers in such issues as potency and act (Suárez would have said that pure potentiality is inconceivable and that prime matter must therefore be somehow actual), substance and accident, and others.

The importance of Suárez as a theologian, however, does not lie in his great metaphysical ability, but rather in that he took the entire scholastic tradition and, while being faithful to Thomas in most of his theology, developed a system that responded to new challenges. Thus, the first thing to be said about Suárez' theology is that here, as in his metaphysics, he showed the result of tireless scholarhip and wide erudition. While following Thomas closer than any other theologian, Suárez was not bound to him by ignorance of other alternatives. His work, then, reads not only like a vast summa, but even like a summa of scholastic summae. His way of handling Thomas may be seen in the manner in which he dealt with Thomas' proof of the existence of God from the fact of movement (*ex parte motus*).[43] Suárez pointed out that this argument requires the principle that everything that moves is moved by another. Although this is true in physics, it is not a metaphysical truth, and therefore Suárez would have preferred to say that whatever is made is made by another.[44] The difference may seem slight, but it shows that Suárez had heeded the criticism of Scotus to the five ways of Thomas.[45] Likewise, on the question of the reason for the incarnation, Suárez followed the

---

[43] See vol. 2 of this *History*, p. 266.
[44] *Disp.*, 29. 1. 20 (Paris edition, 26:27).
[45] See above, 2:309-11.

Franciscan school in asserting that, even if Adam had not sinned, Christ would have become incarnate.[46] He also followed the Franciscans over Thomas and his followers in affirming the immaculate conception of Mary.[47] Therefore, it would not be entirely inappropriate to say that Suárez' system is a post-Scotist and post-nominalist form of Thomism. The same may be said of his doctrine of grace, which he developed by adapting Thomism in response to Molinism—or by modifying Molinism and making it agree with Thomism. This doctrine of grace, as most of Suárez' theology, has become the accepted doctrine in the Society of Jesus.[48]

The Controversies on Grace, Predestination, and Free Will

Although these controversies took place after the Council of Trent, their connection with the doctrinal developments that we have been discussing is so close that it seems best to discuss them before turning our attention to the council itself. But a word about that council's actions on the question of grace is also necessary in order to understand the background of the controversy. In its sixth session, the council had taken up the question of justification, which was one of the crucial issues that stood between the Catholic Church and Protestantism. In response to the views that Luther had proposed, the council declared that one cannot turn toward God without prevenient grace, which is given quite apart from any merits that one might have, but that the human will can and must cooperate with grace by accepting it and by collaborating with it in good works. It then went on to anathematize those who teach that prevenient grace is not necessary, and those who claim, on the other hand, that the will can neither prepare itself to receive justification nor reject grace when it is offered.[49]

These views were also shared by Ignatius, who had instructed his followers that they should speak of divine grace, and praise the

---

46 *Disp. in tertiam partem D. Thomae,* 1. 3. 4 (Paris ed., 19:11).

47 *De ultimo fine hominis,* 5. 9. 4. 8 (Paris ed., 4:614).

48 One should add, however, that his opinions were not always accepted without question. In 1591 a controversy broke out between Suárez and Gabriel Vásquez (1551–1604) on the question of God's justice. Suárez affirmed that God's dealings with the world were just, whereas Vásquez claimed that in the strict sense there can be no justice between God and creatures. The controversy ended when the general of the order imposed silence on both parties. Suárez also was condemned by the Inquisition in 1603 for holding that confession at a distance was valid. Finally, when he affirmed in his *Defense of the Catholic and Apostolic Faith* that tyrannicide is justified under some circumstances, this brought upon him—and, by extension, upon the Society—the wrath of more than one crowned head.

49 *Denzinger* (Rome: Herder, 1957), 792-843.

divine majesty for it, but that this should not be done "especially in our very dangerous times, in such a way that good works and free will may be injured, or taken for naught."[50] In writing such words, he was obviously thinking of the doctrines of Luther and Calvin, and making certain that such views would not find acceptance among his followers. Thus, even before the controversy broke out, there was a tacit tradition among the Jesuits—represented by theologians such as Pedro de Fonseca and Bartholomew Camerarius—which insisted on the freedom of the will and sought ways to coordinate it with the doctrines of grace and predestination.

In Salamanca, however, another view seems to have prevailed since the times of Medina. The earlier teachers of that school—Vitoria, Cano, and Soto—had said that one chooses whether or not one will listen to the divine call. But Medina, and especially Báñez, were of the conviction that there was danger in granting too much to human powers, and thus diminishing the work of grace. Medina said that good works do not prepare us for the reception of grace, and that God may decide to grant grace quite apart from our preparation for it through works. Báñez went much further. In a passage that is strangely reminiscent of Zwingli,[51] Báñez argues that the divine nature is such that nothing outside of it can be the cause of its actions, and that it is the cause of all things and events, including sin. God knows all future contingent events, for God knows all causes, and the same is true of sin. But the actual cause of conversion is help from on high, and the cause of unbelief is the lack of such help. Thus, God grants efficacious grace to the elect, and withholds it from the reprobate, who nevertheless are justly condemned for their sins.

That these views were not well received by all at the University of Salamanca may be seen in the fact that in 1582, in a debate having to do with the merits of Christ, Báñez argued that, even if Christ had been predestined to suffer, his death would still have been meritorious, and immediately a number of colleagues took issue with him. His best known opponent on that score was Fr. Luis de León, who also accused Báñez of holding unorthodox views on the eucharist. The affair eventually became so bitter that it was taken to the Inquisition, which after two years decided in favor of Báñez,

---

[50] *Ejercicios espirituales* (*BAC*, 86:238).
[51] *Schol. Comm. in I*^am^, q. 19, a. 1-9 (ed. Urbano, pp. 409-37).

though not on the question of predestination, but on that of the merits of Christ.

Similar developments were taking place at the University of Louvain, where Michael Baius (1513–1589) was teaching that through the fall we had lost, not a supernatural gift, but something of our very nature, which was now corrupted.[52] As a result, we cannot turn to God, for we lack the power and the real desire to do so. Our corrupted free will cannot desire the good. Seventy-nine propositions held by Baius were condemned by Pius V in 1567. Baius submitted to the papal decree but soon was teaching a new version of his doctrines, and Gregory XIII found it necessary to condemn his views again in 1579. The university supported its professor, who was later elected chancellor. When the Jesuit Lessius attempted to refute the views held by Baius, the university condemned the theses proposed by the Jesuit, who in turn replied by publishing a defense of his position.[53] The lines were clearly drawn. The faculty accused Lessius of Pelagianism, and he in turn accused them of Calvinism. On every aspect of the controversy, the views of the two parties were clearly opposed. The faculty said that God determines the action of the will in conversion; Lessius said that the will determines itself. The faculty said that only some receive from God an efficacious aid for salvation; Lessius held that such aid is given to all. The faculty affirmed that divine predestination is absolutely independent of God's foreknowledge of a person's merits; Lessius asserted that predestination depends on the merits that God foresees in the elect. Finally the affair was brought to the attention of Sixtus V, who appointed a commission of cardinals to study the matter and pronounce judgment. The cardinals could find no fault in the teaching of Lessius, and the pope ordered that the dispute be settled. But the positions of the two parties were too fixed and too diametrically opposed to be brought together by compromise. Therefore, the papal emissary simply ordered each party to refrain from attacking the other.

So matters stood when the Jesuit Luis de Molina (1536–1600) published in Lisbon his treatise on *The Agreement of Free Will with the*

---

[52] F. X. Jansen, *Baius et le Baianisme: Essai Théologique* (Louvain: Museum Lessianum, 1927); H. de Lubac, *Agustinianism and Modern Theology* (New York: Herder and Herder, 1969), pp. 1-33.

[53] C. van Sull, *Léonard Lessius de la Compagnie de Jésus (1554-1623)* (Louvain: Museum Lessianum, 1930)

Gifts of Grace (1588).[54] Hardly was the book off the press before the Dominicans began questioning its orthodoxy. The sale of the book was stopped, and Báñez wrote a series of objections to it. When the book was finally released for sale, it included in an appendix the objections raised by Báñez and Molina's response to them. Thus, by its very format, the book was bound to be controversial.

As its title announces, the purpose of the book is to show the agreement—*concordia*—that exists between free will on the one hand, and grace, foreknowledge, and predestination on the other. Its aim is clearly apologetic, for Molina is trying to respond to the accusation made by Protestants that the Catholic doctrine of free will and merits is a Pelagian denial of the primacy of grace. Its perspective is Thomistic, for it claims to be no more than a commentary on certain brief sections of the *Summa* that deal with the issues at hand. Finally, its basic outline is relatively simple, for it is divided into four parts, dealing with the knowledge of God, God's will, providence, and predestination.

Thus, Molina sets out by discussing the knowledge of God. The first question to be posed in this context is whether God's knowledge is the cause of creatures. Molina's answer is that one must distinguish between God's "natural" and "free" knowledge. God's natural knowledge includes all possible things, even those which God has not willed to create, and therefore it is not the cause of things. But God's free knowledge is determined by the divine will, and extends only to those things which God has willed. Therefore, the free knowledge of God is the cause of creatures.

This distinction in the knowledge of God reflects what Molina understands by freedom. Freedom is not only "freedom from coercion," but also and above all "freedom from necessity." A stone that falls, simply because it is in its nature to fall when released in mid-air, is not coerced into falling; but it is not free, for it falls out of necessity. When Protestants assert that one chooses freely what God has predestined, what they mean is that one is not coerced into a choice, and they are therefore confusing lack of coercion with freedom. If one is to be free, one must choose, not out of necessity, but out of one's own free will. What is free is by definition contingent,

---

[54] In this entire section, we follow the article by E. Vansteenberghe, "Molinisme," *DTC*, 10:2098-2187.

and therefore the carrying out of an eternal degree of predestination cannot be said to imply freedom on the part of the human being.

When Adam was created, he was given the supernatural virtues of faith, hope, and love, and also "original justice," which aided and strengthened his natural freedom so that he could obey God and merit eternal life. Thus, Adam was not simply "natural man," for to his natural powers were added supernatural gifts, which enabled his free will to make the right choices. What happened to him as a consequence of the fall was that he lost both the supernatural virtues and original justice. Strictly speaking, original sin did not affect human nature but affected only the supernatural gifts that had been added to it. Therefore, when traditional anti-Pelagian theology says that sin has weakened human freedom, what it in fact means is not that natural human freedom has been injured, but that it now lacks the supernatural aid with which it was originally endowed.

In our present state, we are still free in the same sense in which we were free before the fall. Faced with each decision, we are free to choose our own course of action. But we are not free to choose by ourselves those things which lead to our supernatural destiny, for such things demand powers that are—and always have been—beyond our nature. Now, as before, we need the help of God. In order to believe, however, the "general help of God," which is offered to every human being, is sufficient. Therefore, although it is not true that one believes simply because one has decided to believe, it is true that the difference between belief and unbelief lies in the free choice of the will, and not in God.

Although justifying faith is much more than assent or belief and does require the prevenient and stimulating grace of God, it too depends on a free action of the will, commanding the intellect to believe. That first act of faith is then followed by the "supernatural habit of faith," which God grants the believer and which henceforth makes it possible to perform the act of faith with no more than God's "general help." If God adds to that habit further gifts of the Spirit, this is not because they are necessary for the act of faith, but because they strengthen it. Thus, the *initium fidei*—the beginning of faith—is in God's action, as Augustine asserted; but our free will still plays an important and necessary role. Furthermore, God has decided that prevenient grace will normally be granted to those who do everything within their power to believe and to renounce sin, and therefore one can say, loosely speaking, that grace and salvation are always at hand for those who wish to choose them. To claim that the reason some are saved and some are not lies in the will of God, or in the gift of a supposedly irresistible grace, is to deny the universal salvific will of God. One must say rather that the original difference between those who choose to believe and those who choose not to believe lies in their free use of their will.

Molina's theories on grace and predestination are closely connected with his understanding of the relationship between God's action and the action of secondary causes. Molina affirms that God is *simultaneously* active in secondary causes—in contrast with the theory of *physical premotion* of Báñez and other Thomists. When fire produces heat, there is a single action in which the secondary cause, fire, and the primary cause, God, work together. The two, however, are very different, for the action of the fire in heating is "particular," whereas God's action is a "general aid" to secondary causes. What in fact has happened is that God has decided from the moment of creation that certain things will be secondary causes of others, and that, knowing they would be unable to act of themselves, God has decided that a "general aid" would work simultaneously with secondary causes whenever such causes would be active. The same is true with reference to free will as applied to those decisions which do not go beyond the realm of the natural and into the supernatural. When we make a decision, God supports that decision by means of a general aid. This does not make God responsible for evil acts, for it was decided from all eternity that God would grant this general aid to our wills. Thus, although power to do evil—and good—is due to the divine aid, such general aid, promised by God to all creatures from all eternity, is not in itself the cause of evil. The only cause of evil, in the moral sense of being responsible for it, is the will that chooses evil.

When it comes to supernatural acts, the same simultaneous collaboration still exists between God's general help and the will, but to these is now added prevenient grace, which can also be called God's "special" aid. What this does is to enable the will, with the help of the general aid, to perform acts of supernatural significance, such as faith. Thus, there is only one act in which three elements are at work: the will, the general aid, and the special aid of God. Thus, grace—just as the general aid—acts not *upon* the will, but *with* it. This means that the difference between prevenient grace and cooperating grace is not that which would exist between two different sorts of graces, but is a way of showing that the will cannot perform a supernatural act without the special aid. Cooperating grace is simply prevenient grace to which the will assents. Once this assent takes place, the supernatural habits—faith, hope, charity—are infused in the believer, who can now perform supernatural acts with the general aid of God.

If we now return to the original question, regarding God's knowledge, we shall find it necessary to posit, besides the natural and the free knowledge, which we have already discussed, a "mixed" or "intermediate" knowledge—*scientia media*. The reason for this is obvious, for there are future contingent realities and events that God knows, not as possible nor as willed by God, but as willed by other free wills that God has decided to create. Thus, the *scientia media* is that knowledge by which God knows future contingents that will be caused by free creatures. In brief, God has a natural knowledge of all possible things, a free knowledge of those things which God has willed, and an intermediate knowledge of those things which other wills shall decide. Therefore, future contingent events do not depend on divine foreknowledge. On the contrary, God foreknows that which free creatures will freely decide. Nor is everything willed by God in the absolute sense, for one must distinguish between God's absolute or efficacious will and God's conditional will. Whatever God wishes according to absolute will necessarily takes place, but what God wishes according to conditional will takes place only if other free causes act to fulfill that will. God's universal salvific will is conditional. Although God wishes that all would be saved, only those who accept the offer of salvation will actually be saved.

Given these premises, the question of election and reprobation can be answered in such a way that it agrees with freedom of the will. Predestination depends on divine foreknowledge, not in the sense that God has decided to withhold divine aid from those who will reject it, but in the sense that God knows who will freely decide to make proper use of the aids granted to all. As grace is not irresistible, the granting of grace—or, in other words, of special aid—does not guarantee salvation. All grace is efficacious and sufficient unto salvation, but it becomes so only by our free decision to accept it.

The opposition of Báñez and other Dominican theologians to

Molina's system was immediate, bitter, and unflinching. Báñez himself attempted to include Molina's work in the *Index* when the faculty at Salamanca was appointed to prepare a list of forbidden books among recent publications. The controversy finally broke out in Valladolid, the capital of Castile, where both the Jesuits and the Dominicans had important schools. For some time the Dominicans had been criticizing Molina in their lectures, when the Jesuits brought the matter to light by holding a public disputation (1594). The Dominicans declared Molina's views heretical, and asked for the judgment of the Inquisition on the subject. Pulpits were used by the Dominicans to attack the Jesuits, who in turn used their influence in court to have the offending preachers removed from their posts. Finally, after a second debate, which bordered on a riot and of which each of the parties gave a different account, Molina was accused before the Inquisition by the Dominicans, and he in turn accused Báñez and another member of his order. The Spanish Inquisition felt unable to render judgment between such influential parties, and the authorities feared that a schism might result from the debate. Therefore, the entire matter was referred to Rome.

The Dominicans opposed Molinism because they correctly felt that the Jesuit's understanding of grace contradicted what they found in Thomas and Augustine. The main issue was the difference between sufficient and efficacious grace. The Molinists, as we have seen, taught that there is no difference between these, and that what makes sufficient grace be efficacious is the action of the will. This the Dominicans could not accept, for it meant that grace received its efficacy *ab extrinseco,* that is, from the will. It was clear to them that Augustine—and Thomas after him—had taught that grace is efficacious in itself, *ab intrinseco.* Furthermore, they conceived of the relationship between grace and the will in terms that were radically different from Molina's. The latter's notion of a simultaneous aid did not seem to them to express adequately Augustine's notion of grace operating on the will. Therefore the Dominicans preferred to speak of a *physical premotion* of the will by grace. This the Molinists saw as a denial of freedom, for a will that is moved by another is not acting freely—here one must remember Molina's understanding of freedom as freedom not merely from coercion, but also from necessity. Thus, the issues at stake were very similar to those involved in the debate between Luther and Erasmus.

Aware of the gravity of the debate, and of its possible disastrous consequences, Clement VIII decided to take matters in his own hands. He ordered that the controversy be halted and that each order send to him a summary of its position. Meanwhile, the opinions of a number of universities and of several ecclesiastical leaders were requested. This temporary solution did not please the Dominicans, who now found their traditional views treated on a par with the "innovations" of the Jesuits. As the Dominicans then seemed to be closer to the ear of the pope, they finally succeeded in persuading Clement that a commission should be appointed to examine Molina's book. This commission was appointed in 1597, and thus began a long series of theological conferences on the matter of divine succor to human freedom—the *congregationes de auxiliis*. In 1598, the commission decided that Molina's views were opposed to those of Augustine and Aquinas, and that in many points they agreed with the opinions of the Pelagians. Molina's condemnation seemed imminent, and the Dominicans were already celebrating their victory, when a number of influential persons pleaded that the matter be handled more cautiously. When such pleas arrived from the king of Spain as well as from the emperor's mother and from a number of church leaders, Clement decided to change his tactics and call for a series of conversations between representatives of both factions, hoping that a compromise might be reached. Such conversations were not successful, and once again Clement was ready to condemn Molina. In Spain, some Jesuits at the University of Alcalá were beginning to question the authority of the pope. Clement then called a new series of conferences, over which he himself presided. These new encounters began in 1602, and were still in progress with no significant results when Clement died in 1605. His successor, Paul V, continued presiding over the assemblies until 1606, when he decided that the best solution to the controversy was not to decide at all. He declared that neither the Dominicans nor the Molinists were teaching opinions contrary to the Catholic faith. The views of the Dominicans were not Calvinistic—as the Molinists claimed—for they said that grace perfects freedom, and does not destroy it. As to the Molinists, they were not Pelagians—in spite of such accusations by the Dominicans—because they placed the *initium fidei* in divine grace, and not in the human will. Therefore, both views could be held and taught, as long as each refrained from accusing the other of heresy. Five years later, Paul V reinforced this decision by ordering that all future works on grace be presented to the Inquisition before their publication. This prohibition was repeated and made more stringent several years later by Urban VIII (in 1625 and 1641). In spite of such prohibitions, however, both Molinists and Dominicans continued their debate for several centuries.

What forced the Molinist controversy into the background was another debate, dealing with essentially the same issues but revolving now about a man whose views were diametrically opposed to Molina's: the Dutch theologian Cornelius Jansenius (1585–1638).[55] As we have already seen, the University of Louvain, under the leadership of Baius, had held that predestination is prior to foreknowledge, that we have lost our freedom to turn to God, and that grace moves the will in the act of conversion. Although the Molinist controversy had drawn attention away from Louvain and toward Spain, the views held by Baius—repeatedly condemned by Rome—continued to circulate in the Netherlands. They came to the surface again in Jansenius' main work, the *Augustinus*, published posthumously at Louvain in 1640.

The *Augustinus* was a voluminous and scholarly attack on the views of Lessius and Molina. Its first volume studies Pelagianism, emphasizing its views on original sin and the power of human freedom after the fall. The second volume expounds Augustine's doctrine on grace, free will, and predestination; and the last volume attempts to show that Molinism and other similar views agree with Pelagius rather than Augustine.

It is possible to characterize the *Augustinus* in a single sentence by saying that it refutes Molinism, not on the basis of the mitigated Augustinianism of the Dominicans and the entire medieval tradition, but by going beyond that tradition back to Augustine, who is interpreted in the most extreme way. According to Jansenius, the

---

[55] N. Abercrombie, *The Origins of Jansenism* (Oxford: Clarendon, 1936); H. de Lubac, *Augustinism*, pp. 34-92; J. van Bavel and M. Schrama, *Jansénius et le Jansénisme dans les Pays-Bas* (Louvain: University Press, 1982); J. Carreyre, *Le Jansénisme durant la régence*, 3 vols. (Louvain: Bureaux de la Revue, 1929-33); A. Gazier, *Historie générale du mouvement Janséniste, despuis ses origines jusqu'à nos jours*, 2 vols. (Paris: Honoré Champion, 1923-24); L. Willaert, *Bibliotheca Janseniana Belgica*, 3 vols. (Namur: Bibliothèque de la Faculté de philosophie et lettres, 1949-50). On the work of Baius, see F. X. Jansen, *Baius et le Baianisme: Essai théologique* (Louvain: Musaeum Lessianum, 1927).

method of theology is radically different from that of philosophy. Philosophy is based on reason, and is unable to go beyond vain disputes. Theology is based on authority, and its knowledge is certain. It is interesting to note that Jansenius, who claims to be interpreting Augustine, here takes a position that was typical of the early opposition to Augustinianism. The reason for this is that Jansenius is interested not in expounding the entire system of the bishop of Hippo, but rather in setting up his views on grace and predestination as an authority in the current debates. In any case, the main point that Jansenius is trying to make through his appeal to Augustine is that the results of the fall are such that the freedom of the will has been severely limited. Although Adam before the fall had an "indifferent" freedom, in the sense that he could choose either to sin or not to sin, this indifference has been destroyed by original sin. The grace that sufficed to lead innocent Adam to God is now insufficient. If one loses his vision, mere light will never suffice to make one see. What one needs is a different sort of help, one that will cure the eyes. Similarly, our will has now been made a slave to sin and has become incapable of doing good. We can love nothing but ourselves and other creatures. We are incapable of loving God. Although we can obey the commandments in an outward fashion, we can only do so out of pride or out of fear, never out of love. Although we can still perceive something of the will of God through natural law, obedience to such law is no virtue, but only the empty shell of goodness.

Thus interpreting the human predicament, Jansenius believes the main task of grace is to liberate us from our slavery to concupiscence. Grace is necessary not only to enable the will to perform supernatural acts, but also to enable the will to do even the least good. Apart from it, the will can do nothing but evil—although it is free to choose which evil it is to do. Furthermore, as our predicament is similar to that of a blind person, the grace that was sufficient for Adam cannot help us. Molina's error consists precisely in not distinguishing between free will as it was before the fall and free will as it is now. He seems to think that all that the will needs is the help of grace—which would be like prescribing more light for a blind person. Against this interpretation of our predicament, Jansenius argues that whereas Adam needed no more than a grace that would strengthen his will, we need a grace that will determine our will, directing it toward God. This grace, which Jansenius calls "healing grace," becomes the sovereign master of the human will, leading it to God with such gentleness that the will itself does not know it is being led. It is irresistible and infallible. Therefore, whoever receives it must of necessity turn toward God, although this is done willingly. Here again Jansenius rejects Molina's views, for the Jesuit had said that true freedom excludes not only coercion, but also necessity. Jansenius, on the contrary, affirms that any act performed willingly is free, even if it is born out of an inner necessity. Predestination is absolute and double—some are predestined to salvation, and some to eternal damnation. This follows from the fact that, without grace, humankind is nothing but a "mass of damnation," and that those who receive grace must necessarily accept it. Therefore, the difference between the saved and the damned depends not on the choice of each, but on the eternal decrees by which God has decided to grant grace to some and to withhold it from others.

Jansenius claims that this is not Calvinism, for Calvin makes freedom the consequence of grace, while the fact is that freedom is precisely in the consent of the will to grace, which at once calls it and moves it. But in spite of these attempts on Jansenius' part to show how he differed from Calvin, he and his followers were repeatedly accused of being secret followers of Protestantism.

The publication of the *Augustinus* was followed by the treatise *On Frequent Communion,* by Antoine Arnauld (1612–1694),[56] which applied to the field of practical piety and ecclesiastical discipline the principles proposed by Jansenius. The movement thus began taking that shape of resistance to ecclesiastical authority which would characterize its later stages. Even before the *Augustinus* appeared, the Jesuits at Louvain had tried to prevent its publication. After its publication, a number of professors at Louvain supported the views of Jansenius against the six theses that the Jesuits opposed to them. The *Augustinus* was then reprinted in Paris, where it had the support of some professors at the Sorbonne. The affair thus became international and threatened to repeat the near schism of the *de auxiliis* affair. The Inquisition banned the reading of the *Augustinus* in 1641; but the faculty at Louvain refused to accept the decree, and

[56] His collected works, in 43 vols., were reprinted in 1964-67 (Brussels: Culture et Civilisation). Vol. 43 includes the classical life of Arnauld by N. de Larriere. See also M. Escholier, *Port-Royal: The Drama of the Jansenists* (New York: Hawthorn Books, 1968).

was supported in that position by growing numbers in France. In 1643, Urban VIII condemned the *Augustinus* in his bull *In eminenti*. As this did not end the debate, Innocent X reiterated the action by condemning in 1653 five propositions that supposedly reflected the views of Jansenius. The Jansenists, however, claimed that the five propositions were not accurate reflections of Jansenius' thought, and that they could therefore continue holding the views of Jansenius while agreeing to the condemnation of the five propositions.

The controversy led to schism. The Cistercian abbey of Port-Royal, led by Arnauld, refused to submit. Arnauld had to hide and go into exile, but the torch was picked up by Blaise Pascal (1623–1662),[57] whose *Provinciales,* written in defense of Arnauld, overshadowed the *Augustinus* in their impact and popularity. A "Formulary" was then prepared, to be signed by all French clergy, expressly stating that the five propositions were indeed to be found in Jansenius and that they were justly condemned. Many refused to sign. As the state—especially during the time of Louis XIV—supported the condemnation of the Jansenists, the movement became increasingly politicized. By the beginning of the eighteenth century, it was clearly the ally of Gallicanism. In 1713, Clement XI again condemned Jansenism—in his bull *Unigenitus.* In Holland a permanent schism resulted from further attempts to suppress the movement. In France, Jansenism joined the forces that eventually led to the revolution, and its last exponent may be said to have been the abbot Henri Gregoire (1750–1831), a zealous Jacobin in whom political ends eclipsed the religious concerns that had been dominant in Jansenius, Arnauld, and Pascal.

The Council of Trent

The Roman Catholic reformation had its most important roots in Spain. When the program of Ximenes was already well under way in Spain, Rome was still ruled by a series of unworthy popes. Most of the popes of the first half of the sixteenth century had other interests at heart than the reformation of the church. Alexander VI, who ruled at the turn of the century, is well known for the manner in which he directed his policy to the aggrandizement of his son Cesare Borgia (1475–1507). After the very brief reign of Pius III, the papal tiara

---

[57] J. Miel, *Pascal and His Theology* (Baltimore: Johns Hopkins, 1969); R. Hazelton, *Blaise Pascal: The Genius of His Thought* (Philadelphia: Westminster, 1974).

was worn by Julius II (1503–1513), who as Giuliano della Rovere had been the most implacable enemy of the Borgias. Although Julius took several measures for the reform of the church and was a promoter of missions to the New World, Asia, and Africa, he also set out to undo the results of Alexander's international policy. In order to do this he became more like a soldier than bishop. Apart from his military and political interests, Julius devoted his attention to the embellishment of Rome. It was he who laid the first stone for the new basilica of St. Peter. Although not a military man, Giovanni de Medici, who became Leo X (1513–1521) after the death of Julius, had most of the weaknesses and few of the strengths of his predecessor. Captivated by the spirit of the Renaissance, he supported a number of artists and scholars, but did little for the care of his flock. It was he who had to deal with the early stages of the Lutheran reformation. Adrian VI (1522–1523), the last non-Italian to occupy the throne of Peter before the twentieth century, may be said to have been the first of the reforming popes, although his very short reign did not permit him to implement his entire program of reformation. Clement VII (1523–1534) was a moderate reformer, but the two most significant events of his pontificate were the sack of Rome by the troops of Charles V and the loss of England for the Roman Church over the marriage of Henry VIII and Catherine of Aragon. Paul III (1534–1549) was also a moderate reformer, although somewhat inclined to nepotism.

In spite of the shortcomings of Paul III, it was with him that the reforming spirit took possession of Rome. Several of the cardinals whom he appointed were ardent advocates of the cleansing of the church. One of them, Caraffa, would later become Paul IV, and as such would carry forth the task of reforming and strengthening the church. But Paul III's greatest contribution to the new shape of the Catholic Church was that he named a commission to delineate a program of reform, and he then convened the Council of Trent, which would take steps toward that reformation and at the same time would define the faith of the Catholic Church vis-à-vis the tenets of Protestantism. Although the reign of Julius III (1550–1555) was a disappointment to the reforming party, most of the later popes of the sixteenth century took the reformation to heart—Paul IV (1555–1559), Pius IV (1559–1565), Pius V (1566–1572), Gregory XIII (1572–1585), Sixtus V (1585–1590), and Clement VIII (1592–1605).

The reformation that these popes undertook had several features that should be noted before discussing the actions of the Council of Trent. The first characteristic of this reformation is that it was centered on the power of the pope. This seemed necessary in order to avoid the divisiveness that Protestantism was showing. Paul IV made claims for the authority of the pope that were reminiscent of the great days of Innocent III. As we have seen, Sixtus V planned to include Vitoria and Bellarmine in the *Index* of forbidden books because they denied that the pope had direct temporal authority over the entire world. This emphasis on centralization would later produce friction between the popes and several monarchs whose ancestors had had a great deal of influence in the affairs of the church in their domains. One should also note that this reformation was conceived as moving down from the head of the church to its members. It was at this point that the Jesuits proved to be the strongest instrument in the hands of the reforming popes. They were an army willing to carry out its instructions with military precision. Without them, the Roman Catholic reformation is inconceivable. Then, one should note that this reformation intended to be strictly orthodox. The traditional faith of the church—and even those traditions which had developed during the last centuries of the Middle Ages—was not to be reformed. What was in need of change was the moral and religious life of the church and its members, and not the institution or its doctrines. The reader may have noticed that most of the leading theologians of the Catholic reformation had troubles with the Inquisition. This resulted from a strong consensus that orthodoxy was to be preserved on every detail and at all costs. The Inquisition was revived and strengthened. It now developed a new instrument for the preservation of orthodoxy: the *Index librorum prohibitorum*. Although the practice of condemning certain books was very old, the invention of the printing press, and the consequent bibliographical explosion, made it seem advisable to publish a list of books that Catholics were forbidden to read. The *Index* was first published in 1559 by the Roman Inquisition and went through a continuous process of revision and addition until Paul VI finally suppressed it in 1966—a year earlier, he had transformed the Holy Office of the Inquisition into the Congregation for the Doctrine of the Faith, whose power and aims were more limited. Finally, one should note that this limited understanding of reformation can be seen in the fact that the Council of Trent did not attempt to modify the liturgy so as to make it more relevant to modern times. This task was left to the Second Vatican Council and the reformation that it set in motion. In the sixteenth century, it was considered sufficient to condemn Protestantism by defining the faith of the Catholic Church, and to reform and regulate the moral life of the church.

The history of the Council of Trent (1545–1563)[58] is long and complex. Although we cannot recount that history here, one should note that the final outcome of the council was the result of a long process in which a series of political and theological difficulties were overcome. Politically, the main difficulty was that the emperor and the pope vied with each other for control of the council. Theologically, the main difficulty was the tension between those who thought that the council should attempt to win back at least some of the Protestants by granting some of their demands, and those who felt that the task of the council should be simply to condemn Protestantism and set its own agenda for reformation. Both sides had strong political support, and even among those who wished to see the Protestants condemned there were those who wished the council to introduce into the Roman Catholic Church some of the changes urged by the Protestants. Thus Charles V, for instance, was hoping that the council would allow priests to marry, to offer communion in both kinds, and to celebrate part of the liturgy in the vernacular. As a result of these tensions, the council was frequently interrupted, and was just nine days short of lasting eighteen years. The final outcome was the modern Catholic Church.

The Council of Trent acted in two basic directions: the reformation of the customs and laws of the church, and the clear definition of dogma against Protestant views. The decrees concerning reform attempted to correct some of the abuses against which both Protestant and Catholic advocates of reform had protested, such as absenteeism,[59] pluralism,[60] ignorance of Scripture,[61] irresponsible ordination,[62] etc.

---

[58] H. Jedin, *A History of the Council of Trent* (London: Thomas Nelson and Sons, 1957); C. J. Hefele, *A History of the Christian Councils from the Original Documents* (Edinburgh: T. & T. Clark, 1872—), vols. 9-10; J. D. Mansi, *Sacrorum Conciliorum nova et amplissima collectio*, reprint (Graz, Austria: Akademische Druckund Verlagsanstalt, 1961), vol. 33; C. S. Sullivan, *The Formulation of the Tridentine Doctrine on Merit* (Washington: Catholic University of America, 1959).

[59] *Mansi*, 33:45, 140-42.

[60] *Ibid.*, pp. 55-56.

[61] *Ibid.*, pp. 29-30.

[62] *Ibid.*, pp. 142-46. Chapter xviii of this Decree on Reformation (*ibid.*, pp. 146-49) deals with the

The doctrinal issues taken up by the council were basically those raised by the Protestant reformation: the authority of Scripture, the nature and consequences of original sin, justification, the sacraments, purgatory, and the veneration of saints and their relics. In practically all these matters, the council took a position that was diametrically opposed to that of the Protestant reformers. Thus, the Protestant reformation had a contrary effect on the Catholic Church, which now felt compelled to define many matters that until then had remained undefined.

Such was the case with the question of the authority of Scripture and its relationship with the authority of tradition. Reacting to the Protestant principle of *sola scriptura*—Scripture alone—the council not only affirmed the authority of tradition, but went much further by putting it on a par with Scripture.

> It [the Council] also clearly perceives that these truths and rules are contained in the written books and in the unwritten traditions, which, received by the Apostles from the mouth of Christ Himself, or from the Apostles themselves, the Holy Ghost dictating, have come down to us, transmitted as it were from hand to hand. Following, then, the examples of the orthodox Fathers, it receives and venerates with a feeling of piety and reverence all the books both of the Old and New Testaments, since one God is the author of both; also the traditions, whether they relate to faith or to morals, as having been dictated either orally by Christ or by the Holy Ghost, and preserved in the Catholic Church in unbroken succession.[63]

Then, after listing the canonical books, the council went on to anathematize any who would refuse to accept the authority of such books "as they have been accustomed to be read in the Catholic Church and as they are contained in the old Latin Vulgate Edition."[64] Consistent with the parity of tradition and Scripture as sources of authority, the Council decreed that no one should interpret Scripture "contrary to that sense which holy mother church, to

---

establishing of seminaries, and would have vast consequences in providing the Catholic Church with a well-educated clergy.

[63] H. J. Schroeder, trans., *Canons and Decrees of the Council of Trent* (St. Louis: B. Herder, 1941), p. 17 (*Mansi*, 33:22).

[64] *Ibid.*, p. 18 (*Mansi*, 33:22).

whom it belongs to judge of their true sense and interpretation, has held and holds."[65] And, in order to guarantee that this order was obeyed, it further directed that no book was to be published without the approval of ecclesiastical authorities, and that such approval was to appear in writing at the beginning of the book. This procedure was to be done at no cost to the author or the publisher—and here one can see the genuine concern of the council for abolishing anything resembling simony.

The fifth session of the council took up the question of original sin. After asserting the reality of original sin, its consequences for both body and soul, and its transmission from Adam to his progeny, it went on to condemn those who rejected infant baptism, as well as anyone who claimed that through the grace of baptism the guilt of original sin is not remitted, "or says that the whole of that which belongs to the essence of sin is not taken away, but says that it is only cancelled or not imputed."[66] Against such a view, Trent asserted that those baptized are made "innocent, immaculate, pure, guiltless," and that all that remains in them is "an inclination to sin."[67]

The decree on original sin may be said to be a foreword to the decree on justification, issued by the sixth session (January, 1547). The decree on justification is without any doubt the heart of the theological work of the council.[68] It consists of sixteen chapters, followed by thirty-three canons of anathema.[69] The decree introduces the subject by declaring that fallen humanity cannot attain justification, and that this is true of the Jews as well as of the gentiles, for neither the law nor human nature suffices for justification (chapter 1). This was the reason for the coming of Christ (chapter 2), so that those to whom the merits of Christ are communicated may be justified (chapter 3), and be translated from their wretched state as children of Adam to the blessed state of adopted children of God through the second Adam (chapter 4).

After this general introduction, the issues debated between Protestants and Catholics—and even among Catholics themselves— are taken up. Chapter five asserts that justification begins with

---

[65] *Ibid.*, p. 19 (*Mansi*, 33:23).
[66] *Ibid.*, p. 23 (*Mansi*, 33:28).
[67] *Ibid.*
[68] See H. Rückert, *Die Rechtfertigungslehre auf dem tridentinischen Konzil* (Berlin: A. Marcus und E. Weber, 1925).
[69] *Mansi*, 33:32-43.

prevenient grace, quite apart from any merits; but it also affirms that free will must then accept or reject the salvation that is offered to it.

> It is furthermore declared that in adults the beginning of that justification must proceed from the predisposing grace of God. . . . Without any merits on their part, they are called; that they who by sin had been cut off from God, may be disposed through His quickening and helping grace to convert themselves to their own justification by freely assenting to and cooperating with that grace; so that, while God touches the heart of man through the illumination of the Holy Ghost, man himself neither does absolutely nothing while receiving that inspiration, since he can also reject it, nor yet is he able by his own free will and without the grace of God to move himself to justice in His sight.[70]

The manner in which adults are prepared to receive justification is by faith, hope, and love. First of all, they receive faith by hearing. This results in their viewing themselves as sinners and being moved to hope that God, for Christ's sake, will look upon them with favor. This makes them trust and love God as the source of justice, and come to hate sin. This hatred of sin is called repentance, and—in adults—must take place before baptism (chapter 6).

After this preparation comes justification itself, which is described in terms that are clearly antithetical to Luther's understanding of the matter. Justification "is not only a remission of sins but also the sanctification and renewal of the inward man through the voluntary reception of the grace and gifts whereby an unjust man becomes just."[71] And "not only are we reputed just but we are truly called and are just, receiving justice within us."[72] "For faith, unless hope and charity be added to it, neither unites man perfectly with Christ nor makes him a living member of his body."[73] Thus, justification is declared to be, not the imputation of Christ's justice to the believer, but the act by which God, with the collaboration of human free will, makes the believer just. The prelates and theologians at Trent clearly perceived that this was one of the crucial issues separating Protestants and Catholics, and addressed themselves directly to it.

---

[70] Schroeder, *Canons*, pp. 31-32 (*Mansi*, 33:33-34).

[71] *Ibid.*, p. 33 (*Mansi*, 33:34-35).

[72] *Ibid.* (*Mansi*, 33-35).

[73] *Ibid.*, p. 34 (*Mansi*, 33:35).

The rest of the decree on justification is simply an elaboration of this point. When Paul speaks of justification by faith, what he actually means is that the beginning of justification takes place by faith and not by merits (chapter 7). It is not necessary to know that one has been justified; justification can be a reality even without one's knowledge thereof, for one can never be certain of having received grace (chapter 9). Justification, being an objective reality in the believer, can be increased by good works (chapter 10). The notion that the justified sin even in their good works—*simul iustus et peccator*—must also be rejected, for the justified, having in themselves an objective justice, can and must do good works, even though they will occasionally fall into venial sin (chapter 11). Except by a rare special revelation, we cannot know of our own predestination, and therefore should not presume on it (chapter 12). Likewise, those who are prone to trust in the gift of perseverance would do better to take heed lest they fall, and devote themselves with fear and trembling to good works (chapter 13). Chapter 14 shows how this understanding of justification is related to the penitential system, for those who have sinned after the grace of baptism must now seek to recover through the sacrament of penance the grace that they have lost. The sacrament—or the desire to receive it—serves for the remission of eternal punishment for sin; but the temporal punishment must be dealt with through satisfaction.

> Hence, it must be taught that the repentance of a Christian after his fall is very different from that at his baptism, and that it includes not only a determination to avoid sins and a hatred of them . . . but also the sacramental confession of those sins, at least in desire, to be made in its season, and sacerdotal absolution, as well as satisfaction by fasts, alms, prayers and other devout exercises of the spiritual life, not indeed for the eternal punishment, which is, together with the guilt, remitted either by the sacrament or by the desire of the sacrament, but for the temporal punishment which, as the sacred writings teach, is not always wholly remitted, as is done in baptism, to those who, ungrateful to the grace of God which they have received, have grieved the Holy Ghost.[74]

Mortal sin causes the loss of grace, although not of faith—except in the case of religious infidelity, in which both are lost. Therefore,

---

[74] *Ibid.*, p. 39 (*Mansi*, 33:38).

those who are in mortal sin, although they may have faith, will not be saved (chapter 15).

Finally, those who have thus been justified must abound in the fruits of justification, which are good works and their merits. Thus, the believer receives eternal salvation "both as a grace mercifully promised to the sons of God through Jesus Christ, and as a reward promised by God himself, to be faithfully given to their good works and merits."[75] The justified, through their good works, can fully satisfy the divine law, and thus merit eternal life.

The anathemas at the end of the decree are too long and detailed to discuss here. In general, after three anathemas simply conforming the condemnation of Pelagianism, the rest are aimed at the Protestants. They are not limited to the question of justification, but deal also with such related matters as grace, free will, and predestination. Some of them are aimed at views voiced only by some of the reformers, and others clearly respond to exaggerations or caricatures of Protestant teaching. But in general they show an accurate understanding of the issues separating the two camps. These anathemas are so crucial for the final parting of the ways that it will be well to quote a few of the more representative.

> Can. 9. If anyone says the sinner is justified by faith alone, meaning that nothing else is required to cooperate in order to obtain the grace of justification, and that it is not in any way necessary that he be prepared and disposed by the action of his will, let him be anathema.
>
> Can. 11. If anyone says that men are justified either by the sole imputation of the justice of Christ, or by the sole remission of sins, . . . or also that the grace by which we are justified is only the good will of God, let him be anathema.
>
> Can. 17. If anyone says that the grace of justification is shared by those only who are predestined to life, but that all others who are called are called indeed but receive not grace, as if they were by divine power predestined to evil, let him be anathema.
>
> Can. 18. If anyone says that the commandments of God are, even for one that is justified and constituted in grace, impossible to observe, let him be anathema.
>
> Can. 25. If anyone says that in every good work the just man sins

---

[75] *Ibid.*, p. 41 (*Mansi*, 33:39).

at least venially, or, what is more intolerable, mortally, and hence merits eternal punishment, and that he is not damned for this reason only, because God does not impute these works unto damnation, let him be anathema.

Can. 30. If anyone says that after the reception of the grace of justification . . . no debt of temporal punishment remains to be discharged either in this world or in purgatory . . let him be anathema.

Can. 31. If anyone says that the one justified sins when he performs good works with a view to an eternal reward, let him be anathema.[76]

The rest of the doctrinal work of the council had to do with the sacraments, which the prelates felt ought to be discussed as the completion of the Catholic doctrine of justification. The seventh session was able to produce only a list of anathemas that did little more than fix the number of sacraments at seven, insist on the objective value and the necessity of the sacraments, and reject the views of the Anabaptists and others on baptism and confirmation.[77] Various political and practical difficulties prevented the council from discussing the eucharist any further, until four years later, when the thirteenth occasion met in 1551. Then, after a pause of almost eleven years, the sacrament of the altar was taken up again in the twenty-first and twenty-second sessions, in 1562. During the interim, some other issues had occupied the attention of the council, although most of the time it had not been able to gather. Therefore, the decrees on the eucharist were produced during a lengthy period, and the legates who participated in the first decree were in many cases different from those who participated in the last two.[78] In general, however, Trent simply affirmed the beliefs and practices that by then had become traditional. The doctrine of transubstantiation, which had already been defined, was reaffirmed. The sacrament is to be both preserved and venerated with the worship of *latria*—that reserved only for God—for God is present in the reserved sacrament. Before communion, both the laity and the priest ought to confess their sins sacramentally, although the priest who does not have the opportunity to do so may celebrate the eucharist in

---

[76] *Ibid.*, pp. 43-46 (*Mansi*, 33:40-43).
[77] *Mansi*, 33:51-55.
[78] *Mansi*, 33:80-85, 121-24, 128-33.

a case of urgent necessity. Communion in both kinds is not necessary for the reception of both the body and blood of Christ. Although it is true that in ancient times communion in both kinds was the usual practice, the church has authority to determine the form in which communion is to be given, and her current law of withholding the cup from the laity should be obeyed, at least until the church herself decides otherwise.[79] The mass is a sacrifice in which Christ is offered anew, although in an unbloody fashion. This sacrifice propitiates God, for "appeased by this sacrifice, the Lord grants the grace and gift of penitence and pardons even the gravest crimes and sins."[80] Although the council prefers that at communion all present participate, masses in which only the priest partakes of the elements are declared to be valid. All the rites instituted by Mother Church in connection with the mass have been established for the welfare of believers, and must be obeyed. This includes the prohibition to say mass in the vernacular, although priests are enjoined to explain the mysteries of the mass to the people. Parallel to these positive affirmations, the council anathematized those views which it considered opposed to the Catholic faith.

As to the other sacraments, Trent reaffirmed again the traditional doctrine of the Catholic Church. In connection with that reaffirmation, such other issues as the existence of purgatory, the value of the relics of saints, and the authority conferred in the act of ordination were also discussed. In each case, the decision of the council was to reassert what was either a doctrine already defined, or simply the general consensus of the medieval church. In every one of them, however, and especially in the context of matrimony and ordination, the council legislated against the various abuses that had become the object of attack by Protestants.

Thus, the Council of Trent responded to the Protestant challenge, and to the general cry for reformation, in a twofold way. In matters of doctrine, it consistently took the conservative side. Whatever had become the accepted belief the Western church, and whatever the Protestants attacked, now became official and final doctrine of the Catholic Church. But in matters of morality and the spiritual care of

---

[79] On this point, the council left the door open for future decisions to be made by the pope. *Mansi,* 33:123-24, 137.

[80] Schroeder, *Canons,* p. 146.

its flock the council took the route of strict reformation. Simony, absenteeism, pluralism, and the violation of the vows of celibacy would no longer be tolerated. The spirit of Trent is the same as that of the Society of Jesus and of the Inquisition: strict adherence to traditional dogma, an austere moral life, and a sincere concern that the ministrations of the church be made available to all her children.

This is one of two reasons that Trent may be said to symbolize the Catholic reformation and therefore the beginning of the modern Roman Catholic Church. The other reason is that during the extended lifetime of the council significant changes took place as far as the authority of the pope was concerned. When the council was to be convened one of the issues at stake was the authority of the pope. It was not merely a matter of the Protestants having denied that authority; it was also that the pope found himself in a position where his authority was questioned by good Catholics. The reason that a council was considered to be necessary was that the pope's voice would not be heeded. The principal reason that it took so long to convene the council and that it then found it so difficult to continue working without lengthy interruptions was that a number of Catholic monarchs—notably Charles V during the early negotiations—felt that they must have a measure of control over the assembly, and therefore did not always collaborate with the pope in his efforts to call the council. At the end of the gathering, however, conditions had changed radically. Pius IV was without any question master of the council, which in its last session petitioned him for a confirmation of all the decrees that it had issued, not only during his reign, but also under Paul III and Julius III. This Pius did in a bull in which he declared the council to have been ecumenical and binding on all, and in which he also decreed that no one was to publish commentaries or other interpretations of the conciliar decisions without the express approval of the Holy See.

The pope was thus made at once the source of the council's authority and its final interpreter. The conciliar movement of the late Middle Ages had come to an end. The modern Roman Catholic Church was born.

IX

The Theology of Lutheran Orthodoxy

In Continental Europe the seventeenth century was a period of confessional orthodoxy. Lutheranism, as well as the Reformed tradition and the Roman Catholic Church, went through a process of systematization and clarification of the doctrinal positions that each of these bodies had taken during the previous century. In England the situation was somewhat different, for during the seventeenth century the controlled reformation advocated by Elizabeth and her ministers broke its bounds, and new and more radical movements came to the foreground. Both on the Continent and in Britain, and among Protestants as well as among Catholics, philosophy developed an increasingly independent status. Although most of the philosophers of the period declared themselves to be sincere Christians, their work was carried on apart from that of theologians. The result was that theology moved for the time being along conservative lines, looking back to the founders of each confession and to its basic documents. Philosophy, on the other hand, profiting from the end of scholasticism, sought new paths to follow, and thus looked to the future. The history of Christian theology from the seventeenth to the nineteenth century is a process in which, after a period of unflinching orthodoxy, theology began to take cognizance of the work of the philosophers and scientists, and thus departed from strict orthodoxy and moved toward rationalism.

From this follows the outline for this and the next two chapters.

Here we shall show what was the nature of Lutheran orthodoxy during the seventeenth century. In the next chapter we shall turn to the parallel events in the Reformed tradition. Finally, we shall review philosophical developments that would later have a great importance for theology. In the latter part of this volume, we shall see how these various trends interacted in several ways in the eighteenth and nineteenth centuries.

Lutheran orthodoxy in the seventeenth century is not to be confused with the strict Lutheranism of the sixteenth. It is true that on most of the points that had been discussed in the previous century the orthodox theologians agreed with the strict Lutherans. But their entire theological outlook was very different. Whereas the strict Lutherans interpreted Luther and Melanchthon in opposition to each other, the orthodox theologians felt that a great deal of what Melanchthon had to say was of great value, and therefore sought to harmonize his views with those of Luther. Many of them acknowledged that they were deeply indebted to Melanchthon, and used his *Loci* as textbook in their classes. Their use of metaphysics— and especially of Aristotle—as the century progressed was another significant departure from the theology of strict Lutheranism. Therefore, Lutheran orthodoxy merits separate consideration in the history of Christian thought.

On the other hand, however, Lutheran theology during the seventeenth century—like most other orthodoxies—did not produce a single figure whose work towers above its contemporaries. Therefore, the best way to expound the theology of the period seems to be to begin with a brief paragraph of introduction to each of the main theologians, showing something of the development that took place, and then to turn to a more systematic exposition of the main tenets of the movement as a whole.

Principal Theologians

The great forerunner of Lutheran orthodoxy was Martin Chemnitz (1522–1586), whom we have already mentioned in connection with his Christology and his participation in the drafting of the *Formula of Concord*.[1] He also wrote a work in four volumes in

---

[1] R. D. Preus, *The Theology of Post-Reformation Lutheranism: A Study of Theological Prolegomena* (St. Louis: Concordia, 1970), pp. 47–49. This book contains an excellent summary of the life and works of

which he attempted to show that the Council of Trent had abandoned not only the faith to be found in Scripture, but also the earlier Christian tradition. Chemnitz thus became Bellarmine's Lutheran counterpart, and a great deal of Roman Catholic polemics against Protestantism in later years was a refutation of his charges. He also made a vast attempt to systematize biblical theology. This was published posthumously under the title of *Loci theologici*. We have already mentioned his treatise *On the Two Natures of Christ,* which was to be very influential in later christological discussions. But the reason that Chemnitz can be said to be the forerunner of Lutheran orthodoxy is that he set for himself the great task of reconciling the opposing factions within the Lutheran tradition. While accepting many of the tenets of the strict Lutherans, he nevertheless was very appreciative of Melanchthon, from whom he derived a great deal of his method and style. Therefore, with Chemnitz—and with the most significant of his achievements, the *Formula of Concord*—the Lutheran tradition entered into a new period in which theology would be more positive, and polemics would be generally directed toward non-Lutherans.

Aegidius Hunnius (1550–1603), after a period of teaching at the University of Marburg, joined the faculty of Wittenberg, and is credited with having begun the tradition of Lutheran orthdoxy in that university.[2] Although he wrote no great systematic compendium, he dealt with the most pressing theological issues of his time. He also wrote extensive biblical commentaries that were later used by other more systematic theologians.[3] He was the father of Nikolaus Hunnius, another orthodox theologian whom we shall meet further on. This is significant, for it has been pointed out that during the period of Lutheran orthodoxy the main chairs of theology were occupied by veritable dynasties, and that theology became an occupation passed from father to son, as any other trade.[4]

the main theologians of Lutheran orthodoxy. I refer the reader to it for further details and bibliography on the theologians whom I discuss, as well as for a longer list of theologians of the period, many of whom I have not included in my brief summary; on Chemnitz, see L. Poellet, ed., *Ministry, Word, and Sacrament: An Enchiridion* (St. Louis: Concordia, 1981). Cf. Jungkuntz *Formulators,* pp. 46-68.

2 F. Lau, "Hunn(ius), Aegidius," *RGG,* 3:46-87; Preus, *The Theology of Post-Reformation Lutheranism,* pp. 50-51; G. Adam, *Der Streit um die Prädestination im augsenhenden 16. Jahrhundert: Eine Untersuchung zu den Entwürfen von Samuel Huber und Aegidius Hunnius* (Neunkirchen: Neunkirchener Verlag, 1970).

3 Adam, *Der Streit,* pp. 213-15, lists all his works.

4 E. G. Léonard, *Histoire générale du protestantisme* (Paris: Presses Universitaires de France, 1961), 2:186-88.

Leonard Hütter (1563–1616) was also a professor at Wittenberg, where he contributed to the work that Hunnius had already begun in favor of Lutheran orthodoxy.[5] Whereas Hunnius did most of his work in biblical studies, Hütter devoted his attention to dogmatics and to the study of creeds and confessions. Together with Gerhard, he developed a theory of the inspiration of Scripture that would become normative for the entire period of Lutheran orthodoxy. Although his best-known systematic work, *Loci Communes Theologici*, was influenced by Melanchthon in many ways, he was closer to Luther than to Melanchthon. Following Luther's lead, he distinguished clearly between theology and philosophy and attempted to develop his theological system on the basis of Scripture and the confessions, and quite apart from philosophical or metaphysical considerations. The importance that he gave to the Lutheran confessions may be seen in the title of what was perhaps his most important work, *A Summary of Theological Themes Gathered from Sacred Scripture and the Book of Concord*. He was also involved in polemics with Catholic and Reformed theologians. Against the Catholics he wrote *Twenty Disputations against Bellarmine*, where he attempted to refute the arguments of the famous cardinal. His main polemical work against the Reformed was his defense of the *Formula of Concord* against the Zurich theologian Rudolph Hospinian.[6]

The greatest theologian of Lutheran orthodoxy was without any doubt Johann Gerhard (1582–1637), who studied at Wittenberg and Jena, spent a number of years in administrative ecclesiastical work, and finally returned to Jena as a professor in 1616.[7] His main work of biblical scholarship was the completion of a *Harmony of the Evangelists*, which Chemnitz had begun. The purpose of this work was not simply to show the literary parallels between the various Gospels, but rather

[5] F. Lau, "Hütter (Hutterus), Leonhard," *RGG*, 3:468; Preus, *The Theology of Post-Reformation Lutheranism*, pp. 1-52; Ritschl, *Dogmengeschichte*, 4:257-61.

[6] Hospinian had attacked the *Formula of Concord* in 1607, under the witty title of *Concordia discors*. Hütter responded seven years later with his *Concordia concors*. Cf. O. E. Strasser, "Hospinian (Wirth), Rudolph," *RGG*, 3:458.

[7] F. Lau, "Gerhard, Johann," *RGG*, 2:1412-13; Preus, *The Theology of Post-Reformation Lutheranism*, pp. 52-53; Ritschl, *Dogmengeschichte*, vol. 4, *passim*; B. Hägglund, *Die Heilige Schrift und ihre Deutung in der Theologie Johann Gerhards: Eine Untersuchung über das altlutherische Schriftverständnis* (Lund: W. Gleerup, 1955); R. P. Scharlemann, *Thomas Aquinas and John Gerhard* (New Haven: Yale University Press, 1964); Kirste, *Das Zeugnis*, *passim*; R. Schröder, *Johann Gerhards lutherische Christologie und die aristotelische Metaphysik* (Tübingen: Mohr, 1983). Cf. J. Wallman, *Der Theologiebegriff bei Johann Gerhard und Georg Calixt* (Tübingen: Mohr, 1961), pp. 5-84.

to show their inner theological coherence. Thus, it is not so much a book of biblical scholarship as a book of biblical theology. But Gerhard's main work is his *Loci theologici*, whose vast nine volumes—a later edition published it in twenty-three—became the great systematic theology of Lutheran orthodoxy. In spite of its title, Gerhard's work follows a methodology that is very different from the earlier *Loci* of Melanchthon. What he attempts to do is not merely to expound a series of loosely connected theological themes, but rather to show the inner systematic connection of the entire body of theological knowledge. Gerhard thus made a significant contribution to what would later be called systematic theology. He also felt that such systematic theology should have a sound metaphysical undergirding, and he sought this in Aristotle, especially as he had been interpreted by the Spanish metaphysicians at Salamanca and by Suárez. This was a clear departure from Luther, who had claimed that no one could become a theologian with Aristotle; but most Lutheran orthodox theologians soon followed Gerhard's lead, and the use of Aristotelian metaphysics became one of the characteristics of Lutheran orthodoxy. He also attacked the "syncretism" of George Calixtus, although the fact that this controversy developed toward the end of his life did not allow him to develop his entire theological system in the light of this issue, as did some of the later theologians. As Gerhard will be one of the main sources in our exposition of Lutheran orthodox theology, we shall not dwell here on the specific content of his theology. It should be noted, however, that in matters such as the inspiration of Scripture and Christology his thought was very influential.

Nikolaus Hunnius (1585–1643),[8] the son of Aegidius, followed Hütter as a professor of theology at Wittenberg and also occupied several ecclesiastical posts of importance. His significance is twofold, for he contributed both to the development of Lutheran orthodoxy and to its divulgation among the laity. His main contribution to Lutheran orthodoxy was his clear distinction between fundamental and secondary articles of faith. By developing a series of criteria for distinguishing between the two, he made it possible for his successors to remain united in spite of minor theological differences. It should

---

[8] W. Jannasch, "Hunn(ius), Nikolaus," *RGG*, 3:491; Preus, *The Theology of Post-Reformation Lutheranism*, p. 56; Ritschl, *Dogmengeschichte*, 4:306-42. This latter work includes a thorough study of the distinction between fundamental and secondary articles of faith.

be pointed out, however, that this was by no means an attempt to reduce Christianity to a sort of common denominator, for what Hunnius took to be fundamental was a great deal of traditional Lutheran theology, and he therefore argued that the differences between Lutheran and Reformed had to do with fundamental issues and could not be mediated. Hunnius also helped popularize Lutheran orthodoxy among the laity through the publication of his *Summary of Those Things Which Are to Be Believed,* which he wrote in German and soon became one of the most widely read religious treatises of its time.

Johann Konrad Dannhauer (1603–1666)[9] was probably the most famous preacher of Lutheran orthodoxy. His sermons, published in a collection of ten volumes, became very influential in later Lutheran preaching. As a professor at Strasbourg, he also wrote against Roman Catholicism, Calvinism, and the Protestant "syncretism" advocated by Calixtus. His *Open Book of the Conscience* dealt with ethics, and his *Wisdom of the Way* discussed the Christian life as a pilgrimage. But Dannhauer's importance for the history of Christian thought lies in the fact that he was Spener's teacher, and that he was therefore a link between Lutheran orthodoxy and Pietism. Thus, although it is true that Pietism was in many ways a reaction against the cold orthodoxy of the seventeenth century, it is also true that there were within the bounds of that orthodoxy persons such as Dannhauer, whose profound piety and concern for the life of the church was one of the sources of Pietism.

Abraham Calov (1612–1686)[10] was the most important theologian of the latter period of Lutheran orthodoxy. A native of Prussia, he began his studies as well as his teaching career at the University of Königsberg, and later joined the faculty at Wittenberg. As in the case of most other theologians of Lutheran orthodoxy, he was also involved in various administrative responsibilities within the church. His literary production was enormous, and therefore of uneven quality and often repetitious. His *Biblia Illustrata,* a vast commentary on the entire text of Scripture, was the result of the very popular lectures that he delivered at Wittenberg on biblical exegesis. Between

---

[9] M. Schmidt, "Dannhauer, Johann Konrad," *RGG,* 2:32; Preus, *The Theology of Post-Reformation Lutheranism,* pp. 57-59; Ritschl, *Dogmengeschichte,* 4:36-39.

[10] F. Lau, "Calov, Abraham," *RGG,* 1:1587; Preus, *The Theology of Post-Reformation Lutheranism,* pp. 59-61; Ritschl, *Dogmengeschichte,* 4:217-24, 427-49, 440-44.

1655 and 1677 he published the twelve volumes of his *System of Theological Themes,* which soon became, after Gerhard's *Loci,* the most influential systematic theology of Lutheran orthodoxy. But where Calov was really at home was in the field of polemics. He was involved in practically every controversy of his time, and wrote copiously on each of them. To the syncretistic controversy, for instance, he devoted twenty-eight works. He was also involved in polemics against the Catholics, Calvinists, Arminians, Socinians, spiritualists, rationalists, and others. Just looking at the list of his works gives the impression that Calov was a computer programmed for controversy. This impression is reinforced when one looks at the manner in which he related to those around him and to his family—he survived five wives. In Calov, therefore, Lutheran orthodoxy reached its high point, both in its best and in its worst features. Calov was without any doubt a serious student of Scripture, and his intellectual ability was staggering.[11] He was also deeply committed to his faith, and saw himself as a "Christian athlete." But on the other hand that very commitment and that very ability led him to a dogmatic rigidity and a polemical attitude that were hardly compatible with the gospel to which he was attempting to witness.

Johann Andreas Quenstedt (1617–1688)[12] presents a marked contrast with Calov. Although Quenstedt was also involved in polemics—every theologian of his time had to be—his approach was much more irenic than Calov's. His family ties reveal what we have already said about the relationships between Lutheran theologians during the age of orthodoxy, for he was Gerhard's nephew, one of Calov's numerous fathers-in-law, and the son-in-law of another theologian—Johann Scharf. Although he was not an original thinker, his erudition and systematic ability allowed him to bring together the best of the Lutheran orthodox tradition in his *System of Theology,* published in 1683. This work is the systematic culmination of Lutheran orthodoxy. Although still couched in terms of opposition to Catholicism and Calvinism, it is never dominated by polemical considerations, as were so many of the earlier writings of the period, in which the impression was often given that the agenda

---

11 In his *Gnostologia* (1633) and *Noologia* (1650) Calov developed a theory of knowledge that may be said to be a forerunner of Kant.

12 F. Lau, "Quenstedt, Johann Andreas," *RGG,* 5:735; Preus, *The Theology of Post-Reformation Lutheranism,* pp. 62-63; J. Baur, *Die Vernunft zwischen Ontologie und Evangelium: Eine Untersuchung zur Theologie Johann Andreas Quensteds* (Gütersloh: Gerd Mohn, 1962).

was set by the opponents of Lutheranism. While the results of earlier theological work—especially among Lutherans—are carefully noted and brought to bear, the general style of the work remains clear and concise. For these reasons, Quenstedt's work came to occupy a place, jointly with those of Melanchthon, Chemnitz, and Gerhard, in the basic library of Lutheran orthodoxy.

David Hollaz (1648–1713)[13] is usually considered the last theologian of Lutheran orthodoxy. He never became a university professor, but remained a pastor—and a teacher of youth— throughout his life. A disciple of Calov and Quenstedt, he was well versed in Lutheran orthodoxy, and it was this that he attempted to summarize for his young students in his *Theological Examination* (1707). Here he followed the method and order of the great systematic treatises of Lutheran orthodoxy, but frequently included personal digressions in which he attempted to show the importance of a particular doctrine for the Christian life. In this, and in his insistence on the importance of a life of true piety, he was influenced by emerging Pietism, and in turn contributed to it. In this he was followed by his son and grandson, both also named David. Thus a connection may be seen between Lutheran orthodoxy and the development of Pietism, although the two eventually saw themselves in opposition to each other.

George Calixtus and the Syncretistic Controversy

The Melanchthonian and crypto-Calvinistic elements within the Lutheran churches had not been entirely destroyed by the debates of the sixteenth century. Although the *Formula of Concord* was able to achieve a measure of reconciliation within those churches, there were still those who felt that strict Lutheranism was in fact a denial of the freedom that Luther himself had discovered in the gospel. As the *Formula of Concord* was accepted and made binding in various parts of Germany, those who favored greater flexibility tended to move to Helmstedt, whose university opposed the *Formula*. The Lutherans at Helmstedt, being of a more Melanchthonian persuasion, favored studies in the humanities and especially in philosophy. Indeed, it was at Helmstedt that Aristotle and his metaphysics were reintroduced

---

[13] E. Wolf, "Hollaz (Hollatius), David," *RGG*, 3:433-34; Preus, *The Theology of Post-Reformation Lutheranism*, p. 65; Ritschl, *Dogmengeschichte*, 4:223-25.

into Lutheran Germany.[14] Therefore, ironically, the University of Helmstedt, which opposed the strict Lutheranism of the sixteenth century as well as the rigid orthodoxy of the seventeenth, contributed to that orthodoxy the Aristotelian metaphysics that undergirded much of it.

It was at this university that George Calixtus (1585–1656)[15] received his humanistic and theological education. It was also there that he later became a professor and first expounded his views regarding the unity of the church. He had also traveled extensively in Western Europe, and had thus had the opportunity to see various forms of Christianity as it was practiced and believed by people of different confessions. His education at Helmstedt, his travel experience, and even his parentage—his father had studied under Melanchthon at Wittenberg—provided Calixtus with an excellent background for the task that he set for himself: calling the various traditions in Christianity to recognize one another as genuine Christian churches.

The manner in which Calixtus hoped to achieve this was by means of the distinction between the fundamental and the secondary articles of faith. As we have already seen in the case of Nikolaus Hunnius, some of the orthodox theologians acknowledged such a distinction, but did not attempt to use it in order to bring about a rapprochement with other theological traditions. Calixtus argued that this distinction should allow Christians of various confessions to recognize one another as fellow Christians, for all that should be required for such recognition is adherence to the fundamentals of the faith, even though there may be significant disagreement on other issues.

Those things are fundamental which are required for salvation. Everything else is secondary. This does not mean that one should be indifferent about secondary issues. On the contrary, secondary articles of faith are also part of Christian truth, and one should endeavor to serve truth in the secondary as well as in the fundamental. The various views regarding the presence of Christ in the Lord's Supper, for instance, are important, and obviously no

---

14 Scharlemann, *Thomas Aquinas and John Gerhard*, pp. 19-21.

15 Ritschl, *Dogmengeschichte*, 4:245-68, 363-423; H. Schüssler, *Georg Calixt, Theologie und Kirchenpolitik: Eine Studie zur ökumenizität des Luthertums* (Wiesbaden: Franz Steiner, 1961); Wallman, *Der Theologiebegriff*, pp. 85-161; P. Engel, *Die eine Wahrheit in der gespaltenen Christenheit: Untersuchung zur Theologie Georg Calixts* (Göttingen: Vandenhoeck und Ruprecht, 1976).

more than one of them can be correct. Theologians and Christians in general should seek to discover which is the correct opinion, and hold fast to it. Calixtus himself believed that Luther's view was, in general, closer to the truth than any of the others. But the precise manner of the presence of Christ in the eucharist was not a fundamental article of faith, for it was not necessary for salvation. Therefore, Lutherans should acknowledge Catholics and Reformed as fellow Christians, even while disagreeing with them on the question of the Supper.

How does one know what are the fundamental articles of faith to be believed by all Christians? Being a patristic scholar, Calixtus answered in terms of what he called the *consensus quinquasaecularis*— the consensus of the first five centuries. Tradition has a function in theology, jointly with Scripture. The Bible is the only source of Christian doctrine, and in it is to be found everything that is necessary for salvation. But the Bible reveals more than is necessary for salvation, for a number of doctrines that have sound biblical basis are indeed true, but are not necessary for salvation. Indeed, even the doctrine of justification by faith, which is certainly scriptural and therefore true, is not generally found in the patristic period, and if one were to claim that it is necessary for salvation one would be forced to conclude that most early Christians were not saved. How then can one distinguish fundamental scriptural truth from those other truths which are also derived from Scripture, but which are not necessary for salvation? It is here that the early tradition of the church—the *consensus quinquasaecularis*—plays an important role, for it allows us to distinguish between fundamental and secondary truths. Only that which was part of the earliest tradition must be required of all. The rest is important because all truth is important; but it is not fundamental. At times Calixtus would go even beyond the *consensus quinquasaecularis,* and assert that all that was necessary for salvation could be found in the Apostles' Creed. But in any case, what is significant here is that, by reaffirming the value of tradition, Calixtus was already making an overture to the Catholic Church—although, let it be stated once again, he insisted on the Lutheran position that tradition is not to be seen as a source of doctrine.[16] This reintroduction of tradition would obviously be one of the reasons

---

[16] Cf. Schüssler, *Georg Calixt,* pp. 71-79.

why more strictly orthodox Lutheran theologians would attack him.

From this distinction between the fundamental and the secondary follows the conclusion that there is already a sort of union among Christians. This "inner communion" must be acknowledged if one is to have an adequate understanding of the true nature of catholicity. In a sense, Christians are already one, even though theological differences separate them. This, however, is not sufficient to achieve "outward communion," for each of the various confessions is accusing the others of erring in fundamental issues. If, on the other hand, the various churches were to acknowledge that their differences, although important, are not fundamental and essential for salvation, it would be possible to achieve an "outward communion," which would include joint participation in the Lord's Supper. In order to achieve this, the churches must see that there is a difference between heresy and error. Heresy is departure from a fundamental article of faith, whereas error has to do with the many other truths of Christianity, which are not necessary for salvation. Heretics are not part of the universal church, and true Christians have no communion with them—neither "inward" nor "outward." But it is possible to believe that someone is in error and still agree on the fundamental articles of the faith. At this point, Calixtus made himself an easy target for his opponents, for in his efforts to reduce the fundamentals to a minimum expression he asserted that only those who reject the clear teaching of the Apostles' Creed are true heretics. His opponents then replied that by such standards those who deny the doctrine of the Trinity are not heretics, for the Trinity is not clearly expressed in the Apostles' Creed—the three persons are affirmed, but their eternal coexistence is not. By emphasizing this, however, his opponents were focusing only on a peripheral issue in Calixtus' views, and one on which he was not always consistent, for the *consensus quinquasaecularis* is obviously a larger criterion than the mere text of the Apostles' Creed.

The proposals that Calixtus put forth met with the almost unanimous opposition of Lutheran theologians. His only success was in Poland, where King Ladislaus IV convened the "amicable colloquy" of Thorn, which met in 1645.[17] But this attempt at reunion

---

[17] *Ibid.*, pp. 122-33.

came to naught. In Germany itself, Lutheran orthodoxy saw the proposals of Calixtus as a denial of its dearest principles. But even so, orthodox Lutherans were not entirely agreed on how and to what extent they were to oppose his views. This disagreement among Lutherans can be seen by comparing Calov's refutation of Calixtus with that of the Jena theologian Johannes Musäus.

Calov's attitude was typical of his temperament and theological stance. He simply rejected the notion that anything could be revealed in Scripture and not be fundamental. Every revealed truth is necessary for salvation. What the creeds of the early councils had done was essentially the same thing that the Lutheran confessions did, namely, to spell out truths contained in Scripture that at the time were being denied by some. The Lutheran confessions, therefore, were not only statements of truth, but statements of fundamental truth. To reject them was not merely to be in error, but to be a heretic. What was needed then was a new confession, stating clearly that all revealed truth is fundamental and necessary for salvation, and condemning as heretics those who hold the opposite—namely, Calixtus and the "Helmstedt school," which followed him. In order to fulfill this need, Calov wrote and proposed his *Consensus repetitus,* a rigid confession of faith that left little freedom for disagreement among Christians and almost equated disagreement with heresy. It was so extreme that, although Calov published more than two dozens works to try to persuade his fellow Lutherans of the need to accept it, and in spite of the fact that his personal influence was great, no Lutheran church adopted it as its official faith. To give some idea of its general tenor, it not only condemned Catholics and Calvinists as heretics, but even condemned those who would affirm that Catholics and Calvinists can be saved. Similarly, the opinion that in John 6 Jesus was referring to the Lord's Supper would have been condemned as heresy, and the same fate was reserved for the assertion that theology does not have to prove the existence of God. In summary, Calov—and the Wittenberg theologians in general—by rejecting every distinction between the fundamental and the secondary, placed themselves in a position where every detail of doctrine seemed to be as important as every other, and where practically every minor disagreement had to be considered a heinous heresy.

At Jena, however, the noted professor Johannes Musäus

(1613–1681)[18] took a different tack. He was no more willing to accept Calixtus' "syncretism" than was Calov. But he felt that it was possible to reject syncretism without going to the extreme rigidity that Calov advocated. "Syncretism" he rejected because it would have seemed to imply that the Lutheran Church did not really believe that its doctrines were to be found in Scripture, and that their denial was a serious error. The church must witness to the truth that has been revealed in Scripture, even if that means accusing other churches of having fallen into error. It is true that in those other churches there may be many who are sincere in their error, and whom God will save; but this does not mean that the Lutheran Church should accept those other bodies as genuine and evangelical churches. If God had not wished for all Christians to hold the truths revealed in Scripture, they would not have been revealed. On the other hand, Calov erred in that, in his reaction against Calixtus, he simply failed to see that a distinction must indeed be made between fundamental and secondary truths. If such a distinction is obliterated, theological disagreement in matters of detail becomes heresy, and theological inquiry is stifled. Musäus thus brought the University of Jena to a form of Lutheran orthodoxy that was much more open than its counterpart at Wittenberg. This tradition was continued at Jena by Musäus' successor—and son-in-law—Johann Wilhelm Baier (1647–1695),[19] whose *Compendium of Positive Theology* attempted to show that Jena's brand of Lutheran theology was not syncretistic.

Although the syncretistic controversy eventually died out, it performed two functions in the history of Christian thought. First, it contributed to the development of a rigid Lutheran orthodoxy. Second, the ideas of Calixtus, in spite of his rather simplistic approach to questions of inter-confessional relations, persisted after his death, and can be traced up to the ecumenical movement of the twentieth century. His disciple Gerard Walter Molanus (1633–1722)[20] took up the torch of Christian unity, and worked to that end in a movement that included such illustrious thinkers as Leibniz and Bossuet.

---

[18] F. Lau, "Musäus, Johannes," *RGG*, 4:1193; K. Heussi, *Geschichte der theologischen Fakultät zu Jena* (Weimar; Hermann Bochlau, 1954), pp. 137 ff.

[19] F. Lau, "Baier, Johann Wilhelm," *RGG*, 1:846; Preus, *The Theology of Post-Reformation Lutheranism*, pp. 64-65.

[20] M. Schmidt, "Molanus, Gerard Walter," *RGG*, 4:1087.

A Brief Exposition of Orthodox Lutheran Theology

As it is obviously impossible to expound here every system of theology that was proposed during the period of Lutheran orthodoxy, I have chosen a method of presentation that will, I hope, give the reader a general idea of the character of that orthodoxy and the main issues discussed by its theologians. This method will consist in a brief exposition of the theology of the period, drawing from various theologians without attempting to distinguish among them.

Given Luther's principle of *sola scriptura,* it was unavoidable that orthodox Lutheranism in the seventeenth century would devote a great deal of attention to the origin, inspiration, and authority of Scripture. Indeed, that doctrine often became the heart of the prolegomena to theology, for if Scripture is the sole source of theology these issues must be clarified before any other theological question can be broached. Although Luther and his early companions had insisted on the sole authority of Scripture, they had not developed a theory of its origin and inspiration, which was taken for granted. During the seventeenth century, therefore, Lutheran orthodoxy, eager to respond to all the major issues raised by the Reformation, would seek to develop a fuller theory of Scripture.

Interestingly enough, a great deal of this doctrine of Scripture was built on the basis of Aristotelian metaphysics, which, as we shall see, gained widespread acceptance among the theologians of Lutheran orthodoxy. In order to avoid the charge of bibliolatry, these theologians applied to Scripture the Aristotelian distinction between matter and form, which by then had become traditional in sacramental theology. The matter of Scripture is the text itself, composed as it is of letters, words, and phrases. The form is the meaning of the text, the message that God wishes to communicate through it. Therefore, it is not strictly correct to say that the text of Scripture is the word of God, as if the matter of Scripture by itself were that Word.[21] On the other hand, however, these theologians wished to make certain that the distinction between matter and form did not lead to an excessive spiritualization of Scripture, and therefore they were quick to add that this distinction is conceptual

---

[21] Preus, *The Theology of Post-Reformation Lutheranism,* pp. 267-68. It is significant, however, that Preus quotes—seemingly inadvertently—a text in which Gerhard uses "form" and "matter" in a way contrary to the typical use of his time. Cf. Hollaz, *Examen theol. acroamaticum,* prol., 3. 13-14.

rather than real.[22] In other cases the distinction was made between inner and outer form.[23] But the main concern was always to show that, although there is a distinction between the physical text of Scripture and the Word of God, this distinction is not such that the two can really be separated.

The text of Scripture was inspired by the Holy Spirit. Inspiration is not a general illumination of some believers, such as prophets and apostles, who then write down their thoughts. Inspiration is a special act of the Spirit, connected specifically with the writing of the text. Inspired writers were such only while writing, and none of their other actions or words can claim the authority of the words that they wrote under the guidance of the Spirit. This was an important point for Lutheran orthodoxy, for otherwise the Catholic view of tradition could have been supported by saying that the apostles, who were generally inspired, wrote some things in Scripture, and passed others on to their successors, thus guaranteeing the infallible authority of tradition. Against such claims, the Lutherans argued that inspiration includes both the content of what was written and the command to write it. Therefore, whatever was inspired by the Spirit was also written and is now part of Scripture.[24]

The inspiration of Scripture is full and verbal. It is full because everything was written by divine inspiration. This is true of the highest mysteries as well as of the most simple and commonplace assertions. It is true that when Moses wrote his five books there were some things that he could know only by divine revelation, such as creation, the tower of Babel, and the ten commandments, whereas there were many others that he knew in and of himself, such as the events connected with the flight from Egypt. But when it came to the act of writing the text of Scripture, he wrote both what he knew and what he did not previously know under the inspiration of the Spirit. Therefore, the Spirit inspired Moses to write about creation, which he could not have known apart from revelation, and also inspired him to write about the Exodus, which he knew from personal experience. And in both cases that inspiration included both the

---

[22] Gerhard, *Loci theologici*, 1. 1.7; cf. 1. 2. 16.
[23] Gerhard, *Loci*, 1. 12. 305-6; Hollaz, *Ex. theol. acro.*, prol., 3. 15.
[24] Gerhard, *Loci*, 2. 33; Calov, *Systema*, I. 543-45; Quenstedt, *Systema*, 1. 4. 2. 2-3.

command to write about a particular theme and the exact words to be used in such writing.[25]

The doctrine of the full inspiration of Scripture leads to verbal inspiration. The Holy Spirit did not simply give the authors of Scripture general guidelines as to what they were to write, but actually guided them in the writing of every word. In this sense, the writers were no more than amanuenses of the Spirit. On the other hand, however, the Spirit did take into consideration the various personalities and situations of the writers, and thus their contributions to the canon show differences of style, personality, and situation. As the seventeenth century progressed, the claims of verbal inspiration for Scripture were made more and more sweeping. By the end of the period, Hollaz claimed that the Masoretic vocalization signs in the Old Testament were as old as the text itself, and as inspired as the consonants.[26]

Scripture is the first principle of theology, although there is also a natural theology, grounded on the common reason imprinted by God in everyone, and developed by the observation of visible creatures.[27] Theology is not a science, but a doctrine of faith. What this means is that it is not the sort of objective discipline that could be mastered by any unbeliever by simply examining the text of Scripture. As the subject matter of theology is none other than Christ himself, and as he can be known only in faith, theology can be done only by those who believe in Christ.[28] Its task is practical, not in the sense that it is reduced to ethics, but in the sense that its purpose is to produce correct belief and piety leading to salvation. Theology, therefore, is not a theoretical discipline in which knowledge is sought for the mere value of knowledge itself. On this basis orthodox Lutheranism rejected all attempts to develop a theology out of curiosity, or to inquire into matters that God has not revealed in the call to salvation.

Although Scripture was seen as the first principle of theology, this did not mean that there was no place for philosophy in the

---

[25] See Preus' excellent summary of this theory, *The Theology of Post-Reformation Lutheranism*, pp. 278-81. This includes abundant references to primary sources.

[26] A collection of pertinent texts on the entire theory of Scripture may be found in R. G. Grützmacher, *Textbuch zur deutschen systematischen Theologie und ihrer Geschichte vom 16. bis 20. Jahrhundert* (Bern: Paul Haupt, 1961), 1:13-15; C. H. Ratschow, *Lutherische Dogmatik zwischen Reformation und Aufklärung*, 2 vols. (Gütersloh: Gerd Mohn, 1964), 1:71-137.

[27] Quenstedt, *Systema*, 1. 1. 1. 13.

[28] Preus, *The Theology of Post-Reformation Lutheranism*, p. 111.

theologian's task. On the contrary, late in the sixteenth century an Aristotelian revival had begun at Helmstedt and from there passed on to almost every other German university. After its initial steps, much of this Aristotelian revival began drawing on Suárez and other Spanish metaphysicians. Finally, Gerhard reintroduced metaphysics into theology, drawing on Suárez and his German followers. Thus, at a time when the controversy between Lutherans and Jesuits reached its apex of bitterness and misunderstanding, both parties were still working on the same metaphysical foundation. This is one of the reasons that the theology of Lutheran orthodoxy is often called "Protestant scholasticism."

On the other hand, however, Lutheran orthodoxy felt compelled to avoid the pitfall of rationalism, exemplified at that time by Socinianism. As we have already seen, the most characteristic tenet of Socinianism was the denial of the Trinity on the basis of a rationalistic critique. The same was true of their entire approach to religious matters, all of which were interpreted in rationalistic and humanistic terms. This was seen by Lutheran orthodoxy as a great threat to the faith, not simply because it denied individual dogmas, but especially because it made human reason the supreme arbiter in matters of faith. In response to this threat, Lutheran theologians continually insisted on the revealed basis of dogma, and on the need to accept every dogma in order to avoid the sin of pride. This, coupled with the constant opposition to the syncretism of Calixtus, led orthodox theologians to develop rigid and detailed systems.

It is the existence of such detailed systems, usually formulated from chairs of theology at German universities, that has given rise to the title of "Protestant scholasticism" to refer to the seventeenth century. Usually, this title is given a pejorative connotation, implying that the theology of the seventeenth century somehow lost Luther's great discoveries and fell back on goals and methodologies that reproduced some of the worst elements of medieval scholasticism. There is no doubt that there is some truth in such a judgment, but there is also a great deal of falsehood. Lutheran orthodoxy certainly lacked the freshness and freedom of Luther and the early reformers. Its attempt to systematize everything often approached a legalism that Luther himself would probably have rejected. Its use of Aristotelian metaphysics—another reason that it has been called "scholastic"—was something that Luther would have deplored. Its understanding of justification by faith often sounded like just another sort of justification by works. And yet, in its very systematization and by its very attention to matters of detail, it kept alive the inheritance of the Lutheran tradition. Its insistence on the need for revelation certainly made it more akin to Luther than the rationalists who in the eighteenth century accused it of having abandoned Luther's insights. In summary, orthodox Lutheran theologians were to Luther what his epigones were to Alexander: members of a later generation, lacking the genius of the founder, but without whom the founder's work would have been in vain.

X

Reformed Theology After Calvin

Although Reformed theology is usually equated with Calvinism, that equation is not altogether exact. Some of the traits of Reformed theology were already developed by Zwingli, Bucer, Oecolampadius, and others who came before Calvin. During Calvin's lifetime, a number of theologians were making contributions to the Reformed tradition in relative independence from the author of the *Institutes*. The name by which they described themselves was "Reformed," and the title of "Calvinist" was first applied to them as a sign of heresy by their opponents—Lutheran as well as Catholic. Furthermore, what eventually came to be called "Calvinism," although chiefly derived from Calvin himself, in some subtle ways differed from the theology of the *Institutes*. In order to show how this development took place, and how it affected the final shape of Calvinism, we shall begin this chapter with a brief survey of the development of Reformed theology during the sixteenth century, both apart from Calvin and after him. We shall then see how Reformed theology, to which the name of "Calvinism" was applied with increasing frequency, developed in various parts of Europe—Switzerland, Germany, the Netherlands, France, Scotland, and England, in that order. I hope this survey will serve to show to what extent what was called "Calvinism" was in fact faithful to Calvin himself, and to what extent it was not.

Reformed Theology During the Sixteenth Century

The undeniable greatness of Calvin as a theologian, an organizer, and a church leader has tended to obscure the significance of a number of lesser lights that shone in Switzerland and elsewhere before, during, and after Calvin's lifetime. This is clearly the case with Zwingli, who was without any doubt the first great Reformed theologian, and is usually eclipsed by Calvin. After the *Zurich Consensus* of 1549, as Calvin's views on the eucharist were increasingly accepted by Swiss Protestantism, Zwingli's theology receded into the background. And yet, on one crucial point much of the later "Calvinism" was closer to Zwingli than to Calvin. This point was the doctrine of predestination, which Zwingli had discussed in connection with providence and creation, while Calvin had placed it within the framework of soteriology. As we shall see, this resulted in the development of a "Calvinistic" doctrine of predestination that went significantly beyond Calvin's own doctrine. We have already had opportunity to show Bucer's influence on Calvin, especially on the eucharist and ecclesiology. John Oecolampadius (1482–1531),[1] the Basel reformer, supported Zwingli in both his theology and foreign policy. His patristic and biblical studies were an important contribution both to Calvin and to other Reformed theologians. Wolfgang Fabricius Capito (1478–1541),[2] Bucer's supporter at Strasbourg—an erudite person who held doctorates in medicine, law, and theology—was active in spreading Reformed theology in southern Germany; and a great deal of the supposed Calvinism that Lutherans deplored in that region was in reality the work of Capito. Therefore, Calvin had a number of predecessors whose work eventually flowed into the great stream of what is usually called Calvinism.

In a description of the movement of Reformed theology beyond Calvin during the sixteenth century, four names stand out as most important and representative: Peter Martyr Vermigli, Jerome Zanchi, Theodore Beza, and Zacharias Ursinus.

---

[1] H. R. Guggisberg, "Oekolampad, Johannes," *RGG*, 4:1567-68; E. G. Rupp, *Patterns of Reformation* (London: Epworth Press, 1969), pp. 3-46; cf. E. Staehlin, *Oekolampad-Bibliographie* (Nieuwkoop: B. de Graaf, 1963).

[2] R. Stupperich, "Capito, Wolfgang," *RGG*, 1:1613; J. M. Kittelson, *Wolfgang Capito: From Humanist to Reformer* (Leiden: Brill, 1975).

Peter Martyr Vermigli (1499–1562)[3] was a native of Florence who came under the influence of Juan de Valdés at Naples. After several unsuccessful attempts at reformation in Italy, he fled to Zurich and then to Strasbourg, where he became professor of theology. In 1547, at the request of Archbishop Cranmer, he went to England to serve as a professor of theology at Oxford. It is possible that his views may have influenced the *Prayer Book* of 1552, as well as the Forty-two Articles of the following year. In 1553 he returned to Strasbourg, and three years later he became professor of Hebrew at Zurich. He held this post until his death in 1562.

The importance of Peter Martyr Vermigli for the development of Reformed orthodoxy lies more in matters of methodology than of actual content. The reason for this is that, although in the content of his theology Vermigli was very close to Calvin and Bucer, his methodology showed the influence of Aristotle to a greater degree than any other Reformed theologian of his time. He had spent at Padua eight years of study, and the university of that Italian city was the center of a great revival of Aristotelianism. While still in Italy, he established a school at Lucca, where Scripture and Aristotle were both studied in an effort to bring about a reformation of the church. It was at that school that Zanchi received a great deal of his theological formation. Later, when Peter Martyr was a professor at Strasbourg, he included among the subjects on which he lectured the *Ethics* of Aristotle.

Peter Martyr Vermigli thus introduced into Reformed theology a methodological approach that would have profound influence on the later development of that theology. Whereas Calvin started from the concrete revelation of God, and always retained an awesome sense of the mystery of God's will, later Reformed theology tended more and more to proceed from the divine decrees down to particulars in a deductive fashion. Thus, although Peter Martyr himself did not enter into such a debate, the later controversy between infralapsarians and supralapsarians was the result of the method that he introduced into Reformed theology. The same

---

[3] J. C. McLelland, *The Visible Words of God: An Exposition of the Sacramental Theology of Peter Martyr Vermigli, A.D. 1500-1562* (Grand Rapids: Eerdmans, 1957); P. McNair, *Peter Martyr in Italy: An Anatomy of Apostasy* (Oxford: Clarendon Press, 1967); K. Sturm, *Die Theologie Peter Martyr Vermiglis während seines ersten Aufenhalts in Strassburg (1542-1547)* (Neukirchen-Vluyn: Neukirchener Verlag, 1971); J. C. McLelland, ed., *Peter Martyr Vermigli: An Italian Reformer* (Waterloo, Ont.: Wilfrid Laurier University Press, 1980).

methodological approach is the reason that later Reformed theologians placed the doctrine of predestination under the heading of the doctrine of God, thus abandoning Calvin's practice of placing it under the heading of soteriology.[4]

Jerome Zanchi (1516–1590) was also an Italian, and a disciple of Peter Martyr Vermigli. In 1550, a few months after Vermigli left Italy, Zanchi was forced to do likewise for fear of his life. After a brief stay at Geneva, he became a professor of theology at Strasbourg, where he remained almost eleven years. During most of that time he was regarded askance by the more strictly Lutheran religious leaders of that city. The pressure was such that he eventually subscribed to the *Augsburg Confession*, although stating that he was interpreting it "in an orthodox fashion." These and other controversies eventually led him to leave Strasbourg, first to become a pastor and, after four years, to succeed Ursinus in the chair of theology at Heidelberg. It was there that he wrote most of his theological works, having to do with issues such as predestination and the doctrine of the Trinity.[5]

From the foregoing it should be clear that Zanchi was not a person overly given to rigid orthodoxies or a hunter of heretics. He was too much a lover of peace for that. And yet, when it comes to his view of presdestination, he too was involved in the process of schematization that marks the difference between Calvin and the later Calvinists.

Zanchi's doctrine of predestination is very systematically expounded in his treatise on *The Doctrine of Absolute Predestination Stated and Asserted*.[6] The manner in which he understands this doctrine, and its relation to the entire system of theology, may be seen in the fact that he begins his treatise with a series of "observations on the divine attributes, necessary to be premised, in order to our better understanding the doctrine of predestination."[7] At the very outset, Zanchi states that the basis for the doctrine of predestination is God's foreknowledge, for "God is, and always was so perfectly wise, that nothing ever did, or does, or can elude His knowledge. He knew,

---

[4] See J. C. McLelland, "The Reformed Doctrine of Predestination (According to Peter Martyr)," *SJT*, 8 (1955): 255-71.

[5] *Opera omnia* (S. Crispin, 1619), 8 vols.

[6] There is an English translation: J. Zanchius, *Absolute Predestination* (Evansville, Ind.: Sovereign Grace Book Club, n.d.).

[7] On the relationship between Zanchi's doctrine of God and his understanding of predestination, see O. Gründler, *Die Gotteslehre Girolami Zanchis und ihre Bedeutung für seine Lehre von der Prädestination* (Neukirchen: Verlag des Erziehungsvereins, 1965).

from all eternity, not only what He Himself intended to do, but also what He would incline and permit others to do."[8] The divine omniscience, joined with the divine omnipotence, implies that everything—and not only the eternal destiny of human beings—has been predetermined by God. "Whatever comes to pass, comes to pass by virtue of this absolute omnipotent will of God, which is the primary and supreme cause of all things."[9] Within this context, "predestination"means not only the divine decision by which some are saved and some are not, but also the divine rule over all things by which all events are predetermined.[10] Given such premises, the typically Calvinistic doctrine of the restricted atonement cannot be refuted: "As God doth not will that each individual of mankind should be saved, so neither did He will that Christ should properly and immediately die for each individual of mankind, whence it follows that, though the blood of Christ, from its own intrinsic dignity, was sufficient for the redemption of all men, yet, in consequence of His Father's appointment, He shed it intentionally, and therefore effectually and immediately, for the elect only."[11]

Significantly, after having established with such cold and inexorable logic the doctrines of double predestination and of limited atonement, Zanchi turns to the task of attempting to show the pastoral and devotional value of these doctrines. What we have here is not therefore a cold and inhuman rationalism. But the fact still remains that Zanchi has changed Calvin's doctrine of predestination not so much in its content as in its tone, making it a doctrine that can be inferred from the nature of God rather than one by which the theologian attempts to express the experience of grace.

Theodore Beza (1519–1605) was called by Calvin to teach at the Academy of Geneva, and after Calvin's death became a leader of the Reformed movement, both in Geneva and throughout Switzerland.[12] Although he was an able New Testament scholar—his edition of the Greek New Testament set new standards for scholarship and textual

---

8 *Absolute Predestination*, pp. 24-25.

9 *Ibid.*, p. 30.

10 *Ibid.*, p. 63.

11 *Ibid.*, p. 33.

12 F. L. Gardy, *Bibliographie des oeuvres théologiques, littéraires, historiques et juridiques de Thèodore de Bèze* (Geneva: Droz, 1960). See in particular W. Kickel, *Vernunft und Offenbarung bei Theodore Beza: Zum Problem des Verhältnisses von Theologie, Philosophie und Staat* (Neukirchen-Vluyn: Neukirchener Verlag, 1967); T. Maruyama, *The Ecclesiology of Theodore Beza: The Reform of the True Church* (Geneva: Droz, 1978).

criticism—he interests us here mostly as a theologian. As such, his main works were his *Confession of the Christian Faith* (1560) and his *Theological Treatises* (1570–82). Beza's theology is very similar to Zanchi's in that, while claiming to be no more than an exponent and continuator of Calvin's views, he distorted those views in subtle yet decisive ways. For instance, he too placed the doctrine of predestination under the heading of the divine knowledge, will, and power, and thus tended to confuse it with predeterminism.[13] Like Zanchi, he insisted on the theory of limited atonement—again, a conclusion that could be drawn from some of Calvin's premises, but that Calvin himself refused to draw. The presbyterian church order, which Calvin and others had developed in Geneva but which they never claimed to be essential, Beza said was required by the clear teaching of Scripture. Calvin had gone beyond Luther in asserting the right to resist tyrannical rulers, but he had always insisted on the traditional doctrine that such resistance is the prerogative and obligation of the lesser authorities, and that individuals are not to take it upon themselves; Beza came very close to inciting all subjects of tyrants—which to him meant Catholic rulers—to rebellion.

In short, then, Beza was in many ways a clear and consistent exponent of Calvin's theology, but this very clarity and consistency meant that he lost a great deal of the sense of mystery and the freshness that was to be found in the work of his predecessor. For him the Bible became a series of propositions, all equally inspired and therefore all equally important, and these propositions were bound together in the Calvinistic system of theology. Where Calvin had always refused to spell out a clear and precise doctrine—the inspiration of Scripture, supralapsarianism, limited atonement, etc.—Beza simply carried the Calvinistic system to its ultimate consequences.[14]

Zacharias Ursinus (1534–1583) spent most of his youth at Wittenberg, where he was a disciple and friend of Melanchthon. He

---

[13] "God is immutable in his counsels, and cannot be wrong in them, or be impeded in any manner from executing them, from which it follows that all that happens to men has been eternally ordained by him, according to what we have said regarding providence." Beza, *Confession de la foy chrestienne*, 6th. ed. (Geneva: François Iaquy, 1563), p. 5.

[14] There is a brief but excellent comparison of Calvin and Beza in B. Hall, "Calvin against the Calvinists," in G. E. Duffield, ed., *John Calvin* (Grand Rapids: Eerdmans, 1966), pp. 25-28. J. Raitt, *The Eucharistic Theology of Theodore Beza: Development of the Reformed Doctrine* (Chambersburg, Pa.: American Academy of Religion, 1972), shows that also with reference to eucharistic doctrine Beza stands between Calvin and the later Calvinists.

also traveled extensively, and his visits to Switzerland may well have strengthened his inclinations toward a "Calvinist" view of the Lord's Supper. In any case, when the controversies that we studied earlier broke out in the Lutheran camp, he was accused of being a crypto-Calvinist and eventually was forced to seek refuge in the Palatinate, where he was called through the intervention of Peter Martyr Vermigli. As the distance between Lutherans and Calvinists widened, especially on the question of the mode of Christ's presence in the eucharist, Ursinus was called upon—jointly with Caspar Olevianus—to compose what eventually became known as the *Heidelberg Catechism* (1563), which became the confession of faith of the German Reformed Church.[15]

Ursinus stood in sharp contract to Vermigli, Zanchi, and Beza. This obviously had a great deal to do with the political and ecclesiastical conditions of the Palatinate, where it was necessary to be moderate and irenic. But in any case, he not only was less dogmatic than his other Calvinistic contemporaries, but he even seems to have understood Calvin—at least on some points—better than they did. Thus, for instance, the *Heidelberg Catechism*—which scholars agree is mostly his work—does not attempt to prove predestination as a consequence of the nature of God, but rather places it after the doctrine of the church, as an expression of the experience of salvation. Commenting on the *Catechism,* Ursinus again does not try to prove what that confession says by relating predestination to the divine attributes—as Zanchi so clearly does—but rather tries to show the pastoral importance of predestination. "In relation to reprobation no one ought to determine any thing with certainty, either concerning himself, or another before the end of life, for the reasons that he who is not yet converted, may be before he dies. Hence no one ought to decide concerning others that they are reprobate, but should hope for the best. In regard to himself, however, every one ought to believe with certainty that he is one of the elect; for we have a universal command for all to repent, and believe the gospel."[16]

Thus, shortly after Calvin's death—and even before—his theology

---

[15] On the historical development of his theology, and the influences and circumstances that guided that development, see E. K. Sturm, *Der junge Zacharias Ursin: Sein Weg vom Philippismus zum Calvinismus (1534–1562)* (Neukirchen: Verlag des Erziehungsvereins, 1972). A good study of some of the essential elements of his theology is W. Metz, *Necessitas satisfactionis? Eine systematische Studie zu den Fragen 12-18 des Heidelberger Katechismus und zur Theologie des Zacharias Ursinus* (Zurich: Zwingli Verlag, 1970).

[16] *Commentary on the Heidelberg Catechism* (Grand Rapids: Eerdmans, 1954), p. 301.

was being schematized by such theologians as Vermigli, Zanchi, and Beza, in spite of the fact that there was also an Ursinus who seems to have understood something of the dynamism and freshness of Calvin's system. This process of hardening, which set in so early, was further aided during the seventeenth century by the various controversies in which Calvinism found itself involved. To these controversies and further development of Calvinism we must now turn, and the order of our discussion will be as follows: First we shall study the further history of Calvinism in Switzerland and Germany. Then we shall turn to the Netherlands, where events were taking place whose significance merits separate consideration. This will be followed by a brief section on the very interesting shape that French Calvinism took. Finally, we shall study the history of Calvinism in Great Britain—first in Scotland, and then in England.

Calvinism in Switzerland and Germany

The most significant and influential theological document produced in Switzerland after Calvin's death was the *Second Helvetic Confession*. As we have already noted, the *Zurich Consensus* of 1549, to which Calvin and Bullinger agreed, joined the forces of Calvinism and Zwinglianism in a single Reformed tradition. But this *Consensus* was never to become a confessional statement generally accepted by the various branches of the Reformed Church. That distinction was to be reserved to the *Second Helvetic Confession,* which strictly speaking was composed not by a Calvinist, but by the Zwinglian Bullinger. Bullinger had written most of the text of this confession in 1561, but had not given it wide circulation until he was requested by Frederick III, Elector of the Palatinate, to prepare a Reformed confession similar to what the Lutherans had presented before the Diet of Augsburg. The reason that Frederick needed this was that a Diet of the Empire was about to convene, and he feared that it would be necessary for him to show that the theology that the church in his domains had espoused was not a departure from the authentic tradition of the church. When Bullinger received the elector's request, he felt that the text that he had written several years earlier would be an adequate response, and he therefore sent it to the elector. At the same time, he sent it to Geneva and to Bern in order to receive the reactions and evaluations of Reformed churches in those cities. After some correspondence and some minor changes—specifically in the preface, which was entirely rewritten—the *Second Helvetic Confession* was accepted and subscribed to by almost all the Reformed churches in Switzerland (1566)—the most significant exceptions were Neuchâtel, which signed two years later, and Basel, which did not subscribe to the *Confession* until the following century. The very year of its publication it was adopted by the Scottish Synod at Glasgow, and the following year the Hungarian Reformed Church subscribed to it. The *Polish Confession,* promulgated by the Reformed Church of Poland in 1570, is no more than a revision of the *Second Helvetic*. Although the French Reformed did not accept it as their confession of faith, the reason for this was simply that they already had their own confession, and therefore in 1571, at the synod of La Rochelle, they declared the *Second Helvetic* to be a true confession of correct Christian doctrine.[17]

The *Second Helvetic Confession,* written as it was by Bullinger—who was not, strictly speaking, a Calvinist—with the purpose of conciliation, was in many ways a moderating influence in the movement toward rigid Calvinistic orthodoxy. Indeed, most of the areas where this confession was promulgated avoided the most extreme consequences of that orthodoxy.

There is no doubt that this is a Reformed document, with strong Calvinistic influence. The Lord's Supper is understood, in accordance with the *Zurich Consensus,* in typically Calvinistic terms (chapter 21). On predestination, this confession stands between Calvin himself and the later Calvinist divines whom we have been studying in the previous section; for it places that doctrine, as they do, at the end of the doctrine of God, so that it appears almost as a preface to the doctrine of salvation. Therefore, the doctrine of predestination of the *Second Helvetic Confession* may be said to be a link between Calvin himself and the later Calvinists.

The other point at which the *Second Helvetic Confession* appears as a bridge between Calvin and Calvinistic orthodoxy is the doctrine of the inspiration of Scripture. Calvin did believe that Scripture was inspired. But he did not begin his theology with a discussion of that inspiration. As a matter of fact, he never did discuss biblical

---

[17] On the history, text, and authority of the *Second Helvetic Confession* see J. Courvoisier's introduction in *La confession helvétique postérieure* (Neuchâtel: Delachaux & Niestlé, 1944), pp. 7-23. On its content, see E. Koch, *Die Theologie der Confessio Helvetica Posterior* (Neukirchen-Vluyn: Neukirchener Verlag, 1968).

inspiration fully, and he even seems to have been aware of the dangers of extreme biblical literalism. The *Second Helvetic Confession*, on the other hand, sets out in its very first chapter by proclaiming that Holy Scripture is the Word of God, wholly inspired by God. This change in the structure of theology, again, does not seem to affect greatly the content of this *Confession* itself. But it is the beginning of a tendency to set up the Bible as the book of the divine decrees from whose text theology is then drawn out as a series of propositions. As we shall see later on, in this respect the *Second Helvetic Confession* is a forerunner of the *Westminster Confession*.

In Geneva itself, however, the influence of Beza was great, and through him his own brand of Calvinism gained ground in other parts of Switzerland. This may be seen in the affairs of Samuel Huber and Claude Aubery. Samuel Huber accused pastor Abraham Musculus, who taught the supralapsarian form of predestination, of going beyond what Calvin had taught.[18] He had also critized Beza for having written that the plague was contagious and that it was licit for Christians to flee from it. After a series of debates that it is not necessary to relate here, he was condemned by the Grand Council of Bern in 1588—the same Grand Council that two decades earlier had forbidden all discussion of the divine decrees and had banished the *Institutes* from the Academy of Lausanne.[19] Claude Aubery's case was theologically different, but the outcome was the same. The views he held were similar to those of Andrew Osiander—that is, that justification is not the imputation of divine justice, but that Christ somehow resides or "inheres" in us, and it is his justice in us that God sees. He too was condemned on the same date and by the same authorities, partially through the influence of Beza and the authority of Calvin.[20] Thus, the power of Calvinism—and especially of Calvinism as Beza understood it—was expanding throughout Switzerland, where that expansion had originally been resisted by many.

After the death of Beza, the most significant leaders of Calvinist orthodoxy in Switzerland were Benedict and François Turretin, father and son. Benedict Turretin—or Turrettini—(1588–1631) was

---

[18] G. Adam, *Der Streit*, pp. 50-90.

[19] H. Vuilleumer, *Historie de l'Eglise Réformée du Pays de Vaud sous le régime bernois*, tome II: *L'orthodoxie confessionnelle* (Lausanne: Éditions La Concorde, 1928), pp. 131-34.

[20] *Ibid.*, pp. 134-41. Vuilleumer then goes on to show that the influence of Aubery did not die out immediately.

an Italian by birth, and was part of the same school of extreme predestinarians that we have already found represented in Vermigli and Zanchi. He was instrumental in gaining the support of the Swiss Reformed for the decisions of the Synod of Dort, which condemned the Arminians and which we shall study further on in this chapter. However, it should be noted that in his later years he advocated leniency and moderation toward the Arminians.

Benedict's son François (1623–1687) was probably the most important systematic theologian of Calvinist orthodoxy on the Continent.[21] Although he took part in the controversies raised by the theology coming out of Saumur in France—to which we shall turn shortly—his main claim to fame is his *Institutiones theologiae elenchticae,* in three volumes, published between 1679 and 1685. These are probably the most systematic and thorough treatise on doctrinal theology in the Reformed camp after Calvin's *Institutes,* and a brief examination of some of its *loci* will suffice to show the nature of seventeenth-century Continental Calvinism.

After a series of prolegomena that are very similar to what would be found in any other scholastic theology, Turretin turns to the question of the authority of Scripture. His concern here is to show that Scripture is the sole authority of Christian theology, and that tradition is not to be placed alongside it. This is traditional Protestant theology, which he draws from the reformers of the sixteenth century. But he then goes on to discuss such details as whether or not the Septuagint is inspired, and whether or not the text of Scripture has somehow been corrupted by manuscript tradition. In both cases his response is negative; but it is significant that his argument with reference to the possible corruption of the text is based on the authority of the text itself: one must affirm that the text of Scripture has been preserved in its pristine purity because to deny it would be a denial of divine providence. Indeed, God has willed to reveal to us in Scripture all things that are necessary for our salvation, and God has also willed that there would be no other revelation beyond that. If God were then to allow the text of the revealed Word to be corrupted by copyists this would be a failure in providence.[22] This manner of

---

[21] See the bibliography in J. W. Beardslee, ed., *Reformed Dogmatics* (New York: Oxford University Press, 1965), pp. 460-63.
[22] *Inst. theol. elench.,* 2. 10. 5.

placing the doctrine of Scripture at the beginning of systematic theology, and then proceeding to define and clarify the absolute inerrancy of Scripture, is typical of later Calvinism, and not to be found in Calvin himself. This tendency reached its peak in the *Helvetic Consensus* of 1675, composed by Turretin and two other theologians, which claimed that the vowel points of the Hebrew text were divinely inspired and therefore inerrant.

When it comes to the doctrine of predestination, Turretin is typical of later Calvinism. His father was an ardent defender of the decrees of Dort. Now in his *Institutiones* François places the doctrine of predestination precisely where we have seen other orthodox Calvinists place it: after the doctrine of God, almost as a corollary drawn from the divine nature. As in the case of others whom we have already studied—Zanchi, Vermigli, et al.—this implies that his discussion of predestination becomes more an exercise of reading the mind of God than a proclamation of God's undeserved grace. Thus he, like most later Calvinists, is drawn into the question of the order of the divine decrees, and whether or not God decreed the fall. Calvin had not seen fit to discuss these issues in detail, for they seemed to be beyond the limits of mystery. Turretin—and many others with him—devotes long pages to these questions. His conclusion is that supralapsarianism—the opinion of those who hold that the decree of election and reprobation was prior to the decree concerning the fall—is "repugnant to the basis of salvation."[23] His own position is that God decreed first to create humankind; second, to permit the fall; third, to elect some out of the mass of perdition, while allowing others to remain in their corruption and misery; fourth, to send Christ to the world as the mediator and savior of the elect; and finally, to call these to faith, justification, sanctification, and final glorification.[24] This is, strictly speaking, the original understanding of "infralapsarianism." What Turretin is here saying is not that God decreed predestination after the event of the fall, or even that God did not decree the fall—although by a permissive rather than an active decree—but rather that in the order of the divine decrees predestination follows the fall, and not vice versa. Later usage of the term "infralapsarian," however, would become ambiguous, for it would come to mean both the view here espoused

---

[23] *Ibid.*, 4. 18. 5.
[24] *Ibid.*, 4. 18. 22.

by Turretin and the opinion that the decree of election follows God's foreknowledge of the fall—or sometimes even the actual fall.

As to the question of whether or not Christ died for all humankind, Turretin follows the by then established Calvinistic view that he died only for the elect, although his death would have been in itself sufficient for the redemption of all if God had so willed it.[25] In practically every other single issue, including the manner of the Lord's presence in the Supper,[26] his views are typically Calvinistic. It is significant, however, that he devotes to the Lord's Supper much less space and attention than to some of the questions regarding predestination and limited atonement. This is a sign of something that we shall find to be generally true of Calvinistic orthodoxy, namely, that the question of the Lord's Supper, which was originally the main mark of distinction of Calvinism, soon was overshadowed by matters of predestination, limited atonement, total depravity, and the like.

On still another point Turretin is a typical exponent of Protestant orthodoxy, and that in his scholastic style and methodology. Here again we find the endless and subtle distinctions, the rigid outlines, the strict sytematization, and the propositional approach that had been characteristic of late medieval scholasticism. Therefore, there is ample reason to call Turretin and his contemporaries "Protestant scholastics."

That this sort of strict Calvinism did not go unchallenged even in Geneva, however, may be seen in that Jean-Alphonse Turretin, the son of François, led a liberal reaction that by 1725 would succeed in having the decrees of Dort, as well as the *Second Helvetic Confession,* abolished in Geneva.[27]

The history of Calvinism in Germany during the sixteenth and seventeenth centuries is practically coextensive with the complicated political history of that nation. That history we cannot retell here. Let it suffice to say that Calvinism was constantly under pressure in Germany, for the measure of tolerance that had been granted to Lutheranism was not accorded to it. Therefore, regions where

---

[25] *Ibid.,* 14. 14. 9-12.

[26] *Ibid.,* 18. 28. M. Heyd, "Un rôle nouveau pour la science: Jean-Alphonse Turretini et les débuts de la théologie naturelle à Genève," *RThPh,* 112 (1980): 25-42.

[27] J. H. Bratt, *The Rise and Development of Calvinism: A Concise History* (Grand Rapids: Eerdmans, 1959), p. 39; E. G. Léonard, *Histoire générale du protestantisme,* tome II: *L'établissement (1564-1700),* p. 244.

Calvin's influence had been strong—notably Strasbourg—eventually joined the ranks of the Lutheran confession. Given these circumstances, the most significant center of Calvinism during the sixteenth century was the Palatinate and its capital Heidelberg, where, owing to particular political conditions, the Reformed faith was favored by the elector. The *Heidelberg Catechism* soon became the most characteristic document of German Calvinism. The Heidelberg theologians, however, were often accused by other Calvinists of having introduced innovations in their theology. In this respect, Thomas Erastus is significant.

Thomas Erastus (1524–1583)[28] was a Swiss-born professor of medicine at the University of Heidelberg, and a member of the church consistory. A Zwinglian in theology, he tried to counteract the influence of Lutheranism in eucharistic theology, and of Calvinism in matters of church order. In 1570 he was accused of Socinianism and excommunicated by the church in Heidelberg. His fame, however, derives from a work published posthumously, consisting of a series of theses on excommunication in which he held that it was the task of the civil authorities to punish Christians who sinned, and that the church itself had no authority of excommunication.[29] Eventually, his name became associated with the view that the state is to be sovereign over the church, even in matters of ecclesiastical discipline—an opinion that has received the name of "Erastianism."

Calvinism in the Netherlands

It was in Holland, early in the sixteenth century, that one of the most significant developments of Calvinist orthodoxy took place. This centered on the teachings of Jacobus Arminius and his followers, and on the synod of Dort, which eventually condemned them.

Arminius (1560–1609)[30] was Dutch by birth, and his theological

---

[28] R. Wesel-Roth, *Thomas Erastus: Ein Beitrag zur Geschichte der reformierten Kirche und zur Lehre von der Staatssouveränität* (Lahr, Baden: Moritz Schauenburg, 1954).

[29] There is an English translation: *The Theses of Erastus Touching Excommunication* (Edinburg: Myles MacPhail, 1844).

[30] An excellent biography has been written by Carl Bangs, *Arminius: A Study in the Dutch Reformation* (Nashville: Abingdon Press, 1971). This includes a thorough bibliography, pp. 361-68. The writings of Arminius have been published in English translation: J: Nichols and W. R. Bagnall, eds., *The Writings of James Arminius,* reprint (Grand Rapids: Baker Book House, 1956), 3 vols.

formation had taken place mostly at the University of Leyden and at Geneva. He was a convinced Calvinist, and he remained one throughout his life, although on many of the points debated he obviously and consciously departed from the teachings of Calvin. Therefore, although eventually "Arminian" came to be a synonym of anti-Calvinist, the reason for this is not that Arminius was opposed to Calvin's teachings in general, but that both he and orthodox Calvinism so centered their attention on the issues of predestination, limited atonement, and the like, that they lost sight of the fact that the controversy, rather than being a debate between Calvinists and anti-Calvinists, was a disagreement between two different groups both of which were deeply influenced by Calvin.

As a young Calvinist scholar, Arminius was influenced by the views of Dirck Koornhert, who found the doctrine of predestination as taught by strict Calvinists to be unacceptable and a denial of the justice of God. While studying the objections of Koornhert, Arminius became convinced that in many points he was right. This, however, would not have caused any great controversy had it not been that four years later (1603) Arminius was appointed professor of theology at Leyden, where his views soon clashed with those of his colleague Franciscus Gomarus (1563–1641).

Gomarus[31] was not only a strict Calvinist, but also a supralapsarian. According to him, God decreed the election of some and the reprobation of others, and then decreed to permit the fall as the manner in which that election and reprobation would take effect. Furthermore, after the fall, all human nature is totally depraved; and Christ died only for the elect. His reaction to the teachings of Arminius was not slow in coming, and his anger was exacerbated when, after the death of Arminius (1609), the vacant chair was filled by Simon Bisschop (1583–1643), whose convictions followed the same general lines as those of Arminius. When Gomarus—who was no longer at Leyden—and his followers attempted to bring pressure to bear for the removal of all Arminians from their teaching positions, forty-six pastors signed the *Remonstrance* (1610). This was a document, probably composed by John Uyttenbogaert—although sometimes attributed to Bisschop—that rejected both supra and infralapsarianism, the doctrine that the elect could not fall from

---

[31] See G. P. Van Itterzon, *Franciscus Gomarus* (The Hague: M. Nijhoff, 1930).

grace, and the theory of limited atonement—that is, that Christ did not die for all.

In all these points, the Remonstrants—as they were called after that time—were simply taking a stand on what had been the teachings of Arminius, and for this reason they are properly called Arminians. Thus, in order to understand their views, it may be well to pause to state what Arminius had taught with reference to the main points of the debate.

On predestination, Arminius had begun by disagreeing with the extreme supralapsarianism of Gomarus, but had concluded that infralapsarianism was also in error. Although it is true that in many ways he was a rationalist, one should point out that his opponents were also rationalists in the sense that they attempted to prove predestination as a consequene of the nature of God, and that Arminius was deeply concerned that any doctrine of predestination must be Christocentric and serve to edify the faithful. Thus, arguing against the extreme supralapsarian form of predestination, he adduced two reasons—among many others—that he must disagree with it: "(1) For this predestination is not that decree of God by which Christ is appointed by God to be the Savior, the Head, and the foundation of those who will be made heirs of salvation. Yet that decree is the only foundation of Christianity. (2) For the doctrine of this Predestination is not that doctrine by which, through faith, we as lively stones are built up into Christ, the only corner stone, and are inserted into him as the members of the body are joined to their head."[32]

His own doctrine of predestination, then, disagrees with what was being taught by the Gomarists on two basic points. First of all, it is more strictly Christocentric—on which point he came closer to Calvin than did Gomarus. And, second, it is predestination based on God's foreknowledge of the future faith of the elect. Thus, Arminius claims that the very first "absolute decree of God concerning the salvation of sinful man, is that by which he decreed to appoint his Son, Jesus Christ, for a Mediator."[33] The second and third divine decrees were that God would save those who would repent and believe, and that God would provide the means by which such

---

[32] Nichols and Bagnall, *The Writings of James Arminius,* 1:216-17.
[33] *Ibid.,* 1:247.

repentance and belief would be made available. Then Arminius comes to the fourth decree, which clearly shows what he understands by predestination: "To these succeeds the FOURTH decree, by which God decreed to save and damn certain particular persons. *This decree has its foundation in the foreknowledge of God,* by which he knew from all eternity those individuals who would, through his preventing [i.e., prevenient] grace, believe, and, through his subsequent grace would persevere, according to the before described administration of those means which are suitable and proper for conversion and faith; and, by which foreknowledge, he likewise knew those who would not believe and persevere."[34]

Therefore, the strict Calvinists were right when they claimed that Arminius' understanding of predestination destroyed the very objective of that doctrine, namely, that none may be able to boast of their own salvation. Indeed, if the cause of our election is God's foreknowledge of our repentance and faith, it follows that the determining factor in our salvation is our own response to the call of the gospel, that is, our own faith, and not God's grace.

In order to avoid this consequence, Arminius had recourse to what he called "preventing grace." According to him, this preventing (or prevenient) grace has been conferred by God on all, and that grace is sufficient for belief, in spite of our sinful corruption, and thus for salvation. The difference between the elect and the reprobate lies, then, in that some believe and some do not, and also in that God has always foreknown what each one's decision will be. Therefore, "the grace sufficient for salvation is conferred on the Elect, and on the Non-elect; that, if they will, they may believe or not believe, may be saved or not be saved."[35] Grace, then, is not irresistible, as the Gomarists insisted.

This in turn implies that Christ died for the entire human race, and that the doctrine of limited atonement must be rejected.

> The point in dispute is . . . whether it can be truly said that, when God willed that His own Son should become a man and die for sins, He willed it with this distinction, that he should assume, for a certain few only, the human nature which he had in common with all men; that he should suffer for only a few the death which could

---

[34] *Ibid.,* 1:248. Italics are mine.
[35] *Ibid.,* 1:367.

be the price for all the sins of all men, and for the first sin which all committed alike in Adam. . . . This, I assert, is the question: you reply affirmatively to this question, and therefore, confess that the allegation is made, with truth, against your doctrine.[36]

Finally, Arminius argued that, precisely because grace is not irresistible, it is possible to fall from grace, or, as he would put it, that "it is certain that the regenerate sometimes lose the grace of the Holy Spirit."[37] This opinion seemed especially injurious to those Calvinists who felt that the greatest asset of the doctrine of predestination was the assurance of salvation that followed from it.

When the *Remonstrance* was published, the whole controversy became involved in a host of political and social issues. Most of the maritime provinces, and especially the bourgeoisie, which was numerous and powerful in those provinces, took the Arminian position. The lower rural classes, as well as those from the islands who lived by fishing, supported the strict Calvinism of Gomarus, and were joined in this position by vast numbers of foreign exiles for whom the purity of the faith was essential. As the maritime provinces supported John Barneveldt in his opposition to the rising power of Maurice of Nassau, the Arminians counted on the support of Barneveldt, while Maurice was in favor of the Gomarists. When Rotterdam opted for the Remonstrant position, Amsterdam, which had long been its rival, took the opposite tack. In any case, by 1618 Maurice of Nassau and his party had consolidated their power, and therefore when the Synod of Dort was called it was clear that it would condemn the Remonstrant position.[38]

In order to see how Dort responded to the various Remonstrant tenets, we shall take each of these, show the position of the *Remonstrance,* and then proceed to show what Dort decided on the matter.[39]

The first article of the *Remonstrance* deals with predestination. It does not deny it, but on the contrary, affirms it. It does not even

---

[36] *Ibid.,* 3:452-53.

[37] *Ibid.,* 3:505.

[38] On the theological reflection on the relationship between church and state prompted by this situation, see E. Conring, *Kirche und Staat nach der Lehre der niederländischen Calvinisten in der ersten Hälfte des 17. Jahrhunderts* (Neunkirchen: Verlag des Erziehungsvereins, 1965).

[39] The five points at issue, and the decision of Dort regarding them, are usually remembered by English-speaking students by means of the mnemonic device "TULIP." Each letter in the name of this typically Dutch flower represents one of the five "heads of doctrine" of Dort: Total depravity, Unconditional election, Limited atonement, Irresistible grace, and Perseverance of the saints.

attack supralapsarianism, although the wording is such that an infralapsarian interpretation seems most natural, for it is said that by an eternal and unchangeable decree God "determined to save, out of the human race which had fallen into sin" those who would be saved, and to leave under sin "the contumacious and unbelieving." Thus, what the *Remonstrance* does at this point is simply to explain predestination in such a way that it could be understood in infralapsarian terms, and it could also be interpreted as the result, not of God's initiative, but of divine foreknowledge regarding those who would believe and those who would not.[40]

The response of Dort to this understanding of predestination leaves no room for doubt. Election is totally unconditional, and therefore is based not on foreknowledge, but only on God's sovereign decision. "The good pleasure of God is the sole cause of this gracious election; which doth not consist herein that God, foreseeing all possible qualities of human actions, elected certain of these as a condition of salvation, but that he was pleased out of the common mass of sinners to adopt some certain persons as a peculiar people to himself, as it is written."[41]

The second point of the *Remonstrance,* again following the teachings of Arminius, affirmed that Jesus "died for all men and for every man, so that he has obtained for them all, by his death on the cross, redemption and the forgiveness of sins."[42] This does not mean the Remonstrants were universalists, in the sense that they believed that all would eventually be saved. On the contrary, they clearly asserted that "no one actually enjoys this forgiveness except the believer."[43] What was discussed was not how many would be saved, but rather whether or not the death of Christ had been for all humankind.

Over against this view, the Synod of Dort affirmed the distinction, made earlier by Gomarus and other Calvinists, between the sufficiency of the merits of Christ in themselves and their efficacy in the divine will. Thus, the death of Christ "is of infinite worth and

---

[40] In this entire section, both the *Remonstrance* and the Canons of Dort are quoted from the English text to be found in R. L. Ferm, ed., *Readings in the History of Christian Thought* (New York: Holt, Rinehart, and Winston, 1964), pp. 397-406.

[41] Ferm, *Readings,* p. 401.

[42] *Ibid.,* p. 397.

[43] *Ibid.,* p. 397-98.

value, abundantly sufficient to expiate the sins of the whole world."[44] But still, "it was the will of God, that Christ by the blood of the cross . . . should effectually redeem . . . all those, and only those, who were from eternity chosen."[45] This is the doctrine of limited atonement, which would become one of the distinctive marks of later orthodox Calvinism.

On the issue of total depravity, both the Remonstrants and the Synod of Dort have often been misrepresented. The commonly held notion, that the Remonstrants denied such depravity and that Dort affirmed it, is not quite accurate. The Remonstrants actually affirmed "that man . . . in the state of apostasy and sin, can of and by himself neither think, will, nor do anything that is truly good."[46] Dort, on the other hand, affirmed that "there remain, however, in man since the fall, the glimmerings of natural light, whereby he retains some knowledge of God, of natural things, and of the difference between good and evil, and discovers some regard for virtue, good order in society, and for maintaining an orderly external deportment."[47]

This is not say that they wholly agreed on the issue. But their divergence was much more subtle than the mere question of whether humans are totally depraved or not. The difference was rather that, whereas the *Remonstrance* refused to link such human depravity with irresistible grace, Dort did establish such a connection, for only a grace that is irresistible can move the heart of a totally depraved sinner.

On the question of irresistible grace, however, the two groups absolutely parted company. The *Remonstrance* said that "as respects the mode of the operation of this grace, it is not irresistible."[48] Against such a claim, the Synod of Dort affirmed that the depravity of humankind is such that God must move the will in order to lead anyone to faith.

Faith is therefore to be considered as the gift of God, not on account of its being offered by God to man, to be accepted or rejected at his pleasure, but because it is in reality conferred,

---

[44] *Ibid.*, p. 402.
[45] *Ibid.*
[46] *Ibid.*, p. 398.
[47] *Ibid.*, p. 403.
[48] *Ibid.*, p. 398.

breathed, and infused into him; nor even because God bestows the power or ability to believe, and then expects that man should, by the exercise of his own free will, consent to the terms of salvation, and actually believe in Christ; but because he who works in man both to will and to do, and indeed all things in all, produces both the will to believe and the act of believing also.[49]

Finally, on the question of the perseverance of the saints the Remonstrants have again been misrepresented. They did not claim that such a doctrine was incorrect. They did not even attack it. What they in fact did was to refuse to teach the opposite doctrine—that of the possibility of falling from grace or "backsliding"—without further scriptural proof. Obviously, such a statement implies that they were not totally convinced of the theory of the perseverance of the saints. But they clearly did not make the opposite theory one of the pillars of their theology. It was the Synod of Dort that made the doctrine of the perseverence of the saints a necessary mark of true Christian faith, and thus led later Arminians to defend the possiblity of falling from grace. The words of Dort leave no doubt as to the importance of the doctrine of perseverance:

> The carnal mind is unable to comprehend this doctrine of the perseverance of the saints, and the certainty thereof, which God hath most abundantly revealed in his Word, for the glory of his name and the consolation of pious souls, and which he impresses upon the hearts of the faithful. Satan abhors it; the world ridicules it; the ignorant and hypocrite abuse, and heretics oppose it. But the spouse of Christ hath always most tenderly loved and constantly defended it, as an inestimable treasure; and God, against whom neither counsel nor strength can prevail, will dispose her to continue this conduct to the end.[50]

In summary, the Arminian controversy and the resultant Synod of Dort are another episode in the process by which the theology of the Reformation was schematized into a strict orthodoxy. By sixteenth-century standards, Arminius and the Remonstrants would have been seen as Calvinists by both Catholics and Lutherans. Their eucharistic doctrine, as well as their understanding of the nature of the church,

---

[49] *Ibid.*, p. 404.
[50] *Ibid.*, p. 406.

were typically Calvinistic. And yet, in less than a century the doctrine of predestination—which Luther had advocated at least as ardently as Calvin—had become the touchstone of orthodox Calvinism. This change is seen as all the more significant when one takes into account that Calvin's most important contribution to Protestant theology was precisely that he did not focus his attention primarily on soteriological questions, as Luther had done.

Before we leave the Netherlands, two other significant Dutch theologians merit specific mention, owing to their influence far beyond the limits of their country. These two are Hugo Grotius and Johannes Cocceius. Grotius (1583–1645)[51] was an Arminian and in general a defender of tolerance and moderation. For this reason, and because his own nation was divided by bitter political and religious struggles, he spent much of his life in exile. His two most influential writings were *On the Truth of the Christian Faith* (1622) and *On the Law of War and Peace* (1625). The first of these works was an exposition of the basic tenets of the Christian faith, grounding them as much as possible on natural theology, and in any case emphasizing the common Christian tradition rather than the various confessional positions. For this reason it gained a high degree of popularity, especially among those engaged in missionary work. The treatise on war and peace attempts to ground the law of nations on natural theology, and therefore constitutes a significant link in the chain from Vitoria to modern international law.[52] Finally, Grotius developed an interesting theory of atonement, affirming that the reason that Christ had to suffer was not to pay for the sins of humankind or to give us an example, but rather to show that, although willing to forgive us, God still considered the transgression of divine law a serious offense that could not go without consequences.

Johannes Cocceius (1603–1669)[53] developed in his *Summa doctrinae de foedere et testamento dei* the classical statement of what has come to be known as "covenant" or "federal" theology. According to this view, the hermeneutical principle that is to serve as the guiding point for the interpretation of Scripture is that God establishes a covenantal relationship with humankind. This relationship is based on a

---

[51] W. S. M. Knight, *The Life and Works of Hugo Grotius* (London: Grotius Society, 1925).

[52] See J. D. Tooke, *The Just War in Aquinas and Grotius* (London: S.P.C.K., 1965).

[53] C. S. McCoy, "Johannes Cocceius: Federal Theologian," *SJT*, 16 (1963):352-70; G. Schrenk, *Gottesreich und Bund im älteren Protestantismus, vornehmlich bei Johannes Coccejus* (Gütersloh: C. Bertelsmann, 1923).

pre-existent covenant beteen the Father and the Son. At the point of
creation, God established with Adam a covenant of works. After the
fall, God established a new covenant of grace, which has two phases:
the Old and the New Testaments. This view, which was a further
development of positions held earlier by Ursinus, was later common
among the Puritans.

Calvinism in France

The story of Protestantism in France is dominated by the fact that
its very survival was often at stake. It was in 1559 that the French
Protestants—who by then were mostly of the Reformed persuasion—organized a French national synod. Two years later they were
involved in a war against the crown. The *Confession of La Rochelle*
(1571), which was Calvinistic in inspiration, was not always strictly
applied to those who wished to join the Huguenot ranks, for
numbers were sorely needed. It was not until 1598, with the Edict of
Nantes, that the Huguenots were guaranteed the right to worship
and believe as they saw fit—and even then only within certain cities
and estates so designated. In order to guarantee this freedom, Henry
IV—a former Protestant who had changed his religion seven
times—gave the Huguenots two hundred armed strongholds and
the right to keep an army. The eventual result of this, however, was
that the Reformed Church became a state within the state, and as
such was regarded askance by those—Cardinal Richelieu among
them—who wished to see a powerful and centralized monarchy
develop in France. As a result, the wars of religion broke out again
early in the seventeenth century, and when they concluded in 1629
the political and military power of the Huguenots had been broken.
In 1659 the crown abolished the national synod, seemingly in an
attempt to fragment the Reformed Church. Finally, in 1685 Louis
XIV revoked the Edict of Nantes, believing that the Huguenots had
become an insignificant minority, and was surprised to see nearly
half a million of his subjects leave his domains. By then the
Huguenots had become a rich merchant class, and their departure
was a significant economic loss to France.

It is a well-known fact that French Protestantism never accepted
the strict Calvinistic orthodoxy of the seventeenth century. The most
common interpretation is that this was due at first to the insecurity

caused by the wars, and later to the economically comfortable position of the Huguenots.[54] This may well be true in part. But it is also true that in many ways French Protestantism remained closer to the original theology and inspiration of Calvin than did the Calvinistic orthodoxy of Geneva and Dort, and that therefore the main reason for its refusal to follow the route of seventeenth-century orthodoxy was its more accurate understanding of Calvin's theology.

This is certainly the case of France's most notable Protestant theologian of the seventeenth century, Moïse Amyraut (1596–1664), whose views so differed from traditional Calvinism that he was dubbed "Beza's scourge." That his views were by no means universally accepted in the French Reformed Church may be seen in that he was accused and tried for heresy at the synod of Alençon in 1637. However, his acquittal shows that many were at least sympathetic to his teachings.

What is most interesting in the case of Amyraut is that he was probably the most assiduous and penetrating student of Calvin in his time, and that he claimed that what he was doing was for the most part insisting on Calvin's teachings over against the incorrect emphases and interpretations of those who claimed to be more strictly Calvinistic. Thus, for instance, he rejected the orthodox doctrine of limited atonement, and showed with an abundance of quotations that Calvin himself never held such a doctrine, but quite the contrary. By drinking at the same sources where Calvin had found his humanistic inclinations, he also preserved the spirit of Calvin at this point, which had been totally neglected by Calvinistic scholasticism. And, with reference to the doctrine of predestination, he insisted—quite correctly—that the so-called orthodox Calvinistic tradition had done Calvin a disservice by attempting to prove predestination by deriving it from the doctrine of God, and taking it out of the soteriological context in which Calvin had placed it.[55] On all

---

[54] See, for instance, Charles Miller in J. H. Bratt, *The Rise and Development of Calvinism* (Grand Rapids: Eerdmans, 1959), pp. 51-55.

[55] B. G. Armstrong, *Calvinism and the Amyraut Heresy: Protestant Scholasticism and Humanism in Seventeenth-Century France* (Madison: University of Wisconsin Press, 1969), p. 266: "Above all Amyraut claimed that predestination had been given a place of prominence in the structure of theology which it should not have had. Therefore, following Calvin, he argued strongly and emphatically for a removal of predestination from the doctrine of God. He insisted that this doctrine is only legitimate in theology as an *ex post facto* explanation of the work of God in salvation, that to discuss theology in the light of this doctrine is to do violence to Scripture, the theology of Calvin, and even the Canons of Dort." This study of Amyraut's theology is fascinating, not only for its insights into that theology, but also and especially for what it implies for our traditional understanding of the relationship between Calvin and orthodox Calvinism. Cf. J. Moltmann, "Prädestination und Heilsgeschichte bei M. Amyraut," *Zschrkgesch,* 65 (1953-54): 270-303.

these points—as well as on several other minor ones—Amyraut, often interpreted by the orthodox Calvinistic tradition as an opponent of Calvin's theology, showed that he had a clearer understanding of that theology than did his detractors.

It thus seems clear that, at least on some points, French Calvinism, which has usually been interpreted as having abandoned the views of its founder, was closer to those views than many of the more ardent defenders of Calvinism.

Calvinism in Scotland

During the early years of the Protestant Reformation in Europe, the political situation of Scotland had been, to say the least, unstable. This instability was aggravated by the fact that Scotland, being a relatively small kingdom, wavered in its foreign policy between the sphere of influence of France and that of England. Inner politics were often overshadowed or at least complicated by the conflicting interests of the Anglophile and the Francophile parties. As England had become Protestant by now, while in France the Catholic party had gained the upper hand, Anglophile interests in Scotland tended to be united with Protestant inclinations, whereas the most ardent Catholics were also members of the pro-French party. Above every other sentiment, however, the dominant one in Scotland was a staunch sense of independence, which seemed to be threatened at various times by either France or England. Thus, when England seemed to be gaining the upper hand many felt inclined to favor both Catholicism and the French party; and the opposite was true when France appeared to be growing too influential in Scotland.

It is not necessary to recount here the long series of political vicissitudes that eventually led to the final triumph of Protestantism in Scotland—and, ironically, to the succession of a Scottish king to the joint thrones of England and Scotland. Suffice it to say that in 1557 a group of Protestant and anti-French nobles bound themselves in a covenant that earned them the title—at first somewhat pejorative—of "Lords of the Congregation." It was through the influence of these lords, the political and marital vagaries of Mary Stuart, the aid of England, popular rebellion, and the zealous and unbending leadership of John Knox, that the reformation finally won the day in Scotland.

John Knox (*ca.* 1513–1572) is credited with having been the shaper of Scottish Calvinism, and through it of the presbyterian tradition in various parts of the world. His fascinating and daring life has been the subject of a number of excellent biographies,[56] especially as so many persons in various parts of the world count him among their spiritual ancestors. However, what interests us here is his place in the history of Christian thought, and more specifically of Calvinism.

Knox is usually represented as Calvin's interpreter to Scotland and therefore to a vast segment of the English-speaking world. There is a great measure of truth in this, for Knox did spend some time in Geneva, where he was profoundly influenced by Calvin's theology. Furthermore, he clearly believed that Calvin had been one of the most significant influences in his life, and he did encourage the study of Calvin's theology in Scotland. However, the traditional view of the relationship between Calvin and Knox must be corrected in a manner similar to that in which we have attempted to correct the traditional understanding of the relationship between Calvin and other forms of Calvinism.

As is the case with other Calvinists, the study of Knox's doctrine of predestination will prove illuminating at this point, for such a study will show that in some ways Knox was more influenced by Zwingli—through Bullinger, with whom he spent some time in Zurich—than by Calvin.[57] It was on this subject that Knox wrote his only major theological treatise, and in it we find once again—although not as markedly—what we have already found in Beza, Zanchi, Vermigli, and others—namely, the doctrine of predestination defended on the basis of the divine nature rather than on the basis of the experience of grace.

The influence of Zwingli and Zurich on Knox can also be seen in his attitude toward civil authority. On this point, Calvin had been much more conservative than Zwingli. Calvin's attitude toward royalty, especially, was always respectful. Given the circumstances in

---

[56] See J. Ridley, *John Knox* (New York: Oxford University Press, 1968); W. S. Reid, *Trumpeter of God: A Biography of John Knox* (New York: Scribners, 1974).

[57] A point that has been made, among others, by Basil Hall in G. E. Duffield, ed., *John Calvin*, pp. 33-34: "John Knox himself, contrary to the received opinion about him, leaned more to Zurich than to Geneva in his theology and something of his practice, and he had been the disciple of George Wishart, whose theological interests were entirely German Swiss." On this question, see also Ridley, *John Knox*, pp. 291-98. An excellent approach to Puritanism by way of its sacramental theology is E. B. Holifield, *The Covenant Sealed: The Development of Puritan Sacramental Theology in Old and New England, 1570-1720* (New Haven: Yale, 1974). Abundant bibliographical references to this period in pp. 28-138.

Scotland, and the opposition of Mary Stuart to the cause of the reformation, Knox borrowed many a page from Zwingli.

In spite of this, however, Knox is probably the most genuinely Calvinistic reformer of the second half of the sixteenth century, and the *Scottish Confession* of 1560, which seems to have come mostly from his pen, is without any doubt closer to Calvin's original thought than the more famous *Westminster Confession*.

The Puritan Movement

The Elizabethan settlement did not satisfy vast numbers of pious and zealous persons in England who felt that the task of reformation had not been carried as far as it ought to have been. Because these persons wished to purify the church of all nonbiblical beliefs and practices, they were called "Puritans." The essence of the disagreement between the early Puritans and the Anglicans may be seen in a letter that Bishop Grindal wrote to Bullinger in 1566, where he says that "it is scarcely credible how much this controversy about things of no importance has disturbed our churches, and still, in great measure, continues to do."[58] What was of no significance to the bishop was of the very essence of the gospel to those who insisted on a thorough reformation and believed that such reformation required strict adherence to the practices of the New Testament in every respect. In a way, they were simply following the teaching of the earlier English reformers to their final consequences—and there is no doubt that on some points they could claim the inheritance of such theologians as Bishop Hooper, and to a lesser degree even of Cranmer and others. But it is also true that their spirit was very different from that of the earlier English reformers. They felt that a reformation that attempted to reconcile the tradition of the church with the biblical record would needs be unfaithful to the latter. Therefore, their difficulties with the queen arose out of a conflict of interests: whereas Elizabeth sought to reach a happy medium to which most of her subjects could subscribe, for the Puritans the only criterion for the life of the church was obedience to the Word of God as they understood it, and on this no compromise was possible.

---

[58] Quoted in C. Burrage, *The Early English Dissenters in the Light of Recent Research* (Cambridge: The University Press, 1912), 1:79.

The Puritans did not set out to destroy the Anglican Church. On the contrary, they agreed with Anglicanism in that there was to be a state church. Their original goal was not to abolish the Anglican union of church and state, or even to create another church alongside it. What they tried to do at first was to bring about radical change in the established Church of England. In spite of this, however, these advocates of further reformation were subversive to the Elizabethan settlement in more ways than one. Many of them adhered to a covenant theology that held that according to Scripture God enters into covenants with a people, and that the latter must obey such covenants if God is to keep the agreement. This covenant theology also had its Continental advocates in Ursinus and—in the seventeenth century—in Johannes Cocceius. But what made it particularly subversive in England was that many Puritans came to the conclusion that the state itself exists in the form of a covenant. This in turn could serve as a basis for attempting to modify, or even to change radically, the structure of government. Although this revolutionary trait was hardly discernible—if at all present—in the early Puritans, it would eventually cost Charles I his head. Others among the early Puritans held that the true government of the church should be presbyterian, and that the episcopacy should be abolished. Some took a middle position and accepted ordination by the episcopacy, but would not take charge of a congregation unless they were called by it. Still others went further and, having become convinced that the established church would never be reformed in the way the word of God required, formed their own separate churches. One such person was Robert Browne (*ca.* 1550–1633), formerly a Puritan member of the clergy who had been disenfranchised by the Anglican Church because of his Puritan ideas. In 1581, Browne founded in Norwich the first congregational church in England and became its pastor. This and a number of similar cases were the beginnings of the separatist movement, which in the following century would become one of the most significant religious forces in England. But already in the sixteenth century these various attempts to change the polity of the church were not viewed with sympathy by the Elizabethan authorities, for they would alienate the more conservative, and would also undercut the close collaboration between church and state that was one of the goals of Elizabeth's policy.

Although the Puritan movement had profound roots in Lollardy and in the various reforming trends of the early sixteenth century, very soon it became closely associated with Calvinism. This was partly owing to the return from exile, on the death of Mary Tudor, of many who had sought refuge in Geneva, Frankfurt, and other cities where Calvin's influence was great. It was further strengthened by the many disciples whom Martin Bucer had acquired at Cambridge, where he had taught during the reign of Edward VI. Therefore, the Puritans tended to interpret the Elizabethan settlement as a halfway measure standing between Rome and Geneva or—what seemed to be the same—between Rome and scriptural Christianity. Then, partly owing to the success of the Reformation in Scotland, and to the shape that the Protestant church took in that neighboring country, the Puritans became increasingly convinced that the presbyterian form of government was part of scriptural Christianity.

As true Calvinists, the Puritans were predestinarians. For them, however—at least in the earlier stages of the movement—the doctrine of predestination was not something to be drawn or concluded from the nature of God, but was rather an expression of the experience of grace. Predestination was not something that could be understood by all—believers and unbelievers alike—but was rather a doctrine spoken within the context of faith.

This doctrine of election in no way produced the quietism or the complacency that so many detractors of predestination have claimed is its necessary consequence. On the contrary, the Puritans were convinced that God had elected them, not only for eternal salvation, but also to collaborate with the divine plan for humankind. Therefore, activism—and sometimes success in that activity—became a sign of election. No time, money, or energy was to be wasted in frivolous matters that seemed to have little to do with the seriousness of the divine purpose. As many of these Puritans were members of the emerging middle class, these views soon became connected with, and contributed to, the emerging capitalist economies of England and her American colonies.

Although all Puritans agreed on the need to conform church order to scriptural Christianity, there soon developed among them various views as to the exact content of such Christianity. Most remained faithful to the presbyterian view. But others—Browne among them—felt that the organization of the church in the New

Testament was congregationalist, and that presbyterianism therefore was just another compromise. Still others went further, and claimed that Calvin and the main reformers had conceded too much to tradition. The New Testament church, they claimed, was strictly a gathered community of believers, bound together by a covenant with one another and with God. This church had to be free of all connections with the state, which was not a voluntary community. Its members had to make a personal choice to belong to it, and therefore could only join it as adults. In consequence, infant baptism was rejected. Given the need to conform to scriptural practice in every detail, eventually only baptism by immersion was accepted by these groups, which were given the name "Baptists." While the so-called General Baptists rejected the strict Calvinistic understanding of predestination, others—the Particular Baptists—remained Calvinistic on that score.

Puritan hopes were high when it became increasingly evident that Elizabeth would be succeeded by James VI of Scotland. These hopes, however, were shattered when James refused to grant the requests of a rather moderate Puritan petition—he agreed only to authorize a new version of the Bible, and the result was the King James version of 1611. It soon became clear that James was not about to encourage any move that would model the more malleable Church of England after the rather intractable Church of Scotland. By the time James was succeeded by his son Charles I, discontent among the Puritans was about to reach its boiling point.

The religious policies of Charles were unwise. In Scotland, his father had managed to overcome presbyterianism by catering to the nobility. Charles now reversed the policies of James, and presbyterianism once again gained the support of the aristocracy. In England, he took William Laud as his chief advisor in religious matters, and eventually made him Archbishop of Canterbury. Laud was an honest and pious man who was convinced that the new Puritan tide must be stopped, and that the Church of England must somehow make its peace with Rome. He himself was not a Roman Catholic, but his overtures to the Roman Catholic Church were such that he was even offered a cardinal's hat. He was also staunchly anti-Calvinist, and consistently favored those who had been accused of Arminian leanings. For all these reasons he was very much disliked by the Puritan party. As Parliament was somewhat favorable to the Puritan position, Charles dismissed it in 1629. But in 1638 Scotland revolted in response to his attempt to force uniformity of worship upon it. By 1640, the king was forced to convene Parliament in order to request its support for the war with Scotland. Parliament then seized the opportunity to promote the Puritan position. Among the many acts of this "Long Parliament," the most significant for the history of Christian doctrine was its calling of the Westminster Assembly, a group of one hundred and fifty-one persons whose task it was to advise Parliament on religious matters. This assembly produced, among other documents, the famous *Westminster Confession,* and the *Shorter and Larger Catechisms.* These documents—especially the *Confession*—have become one of the hallmarks of presbyterian Calvinism.

Given its significance and the fact that it has often been interpreted as representative of Calvin's theology, the *Westminster Confession* deserves some detailed consideration, as well as a comparison with the theology of Calvin himself.

The *Westminster Confession* begins with a chapter on Holy Scripture. Here it is asserted that the Greek and Hebrew texts of the Old and New Testaments, which have been kept pure throughout the ages, are "immediately inspired" by God. The infallible rule for interpreting Scripture is no other than Scripture itself, in which the elements necessary for salvation are clearly stated—even though lesser matters may be more difficult for the unlearned to interpret. Although Calvin would agree with the importance that the *Confession* gives to Scripture, there are two points on which this document differs from him. The first is the placement of the doctrine itself within the structure of theology. Calvin took the human condition and the goal of human existence as the starting point for his theology. Within this structure, Scripture was important as a means of helping us attain the goal for which we were created. In the *Confession,* on the other hand, Scripture becomes almost a book of jurisprudence in which texts are to be found to prove and support various points—including the proper understanding of what it means to be human. On this point, it is interesting to note that the two catechisms produced by the Westminster Assembly—drawn up by different persons—agree with Calvin rather than with the *Confession.* The other point on which the *Confession* differs from Calvin is in its emphasis on scriptural inerrancy. Although Calvin believed in the divine inspiration of Scripture, he never spelled out this doctrine in any detailed or mechanistic way. Calvin's emphasis was on the use of Scripture by the Holy Spirit in the community of faith, especially in the act of preaching. The *Confession* deals with the sacred text in a more individualistic fashion, as a guide for the faith of each Christian.

The *Westminster Confession* coincides with most later Calvinists in placing the doctrine of predestination in such a place in the structure of theology that it seems to be derived from the nature of God rather than from the experience of grace within the community of belief. This may be seen in that, immediately after affirming the authority of Scripture, the *Confession* goes on to discuss the Godhead in its second chapter, and the eternal decrees of God in the third.

Two clear examples of the way in which Puritanism differed from Calvin's theology may be seen in the manner in which the *Confession* deals with prayer and the Sabbath. On prayer, Calvin says that it is the moment in which we most closely approximate our intended end. In prayer we glorify God and relate to the Divine in such a way that we clearly expect God to be the source of all that we are and need. The *Confession* approaches prayer in a rather legalistic fashion, affirming that it is "required of all men," that it ought to be in the name of the Son, in a known tongue, and not for the dead. Regarding the Sabbath, the same chapter of the *Confession* adopts a position diametrically opposed to that of Calvin. The Genevan reformer affirms that the Sabbath was a figure of things to come, and has therefore been abolished by Christ, whose resurrection is the beginning of the final Sabbath. The celebration of Sunday, then, is not a new form of keeping a "superstitious observance of days," but is rather a practical means of enabling the church to worship together, and of giving rest to those who labor. In a way, all Christians now are in the day of rest, for we are no longer dependent on our own works.[59] The *Confession,* on the other hand, affirms that God

in His Word, by a positive, moral, and perpetual commandment, binding all men, in all ages, He hath particularly appointed one day in seven, for a Sabbath, to be kept holy unto Him: which, from the beginning of the world to the resurrection of Christ, was the last day of the week; and, from the resurrection of Christ, was

---

[59] *Inst.,* 2. 8. 28-34.

changed into the first day of the week, which, in Scripture, is called the Lord's Day, and is to be continued to the end of the world, as the Christian Sabbath.

This Sabbath is then kept holy unto the Lord, when men, after a due preparing of their hearts, and ordering of their communion affairs beforehand, do not only observe an holy rest, all the day, from their own works, words, and thoughts about their worldly employments, and recreations, but are also taken up the whole time in the public and private exercises of His worship, and in the duties of necessity and mercy.[60]

This marked contrast between Calvin and the *Westminster Confession* may be seen as following from the manner in which the two deal with Scripture, which has been discussed above.[61]

Calvin's influence may be seen in the *Confession* where it states that both law and gospel belong to the covenant of grace. By saying this, the *Confession* avoids the marked contrast between law and gospel that was characteristic of Luther and that Calvin had tried to avoid. But then the *Confession* goes on to state that Adam, as originally created, was under a "covenant of works" and that it was only later, after the fall, that the "covenant of grace" was established. Calvin would never have said this, as it would seem to make faith a substitute for the works that we can no longer perform. If faith belongs to a new covenant, it follows that it was not required of Adam and Eve as it is required of human beings in all later generations.

Thus, the *Westminster Confession,* as so much of seventeenth-century Calvinism, so schematized the theology of Calvin that a great deal of its original spirit was lost.

In summary, what we have just said about the *Westminster Confession* can also be said about most seventeenth-century Calvinism—with the notable exception of Amyraut and his circle in the French Reformed Church. This is the reason that historians often refer to that period as one of "Calvinist orthodoxy." This orthodoxy usually centered on the question of predestination, which now

---

[60] *West. Conf.,* 21. 7-8.
[61] Similar differences may be seen in such issues as the perseverance of the saints, the assurance of salvation, the understanding of union with Christ, and eucharistic doctrine. But the issues we have singled out suffice to show that the *Confession*, while being very close to Calvin on many points, does differ from him significantly.

became the touchstone of Calvinism. This is all the more interesting since during the sixteenth century the major point of divergence between Calvinists and Lutherans had not been predestination—on which both groups agreed—but rather the manner of Christ's presence in the Lord's Supper.

Calvinist orthodoxy did a disservice to true Calvinism inasmuch as later generations believed that it was an accurate expression of Calvin's views, and therefore tended to see him as more rigid than he in fact had been. This in turn meant that the Genevan reformer received a much less sympathetic ear than he deserved.

XI

New Awakenings in Personal Piety

Protestant orthodoxy did a great service to the development of Protestant theology, for it served to spell out some of the implications of the great insights of the sixteenth century. At first, it was deeply religious, for it was an attempt to set down with as much detail and clarity as possible what were matters of personal religious significance for those involved in the movement. However, as succeeding generations inherited the theological work of their ancestors, that work became increasingly stale and objectified, as if the significance of theology were to be found primarily in a series of truths that could be formally stated in propositions to be transmitted from one generation to another.

Two different reactions opposed this rather barren orthodoxy. One, rationalism, questioned many of the intellectual foundations of orthodoxy. This rationalism was not a new movement, but rather an outgrowth and blossoming of the thought of the Renaissance, which had both assisted and resisted the Reformation of the sixteenth century. In the seventeenth and eighteenth centuries, rationalism had its strength in France and England. However, as we shall see in the next chapter, it did not have a great effect in Germany until the late eighteenth century. In contrast, Pietism, the other main reaction to strict orthodoxy, began in Germany in the seventeenth century, and it was only in the following century that it had its English counterpart—Methodism. Rationalism and Pietism were therefore concurrent movements, although their chronological relationship varied from country to country. In England, rationalism preceded Pietism, whereas the reverse was true in Germany. It is therefore difficult to choose which movement to discuss first. However, since much of nineteenth-century Protestant theology is best understood immediately after a discussion of the final outcome of rationalism in Kant's philosophy, it seems best to postpone the study of the new philosophical currents, and to turn first to the renewed emphasis on personal piety that appeared as one of the main reactions to Protestant orthodoxy.

As a reaction to the orthodox understanding of the function of theology in Germany, and later to cold rationalism in England, several interrelated movements appeared. Although these movements differed in the shape that they took in each different land, it is clear that they are connected by a feeling that the Christian faith is much more vital than the disquisitions of scholastic theologians or the speculations of philosophers, and that ways must be found to recover that vitality.

These movements claimed that they were not questioning the generally accepted orthodoxy of their times. What they were attempting to do was rediscover the profound personal implications of the Christian faith. Had they actually done just that, they would hardly merit a place in a history of Christian thought, which of necessity must deal with other kinds of issues. But such a clear distinction between theology and the actual practice of the Christian life is not really possible. At first some of the orthodox theologians saw the movement with sympathy, only to discover later that there were indeed far-reaching theological implications and presuppositions in it, and that in many ways the new trends in practical Christian life questioned much of the perspective of orthodox theology. This is one of the reasons that these movements merit a place in the history of Christian thought. The other reason is that vast numbers of twentieth century Protestants are heirs of these movements, while both theology and philosophy have been profoundly influenced by them.

The movements that we shall here study are Pietism, the Moravians, Methodism, and the Great Awakening in the English Colonies in North America.

Pietism

The founder of German Pietism was Philipp Jakob Spener (1635–1705),[1] who had been raised in a devout Lutheran family but saw little connection between the faith that he had received in the home, which was very vital to him, and the theology taught at the universities. In a journey to Switzerland he came in contact with the teachings of Jean de Labadie, a former Jesuit who insisted that the immediate inspiration of the Holy Spirit was necessary for the proper understanding of Scripture.[2] Although Spener never accepted all the doctrines of Labadie—especially regarding the marriage of a Christian with an unbeliever, which the former Jesuit held to be invalid—he was impressed by the vitality of the faith that he saw in the Labadist movement, and determined that he would attempt to awaken in the Lutheran Church a similar fervor. Upon his return to Germany, he served as pastor first at Strasbourg and later at Frankfurt. It was in Frankfurt that he began experimenting with small groups that met at his house for devotions. Also while at Frankfurt, he published (1675) his short but influential book *Pia desideria*,[3] which may be seen as the actual beginning of the Pietist movement. He later became court preacher at Dresden, where he enrolled August Hermann Francke as a follower of his views. The opposition of Lutheran orthodoxy to Pietism was not slow in coming.[4] Soon Spener and Francke were involved in controversy with the theologians of the universities of Leipzig, Wittenberg, and others. J. Deutschmann, one of the Wittenberg theologians, charged them with two hundred and eighty-three heretical teachings, and most orthodox theologians concurred on many of these.[5] As a result, the Pietists were forced to found the University of Halle (1694), which soon became a center out of which their inspiration spread

---

[1] P. Grünberg, *Philipp Jakob Spener*, 3 vols. (Göttingen: Vandenhoeck & Ruprecht, 1893–1906); H. Bruns, *Ein Reformator nach der Reformation: Leben und Wirken Philipp Jakob Speners* (Marburg an der Lahn: Spener-verlag, 1937); J. Wallmann, *Philipp Jakob Spener und die Anfänge des Pietismus* (Tübingen: Mohr, 1970); D. Blaufuss, *Spener-Arbeiten: Quellenstudien und Untersuchungen zu Philipp Jakob Spener und zur frühen Wirkung des lutherisches Pietismus* (Bern: Lang, 1980).

[2] Although written in the last century, the best study of Labadie that I know is still H. Heppe, *Geschichte des Pietismus und der Mystik in der reformierten Kirche* (Leiden: E. J. Brill, 1879), pp. 240-374.

[3] There is an English translation: *Pia desideria* (Philadelphia: Fortress Press, 1964).

[4] At first, however, some orthodox theologians reacted positively to Spener's *Pia desideria*. B. Hägglund, *History of Theology* (St. Louis: Concordia, 1966), p. 325.

[5] K. Depperman, *Der hallesche Pietismus und der preussische Staat unter Friedrich III* (Göttingen: Vandenhoeck & Ruprecht, 1961), pp. 69-87.

throughout Germany and even—through the Pietists' interest in missions—to the rest of the world.

The six "pious desires" that gave the title to Spener's *Pia desideria* were the program of the entire movement. The first such desire was that Christians might be moved to a clearer and deeper understanding of Scripture through their devout study in small conventicles or house meetings, which Spener called *collegia pietatis*—hence the name of Pietists given to his followers by their opponents. Second, Spener wished to have the laity rediscover the universal priesthood of believers by giving lay persons positions of responsibility in these conventicles. Third, he urged all to see that the nature of Christianity is such that it cannot be contained in doctrinal formulations, but that it is rather a total experience of faith, and an attitude in the whole of life. Doctrines are important—and Spener affirmed repeatedly that he accepted all the orthodox doctrines—but much more important is the actual experience and practice of the Christian life. In the fourth place, and as a consequence of his third wish, Spener hoped that all controversies—for he did not doubt that there are moments when controversy is required—might be carried out in a spirit of charity, for to deny such a spirit is a sin at least as grave as doctrinal error. Next, Spener wished that the training of pastors would go beyond cold logic and orthodox theology, and include a profound immersion in devotional literature and practice as well as some training and experience in the actual work of shepherding the flock. And finally, as a result of this newly trained clergy, Spener wished to see the pulpit regain its original purpose of instructing, inspiring, and feeding the believers, rather than being used for learned disquisitions on obscure or irrelevant points of doctrine. Thus, the *Pia desideria* already showed what would be the main marks of Pietism: an emphasis on personal piety; the practice of forming small groups to promote that piety, while at the same time implying that the church at large was incapable of performing that duty; the stress on personal reading of Scripture; the feeling that the core of Christian doctrine must be simple, and that it is the theologians who complicate it; and the emphasis on the ministry of the laity. All of this was placed within an epistemological context in which personal experience was more important than communal faith, and sometimes even more important than historical revelation.

Spener's friend and follower, August Hermann Francke (1633–

1727),[6] gave the movement institutional continuity by founding charitable centers such as a school for poor children and an orphanage. When he joined the newly formed University of Halle, he turned it into a center for the training of Pietist leaders who were soon to be found throughout Germany and even overseas. He carried Spener's emphasis on personal experience much further, claiming that true believers must be able to point to their own "struggle of repentance," in which, being confronted by the law and their own sinfulness, they have finally had an experience of conversion, at a time and place to which they can point. He also emphasized the importance of reading Scripture with a simple mind, to the point that at times he seemed to be opposed to excessive learning. "We may safely assure those who read the word with devotion and simplicity, that they will derive more light and profit from such a practice, and from connecting meditation with it . . . than can ever be acquired from drudging through an infinite variety of unimportant minutiae."[7]

While none will doubt that this statement is essentially correct, such a position did arouse opposition among the orthodox theologians and the ecclesiastical leaders—although not so much for what it in fact said as for what it did not say. The emphasis here falls entirely on individual believers and their relationship with God, and the church seems to be entirely bypassed. Although Luther had indeed asserted that a Christian with the Bible had more authority than a council or a pope without it, he still had given a great deal of attention to the church and the sacraments, which he believed to be indissolubly linked with the gospel. This tendency to set aside the church and her ministrations was one of the main reasons why the orthodox Lutheran theologians attacked the Pietist movement.

Another significant difference between Pietism and orthodox Protestantism lay in their diverging attitudes toward world missions. For a number of reasons, having to do mostly with their historical and political circumstances, none of the major Protestant leaders of the sixteenth century had been favorable to missions, and some had even opposed them altogether. On this point, as in most others, they

[6] F. Ernest Stoeffler, *German Pietism during the Eighteenth Century* (Leiden: E. J. Brill, 1973), pp. 1-38; E. Peschke, *Studien zur Theologie August Hermann Franckes*, 2 vols. (Berlin: Verlagsanstalt, 1964–66). An introductory biography: E. Beyreuther, *August Hermann Francke (1633–1727) Zeuge des lebendigen Gottes* (Marburg an der Lahn: Francke-Buchhandlung, 1956).

[7] *A Guide to the Reading and Study of the Holy Scriptures* (Philadelphia: David Hogan, 1823), p. 83.

were strictly followed by Protestant orthodoxy. Gerhard, for instance, stated that the difference between the apostles and present-day Christians was, among others, that the apostles were commanded to go from place to place, whereas Christians must now stay where God has placed them.[8] Against this view, both Spener and Francke claimed that the Great Commission had been given by Christ to all Christians, and that all were responsible for the conversion of unbelievers. Therefore, the University of Halle became also a center for the training of missionaries. Thus, when Frederick IV of Denmark decided to found a mission in India, he could not find among the orthodox Lutherans in his country any qualified person to head the mission, and had to appeal to the University of Halle to send him missionaries whom he in turn would send to India.[9] This interest of Pietism and its various kindred movements in missions is one of the reasons that their influence is so great even in the twentieth century in the younger churches throughout the world.

Zinzendorf and the Moravians

Count Nikolaus Ludwig von Zinzendorf (1700–1760) was a man of profound religious conviction who had studied at the University of Halle.[10] There he had been influenced by Pietism, and it was from that perspective that he always understood the nature of Christianity.[11] In 1722 a group of Bohemian Brethren who were undergoing persecution accepted his invitation to settle on one of his estates in Saxony. At first Zinzendorf was not even a member of the community; but eventually his sincere religiosity, jointly with his own personal gifts, made him the leader of the community. Because of their origin, these Bohemian Brethren came to be known as "Moravians"—and also as "Herrnhuters," after the village of Herrnhut, which they founded in Zinzendorf's territory.

[8] *Loci theol.*, 24. 5. 221-25.

[9] Pedersen, *Pietismes Tid: 1699–1746*, vol. 5 of H. Koch and Bjorn Kornerup, *Den Danske kirkes historie* (Copenhagen: Gyldendal, 1951), pp. 36-40.

[10] Stoeffler, *German Pietism during the Eighteenth Century*, pp. 131-67; J. R. Weinlick, *Count Zinzendorf* (Nashville: Abingdon Press, 1956); E. Beyruether, *Der junge Zinzendorf* (Marburg an der Lahn: Francke-Buchhandlung, 1957); S. Hirzel, *Der Graf und die Brüder: Die Geschichte einer Gemeinschaft* (Gotha: Leopold Klotz, 1935); H. Plitt, *Zinzendorfs Theologie*, 3 vols. (Gotha: Friedrich Andreas Perthes, 1869-74); L. Allen, *Die Theologie des jungen Zinzendorf* (Berlin: Lutherisches Verlaghaus, 1966); H. C. Hahn, *Quellen zur Geschichte der Brüder-Unitat von 1722 bis 1760* (Hamburg: Wittig, 1977).

[11] Bergmann, *Grev Zinzendorf og hans Indsats i Kirkens og Missionens Historie* (Copenhagen: Gyldendal, 1953), pp. 19-24.

Like most Pietists, Zinzendorf was a true Lutheran and orthodox in his beliefs, although reacting at the same time against the rigid spirit of Lutheran orthodoxy. Therefore, the Moravians came to accept the *Augsburg Confession* as a statement of their faith, but they always insisted on the primacy of devotional and moral life over theological formulations. This devotional life was centered on the contemplation of Christ and of his suffering on the cross. In him they found the sum total of theology, for the Divine was not to be known by any natural or philosophical means, but only through revelation in Christ. This assiduous contemplation of Christ led the believer to complete trust in the Lord for the forgiveness of sins, as well as for the whole of life. This was the reason that the Moravians whom Wesley met during a stormy Atlantic crossing so impressed him by their trust in God.

Given their very limited numbers, the Moravians could have been of scant importance for the history of Christianity. However, their significance is out of all proportion to their numbers. Their interest in missions resulted in their spreading the faith to various parts of the world,[12] where they have influenced not only their own direct spiritual descendants, but also other Protestant churches that have existed alongside them. Their impact on Wesley can be seen not only in Wesley himself, but also—although less directly—in the entire Methodist tradition. Through their influence on Friedrich Schleiermacher, they made a significant contribution to nineteenth- and twentieth-century theology.

Wesley and Methodism

While the Pietists and Moravians on the Continent were trying to offer an alternative to cold, propositional orthodoxy, many in England were also finding that the traditional form of Christianity that they had received failed to speak to them and to the masses. It was a time of great movements of population from the rural areas to the cities, to which seeming economic opportunities attracted many among the rural poor. But this produced large masses of unchurched people to whom the formal life and worship of

---

[12] By the end of the eighteenth century, they had sixty-seven missionaries in the West Indies, ten among the Indians of North America, twenty-five in South America, eighteen in Greenland, twenty-six in Labrador, ten in the Cape of Good Hope, and five in India. *Periodical Accounts of the Missions of the Church of the United Brethren Established among the Heathen (1797–1800)*, 2:502.

traditional Anglicanism seemed to have little to say. Anglicans as well as Dissenters seemed content with a bland form of Christianity that rested on ritual and outward observances, but that did little to nurture the faith of the believer. Preaching had often become little more than moral exhortation. To this was added the influence of rationalism—which we shall study in the next chapter—whose consequence was a commonly held "natural theology" that had little to say about Jesus Christ, except perhaps as a moral example.

Therefore, the question being asked in England, although of different origin, was essentially the same as that being asked on the Continent, namely, how can this traditional, seemingly cold Christianity be made to speak to the masses, to whom it says so little? How can the gospel be presented in a simple, yet compelling—and theologically correct—manner?

Answers to this question came from many quarters. What is especially interesting, however, is the fact that most of these sources had resort to devices similar to Spener's *collegia pietatis*. Thus, for instance, in 1678 the first of a series of religious societies was founded in London. The purpose of these societies was not to take the place of the church, but rather to supplement the worship of the church with the devotion, study, and experience of smaller groups. As was the case also with the Pietist groups in Germany, they soon became involved in acts of mercy by which they tried to alleviate the suffering of those caught in the social evil of the times—poverty, imprisonment, lack of roots, etc. A similar phenomenon appeared among the Presbyterians in Scotland, where societies of prayer became quite popular early in the eighteenth century.

It is from one of these small groups of Christians that Methodists derive their name. As early as 1702, Samuel Wesley, John Wesley's father, had organized a religious society in his parish at Epworth. Years later, when John Wesley (1703–1791) and his brother Charles (1707–1788) were students at Oxford, they were members of a small club, originally organized by Charles and others to help one another in their studies.[13] This club, however, soon became similar to the

[13] The bibliography of the Wesleys and their movement is too extensive to review here. See F. Baker, "Wesley and Methodism," *The Duke Divinity School Review*, 37 (1972): 82-83; R. J. Rogal, "The Wesleys: A Checklist of Critical Commentary," *Bulletin of Bibliography*, 28 (1971): 22-35. For older materials, see G. Osborn, *Outlines of Wesleyan Bibliography* (London: Wesleyan Conference Office, 1869).

collegia pietatis advocated by Spener—with the notable difference that this original Methodist club continued being also a center of academic and scholarly activity. As their activities became known among their fellow students, they were dubbed first "the holy club," and eventually "Methodists."

John Wesley, who soon became the leader of the Methodist club, was a very able student whose scholarship earned him the position of Fellow of Lincoln College. He was also an earnest person who had derived from his father, Samuel, a profound commitment to high Anglicanism, and from his mother, Susanna, a similar commitment and an acute sensitivity and deep devotion. He was also a man of boundless energy, a born activist who shared with the Puritans a driving urge to be constantly doing something positive for the service of God. He became an Anglican deacon in 1725, and a priest in 1728. Seven years later, he went as a missionary to the colony of Georgia, and it was on his voyage across the Atlantic, when a storm threatened the ship, that he was able to see the tranquil trust in God of a group of Moravians who were part of the company. In Georgia it soon became obvious that he was unfit for the task which he had undertaken. His punctiliousness in Anglican worship and discipline—often carried beyond what was the actual practice in England—soon gained him a number of enemies. He was almost engaged to be married when he decided to cast lots on the issue—there was always a streak of superstition in him—and on that basis he broke off the relationship. When the woman married another and ceased attending the small religious circle that Wesley—in imitation of his father and of the "holy club"—had founded, he refused to give her communion on the basis that she was not prepared to receive it. This and many similar incidents made him the object of several civil suits. Under such circumstances, convinced that he had failed as a minister, Wesley decided to return to England. Back in Britain, he again established contact with the Moravians, who helped him in his struggle for faith and self-worth. Finally, on May 24, 1738, the famous Aldersgate experience took place: "In the evening I went unwillingly to a society in Aldersgate-Street, where one was reading Luther's preface to the Epistle to the Romans. About a quarter before nine, while he was describing the change which God works in the heart through faith in Christ, I felt my heart strangely warmed. I felt I did trust in Christ, Christ alone for salvation: And an assurance was given me, that he had taken away *my* sins, even *mine*, and saved *me* from the law of sin and death."[14]

As the Moravians had impressed him on a number of occasions, Wesley then decided to travel to Germany, where he met with Zinzendorf and visited Herrnhut. As before, he was moved by the depth of conviction of the Moravians, and by their moral and religious life. However, he was not entirely convinced that he ought to follow them in all things, especially in what to his active temperament seemed an unwarranted quietism, and in their mystical inclinations. For some time after his return to England, he maintained friendly relations with the Moravians. But eventually he was forced to enter into controversy with them, and to distinguish his movement from theirs. From the beginning, he had objected to Moravian quietism and mysticism. In his final break with them he published sections of his Journal in which he had written some of his objections to the Moravians—especially as they existed in England. It is clear that what Wesley here presents is a caricature of Moravian belief. But in any case it may be helpful to quote his words, in order to see the nature of his objections.

> As to faith, you believe,
> 1. There are no degrees of faith, and that no man has any degree of it, before all things in him are become new, before he has the full assurance of faith, the abiding witness of the Spirit, or the clear perception that Christ dwelleth in him.
> 2. Accordingly you believe, that there is no justifying faith, or state of justification, short of this. . . .
>
> Whereas I believe,
> 1. There are degrees in faith; and that a man may have some degree of it, before all things in him are become new; before he has the full assurance of faith, the abiding witness of the Spirit, or the clear perception that Christ dwelleth in him.
> 2. Accordingly, I believe there is a degree of justifying faith (and consequently, a state of justification) short of, and commonly antecedent to, this. . . .

---

[14] *The Works of John Wesley*, photographic reprint of edition of 1872 (Grand Rapids: Zondervan, 1958–59), 1:103.

As to the way to faith, you believe,
That the way to attain it is, to wait for Christ, and be still; that is,
Not to use (what we term) the means of grace;
Not to go to church;
Not to communicate;
Not to fast;
Not to use so much private prayer;
Not to read the Scripture;
(Because you believe, these are not means of grace; that is, do
not ordinarily convey God's grace to unbelievers; and,
That it is impossible for a man to use them without trusting in
them);
Not to do temporal good;
Nor to attempt doing spiritual good.
(Because you believe, no fruit of the Spirit is given by those who
have it not themselves;
And, that those who have not faith are utterly blind, and
therefore unable to guide other souls.)

Whereas I believe,
The way to attain it is, to wait for Christ and be still;
In using all the means of grace.
Therefore I believe it right, for him who knows he has not faith,
(that is, that conquering faith,)
To go to church;
To communicate;
To fast;
To use as much private prayer as he can, and
To read the Scripture;
(Because I believe, these are "means of grace;" that is, do
ordinarily convey God's grace to unbelievers; and
That it is possible for a man to use them, without trusting in
them;)
To do all the temporal good he can;
And to endeavour after doing spiritual good.
(Because I know, many fruits of the Spirit are given by those
who have them not themselves;
And that those who have not faith, or but in the lowest degree,
may have more light from God, more wisdom for the guiding of
other souls, than many that are strong in faith.)[15]

---

[15] *Works,* 1:256-58.

In these objections one can see a great deal of the nature of Wesley's piety and theology. It was not his purpose to set up his "Methodist societies" in opposition to or competition with the Church of England. On the contrary, he always believed that the sacraments administered within that church were valid and effective means of grace, and that those who were members of it, and not of the Methodist movement, were true Christians who did have justifying faith, although they might lack the degree of faith and the assurance that he had found in the Aldersgate experience and that he hoped his preaching and his societies would foster. He saw himself not as preaching the gospel in a heathen country, but rather as working among fellow Christians for the renewal and strengthening of their faith.

Furthermore, although Wesley was a man of profound and sincere devotion, he objected strongly to any mysticism that attempted to bypass the historic means of grace—the sacraments and ministrations of the church as well as the biblical revelation and the incarnation of God in Jesus Christ.

Given these considerations, it was to be expected that Wesley's theology would generally agree with that held by the Church of England. And indeed it did, for Wesley always affirmed the doctrines of the Thirty-nine Articles and commended the *Book of Common Prayer* to his followers. On two points, however, his theology merits special attention. These are his doctrine of the Christian life and his ecclesiology.

Wesley had to clarify his understanding of the Christian life and the process of salvation when he was accused of being an Arminian. To this charge he readily agreed, although objecting to the senseless name-calling between Arminians and Calvinists and making it clear that Arminianism had been much maligned by the defenders of the Synod of Dort—of which he said, with a note of sarcasm, that it was "not so numerous or learned, but full as impartial, as the Council or Synod of Trent."[16] In spite of all the accusations to the contrary, he claimed that neither he nor the Arminians denied original sin or justification by faith. The three points at issue, according to Wesley, were whether predestination is absolute or conditional, whether grace is irresistible, and the perseverance of the saints. In the final

---

[16] *Ibid.*, 10:359.

analysis, Wesley claimed, there is only one issue, that of predestination, for the other two are but its corollaries. The only sense in which Wesley accepted an absolute and unconditional predestination was in the sense that at times God chooses certain individuals for particular tasks, and these cannot be avoided. But in that sense which has to do with eternal salvation, predestination is always conditional, and depends on the person's belief.

> I will tell you in all plainness and simplicity. I believe it [election] commonly means one of these two things: First, a divine appointment of some particular men, to do some particular work in the world. And this election I believe to be not only personal, but absolute and unconditional. Thus Cyrus was elected. . . .
>
> I believe election means, Secondly, a divine appointment of some men to eternal happiness. But I believe this election to be conditional, as well as the reprobation opposite thereto. I believe the eternal decree concerning both is expressed in these words: "He that believeth shall be saved; he that believeth not shall be damned." And this decree, without doubt, God will not change, and man cannot resist.[17]

Unconditional election he could not accept because it would necessarily imply unconditional reprobation, and this seemed to him to be contrary to the witness of Scripture regarding the nature of God. As to the biblical passages that speak of an election "before the foundation of the world," Wesley claimed that, because God is eternal, from the divine perspective all things are seen as happening before they actually take place, as when God calls Abraham "the father of many nations."

This obviously means that, although in some rare cases grace may have been irresistible, this is the exception rather than the norm,[18] and one cannot claim not having been offered irresistible grace as a reason for not believing. The reason for unbelief is precisely resistance to grace.[19]

How, then, did Wesley avoid claiming that the first movement of faith, the *initium fidei,* is on the human side? Such a claim he indeed had to avoid, for otherwise he would have been rightly accused of

---

[17] *Ibid.,* pp. 209-10.
[18] *Ibid.,* 6:280.
[19] *Ibid.,* 10:254-55.

Pelagianism, and of making the grace of God unnecessary or the result of human merit. His response to this question was simply that there is a universal prevenient grace. As this grace is given to all, all are capable—not in themselves, but through the working of grace in them—of accepting the further grace of belief, which will lead them to justifying faith and—eventually—to the assurance of their salvation.

> For allowing that all the souls of men are dead in sin by *nature*, this excuses none, seeing that there is no man that is in a state of mere nature; there is no man, unless he has quenched the Spirit, that is wholly void of the grace of God. No man living is entirely destitute of what is vulgarly called *natural conscience*. But this is not natural: It is more properly termed, *preventing* [i.e., prevenient] *grace*. Every man has a greater or less measure of this, which waiteth not for the call of man. . . . So that no man sins because he has not grace, but because he does not use the grace which he hath.[20]

Another element in Wesley's view of the Christian life that caused some controversy among his contemporaries, and that has been debated by Methodists ever since, was the doctrine of sanctification. Wesley did not understand sanctification as something that happens after justification, or as something having to do with works, while justification has to do with faith. "We are sanctified as well as justified by faith," and "no man is sanctified till he believes: every man when he believes is sanctified."[21] Strictly speaking sanctification is the effect on us of our having been pronounced just, for by a single act God both justifies and begins to sanctify the sinner. But this is not instant sanctification. On the contrary, sanctification is a process, a pilgrimage on which every believer must set out. Its goal is entire sanctification, or Christian perfection. This perfection does not mean that the Christian who has attained it no longer errs, or no longer needs the grace and sustenance that come from God. What it actually means is that the person who has attained it no longer willfully breaks the law of God, but rather acts out of love. Wesley did not believe that every Christian achieves this state during the course of this life. But he did believe that it ought to be preached, both as a

---

[20] *Ibid.,* 6:512.
[21] E. H. Sugden, ed., *Wesley's Standard Sermons* (London: Epworth Press, 1961), 2:453.

preparation for the coming kingdom, and as a way of keeping it constantly as a goal before all believers, so that they might steadily move toward it. For, he insisted, when salvation and the Christian life stand still, they begin to recede.

This brings us to the last element in Wesley's understanding of the Christian life to be discussed here: his view of Christian assurance. Having rejected the doctrine of unconditional predestination, he had to reject the Calvinist theory of the perseverance of the saints, which he saw as simply a corollary of predestination. This doctrine, however, played an important role in Calvinism, and especially in Puritanism, for it assured the faithful that, if they were among the elect, they no longer had to fear for their salvation. A similar role is played in Wesley's theology by the doctrine of Christian assurance, or of the witness of the Spirit. What this means is that the Spirit testifies to the human spirit that we are forgiven and adopted as children of God. There is no doubt that in developing this doctrine Wesley was influenced by his Aldersgate experience, which consisted precisely in being suddenly convinced that his sins were forgiven. But he did not make this particular form of his experience normative for all Christians. "I do not deny that God imperceptibly works in some a gradually increasing assurance of his love; but I am equally certain, he works in others a full assurance thereof in one moment."[22]

This assurance, however, differs from the Calvinistic doctrine of the perseverance of the saints in that Wesley did not believe that it guarantees that the person who has such assurance will remain steadfast. The Calvinistic doctrine of perseverance, being grounded on one's election, guarantees both one's present state of redemption and one's future permanence in that state. Wesley's doctrine of assurance simply tells us that all our sins are forgiven; but it says nothing about the ever-present possibility of falling from grace.

If Wesley had been content to preach these doctrines, the Methodist movement would never have become a separate denomination within the Christian church. Indeed, Wesley did not wish such separation to occur, and always insisted on his membership in the Church of England. Even Wesley's enthusiastic preaching, although regarded askance by Anglican authorities, would not have

---

[22] *Works*, 19·60.

given birth to a separate group. The reasons that led Methodism to become a separate denomination were Wesley's decision to ordain clergy for his followers and his ability as an organizer. At first, he relied on the Anglican clergy to administer the sacraments to his people; and he always insisted that his societies were by no means substitutes for the established church, but were rather complementary to it. But when he found that very few clergymen shared in the movement, and that some leaders had to be sent to the New World to supervise Methodism in the colonies, he and a few others ordained such leaders. His theological and historical justification for such a step was that in the early church there was no distinction between presbyters and bishops, and that therefore, as he was ordained a presbyter, he could ordain others to the same function. His argument was probably correct historically. But in practical terms it meant that the break with the Anglican tradition would not be easy to heal. Thus, while claiming that he had not founded a new church, Wesley took steps that in fact did lead to the founding of such a church.

This ambiguity was later reflected in the ecclesiology of the Methodist Church. The societies that Wesley founded were not churches to him, and therefore he could retain most of his high-church ecclesiology while not necessarily having that ecclesiology give shape to the societies. Methodists were Anglicans, and their church was the Church of England. With the eventual separation of the two bodies, however, Methodism became an organization that closely resembled other free-church traditions and at the same time inherited in the theology of its founder views of the church that were very different from its actual practice. Different attempts at resolving this ambiguity account in part for the difference between English and American Methodism.

Before we leave the Methodist movement, some mention must be made of the contribution of George Whitefield (1714–1770), who was a member of the Oxford "holy club," and whose work was in many ways parallel to Wesley's although the two differed in their theological outlook. The importance of Whitefield for the history of Christian thought lies simply in that, while being in every other respect a Methodist, he nevertheless was staunchly Calvinistic rather than Arminian in his theology—although he himself denied ever having read Calvin.[23] His contemporaries considered him a more persuasive preacher than John Wesley, and his work eventually resulted in the Welsh Calvinistic Methodist Church. His success as a preacher belies the easy assumption that Arminianism is somehow more "preachable" than strict Calvinism.

The Great Awakening

The British colonies in North America saw during the eighteenth century a series of movements that were in many ways similar to the revivals of personal piety that we have just seen in Europe. There was some connection between the two, for George Whitefield was one of the most influential preachers in the New World,[24] and Francis Asbury and others also brought Wesleyan Methodism across the Atlantic. But there were also conditions in the colonies that in many ways prompted answers similar to those of the Pietists, Moravians, and Methodists. Here too religion had become stale and contained within the churches and their orthodoxies, while vast numbers who still had some sort of Christian faith had little to do with organized religion. The response to this situation was a movement similar to its European counterparts in its insistence on personal piety and salvation, but different in that it cut across all denominational lines and thus contributed to the shape of Protestant Christianity in what eventually would become the United States.

In their theology, the various movements included under the common title of "Great Awakening" presented every conceivable shade of opinion. In practice, however, they were similar in their emphasis on conversion, personal experience, private reading of Scripture, and a tendency toward enthusiastic worship.

The most significant theologian of the American Awakening was Jonathan Edwards (1703–1758).[25] As a student at Yale in 1717, Edwards had come under the influence of Locke's philosophy—which we shall discuss in the next chaper—and even after his interest turned to theology, the impact of that English philosopher could be seen in his methodology. Years later he had an experience of

---

[23] S. C. Henry, *George Whitefield: Wayfaring Witness* (Nashville: Abingdon Press, 1957), p. 96.

[24] See J. C. Pollock, *George Whitefield and the Great Awakening* (Garden City, N. Y.: Doubleday, 1972).

[25] D. Levin, ed., *Jonathan Edwards: A Profile* (New York: Hill & Wang, 1969); P. Miller, *Jonathan Edwards* (Toronto: William Sloane, 1949); A. C. McGiffert, *Jonathan Edwards* (New York: Harper, 1932).

conversion similar to that of Wesley, although more centered on the overpowering glory of God. This experience, as well as his upbringing, made him a convinced Calvinist, especially on the doctrine of election, for he felt that unconditional predestination such as was taught by Calvinism necessarily followed from God's sovereignty. As a Congregational minister at Northampton, Massachusetts, and as one of the Awakening's most eloquent orators, he preached the doctrine of divine election as the clue for a proper understanding of the Christian life. His Puritan Calvinism, however, led him to apply the discipline of the church so stringently that he was removed from office by his congregation. During his last years as a pastor, he had written his *Treatise concerning Religious Affections* (1746),[26] in which he attempted to strike a balance between those who condemned the emotional manifestations of the Awakening, and those who attempted to foster these manifestations and exploit them. In order to lead his readers on this matter, he suggested a number of criteria by which those "affections" which were the result of the working of the Spirit could be distinguished from those which were not. After his dismissal from his congregation, he wrote *A Careful and Strict Enquiry into the Modern Prevailing Notions of that Freedom of the Will Which is Supposed to be Essential to Moral Agency, Vertue and Vice, Reward and Punishment, Praise and Blame* (1754).[27] Here he defended unconditional election, which had come to be the trademark of Calvinism. According to him, this election does not destroy freedom, which consists in being able to do what one wills, for what the irresistible grace of God does is precisely to lead the will to a proper choice. Therefore, although one wills because grace acts, one is still free to choose and do that which one wills.

As time passed, the Great Awakening took on more emotional overtones. Although it appeared first among Presbyterians and Congregationalists, it soon spread to Methodists and Baptists, among whom it took root and for whom it became a formative experience. For years to come, and especially among Baptists and Methodists, the experiences of the Awakening would influence much of the life of the churches, and of their understanding of their mission.

---

[26] Ed. J. E. Smith (New Haven: Yale University Press, 1959).
[27] Ed. P. Ramsey (New Haven: Yale University Press, 1957).

XII

The Changing Philosophical Setting

The first chapter of this volume attempted to provide a brief outline of the ferment that existed in Europe at the beginning of the sixteenth century. For obvious reasons, we have centered our attention on the Protestant and Catholic Reformations and on the various theological views that appeared within them. But the great unrest of the sixteenth century could not be contained within the confines of ecclesiastical theology, be it Protestant or Catholic. When the Reformation appeared on the scene many new interests besides the religious were captivating the imagination of Europe. These were basically of two orders: the discovery of the natural world, and the discovery of the powers of the mind. The natural world was increasingly attracting the attention of the sixteenth century. Columbus had opened an entire new world. In the old, new discoveries such as the printing press, the compass, and gunpowder were showing that there were in the universe vast resources that had scarcely begun to be tapped. Thus the sixteenth century saw a growing interest in technology. Leonardo da Vinci was a symbol of the new age in that he was not only a painter and a mathematician, but also a physicist and an engineer. At the same time, others were discovering other powers of the mind. Sometimes this discovery was connected with new technical developments. In some cases it was related to the great wealth of philosophical materials that was being introduced into the Latin world by the Byzantines and by the

318

humanists. Thus, already in the sixteenth century, philosophy was once again moving along its own paths, paying little attention to the debates and dictates of the theologians.

Interest in the world and in the human mind thus constituted two currents of thought that would meet, entwine, and part repeatedly during later generations. These two currents were well represented in the seventeenth century—the first by Galileo and Bacon, and the second by Descartes. As they were influential in the further development of theology, we must pause to discuss them briefly.

Galileo Galilei (1564–1642) was a man entirely devoted to the observation of the universe. This observation, however, was not simply that of the curious naturalist who observes and takes notes. Galileo was a mathematician at heart—in fact, for many years he taught mathematics, first at the University of Pisa and then at Padua—and he firmly believed that "the book of nature is written in mathematical language." According to him, there is no source of knowledge other than experience, which constitutes a veritable revelation of the world to humankind. If there is a seeming error in experience—as when a partially submerged cane seems to be broken—the error is not in the empirical datum itself, but in the manner in which the mind interprets it. Experience, then, must be the source of true philosophy. Galileo had little use for the "philosophers" who attempted to discover the nature of the universe by reading Aristotle. Their "paper world" would never reveal the real world, and the observation of any fool could show the ancient authors to have often been wrong. But experience must be reduced to mathematics in order to be true knowledge. Qualitative language does not describe the world adequately. Only that which can be expressed in quantitative terms is properly understood. This was the basis for the episode in the cathedral of Pisa—which may well be a legend—when the observation of a swinging lamp led Galileo to the conclusion that the movement of a pendulum is always isochronal. The same is true of the observations that he made from the tower of Pisa, regarding the speed of falling bodies. But once one has this quantitative knowledge, one can apply it to the discovery of new knowledge; and thus Galileo invented the telescope, and through his observations concluded that Copernicus was right, and that the earth revolved around the sun. In summary, what Galileo proposed was a strictly empirical and mathematical method for the observation of the universe. This was probably his greatest contribution to the development of modern science.

Francis Bacon (1561–1626) went beyond Galileo in that he conceived of science not only as a means to understand the universe, but also and primarily as a means to rule nature. If one manages to understand the principles that rule natural phenomena, it will be possible to control those phenomena by obeying and applying their principles. The method by which such knowledge is achieved is expounded in the *Novum organum*, which Bacon wrote in opposition to the *Organum* of Aristotle. This was part of a great work that he planned, but never wrote, and that was intended to be a vast encyclopedia of science. The method here proposed is basically that of experimentation. Mere experience is insufficient, for one must observe phenomena in a certain order. Through experimentation—and by means of a very elaborate series of steps—it is possible to discover the "forms" that underlie phenomena.

The main obstacles that one finds in this quest are what Bacon calls "idols." These are of four kinds: idols of the tribe, idols of the cave, idols of the marketplace, and idols of the theater. The first are those which are common to the entire human race, such as the tendency to jump from a few particular instances to general conclusions. The idols of the cave have to do with the particular temperament of each person, for everyone is prone to see things in a particular way. The idols of the marketplace arise because the language used for communication imposes itself on the mind and usurps the place of reality. Finally, the idols of the theater come from earlier philosophical systems and their erroneous and fallacious arguments. Of all these, the ones that Bacon attacks with most vigor are those resulting from received opinions. Why should older opinions be necessarily better? In fact, if one gives the matter some consideration, it will be apparent that the so-called older views are in fact younger, for they are the product of a younger world. As the world becomes older, the new opinions reflect greater maturity and experience and should therefore be preferred to the older views. This can be seen in the manner in which the idols of the theater are still accepted when in fact they are wrong. If it were not for these idols, people would acknowledge that Aristotle was little more than a sophist who was more interested in giving verbal definitions of things than in seeking truth, and that Plato's work is no more than a superstitious mixture of philosophy with theology. If all this false knowledge of antiquity were left behind, humankind could march confidently toward the *New Atlantis*—a mythological island that Bacon conceived as a society benefiting from, and totally devoted to, the discovery of the principles that rule nature.

Although Bacon's methodology was never entirely applied to scientific research, his work—and that of Galileo—is significant in that it shows that late in the sixteenth century, and early in the seventeenth, the foundations were being laid for modern technology. The method and the means may not have been developed yet, but the goals and the implicit values were already present at that time. Furthermore, Bacon's criticism of received knowledge, which was shared by many intellectuals in his time, necessarily led in the direction of seeking new means of inquiry—methods that would not be vulnerable to the criticisms raised against the ancient philosophers. What Bacon attempted in the field of natural phenomena, Descartes would attempt in the field of metaphysics, developing a rationalist idealism as a basis for understanding the whole of reality.

Descartes and the Rationalist Tradition

René Descartes (1596–1650)[1] was, like Galileo, a man of profound curiosity. After having received a traditional scholastic education under the Jesuits, Descartes felt that he must gain wider experience of the world, and to that end he joined the armies of Maurice of Nassau and, later, of Maximilian of Bavaria. While in the Netherlands he met a medical doctor whose studies and experiments in science and mathematics he found fascinating, and from that moment on Descartes would devote a great deal of his time to the study of mathematics and of physical phenomena. It was, however, on the tenth of November, 1619, while he was in a small village in Germany, that he made his great philosophical discovery. He himself describes this experience in terms similar to those used by Augustine in relating his experience in the garden in Milan or by Wesley concerning Aldersgate.[2] Although we do not have a contemporary account of the content of that discovery, one can safely assume that it

---

[1] Besides the general histories of philosophy, and the works of Descartes himself, I have found the following useful: D. Cochin, *Descartes* (Paris: Félix Alcan, 1913); O. Hamelin, *Le système de Descartes* (Félix Alcan, 1911); J. Laporte, *Le rationalisme de Descartes* (Paris: Presses Universitaires de France, 1950).

[2] *Oeuvres de Descartes*, ed. Ch. Adam and P. Tannery (Paris: Léopold Cerf, 1913), 10:179.

was the method that he later outlined and applied in his *Discourse on Method* (1637) and his *Meditations on Philosophy* (1641). That he did not understand his discovery as in any way opposed to Christian doctrine may be seen in the fact that as an act of gratitude he vowed to visit the sanctuary of the Virgin of Loreto. Although he was clearly aware that his philosophy was very different from what he had been taught at the Jesuit school of La Flèche, he was convinced that it was perfectly consonant with the Catholic faith, and he expected that philosophers and theologians alike, being persons of good will, would receive it gladly. He was surprised when the views of Galileo were condemned by the Inquisition, for those views formed much of the background of the *Treatise on the World*, which he had been preparing for publication—and which he then prudently kept to himself. And he was dismayed when his views were so opposed by theologians at Utrecht that in 1642 it was forbidden to teach or discuss them. In subsequent years other universities and centers of learning took similar steps, while Descartes protested and explained his views to no avail.

The method that Descartes proposed consisted of four points. First, not to accept as true anything that has not been clearly proven to be so. Second, to analyze and divide each difficulty found in the way, so as to be able to solve the difficulties in various parts. Third, to order one's thoughts from the simplest to the most complex. Fourth, to make certain that everything is so enumerated and listed that nothing is omitted. These four points, however, can best be understood if one keeps in mind that for Descartes there is no knowledge more certain than mathematical knowledge, for it derives not from empirical observation, which may err, but from the very nature of reason. Mathematical knowledge is true even apart from the physical objects to which it can be applied. Empirical knowledge, on the other hand, is not absolutely certain, for we can all remember occasions on which our senses have deceived us—and, if they have deceived us once, how can we know that they do not deceive us all the time?

Thus the starting point of the Cartesian method—Descartes' name in Latin was Cartesius, and therefore his philosophy is often called Cartesianism—is doubt of all knowledge derived from the senses, combined with the absolute certainty of purely rational knowledge. This he himself shows in the first principle of his method, namely, that nothing is to be believed as true until it has been proven beyond the shadow of a doubt. And this is also the reason that, when attempting to build his own philosophical system, he began by an attitude of universal doubt.

This Cartesian doubt was misunderstood by many of his contemporaries as sheer skepticism. But in fact it differs greatly from what is usually known by that name. His doubt does not stem, as in the case of skepticism, from the notion that all knowledge is doubtful and that there can be no certainty.

On the contrary, he resolves to doubt because he believes that absolute certainty is a possibility, but that such certainty can only be attained by distinguishing between the probable and the indubitable. This is precisely the function of Cartesian doubt, for it serves as a strainer through which only the absolutely certain can pass.

Given this attitude of universal doubt, the philosopher's quest for truth must begin with the mind itself. It is for this reason that Descartes begins evolving his system out of his famous *cogito, ergo sum*—I think, therefore I am. When the mind resolves to doubt all things, there is one thing that it cannot doubt, namely, its own act of doubting. And it is obvious that in order to doubt it must exist.

Characteristically, Descartes then does not go on to attempt to prove the existence of empirical reality. Before he can prove that existence, he must prove the existence of God. This obviously he cannot do by following any of St. Thomas' "five ways," for all these take the existence of contingent beings as their starting point. He therefore follows a path similar to that of St. Anselm, attempting to prove the existence of God on the sole basis of ideas that are certain. But the argument that Descartes offers differs from Anselm's, in that he does not attempt to show that the idea of God logically includes existence. What he does is to look at the idea of God in his mind and then try to discover what can be the origin of that idea. In thus arguing from the contingent—his own idea of God—to the necessary, his argument is similar to that of St. Thomas, and he therefore stands between Thomas and Anselm on this point. His argument is simple, although he repeats it in different ways in various passages.[3] What he says is, in essence, that he discovers within his mind the idea of an infinite and perfect being. This idea he

---

[3] *Oeuvres*, 3:297; 7:34-52; 9:209-11.

attempts to doubt; but he finds that he cannot, for he must explain its existence somehow, and the only way in which the idea of a perfect being can have been placed in his mind is by such a being. His finite mind certainly cannot of itself have conceived such an idea, which is clearly greater than itself. Can one then not claim that the mind has simply brought together several elements, and put them together in a way that does not conform to reality, as in the case when the ideas of a horse and a man are put together to form a nonexistent centaur? Certainly not, for the idea of God is absolutely simple and cannot be explained as a conglomerate of discrete notions. Furthermore, the existence of God can also be proven from the fact that we are somehow able to order our ideas according to their degree of perfection, and if there are degrees there must be an absolute standard, namely, God—and here Descartes approaches the traditional argument *ex gradibus*, although applying it not to things, but rather to ideas.

The *cogito, ergo sum* has already served Descartes to prove the existence of himself as a "thinking thing"—*res cogitans*. But, can he be as certain of the existence of his body? It is clear that the existence of the body—and of the physical world in general—is not a purely rational truth that the mind knows in a direct and indubitable fashion. Are we then condemned to remain in doubt as to the existence of our own bodies and of the world? Absolutely not, for we are now certain of the existence of God, and it is inconceivable that God would induce us to believe such a great falsehood. Thus, interestingly, Descartes proves the existence of the body and the world starting from the existence of the soul and of God.

The most clear conception we can have of our body is its extension, that is, that it occupies space, and has dimensions such as those studied by geometry. Therefore, Descartes refers to the human body as a "thing with extension"—*res extensa*—in contrast to the "thinking thing," which is the soul. What he never clarifies is how these two substances are related to each other. The question, then, is, How can thought act on body, and vice versa? When my mind produces a thought, how does it communicate it to my body? When something happens to my body, how does my mind learn of it? This is the question of the "communication of the substances," which would draw the attention of later Cartesians.

Descartes was always careful not to incur the displeasure of ecclesiastical authority. As we have already said, when he heard that the views of Galileo had been condemned he refrained from publishing his own work, which set forth similar views (he later published some sections of it that he thought would not offend the orthodox). Furthermore, this was a matter not only of prudence, but of profound conviction. Throughout his life he remained a devout man who—except for some connection with theosophic groups —was strictly faithful to orthodox belief. And yet, he and his followers were often regarded askance by ecclesiastical and academic authorities, and his writings were banned from more than one university. The reasons for this should be obvious if one takes into consideration that Descartes was advocating a system in which the final authority was not revelation, but reason. Indeed, within the Cartesian framework, if one believes in the value of historical revelation, this belief is only possible after a rational process that proves that things and events in the physical world can be trusted. Thus, although Descartes himself believed that he was actually showing the rationality of the Christian faith, many saw in the very proof of that rationality the implication that revelation was no longer to be trusted. After him, philosophers tended to attempt to build their entire systems on the basis of reason alone, and theologians often found themselves facing the alternative of either building on the foundations of rationalistic philosophies or claiming that reason by itself was not a valid instrument for knowledge of eternal realities and that the rationalist philosophers were therefore wrong.

Cartesianism soon had many followers throughout Europe. Although most Cartesians were more interested in the physics, mathematics, and physiology of Descartes than in his metaphysics, there were a number of theologians who took up his philosophy as a tool for their endeavors. Adriaan Heerebord and Jacques du Roure tried to present his theses in traditional scholastic form. Among Roman Catholics—and especially among French Oratorians—there were numerous attempts to show substantial agreement between Descartes and Augustine—often by collating texts from both authors. In the Netherlands a number of Protestant theologians saw in Cartesianism the possibility of showing the essential rationality of orthodox Calvinism, especially since a mathematical approach to reality seemed to corroborate the determinism into which Calvin's doctrine of predestination had evolved. The most notable among these was Christoph Wittich, who in 1659 published a treatise in which he sought to demonstrate the agreement of scriptural truth with the "philosophical truth discovered by Descartes."

The most characteristic form that Cartesianism took in theology, however, may be seen in the work of the Oratorian Nicolas de Malebranche (1638–1715),[4] who can hardly be called a Cartesian, for he combined philosophy with a strong mystical bent of Augustinian inspiration. However, as he influenced—and was refuted by—such distinguished French scholars as Bossuet and Fénelon, it was his brand of Cartesianism that became most current in France, and would give the French Catholic Church the particular flavor for which it was noted in the nineteenth century.

Malebranche's mysticism led him to center his entire philosophy on God. Here his most significant contributions were two: his notion that all ideas are known in God, and the claim that God is the only efficient cause of all things. On both of these points he obviously went beyond Descartes. The first means that God is not only the guarantee—which Descartes had already said—but also the object of all knowledge. When we think that two and two make four, it is in God that we see this truth, for it is in the divine light that we see every truth, and God sees what we do.[5] This view he based on his own interpretation of Augustine's theory of illumination. Although this interpretation was historically incorrect, it served to set the tone for a great deal of French mysticism in the eighteenth century.

Malebranche's claim that God is the efficient cause of all things had to do with the question of the communication of the substances, which we have already mentioned as one of the problems with which later Cartesianism had to deal. Descartes had implied that the soul—res cogitans—communicates directly with the body—res extensa. But the manner in which he had contrasted the two made it difficult to see how such communication could take place. Malebranche solved this problem by claiming that the soul and the body communicate not directly with each other, but only through God. When my soul seems to make my body perform an action, what in fact happens is that God, in view of my soul's desire, makes by body

4 A. Cuvillier, Essai sur la mystique de Malebranche (Paris: J. Vrin, 1954); L. Labbas, L'idée de science dans Malebranche et son originalité (Paris: J. Vrin, 1931); B. K. Rome, The Philosophy of Malebranche: A Study of His Integration of Faith, Reason, and Experimental Observation (Chicago: Regnery, 1963); M. E. Hobart, Science and Religion in the Thought of Nicolas Malebranche (Chapel Hill: University of North Carolina, 1982).
5 Recherche de la vérité (éclaircissement 10) Oeuvres, 21 vols. (Paris: J. Vrin, 1962–1970), 3:127-43.

perform the corresponding action. The same is true when my body seems to communicate with my soul, and even when one body seems to act upon another—as in the case of two billiard balls. In all these instances—and in every conceivable instance—God is the efficient cause of every effect. Here again one sees Malebranche's interest in centering everything on God, for he claimed that to attribute efficacy to any secondary cause would grant it some measure of divinity.

How, then, can one avoid the conclusion that there is no order in the universe? How can one explain the fact that there seem to be natural laws, and that similar bodies under similar circumstances seem to react in similar ways, as if those circumstances were the cause of their action? The answer is simple: God is not capricious. On the contrary, God has established an order that will normally direct the divine action upon a creature *on the occasion* of another creature's action. Thus, for instance, God has determined that on the occasion of one body coming to the place occupied by another God will cause that other body to move in a certain way. For this reason, the billiard ball that hits another may be said to be the *occasional cause* of the movement of the other; but the efficient cause is always and only God.

A slightly older contemporary of Descartes was the Englishman Thomas Hobbes (1588–1679),[6] who developed an entirely different sort of rationalistic system. Hobbes, too, wished to construct his philosophy on totally rational bases, but his point of departure was sense perception rather than the ideas that the mind discovers within itself. On this point he was the forerunner of English empiricism, which we shall study later in this chapter. But his emphasis on deductive thought as the goal of science places him near Descartes. In any case, for Hobbes the starting point of his philosophy is that nothing can be perceived by the senses unless there is a "change in motion." That which is just as it was before cannot impress our senses, and therefore cannot be known through them. The laws of motion are inertia, causation, and the conservation of matter. On these laws Hobbes builds a naturalistic system that includes not only

---

[6] F. Brandt, *Thomas Hobbes' Mechanical Conception of Nature* (Copenhagen: Levin & Munksgaard, 1928); T. E. Jessop, *Thomas Hobbes* (London: Longmans, 1960); J. Laird, *Hobbes* (London: E. Benn, 1934); B. Landry, *Hobbes* (Paris: Félix Alcan, 1930); Z. Lubienski, *Die Grundlagen des ethisch-politischen Systems von Hobbes* (Munich: E. Reinhardt, 1932); R. Polin, *Politique et philosophie chez Thomas Hobbes* (Paris: Presses Universitaires de France, 1953); T. A. Spragens, *The Politics of Motion: The World of Thomas Hobbes* (Lexington: University of Kentucky Press, 1973).

physics, but also ethics, psychology, and political theory. For these reasons, he has often been credited with being the forerunner of modern psychology, sociology, and political science. For the history of theology, however, he is significant in that he illustrates the rationalistic mood in his effort to derive all these things from natural knowledge. The entirety of his ethics and political theory, for instance, is grounded on the universal impulse for self-preservation. God he considers to be totally unrelated to true knowledge, for if what the theologians say is true, and there is no change of motion in God, it follows that there is no way in which we can know God. Although with different content, this naturalistic and rationalistic attitude would be common among philosophers throughout the eighteenth century, and would pose a challenge for theology.

Although certainly not a Cartesian, Baruch Spinoza (1632–1677)[7] was deeply influenced by the works of Descartes and, to a lesser degree, of Hobbes. A Jew born in Amsterdam from Portuguese crypto-Jewish parents who had gone to the Netherlands fleeing the Inquisition, Spinoza was a man of profound mystical inclinations. The notion of the supreme and only God, which he had been taught at home and in the synagogue from an early age, continued informing his philosophy long after he had been expelled from the synagogue—on grounds of heterodoxy—in 1656. Spinoza felt that Cartesianism was a good preliminary discipline to his own philosophy, for he agreed with Descartes that the best method of attaining true knowledge was that followed by mathematics. But he carried this mathematical methodology much further than did his French counterpart. In fact, his principal work, *Ethics Proven by the Order of Geometry* (published posthumously in 1677), is composed of a logically connected series of theorems whose demonstration follows the strict principles of geometry.

But his disagreement with Descartes went far beyond this. He felt that Descartes had established an unwarranted distinction between

---

[7] D. Bidney, *The Psychology and Ethics of Spinoza: A Study in the History and Logic of Ideas* (New York: Russell & Russell, 1962); L. Browne, *Blessed Spinoza: A Biography of the Philosopher* (New York: Macmillan, 1932); V. Delbos, *Le spinozisme* (Paris: J. Vrin, 1926); J. Martineau, *A Study of Spinoza* (London: Macmillan, 1883); L. Roth, *Spinoza, Descartes, and Maimonides* (Russell & Russell, 1963); H. H. Joachim, *A Study of the Ethics of Spinoza* (Russell & Russell, 1964); J. A. Picton, *Spinoza: A Handbook to the Ethics* (London: A. Constable, 1907); R. Kennington, *The Philosophy of Baruch Spinoza* (Washington: Catholic University of America Press 1980); A. van der Linde, *Benedictus Spinoza: Bibliographie* (Nieuwkoop: A. de Graaf, 1961).

the *res cogitans* and the *res extensa*. These are not in reality two different substances, but two attributes of a single substance. In fact, all reality is but a single divine substance—and for this reason Spinoza's philosophy is correctly interpreted as the rationalist expression of pantheism. This substance has infinite attributes. Thought and matter are two of these attributes, and the only reason that we believe that they comprise all of reality is that they are the only two that we are equipped to know. God is the one substance of reality, the one nature of all things—which appears as creative nature in what we usually call "God," and as created nature in the world. As for the philosopher—or any human being, for that matter—the goal in life should be no other than so to understand this pervasive reality, and so to be attuned to it, that all passions subside and one is reconciled to one's present condition and destiny. This present condition is not one of freedom, for everything is predetermined, and freedom is no more than an illusion due to our partial perspective on reality. Our destiny consists simply in returning to the One, as a drop of water returns to the ocean.

Gottfried Wilhelm Leibniz (1646–1716),[8] was a man of vast erudition who must be credited with having discovered—independently of Newton—the mathematical principles of integral calculus. His theological work, although much less significant than his philosophy, was geared toward the reunion of Catholics and Protestants, on the basis of that sort of "common-sense theology" which is characteristic of rationalism. His philosophy, on the other hand, seeks to avoid some of the problems of Spinoza, and especially of Cartesianism. What he found objectionable in Spinoza's philosophy was the notion that everything, including the world, happens out of necessity, as the necessary consequence of the divine nature. This—and the closely related doctrine of pantheism—Leibniz found unacceptable. Against Spinoza, Leibniz proposed a distinction

---

[8] R. W. Meyer, *Leibnitz and the Seventeenth-century Revolution* (Cambridge: Bowes & Bowes, 1952); C. A. Thilo, *Leibniz's Religionsphilosophie* (Langensalza: Hermann Beyer and Söhne, 1906). Of special interest is Bertrand R. Russell, *A Critical Exposition of the Philosophy of Leibniz with an Appendix of Leading Passages* (London: G. Allen & Unwin, 1937); H. G. Frankfurt, ed., *Leibniz: A Collection of Critical Essays* (Garden City, N.Y.: Doubleday, 1972); R. McRae, *Leibniz: Perception, Apperception and Thought* (Toronto: University of Toronto, 1976); J. Jalabaert, *La théorie leibnizienne de la substance* (New York: Garland, 1985).

between "truths of reason" and "truths of fact." A truth of reason is
necessary truth, for the predicate is contained in the subject. Thus,
for instance, when I say that the angles in a triangle add up to one
hundred eighty degrees, what I am doing is simply making explicit
what was already contained in the notion of a triangle, and therefore
this is a necessary truth, whose contrary is impossible. But when I say
"this particular thing exists thus and thus," that is a truth of fact. It is
contingent truth, for its contrary is quite thinkable. Furthermore, in
the actual world of reality we never encounter such nude necessity as
that implied by truths of reason. Truths of reason belong in the field
of logic, whereas truths of fact belong in the field of reality.
Therefore, the actual order of the world is not a necessary order.
The reason for the existence of the world—and of this particular
world—is not a *necessary reason*. God could just as logically have made
another world, or no world at all. But there is a *sufficient reason* for the
existence of the world, namely, that God willed to make the best of all
possible worlds, and this is it. In consequence, the relationship
between God and the world, while being rational, is not necessary—
and thus Spinoza's pantheism is rejected.

Leibniz then turns to the familiar Cartesian problem of the
communication of the substances. This he solves by the twofold
device of denying that there are two different sorts of substances,
and denying also that there is any communication between body and
soul. There are not two sorts of substance, because all that exists is
spiritual. Matter is no more than a conglomerate of individual
substances, each of which is spiritual. Each of these substances, which
Leibniz calls *monads,* is both complete and self-contained. As Leibniz
says, monads have no windows; they do not communicate with other
monads. But each of them contains a representation, from its own
perspective, of the entire universe—that is, of all other monads. God
is a monad, although differing from other monads, first, in that God
is the only one whose existence is a necessary truth—and here
Leibniz offers his own version of the ontological argument—and,
second, in that God has a universal perspective over the entire
universe.

If these monads "do not have windows," and therefore cannot
communicate with one another or be influenced from the outside, it
follows that what we usually call "communication of the substances"
is in reality a pre-established harmony.

We have now to inquire how the soul is conscious of the motions of its body, since we can see no way of explaining by what channels the activity of an extended mass can pass into an indivisible being. Ordinary Cartesians declare that no explanation of this union can be given. . . . For my part I explain it in a natural way. From the notion of substance or concrete being in general, which declares that its present state is always a natural consequence of its preceding state, it follows that the nature of each individual substance, and consequently of every soul, is to express the universe. Each has been from the first created such that, in virtue of the laws of its own nature, it must happen that it is in harmony with what takes place in bodies, and especially in its own body. We need not then be surprised to find that it has the power of representing to itself the pinprick, when this takes place in its body.[9]

In another passage, Leibniz argues that the soul and the body are to be seen as two clocks, both constantly keeping the same time. The theory of the direct communication of the substances would be like imagining that the two clocks must be connected with each other in order to be able to keep the same time. The theory of occasional causation by God would be like saying that the clockmaker has to tamper continually with the clocks. The theory of pre-established harmony simply affirms that God is like a perfect clockmaker, whose creation is such that each part keeps perfect pace with the other, even though there is no real connection between them.[10] Thus, "according to this system bodies act as if (to suppose the impossible) there were no souls, and souls act as if there were no bodies, and both act as if each influenced the other."[11]

Given his theory of monads, so that the human soul has no windows through which it can learn from the outside world, it follows that for Leibniz all ideas are innate. This includes not only the "truths of reason"—which Descartes and the entire Cartesian tradition would agree are indeed innate—but also the "truths of fact." The mind learns nothing through experience, for it cannot have any experience of anything outside itself. Rather, what seems to

---

[9] From a letter to Arnauld (1687), quoted in R. Latta, ed., *The Monadology and other Philosophical Writings* (London: Oxford University Press, 1951), p. 200.

[10] "Third explanation," in *Monadology* (ed. Latta, pp. 333-34).

[11] *Monadology*, 81 (ed. Latta, p. 264).

be a perception of the outside world is no more than the unfolding of the mind's own nature, as it was created by God. From this perspective, Leibniz—who did not consider himself a Cartesian—was the culmination of the trend begun by Descartes, which sought to discover true knowledge in the innate ideas to be found within the mind, rather than in the world of sense experience.

In a sense, the philosophy of Leibniz is the natural conclusion of the methodology proposed by Descartes. Descartes set out by doubting the existence of all reality, and then proving that he could not deny the reality of his own thinking self. The most typical characteristic of the tradition of philosophical idealism that he founded is that the mind and its ideas become the primary reality. Descartes then went on to show, on the basis of the idea of God in our mind, that the sensory world and the body do indeed exist. But those who followed his inspiration always had difficulties explaining how it was that the two realities—the mind and the body—communicate with each other. Malebranche proposed his theory of God as the occasional cause of all motion. Spinoza suggested that in fact mind and body are but two attributes of a single all-encompassing being. Now Leibniz cut the Gordian knot by simply saying that there is no such communication. Monads have no windows. What appears to us as an impression of the outer world on our minds is no more than the unfolding of what was already in us. Therefore, strictly speaking, there is no knowledge, for knowledge implies a connection between the known and the knower. Such was the impasse in which the tradition of idealism found itself with Leibniz, and out of which it would not come until it found new directions in the work of Kant and his successors. But before we turn to these later philosophers we must pause to consider the work of the empiricists, who attempted to offer an alternative to idealism—and who, with Hume, found themselves in an impasse similar to the one in which idealism found itself with Leibniz.

The British Empiricist Tradition

At the beginning of this chapter, we pointed out that one of the factors giving birth to rationalism was the plethora of discoveries that were taking place during the modern age. These discoveries showed that in many ways the structures of reality correspond to the structures of the mind, and thus served as an inspiration for the Cartesian method, which attempted to ground the knowledge of the world on the knowledge of the mind. But these discoveries also showed that careful observation of natural phenomena serves to correct many misconceptions otherwise accepted by the mind as true. This was the thrust of the work of Francis Bacon, whom we have already discussed. We have also shown how Thomas Hobbes attempted to build a rationalist system on the basis of sense perception. Both Bacon and Hobbes exemplify the early stages of that empiricism which would later become the British alternative to Continental idealism. This empiricism would exert a great influence on British theology, which would repeatedly attempt to build rational systems on the basis of the empiricists' understanding of reason. Later, as we shall see, it also exerted a very significant influence on Continental theology—although this was mostly an indirect influence through Kant and his attempt to provide an alternative to the cul-de-sac in which empiricism found itself with David Hume.

Although British empiricism had its forerunners in Bacon and Hobbes, John Locke (1632 1704)[12] is usually credited with giving that system its most cogent expression. This he did in 1690, in his *Essay Concerning Human Understanding*. Here he asserted that, apart from perceptions, the mind is like a clean slate, for there are no innate ideas. The notion of innate ideas, espoused by Descartes and his followers, had recently found new and forceful expression in the work of the Cambridge Platonists. Ralph Cudworth (1617–1688), for instance, had published in 1678 *The True Intellectual System of the Universe*,[13] in which he attempted to show that the idea of God, the basic moral principles, and the notions of freedom and responsibility are all innate, and that Christianity is therefore the most rational religion. Locke did believe in the reasonableness of Christianity; but he had a different view of reason itself, and he believed that the very notion of reason and its function should be clarified before attempting to show that reasonableness. Attempts to found systems on so-called innate ideas are doomed to failure, for they accept

---

[12] R. I. Aaron, *John Locke* (3d ed., Oxford: Clarendon Press, 1971); K. MacLean, *John Locke and English Literature of the Eighteenth Century* (New York: Russell & Russell, 1936). His works have been published in four volumes (London: W. Straham, 1777). The *Essay* is available in countless editions.
[13] Reprint (London: R. Priestley, 1820).

unproven principles as necessarily valid. On the contrary, one must begin by rejecting all preconceived and unproven notions—which is what "innate" ideas really are—and recognize that all knowledge comes from experience. This does not mean, however, that all knowledge comes from the external information provided by the senses, for there is also an inner experience of ourselves and of the functioning of our own minds.

> Let us then suppose the mind to be, as we say, white paper, void of all characters, without any ideas; how comes it to be furnished? . . . To this I answer in one word, from experience; in that all our knowledge is founded, and from that it ultimately derives itself. Our observation employed either about external sensible objects, or about the internal operations of our minds, perceived and reflected on by ourselves, is that which supplies our understandings with all the materials of thinking. These two are the fountains of knowledge, from whence all the ideas we have, or can naturally have, do spring.[14]

This is not to say that Locke was a skeptic on religious matters. On the contrary, he believed that, even while doing away with innate ideas and first principles, he could still hold the essential doctrines of traditional Christianity. Moreover, ridding theology of innate ideas and showing that all knowledge must be grounded on experience would help restore Christianity to its original reasonable simplicity and do away with the endless and futile speculations of all sorts of theological scholasticism. Therefore, he attempted to show that the doctrine of the existence of God, for instance, would not suffer from his denial of innate ideas. Naturally, his argument for the existence of God took the form of the traditional cosmological argument—that is, he began with things perceived and moved back to their original cause. Furthermore, Locke did not deny revelation as a source of knowledge. What he meant by "experience" was not only ordinary sense experience. Revelation is also an empirical reality, not in the sense that it can be controlled and examined in a laboratory—which in any case is not what Locke meant by "empirical"—but in the sense that it, too, comes to humankind as an experience.

From this perspective, Christianity—once divested of all its

---

[14] *Essay*, 2. 1. 2.

scholastic baggage—can be shown to be the most reasonable form of religion. Christianity consists essentially in belief in God and in Christ as the Messiah, who has been sent to reveal God and God's will for us. This divine mission of Christ was attested by his many miracles—and Locke did not deny miracles, although he showed clearly that the perception of a miracle as a revelatory occasion requires certain conditions in the beholder.

Locke's attempt to simplify Christianity while at the same time retaining that which he thought was essential to it had a very practical purpose. He saw his nation divided by theological controversies dealing with what seemed to him insignificant and often inscrutable matters. Therefore, to show the futility of theological inquiry beyond certain limits, and to define the essence of Christianity, seemed to him a very important task in the process of reconciling the nation, and Christians within it. This can be seen most clearly in his *Letters concerning Toleration*, where he advocated religious freedom for all except Catholics and atheists—whom he considered subversive to the state.

The empiricism that Hobbes and Locke advocated in philosophy found theological expression in Deism.[15] In this context, the term does not mean, as it later came to mean, the view that, while there is a God, this God is not concerned with present human affairs. It means, rather, the attempt to reduce religion to its basic, most universally held, and most reasonable elements. In this sense, the main forerunner of Deism was Lord Herbert of Cherbury (1538–1648), who rejected the notion of special revelation and attempted to show that all religions have five points in common: the existence of God, the obligation to worship the Divine, the moral character of this worship, the need to repent for sin, and an afterlife of reward and punishment. These were the basic tenets of the English Deists of the eighteenth century, whose hand was strengthened by Locke's criticism of dogmatic theology, as well as by his insistence on the reasonableness of Christianity.

The Deists, however, went far beyond attempting to show the reasonableness of Christianity. Their theme was the reasonableness

---

[15] J. Orr, *English Deism: Its Roots and Its Fruits* (Grand Rapids: Eerdmans, 1934); P. Gay, *Deism: An Anthology* (Princeton: Van Nostrand, 1968); W. L. Craig, *The Historical Argument for the Resurrection of Jesus during the Deist Controversy* (Lewiston, N.Y.: E. Mellen, 1985).

of natural religion, to which all religion must conform. Inasmuch as Christianity agrees with natural religion, it is true and reasonable; but when it attempts to add an element of special or positive revelation, it lapses into superstition. Such was the view expressed by John Toland (1670–1722) in his book *Christianity not Mysterious*, where he attempted to show that all that is valuable in Christianity can be understood by the human mind, that revelation is not necessary, and that all the elements of mystery to be found in traditional Christianity are either borrowed from paganism or inventions of the clergy. Similarly, Matthew Tindal (1655–1733) wrote a book, *Christianity as Old as Creation*, in which he claimed that the purpose of the gospel was not to bring an objective redemption—not even to give a new revelation—but simply to show that there is a universal natural law that is the basis and content of all religion, and thereby to free humankind from superstition.

The supposedly universal religion of the Deists was in fact a selection of those traditional Christian doctrines which they found most congenial, and which they believed could be supported by the proper use of reason. Thus, for instance, they often proved the existence of God by the order of causation—something that traditional theologians had been doing for a long time—and the God whose existence they thus proved turned out to be very similar to the God of Christian orthodoxy. Likewise, they believed that they could show the soul to be immortal, and that they could prove retribution after death for sin and virtue. Their ethics owed a great deal to Stoicism, in which the notion of natural law had already played a very important role; and the ethical injunctions of the New Testament were therefore interpreted in terms of the Stoic theory of natural law—for which in any case there was ample precedent within the Christian tradition.

Although it was in Britain that Deism found its most fertile ground, it soon had spread to other parts of the world. It had a formative influence in the early days of the United States through such figures as Benjamin Franklin, Thomas Jefferson, and Thomas Paine—who declared "I believe in one God and no more."[16] In France, it took a peculiar character in the person of Voltaire, who

---

[16] G. A. Koch, *The Religion of the American Enlightment* (New York: Thomas Y. Crowell, 1968); H. M. Morais, *Deism in Eighteenth Century America* (New York: Russell and Russell, 1960).

poked fun at the English Deists for claiming to know more than is humanly possible.

Deism drew numerous attacks from those who saw it as a threat to the Christian faith. Most of these attacks did not deal with the arguments and objections of the Deists, but simply resorted to biblical revelation as a way of refuting them. It was Joseph Butler (1692–1752) who, in his *Analogy of Religion,* offered the most cogent response from the point of view of orthodoxy.[17] In the first part of this work, Butler dealt with natural religion. Here he agreed with the Deists, and even repeated their arguments for the existence of God, the immortality of the soul, reward and punishment after death, etc. It was in the second part, which dealt with revealed religion, that Butler attempted to show that the Deists erred in rejecting the data of revelation. Here he did not try to prove that the content of revelation is essentially reasonable. Rather, he conceded that there are difficulties in the notion of a special revelation; but he then added that there are also difficulties in the view that the universe is a coherent and orderly system. In both cases one must be guided by probabilities. All life is guided by this sort of probability, and in like fashion our trust in revelation must follow the same path. Having thus reinstituted revelation, Butler went on to show that there were a number of elements in Christianity that the Deists either rejected or ignored, but that were fundamental to true religion. Butler's book soon became popular as an instrument for refuting the Deists. Such attempts to refute Deism took the form of a "rational supernaturalism," in which it was hoped to prove by rational argument that the Deists were wrong, and that reason forces us to posit the supernatural, and in particular the doctrines of creation and revelation, and the miracles of the New Testament. Chief among the exponents of this position was William Paley (1743–1805), who popularized the argument that the complexity of creation points to a Creator, just as a watch requires that there be a watchmaker.[18] Although such arguments became popular at once, and were used well into the nineteenth and even in the twentieth centuries, they

---

[17] W. E. Gladston, *Studies Subsidiary to the Works of Bishop Butler* (Oxford: Clarendon Press, 1896); E. C. Mossner, *Bishop Butler and the Age of Reason: A Study in the History of Thought* (New York: Macmillan, 1936); W. J. Norton, *Bishop Butler: Moralist and Divine* (New Brunswick, N. J.: Rutgers University Press, 1940).

[18] See D. L. LeMahieu, *The Mind of William Paley: A Philosopher and His Age* (Lincoln: University of Nebraska, 1976).

soon were put aside by intellectuals who realized the full impact of Kant's work.

The most severe blow to Deism, however, came not from the theologians who opposed it, but from the philosopher David Hume (1711–1776).[19] Taking Locke's empiricism as his starting point, Hume carried it to its final consequences, and in so doing showed the inadequacies of empiricism itself. In his *Inquiry Concerning Human Understanding*, Hume agreed with the empiricist tradition in that nothing can be known that has not previously been experienced. The mind is a clean slate in which there are no innate ideas. But this then means that we do not really know a number of things whose existence we take for granted. In particular, we know neither causality nor substance. We have never experienced an event causing another. What we have experienced is that, in the past, a certain event has always been followed by another particular event. We then tell ourselves that, as event A is the cause of event B, another event similar to A will result in something similar to B. Here we err on two counts. First, we have not really seen event A causing event B. All that we have experienced is a coincidence of the two events, and never a connection. Second, we presuppose the future continuation of an order—and that is obviously something that we have not experienced. Causality, therefore, may be a useful category in daily life—indeed, we could not order our lives without taking it for granted—but it is neither an empirical reality nor a rational certainty. Similarly, substance is something that we have never experienced, but that we however take for granted. All that we perceive is a series of impressions—size, color, smell, etc.—and we then attribute all these to a "thing" or substance that we have never experienced. I may well perceive qualities such as size, color, etc.; I may also perceive that there is a coincidence of time and space among them; and then I posit a substance X, of which I say that it smells thus, has such size, etc. Once again, it may be absolutely necessary in our daily lives to posit the existence of such substances. But let no one claim knowledge of a substance, for knowledge comes from experience, and no one has ever experienced nor can ever

[19] E. C. Mossner, *The Life of David Hume* (London: Thomas Nelson, 1955); H. H. Pierce, *Hume's Theory of the External World* (Oxford: Clarendon Press, 1940); V. C. Chappell, *Hume* (Garden City, N.Y.: Doubleday, 1966); J. H. Noxon, *Hume's Philosophical Development: A Study of His Methods* (Oxford: Clarendon, 1973); B. Stroud, *Hume* (London: Routledge and Kegan Paul, 1977).

experience substance. Furthermore, this is true not only of substances supposedly related to outer perceptions, but also of the mind. We have never perceived our own minds. What we have perceived are a number of operations that we ascribe to a supposed substance called "mind."

The significance of Hume is twofold, for he showed at once the difficulties inherent in Deism and the impossibility of a purely empiricist epistemology.

Hume sounded the death knell for Deism by pointing out that the arguments by which it attempted to prove the reasonableness of natural religion were not as rational as they had originally seemed. The cosmological argument for the existence of God, for instance, was based on the notion of causality, which Hume now showed to be little more than a convenient fiction. And the arguments for the immortality of the soul, based as they were on the notion of the soul as an immaterial substance, lost a great deal of their power when the very notion of substance was brought into question.

As to empiricism, Hume played with regard to it a similar role to that played by Leibniz with regard to the early stages of idealism: he carried it to an impasse. If it is true that we can experience neither substance nor causality, and that thought is impossible without such categories, it is obvious that a strictly empiricist epistemology is inadequate as an explanation of human cognition. The task of leading philosophy out of the difficulties in which it found itself with Hume's empiricism, as well as with the idealism of Leibniz, would be left to Immanuel Kant.

Kant and His Significance for Modern Theology

Immanuel Kant (1724–1804)[20] lived his entire life in East Prussia, mostly in the city of Königsberg. The provincialism of his life makes the universal scope of his work astounding. He drew from widely different sources throughout Europe, including the philosophies of

---

[20] E. Caird, *The Critical Philosophy of Immanuel Kant* (Glasgow: J. Maclehose & Sons, 1909); R. Kroner, *Kant's Weltanshauung* (Chicago: University of Chicago Press, 1956); W. Schultz, *Kant als Philosoph des Protestantismus* (Hamburg: Herbert Reich, 1960); H. J. de Vleeschauwer, *The Development of Kantian Thought: The History of a Doctrine* (London: Thomas Nelson, 1962); R. M. Wenley, *Kant and His Philosophical Revolution* (Edinburgh: T. & T. Clark, 1910); C. D. Broad, *Kant: An Introduction* (Cambridge: University Press, 1978); E. Cassirer, *Kant's Life and Thought* (New Haven: Yale, 1981); H. E. Allison, *Kant's Transcendental Idealism: An Interpretation and Defense* (New Haven: Yale, 1983). Of special interest is Martin Heidegger, *Kant and the Problem of Metaphysics* (Bloomington: Indiana University Press, 1962).

Hume and Leibniz, the physics of Newton, and the religiosity of the Pietists. He then bound these together in an epistemology and critique of earlier philosophy that would in its turn change the thought patterns of succeeding generations in an equally wide variety of contexts.

Like many of his contemporaries, Kant was initially influenced by the rationalism of Descartes and Leibniz. But, as he would later say, he was awakened from his "dogmatic slumber" by Hume.[21] He could not accept the skepticism that had been Hume's conclusion. On the other hand, he agreed with Hume that experience can never know causality and substance. Furthermore, he soon discovered that these two were not the only elements of knowledge that could not be accounted for by experience. He then proceeded to list these elements and to seek an explanation for them. The results of this search he set down in his monumental *Critique of Pure Reason* (1781)[22] and in the *Prolegomena to Any Future Metaphysics* (1783).

Kant accepted the empiricist claim that all the data of knowledge are derived from experience. He also saw, with Hume, that one can never experience the very being of an object—what he termed the "noumenon," in contradistinction to the "phenomena." All that is ever given to us by sense perception is a series of phenomena. These, however, do not come to us in an organized fashion, for to claim such order in the universe would be to fall prey once again to the objections that Hume had raised. How, then, can one explain the transition from the chaotic data of the senses to the ordered and significant idea that we call knowledge?

Such explanation cannot be found in the innate ideas that Cartesianism and other forms of idealism advocated. Nor can it be found in the empiricist notion of the mind as a blank slate. The significance of Kant's philosophy lies precisely in having paid heed to the valid points raised by both sides, and then having offered his own unique solution. This solution consisted in asserting that, while all the data of knowledge have an empirical origin, there are structures in the mind itself that it must necessarily employ in receiving and organizing such data. The mind can know phenomena only by placing them in the basic structures of time and space. Time and

---

[21] *Prolegomena to Any Future Metaphysics* (Indianapolis: Bobbs-Merrill, 1950), p. 8.
[22] He published a revised edition in 1787.

space are not to be found "out there," as objects of knowledge. They are rather within us, as innate patterns in which the chaotic data of the senses are organized. If there are phenomena that do not fit these patterns, the mind can never know them, for they fall outside the range of human cognition and experience—like the high-pitched dog whistle that the human ear cannot hear. Furthermore, besides time and space, there are other structures of cognition, which Kant calls "categories." The categories are twelve, divided into four groups: of quantity (unity, plurality, and totality), of quality (reality, negation, and limitation), of relation (substance, cause, and community), and of modality (possibility, existence, and necessity). These are basic structures present in every human mind. They are universal and unalterable.

What sense perception offers to the mind ought not to be called "experience." The senses provide no more than an amorphous jumble of perceptions, with no relationship among themselves. "Experience consists in the synthetical connection of phenomena (perceptions) in consciousness, so far as this connection is necessary."[23] Experience is the result of the process by which the mind orders the data of perception. Had Kant lived two centuries later, perhaps he would have used the illustration of a computer, into which certain structures are programmed. This computer is capable of receiving, organizing, and employing various sorts of data furnished to it, but only to the extent that such data are compatible with its program. There are therefore very significant limitations to the human mind—limitations given by its very structure. But there is also a sense in which the mind, as Kant understands it, is given a much more positive and creative role than the empiricists had been willing to grant to it.

Kant's philosophy had enormous implications for the future development of theology as well as of philosophy. In the field of philosophy, his work has been compared with the Copernican revolution in astronomy. The theological significance of his philosophy went far beyond what he himself foresaw—and to that significance we shall have occasion to return. First, however, we must take note of what he did actually write in the field of theology, for on

---

[23] *Prolegomena to Any Future Metaphysics*, p. 52.

this score his work, more than the beginning of a new era, is the culmination of eighteenth-century rationalism. Because he did approach his theological undertakings with the same systematic thoroughness with which he approached the question of epistemology, his theological thought deserves some attention here, as a cogent expression of theological rationalism.

In typical rationalistic fashion, Kant sees religion as having the sole function of assisting in the moral life. This does not mean that religion is the source of our knowledge of moral responsibility. To claim such a function for religion would imply that those who are not religious may be excused if their moral life leaves something to be desired. The basic principle of morality, which Kant calls "the categorical imperative," is universally known. It simply tells us that the principle of our actions must be such that we would be willing to see those principles raised to the level of universal rules for all humankind. Reason, and not religion, is the source of our knowledge of this imperative. The function of true religion is to aid in the fulfillment of this obligation. Whatever in religion detracts from this, or is not aimed toward it, is mere superstition. Furthermore, true religion is universal and natural religion. It is based not on a particular or historical revelation, but rather on the very nature of human life.

In a sense, this true religion is rational. But this does not mean that its tenets can be demonstrated by reason. When it comes to religious matters, such as the existence of God, the immortality of the soul, and the freedom of the self, pure reason can reach no more than antinomies—that is, situations in which both the affirmation and the negation seem to be equally rational. The reason for this is that these are matters on which there are no empirical data, and therefore there can be no knowledge in the strict sense. And yet, there are valid reasons for affirming the existence of God, the immortality of the soul, and the freedom of the self. The ground for such affirmations is to be found beyond the limits of pure reason, in what Kant calls "practical reason." In his *Critique of Practical Reason* (1788), Kant argued that there are certain tenets that must be regarded as true because they are the foundation of the moral life. Therefore, it is practically rational to affirm the existence of God as the judge of moral actions, the afterlife of the soul as the occasion for retribution, and the freedom of the self as a responsibile agent. These constitute the core of true, natural religion, of which Christianity is an expression.

Although Christianity is an expression of natural religion, it is also a historical, particular religion. It has certain characteristics that no other religion possesses. Jesus of Nazareth did not found a religion. The true religion, being natural and universal, cannot be founded by any one person. Jesus simply taught this true religion. He did, however, found a church. Christianity is the true religion combined with ecclesiastical, historical elements that were meant to be solely geared to the fulfillment of the universal ethical vocation. These ecclesiastical elements include such "means of grace" as private prayer, churchgoing, baptism, and communion. Proper private prayer helps us to consider our duty, and strengthens our resolve to perform it. Churchgoing places us within the context of a fellowship devoted to true religion, and also gives public witness to the need for serious moral commitment. Baptism is the initiatory act by which we join the fellowship. And communion maintains and strengthens the bonds of community within the church. All of these, when properly used, are very helpful to the moral life; but they must never be allowed to become ends in themselves.

The extent to which his moral interest determines Kant's understanding of religion may be seen in the manner in which he deals with the subject of grace. He does have a concept of grace, which he believes to be necessary, for otherwise those who have sinned would come to the conclusion that any attempt to correct their lives would be pointless. Grace thus assures the believer that all evil actions performed before the decision to follow the moral life can be counted as forgiven. Also, even after that decision, no life is perfect, and therefore grace plays a role here assuring us that if we do our utmost God will provide for our deficiencies, and our reward will not be lost. This moralistic understanding of grace, so similar to that against which Luther was protesting, results in the assertion that "it must be inculcated painstakingly and repeatedly that true religion is to consist not in the knowing or considering of what God does or has done for our salvation but in what we must do to become worthy of it."[24]

---

[24] *Religion within the Limits of Reason Alone*, 3. 2. English translation by T. M. Greene and H. H. Hudson (New York: Harper, 1960), p. 123. Cf. R. M. Green, *Religious Reason: The Rational and Moral Basis of Religious Belief* (New York: Oxford University Press, 1978).

The impact of Kant's work on the later development of philosophy and theology was enormous. Even in the field of theoretical physics, Albert Einstein has paid tribute to Kant's influence on his thought.[25]

The first thing to be said about Kant's importance for theology is that his work spelled the end of the shallow and facile rationalism that had been so dominant during the preceding generations. By claiming that the mind cannot pierce beyond the phenomena to the noumenon, he brought into question all language about substance, God, the soul, freedom, etc. Furthermore, on such issues as the existence of God, the immortality of the soul, and moral freedom, he showed that the mind can reach two sets of contradictory conclusions, and that the reason for this is that in such cases the mind is attempting to grapple with questions that lie beyond its grasp. All the traditional arguments attempting to prove the existence of God seemed to have lost their value. Therefore, that Deism which we found flourishing in England in the eighteenth century was shown to be rationally as questionable as any appeal to revealed truth. This in turn meant that a number of options were open to later thinkers on such matters.

The first and most obvious option was to attempt to ground religion on some faculty of the mind other than pure reason. Kant himself, in his *Critique of Practical Reason* and in *Religion within the Bounds of Reason Alone,* followed this direction. For him, the proper locus of religion was not the purely rational, but the ethical. Humans are by nature moral beings, and that morality argues in favor of the existence of God, the immortality of the soul, and the freedom of the self. What Kant has done therefore is simply to attempt to salvage something of the rationalist tradition in religion, and to do so by appealing not to pure reason, but to practical or moral reason. In the nineteenth century, some—notably Ritschl and his school—would follow this lead, attempting to ground religion on moral values. Others, while rejecting the attempt to base religion on ethics, would still try to find some locus in the human mind different from both speculative and moral reason. In this sense, Schleiermacher may be seen as a response to Kant.

The second option was to return to revelation. If pure reason is

---

[25] "Remarks concerning the Essays Brought Together in This Co-operative Volume," in P. A. Schilpp, ed., *Albert Einstein: Philosopher-Scientist* (Evanston, Ill.: The Library of Living Philosophers, 1949), p. 674.

shown to be incapable of dealing with the most important religious questions, it can no longer point its finger at those who affirm belief in divine revelation. Reason can no longer be the supreme judge. Ultimately, it is a question of a decision of the will. If one opts for belief in revelation, reason can no longer declare that such belief is untenable. If, on the other hand, one opts for disbelief, there is nothing reason can do to prove the validity of revelation. This was the option followed by Søren Kierkegaard in the nineteenth century, and by Karl Barth in the twentieth. And yet, after Kant this could no longer be a simplistic return to earlier theological formulations. If, as Kant had shown, the mind plays an active role in knowledge in such a way that it actually shapes and determines what we can know, it follows that it also plays a role in that type of cognition which is connected with revelation. Therefore, the nature of revelation is no longer determined by God alone. We, the recipients, are also shapers of revelation, not in the sense that we create it, but in the sense that revelation will always be God speaking in human terms. The Godhead itself—as any noumenon—cannot be known. God can be known only in revelation. It is obvious that there is a great affinity between this and Luther's theology of the cross—and therefore we should not be surprised that there has been a revival of studies on Luther during the last hundred years.[26]

The third option was to agree with Kant that the mind plays an active role in knowledge, but then to extend this by asserting that rationality is the very nature of things—that the universe and its history behave like a vast cosmic mind. This was the route followed by Hegel and German idealism.

We thus come to the end of our very rapid survey of the changing philosophical setting that will be the background of nineteenth-century theology. This survey must needs be limited. And yet, it should suffice to show the origin and importance of the one great issue with which modern theology would be forced to struggle. The philosophical evolution that we have described brought into question, in the name of reason, the traditional view of Christianity as divinely revealed. Yet, toward the end of the eighteenth century that very reason began questioning its own presuppositions.

---

[26] It is interesting to point out the parallel between Kant's critique of earlier philosophy, and the nominalists' critique of earlier scholasticism. Given that parallel, Luther and Barth can be seen as similar responses to similar situations.

Rationalism, like the French Revolution, was devouring its own children. How, then, are we to understand the human situation, and what is the place of Christianity in relation to it? Have we surpassed the religious state of humanity, and has all religion thus become obsolete? Or is there some dimension to being human that requires religion, in spite of all our progress and our doubts about dogma and revelation? This was the one crucial issue behind nineteenth-century theology.

XIII

Protestant Theology in the Nineteenth Century

The nineteenth century was a period of contrast that is difficult to characterize. It was a time when political, economic, and cultural circumstances seemed to spell doom for the Christian faith—at least in its traditional form. The French and American revolutions, which ushered in the century, were the beginning of a process whereby an ever increasing number of states would divest themselves of any obligation to support the church. The industrial revolution resulted in such a thorough dislocation of previous sociological patterns that there was ample reason to doubt that the old structures of the church would continue being relevant. That industrial development itself was based on a series of scientific discoveries that brought into question much of the Christian world-view—creation in six days, heaven above and hell below, etc. The era of plenty that the new technology seemed to promise produced drastic changes in the goals of human life—changes that were not seen with enthusiasm by most ecclesiastical leaders. And yet, the nineteenth century was also a period of great religious awakening within the Protestant churches—the very churches where the new conditions had greatest impact. This was the great century of Protestant missions, which encircled the globe in a few decades. It was the time when the Christian conscience was aroused against the slave trade, and vowed to put an end to it. And it was also the period of the most active and original theological work within Protestantism since the sixteenth century.

This theological work was so vast and varied that it is impossible to summarize it here. It ran the whole gamut, from Feuerbach's attempt to show that all Christian doctrine is the result of human projection, to the most obscurantist attempt to suppress and ridicule the theory of evolution. Furthermore, this theological activity was paralleled and supported by significant developments in such ancillary disciplines to theology as historiography, archeology, philology, etc. Theology did not escape the great explosion of knowledge that took place during the nineteenth and twentieth centuries.

In the midst of this complexity, however, there are a few theologians who seem to be the most significant for the development of Christian thought, and who also exemplify various possible ways of doing theology after Kant. Of these, I have chosen four as the most significant, and to each of them in turn I shall devote a section of this chapter: Friedrich Schleiermacher (1768–1834), G. W. F. Hegel (1770–1831), Søren Kierkegaard (1813–1855), and Albrecht Ritschl (1822–1889). Then, I shall turn to other questions and movements that merit some consideration.

Schleiermacher's Theology

Friedrich Daniel Ernst Schleiermacher[1] was the son of a Reformed army chaplain who was converted to the Moravians, and who believed that young Friedrich's excessive self-confidence should be dampened by sending him to a Moravian school. In the atmosphere of this school, Schleiermacher developed a profound sense of sin, and of the necessity and availability of grace. He then went to seminary, where he found that the arguments of the orthodox against religious skepticism were weak, and lost his faith in the divinity of Christ and in atonement by his blood. He then went to the University of Halle, where, being at the same time deeply influenced by Kant's philosophy, he began to develop his own understanding of the Christian faith. In 1794 he was ordained as a Reformed pastor,

---

[1] I know no better introduction than M. Redeker, *Schleiermacher: Life and Thought* (Philadelphia: Fortress Press, 1973). This includes a good bibliography. See also C. Welch, *Protestant Thought in the Nineteenth Century* (New Haven: Yale University Press, 1972), 1:92-93; B. A. Gerrish, *A Prince of the Church: Schleiermacher and the Beginnings of Modern Theology* (Philadelphia: Fortress Press, 1981); A. B. Blackwell, *Schleiermacher's Early Philosophy of Life: Determinism, Freedom, and Phantasy* (Chico, Cal.: Scholars Press, 1982); K. Barth, *The Theology of Schleiermacher* (Grand Rapids: Eerdmans, 1982).

and while serving in that capacity in Berlin he was influenced by the Romantic movement. In 1799 he published his *On Religion, Speeches to Its Cultured Despisers,* where the broad outlines of his theological system already appear, although the influence of Romanticism on his thought is much stronger than it would later be. Finally, in 1821 and 1822, he published *The Christian Faith* (and a revised edition in 1830), where he expounded his mature theological thought.

The *Speeches* of 1799 were extremely well received throughout Europe. What Schleiermacher had attempted to do in them was to secure a place for religion by showing that its proper locus is neither knowledge nor morality. To the "cultured despisers" of religion, he says: "In order to make quite clear to you what is the original and characteristic possession of religion, it resigns, at once, all claims on anything that belongs either to science or morality. Whether it has been borrowed or bestowed it is now returned."[2] The proper realm of religion, then, is feeling—and here we see the Moravian Schleiermacher making use of the Pietist tradition to appeal to his Romantic readers. Religion is the feeling of unity with the Whole, and the sense of wholeness that comes with this feeling. It is an immediate consciousness, and not a series of intellectually held doctrines or a system of morality. Therefore, in the *Speeches* Schleiermacher has little use for theology as an intellectual discipline, for the tradition of the church, or for religious ethical principles.

The very success of the *Speeches,* however, forced their author to give more consideration to elements in the Christian faith that he had not included in his now famous work. As his theology matured he came to a position in which, while still claiming that feeling was the proper locus for religion, he sought to clarify the meaning of feeling and its relationship to the other two spheres of life—knowledge and morality. The result was *The Christian Faith,* which was probably the most influential theological work of the nineteenth century.

Two significant new elements stand out in the first few pages of *The Christian Faith.* The first of these is the greater clarity and precision with which the religious feeling is described. The second is the importance now given to the church, and to intellectual formulations of its faith.

---

[2] *On Religion: Speeches to Its Cultured Despisers,* trans. J. Oman (New York: Harper, 1958), p. 35.

In the *Speeches,* religious feeling had been described in imprecise ways. It was a sense of unity with the Whole. Now, in *The Christian Faith,* we are clearly told that religious feeling, which he terms piety, is "the consciousness of being absolutely dependent, or, which is the same thing, of being in relation with God."[3] This awareness of absolute dependence is the nature of piety in all religions—even in those which are not organized. Schleiermacher further describes piety as an "immediate self-consciousness,"[4] by which he means that it is not based on intellectual reflection, but is of the category of "feeling"—*Gefühl.* This is not, as our everyday use of the term "feeling" would seem to convey, passing emotion. It is rather our constant, profound awareness of an Other whose presence is the source and basis of all that is—incuding ourselves.

However, here Schleiermacher is no longer primarily interested in religion in general. What he is attempting to do is to describe the Christian faith—more particularly, the Protestant faith. In the fourth of the *Speeches* he had pointed out the importance of specific communities for the growth and development of religious affections. This insight underlies the entirety of *The Christian Faith,* in which Schleiermacher sets out to describe in precise intellectual terms the doctrines by which the Protestant church expresses its particular experience of absolute dependence upon God. The doctrines of the church are important because they help to maintain the purity of the original experience that gave rise to the community. For Protestants, there are two crucial historical moments, and the task of doctrine is to express their significance. The first of these is the impact of Jesus of Nazareth on his immediate followers. The New Testament is the direct witness to this impact. The second crucial moment for the Protestant church is the reformation of the sixteenth century, which gave rise to several doctrinal statements expressing the distinctive essence of Protestantism. On this basis, it is clear that the Old Testament cannot be a fundamental authority for the Christian community.[5] It is also clear that the first source for Protestant systematic theology is the confessional statements of Protestantism, and only when these are inadequate is there need to

---

[3] *The Christian Faith,* trans. of the 2nd ed. (Edinburgh: T. & T. Clark, 1928), p. 12.
[4] *Ibid.,* p. 5.
[5] *Ibid.,* p. 115.

go back to the New Testament.[6] This shows an appreciation for tradition that was to be found neither in rationalist nor in Pietist theology.

Schleiermacher defines Christianity as "a monotheistic faith, belonging to the teleological type of religion, and is essentially distinguished from other such faiths by the fact that in it everything is related to the redemption accomplished by Jesus of Nazareth."[7] This is a carefully thought out definition. Christianity is monotheistic because in it our feeling of dependence is directed toward a single source. It is teleological because it leads to purposeful activity within the world, with an end to establishing the kingdom of God. This purposeful activity is the content of Christian ethics—and here we see a closer connection between piety and ethics than was to be found in the *Speeches*. Last, everything in Christianity is related to Jesus of Nazareth because he is the source of the new religious consciousness—the specific piety—that is characteristic of the Christian faith. This faith is based on the experience of redemption, which is an element not common to all religions. More than a teacher, Jesus is our redeemer, because through his person and his interaction with us we are brought into the new level of existence that is the Christian life. By thus emphasizing the person of Jesus, and making him more than a mere teacher, Schleiermacher challenged the rationalist tradition of the eighteenth century, which viewed Jesus as primarily a teacher of enlightened natural morality.

The structure of *The Christian Faith* is determined by Schleiermacher's understanding of human consciousness in general, and of Christian consciousness in particular. There are three levels of human selfconsciousness. The first, Schleiermacher terms "the animal grade." We all begin at this level. Here there is no distinction between self and world. But as the human creature develops, two distinct processes occur. First, there is an increasing distinction between self and world. This distinction, however, is not a simple opposition, for what actually happens is that our sense of world develops in the same measure in which our sense of self grows, and vice versa. Here one can see the influence of Kant on Schleiermacher, for the "world" is not simply "out there," but is determined

---

[6] *Ibid.,* p. 112.
[7] *Ibid.,* p. 52.

by our ability to organize our sense perceptions into a meaningful whole. This understanding of the "world" is very important for Schleiermacher, since monotheism can arise only within a cultural setting in which the world is seen as a unified whole and therefore the result of the creative work of a single deity. Second, as the distinction between self and world increases, our sense of freedom vis-à-vis the world—that is, of our ability to affect the world—also increases. The same is true, on the other hand, of our sense of dependence upon that world. This is the nature of finite freedom. The world is given, and we cannot change that givenness. But at the same time that very world is the field in which we exercise our freedom. As finite beings, we can neither experience nor imagine absolute freedom—that is, freedom within a context entirely created by us. Since this second level of consciousness is so closely related to sense perception, value judgments made purely at this level are determined by the antithesis of pleasure and pain. As this second level is attained—which normally happens in the natural course of human development— the previous animal level is gradually superseded. The second level, however, is a constant element that will always remain in this life.[8]

The third level of human consciousness—which is God-consciousness—is the specifically religious. It has to do not with freedom, but with dependence. Whereas it was not possible, at the second level, to speak of absolute human freedom, it is possible—indeed necessary—at this third level to speak of absolute human dependence. Here we are aware that both the self and the world are absolutely dependent upon an Other that neither we nor the world can affect. This Other has absolute freedom. In the face of this Other we are totally passive. In regard to the world, however, we are still called to activity.

The religious self-consciousness thus determines the fact that systematic theology will have to deal with three main themes: the self, the world, and God. Since the second level of consciousness is never overcome, and at that level all is based on the antithesis of pleasure and pain, the third level—within the Christian faith—now judges the previous existence and the continuation of that second level as sin. But the Christian faith is centered on the experience of redemption, and therefore, from the perspective of this third level, sin itself is seen within the context of grace.

---

[8] *Ibid.*, pp. 20-25.

Schleiermacher's *Christian Faith* thus deals with three main themes: the self, the world, and God. These are considered first in general in a brief introductory section. Then they are considered again from the perspective of the antithesis of sin and grace—in that order—which is the specific content of Christian religious consciousness.

In the introductory section, Schleiermacher discusses, first, the doctrines of creation and preservation; second, those attributes of God which have to do with creation and preservation; and, third, the original perfection of the world and of humanity. The doctrine of creation states that God is the source of all that exists, and that our dependence upon God is therefore to be absolute. Creation does not deal with prehistory or with the chronological origin of the world, for this is not included in our present religious experience. The doctrine does assert, however, creation out of nothing, for this is necessary in order to safeguard our absolute dependence. The doctrine of preservation is not separate from that of creation. Preservation has to do with God's continuing support of all that exists and its total interrelatedness. The relationships of cause and effect that exist in the world—the fact that everything is related to everything else, no matter how minutely—is to be seen as God's continuing work of creation. Therefore, no distinction can be made between the natural and the supernatural. God is equally related to all things at all times. In their interest in the relationships of cause and effect in the world, piety and science thus coincide. "In each and every situation we ought to be conscious of, and sympathetically experience, absolute dependence on God just as we conceive each and every thing as completely conditioned by the interdependence of nature."[9] With these words, Schleiermacher is opposing the "God of the gaps" view, which forces us to choose between natural and supernatural causes of events. On this point, while opposing the rationalists, he is showing the effect of Kant.

The attributes of God that have to do with creation and preservation are eternity, omnipresence, omnipotence, and omniscience. It is obvious that these are directly related to our sense of absolute dependence upon God in every time and place.

One of the most interesting sections in *The Christian Faith* is that

---

[9] *Ibid.,* pp. 170-71.

which deals with the doctrine of the original perfection of the world and of the human creature. As we have seen, self-consciousness in its second level is based upon a passive and active—a dependent and free—relationship between the self and the world. The doctrine of original perfection states that the world has always been, and still is at every moment, providing us with sufficient stimuli for God-consciousness to develop. It is in this sense that the world is perfect: it is sufficient to lead us to God-consciousness. At the same time, we are active toward that world, and it has always been sufficiently malleable for us to shape it on the basis of God-consciousness. It is a proper sphere for the full play of that consciousness. The Christian self-consciousness therefore tells us two things: first, that our failure to develop God-consciousness before we did was sin on our part, for everything we needed to that effect was provided; second, that our failure to shape the world into the kingdom of God—or at least to begin this process—is also sin on our part, for the world has always been receptive to our action as a whole human family. The doctrine of the original perfection of the human creature likewise means that we have always been capable of God-consciousness, and that our lack of it is sin. The stories about Eden, therefore, are not to be interpreted as historically true; but they are to be seen as valid expressions of God-consciousness, and not to be ignored.

Schleiermacher then turns to the consideration of the self, the world, and God from the perspective of the consciousness of sin, and later from the perspective of the consciousness of grace. The reason for this is that "the distinctive feature of Christian piety lies in the fact that whatever alienation from God there is in the phases of our experience, we are conscious of it as an action originating in ourselves, which we call Sin; but whatever fellowship with God there is, we are conscious of it as resting upon communication from the Redeemer, which we call Grace."[10]

Regarding the self, we have already seen that God-consciousness will call the entire life preceding its development sin. It is also true that the continued resistance to the growth of God-consciousness after it has begun will be labeled sin on the basis of that very consciousness. But the highest degree of awareness of sin comes to us as we view Jesus the redeemer. He shows us what life would have

---

[10] *Ibid.*, p. 262.

been like for us had we from the very beginning lived out the possibilities of perfection. It is by looking at Jesus—rather than at some prehistoric garden—that we see the real character of original perfection. The doctrine of original sin expresses the fact that we know ourselves to possess a resistance to God-consciousness, which is the basis for our actual sins. It also points to the corporate solidarity of sin that exists in the world because all actions are interrelated. My sin will ultimately affect the whole world, and I am affected by the sins of the entire world.

From the perspective of sin, the world is seen as preventing God-consciousness. The negative elements in the world—those which cause pain in the second level of consciousness—are now considered punishment given by God because of our guilt. This does not imply that all those elements would not exist without sin, but simply means that their existence would be interpreted differently. They could just as easily be perceived as stimuli for the further growth of God-consciousness. "Natural evils, therefore, objectively considered, do not arise from sin; but as man, were he without sin, would not feel what are merely hindrances of sensuous functions as evils, the very fact that he does so feel them is due to sin, and hence that type of evil, subjectively considered, is a penalty of sin."[11]

There are two divine attributes directly based on the consciousness of sin. These are holiness and justice. The holiness of God relates to our sense of inadequacy in the face of the goodness of God's commands. God's justice is based on our awareness of our lack of conformity to the divine will and our sense of the evil in the world as punishment for our sin. At this point Schleiermacher adds that "mercy" is not a useful term in dogmatics, for it seems to imply that God acts in accordance with the second level of consciousness, to augment our pleasure and limit our pain.

Finally, Schleiermacher turns to the consideration of the self, the world, and God from the perspective of the consciousness of grace.

When viewing the self under the consciousness of grace, two subjects are to be discussed; the person and work of Christ as the cause of grace, and the transformation of the self through grace. The redemptive activity of Jesus is due to his sinless perfection—that is to say, his absolute God-consciousness, which was never in conflict with

---

[11] *Ibid.*, p. 319.

his second level of consciousness. This perfection cannot be explained as being caused by its antecedents in human history, for what was there was sin. It can be explained only by the existence of God in him. Jesus Christ is both divine and human. "In the uniting of the divine nature with the human, the divine alone was active or self-imparting, and the human alone passive or in process of being assumed; but during the state of union every activity was a common activity of both natures."[12] In this statement once again we see the human defined as totally passive in regard to God, and God as totally active in regard to the human. The fact that Jesus as human is totally passive—and therefore absolutely dependent—is his sinless perfection. It is also the means by which God can be seen as totally active in him, and the union takes place. Thus understood, the traditional statement of the union of two natures in Jesus is acceptable for Schleiermacher.[13] This union, however, is not dependent upon the doctrine of the virgin birth, which is not to be taken literally. The same is true of the doctrines of the resurrection, the ascension, and the return in judgment, which are not necessary expressions of Christian consciousness. The disciples knew Jesus to be the redeemer without these doctrines. It is obvious that here we find in Schleiermacher some common elements of earlier rationalism, which would persist in a great deal of the theology of the nineteenth century.

The work of the redeemer is based upon this definition of his person. This work is the communication of his absolute God-consciousness to other human beings. He does this by assuming believers into his own God-consciousness. The redeemer is active in us, as God is active in him; we are passive in regard to him, as he is passive in his humanity in regard to God. His redemptive activity is the work of God through him in us. Paradoxical as it may sound, our action in our redemption is to be passive, just as Jesus was united with God through his own human act of passivity. We become unconscious of our own life and become conscious of his life. This is the passage from sin to perfection. It is an act of freedom for us as well as for the redeemer. We are formed as new persons in him and thus become part of the new creation, which expresses the original perfection.

---

[12] *Ibid.*, p. 398.

[13] The doctrine of the *communicatio idiomatum*, however, is not acceptable, for it implies a divine nature whose attributes can be described apart from human God-consciousness. *Ibid.*, pp. 411-13.

This is our state as believers from the perspective of the consciousness of grace, but we must remember that the antithesis of sin and grace is still present in the Christian life. Even so, however, we now have a new perspective upon evil, for it appears no longer as punishment for sin, but rather as the occasion for our activity within the world. Our consciousness of being forgiven causes us to see the negative stimuli, which we previously considered punishment, as calls to ethical activity within the world.[14]

In typical Reformed fashion, Schleiermacher discusses the work of Christ under the headings of the three offices of Christ as prophet, priest, and king. As prophet, Christ announces the kingdom of God. But one must remember that he also ushers in the kingdom that he announces, and that he is thus also the end of prophecy. One cannot separate his teachings from his person and work—and here Schleiermacher is reacting against the rationalist tradition, which made Jesus no more than a teacher and made a radical distinction between the teachings of Jesus and teachings about him.[15] As priest, the redeemer received upon himself the burden of the sins of the entire world. This does not mean, in the literal sense, that he died in our place. What it means is that, because his sinless perfection was a judgment upon us, he suffered the hostility of the entire world, and died for it. Since he responded to this situation out of total God-consciousness, and not out of sin, he opened a new possibility in our world and our history—the possibility of love, forgiveness, and reconciliation.[16] His suffering is therefore the necessary culmination of his work as our redeemer, and ends all priesthood, except that which is a continuation of his redeeming work.[17] In these statements Schleiermacher is opposing all views of atonement that would center the work of Christ on a particular moment of his life. As king, the redeemer creates a people whom he still rules through the ordinances that he established.[18] He is the provident ruler who gives us all things that are necessary for our life as his people.[19] The conclusion to be drawn from this is that there can be no political religion, no theocracy, and no union of church and state.[20]

---

[14] *Ibid.*, p. 432.
[15] *Ibid.*
[16] *Ibid.*, pp. 452-53.
[17] *Ibid.*, pp. 465-66.
[18] *Ibid.*, p. 468.
[19] *Ibid.*, p. 466.
[20] *Ibid.*, p. 473.

Schleiermacher then turns to a discussion of the transformation of the self through grace. Obviously, a great deal of what has just been said under the heading of the person and work of Christ touches on this subject. This section of *The Christian Faith* consists of definitions of traditional doctrines from the point of view of God-consciousness. The discussion includes terms such as regeneration, justification, conversion, repentance, faith, forgiveness, adoption, sanctification, and perseverance. Through the transformation of the self to which these terms refer, we become active instruments within the world through which the redemptive activity of Christ is brought to others.

Just as in the second level of consciousness there could be no sense of self without a sense of "world," so from the perspective of grace there can be no new self without a transformation of the context within which that self exists. Furthermore, since the definition of Christianity relates the new God-consciousness to the person and work of Jesus of Nazareth, there must be a community historically linked with the redeemer that provides the present context for the life of the Christian self. This community is the church. Therefore, the section in *The Christian Faith* that deals with the world from the perspective of grace comprises the doctrine of the church. Summarizing the contents of this lengthy section, Schleiermacher states that "in a comprehensive summary of what our Christian self-consciousness has to say about the fellowship of believers, we must first treat of the origin of the Church, the way in which it takes shape and disengages itself from the world; then the way in which the Church maintains itself in antithesis to the world; and finally the abrogation of this antithesis, or the prospect of the Church's consummation."[21]

The insight that Schleiermacher had in the *Speeches*, that there is no such thing as solitary faith, is continued and developed here. Although Jesus founded a fellowship, the church did not become an organized, corporate entity until his personal activity ended. The beginning of this new entity is what is meant by the giving of the Spirit. The Spirit was given only after the departure of Christ, because in his presence the disciples had to be passive, and the task of the Spirit is to develop spontaneous activity based on our

---

[21] *Ibid.*, p. 528.

God-consciousness.[22] A true community is formed at this point precisely because no one is directly dependent on any other, but all are related to all, and the whole to the redeemer. The entire church is the image of Christ, and each person a necessary part of it.[23]

There are both mutable and immutable elements within the church. The reason for this is that the church is a community within history and yet, throughout that history, it has maintained the same unchangeable, absolute God-consciousness of the redeemer. The mutable elements are the effect of the world and of our human nature. The immutable elements are the result of the constant activity of Christ.[24] These constant features are six in number. The first two—Scripture and the ministry of the Word of God—can be viewed both as the witness to Christ within the community and as the continuing prophetic activity of the redeemer within his church. The next two—baptism and the Lord's Supper—are at the same time ways by which the community has fellowship with Christ and ways by which the priestly activity of Christ is continued within the community. Because he stresses the fellowship with Christ that occurs in the Lord's Supper, Schleiermacher rejects both the Catholic view of transubstantiation and the extreme Protestant view which denies the real presence. The last two immutable elements in the life of the church—the power of the keys, and prayer in the name of Jesus—are means by which the individual and the community are interrelated, and they are also the channels through which the kingly activity of Christ continues in the church. The power of the keys—traditionally called the power of excommunication—is the community's discrimination between those who are within it and those who are not. "The Power of the Keys is the power in virtue of which the Church decides what belongs to the Christian life, and disposes of each individual in the measure of his conformity with these decisions."[25] This statement—which may seem surprising in the "father of liberal theology"—means that the community, and not the individual, is the judge of the nature of the Christian life. Prayer

---

[22] *Ibid.,* pp. 565-69.

[23] *Ibid.,* p. 578. It is interesting to note that it is at this point that Schleiermacher introduces the doctrine of predestination. Although the content that he ascribes to this doctrine is very different from Calvin's, he has restored it to the place that it originally had in Calvin's theology—that is, under the heading of redemption.

[24] *Ibid.,* pp. 582-84.

[25] *Ibid.,* p. 662.

must be understood not as a means by which the believer affects the mind of God, but rather as a process by which we make ourselves more ready for the transforming activity of the redeemer. For this reason, true Christian prayer is prayer in the name of Jesus, that is, prayer that is consonant with the God-consciousness of the church as a community. It does affect the world inasmuch as it alters our perception of reality, and the world is precisely a construct formed from such perception.[26]

The mutable elements of the church are divisions, error, and sin. All these exist in the church in its present state. However, they have no place in the true nature of the church, and therefore the Christian community will constantly be striving to overcome divisions by unity, error by truth, and sin by grace. Schleiermacher uses the traditional distinction between the visible and invisible church, although he warns that the truest Christians are usually the most visible in their action in the world.[27]

The doctrines relating to the consummation of the church are four: the return of Christ, the resurrection of the flesh, the last judgment, and eternal blessedness. These point to a goal beyond history, when all the mutable elements of the church will be gone, and its God-consciousness will be fulfilled. The literal understanding of these doctrines is due to an uncritical use of tradition.

Finally, the attributes of God viewed from the perspective of the consciousness of grace are two: love, which is God's desire to be united with us, and wisdom, that all things are so ordered that this will be accomplished.

In the twentieth century, after the work of Karl Barth and neo-orthodoxy, it seems a rather simple matter to criticize Schleiermacher. He has been accused of being the starting point of the "undercover apotheosis of man"[28] planned by liberal theology. The point at which he has been most severely criticized is his concentration on human God-consciousness rather than on revelation, and his willingness on this basis to forsake the radical "otherness" of the Christian gospel. On this basis, one of his critics has written that "it would be roughly true to say that he has put

---

[26] *Ibid.*, pp. 671-75. Here again, one can see the influence of Kant on Schleiermacher.
[27] *Ibid.*, p. 677.
[28] K. Barth in "An Introductory Essay" to L. Feuerbach, *The Essence of Christianity* (New York: Harper, 1957), p. xxii.

discovery in place of revelation, the religious consciousness in the place of the word of God, and the mere 'not yet' of imperfection in the place of sin."[29] The same critic also affirms that "it is only in a relative sense, therefore, that we can speak of the *Dogmatic* of Schleiermacher as an authentically Christian book."[30]

And yet, such criticism often fails to see Schleiermacher within his situation, or to take account of the degree to which twentieth-century theology is indebted to him. Barth himself paid tribute to this indebtedness by hanging a portrait of Schleiermacher in his study at Basel. Seen within the context of the early nineteenth century, the contribution of Schleiermacher to Protestant theology was of enormous significance, and can be felt to this day. Coming out of a Pietist background, he nevertheless overcame the individualism of Pietism by his emphasis on the importance of the church. While starting out as an apologist for Christianity amidst the followers of Romanticism, he avoided the subjectivism of the Romantics by the same emphasis on corporate experience and on its reflection in tradition. Though greatly influenced by the rationalists and by Kant, he corrected the rationalist position by insisting on the centrality of the person of Jesus for the Christian faith, and that faith is not a mere endorsement of civil morality.

Although it is true that liberal theology took its starting point from Schleiermacher, it is no less true that in the twentieth century, even after the demise of classical liberalism, his influence can still be felt in many positive ways. The Christocentricity of much of contemporary theology, as well as its emphasis on the church, is the legacy of Schleiermacher. The same is true of the importance that is now given to the category of redemption. Schleiermacher's positive valuation of tradition—which led some to accuse him of "Romanism"—has been a valuable contribution to the ecumenical movement. His insistence on the corporate nature of sin and on the obligation of Christians to be active in the world is behind the modern theological concern for the social dimensions of the gospel. In more ways than one, we are still doing theology under the shadow of Schleiermacher.

---

[29] H.R. Mackintosh, *Types of Modern Theology: Schleiermacher to Barth* (New York: Scribner's, 1937), p. 100.

[30] *Ibid.*

Hegel's Philosophy

Georg Wilhelm Friedrich Hegel (1770–1831)[31] began his academic career as a student of theology at Tübingen. There he dealt with two issues that would later prove to be determinative for his system.[32] The first was the historical nature of Christianity, and how a religion so related to particular events could claim universal validity. The other—in which he saw a partial answer to the first—was the role of love as taught by Jesus. Here he saw a reconciliation of opposites, so that in the love of God the legalistic opposition of sin and virtue is overcome, and a new life of freedom ensues.

Hegel always considered himself a theologian. The theology after which he was seeking, however, was no mere exposition of Christian doctrine as expressed in traditional formulas, but rather a sweeping understanding of the nature of reality, including the place of Christianity within that totality.

In a sense, what Hegel actually did was to carry Kant's vision of the active role of the mind to its final consequences, while abandoning other elements of Kant's system. Hegel therefore saw reality not primarily as something that reason has to grasp, but rather as the unfolding of the very principle of rationality in the universe—what he called the Spirit. Not only is reality logical, but logic is reality. This logic, however, is not the static logic of Parmenides or the rationalists of the Enlightenment. It is rather a dynamic logic, one that moves through a dialectic, always seeking new and fuller truth. It is within this context that Hegel's famous triad of thesis, antithesis, and synthesis must be understood. This is not a rigid pattern that all thought must follow—actually, what Hegel meant by these three terms is not always consistent. The dialectic is rather the affirmation that reality—and reason with it—is dynamic.

It was this intuition of the dynamic nature of reason and of reality that allowed Hegel to develop his very impressive philosophy of history. All of history is the unfolding of the Spirit through the logical process in which a thesis is posed, only to find an antithesis

---

[31] E. Caird, *Hegel* (Edinburgh: W. Blackwood and Sons, 1901); W. A. Kaufmann, *Hegel: Reinterpretation, Texts and Commentary* (London: Weidenfeld and Nicolson, 1966); H. Küng, *Menschwerdung Gottes: Eine Einführung in Hegel's theolog. Denken* (Freiburg im Breisgau: Herder, 1970); W. Wallace, *Prolegomena to the Study of Hegel's Philosophy and Especially of His Logic* (Oxford: Clarendon Press, 1894); E. L. Fackenheim, *The Religious Dimension in Hegel's Thought* (Bloomington: Indiana University Press, 1967); Q. Lauer, *Hegel's Concept of God* (Albany: State University of New York, 1982); J. N. Findlay, *Hegel: A re-examination* (New York: Oxford University Press, 1976).

[32] C. Welch, *Protestant Thought*, 1:92-93.

within itself, and to resolve the two in a synthesis. But the new synthesis is never final, for it too is a thesis with its own antithesis. And so the process goes on. Hegel has been severely criticized for falsifying history in his attempt to include everything within his conceptual framework. There is no doubt that his system did tend to oversimplify the complex realities of history. But let it be said in his favor that his understanding of the relationship between history and reality gave great impulse to historical studies. Hegel did not see history as revealing a hidden truth behind or beyond it. On the contrary, history itself was truth—dynamic truth, dialectical truth. Therefore, the study of history became the study of ultimate, purely logical reality. No longer was it a matter of seeking pure essences behind historical particularities. Historians could now seek to understand events with confidence that they were studying the very nature of the universe. It is no coincidence that modern historical research—especially on theological matters—began at Tübingen under the leadership of such Hegelians as F. C. Baur (1792–1860) and D. F. Strauss (1808–1874). Although a great deal of this historical research would question much of traditionally accepted Christian orthodoxy, it would eventually push Christian theology back to its historical sources.

Within the framework of this philosophy of history, Hegel went on to reinterpret Christianity in such a way that it was seen as the culmination of the unfolding of the Spirit—and therefore as the Absolute Religion. He rejected the rationalist theory of a universal natural religion underlying all positive religions and obscured by them. All religions reveal the ultimate nature of reality, although they must all be seen in the historical process of the unfolding of the Spirit. This process culminates in the Christian religion, whose often despised dogmas are in truth profound representations of the very nature of reality. Thus, for instance, the doctrine of the incarnation is the religious expression of the final coming together of God and humanity, which are no longer to be considered antithetical. And the doctrine of the Trinity is the assertion of the dialectical character of ultimate reality itself.

Hegel's significance for the later development of Christian theology went far beyond his having produced such an impressive system. As a matter of fact, the system itself soon collapsed, for its very inclusiveness made it vulnerable to attack from various quarters. But different elements of Hegel's thought were later taken up by others whose influence on Christian theology was great. Two such cases are the evolutionist views of Charles Darwin (1809–1882) and the dialectic materialism of Karl Marx (1818–1883). Hegel's view of the progressive unfolding of the Spirit was part of the background of Darwin's theory of evolution—and the impact of that theory on popular theology is well known. Marx's dialectic is a transposition into a materialist framework of Hegel's idealist dialectic.[33] Although Marx was generally ignored by theologians during the nineteenth century, his influence on twentieth-century theology is clear at least on two counts. The first is the constant dialogue between Christianity and Marxism, given the fact that the latter has become a political and ideological power in the modern world. The second is our increasing awareness that, as Marx pointed out, our ideas and ideals are affected by economic, social, and political circumstances—just as Freud has made us aware of the unfathomable psychological depths of such ideas and ideals.[34]

The Theology of Kierkegaard

Søren Aabye Kierkegaard (1813–1855)[35] is at once the most attracting and the most repelling theologian of the nineteenth century. In a sense, this is precisely as he wished it to be. His life was the drama of a highly gifted man who was aware of his genius, but who also disliked himself intensely and made every effort to inspire in others similar feelings about himself. His self-deprecating comments are illuminating at this point. He said that the year he was born the government went bankrupt and that he was like one of the bills circulating at the time, having some vestige of greatness, but in fact lacking in value. He compared his voice to the screeching of a

---

[33] R. Cooper, *The Logical Influence of Hegel on Marx* (Seattle: University of Washington Press, 1925); S. Hook, *From Hegel to Marx: Studies in the Intellectual Development of Karl Marx* (New York: Humanities Press, 1958).

[34] While much of nineteenth-century philosophy and theology was concerned with the nature of consciousness, and particularly of self-consciousness, Sigmund Freud (1856-1939) brought to the fore the unconscious forces that shape human life. He pointed to the irrational basis of much of human "rational" activity. Although his writings included some works on religion, it is the whole trend of his thought—as with Kant, Hegel, and Marx—that has had great impact on theology, particularly in the twentieth century.

[35] For general introductions, see W. Lowrie, *Kierkegaard*, 2 vols. (New York: Harper, 1962), and R. Jolivet, *Introduction à Kierkegaard* (Paris: Editions de Fontenelle, 1946). There is an excellent bibliography in Lowrie, 2:619-25. See also F. E. Wilde, *Kierkegaard and Speculative Idealism* (Copenhagen: C. A. Reitzel Boghandel, 1979); J. D. Colling, *The Mind of Kierkegaard* (Princeton: Princeton University Press, 1983).

seagull. His body was ill-formed, and he was aware of it. He expected to die before his father, for several of his brothers and sisters had already died and his father had told him that the family was cursed and all his children would die before him. When the prophecy failed to be fulfilled, Kierkegaard began speaking of himself as an unlikely and unworthy survivor. On the other hand, he was well aware of his intellectual brilliance, and he often referred to himself as a genius. He was certain that he had been given his enormous capabilities in order to carry out a great mission, and he eventually came to the conclusion that this mission was to make clear the tremendous difficulty involved in being a Christian. He was engaged to be married to Regina Olsen, a young woman with whom he always claimed he was very much in love, but whom he gave up for reasons as confused as his own personality—he should not burden her with his sick melancholy; she could not live at the same level of intense and passionate religion as he was dedicated to live; he had sacrificed her as Abraham had sacrificed his beloved Isaac on the basis of a nonethical commandment from on high, etc.[36] While he acted as if he did not care what opinions others might form about him, he went to ridiculous extremes to create the image of an almost miraculous genius. Thus, for instance, he would appear at the opera, let himself be seen, and go home to work as soon as the lights went out. He would then return just before the performance ended, in order to amaze all by his seemingly effortless literary production.

Although Kierkegaard has been hailed as a great philosopher and the founder of modern existentialism, he saw himself not as a philosopher, but rather as a knight of faith who had been given the mission of making Christianity difficult.[37] What he means by that is not that he wishes to keep others from becoming Christians, but, on

---

[36] A comparison with Schleiermacher is illuminating at this point. Schleiermacher was convinced of the significance of family life for the full development of human personality in community. He was in love with Eleonore Grunow, a married woman who, after a long struggle, decided against divorce. Schleiermacher later married someone else. His writings on marriage stress the need for the development of individuality within it. His view of the family as the means by which piety is communicated to children is to be found both in the *Speeches* and in his brief writing, *Christmas Eve: Dialogue on the Incarnation* (Richmond: John Knox Press, 1967). In contrast, marriage and family life appeared to Kierkegaard as a temptation by which we avoid the difficult realization of individuality. His rejection of Regina Olsen, therefore, is also related to his sense of vocation as "the solitary individual."

[37] *The Point of View for My Work as an Author*, trans. W. Lowrie (London: Oxford University Press, 1939), p. 95. Here he ironically comments, after explaining the reason for his entire literary production: "And now—now I am no longer interesting. That the problem of becoming a Christian, that this *really* should be the fundamental thought in my whole activity as an author—how tiresome!"

the contrary, that he wishes to show what a strenuous and life-consuming thing Christianity is, in order to challenge great souls to embrace it. The "Christianity of Christendom" is not real Christianity. In his Lutheran Denmark, where all were called Christians by reason of birth, and where Hegelianism and rationalism had become popular ways of showing that after all Christianity was the most rational form of religion, Kierkegaard felt called to use the power of his pen to destroy the notion that the Christian life is identical with the good, profitable, decent life of an exemplary citizen. In a short article published in 1854, he attacked the popular and successful ministers of his time by saying that "to represent a man who by preaching Christianity has attained and enjoyed in the greatest measure all possible worldly goods and enjoyments, to represent him as a witness to the truth is as ridiculous as to talk about a maiden who is surrounded by her numerous troop of children."[38] And elsewhere he makes clear the radical impact that true Christianity must have on the person who embraces it:

> As an individual, quite literally as an individual, to relate oneself to God personally is the formula for being a Christian. . . . If once this occurs, then it is an event incomparably more important than a European war and a war which involves all the corners of the earth, it is a catastrophic event which moves the universe to its profoundest depths. . . . He whose life does not present relative catastrophes of this sort has never, not even in the remotest approximation, had recourse as an individual to God—that is just as impossible as to touch an electrical machine without receiving a shock.[39]

The manner in which one then makes Christianity difficult is by showing that there is an enormous gap between the highest level of human decency and the Christian life. There are indeed three "stages on life's way"—the aesthetic, the ethical, and the religious. These three are not continuous, and therefore the passage from one to the other does not take place simply as the culmination of a lower stage. On the contrary, such passage requires a "leap"—a very important category in Kierkegaard's thought. This is not the Hegelian "mediation" in which a higher stage is achieved through

---

[38] *Attack upon "Christendom,"* trans. W. Lowrie (Boston: Beacon Press, 1956), pp. 10-11.
[39] *Ibid.*, p. 274.

the logical resolution of a previous conflict. Hegel's mediation, and indeed the entire Hegelian system, substitutes abstract reasoning for genuine human existence. The "System"—as Kierkegaard ironically calls it—gives the impression that everything makes sense, that everything falls into place. All problems seem to be solved "now that the System is almost finished, or at least under construction, and will be finished by next Sunday."[40] But the one problem that the System does not solve—the one problem that it cannot even see—is the problem of existence. Hegel's impressive construction is like a beautiful castle that someone builds and then spends the rest of life looking at from the barn.

Hegel and his followers must ignore the discontinuity of the stages on life's way, because the System has priority for them. Kierkegaard argues that existence is primary, and that any attempt at systematizing reality must necessarily do away with existence. It is possible to create a logical system, as Hegel has done. But "nothing must then be incorporated in a logical system that has any relation to existence, that is not indifferent to existence."[41] On the other hand, "an existential system cannot be formulated. Does this mean that no such system exists? By no means; nor is this implied in our assertion. Reality itself is a system—for God; but it cannot be a system for any existing spirit."[42] Actual human existence is always involved in paradox and pathos and these are two categories that abstract logic cannot encompass.

The three stages on life's way, then, do not stand in a logical relation to one another. There is no way in which the ethical can evolve out of the aesthetic. Likewise, it is impossible for the religious to result out of the exaggeration of the ethical. This in turn means that a direct call from a person living in the religious stage to another living in the aesthetic or the ethical will not be heeded. The person living in one of these other stages may well believe that he or she is already a Christian. In that case, the task of "making Christianity difficult" must be performed indirectly. "No, an illusion can never be destroyed directly, and only by indirect means can it be radically removed. If it is an illusion that all are Christians—and if there is

---

[40] *Concluding Unscientific Postscript*, trans. D. F. Swenson and W. Lowrie (Princeton: Princeton University Press, 1941), p. 97.

[41] *Ibid.*, p. 100.

[42] *Ibid.*, p. 107.

anything to be done about it, it must be done indirectly, not by one who vociferously proclaims himself an extraordinary Christian, but by one who, better instructed, is ready to declare that he is not a Christian at all. That is, one must approach from behind the person who is under an illusion."[43]

The need thus to catch his readers off their guard was one of the reasons for the pseudonymity of a vast part of Kierkegaard's literary production. The many books that he published pseudonymously are written from the perspective of the aesthetic and ethical stages, and attempt to incite readers in those stages to take the leap that would eventually lead them to the religious stage. The other reason for pseudonymity was to draw attention away from himself, so that readers could not say "this is Kierkegaard's opinion," but would have to confront truth directly and by themselves. In his typically ironical style, Kierkegaard says "if anyone were to be so polite as to assume that I have an opinion, and if he were to carry his gallantry to the extreme of adopting this opinion because he believed it to be mine. I should have to be sorry for his politeness."[44] For this reason, Kierkegaard's literary production is like "a marionette theatre" in which Victor Eremita, John the Seducer, Johannes de Silentio, Johannes Climacus, Anti-Climacus, and others express different views that are often not Kierkegaard's—although it was common knowledge that he was the author—but that show different perspectives on life.[45] At the same time as he was publishing these pseudonymous works, he was also publishing, under his own name, a series of *Edifying Discourses* from the religious viewpoint.

If we now return to the stages on life's way, we shall see that the entirety of Kierkegaard's work consists precisely in a vast attempt to call his readers to take the successive leaps that will take them to the true Christian life. It was in that manner that he described his literary production in *The Point of View for My Work as an Author,* although he made it clear that the exact place of some elements in this vast plan were not evident to him at the time he wrote them, and that it was Providence that guided him along the way.[46] This was especially true of the books that he wrote "because of her"—Regina Olsen.

The first of the three stages is the aesthetic. Those who live at this

---

[43] *The Point of View,* pp. 24-25.

[44] *Philosophical Fragments,* trans. D. F. Swenson (Princeton: Princeton University Press, 1936), p. 3.

[45] T. H. Croxall, *Kierkegaard Commentary* (New York: Harper, 1956), pp. 254-55.

[46] *The Point of View,* p. 92.

level have no goal but the pursuit of pleasure. They live for the moment, for it is in it that they enjoy pleasure. This pleasure, however, is not limited to crass sensual titillation. It includes also the refined artist who seeks after beauty, and even the philosopher who enjoys playing with ideas. It is therefore possible to think aesthetically about ethics and religion while being neither ethical nor religious. The philosopher and the artist may not like being classed together with the Epicurean. But all three live at the same level in that they live for the pleasure that a moment can give. Precisely in order to make it clear that the aesthetes to whom he is referring are not only those who live in debauchery, Kierkegaard centers his attention at this point on the higher forms of the aesthetic life. The final outcome of this sort of life is despair. To live for the moment eventually means that the moment itself is meaningless. Life becomes no more than a series of sensations, and even these sensations lose their attractiveness in that the aesthete is constantly thinking ahead about future sensations, or remembering past ones. Despair, then, is the necessary consequence of the aesthetic life. This despair, however, is not always conscious. Some aesthetes are still at such a point that they do not even perceive their own despair. These are the most hopeless, for none can be saved out of unacknowledged despair. Others—the majority—keep their despair to themselves, and try to hide it by presenting a joyful façade. Despair, however, is not entirely negative, for it is precisely the questioning of the aesthete's life that leads to the leap to the ethical stage.

Kierkegaard has many positive things to say about the ethical stage. The person who lives at this level follows principles that are universally true, and in making life conform to those principles finds a measure of authenticity. The aesthete is lost in the atomization of successive moments of pleasure. The ethical life involves finding oneself in one's own individual application of the general. "Ethically the highest pathos is interested pathos, expressed through the active transformation of the individual's entire mode of existence in conformity with the object of his interest; aesthetically the highest pathos is disinterested. When an individual abandons himself to lay hold of something great outside him, his enthusiasm is aesthetic; when he forsakes everything to save himself, his enthusiasm is ethical."[47]

---

[47] *Concluding Unscientific Postscript*, p. 350.

Thus, in the ethical life one follows the normal pattern of what is considered decent and good in the community. It is the life of duty and responsibility. One is a good parent and a good spouse, an honest citizen, and a responsible employee. This stage, unlike the aesthetic, involves the recognition that other lives have a claim upon oneself. The ethical life is not to be disparaged, for it is the basis on which most people live, and the only basis on which society is possible.

But the ethical also leads to despair. It cannot cope with the facts of sin and repentance. What does one do when one has failed to apply the ethical principles in a concrete situation? What does one do when one realizes that such failure is not a mere mistake, but part of one's own constitution? This is the source of the despair that can push one to the leap of faith into the religious stage. At this point, Kierkegaard is rejecting the entire rationalist tradition—including Kant—which saw in religion no more than an aid or a guide to morality.

The leap of faith out of the ethical is a frightening experience. It takes place when one perceives the ethical no longer as one's guide for action, but as the temptation to trust in one's moral rectitude rather than in God—or in universal principles rather than in individual vocation. Absolute trust in God, which is the mark of the "knight of faith," means that, while one still sees ethical principles as universally valid, one sees the possibility that, for a particular situation, they may be overcome by a higher commandment. There is little doubt that Kierkegaard had in mind the unethical way in which he had behaved in his engagement with Regina, when he wrote in *Fear and Trembling* that "the ethical expression of what Abraham did is, that he would murder Isaac; the religious expression is, that he would sacrifice Isaac; but precisely in this contradiction consists the dread which can well make a man sleepless, and yet Abraham is not what he is without his dread."[48] What adds to this dread is precisely that there is no outward sign to show the world that one is really acting on the basis of a divine "teleological suspension of the ethical." What thus seems to be highly religious may simply be grossly unethical! Abraham may have been about to murder his own son. Kierkegaard may have been no more than irresponsible toward Regina. There is no way in which the knight of

---

[48] *Fear and Trembling* (Garden City, N. Y.: Doubleday, 1954), p. 41.

faith can avoid this dread—indeed, it is precisely this dread that shows that one is not simply acting at the aesthetic level. The only recourse is to faith—which by its very nature remains always problematic. This is why it is difficult to be a Christian.

The religious stage can only be reached out of the consciousness of sin produced by the ethical stage. But it is not the necessary consequence of the despair to which the ethical life leads. Between the ethical and the religious there is no continuity, no Hegelian mediation, but a dreadful gap that can be crossed only by a leap of faith. The crucial difference between the ethical stage and the religious is that in the former stage one's life was guided by universal principles, whereas in the latter the Absolute rules supreme. The universal is not to be equated with the Absolute, for the Absolute grasps the individual in a concrete and unique situation, and there makes its singular demands. The person who lives at the religious level knows that the laws of God are not identical with God. It is true that the laws are from God, and therefore the universal principles are generally binding. But knowing that God stands above laws means that the theological content of this third stage on life's way is the forgiveness of sins. Faith is related directly to God, and not to law. For this reason, the ethical person knows of the commandments of God, but not of God's forgiveness. The religious person, on the other hand, knows both that God commands and that God forgives. Whereas the ethical person lives in despair and knows nothing but good and evil, the religious holds to faith, which overcomes despair. Faith is indeed the opposite of despair, and therefore the only real sin is despair. It is not virtue that finally overcomes sin, for virtue and sin are both elements of the ethical stage. What overcomes sin—the real opposite of sin—is faith. Virtue does not save. Only faith—the individual's direct relationship with the Absolute—can save.[49] Thus, it is clear that Kierkegaard is arguing against the entire rationalist tradition—Kant included—which saw in faith little more than an aid to virtue. It is also clear that Kierkegaard has been profoundly influenced at this point by Luther, whose understanding of faith, law, and salvation are starkly reaffirmed by Kierkegaard after long neglect in much of the Lutheran tradition.

Kierkegaard, however, is not arguing for some diffuse form of

---

[49] *The Sickness unto Death* (Princeton: Princeton University Press, 1941), p. 204.

general religiosity. He considers himself a Christian, calling others to accept the demands of the Absolute as revealed in Christ. The problem then is, how can a person living in the nineteenth century relate to someone who lived so long ago? Is it merely through the succession of followers of Jesus who have existed through the ages, and who have kept his message alive? If this is the case, does it not follow that the strength of the original message must have weakened through the generations, and that we are therefore at a disadvantage when compared with the contemporaries of Jesus? This is the question to which Kierkegaard addresses himself in the *Philosophical Fragments*. His answer is that, even for those who saw Jesus in the flesh, such factual vision was not necessarily conducive to faith. Seeing Jesus simply made it possible for them to become disciples; but the actualization of that possibility took place only when they made the leap of faith. Likewise, we who live centuries after the fact need the testimony of those who saw Jesus, for without such factual perception it would obviously be impossible to become his disciples. But it is still the leap of faith, and not the convincing power of the testimony, that makes us believers. In both cases, revelation is necessary. "Now just as the historical gives occasion for the contemporary to become a disciple, but only it must be noted through receiving the condition from God himself . . . so the testimony of contemporaries gives occasion for each successor to become a disciple, but only it must be noted through receiving the conditions from God himself."[50]

Once again, becoming a disciple is never an easy matter. It did not suffice to be a Galilean fisherman in the first century, and it does not suffice to be a Danish Lutheran in the nineteenth.

Kierkegaard's age was not ready to hear his message. The elements in the church and the "System" that he attacked were not seen as problems by most of his contemporaries. His influence on the nineteenth century was therefore minimal. But when he was rediscovered in the twentieth, when many of the old certainties of previous generations were collapsing, his impact was great and far-reaching.

In the general field of philosophy, quite apart from his Christian vocation, Kierkegaard has been one of the main sources of modern

---

[50] *Philosophical Fragments*, p. 84.

existentialism. His insistence on the category of human existence, which neither the Hegelian system nor any other human system was able to grasp, was the initial insight that gave rise to the various forms of contemporary existentialism.

In theology, Kierkegaard's most significant contribution was in drawing attention to the discontinuity between history and faith, and between the order of the ethical and the order of the religious. Christianity is not the natural culmination of the best in the human creature. The influences of this insight may be seen in the young Barth's understanding of the relationship between nature and grace. Furthermore, Kierkegaard served to show that Luther's views on the radical otherness of grace had unwittingly been set aside. In this he contributed to the revival of Luther's studies, which has been so characteristic of twentieth-century theology, especially in Scandinavia.

By showing that the opposite of sin is faith, and not virtue, Kierkegaard has alerted twentieth-century theology to the moralism involved in the rationalist approach to faith and ethics, and has forced succeeding generations to face the need to develop Christian ethics in consonance with the doctrine of justification by faith.

Kierkegaard has also pointed out vigorously that orthodoxy does not suffice. Faith is not a matter of doctrinal formulations, but is rather a relationship with God.

Finally Kierkegaard's theory of indirect communication, and his theological and psychological grounding for such communication, have served to stimulate attempts to express the Christian faith through drama, fiction, and other such indirect media.

On the other hand, however, there are some elements in Kierkegaard's thought that must be seen as negative. The most important of these is his exaggerated individualism. Not only was he a solitary figure, but he projected his solitude into the whole of theology. One must face God alone. Faith is an individual decision. At the religious stage, it is impossible to communicate to others the reasons for one's actions. Such an understanding of the life of faith falls short on two counts: first, it leaves little place for a doctrine of the church; second, it ignores the corporate nature of sin and injustice, and thus does not serve to call the believer to action in the sphere of society. Since the twentieth century has been forced to ask anew questions of ecclesiology and of social justice and action, Kierkegaard has not been helpful at this point.

Finally, although there is something admirable in Kierkegaard's lyric description of the religious life, the "knight of faith" is described in such terms that the doctrine of grace is sometimes obscured. What he says is important is to dare greatly, to take the leap, to accept the dread that comes with faith. It is difficult to see how this relates to grace.

In summary, there is much in Kierkegaard that would be difficult to follow in the twentieth century. And yet, perhaps this is his greatest success. For he set out not to make followers for himself, but disciples for Another. He would be pleased to know that his "seagull-like voice" has raised few followers, but many an attentive ear.

The Theology of Ritschl

Albrecht Ritschl (1822–1889)[51] is the fourth representative theologian whom we shall study in this chapter. During his early years he was under the influence of the Tübingen school—of which more will be said in the next section of this chapter—but he soon felt the need to abandon the Hegelianism that lay at the basis of that school's interpretation of early Christianity. The conviction that Hegelianism, as well as any other form of metaphysical speculation, must be expelled from theology, may be seen as the starting point for Ritschl's own theology. He felt that intellectual speculation could never lead to Christian doctrine. The locus of religion is not metaphysical knowledge, but moral value. Religion is essentially practical, and religious knowledge must be distinguished from theoretical knowledge. Whereas the latter expresses being, the former expresses value. This emphasis on the practical character of religion is obviously taken from Kant. The same is true of the rejection of metaphysics. Therefore, in a sense, what Ritschl is doing is going back beyond Hegel to the original Kant, and taking his challenge and opportunity more seriously than had those who simply had seen later idealism as the epitome of philosophy.

On the other hand, Ritschl wished to distinguish his position as clearly as possible from that of Schleiermacher. What he saw in Schleiermacher was a Romantic attempt to bypass the challenge

---

[51] P. J. Hefner, *Faith and the Vitalities of History: A Theological Study Based on the Work of Albrecht Ritschl* (New York: Harper, 1966); D. L. Mueller, *An Introduction to the Theology of Albrecht Ritschl* (Philadelphia: Westminster Press, 1969).

posed by Kant. He tended to disregard all that Schleiermacher had said about the importance of the historical Jesus and of the community, and therefore saw his theology as plagued with a subjectivism that ran the risk of leaving the way open for mysticism. And mysticism Ritschl considered one of the worst possible perversions of Christianity, for it leads the individual away from the world and moral responsibility, and destroys the sense of community among believers. For these reasons, Ritschl's writings are full of attacks on Schleiermacher. And yet, when one now reads those writings from the perspective of a later age, it is clear that his debt to and agreement with that earlier theologian were greater than he knew.

The method and general tenor of Ritschl's theology are best seen in his three large volumes on *The Christian Doctrine of Justification and Reconciliation*, which he began publishing in 1870. Here he states that Christianity is not like a circle that can be described from a single center, but rather like an ellipse with two focuses: redemption and the kingdom of God.[52] The relationship between these two is so close that they can never be separated. Too often theologians have attempted to speak as if the first of these two focuses were the proper field of theology, and the latter were the basis for ethics. This is an error, for each of the two focuses can only be properly understood "under the constructive influence of the other."[53]

Forgiveness of sins means that the penalty of separation from God has been removed.[54] This does not imply, however, that Christ has performed an objective act of expiation for our sins. What actually happens is rather that the consciousness of guilt for not fulfilling the moral destiny set by God for us loses its power to separate us from God.[55] God does not need to be reconciled with us; we are the ones who stand in need of reconciliation. Here, Ritschl rejects the "objective" or "juridicial" theory of atonement usually connected with the name of Anselm in favor of a modernized version of Abelard's "subjective" theory. The main difference between Ritschl and Abelard at this point is that one does not find in Ritschl the emphasis on the supernatural and on the essential divinity of Christ,

---

[52] *The Christian Doctrine of Justification and Reconciliation* (New York: Scribner's, 1900), 3:11-13.
[53] *Ibid.*, p. 14.
[54] *Ibid.*, p. 53.
[55] *Ibid.*, p. 79.

which is so clear in Abelard. Otherwise stated, Ritschl's theory of atonement is an exaggerated version of Luther's "imputed justice," which has become one-sided because Ritschl believes that any talk of the "justice" or "wrath" of God would contradict the central divine attribute, which is love.

Reconciliation implies more than justification, for whereas the latter speaks only of the forgiveness of sins, the former refers to the new life based on that forgiveness.

> By the idea of justification sinners are merely passively determined, and it fails to inform us what stimulus is acted upon them by the Divine treatment of their case. On the other hand, the idea of reconciliation is expressive of the fact that those who formerly were engaged in active contradiction to God have, by pardon, been brought into a harmonious direction towards God, and first of all into agreement with the intention cherished by Him in acting thus. From this point of view we may count on it that the justification which is successfully dispensed by God finds its manifestation and response in definite functions of the persons reconciled.[56]

It is here that the kingdom of God comes into play, for the new relationship with God brought about by reconciliation is not a purely individualistic matter. It is corporate both in that it originates in the community of faith, and in that it is directed toward the kingdom of God. This kingdom is not a supernatural order that will come about through an intervention from on high at some future time. It is rather the new order that has been begun by Jesus, whose personal vocation was precisely the founding of the kingdom. In content, the kingdom is a corporate state of life in which spirit rules over nature, and there is a loving and free mutual service among human beings. In this kingdom, each person has a particular vocation, and therefore moral responsibility—which is the essence of religious life—consists in fulfilling that vocation.

Ritschl's significance—in contrast to Schleiermacher and Kierkegaard—is to be found not so much in what is strictly his theology, as in the manner in which he reflects the direction that theology was taking in the latter half of the nineteenth century. This may be seen

---

[56] *Ibid.*, p. 78.

at least on four points. First, his emphasis on the love of God, to the point of rejecting divine justice and wrath, is characteristic of the period. The transcendence of a God who judges and calls into question all human activity was greatly lost in the liberal theology of the period preceding the First World War. Second, as a consequence of the first point, both sin and grace were significantly reduced in importance. Sin originates in ignorance, and consists in evil acts rather than in a state of being. Grace is little more than our awareness of God's love. Third, the best approach to the study of the essential nature of Christianity is through historical study. This emphasis was directly connected with the historical studies that we shall mention in the following section, and in a sense was the result of Schleiermacher's stress on the centrality of Jesus and on the faith of the community as the proper subject of systematic theology. Finally, Ritschl's emphasis on morality as the seat of religion, which he drew from Kant, was increasingly important in this period. Ritschl himself so identified Christian morality with what was current in his time that it has been said of his ideal of the Christian life that it is "the very epitome of the national-liberal German bourgeois of the age of Bismarck."[57] Therefore, his theology led easily to the identification of German culture with Christianity that had such tragic consequences in the twentieth century. On the other hand, his emphasis on judgments of moral value, and on the application of such judgments to the kingdom of God, led to the social gospel of Walter Rauschenbusch, as well as to more recent applications of the Christian faith to the task of reordering society. For more than an entire generation, however, Ritschl was the leading figure of German theology, and it is to his followers that the name "liberal theologians" is most strictly applied by historians of theology.

The Question of History

One theme that pervaded theological inquiry in the nineteenth century was history. This was partly the result of Hegel's attempt to put history at the center of reality, partly a reflection of the optimism of the time and its confidence in progress, and partly the result of critical studies in the field of history. Already in the eighteenth

---

[57] K. Barth, *From Rousseau to Ritschl* (London: SCM Press, 1959), p. 392.

century the Deists and others had raised questions about the historicity of biblical accounts, particularly regarding miracles. Germany had been shocked by the posthumous publication of portions of the work of Hermann Samuel Reimarus (1694–1767), *Apology for the Rational Worshippers of God*. This had prompted biblical scholars to take up the challenge of a critical study of Scripture. Notable in this enterprise were Johann Salomo Semler (1725–1791), a professor of theology at Halle who became one of the pioneers of the critical historical method in the study of the Bible, and Johann August Ernesti (1707–1781), whose work concentrated on matters of grammar and philology. Also in the eighteenth century, Gotthold Ephraim Lessing (1729–1781) had published *The Education of the Human Race,* in which he argued that the entire process of history is one in which the human race is moving toward higher and more refined religious understanding, and that therefore the time was approaching when the traditional teachings of Scripture and the creeds would no longer be necessary. These had been very important as a step in the educational process of humankind. But such a step should not be absolutized. Only the principle behind it, which humans could increasingly approach by rational means, was to be absolutized.

The nineteenth century took these various trends, all pointing to the centrality of history, and wove them in different ways. We have seen Kierkegaard asking the question of discipleship after nineteen centuries, Schleiermacher underscoring the continuity of the believing community, and Hegel developing an entire philosophy of history.

In Tübingen, F. C. Baur, whom we have already mentioned as a follower of Hegel, sought to apply Hegelian methods to the study of the New Testament. This "Tübingen school" studied the various theological trends that appear in the New Testament, which it considered to be the synthesis of earlier theological views. In particular, the Tübingen school underscored the contrast between a "Petrine theology" and a later "Pauline theology." Echoes of this conflict can be heard in the New Testament, although the formation of the canon itself was part of the synthesis that would bring these together into early Christianity. Later in the United States, Philip Schaff (1819–1893) and the "Mercersburg school" would apply these principles to church history, proposing that Roman Catholicism embodied the Petrine principle and Protestantism the Pauline, and seeking a new synthesis.

In 1835, D. F. Strauss published his *Life of Jesus,* in which he argued that those who took as literal miracles and references to the supernatural erred, and that the same was true of those who simply rejected them as fiction. The New Testament is not simply a chronicle; it is a witness of faith by those who believed in Jesus. Its narratives therefore should not be read as statements of fact. They are in truth "myths." A myth, in the sense in which Strauss uses the word, is not pure falsehood. On the contrary, a myth expresses truth of the highest order. What is therefore important about the New Testament is not Jesus himself, or his miracles, or even his teachings, but the fundamental truth to which these point: the ultimate unity of God and humanity.

This was the context of the long process reviewed in 1906 by Albert Schweitzer in his famous book *The Quest for the Historical Jesus,* whose original full title is "From Reimarus to Wrede, A History of Research on the Life of Jesus." Here Schweitzer pointed out that the views of Jesus, and the manner in which research on his life was conducted, had evolved during the course of the century. At first, debate concentrated on the question of miracles and the supernatural. Then, there were attempts to discover the inner workings of the mind of Jesus, and to present him as the example manifesting what there is of the heroic in all of us. The foremost exponent of this approach was Ernst Renan's *Life of Jesus,* which for many years was a popular best-seller, and provided the majority of educated Europeans with their images of Jesus. The work of Baur and his colleagues then raised questions about the reliability of the factual data that previous authors had taken from the New Testament as the basis for their lives of Jesus—in particular those to be found in the Fourth Gospel. Finally, in 1892, Johannes Weiss published *The Preaching of Jesus on the Kingdom of God,* in which he showed that all of these studies of Jesus had missed the apocalyptic element that is central to understanding his preaching and his life. Earlier "lives" of Jesus had turned him into a nineteenth-century ideal, forgetting that his proper setting was the eschatological expectation of his Jewish milieu. The friendly, polished Jesus of the "lives" had never existed; he was simply a projection of the wishes of his biographers.

Schweitzer himself was convinced that Weiss was right in his emphasis on the eschatological aspect of the teachings of Jesus. He also thought that what was important to rediscover was not the historical Jesus, but rather what he called "the spirit of Jesus." And thus he ended with his now famous paragraphs, which he then sealed with a life of self-giving service in Africa:

> But the truth is, it is not Jesus as historically known, but Jesus as spiritually arisen with men, who is significant for our time and can help it. Not the historical Jesus, but the spirit which goes forth from Him and in the spirits of men strives for new influence and rule, is that which overcomes the world.
>
> It is not given to history to disengage that which is abiding and eternal in the being of Jesus from the historical forms it worked itself out, and to introduce it into our world as a living in-fluence. . . . He comes to us as One unknown, without a name, as of old, by the lake-side, He came to those men who knew Him not. He speaks to us the same word: "Follow thou me!" and sets us to the tasks which He has to fulfill for our time. He commands. And to those who obey Him, whether they be wise or simple, He will reveal Himself in the toils, the conflicts, the sufferings which they shall pass through in His fellowship, and, as an ineffable mystery, they shall learn in their own experience Who He is.[58]

From this quotation, it should be evident that there is a connection between the failure of these attempts to describe Jesus in terms of the modern age, and Barth's vibrant proclamation, just a few years later, of the sovereign Other who speaks a word of grace and judgment. It is also clear that Schleiermacher had been vindicated, and that the attempt to separate the person of Jesus from his teachings, or to go beyond the faith of the Christian community, was doomed to failure. In more recent times, a new search for the historical Jesus has been undertaken; but, in spite of its better tools, this new quest has learned humility from the previous century.

While interest in history was leading the nineteenth century through this quest, it was also manifesting itself in abundant research on the history of Christianity. The most notable figure on this score was Adolf von Harnack (1851–1930), whose *History of Dogmas* stands as a monument to historical research. Harnack was an enthusiastic

---

[58] *The Quest for the Historical Jesus* (New York: Macmillan, 1922), pp. 399, 401.

follower of Ritschl, whom he called "the last of the Church Fathers." Therefore, he thought that the teachings of Jesus could be summarized in three points:

First, the Kingdom of God and its coming.
Secondly, God the Father and the infinite value of the human soul.
Thirdly, the higher righteousness and the commandment of love.[59]

Applying this view to the history of Christian thought, that entire history appeared as a process of increased Hellenization whereby the focus of attention shifted from the teachings of Jesus to his person. This led him to call Protestants away from the dogmatic, liturgical, and ecclesiastical results of that process, returning to the original teachings of Jesus. It also led him to harsh criticism of both the Eastern Orthodox[60] and the Roman Catholic traditions.[61]

Another related development was the *Religionsgeschichtliche Schule* (or History of Religions School), which sought to place Christianity within the context of the history of religions, and in particular of the religions amidst which it was born. It was in this school that the most radical theories appeared about the influence on Christianity of earlier gnostic myths and of mystery religions. J. F. W. Bousset, *Kyrios Christos*, published in 1913, is a typical example of this school's approach, for here Bousset seeks to uncover the process by which the title of "kyrios" (Lord) passed from other religions into Christianity, and how it came to pass that Jesus was raised to the exalted status of Lord.

The most influential author coming out of this school, however, was Ernst Troeltsch (1865–1923).[62] Troeltsch was interested above all in the relationship between religion and culture, or in the place of religion within the totality of life. He opposed Marx's understanding on this score, and insisted that there is a "religious a priori" that influences society, and that is not merely the working out of social and economic interests. At the same time, he felt that the interaction

---

[59] *What is Christianity?* (New York: Harper and Brothers, 1957), p. 51.

[60] "There is no sadder spectacle than this transformation of the Christian religion from a worship of God in spirit and in truth into a worship of God in signs, formulas, and idols." *What is Christianity?* p. 238.

[61] ". . . As an outward and visible Church and a State founded on law and force, Roman Catholicism has nothing to do with the Gospel, nay, is in fundamental contradiction with it." *Ibid.*, p. 264.

[62] There is an excellent introduction to Troeltsch in W. Pauck, *From Luther to Tillich: The Reformers and Their Heirs* (New York: Harper and Row, 1984), pp. 106-38.

between religions and society was in need of further study, and he set out to do this in the context of the Christian religion. Although he held a chair of theology, he felt that books on systematic theology, precisely because they did not take cultural and historical factors into account, were devotional even though they passed for scholarship. He felt that a great deal of the difficulties Germans had in bringing their faith to bear on political and social problems stemmed from the influence of Lutheranism with its sharp distinction between Law and Gospel, and therefore became a student of Calvin, Calvinism, and their relationship with modern society. His most famous work, however, was *The Social Teachings of the Christian Churches*.[63] Here he classified the various Christian groups, according to the manner in which they relate to the surrounding society, into churches, sects, and mystical groups—a classification that has had widespread use among sociologists of religion.

The Social Gospel
and Walter Rauschenbusch

One of the most significant contributions of the United States to the development of Christian thought was the Social Gospel. It arose at the end of the nineteenth century and early in the twentieth, when extreme capitalism was running rampant with few laws to curb it. It was precisely the time when the social problems produced by this mode of industrial and economic development were already being felt, and there was yet little effort on the part of society to respond to the new situation. The new nation, born little more than a century earlier in hopes of "freedom and justice for all," was beginning to be plagued by urban slums that were clearly the result of economic and social injustice. And while this was taking place, churches seemed content with continuing the task of calling individuals to repentance and conversion, often claiming that the conversion of individuals was sufficient for the restructuring of society.

It was against this understanding of the Christian task that the social gospel movement leveled its vigorous protest. Although the movement itself had begun a few years earlier, it found its clearest and most cogent expression in the work of Walter Rauschenbusch

---

[63] First published in 1912. English translation, 2 vols. (New York: Macmillan, 1931).

(1861–1918),[64] and especially in his two books *Christianity and the Social Crisis* and *A Theology for the Social Gospel*. The fact that Rauschenbusch was the son of a German Baptist professor meant that he was able to draw from German liberal theology for his formulation of the social dimensions of the gospel. His experience of eleven years as a pastor in one of the worst sections of New York City gave him profound insight into the nature of the evils afflicting the nation. It was his ability to combine these two elements that made him the unquestioned leader of the movement.

Partly through the influence of Ritschl, Rauschenbusch was aware of the corporate nature of sin and of the importance of the kingdom of God in the New Testament. Joining these insights to the use of scientific tools for the analysis of society, he came to the conclusion that the problems that were so evident in the slums of New York were not to be solved by mere philanthropy or by the conversion of one individual after another. It was necessary to affect the very order of society, its laws and institutions, in order to provide a more just environment for human life.

> Social religion, too, demands repentance and faith: repentance for our social sins; faith in the possibility of a new social order. As long as a man sees in our present society only a few inevitable abuses and recognizes no sin and evil deep-seated in the very constitution of the present order, he is still in a state of moral blindness and without conviction of sin. Those who believe in a better social order are often told that they do not know the sinfulness of the human heart. They could justly retort the charge on the men of the evangelical school.[65]

It is this deep-seated sinfulness in the social order that Christians are called to attack. This is to be done by preaching the gospel. But not the gospel that ends with personal salvation and individualistic morality. The true gospel of Jesus Christ calls all its believers to work for the kingdom of God, which is a kingdom of justice.

This kingdom—like many other facets of the Christian faith—Rauschenbusch understood in essentially liberal terms. Although there was much in his theology that transcended liberalism, this fact

---

[64] D. R. Sharpe, *Walter Rauschenbusch* (New York: Macmillan, 1942); R. Müller, *Walter Rauschenbusch: Ein Beitrag zur Begegnung des deutschen und das amerikanischen Protestantismus* (Leiden: E. J. Brill, 1957). See also: C. H. Hopkins, *The Rise of the Social Gospel in American Protestantism 1865-1915* (New Haven: Yale University Press, 1940).

[65] *Christianity and the Social Crisis* (New York: Macmillan, 1919), p. 349.

was not seen by most of his contemporaries and therefore his thought suffered from the eclipse of liberalism that took place after the First World War. However, in more recent times, as social issues have again come to the foreground of Christian concern, and as his writings have been read from a different perspective, Rauschenbusch has been shown to have been a forerunner of a great deal of twentieth-century theology, and a much more profound theologian than was thought at an earlier time.

The Growth of Neoconfessionalism

In response to these various forms of theology that seemed to challenge many of the traditional assumptions, and also to the individualism of Pietism, there was a renewed emphasis on confessionalism in widely divergent circles at various points in the nineteenth century.[66] In Germany, it took the shape of the neo-Lutheran movement, whose leaders were concerned with the inroads of rationalism into orthodoxy, of Pietism into the corporate understanding of Christianity and of the church, and of liberal and nationalistic ideas into the fabric of society.

In the United States, the new confessionalism was a response to similar challenges: rationalism—in particular Darwin's theory of evolution—the individualism of revivalism, and the growth of political liberalism and egalitarian ideas. In this case, given the confessional pluralism of the nation, the reaction took two distinct roads that at times coalesced. One was a movement among some traditions—in particular the Lutheran, Reformed, and Anglican—to reinforce their confessional stance, often by strengthening ties with the country of origin in Europe. Another was the "fundamentalist" movement, so called because of the five "fundamentals" proclaimed at a conference in Niagara Falls in 1895. These fundamentals were the inerrancy of Scripture and four points having to do with Jesus: his virgin birth, his substitutionary death, his physical resurrection, and his impending return. Although fundamentalism did not stem from neoconfessionalism, and it gained most of its strength from revivalist elements, it did at times join forces with confessionalism, as

---

[66] There is an excellent global study of this movement: W. H. Conser, *Church and Confession: Conservative Theologians in Germany, England and America, 1815-1866* (Atlanta: Mercer University Press, 1984).

when the General Assembly of the Presbyterian Church adopted a slightly revised version of the "fundamentals."

Finally, a word must be said about the Oxford movement.[67] This was an effort, mostly on the part of a group of able and devout scholars in and around Oxford, to counteract the influence of liberalism and evangelicalism in the Church of England. Although liberalism and evangelicalism were opposed in many ways, they coincided in their lack of a sense of tradition, and in their emphasis on the authority of the individual above the community. The "Tractarians"—as the members of the Oxford movement were also called—felt that Protestantism had gone too far in its rejection of tradition and its emphasis on individual judgment. For them, however, this was a matter not merely of abstract theology, but of concrete devotion. By cutting themselves away from tradition, the liberals and evangelicals had lost a great deal of the richness of Christian worship. Their emphasis on the authority of the Bible, lacking any sense of tradition, had led them, quite unwittingly, to place the authority of the individual interpreter above that of Scripture. Tradition would prove to be a corrective to this, for then individual Christians would not be as ready to offer their own particular interpretations. A liturgy that brought to life the patristic tradition of the church would be a means for reinstating the corporate nature of the Christian life to its proper place. This would also be aided by increased contacts between the Church of England and the Eastern churches. Furthermore, the church had a divinely commissioned purpose and authority, and therefore the state should not be allowed to intervene in ecclesiastical matters.

The movement came to light in 1833, when the famous scholar and writer John Keble preached at Oxford against the reduction by Parliament of the number of Anglican bishoprics in Ireland. That same year, the *Tracts for the Times* began appearing. These were publications by a number of scholars attempting to show the value of the genuine Catholic tradition for the Church of England, over against "Popery and Dissent." The first and the last—the ninetieth—were written by John Henry Newman, who soon became the best-known leader of the movement. As the years went by, it was

---

[67] O. Chadwick, ed., *The Mind of the Oxford Movement* (Stanford: Stanford University Press, 1960); C. H. Dawson, *The Spirit of the Oxford Movement* (London: Sheed & Ward, 1945); E. R. Fairweather, ed., *The Oxford Movement* (New York: Oxford University Press, 1964).

obvious that the *Tracts* were becoming increasingly favorable to Roman Catholicism. The last of them, published in 1841, made such concessions to Rome that the bishop of Oxford ordered that the series be ended. Four years later, Newman declared himself a Roman Catholic, and he eventually became a cardinal. Others followed the same path, thus increasing the suspicion of the opponents of the movement.

The vast majority of the members of the Oxford movement, however, remained within the Church of England and there had great influence. To them was due a profound liturgical renewal, the revival of monastic orders, and the awakening of a form of piety more closely related to the tradition of the church at large. Eventually their influence would reach beyond the limits of the Anglican communion and would be felt in several other Protestant bodies. The impact of the movement could also be seen in the contribution that the Church of England would eventually make to the cause of ecumenism. As to Newman, we shall encounter him again as we discuss Roman Catholic theology.

The foregoing is only a brief review of some of the major theologians and movements within Protestantism in the nineteenth century. In the following two chapters, as we survey Roman Catholic and Eastern Orthodox theology during the same period, the vitality and originality of Protestant theology at that time will become increasingly striking. While the other two major branches of the Christian church were struggling to keep traditional orthodoxy untainted by modern times, a number of Protestant theologians were seeking ways to relate theology to the new currents of thought. The urge to develop comprehensive theological systems was one of the most remarkable characteristics of the period. This urge led to radical reformulations of the Christian faith. Protestant theologians attempted to consider not only abstract philosophy and logic, but also the social, political, and economic conditions of the time. While the direct political influence of the church was decreasing through the growth of the secular state, the impact of Protestantism was increasing through greater involvement in the world.

Therefore, although the nineteenth century has often been severely criticized by later theologians, and although there was much in it that could hardly serve as a guide for our time, it still remains—jointly with the sixteenth—one of the two great moments of Protestant theology.

XIV

Roman Catholic Theology to the First World War

As we have seen, during the sixteenth century the Roman Catholic Church went through a period of intense theological activity and profound reformation. It emerged from that period—at least in theory—as a highly centralized body, for after some hesitation Rome had taken the leadership in the movement for reformation. This centralization took place precisely at the time when the emerging European nations were asserting their own autonomy, often under the rule of autocratic monarchs. Such rulers would not regard with favor the existence within their own territories of a church whose loyalty seemed to be directed to another monarch. Therefore, they encouraged those within the Catholic Church who for various reasons felt that the power of the pope ought to be curbed. As a result one of the dominant theological issues during the seventeenth to the nineteenth centuries was the precise nature and scope of the pope's authority. As we shall see, Gallicanism, Febronianism, and Josephism were attempts to limit that authority, whereas ultramontanism was the opposite attitude. In a sense, the First Vatican Council was the outcome of the controversy, with victory going to the ultramontanist camp.

The second concern that occupied the minds of theologians during this period was that of the manner in which the church ought to respond to new trends in the world. The point at which this issue became most acute was the threat that the new science, philosophy, and political ideas seemingly posed to Catholic orthodoxy. On this score, the history of the Roman Church in this period is an almost uninterrupted series of attempts to assert the value of traditional views over against the new—a trend that culminated in the condemnation of modernism in 1907. On the other hand, on the matter of Christianity and social justice, the Roman Church did take a positive attitude under the leadership of Leo XIII.

The two preceding paragraphs will serve as the outline for this chapter. First we shall discuss the issue of papal authority, to its final outcome in the First Vatican Council. We shall then turn to the issues that we have listed as having to do with the relationship between the church and the modern world.

Before we turn to the first of these issues, however, a word must be said about Jansenism. This issue was still very much alive during the early part of the period that we are now studying. Since we have already discussed its progress and final outcome, we shall not return to it here. But I alert the reader to its importance as part of the total picture of Roman Catholicism during the seventeenth and eighteenth centuries.

The Issue of Papal Authority

While Protestantism was attacking the authority of the pope, there were many within the Roman Catholic Church who were also questioning that authority and attempting to set its limits. The conciliar views of the fifteenth century had never completely died out— especially in France, where they continued being taught at the Sorbonne for some time. The nationalist sentiments that contributed to the Protestant Reformation in England, Scotland, Germany, and the Netherlands existed also in Catholic countries such as Spain, Portugal, and France. Catholic rulers were made uneasy by the growing centralization of ecclesiastical authority in Rome. Many prelates shared that uneasiness, for their power and authority were bound to wane as the pope's waxed stronger. In this view they were supported by historical research, which showed that in earlier times the church was not as centralized as Rome now claimed.

Although this opposition to excessive ecclesiastical centralization was quite widespread throughout Catholic Europe, it was strongest in France, and therefore came to be called Gallicanism. Those who opposed the Gallicans, and defended the authority of the pope, were called "ultramontanes"—for they looked "beyond the mountains" (the Alps) for the locus of ecclesiastical authority.

France had ample historical reason for becoming the center of opposition to the power of Rome. During its residence in Avignon, the papacy had made a number of concessions to the French crown—concessions that the kings were eager to retain. Many of the most able leaders of the conciliar movement had been French, and their ideas were still held by many in that land. In 1516, for complex political reasons, Leo X had signed with Francis I a concordat that gave the king and his successors ample powers over the church in their domains. Therefore, when the French referred to the "Gallican liberties" they were speaking not of future goals, but of traditional practices that now seemed threatened.

All these factors may be seen at work in the manner in which the French reacted to the Council of Trent.[1] When the council was being prepared, and even while it was taking place, many in France objected to the manner in which it was conducted. To them, Trent was no more than an Italian council. As a result, the question of the promulgation of the council's edicts in French territories became the central issue in the early stages of the struggle between Gallicans and ultramontanes.

French opposition to the promulgation of the edicts of Trent came from several sources. Those who still clung to conciliarist ideas felt that this particular council had conceded too much to papal authority. Many of the most zealous advocates of reformation among the clergy believed that their goals could best be achieved with the support of the crown, and that the intervention of Rome through its council, and eventually through papal decrees, would hinder their efforts to gain the political support needed for their intended reformation. The kings and their closest supporters feared that the promulgation of the decisions of Trent would be tantamount to declaring the supremacy of Rome over the crown—at least in ecclesiastical matters. But the staunchest opposition came from parliament, controlled as it was by a vast majority of elderly noblemen who would never agree to the enactment of foreign laws on French soil.

---

[1] L. Willaert, *Après le concile de Trente: La restauration catholique* (vol. 18 of Fliche and Martin, *Histoire de l'église* [Paris: Bloud et Gay, 1960]), pp. 375-83.

In 1580, Henry III, following the advice of those who wished to see him take the lead in the reformation of the church, published at Blois a series of sixty-six ordinances on ecclesiastical discipline. These were for the most part taken from the decrees of Trent. But Pope Gregory XIII felt that this was an unwarranted usurpation of power on the part of the civil authorities. According to him and his supporters, what the king was to do was not to decree the reformation of the church, but simply to sign the decisions of Trent. The debate that ensued did little to strengthen the position of Rome in France.

When the assassination of Henry III left the throne vacant and succession in doubt, the pope tried to intervene by declaring who was and who was not eligible for the crown. This aroused the fury of many, and further strengthened the Gallican position. When the ex-Protestant Henry of Navarre became Henry IV, he was already under the ban of excommunication, placed on him by Rome as a relapsed heretic. Technically, therefore, only the pope could restore him to communion. This placed the French church in a difficult position, for it could either accept a heretic as king, or petition the Holy See for the lifting of the excommunication—and therefore agree to the pope's jurisdiction in such matters. What the French clergy did was simply to restore the king to communion on its own authority, without consulting with the Holy See. Rome railed against the French clergy and against the king for this act, and brought such pressure to bear that two years later Henry IV had to petition the pope for his pardon, and to submit symbolically to the discipline of the Holy See. In exchange for his restoration to communion with Rome, the king agreed to sign and promulgate the decrees of Trent. This he tried to do repeatedly, but the staunch opposition of the French parliament never allowed it. When Henry was assassinated, in 1610, by the fanatic François Ravaillac, whose motivations were connected with some ultramontane arguments favoring tyrannicide, a strong Gallican reaction ensued. The result was that the Council of Trent was still not accepted as binding within the French kingdom.

In 1615, the majority of the French clergy—which by now had become generally convinced of the need to have the council be made binding in France—took a momentous step. They decided that, since the crown and the parliament were not about to promulgate the council's edicts, and since in any case these had to do with spiritual matters rather than temporal, they would simply go ahead and declare on their own, as spiritual directors of Christians in the kingdom, that henceforth the decrees of the council would be valid and binding on all Christians. Although this meant that the issue of the authority of the council was now resolved—not without civil opposition—it meant also that this solution had come from the French clergy. Thus, the step taken in 1615 was ambiguous. While most of its supporters were ultramontanes who were attempting to bolster the authority of the pope in France, the very fact that it took an act of the "Gallican church" to do so would eventually serve as a precedent in favor of Gallicanism.

During this early period of Gallicanism, four names are outstanding as the foremost leaders in the opposition to Roman power: Guy Coquille, Pierre Pithou, Edmond Richer, and Jean Duvergier de Hauranne—better known as Saint-Cyran.

Guy Coquille (1525–1603)[2] published a *Treatise on the Liberties of the Church of France* and a *Discourse on the Liberties of the Church of France.* A nobleman, a humanist, and a lawyer, he based his arguments on an aristocratic understanding of the church. The bishops are the ones who do have the authority, and the primacy of the pope is simply one of honor, and not of authority. The popes, therefore, have no authority to depose kings. But the latter do have authority over the clergy, especially in financial and juridical matters.

Pierre Pithou (1539–1596)[3] wrote *The Liberties of the Gallican Church,* a treatise that saw five printings during the controversy. His work was more historically oriented than that of Coquille, and he also made more precise use of jurisprudence—for he too was a lawyer. His thesis was simply that the pope has no temporal authority in the territories of the "most Christian king," and that his spiritual authority is strictly limited by the canons of the ancient councils. The "Gallican liberties" are eighty-three—having to do mostly with the authority of French bishops and synods, and the ecclesiastical authority of the king. Pithou was also one of the moving spirits behind the ordinances of Blois, as well as behind the decision of the French clergy to absolve Henry IV without consulting with the pope.

---

[2] *Ibid.,* p. 385.
[3] *Ibid.* J. Carreyre, "Pierre Pithou," *DTC,* 12:2235-38; H. R. Guggisberg, "Pithou, Pierre," *RGG,* 5:389.

Edmond Richer (1559–1631)[4] changed the tone of Gallicanism. Coquille and Pithou, being lawyers, had discussed the matter mostly from a juridical perspective. Richer, on the other hand, was a doctor from the Sorbonne, and a syndic of the Faculty of Theology. Therefore, whereas the Gallicanism of Coquille and Pithou was mostly political, Richer's was clearly theological. His very brief book—thirty pages—*On Ecclesiastical and Political Power* (1611) became the most influential piece of literature in the entire controversy. In some ways, it is simply a radical denial of the traditional arguments for Roman supremacy, as Bellarmine had expounded them. Richer rejects the notion of the church as a hierarchical entity. Drawing from the earlier arguments of the conciliarists, he claims that the only head of the church is Christ, who has delegated his authority to believers as a whole. These in turn have entrusted their authority to priests and bishops. The priests have been given sacerdotal authority, each in his own parish—and here Richer was accused of approaching presbyterianism. The bishops have been given authority of jurisdiction, which they are to exercise each in his own diocese. Joined together in a council, the bishops are the seat of supreme authority within the church. The pope then is the minister of the council, executing its policies and orders, and reporting periodically to it.

Richer's main opponent was André Duval (1564–1638),[5] who argued in favor of the hierarchical understanding of the church as found in Bellarmine, and in favor of the promulgation of the decrees of Trent. It is significant, however, that in spite of his generally conservative attitude he still defended the "Gallican liberties"—although not as rights that the French church had in and of itself, but rather as privileges that he expected the Holy See to grant in deference to the ancient customs of the Gallican church.

Saint-Cyran (1581–1643)[6] was a friend of Jansenius, and one of the means by which Jansenism gained a strong foothold in France. He approached the Gallican issue, however, from a different angle. Some of the monastic orders, especially the Jesuits, were seen as arms of the papacy in various countries. Owing to their direct connection

---

[4] Willaert, *Après le concile de Trente*, pp. 387-89; H. R. Guggisberg, "Richer, Edmond," *RGG*, 5:1093; J. Carreyre, "Richer, Edmond," *DTC*, 13:2698-2702; R. Golden, *The Godly Rebellion: Parisian Curés and the Religious Fronde, 1652-1662* (Chapel Hill: University of North Carolina Press, 1981), pp. 72-74.

[5] A. Ingold, "Duval, André," *DTC*, 4:1967.

[6] C. Constantin, "Du Vergier ou Du Verger de Hauranne, Jean," *DTC*, 4:1967-75.

with Rome, they were regarded askance, not only by secular princes, but also by a number of prelates. Saint-Cyran took up this issue on the occasion of a debate between the Jesuits and the hierarchy regarding jurisdiction over work in England. In a treatise that he published under the name of Petrus Aurelius, Saint-Cyran defended the authority of the episcopacy against both the pope and the regular clergy. The bishops receive their authority directly from above, and to them belongs all power. They share this with the parish priests, whose authority reflects that of the bishops. In this sense, it can be said that the priests are "lesser prelates." This authority derives from their ordination and not from their vows. The vows and rules of the various orders are mere human institutions, and add nothing to the authority of a priest. Therefore, the seat of authority in the church is in the episcopacy and its clergy, and not in the bishop of Rome or in orders that claim to derive their commission from him.

The next step in the development of Gallican theory took place in the work of Pierre de Marca,[7] archbishop of Toulouse, during the regime of Richelieu. The exact goals of Richelieu's policies are uncertain. But in any case it was to his advantage—in his playing cat-and-mouse with Urban VIII—to have a Gallican statement that at the same time offered the pope some hope for reconciliation. This statement was provided by Pierre de Marca (1594–1662) in his treatise *On the Concord between the Priesthood and the Empire,* written at the king's behest—which is to say, Richelieu's. The details of his theories are not important here. In summary, he argued for the primacy of the pope, rejecting the old conciliarist views, while also insisting on the sovereign authority of the king and on the obligation of the monarch to sustain the particular canons of the French church—which the pope did not have the power to abolish. Thus, in de Marca's work we see an example of what would always be one of the worst temptations for Gallicanism: to become subservient to the dictates of the state, and to turn its defense of the autonomy of the national church into a means for making that church a tool of the policies of the state.

After the death of Richelieu, precisely at the time when France was reaching the apex of her power under Louis XIV, the controversy became more acute. The question of whether or not the pope had the

---

[7] J. Carreyre, "Marca, Pierre de," *DTC,* 9:1987-91; Willaert, *Après le concile de Trente,* pp. 402-3.

right to abolish the particular canons of the Gallican church led some ultramontanes to affirm the infallibility of the pope in starker terms than ever before. In response to this, the authorities simply attempted to use force to suppress such views—opposed as they were to the policies of Louis XIV. Although the question of the authority of the pope was still debated, the policy of suppression was not conducive to creative dialogue. The most significant theological document of the period—significant not for originality, which it lacked, but for its later importance—was the *Six Articles* published by the Sorbonne in 1663. These articles affirmed that, in temporal matters, the king was completely independent from the pope, and that the pope lacked the authority to depose French bishops, according to the ancient Gallican canons. More ambiguously, the articles went on to declare that the faculty at the Sorbonne did not affirm the superiority of the pope over a council, and did not believe that the infallibility of the pope was to be held by all as a dogma.[8] In the very timid and ambiguous nature of these statements, it may be seen that the theologians at the Sorbonne felt that the power of the state was too great to risk its displeasure. Thus the defense of the "Gallican liberties" had resulted in a great loss in the liberty of the church vis-à-vis the state. By 1682, it was evident that Louis XIV was using Gallicanism as a means to bend the church to his will, especially in matters of finances and appointments. At that time, an extraordinary assembly of the clergy, called by the king, granted him his wishes and then proceeded to justify its actions on the basis of Gallican theory. The result was the *Four Articles* of 1682, written by the famous court preacher Jacques Bossuet.[9] These articles affirmed the king's temporal power, limited the pope's authority by asserting that he had to act according to the ancient Gallican liberties, and declared that, although the pope was the head of the church in matters of faith, his judgments were not beyond correction—in other words, denied the infallibility of the pope, at least in its broadest scope. The pope refused to accept these decisions, the Inquisition condemned them, and a number of theologians from other areas wrote treatises against them. Those in France who followed the lead

---

[8] E. Préclin, *Les luttes politiques et doctrinales aux XVIIe et XVIIIe siècles* (vol. 19 of Fliche and Martin, *Histoire de l'église* [Paris: Bloud et Gay, 1955]), p. 152; A. Sedwick, *Jansenism in Seventeenth-Century France: Voices from the Wilderness* (Charlottesville: University Press of Virginia, 1977), pp. 20-46.

[9] English text in H. Bettenson, ed., *Documents of the Christian Church* (New York: Oxford University Press, 1943), pp. 379-80.

of Rome on this matter were brought under heavy pressure. And yet, there was always an undercurrent of opposition, even in France itself, to this new brand of Gallicanism, which had become a veiled form of caesaropapism—although most of this opposition did not take the shape of ultramontanism.

The eighteenth century thus marked the apogee of Gallicanism. By then, however, it had become clear that there were at least two sorts of Gallicanism. One was the genuine attempt on the part of the bishops and some of the clergy to defend the authority and autonomy of the national church. The other was the desire on the part of the king and his court to extend their authority over the church. None of these was essentially democratic in character—as they have been depicted by some liberal historians. In any case, the growing conviction on the part of those who wished a genuine reformation of the church that such reformation would not be produced by the crown was one of the main factors contributing to the eventual decline of Gallicanism. The other factor was the French Revolution.

But before we turn to the impact of the French Revolution on the question of papal authority, a word must be said about two movements that were intimately connected with Gallicanism: Febronianism and Josephism.[10] Febronianism derived its name from Justin Febronius, whose real name was Johann Nikolaus von Hontheim (1701–1790).[11] Febronius published in 1763 a treatise on the legitimate authority of the Roman pontiff that said that sovereigns are not subject to the pope, whose authority derives directly from the whole church. This means that the pope is subject to the entire church, which may judge and depose him in a conciliar gathering. Furthermore, he is not superior to other bishops, and he has no direct authority within dioceses not his own. What authority he has in this respect, he derives solely as the guardian of the canons and the executor of the dictates of the whole church. As will be readily seen, Febronianism was little more than the German counterpart to Gallicanism. As in France, here too the monarchs saw in this sort of doctrine a valuable tool for their policy. Thus Febronianism resulted in Josephism when Holy Roman Emperor

---

[10] Préclin, *Les luttes,* pp. 769-801.

[11] T. Ortolan, "Febronius, Justin (ou Jean-Chrysostome-Nicholas de Hontheim)," *DTC,* 5:2115-24; E. Wolf, "Febronianismus," *RGG,* 2:890-91.

Joseph II decided to apply its theories within the Empire.[12] This was coupled with a series of measures against religious orders, which Joseph saw—with some justification—as papal arms within his domains. When Joseph's brother Leopold applied the same principles in his Tuscan territories, Josephism seemed to be expanding. But in fact it disappeared almost immediately after the death of Joseph, in 1790. Febronianism was condemned by the Inquisition in 1764, and Josephism by Pius VI in 1794.

It was the French Revolution that spelled the end of Gallicanism as well as of Febronianism and Josephism. The overthrow of the Bourbons, the bloodbath of the Revolution, and the general tendency toward separation of church and state in the nineteenth century, all contributed to the decline of Gallicanism. As the eighteenth century saw the apex of Gallicanism, so did the nineteenth see the rapid process through which ultramontanism gained the upper hand. This process began with the works of Joseph de Maistre and F. R. de Lamennais, and culminated in the First Vatican Council with the promulgation of papal infallibility.

Count Joseph Marie de Maistre (1753–1821)[13] embodied the reaction of the French nobility to the Revolution. He saw order as the supreme value in society, and he believed that this order had been established once and for all, in a fixed manner, by God. Since reality is both physical and spiritual, God has set two different hierarchies to rule over the world. Both of these hierarchies are monarchical, for the king is at the head of the temporal power, and the pope is the final authority in spiritual matters. Both king and pope rule by divine authority. However, since in the order of things the spiritual is always above the material, the pope has ultimate authority over the king. He can discipline and depose kings, for he is the representative of Jesus Christ on earth, and he is responsible to none save God. If the king seems to act unjustly, his subjects have no right to oppose or depose him. All they can do is to appeal to a higher court: the pope. Against the pope there is no legitimate resistance, and no court of appeal beyond him.

---

[12] G. Mollat, "Josephisme," *DTC*, 8:1543-47.

[13] S. Rocheblare, *Étude sur Joseph de Maistre* (Strasbourg: Istra, 1922); C. S. Phillips, *The Church in France, 1789-1848: A Study in Revival* (New York: Russell & Russell, 1966), pp. 207-13.

Félicité Robert de Lamennais (1782–1854)[14] had one of the most interesting theological careers of the nineteenth century. His first significant literary efforts were directed against Napoleon's plans to control the church. He then became a supporter of the royalist party in France, although his interest at this point was not so much the institution of royalty itself as the contribution that that institution would make to the true and orderly religion. He saw authority as the principle without which no order and no faith could subsist, and he thus connected Protestantism and Gallicanism with religious indifference and with atheism. Cartesianism he also attacked for its confidence in the mind of the individual. Gallicanism was to him a "system which consists in believing as little as possible without being a heretic, in order to obey as little as possible without being a rebel."[15] In his earlier years, he held that there could be no alliance between Catholicism and democracy, for they follow opposite principles, and in the long run democracy is destructive of society itself. Furthermore, the pope must be declared to be infallible, and in him must all power reside, for without him the Christian faith collapses, and without such faith society cannot subsist. The best possible order would be a theocracy, with the pope at its head.

But then Lamennais carried these doctrines even further. It was precisely the established civil authority that was opposing the power of the pope. Why not then break the traditional alliance of crown and tiara, and join the forces of political liberalism? He had said earlier that subjects should disobey rulers who did not act according to Christian principles. Now he would add that the best policy for Christians to follow was to set out in a great crusade for political freedom, with the pope as their leader. After all, Christianity must guarantee political freedom, and it is precisely the pope's power and authority that guarantee such freedom. In the earlier stages of his career, he had received the support of Leo XII, who probably intended to make him a cardinal. Now he set out for Rome, to secure the support of Gregory XVI for his views and his crusade. But instead the pope condemned his doctrines in the encyclical *Mirari vos*

---

[14] Phillips, *The Church in France, 1789–1848*, pp. 216-58; A. Dansette, *Religious History of Modern France*, vol. 1: *From the Revolution to the Third Republic* (Freiburg: Herder, 1961), pp. 207-26; A. R. Vidler, *Prophecy and Papacy: A Study of Lamennais, the Church and Revolution* (New York: Scribner, 1954); P. N. Stearns, *Priest and Revolutionary: Lamennais and the Dilemma of French Catholicism* (New York: Harper and Row, 1967); J. J. Oldfield, *The Problem of Tolerance and Social Existence in the Writings of Félicité Lamennais* (Leiden: Brill, 1973); L. LeGuillou, *La condamnation de Lamennais* (Paris: Beauchesne, 1982).

[15] Phillips, *The Church in France, 1789–1884*, p. 224.

(1832). Here Gregory said that such ideas incited to sedition, and that the freedom of the press—which Lamennais advocated—was contrary to the maxims of the church. Lamennais accepted the condemnation and retired to his estates in La Chesnai, where he wrote the *Words of a Believer*, replying to the pope. When his opinions were condemned again by the encyclical *Singulari nos* (1834), many of his friends submitted to the pope, but Lamennais left the church.

After that time, Lamennais concentrated his efforts in the political field, and he eventually became a member of Parliament in the revolution of 1848. In the field of theology, he abandoned orthodoxy, denying the supernatural and tending toward pantheism. For his work during this period, he may be said to be a forerunner of modern political ideas as well as of modernism—which we shall discuss later in this chapter.

Although Lamennais was condemned by the pope, the views that were rejected showed a clear insight into what would eventually lead to the triumph of ultramontanism in the Catholic Church. Indeed, as long as the traditional order stood, with its close association of church and state, civil powers would make every effort to secure control of the church within their domains. This had become evident in the Gallican movement, especially in its later stages. But once the church began losing its political power in the various nations the opposition on the part of rulers to ecclesiastical centralization would diminish. Thus, during the nineteenth century two seemingly contrary but really complementary developments were taking place: while the pope was increasing his authority over the entire Catholic Church, the actual power of that church was diminishing.

One of the most important milestones in the development of papal authority was the bull *Ineffabilis Deus* (1854),[16] of Pius IX. For centuries, the question of the immaculate conception of Mary had been debated among Catholic theologians. The question was not whether Mary conceived Jesus without sin—that had been decided by consensus long before—but whether Mary herself had been preserved from any taint of original sin, even at the moment of her conception. Some earlier theologians—Anselm among them—had opposed the growing tendency to exalt the Virgin in this respect, and had said that she was conceived and born in sin. Thomas Aquinas,

---

[16] Portion of the English text in Bettenson, *Documents of the Christian Church*, pp. 380-81. A Latin selection in *Denzinger,* 1641.

and the Dominicans after him, held that the Virgin was conceived in original sin, but sanctified before her birth. Against them, the Franciscans insisted on the immaculate conception. By the late fifteenth century, the debate had grown so bitter that Sixtus IV had to intervene, forbidding any to accuse others of heresy on a matter on which the church had made no dogmatic declarations. The Jesuits agreed with the Franciscans on the immaculate conception of Mary, and through the influence of these two powerful orders that theory had been gaining ground among conservative Catholics. Such was the state of the matter when Piux IX became pope. A similar, but more recent, process had been taking place with reference to the theory of papal infallibility. In the conflict with Gallicanism, many ultramontanes had asserted that the pope was infallible. Some went beyond infallibility on dogmatic questions and claimed that he was also infallible on questions of ethics and politics. Pius IX now decided that the promulgation of the doctrine of the immaculate conception would be a good issue on which to assert his authority on questions of dogma. On this he was right, for the question of whether or not Mary was conceived without original sin was not likely to arouse much interest in the part of political rulers who would normally look with suspicion upon any attempt to strengthen the authority of the pope. Therefore, the bull *Ineffabilis* was generally accepted without a great deal of debate. Here Pius affirmed that, "through a singular grace and privilege of God omnipotent," Mary was preserved immune from any original guilt, and that this doctrine is revealed by God and must therefore be believed by all. The significance of this declaration, however, went far beyond questions of Mariology. Now, for the first time in the history of the church, a pope had defined dogma on his own authority. The fact that there was little opposition or negative reaction to this declaration led the ultramontane party to believe that the time was approaching for the formal dogmatic declaration of papal infallibility. This was to be the main order of business of the First Vatican Council.

The First Vatican Council[17] was formally called by Pope Pius IX in 1868, and began its sessions the following year on the Feast of the

---

[17] R. Aubert, *Vatican I* (Paris: Editions de l'orante, 1964); E. C. Butler, *The Vatican Council* (London: Longmans, Green, 1930); E. Cecconi, *Storia del concilio ecumenico vaticano scritta sui documenti originali*, 4 vols. (Rome: Vaticano, 1873-79); *Actes et histoire du concile oecuménique de Rome MDCCCLXIX*, 7 vols. (Paris: A Pilon, 1870-71).

Immaculate Conception (the eighth of December). It was suspended late in 1870, when the war between Prussia and France made it impossible to continue meeting. Although the council dealt with a number of issues, by far the most important was papal infallibility. On this issue, opinions were divided, although the majority was in favor of declaring papal infallibility to be a dogma of the church. Some of those who favored the definition wished to see no limitation placed on papal infallibility, and the extremists in this party went so far as to affirm that *quando egli medita, è Dio che pensa in lui*—"when he meditates it is God who thinks in him." Others—the majority—felt that papal infallibility ought to be promulgated as a dogma of the church, but that this ought to be done in such a way that the fact that some popes had fallen into heresy—notably Liberius and Honorius—would not be an obstacle for the reception of the council's definition. A substantial number of bishops from lands where Catholics were a minority—especially in eastern Europe—were in favor of the doctrine itself, but felt that the moment was not opportune for its promulgation. Some, such as the bishop of Baltimore, suggested a dogmatic definition in which the word "infallible" was not used. The minority, led by the archbishops of Vienna and Prague, simply opposed the doctrine altogether. Since the opposition to the doctrine itself was small, and since the council had adopted strict rules on closure of debate, it soon became evident that the council would promulgate papal infallibility. This was done on July 18, 1870, with 522 votes in favor, two opposed, and over a hundred abstentions. The definition itself said in part:

> Therefore, faithfully adhering to the tradition derived from the commencement of the Christian faith, to the glory of God our savior, to the exaltation of the Catholic religion, and to the salvation of Christian nations, *Sacro approbante Concilio*, we teach and define that it is a divinely revealed dogma: that the Roman pontiff, when he speaks *Ex Cathedra*, that is, when in discharge of his office of pastor and doctor of all Christians, he defines, in virtue of his supreme apostolic authority, a doctrine of faith or morals to be held by the universal Church, is endowed by the divine assistance promised to him in blessed Peter, with that infallibility with which our divine redeemer willed that the Church should be furnished in defining doctrine of faith or morals; and, therefore,

that such definitions of the Roman pontiff are irreformable of themselves and not in virtue of the consent of the church.[18]

Thus, those who wished to see the doctrine proclaimed had won the day. Although the definition itself made it clear that the pope was not always infallible—and thus made it possible to explain the cases of Liberius and Honorius—it did give him final authority on questions of faith and morals. In another part of the same decree, it was affirmed that the pope had direct jurisdiction over the entire church, not only in matters of faith and morals, but also in discipline and administration. The conciliar movement was finally dead and it was precisely a council that gave it the *coup de grâce*.

The new doctrine was received with little resistance. The Bavarian church historian John Joseph I. Döllinger, who had led the opposition, refused to accept the definition, and was excommunicated. Some in the Netherlands, Germany, and Austria left the Roman Catholic Church, took the name of "Old Catholics," and formed small national churches. The Russian and Greek Orthodox, as well as many Protestants, simply took the doctrine to be a further confirmation of Rome's heresy. But among Roman Catholics themselves there was little turmoil.

Thus Gallicanism and its kindred movements had come to an end. And yet, it was a hollow victory for the papacy, for the main reason that the doctrine of papal infallibility met such scarce resistance was that the church had lost a great deal of influence in the world. Two months after this declaration the pope lost the city of Rome to the Kingdom of Italy. Whether the pope was declared to be infallible or not was now seen by many in traditionally Catholic countries as a largely irrelevant matter. This was partly owing to the manner in which Roman Catholicism had responded to the challenges of the modern world.

The Church and the Modern World

Although it was the nineteenth century, with its new philosophical and political outlook, that most clearly posed the question of the relationship between the church and the world, this question had already arisen at an earlier date in two controversies that usually

---

[18] C. J. Barry, ed., *Readings in Church History*, vol. 3: *The Modern Era: 1789 to the Present* (Westminster, Md.: Newman Press, 1965), pp. 78-79.

receive little attention but that serve to exemplify the delicate issues with which the Roman Catholic Church was having to deal. These two controversies had to do with quietism in France, and with the missionary practices of the Jesuits in China and India.

Quietism was a form of mysticism that developed in France in the seventeenth century.[19] Its origins may be found in quasi-heterodox forms of mystical piety that had appeared in Spain in earlier centuries, partially under the influence of Moslem mysticism. In any case, it was introduced in France by the Spaniard Miguel de Molinos, one of whose disciples, Madame Jeanne-Marie de Guyon, soon made it popular. The main tenet of this form of mysticism was that Christian perfection consists in a continuous state of contemplation in which the believer becomes indifferent to all that is not God. In this state, one is not concerned for salvation, one needs no works of charity, and the entire world is forgotten. Madame de Guyon won her spiritual advisor, François Fénelon, to this form of mysticism. Fénelon was one of the most distinguished ecclesiastical leaders in France, and soon became archbishop of Cambrai. When Bossuet—whom we have already mentioned in connection with Gallicanism—attacked quietism, Fénelon came to its defense, and thus two of the most respected prelates in the country were engaged in a bitter controversy. The affair ended when Rome condemned Fénelon (1699). But the influence of quietism persisted in France. In any case, the significance of the controversy is that it shows that the Catholic Church was not ready to accept the theories of those who advocated total indifference toward the world.

The controversy over the missionary practices of the Jesuits in China had its roots in the policies adopted by Matteo Ricci, who in 1601, after great difficulties, had established a Catholic mission in Peking.[20] He managed to do this by developing great appreciation for Chinese culture, and by thus gaining the confidence of the emperor. Although Ricci himself was hesitant on the matter,[21] his successors felt that most of the Confucian rites practiced by the Chinese were civil and cultural in character, and that therefore Christian converts could continue participating in them without falling into idolatry or

---

[19] Préclin, *Les luttes*, pp. 165-73.

[20] *Ibid.*, pp. 173-92; G. H. Dunne, *Generation of Giants: The Story of the Jesuits in China in the Last Decades of the Ming Dynasty* (London: Burns & Oates, 1962).

[21] *Della entrata della Compagnia di Giesù e Christianità nella Cina*, in *Fonti Ricciane* (Rome: La Libreria dello Stato, 1942–49), paragraphs 55, 129-30, 178, 181, and 609.

superstition. The Dominicans and Franciscans who arrived later did not understand the precarious balance on which missions could exist in China, and were puzzled and scandalized by the Jesuit concessions. In 1645 a Dominican obtained a decision from Rome against the Chinese rites. The Jesuits had the emperor of China make a solemn declaration that the rites in question were not religious, but civil, and this declaration was proclaimed throughout the land. In consequence, the emperor felt personally affronted when some "barbarian" in Rome insisted on contradicting him. The final outcome did not take place until 1742, when the Chinese rites were formally condemned by the Catholic Church.[22] The net result of all this was the almost complete disappearance of what had been a very successful mission. Here we see illustrated, albeit in a somewhat unusual context, the variety of opinions existing within the Roman Catholic Church regarding the manner and degree to which the church ought to accommodate itself to culture.

It was, however, the nineteenth century that posed this question with acute urgency. The new developments in science and philosophy that we have discussed in previous chapters posed grave threats to the Catholic Church. Growing rationalism challenged traditional views of the supernatural and of revelation. Historical studies questioned both the reliability of the Bible and the authority of a tradition whose seamy side was now showing. The infelicitous moments—such as the case of Galileo—when orthodoxy had been an obstacle to scientific progress were constantly pointed out. But above all, where the church felt most threatened was in the spreading notion of a secular state. Roman Catholic leaders saw all these currents as posing the basic issue of authority, and therefore for them the notion of a secular state, with freedom of the press and religious plurality, was the epitome of all that threatened and denied the faith.

There were reasons for this fear on the part of the church. Although the French Revolution had spelled the beginning of the end for Gallicanism, its ideal of a secular state persisted and spread

---

[22] Almost two hundred years later, however, the Sacred Congregation of the Propagation of the Faith declared: "It has become increasingly evident that in the Far East certain ceremonies, which were originaly connected with pagan religious worship, have now become nothing more than civil acts of reverence for the ancestors or a demonstration of love of one's country or courtesy towards one's neighbors." Quoted in Barry, *Readings in Church History*, 3:406. The reason for this was the problem posed by Shintoism in Japan, and its connection with rising Japanese nationalism.

throughout Europe. Most of Latin America became independent early in the nineteenth century, and Rome's support of Spain in the struggle for independence—and afterward—produced strong anti-clerical feelings in many of the ruling classes in the new nations. In 1848 the *Communist Manifesto* was published, and 1864 saw the foundation of the First International Workingmen's Association. Also in 1848, the Second French Republic was proclaimed. The same year Italy began its war of independence. In Rome the people revolted, forced the pope to appoint a democratic minister, and proclaimed the Roman Republic. In 1860, through a plebiscite, most of the papal states were transferred to the authority of the monarchy. Ten years later, the pope lost Rome, and his temporal rule was reduced to the Vatican.

The reaction of the Catholic Church to these threats and losses was simply to defend its traditional position and privileges. Where the authority of the pope and the church was still recognized, that authority was strengthened. In Spain, for instance, a concordat was signed with the pope whereby the Catholic religion was the only legal one, and education and censorship were placed entirely in the hands of the church. The policy of placing books on the *Index* and of condemning individuals who held views contrary to those of the church was now used throughout Europe against liberal and democratic elements. We have already mentioned the case of Lamennais, one of the papacy's staunchest supporters who was condemned when he embraced liberal political ideas, and suggested that it would be in the best interest of the church to support political liberalism.

The church's opposition to the new ideas found its strongest and most sweeping expression in the *Syllabus of Errors,* published by Pius IX in 1864. This is a list of eighty errors held—or supposedly held—by persons of very different persuasions, but all opposed to the authority of the church. The last error condemned in this document could well have been the first, for it expresses the mood of the entire list. This error is that "the Roman pontiff can and ought to reconcile and harmonize himself with progress, with liberalism, and with modern civilization."[23] It is also an error to assert that "the method and principles whereby the ancient scholastic doctors

---

[23] Error 80, in Barry, *Readings in Church History,* 3: 74.

cultivated theology, are not suited to the necessities of our time and to the progress of the sciences,"[24] or even that "the too arbitrary conduct of Roman pontiffs contributed to the Church's division into East and West."[25] It was, however, on the issues arising out of the idea of a secular and pluralistic state that the *Syllabus* placed its emphasis. This may be seen in the following selection of some of the errors condemned in it:

> 45) The whole governance of public schools wherein the youth of any Christian state is educated . . . may and should be given to the civil power; and in such sense be given, that no right be recognized in any other authority of mixing itself up in the management of the schools, the direction of studies, the conferring of degrees, the choice or approbation of teachers.
>
> 47) The best constitution of civil society requires that popular schools which are open to children of every class, and that public institutions generally which are devoted to teaching literature and science and providing for the education of youth, be exempted from all authority of the Church. . . .
>
> 55) The Church should be separated from the state, and the state from the church.
>
> 57) The science of philosophy and morals and also the laws of a state, may and should withdraw themselves from the jurisdiction of divine and ecclesiastical authority. . . .
>
> 77) In this our age it is no longer expedient that the Catholic religion should be treated as the only religion of the state, all other worships whatsoever being excluded.[26]

The *Syllabus*, however, did not reflect the mood of all Catholics. In various parts of Europe—but especially in France and Britain—there were Catholic leaders who showed more openness toward the modern world, and more willingness to work within the increasingly pluralistic setting of the new times. The best known of these at the time of the promulgation of the *Syllabus* was John Henry Newman (1801–1890),[27] whom we have already encountered in our discussion of the Oxford movement. After his conversion to Roman Catholicism in 1845, Newman became one of the most celebrated Catholic

---

[24] Error 13, in *ibid.*, p. 70.

[25] Error 30, in *ibid.*, p. 72.

[26] *Ibid.*, pp. 72-74.

[27] L. Bouyer, *Newman: His Life and Spirituality* (New York: P. J. Kenedy, 1958); C. F. Harrold, *John Henry Newman: An Expository and Critical Study of His Mind, Thought, and Art* (Hamden, Conn.: Archon

leaders in England—as well as in Ireland, where he served as rector of the University of Dublin for four years. In 1858, however, a conflict arose between him and Henry Edward Manning, another Roman Catholic convert from the Oxford movement who had become a spokesman for papal authority and infallibility. As a result, Newman's relations with Rome were already strained when the *Syllabus* appeared. It seems likely that, had he not lived in a Protestant country where he was doing significant apologetic work in favor of Roman Catholicism, he would have been condemned. As it was, Newman practically ignored the *Syllabus* while Rome winked at his liberal tendencies. His most significant works were *Essay on the Development of Doctrine, Apologia pro vita sua,* and *Grammar of Assent.* In the first of these he attempted to show that dogma does indeed evolve—contrary to what was held by most Roman Catholic theologians—but that this evolution takes place under the guidance of the Spirit and is the proper result of the original Christian faith—as a tree grows from an acorn. These views, as well as his opposition to the definition of papal infallibility—a doctrine that he accepted once it was defined—gained him many opponents among traditional Roman Catholics. He was vindicated, however, when Leo XIII made him a cardinal in 1879.

A younger generation of Catholic scholars who also attempted to relate the Catholic faith to modern times arose in the late nineteenth and early twentieth centuries. Since at that time biblical and historical criticism had advanced in Germany to the point of skepticism, their views were much more radical than Newman's, often questioning the historical origins of Christianity and criticizing the "medievalism" that they saw prevalent in the church. These scholars were dubbed "modernists" by the more traditional Catholics, and their views were finally condemned early in the twentieth century.[28] In Italy, Antonio

Books, 1966); M. Trevor, *Newman* (Garden City, N.Y.: Doubleday, 1962); J. H. Walgrave, *Newman the Theologian: The Nature of Belief and Doctrine as Exemplified in His Life and Works* (New York: Sheed & Ward, 1960); M. Misner, *Papacy and Development: Newman and the Primacy of the Pope* (Leiden: Brill, 1976); B. W. Martin, *John Henry Newman: His Life and Work* (New York: Oxford University Press, 1982). For further references see J. R. Griffin, *Newman: A Bibliography of Secondary Studies* (Front Royal, Va.: Christendom Publications, 1980).

[28] J. Rivière, "*Modernisme,*" *DTC,* 10:2009–47; L. da Veiga Coutinho, *Tradition et histoire dans la controverse moderniste (1898–1910)* (Rome: Universitas Gregoriannae, 1954); A. J. Loeppert, *Modernism and the Vatican* (Cincinnati: Jennings and Graham, 1912); M. Ranchetti, *The Catholic Modernists: A Study of the Religious Reform Movement, 1864-1907* (London: Oxford University Press, 1969); A. R. Vidler, *The Modernist Movement in the Roman Church: Its Origins and Outcome* (Cambridge: The University Press, 1934). A selection of texts: B. M. G. Reardon, ed., *Roman Catholic Modernism* (London: A. & C. Black, 1970). G. Daly, *Transcendence and Immanence: A Study in Catholic Modernism and Integralism* (Oxford:

Fogazzaro expressed modernist views in fiction; but his most famous novel, *The Saint*, was placed on the *Index* in 1905. In Britain, Baron Friedrich von Hügel (1852–1925) advocated the critical study of Scripture and sought to reconcile Catholicism with modern culture. Although he was never condemned, his influence in Roman Catholic circles was hampered by the negative attitude of the church, and he was therefore much more influential among Protestants than among his fellow Catholics. Von Hügel's friend, the Jesuit George Tyrrell (1861–1909), did not fare as well. An ex-Anglican with deep and abiding appreciation for Catholic piety and devotion, Tyrrell felt that the dry and dogmatic scholasticism of his age was selling Catholicism short. His repeated attempts to set a new tone for theology, however, caused him to be expelled from the order and eventually excommunicated. In 1908 his book *Medievalism* showed how bitter he had grown toward a church that he had loved but that could not accept the shape of his love.

It was in France, however, that modernism drew its largest following. Its most important leader in that country was Alfred Loisy. Alfred Firmin Loisy (1857–1940)[29] was a biblical and historical scholar who was greatly influenced by German critical studies. From the beginning of his career he was viewed askance by the more conservative elements in the Catholic Church, which suspected him of holding views similar to those which Renan had set forth in his rationalist *Life of Jesus* (1863). Loisy, however, was not really a rationalist in the traditional sense. He believed that the actual constitution of the church, and especially the mass, were valuable and should be kept. He was not seeking a universal and natural form of Christianity, but was rather attempting to rid the present form of the faith from its vulnerability to historical studies. This became clear when he responded to Adolf Harnack's *What Is Christianity?* In his response, under the title of *The Gospel and the Church* (1902), Loisy claimed that whether or not Jesus attempted to found a church or to institute sacraments was immaterial. The essence of Christianity is to be found not by going back to its origins, but by seeing what it has

---

Clarendon, 1980); L. B. Gilkey, *Catholicism Confronts Modernity: A Protestant View* (New York: Seabury, 1975).

[29] The best introduction is Loisy's autobiography, *My Duel with the Vatican* (New York: E. P. Dutton, 1924). See also F. Heiler, *Der Vater des katholischen Modernismus: Alfred Loisy, 1857-1940* (Munich: Erasmus, 1947); M. D. M. Petry, *Alfred Loisy: His Religious Significance* (Cambridge: The University Press, 1944); A. H. Jones, *Independence and Exegesis: The Study of Early Christianity in the Work of Alfred Loisy (1857-1960), Charles Guignebert (1867-1939) and Maurice Goguel (1880-1955)* (Tübingen: Mohr, 1983).

become under the guidance of the Holy Spirit. Needless to say, this book drew the immediate condemnation of ecclesiastical authorities. A year later several of Loisy's writings appeared on the *Index* of forbidden books. In 1908, he was excommunicated, but by then he had become one of the most influential religious writers in France. The thirty-one remaining years of his life were spent in teaching, writing, and research on the origins of Christianity, on mystery cults, and on the history of the modernist movement. Although condemned, Loisy was one of the main factors giving the French Catholic Church its particularly liberal flavor.

In Loisy we see exemplified the main characteristics of the modernist movement. The first and most important of these was the use of the critical methods developed by Protestant biblical and historical scholars in Germany. At this point, it is significant that Loisy attempted not to refute all of Harnack's understanding of Christian origins, but simply to deny its implications. His later studies on the Gospels and on mystery religions drew heavily from contemporary German scholarship. Second, Loisy and the modernists—in opposition to Protestant liberal scholarship—did not feel that these historical studies should lead one to reject the present form of the Christian faith, for they insisted on the work of the Spirit guiding the history of the church according to God's purpose and goals. Finally, the modernists agreed with Protestant liberalism in affirming that there was need for a new sort of theology, different from traditional orthodoxy—and most definitely different from scholasticism. This new theology was to be geared to the actual practice of the Christian life.

The modernists had high hopes when Leo XIII was elected pope, for he was known as a studious man who respected sound scholarship.[30] Leo did indeed issue in 1893 the encyclical *Providentissimus Deus,* which spoke in favor of the use of modern discoveries in biblical studies but at the same time warned against the dangers of misuse of such discoveries.[31] The modernists saw in this encyclical a measure of encouragement from the Holy See, while the traditionalists saw it as a caveat against modernism. In later years, as the traditionalists gained the upper hand, *Providentissimus Deus* was

---

[30] E. T. Gargan, ed., *Leo XIII and the Modern World* (New York: Sheed & Ward, 1961). This volume includes a number of shorter pieces dealing with various aspects of Leo's work.

[31] *Denzinger,* 1941–53.

generally interpreted in the most conservative way. Leo's successor, Pius X, returned to the unambiguously conservative policies of Pius IX. Following the directives of the pope, the Holy Office issued in 1907 the decree *Lamentabili*,[32] in which sixty-seven modernist propositions were condemned. Later in the same year, Pius X confirmed their condemnation in his encyclical *Pascendi*.[33]

The ambiguity of *Providentissimus Deus* regarding modern critical scholarship reflects the attitude of Leo XIII toward the whole range of challenges facing the church at this time. Therefore, although he was by no means a liberal pope, he may be seen as an enlightened moderate, attempting to find ways in which the traditional faith could speak to modern times—and, between the reigns of Pius IX and Pius X, this was in itself a significant respite. His encyclical *Aeterni Patris* (1879)[34] commended the study of Thomas Aquinas; however, the reason for this was not the need for a simplistic return to past times, but the fact that the philosophy of Aquinas seemed best suited to relate Christian doctrine to human science. This was the beginning of a renaissance of Thomistic studies. In opening the archives of the Vatican to scholarly research, he encouraged critical study of Christian origins and history. His encyclical *Rerum Novarum* (1891)[35] is a milestone in the history of ecclesiastical pronouncements on the subject of social justice. This encyclical supported the right of workers—and employers—to organize, and declared that a just wage should be sufficient to allow a worker and his family to live with a measure of comfort. By practicing thrift, such a worker should be able to purchase property of his own. This encyclical also asserted that the place of women was in the home—although this ought not to be seen solely as an attempt to limit the activity of women, but also as a directive for protective legislation against their exploitation. It also affirmed the right to private property and its inheritance—against rising socialism. This encyclical was so significant that forty years later Pius XI, in *Quadragesimo anno*,[36] applied it to new conditions, and John XXIII did likewise on the seventieth anniversary of its proclamation in his *Mater et magistra*.[37] There was, however, one aspect of the modern world that

---

[32] *Ibid.*, 2001-65.
[33] *Ibid.*, 2071-109; Barry, *Readings in Church History*, 3:112-20.
[34] Barry, *Readings in Church History*, 3:79-86.
[35] *Denzinger*, 1938 a-d. There are also many separate English translations.
[36] *Ibid.*, 2253.
[37] *The Encyclicals and Other Messages of John XXIII* (Washington, D.C.: TPS Press, 1964), pp. 250-315.

Leo felt bound to reject. This was the notion of a secular and pluralistic state. In his encyclical *Immortale Dei* (1885)[38] Leo supported the ideal of a Catholic state, asserting that error and truth do not have equal rights and that therefore religious toleration ought to be supported only in non-Catholic countries and then only as an expedient and not as good in itself. Freedom of conscience should exist only for truth, and not for error. This statement had serious repercussions in the United States, where Roman Catholic immigration was increasing, and where many began fearing that, should Catholics ever attain positions of power, they would attempt to implement Leo's ideal of a Catholic state. In the long run, however, the result was the opposite, for the statement on religious freedom of the Second Vatican Council (1965) was partly due to the influence of Roman Catholics from the United States, many of whom had experienced the negative reaction to Leo's views.

This brief survey of Roman Catholic theology should suffice to show that the nineteenth century was—even more than the sixteenth—the most conservative century in the history of Roman Catholicism. In the face of a rapidly changing world the Catholic Church chose—at least officially—to formulate an understanding of itself that reflected conditions no longer existing in the world. In a time of growing skepticism and questioning of every authority, the pope was declared infallible. When the Virgin birth of Jesus, was being doubted, the pope proclaimed the immaculate conception of Mary. Europe was being flooded with new and radical ideas, and the church still relied on the *Index* and the Holy Office to combat those ideas. When modern forms of critical research were developed, Rome condemned those who tried to relate them to religious questions. All this provides some justification for the commonly held view among Protestants that the Catholic Church was one of the most reactionary forces in the world.

And yet, the very condemnations stand as witness that the official conservatism of the church was by no means universal, and that there was still in it a great deal of intellectual vigor. Condemnations of this caliber and insistence are normally issued only against opinions already existing within the church. As we have seen, such opinions were indeed present in a variety of ways in Roman Catholic circles. Against this background, the dramatic changes brought about by John XXIII and the Second Vatican Council are more readily understood.

---

[38] *Denzinger*, 1866–88; Barry, *Readings in Church History*, 3:93-106.

XV

Eastern Theology
After the Fall of Constantinople

The circumstances in which most of Eastern Christianity found itself after the fall of Constantinople (1453) were not conducive to great theological originality. Turkish expansion did not cease with the fall of the ancient patriarchal see, but went on to conquer Greece and to invade Europe as far as Vienna. This political expansion was coupled with a great zeal for Islam, which placed severe limitations on the churches in conquered areas. Although Christians were protected from forced conversion by being a "people of the Book," the Turks placed them under such pressure that many abandoned their faith and became followers of the Prophet.[1] The patriarch of Constantinople often became little more than an officer whose main function was to serve as a liaison between the Sultan and his Christian subjects. The only Eastern church that was able to continue its life under a friendly political power was the Russian Orthodox Church. Other Eastern churches, now further cut off from the West, continued the process of slow decline that had already begun in the Middle Ages.

---

[1] By far the most painful and humiliating measure taken by the Turks against the Christians was the practice of periodically selecting the most promising Christian boys to be taken away from their homes and brought up to become members of a select and fanatical corps of Moslem soldiers known as the Janissaries.

411

Theology in the Greek Orthodox Church

As before, the dominant factor in Greek theology was the question of relations with the West. Given the general decline of most theological schools in Asia Minor and Greece after the Turkish conquests, many Greek theologians were trained in the West. Since the West was bitterly divided during the sixteenth and seventeenth centuries by the conflict between Protestants and Catholics, that controversy and the issues involved in it were transplanted into the Greek Church. Later, when the issues of rationalism and of the relationship between science and theology became paramount in the West, these issues were also introduced into the East. Therefore, although there were a number of other questions discussed in the Greek Church, the two issues that stand out as most significant are, first, the debate over the proper attitude to be taken regarding the Protestant Reformation and, later, the questions posed by the new science.[2] Because the first of these issues came to a head during the patriarchate of Cyril Lucaris, we shall discuss it by centering our attention on his theology and career—with some mention of the final outcome of the controversy. We shall then turn to the influence of modern philosophy and science on Greek theology, and the response of those who opposed such influence.

Cyril Lucaris (1572–1638)[3] may have derived some of his distaste for Roman Catholicism from his older friend and sponsor Meletius Pegas (ca. 1537–1601), patriarch of Alexandria, who wrote against the Romans a treatise On the True Catholic Church and Its True Head. Cyril had come into direct contact with Roman Catholicism as a student in Italy, and especially later when he was sent on a mission to Poland. There Roman Catholicism was making significant inroads among many who had formerly been Eastern Orthodox, and Prince Constantine of Ostrog was attempting to stem the tide by favoring both Eastern Orthodoxy and Protestantism. Lucaris became involved in the prince's maneuvers to such an extent that he was

---

[2] Other more traditional subjects were also revived, but these did not reflect the same level of originality. Thus, for instance, Dositheus of Jerusalem (+ 1707) and Meletius of Athens (+ 1714) wrote historical treatises, while Nicodemus Hagioreites brought about a revival of Hesychasm. Early in the nineteenth century, the question of Greek ecclesiastical independence from Constantinople was debated by Constantine Economos and Theocletus Pharmakides, whom we shall discuss in a different context. B. K. Stephanides, Ἐκκλησιαστικὴ Ἱστορία (Athens: Aster, 1959), pp. 769-70.

[3] G. A. Chatzeantoniou, Protestant Patriarch: The Life of Cyril Lucaris (Richmond: John Knox, 1961); Germanos of Thyateira, Kyrillos Loukaris, 1572-1638: A Struggle for Preponderance between Protestant and Catholic Powers in the Orthodox East (London: S.P.C.K., 1951).

accused of Calvinism, and in 1601 had to produce a confession of faith rejecting such accusations—which, as later events would show, probably were not entirely lacking in foundation.[4] In 1602, having returned to Egypt, Lucaris became patriarch of Alexandria, and in 1620 he was promoted to the see of Constantinople. During his Alexandrine tenure, he followed a policy of attempting to strengthen Protestant influence in the Eastern Church as a means both to counterbalance Catholic influence, and to promote a measure of reformation. As a result, his elevation to Constantinople had the support of the British and Dutch ambassadors, and the opposition of the French, Venetian, and Austrian representatives before the Sultan. The ensuing intrigues cost Lucaris his see and freedom, for he was deposed and sent in chains to Rhodes—according to the French ambassador, so that he could have the leisure to comment on Calvin's *Institutes*. But he was soon returned to his see, thanks to the faithful support of many of his clergy, his own political ability, and the good offices of the Dutch ambassador.

It was during this second period as patriarch of Constantinople that Lucaris published his famous *Confession of Faith* (1629), which caused great uproar in the East as well as in the West. Indeed, it was not an everyday occurrence to have a patriarch of Constantinople publish a Calvinistic confession of faith, as many interpreted this document to be. Here, Lucaris asserts that the authority of Scripture is above that of tradition, for the latter may err, whereas the word of the Holy Spirit through Scripture is infallible. According to Scripture, God has predestined some to salvation and some to eternal damnation, and has done this not in view of divine foreknowledge of future acts of faith, but on the basis of a sovereign and totally unmerited decree. Although Lucaris does not explicitly reject the intercession of the saints, he does affirm that Jesus Christ is "our sole mediator," and the only head of the church. Justification is by faith alone, for the only principle of salvation is the justice of Christ, which is applied in favor of those who repent. But this repentance, again, is the result not of human free will—which no longer exists in the unregenerate—but of predestination. There are only two sacraments—baptism and communion. In the latter, Christ

---

[4] Some authors claim that during this period Lucaris visited Wittenberg and Geneva. But modern research does not seem to support such claims.

is really present, but in such a way that the faithful eat him "not with their teeth, but with the faculties of their souls." Finally, though the art of those who produce religious icons is to be commended, the worship that is rendered to such images must be rejected as superstition.

With the publication of the *Confession,* the intrigues surrounding the patriarchal throne became more acute. Cyril was repeatedly deposed and reinstated—in total, he ascended to the position of patriarch of Constantinople seven times—until he was murdered in 1638. His successor—who, jointly with the Turkish authorities, some Western ambassadors, and perhaps even some Jesuits, was responsible for his death—immediately called a synod that condemned Lucaris and his teachings, and the new patriarch then signed a confession of faith that was submitted to him by the Roman Church. This, however, was not the end of the matter, for the new patriarch was soon murdered, and Lucaris himself began being venerated as a martyr—although some now were claiming that the famous *Confession* was a forgery and that he never held such views. Finally, a synod gathered in Jerusalem in 1672 declared that "if Lucaris was indeed a Calvinistic heretic," he was condemned.

The other point at which it was clear that the West had an enormous influence on Eastern Christianity was the question of the relationship between theology on the one hand and the new philosophy and science on the other. Late in the eighteenth century, Eugenios Bulgaris (1717–1806) introduced the new philosophy into the Greek church when he began expounding the views of Descartes, Locke, and Leibniz.[5] But he was forced to leave his teaching position at Mount Athos, for his efforts found little sympathy among the conservatives who at that time had the upper hand in the church. He then went to Russia in response to an invitation from Catherine the Great, and there he eventually became an archbishop and a member of the Imperial Academy. Nicephoros Theotokis (1736–1800)[6] had similar views and a parallel career, for he too spent the latter part of his life in Russia—which at that time was more open to the new ideas coming from the West.

---

[5] A. Palmieri, "Bulgaris, Eugène," *DTC,* 2:1236-44.
[6] V. Grumel, "Nicéphore Theotokis," *DTC,* 11:467-70.

The issue came to a head in the nineteenth century, in the opposition between Constantine Economos and Theocletus Pharmakides.[7] Economos was convinced that all traditional teaching must be held to be true, lest error creep in and the entire edifice of faith be subverted. In his four-volume work, *On the Seventy Translators of the Old Testament,* he argued in favor of the legendary accounts of the origin of the Septuagint, whose inspiration was thereby attested. To question those accounts would be tantamount to questioning the inspiration of Scripture itself—for the Septuagint is divinely inspired. As a corollary, he opposed the translation of Scripture into modern Greek. He also rejected every attempt to abbreviate the liturgy, all oaths under any circumstances, and the view of those who claimed that, now that Greece had become independent from Turkey, the church in the new country should also be independent from the patriarch of Constantinople—which, after all, was also the Turkish Istanbul.

Pharmakides, who had studied theology at Göttingen, was opposed to Economos in every way. He established a distinction between authentic tradition and that which was no more than later additions completely lacking any basis. The manner in which one could then determine whether or not a given opinion or practice was part of authentic tradition was by scientific historical research. Such research must not be hampered *a priori* by the dictates of commonly held opinion, for in that case one would risk allowing false tradition to continue unquestioned. The Septuagint was not divinely inspired, although God used it to speak to the church; and therefore the modern church would be as justified in translating Scripture into modern Greek as was the ancient church in using the Septuagint. Given the present circumstances, and the pressure of time in the modern world, the liturgy ought to be abbreviated. Finally, since Greece was politically independent from Turkey, the church in the new nation should reflect the new circumstances by becoming independent from the patriarch of Constantinople.

Not all the issues between Economos and Pharmakides were immediately settled. The new political status of Greece, and its growing contact with the West, tended to favor the program of renewal proposed by Pharmakides. Still, the church was conservative

---

[7] Stephanides, Ἐκκλησιαστικὴ Ἱστορία, pp. 772-73.

enough that Pharmakides was transferred from the faculty of theology to that of philosophy. In the long run, although at a very moderate pace, the new scientific world view and the Western philosophical currents of the nineteenth and twentieth centuries became generally accepted by Greek theology.

Russian Theology[8]

As I have already pointed out in the previous volume,[9] the Russian Church was technically united with Rome at the Council of Florence. The manner in which this took place, however, was that the metropolitan of Moscow at the time was a Greek who had been named by the authorities in Constantinople precisely so that he would favor the union to be proposed at Florence—a union that was politically important to the Greeks in the face of the Turkish threat to Constantinople. When the new metropolitan and his court arrived at Moscow, however, their submission to Rome was rejected by the Russians. The fact that the patriarch of Constantinople had signed a document of union with Rome made the Russians feel that the Greek Church had failed and that Russia had now become the guardian of orthodoxy. This feeling was greatly encouraged by the fall of Constantinople in 1453. The second Rome, as well as the first, had succumbed to error and fallen prey to unbelievers. The torch of orthodoxy had now passed on to the third Rome—Moscow. Early in the sixteenth century the monk Philotheus of Pskov developed this theory by placing it within a vast framework of universal history whose purpose was to show, among other things, that Constantine had transferred Rome to Constantinople before Rome was taken by the barbarians, and that now it was the turn of Russia to transfer it to Moscow. In 1547 Ivan IV took the title of czar, by which he claimed to be the successor of the former caesars of Rome and Constantinople. Finally, in 1596 the metropolitan of Moscow became a patriarch. This understanding of its historical destiny was one of the most

---

[8] In this entire section, we follow the excellent article by J. Ledit and M. Gordillo, "Russie (Pensée religieuse)," *DTC*, 14:207-371. Also helpful have been F. C. Conybeare, *Russian Dissenters* (New York: Russell & Russell, 1962), and S. Bolshakoff, *Russian Nonconformity* (Philadelphia: Westminster Press, 1950).

[9] 2:294. Since at that time the Russian Church was under the patriarchate of Constantinople, union with Rome was technically included in the act by which Constantinople acceded to that union. However, given the importance of the Russian Church, the Greeks and Latins were interested in having the metropolitan of Moscow agree personally to the union.

important factors in the life of the Russian church for centuries. It should be pointed out, however, that in the arguments adduced in support of this theory the empire played a more important role than the church. Moscow is the third Rome by reason of her emperor. Orthodoxy is important, for the task of the third Rome is precisely to support orthodox belief. But the mainstay of orthodoxy is the emperor—with little mention being made of the patriarch. As a result of this theory—as well as because of political circumstances and the precedent of Constantinople—relations between church and state in Russia would soon be marked by a high degree of caesaropapism.

In our brief overview of the course of Russian theology during the modern age, we shall begin by looking at the question of relations with other Christians, which seems to have dominated the sixteenth and seventeenth centuries. Then, with the establishment of new theological schools in the eighteenth century, we shall see Russian theology take a more independent course.

Although the Russian church had always produced a fair number of anti-Catholic polemical writings, the issue of relations with Roman Catholicism became crucial during the difficult interregnum (1598–1613) between the end of the Rurikide dynasty and the advent of the Romanovs. At that time the Poles became involved in the wars of succession, attempting to place their own people on the vacant Muscovite throne. Finally they took Moscow and named the son of King Sigismund of Poland as czar. With the Poles came the Roman Catholics, and especially the Jesuits, whose attempts to bring the Russian church into unity and uniformity with the West were bitterly resented. The Polish pretender to the throne of the czars, however, never took possession of his crown, for an insurrection led by Russian monks expelled the Poles from Moscow and elected Michael Romanov as czar (1613), thus ending the period of anarchy that had left Russia at the mercy of her neighbors.

The anti-Catholic reaction was not slow in coming. At a synod gathered in 1620, it was declared that the Romans were heretics and that baptism as practiced by them was not valid. It was claimed that the Romans had subverted the Trinity by including the *Filioque* in the Creed. By so doing, they were proclaiming two separate principles in the Trinity. This is indeed the sin against the Holy Spirit, which Jesus said would not be forgiven. The Romans were Judaizers, for they fasted on Saturdays; and Montanists, for they rejected marriage and took concubines. They had changed the date for the celebration of Easter, and in true Manichaean fashion determined that date by the stars—in some cases they even went to the extreme of celebrating it at the same time as the Jewish Passover! They baptized by infusion instead of by immersion, they did not require penance before absolution, and they celebrated communion with unleavened bread—after the Jewish fashion. Therefore, those who wished to join the true orthodox church and had been baptized in the Western heresies must be baptized anew after recanting all their errors with a series of curses against the Western emperor, a long list of popes, the *Filioque*, the unleavened bread, the authorization for priests to have seven concubines (!), etc.

Russia had now become the guardian of the true faith, and in her new role she simply took for granted that all others had erred in all possible ways, and was willing to believe the worst accusations against other Christians without even hearing their case. Such isolation was the price that she paid for her claim to be the third Rome.

During the early years of the Protestant Reformation, Protestantism penetrated into some of the western provinces of Russia, but it did not become a major issue for the Russian church. In spite of this, already in the first half of the sixteenth century Maximus the Greek—whose origin may have been one of the reasons for his interest in affairs outside of Russia—wrote *Discourse against Luther the Iconoclast*, and *Against Those Who Blaspheme the Most Pure Mother of God*.

By the second half of the century, there was already a Protestant church in Moscow, although its members were mostly German merchants residing in that city. Oddly enough, the most significant piece of anti-Protestant polemics during this period was written by Ivan the Terrible. Ivan had followed a relatively tolerant policy toward Protestants, and this had encouraged the Moravian John Rokita to attempt to convert the czar. To this end he requested an interview, which Ivan granted while guaranteeing the Moravian minister that he would not be punished for expressing his opinions. In that interview, Ivan became enraged by Rokita's opinions, and he later produced a fulminating *Reply from the King* in which he came to the defense of orthodox Christianity with a combination of invectives and scriptural quotations. In spite of his fame and furor, however,

Ivan spared Rokita's life, and was content with ordering him not to teach his heresies within the czar's territories.

In 1620, the same synod that set standards for the baptism of converted Roman Catholics also set similar standards for the baptism of former Protestants. This was part of a reaction to the attempts on the part of Sweden to carry her faith and her influence to several Russian provinces during the interregnum and civil strife of 1598–1613. Here again, it was affirmed that Protestant baptism was not valid, and instructions were given for converts from Protestantism to recant their heresies. As in the case of Roman Catholics, the synod seems to have been grossly misinformed regarding the actual beliefs and practices of Protestants.

Later in the same century Simeon of Polock, a monk from Kiev who had opened a school in Moscow, wrote a series of anti-Protestant works. Simeon had studied in Poland, where he had been so influenced by Roman Catholic scholasticism, that he was later accused of having been a secret follower of the pope. Although such accusations were false, and he always remained a faithful member of Russian orthodoxy, it is true that he viewed Roman Catholicism with great favor, and that he never wrote against it. Given his strong tendency toward Catholic scholasticism, most of his anti-Protestant arguments are taken from the Latins, and there is little in his theology that could be termed a Russian response to Protestantism.

The next stage in anti-Protestant polemics took place when Prince Waldemar of Denmark went to Moscow to marry princes Irene Mikhailovna. Although the Danish prince had been promised that he would be allowed to keep his Protestant faith, no sooner had he arrived in Moscow than he was asked to embrace orthodoxy. He refused, telling the czar that he would be willing to shed his blood for him, but that he would not abandon the Protestant faith. The prince then received a letter from the patriarch—written by the priest Ivan Nasedka—attempting to show him the various reasons why Russian orthodoxy was the true form of Christianity. Waldemar asked his pastor, Matthew Velhaber, to reply, and thus started a series of theological debates and negotiations that eventually led to Waldemar's return to his native Denmark. What is significant in this controversy, however, is the extremes to which a theologian such as Nasedka—and the patriarch with him—would go to refute Protestant views. In one of his letters, Nasedka even claims that the

Fathers of the Church were as inspired as the apostles who wrote the
New Testament, and that their teachings therefore ought to be
received in the same way in which one receives the teachings of
Scripture. Later on he adds to the teachings of the Fathers the oral
tradition in the church. Although he does not actually say that all oral
tradition is as authoritative as Scripture itself, such is the clear
implication of what he does say.

Once again, as the new guardian of the faith, Russian theology put
itself in a position in which it was difficult—if not impossible—for it
to serve for the renewal of the church. The view that Scripture, the
"Fathers," and oral tradition all have equal and infallible authority
would make it very difficult for the Russian church to acknowledge
its errors, even in seemingly inconsequential matters. Such was the
case, although within a different context, of the Patriarch Nikon and
his attempts at liturgical renewal.

When Nikon (1605–1681) became patriarch of Moscow in 1652,
Russia was flourishing and increasing in political power. This
seemed to confirm the thesis that Moscow was the third Rome, and
that she should lead Eastern orthodoxy. But there was a
contradiction implicit in this idea, for the very notion of the third
Rome was based on the theory that Constantinople had erred and
failed; and as long as Moscow insisted on such a negative view of the
Greek Church, that church would not accept Russian leadership.
Czar Alexis had visions of reconquering Constantinople for
Christianity, and once more celebrating the eucharist at Saint
Sophia, with all five patriarchs joining in a great act of thanksgiving.
One of the first steps toward this goal must be to gain the confidence
of other Eastern Christians. And this he could not do as long as the
Russian Church continued acting as if all the rest of Christendom
had fallen into heresy. These were the political considerations
behind Patriarch Nikon's order that the Russian liturgy was to be
modified so as to agree with the practices of the Greeks.

But the opposition to Nikon's orders also had strong political and
social motivations. It was the staunch orthodoxy of the monks and
the lower classes that had helped Russia come out of the period of
anarchy and foreign invasion. As a result, orthodoxy had become the
rallying point of these lower classes, who now had a claim on Russia.
They suspected the aristocracy of favoring precisely that foreign
influence against which they had fought. The fact that Nikon, the

son of a smith, had become patriarch, was a symbol of the new Russia that was being born. But now Nikon himself seemed to have been corrupted by power, and was abandoning the faith that had given Russia her freedom. Moscow, the third Rome, ought not to be catering to the fallen Constantinople and her materially rich but morally bankrupt dignitaries. Let Constantinople adjust her liturgy to Moscow's, and thus come closer to the truth.[10]

Those who opposed Nikon's reforms soon became a strong and numerous party that took the name of "Old Believers"—also called Staroveri and Raskolniks. Their leader was the monk Avvacum, who had in his favor the fact that he was exiled to Siberia and thus carried the aureola of a martyr.[11] A Grand Council of Moscow, gathered in 1666–67, condemned them and asked Simeon of Polock—the same whom we have found refuting Protestantism—to write the official rebuttal of the church against the Old Believers. As Simeon was very much influenced by Roman Catholic Christianity, his work simply served further to infuriate the opposition. Armed force was then used against them. A monastery under siege resisted for several months, and when it was finally taken the monks were massacred. Many among the Old Believers then turned to a fervid eschatological expectation. These were the last times of the great apostasy, for even the third Rome had now fallen into heresy. And in these last times it was better to die than to submit to the Antichrist. In consequence, thousands committed suicide through self-immolation. Others within the movement condemned such practices. From his exile, Avvacum began teaching strange Trinitarian doctrines, and the movement became further confused. All these issues eventually subsided, however, as the more extremist groups disappeared. The one question that continued to divide the Old Believers was the matter of the priesthood. Some accepted the priests who came to them from the patriarch's church, while others simply decided that priests were not necessary. The former were called Popovtsy, and the latter received the name of Bezpopovtsy or priestless. Since the

---

[10] On this point at least, resistance to Nikon was correct, for the influence of Rome in Byzantium had caused the Greeks to introduce a number of liturgical changes, and therefore in the seventeenth century the Russian liturgy was closer than the Greek to the Byzantine ritual of the eleventh century. N. Zernov, *Cristianismo oriental: Orígenes y desarrollo de la Iglesia Ortodoxa Oriental* (Madrid: Guadarrama, 1962), p. 171.

[11] J. Harrison and H. Mirrlees, trans., *The Life of the Archpriest Avvakum, by Himself* (Archon Books; Hamden, Conn.: Shoe String Press, 1963).

Bezpopovtsy continued a complicated process of fragmentation over all sorts of issues, the Old Believers that still exist are of the Popovtsy branch.

Western influence on Russian theology increased with the advent to the throne of Peter the Great (1682), who felt that Russia was a barbaric land and therefore made every attempt to put it in contact with what he considered the more civilized West. Since Peter abolished the patriarchate, and substituted for it a "Holy Synod" of his own creation, the impact of his policies on the church was decisive. Peter himself favored closer ties with the Roman Catholics, and therefore a great deal of Russian theology during his reign and immediately thereafter was dominated by those who, while remaining Russian Orthodox, drew much of their inspiration from Roman Catholic theology. This particular theological orientation was connected with the names of Peter Mogila and the Kievan school. In opposition to them, Theophanes Prokopovic and his followers attempted to draw Russian theology closer to Protestantism. Prokopovic's school reached its apex in the early nineteenth century. At that time a reaction set in that sought to return to traditional orthodox and Russian sources.

We shall now direct our attention to each of these in turn.

Although there had been a school at Kiev before his time, it was Peter Mogila (1596–1646)[12] who gave this school its characteristic orientation. Mogila was an able scholar who had studied and admired the Latin scholastics, but who, however, resisted the efforts that Roman Catholics were making at the time to bring the Ukraine into submission to the pope. In 1633 he became metropolitan of Kiev, and he then took steps to assure that his clergy received the best education possible. Since at that time the anti-Catholic reaction in Russia was at its height, his influence on Muscovite theology was not immediate. His *Orthodox Confession of the Catholic and Apostolic Eastern Church* was accepted by the patriarchs of Constantinople, Jerusalem, Alexandria, and Antioch, and was one of the major sources of Latin influence in the East. His impact upon Russian theology increased at the time of Peter the Great, and continued throughout the eighteenth century.

---

12 M. Jugie, "Moghila, Pierre," *DTC*, 10:2063–81.

Mogila and the Kievan school were strict followers of traditional Russian orthodoxy, but on all matters that were still open to debate they took the Roman Catholic position. Their style and theological methodology were copied after the medieval Latin scholastics. They affirmed the immaculate conception of Mary—which, although still not declared a dogma, was growing in popularity in the West. On the question of when transubstantiation takes place, they rejected the Greek view that it happens at the moment of the epiclesis—the prayer invoking the presence of the Holy Spirit—and agreed with the Romans that it was at the words of institution. Finally, they affirmed the existence of purgatory—a theory by no means common among the Eastern Orthodox at that time. The only two crucial points, then, on which the Kievans were not willing to follow Roman theology were the supremacy of the pope and the procession of the Spirit—the *Filioque* clause.

During the reign of Peter the Great, while Kievan theology was at its height, another school was being formed, which would soon challenge it. This other school, under the leadership of Theophanes Prokopovic, also looked to the West for its theological inspiration. But it found the Protestant divines more congenial than the Roman Catholics. Prokopovic felt that the weight of unquestioned tradition upon the Russian church was too great, and that this tradition included much whose origin was doubtful. Therefore, it was necessary to return to Scripture in order to find pure Christian doctrine. Although he did refer frequently to the ancient Christians writers and their teachings, he did so in a manner similar to that of Luther or Calvin, and never affirming or even implying that their authority was comparable to that of Scripture. Being a good Russian Orthodox, he rejected the Protestant views of the eucharist, and insisted on the veneration of icons and the procession of the Spirit from the Father alone. But on such matters as justification, the nature of good works, the canon of the Old Testament, predestination, and free will his views were clearly akin to those held by Protestants. By 1715, the doctrines of Prokopovic had made such inroads on Russian theology that even the school where Mogila had taught at Kiev was infiltrated by them. Twenty-five years later, the metropolitan see of Moscow was occupied by the Prokopovickian Plato Lefsin. By that time, Catherine II was sitting on the throne of the czars—then at St. Petersburg—and her efforts to bring Russia into closer contact with the rest of the world tended to strengthen the hand of the Prokopovickians.

The early nineteenth century saw the apex of Prokopovickian influence in the Russian church. Jointly with Protestant ideas, the philosophy of the Enlightenment and Romanticism were penetrating Russia. At first all these new ideas overwhelmed the Russians, who seemed to think that their country must become "modernized" in the Western fashion. But by the middle of the nineteenth century a reaction had clearly set in. This reaction took two distinct shapes: the return to the early sources of Russian Christianity, and the attempt to discover, within the framework of philosophical idealism, what it meant to be Russian.

The return to the sources of Russian Christianity took the form of historical inquiry, publication of documents and histories of the church, and attempts to develop a theology more akin to what had been commonly held in Russia before the time of Peter the Great and the upsurge of foreign influence. This movement produced many manuals of theology and of ecclesiastical history, but no outstanding theologian.

The attempt to apply the categories of idealism to the question of Russia's identity gave rise to the Slavophile movement. Its main spokesman was Alexis Khomyakov,[13] who had been profoundly influenced by Hegel and Schelling. Khomyakov set out to develop a view of traditional Russian ecclesiology that would show it to be the synthesis between the Roman Catholic thesis and the Protestant antithesis. Roman Catholics and Kievan theologians alike underline the unity of the church, whereas Protestants and Prokopovickians stress the freedom that the gospel requires. The true orthodox understanding of *sobornost*—catholicity—includes both of these in a perfect synthesis. Protestants have freedom, but no unity. Catholics have unity, but no freedom. Orthodoxy has both, for the unity that its members enjoy is such that the freedom of the gospel is still allowed, and the unity itself is one of love rather than law—and is therefore a free unity. The Russian Church, therefore, does not need to make a choice between the two Western branches of Christianity. It already includes the best of both. Khomyakov's

[13] S. Bolshakoff, *The Doctrine of the Unity of the Church in the Works of Khomyakov and Moehler* (London: S.P.C.K., 1946); A. Gratieux, *A. S. Khomiakov et le mouvement slavophile* (Paris: Éditions du Cerf, 1939); A. Gratieux, *Le mouvement slavophile à la veille de la Révolution* (Paris: Éditions du Cerf, 1953).

theories were not well received by ecclesiastical authorities within Russia, for they seemed to value too highly a spirit of freedom that was not easily assimilable within the actual structures of Russian orthodoxy. As a result, the Slavophiles became critics of the oppressive attitudes of the hierarchy, which they saw as contrary to the genuine spirit of Russian orthodoxy. On this point, their best known and most influential exponent was Fëdor Dostoevski (1821–1881), the famous Russian novelist.

The Russian Revolution of 1917 created new conditions for theology in that country. Let it suffice to say that for the first few decades after the revolution the most significant theological work by Russian orthodox theologians was done in exile—especially in Paris. Later on in the twentieth century, however, the Russian church once again began producing its own theologians, often dealing with the question of the function of Christianity within a Marxist state.

Nestorian and Monophysite Theology

The Mongols took Baghdad in 1258, and the Nestorian community never recovered from that blow. As a result, its theology went into further decline. The Nestorian writings of the fifteenth and sixteenth centuries that have been preserved consist mostly of versifications of earlier hagiographies, chronologies, and other such materials. The only relatively significant theological activity took place among those who submitted to the pope—the "Chaldean Catholics." The most important of these was Joseph II, uniate patriarch of Diyarbakir, who composed a defense of Roman Catholicism under the title of *The Pure Mirror*.[14] In more recent times, the persecutions that the Nestorians have suffered in the Near East have reduced their numbers to a few thousand.

Of all the Monophysite churches, the only one that showed a measure of theological vitality was the Armenian Church. The Coptic Church, already weakened by Arab rule, lost further ground under the Turks (1517–1798). The Church of Ethiopia, which had always had close ties with the Copts, suffered from lack of contact with other Christians. When the Moslems invaded Ethiopia in 1520, the Christian faith became the rallying point for nationalist

---

[14] E. Tisserant, "Nestorienne (L'église)," *DTC*, 11:284-85.

sentiment, and therefore the church emerged from the conflict with greater strength than it had previously had. But in the field of theological literature the very circumstances of the conflict fostered little more than hagiographic material whose goal was to strengthen the faithful in their struggle. After the Turkish advance, the Syrian Jacobites produced little worthy of mention. The Armenian Church also was not spared difficulties, for in the sixteenth century the country was conquered by Persia and has never regained its independence. This, however, resulted in a revival of Armenian theology, for many who went into exile came into contact with new ideas, and then produced works that were later introduced into Armenia. Soon there were Armenian centers of learning and publishing in Vienna, Venice, Moscow, Istanbul, Calcutta, and Jerusalem. The highest point in the Armenian renewal was probably reached in the seventeenth century, when John Agop—or Holov— wrote significant apologetic, exegetical, and systematic works, while in his *Book of Histories* Arakel of Tauriz narrated the sufferings and glories of the Armenian Church. In the nineteenth century, the Armenians in Venice became well known for their very valuable publications of ancient texts, and thus their patristic studies made a modest but significant contribution to theological scholarship. On the whole, however, it is fair to say that theology in the entire Monophysite tradition suffered further decline after the fall of Constantinople.

We thus come to the end of our very brief survey of Eastern theology since the sixteenth century. It is hoped that this survey will have shown that there is much of interest in Eastern theological activity. The story of Cyril Lucaris, for instance, should be of interest to those who are concerned with the history of Protestant influence in various parts of the world, and should also serve to show that in the Greek Church there were those who were seeking to renew that church. The opposition between the schools of Mogila and Prokopovic shows that the same issues were very much alive in Russia. The rise of the Old Believers, and their subsequent history, should interest those who seek to discover the relations that obtain between theology and social struggles. But even more, this entire chapter should remind Western Christians that they are no more than a part of the entire body of Christian believers throughout the world—a reminder that should help them in their relations with the younger churches that have arisen during the last two centuries in Asia, Africa, and Latin America. And yet, even this is clearly said from a typically Western perspective, which sees theological debate and development as a fundamental mark of vitality. It may well be that future times of trial will show Western Christians the importance of the Eastern perspective, with its emphasis on liturgical devotion as the locus of true ecclesiastical vitality. Indeed, as these words are being written it is becoming increasingly clear that the power of their traditions—and in particular of their liturgy—has sustained and will sustain the Eastern churches even in the most trying times. It is also becoming apparent that, as the full consequences of the "end of Christendom" are made manifest in the Western churches, they will have much to learn from their Eastern counterparts.

XVI

Theology in the Twentieth Century

In Europe, the nineteenth century was a period of unprecedented peace and prosperity. With minor interruptions of relatively localized war and attempted revolution, it was a century of progress and expansion. In the United States, with the very dramatic exception of the Civil War, it was also a period of peace within the borders of the new nation, and of continuous expansion of the western frontier. On both sides of the Atlantic, science and technology had begun to solve many of the problems that had plagued humankind since time immemorial. The natural world finally seemed to be coming under human dominion, and to prove itself malleable to human wishes and designs. The harnessing of steam and other forms of power made distances shorter, and made more leisure possible for certain segments of society—precisely those segments in which most theological reflection took place.

On both sides of the Atlantic, it was believed that Western civilization was particularly called to bring about a new age in history, not only in its traditional geographical areas, but also throughout the world. The expansionist tendencies of the times were ideologically justified in the United States with the theory of "manifest destiny," and in Europe with the deceivingly altruistic notion of the "white man's burden." Both meant that it was the God-given mission of Western civilization to be a beacon into the future for the rest of the world. On this basis, the United States took lands from the native

428

Americans and from Mexico with very little protest from Christian leaders within the nation, and Europe's expansion was greatly encouraged by those who saw in it an opportunity for Christian missions.[1]

This was the background of nineteenth-century theology. As we have seen, Roman Catholic and Eastern Orthodox theology generally did not see the new situation and its promise with the same optimism with which Protestants saw it. The lands in which they were strong were not benefitting from the new conditions to the degree to which traditionally Protestant lands benefitted. In contrast to this reticence, or even hostility, from Catholic and Orthodox theology, Protestant theologians tended to view the new circumstances with almost unbounded optimism. Schleiermacher, Hegel, Ritschl and Troeltsch, all agreed that Christianity was the highest form of religion to which all others pointed—that is, Protestant Christianity once it had been purified from superstitions lingering from a by-gone age. Kierkegaard's lone dissenting voice was hardly noticed in the stampede of progress. It was a time of trust in human ability, in technological progress, in the evolutionary process that was bringing humankind to its appointed goal, and in Western civilization as the harbinger of the new age.

Then war broke out. It was the costliest war humankind had ever seen, for it involved the entire globe. It was a war in which precisely those powers whose burden it supposedly was to civilize humanity actually dragged the entire world into their conflict. It was a war in which progress and technology showed their seamy side, multiplying the destructive power of human hatred. And it was a war that solved very little, for a few years after its end the globe was again involved in another armed conflict, distinguished from the first only in that its scope was even wider, and in that the destructive power unleashed by it dwarfed that of the earlier war. The inherent racism of Western civilization—and of Christianity, as understood by much of nineteenth-century theology—was made manifest in the death of millions of Jews and in the decision to use nuclear weapons against Japanese cities. Shortly after the end of this Second World War, it was clear that for the first time it was within human power to destroy the entire species—and much of the Earth with it.

---

[1] See Stephen Neill, *Colonialism and Christian Missions* (London: Lutterworth, 1966).

The wars and their aftermath have also changed the perception of Western civilization by the rest of the world. During the high tide of Western expansion, this had been accepted by many, not only as the result of superior physical force, but also as the result of superior civilization. Western ways and religion were adopted by multitudes in Asia, Africa, and the Pacific, while in Latin America many looked to Britain and the United States as models for their political future. Now, after two wars and several decades of an insane and seemingly unstoppable arms race, it became apparent that there were serious flaws in the much taunted superiority of Western civilization. Nations and individuals began distinguishing various aspects of that civilization, and trying to decide on their own what to keep and what to discard. Politically and economically, the "Third World" strove for independence. In Africa, where only two nations had been independent in 1914, the entire colonial system was dismantled. In Asia, Africa and Latin America, the superpowers, afraid for good reason of confronting each other directly, fought wars by proxy —wars that made terror and famine endemic to entire regions of the globe. As a result, there was a growing feeling in the rest of the globe that Western civilization, far from being the harbinger of a new age of happiness, was dragging the entire world into its inner conflicts, and that these conflicts threatened to destroy all of humanity. Thus the question was posed with increasing frequency and urgency, is it possible to accept some of the technological advances of the West, while humanizing them with the riches of our own culture?

While all this was taking place in the world at large, similar changes were taking place in the church. The most notable change was that Christianity, which until the beginning of the nineteenth century had been closely associated with Western civilization, became truly a world-wide movement. Later in this chapter we shall see that this was one of the reasons behind the new initiatives of the Second Vatican Council. At some point in the second half of the twentieth century, the numerical strength of Christianity passed from the North Atlantic to the southern hemisphere, and from the white race to people "of color"—Africans, Asians, and Latin Americans. People from these various branches of the church began insisting on their right and obligation to do theology from their own perspective and dealing with their own problems and insights. Thus was a truly ecumenical theology born—one in which there was a world-wide dialogue, not always in agreement, but certainly mutually enriching.

Meanwhile, the traditional centers of theological and ecclesiastical activity in the North Atlantic were also undergoing radical changes. Certainly the most momentous of these changes was the "end of Christendom." Ever since the time of Constantine, Christianity had counted on the support of the state and of the culture around it. That part of the world whose rulers and populations called themselves Christian was known as "Christendom." It was here that churches were powerful, monasteries and Christian centers of learning were built, and most theological activity took place. Now, through a process that had begun centuries earlier, much of this was coming to an end. Separation of church and state had earlier become the norm in the United States, in France, and in the countries modeled after their constitutional form of government. In Great Britain, while such separation was not official, the support that the church received from the state was waning. Late in the nineteenth century, when the Kingdom of Italy took the city of Rome, the Papacy lost its last vestiges of temporal power—except for its rule over the Vatican itself. Early in the twentieth century, just as the First World War was drawing to a close, the Russian Revolution put an end to the Czarist regime and to its collaboration with the Russian Orthodox Church. Soon, there were very few countries in which the state officially supported the church.

What was true at the level of political support was also true at the more personal level. In the traditional centers of Christianity, increasing numbers felt that the old faith was no longer tenable. In Western Europe, church attendance and participation in the life of the church dropped drastically. In the United States there was a similar drop, although not as marked nor as constant. On both sides of the Atlantic, it seemed to many that a modern world-view left no place for Christianity—or for religion of any sort. Thus, the increasing secularization of their societies would be one of the many themes that would preoccupy Western theologians during the twentieth century.

This is the background in which Christian theology has developed during the twentieth century. Given such background, it should not surprise us that twentieth-century theology is characterized both by its vitality and by its variety, and that it is difficult if not impossible to organize the various streams of theological thought into a coherent outline or framework. Nevertheless, it does appear clear that one can distinguish between the earlier part of the twentieth century, when theology was still dominated by the traditional centers of theological activity, and a later period, beginning after the Second World War.

A New Beginning: The Theology of Karl Barth

There can be no doubt that during the period between the two world wars the towering figure in Christian theology is Karl Barth (1886–1968). His father was a Reformed theologian of conservative tendencies—although not in political matters—who shaped his earlier studies and for whom he always had the greatest respect and gratitude. After studying at Bern, Tübingen, and Marburg, he became a pastor in his native Switzerland, first in Geneva (to the German-speaking parish in that city), and then in the village of Safenwil (1911). As a result of his theological education, he went to the pastorate convinced of many of the tenets of liberal theology, but soon came to the conclusion that there were other subjects that were more relevant to his work than theology. Although during the early years of his pastorate he continued his theological readings, he later declared that in Safenwil he became so involved in the Social Democratic movement that he read theology only as was necessary for his preaching and teaching, and spent most of his time studying industrial legislation, union organization, and like matters. He was convinced that God was working to bring the Kingdom, not so much through the church, which was lethargic, as through Social Democracy. In 1915, he officially joined the Social Democratic Party.

While he was concerned with the rights of his peasant and laborer flock, the world around him was plunging into disaster. The First World War came to him as a disappointment. His former teachers, and his own contemporaries whom he had come to admire, were carried away by the militaristic spirit. The same was true of many of the socialists with whom he had worked. Furthermore, as the news of the atrocities of the war kept arriving, he found it increasingly difficult to relate the theology he had been taught to the harsh realities of his day. New theological readings, particularly of the works of J. C. Blumhardt, made him aware of the need to recover the eschatological dimension of Christianity. In conversations with his lifelong friend Eduard Thurneysen, he became convinced that it was necessary to revise much of the theology that he had learned.

Eventually, he promised Thurneysen to work on a *Commentary on Romans*, not for publication, but for private circulation among some like-minded friends. The resultant work, however, was published in 1919, shortly after the end of the war, and soon gained wide recognition for its author.

Barth was working on a radically revised edition of his *Commentary on Romans* when he was invited to teach Reformed theology at Göttingen. He took this position in 1921, and thus began a teaching career that took him from Göttingen to Münster, then to Bonn, and eventually—after being forced to leave Germany because of Hitler—to Basel, where he lived for the rest of his life.

What Barth proposed in his *Commentary*, and particularly in its revised second edition, was a theology based, not on the continuity between the human and the divine, but on their discontinuity. Christianity is not, as so much of the nineteenth century had assumed, the highest human achievement. As he would later say, "to speak about God is not the same as to shout about humans." Over against the emphasis of his predecessors on the immanence of God, Barth came to emphasize the divine transcendence to the point that he would refer to God as "the wholly Other"—which led Harnack, now in his last years, to exclaim, "Marcion all over again!"

There is also discontinuity between sin and grace, between human achievement and God's action, between our being under grace and our attempts to express this in systems of theology or of ethics.

> Sin and grace, then, cannot be placed side by side, or arranged in series, or treated as of like importance, any more than death and life can be so treated. There is no bridge across the gulf that separates them. They have no blurred edges which might be run together. The impassable gulf runs starkly through the fissure between good and evil, between what is valuable and what is valueless, between what is holy and what is unholy. . . . The knowledge of God which is the condition of our survey compels us to distinguish clearly between sinners and righteous men; but the human knowledge which emerges is at once dissolved by the very criterion by which it is created. Only because of the power of obedience in which we stand are we able to comprehend and lay hold of the possibility of impossibility.[2]

---

[2] *The Epistle to the Romans* (translated from the sixth edition; London: Oxford University Press, 1933), p. 228.

For this reason, the theological current which Barth founded has been called "Dialectical theology"—although in using this term one should be aware that one is speaking of a dialectic that is closer to Kierkegaard's than to Hegel's. Particularly in its early stages, Barth's theology and that of his associates has also been characterized as a "theology of crisis," in the sense that it emphasized the crisis of humanity as it stands before God. Finally, and especially after the break with existentialism, many have called the new tendency "neo-orthodoxy," for it sought to recover much in traditional Christian teaching that had been left aside by the leading figures of the nineteenth century.

Soon Barth found that there were others who agreed with much of his criticism of liberal theology. His friend Thurneysen, Lutheran theologian Friedrich Gogarten (1887–1967), and others founded in 1922 the theological journal *Zwischen den Zeiten*—Between the Times—which soon became one of the most influential theological publications of its time. One of its frequent collaborators, although not one of its founders, was Reformed theologian Emil Brunner (1889–1966), who taught at Zurich. In those early years, biblical scholar Rudolf Bultmann (1884–1976) was also generally considered to be one of the leaders of the new "dialectical theology."

Barth himself, however, was drawing consequences from his earlier insights that would soon lead to a break with most of these early companions—with the notable exception of Thurneysen, who always remained his close friend and associate.

The first break took place in the 1920's, and was the result of the insistence of Gogarten and Bultmann, on the one hand, on the existential dialectics that had also been Barth's earlier position, and of Barth and Brunner, on the other, on the need to move away from anthropology and into theology proper. If all that we have is "the moment before God," and we can speak of nothing else, as an existentialist theology is inclined to affirm, the task of theology is to study and explicate the experience and understanding of faith. Both Barth and Brunner felt that this reduced theology to the study of a human experience, and were therefore moving towards a theology more firmly grounded on the Word of God, and concentrating particularly on Christology.

In the case of Barth, this was closely connected with his growing conviction that there is a content to the Word of God. It is not merely a matter of an encounter. There is also a "Logos," a rationality, so that the Word leads us to its own understanding. This meant both that existentialist philosophy, with its emphasis on the moment, had to be left behind, and that theology could and should move in the direction of seeking to understand the Word of God, and elucidate its implications, not on the basis of existentialism or of any other philosophy, but on the basis of the "logic of faith." In 1927, Barth published the first volume of what he hoped would be his great systematic work, the *Christian Dogmatics*. But before he published the second volume, his study of Anselm's Proslogion, published in 1931,[3] convinced him that he must move in the direction of the "logic of faith," and that existentialism was not an appropriate tool to this end. Therefore, by 1932 he had abandoned his first attempt at a systematic theology, and published the first volume of *Church dogmatics*.

This new start was a clear indication of an important shift in Barth's thought. This shift had taken place basically in two directions. As indicated above, his study on Anselm, and his own reflection on the significance of the Word of God, had led him to reject the use of any philosophy as a proper tool for theology. The second new direction was a greater emphasis on the role of the church in the task of theology.

> When the word "Church" replaces the word "Christian" in the title of the book, that means . . . that dogmatics is not a "free" science, but one bound to the sphere of the Church, where and where alone it is possible and sensible.[4]

In thus rejecting existentialism, Barth had broken with Gogarten and Bultmann. The next break would be with Brunner, and in some ways would be an extension of the same development of Barth's part. As time went by, Barth came to the conviction that "natural theology" must be rejected. Otherwise, he was afraid that one would again blur the distance between the divine and the human, between reason and revelation.

Although it is possible to see the widening gulf in some earlier articles in *Zwischen den Zeiten*, the actual break began in 1933, when

---

[3] English translation: *Anselm: Fides Quarens Intellectum: Anselm's Proof of the Existence of God in the Context of His Theological Scheme* (Richmond: John Knox Press, 1960).

[4] *Church dogmatics*, I/1, p. ix.

Barth published an article on "The first commandment as a
theological axiom." The debate would soon lead to the demise of the
journal, and to a continuing debate between Barth and Brunner. In
his article, Barth launched a campaign against the "alien gods" that
pervert theology. One thing that all these gods have in common is
that they infiltrate theology by means of the short but most
important conjunction "and." The word "and" implies that there is
something else that can be placed next to God. "And" is the first sign
of idolatry. "And" is the error that has led theology astray.

> Thus the eighteenth century said: revelation *and* reason. Thus said
> Schleiermacher: revelation *and* religious consciousness. Thus said
> Ritschl and his followers: revelation *and* history of religions. And
> thus is it spoken today everywhere: revelation *and* creation,
> revelation *and* protorevelation, the New Testament *and* human
> existence, the commandment *and* the orders of creation.[5]

While the reference to "the new Testament and human existence"
was a reference to his rejection of Gogarten and of Bultmann's
program (to which we shall return), the last pair in this list, "the
commandment and the orders of creation," was a direct rejection of
Brunner, who a few months earlier had published a book under that
title.[6] A few months later, in his article "Abschied"—Farewell—
Barth insisted on his position and broke with *Zwischen den Zeiten*
—which then ceased publication.

In 1934, Brunner responded with his small book *Nature and Grace*.
Its tone was rather conciliatory, although Brunner insisted that
Barth had drawn a number of false conclusions from the doctrines of
the Word of God and of the *sola gratia*: (1) Barth believes that the
image of God in the human creature has been destroyed by sin, while
Brunner would prefer to say that it has been *materially* destroyed, but
is still *formally* in existence; (2) Barth errs in limiting revelation to that
in Christ, for it is necessary to leave room for God's witness to the
pagans; (3) Barth errs in rejecting what Brunner calls a "preserving
grace" and appears therefore to be able to speak only in terms of
instants; (4) likewise, in rejecting the "orders of creation" or "orders
of preservation," Barth rejects one of the crucial bases of Christian

---

5 "Das erste Gebot als theologisches Axiom," *Zwischen den Zeiten,* 12 (1933), p. 308.
6 *Das Gebot und die Ordnungen: Entwurf einer protestantisch-theologischen Ethik.* Eng. trans.: *The Divine
Imperative* (Philadelphia: Westminster, 1947).

ethics; (5) Barth errs in denying the existence of a "point of contact" —*Anknüpfungspunkt*—in human beings and in society for the grace and action of God; (6) finally, Barth misinterprets the relation between the old creation and the new. According to Brunner, this last point is the fundamental issue of the debate. Barth appears to be convinced that any continuity between the old order and the new minimizes human sin and, even more, God's grace. Brunner, on the other hand, wishes to present the Gospel in such a way that it is God's answer to human needs. In this, he adduces that, as Thomas Aquinas declared, *gratia non tollit naturam sed perficit*—grace does not destroy nature, but perfects it. Furthermore, argues Brunner, Barth has misunderstood the title of his recent work, for the "and" there is not the same as the other "ands" that he lists. "It is the 'and' of a problem, of a questioning relationship, not the 'and' of coordination."[7] In any case, concludes Brunner, there may be a place for both his view and Barth's and their differences may be more of temperament than of purpose, for "God uses both the genius of partiality . . . and the spirit of moderation."[8]

Barth, however, would not be mollified. He responded with a short piece under the stark title of *Nein! Antwort an Emil Brunner*—No! Response to Emil Brunner. No, Brunner errs in believing that positing the "and" as a problem is not in itself to posit something next to revelation. No, Brunner errs in seeking a middle way between the way of God and human ways. No, Brunner errs in thinking that one can discuss natural theology without *ipso facto* practicing it. Natural theology is not a proper theological problem, since proper theology knows that its subject matter is none other than the Word of God. "The true denial of natural theology takes place when it does not reach the category of an independent theological problem."[9] Thus, as Barth sees the matter, the entire discussion is not about a particular theological issue, but rather about something that is prior to any theological work, and that must be excluded by definition. Natural theology cannot be part of theology; it cannot be a parallel enterprise; it cannot be a theological question; it must be seen as diametrically opposed to a theology of the Word of God.

---

[7] *Natur und Gnade* (Tübingen: J. C. B. Mohr, 1934), p. 6.
[8] *Ibid.*
[9] *Nein! Antwort an Emil Brunner, Theologische Existenz heute*, 14, p. 12.

Although this debate may give the impression that Barth was simply insisting on his extremism, it will be understood differently if one remembers that this was the time of the rise of the Third Reich. Barth was deeply concerned that the liberal willingness to confuse the Gospel with the highest human achievement would play into the hands of an ideology that sought to use the church for its own ends of world supremacy. He was convinced that, in order to resist the temptations of Nazism, Christians had to be clear that their sole source of authority was the Word of God, and that what he called the theologies of the "and" could be twisted to the ends of the Reich. Indeed, when in 1934 a group of German church leaders, Lutheran as well as Reformed, issued in Barmen the "Declaration" that became the rallying point for the "Confessing Church," there was no doubt that the Barmen Declaration drew much of its strength and inspiration from Barth, as may be seen in the following words from its opening statement:

> Jesus Christ, as he is testified to us in the Holy Scripture, is the one Word of God, whom we are able to hear, whom we are to trust and obey in life and in death.
>   We repudiate the false teaching that the church can and must recognize yet other happenings and powers, images and truths as divine revelation alongside this one Word of God, as a source of her preaching.[10]

The Declaration, and the events that followed, forced Barth to leave Germany and return to his native Switzerland, where he spent the rest of his career at Basel. As a consequence of these upheavals, the second volume (more exactly, the second part of the first volume) of his *Church Dogmatics* appeared six years after the first. From that point on, he continued the regular publication of this great work, until he died while working on part four of volume four.

While it is impossible to offer here even the broadest outline of the contents of the *Dogmatics* (its four "volumes" are really divisions grouping what amounts to thirteen thick volumes)[11] one must at least indicate some of its general characteristics.

The first and most obvious is the very vastness and scope of the

---

[10] J. H. Leith, ed., *Creeds of the Churches*, 3rd edition (Atlanta: John Knox Press, 1982), p. 520.
[11] H. Gollwitzer has published a selection of sections from the first three volumes: Karl Barth, *Church Dogmatics: A Selection* (New York: Harper Torchbooks, 1961).

enterprise. At a time when many thought that the age of the "summas" was past, Barth produced a monument worthy of comparison with the best of the works of the Middle Ages or of the Protestant scholastics. While remaining faithful to his own method and fundamental insight, Barth dealt not only with the doctrine of the Trinity and with creation, but also with angels and other similar topics.

Secondly, the work is remarkable for its coherence. There are indeed developments and changes in emphasis from one volume to another. In particular, Barth slowly mitigated some of his earlier emphasis on the radical "otherness" of God.[12] Still, the main impression is one of continuity. Once Barth had started his *Dogmatics* for a second time, the basic lines of his theology were sufficiently settled that he could continue writing for over three decades while remaining true to himself.

Finally, this work stands out for its "Christological concentration." Although each of its volumes deals with a different topic, in the last analysis they all deal with the revelation of God in Jesus Christ. Rather than successive steps in a ladder, they are like a series of detailed looks at the same subject from different angles. Referring to the subject of the four volumes, it has been said that they

> are not presented as dealing with quite separate topics, such that to move from one to another would be in any sense a change of subject, but rather as four equally fundamental and interlocking dimensions of the same ground-motif that runs throughout: that Jesus Christ is the actualisation and realisation in time and history of God's eternal decision to be God for and with man; he is himself the everlasting covenant of God with us, and in that covenant the meaning and purpose of the created universe is contained; and in him too lies the uncovering and overcoming of man's estrangement from God by the divine "No!" of the cross which leads on the "Yes!" of the resurrection.

This concentration on Christology is of the very essence of Barth's method, but the greatness of his theological achievement lies not simply in the method and form of the whole, but in the way in which he succeeded by this means in re-integrating and casting quite fresh light on all the great leading themes of classical

---

[12] A point which he himself made and explained in 1956. See K. Barth, *The Humanity of God* (Richmond: John Knox, 1960), pp. 37-38.

orthodox belief. Not without reason has his impact on theology been compared with that of Einstein on physics.[13]

This impact is such that it can hardly be overstated. His theology gave impetus, not only to the Confessing Church in Germany, but also to the ecumenical movement that was taking shape at the time. When, shortly after the War, the World Council of Churches was organized (1948), many of its leaders were profoundly influenced by Barth's theology. The same was true of the World Student Christian Federation, which produced much of the leadership for the next generation, both for the ecumenical movement and for churches throughout the world. Among Protestant leaders in the Third World, no theology was as influential as that of Karl Barth—an influence that can still be seen in much of Protestant Third World theology.

Barth developed a theology that went beyond the strictures of orthodoxy without thereby abandoning any of its traditional themes. Likewise, his theology avoided the extreme malleability of liberalism without thereby rejecting the achievements of historical studies, Biblical criticism, and other modern developments. This led to the recovery of much of the inheritance of the patristic period and of the Reformation. It also meant that Barth was widely read and respected by contemporary Catholic theologians, and that his influence can be seen in much of modern Catholic thought.

Rudolf Bultmann and Demythologization

Early in the twentieth century, Rudolf Bultmann became known for his leadership in Biblical studies, particularly in what Biblical scholars call "Form criticism." However, he also counted himself among the proponents of "dialectical theology"—a term which he continued claiming long after his break with Barth and Brunner. While primarily a New Testament scholar, he was particularly interested in interpreting the message of the New Testament in such a way that it could be understood and received by his contemporaries.

In order to reach such an interpretation of the New Testament, Bultmann proposed that the first task was "demythologizing" it. The

---

[13] A. I. C. Heron, *A Century of Protestant Theology* (Philadelphia: Westminster, 1980), p. 91.

New Testament, argued Bultmann, was written within a mythological framework, and it is necessary to distinguish between what is mythical in it and what is the essence of the Christian *kerygma*. This process is what Bultmann calls *Entmythologisierung*—demythologization. Once this has been done, we shall discover that the message of the New Testament is directly addressed to us, even in the midst of our modernity. If, on the other hand, we refuse to follow this process, we turn the New Testament into a collection of ideas, images and events that our contemporaries will justifiably reject. It is true that the Gospel is a scandal and a stumbling block. But if we simply decide that all must take literally all that the New Testament says we shall be placing an entire series of spurious stumbling blocks in the way to faith—such as miracles, demons, the virgin birth, etc.—and these will obscure the true scandal of the Gospel.

It is important, however, to clarify what is meant by "myth," and here critics have pointed out a certain ambiguity in Bultmann's use of the term. On the one hand, when proposing his program, Bultmann characterized the mythological character of the New Testament as follows:

> The cosmology of the New Testament is essentially mythical in character. The world is viewed as a three-storied structure, with the earth in the centre, the heaven above, and the underworld beneath. Heaven is the abode of God and of celestial beings—the angels. The underworld is hell, the place of torment. Even the earth is more than the scene of natural, everyday events, of the trivial round and common task. It is the scene of the supernatural activity of God and his angels on the one hand, and of Satan and his daemons on the other. These supernatural forces intervene in the course of nature and in all that men think and will and do. Miracles are by no means rare. Man is not in control of his life. . . . [14]

In this passage, Bultmann's concern is with the miraculous and the apparently outdated character of the New Testament. In other passages, however, Bultmann offers a different understanding of the mythical, one which is closely related to his own existentialist philosophy. In such passages, he is following existentialist philosopher Martin Heidegger (1889–1976) in affirming that God is first of

---

[14] H. W. Bartsch, ed., *Kerygma and Myth* (New York: Harper Torchbooks, 1961), p. 1.

all existence. Here he is distinguishing, with Heidegger, between two forms of "being": *Dasein*—the being there, in a situation, existing in Kierkegaard's meaning of the word—and *Vorhandenheit*—being in the traditional and static sense. Once this distinction has been established, it is clear that God's being must be spoken of in terms of *Dasein*. The God of the Bible is a personal being. The subject of God's action and revelation is none other than God. To turn God into an object, no matter how slightly, is myth. In this context, the essence of myth is turning divine being and action into objectively verifiable realities. Therefore, the task of demythologization consists in elucidating the true nature of divine action, hidden behind the myths that make God and divine action into objects of observation.[15]

In any case, the program which Bultmann proposed was an effort to make the New Testament believable to his contemporaries. According to Bultmann, modern people can no longer accept the mythological framework of the New Testament. We no longer live in a three-tiered universe, inhabited by spirits. We no longer believe in miracles, but are convinced that all events can be explained by natural causes. The New Testament speaks of a "Spirit" and of sacraments that have no meaning for us. The theory that death is punishment for sin is contrary to all modern thought. The notion that we are all saved through the death of one is contrary to our highest moral sense. And the physical resurrection of Jesus is also plagued with difficulties.

All of this makes the *kerygma* unbelievable for modern people, who are convinced that the mythological view of the world is obsolete. For them, the world is not an "open" entity, subject to mysterious supernatural interventions, but is on the contrary a "closed" entity in which everything takes place through an uninterrupted chain of cause and effect. Naturally, the power of will over the mind can make some of us accept and believe what is rationally unacceptable. But such forced acceptance of the unbelievable moves the accent away from true and existential faith and towards faith as assent to a series of irrational propositions. When this happens, the believer hides behind that assent, and thus avoids the existential encounter with the true message of the New Testament. By depriving us of such cover,

---

[15] See H. P. Owen, *Revelation and Existence: A Study in the Theology of Rudolf Bultmann* (Cardiff: University of Wales Press, 1957), pp. 20-24.

Bultmann hoped to force us to a direct encounter with the Lord of the New Testament.

Since such is his purpose, we must not confuse Bultmann's program with those of the nineteenth century that sought to rid the New Testament of everything that was connected with myth. According to Bultmann, the manner in which such programs were carried forth necessarily had to lead to the abandonment, not only of myths, but also of the very message of the New Testament. The Religionsgeschichtliche Schule, for instance, turned the action of God in Jesus into no more than a symbol of eternal realities. The error of such approaches was in depriving Christianity of its historicity, turning the events of the New Testament into a mere example or demonstration of eternal truths. But in so doing they undid and rejected the very message of the New Testament, that in Jesus God was acting for human redemption.

Bultmann was convinced that the error of these earlier attempts was intimately connected with their philosophical presuppositions, which led them to reject the possibility of a saving event. Over against such earlier attempts, Bultmann believed that, by making use of existentialist philosophy, he could reinterpret the mythology of the New Testament without losing the essential character of the kerygma, for existentialism is not in search of "eternal truths," but rather looks for truth in the concrete, in the historical, in existence.

Bultmann did not claim that he was performing the total task of demythologizing the New Testament. This was a task that, as he thought, would take an entire generation of scholars and theologians. What he did seek to do was to offer an outline of what such demythologization should include. In short, three themes must be part of the demythologized kerygma: life without faith, life with faith, and the event that makes the passage possible from one to the other: Jesus.

Life without faith is what the New Testament calls living "according to the flesh." This does not refer to the physical flesh, to the body and its senses. It means rather that life based on trust in things about us, in the perishable, in ourselves. Those who live "according to the flesh" are preoccupied with themselves, their own security, and fall prey to anxiety. Sometimes we deceive ourselves into thinking that we have somehow gained assurance and safety. It is at this point that we "glory" in ourselves, as Paul would say. But the result is a twisted life—or, in Heidegger's terms, an inauthentic life. For such people, the entire creation becomes what the New Testament calls "this world," that is, a reality peopled and even run by evil powers that rob humans of their freedom and authenticity.

On the other hand, there is "authentic" life, life "based on invisible realities." This implies abandoning all assurance based on ourselves. This is what the New Testament calls living "in the Spirit" or "in faith." In this authentic life, one places all trust in God's grace, which means the forgiveness of sins. We no longer have to seek our own security. We no longer have to put our trust in the world of "objective" reality. We are no longer prey to anxiety and anguish. This is what Paul means when he speaks of being "dead to the world," or of being "new creatures in Christ." And this is also what the existentialist calls an "authentic" life.

Thirdly, we must demythologize the means whereby the step is made possible from inauthentic to authentic life. This is the event of Jesus. This is crucial, for the historical nature of the New Testament message must not be denied. Indeed, the New Testament "claims that faith only became possible at a definite point in history in consequence of an event —viz., the event of Christ. Faith in the sense of obedient self-commitment and inward detachment from the world is only possible when it is faith in Jesus Christ.[16] Here again, however, we must remember that "the New Testament presents the event of Jesus Christ in mythical terms," and that "side by side with the historical event of the crucifixion is the definitely non-historical event of the resurrection."[17] His death was in itself the victory which is expressed in mythical terms when the New Testament speaks of resurrection. By his death, he overcame the power of death, which is also the power of an inauthentic life. Thus, the value of this death for us is not to be understood in mythical terms of payment for our sins, or of overcoming the Devil, but rather in existential terms is an "ever-present reality," whose significance is in that we too can be crucified with him, and thus share in the authentic life and its victory.

How successful Bultmann's efforts at demythologizing were, depends on one's evaluation of his existentialist approach. Indeed, he has been faulted for being too dependent, not only on existentialism, but on one particular form of it—Heidegger's. But

---

[16] *Kerygma and Myth*, p. 22.
[17] *Ibid.*, p. 34.

there is no doubt that by raising the issue of the difficulties involved in translating the imagery and world-view of the New Testament into our times Bultmann has raised a crucial issue for modern theology.

Other Currents in European Protestant Theology

In the same decades in which Barth and his companions of *Zwischen den Zeiten* were seeking to clarify the nature of their theological task, significant developments were taking place in Sweden, in relative independence from the work of Barth. There, what came to be called the "Lundensian school" had deep roots in the study of the history of dogma, as it had been proposed and practiced in the nineteenth century. Indeed, the first major publication of Gustaf Aulén, in 1917, was a history of dogma. Starting from that basis, and in part due to their historical studies, the Lundensians took the lead in a reinterpretation of Luther and in a rediscovery of Irenaeus. In this task, they followed a method characteristic to the Ludensian school, that of *Motivforschung*, or "motif research." What this method sought was the discovery of key motifs or characteristic ideas to be found behind diverse formulations. In the history of religions, as well as in the history of Christianity, such motifs interact, collide, and coalesce. But the historian and theologian must discern among them, in order to disengage those that are essentially Christian from those that are not, and thus to clarify the nature of the Christian faith.

Two well-known works may serve to illustrate the work of the Lundensian school: *Agape and Eros*, published by Anders Nygren in 1930 and 1936,[18] and *Christus Victor*, published by Gustaf Aulén in 1948.[19]

In *Agape and Eros*, Nygren compares two Greek terms, both usually translated into English and modern European languages as "love," and argues that these represent two views of life and of salvation, that they have become confused in Christian history, and that the Reformation—in particular Luther's theology—was an attempt to recover the uniqueness of agape.

Aulén's *Christus Victor* is a similar inquiry into motifs, although now having to do with the work of Christ. For some time, particularly

---

[18] London: S.P.C.K., 1932-39; revised ed., Philadelphia: Westminster, 1953.
[19] New York: Macmillan, 1957.

since Ritschl's work on the subject, it had become customary to contrast two opposing views of the work of Christ, the "objective" theory of Anselm, and the "subjective" of Abelard. Aulén, however, claimed that there was in the ancient church a third view of the work of Christ. This is the "dramatic" or "classical" theory, and it stems from a different "motif" than the other two views. While Anselm's theory sees Christ as offering a substitutionary payment for our sins, and Abelard's sees him as an example for us, the classical or dramatic theory underscores the element of conflict and victory in the work of Christ. Christ is the conqueror of the powers of evil under whose dominion we stood. Aulén rejects the tendency of scholars to interpret ancient texts referring to Christ as the conqueror of the Evil One as mere metaphors. On the contrary, such texts must be taken seriously, for they witness to the early Christian understanding of the work of Christ.

Furthermore, this is not only a matter of historical interest. It has to do with the very heart of the faith, for these various theories manifest different views of the human predicament and of the entire process of salvation. In both the "objective" and the "subjective" views, the power of sin is limited by setting aside the radical opposition of evil to the will of God. In the "classical" theory, in contrast, there is a real "drama of redemption," for there are opposing forces struggling against each other. Therefore, human sin is not something that can be undone by a mere example or a mere payment. It is human enslavement to the powers of evil, which can only be undone by the defeat of such powers.

This leads us to another characteristic of the Lundensian school, its "limited dualism." Without thereby falling into a Manichean dualism, the Lundensians have insisted that the message of the New Testament cannot be understood without taking very seriously the real opposition, conflict and struggle between God and the powers of evil.[20]

Lundensian theology is significant on several counts. Its recovery of the importance of evil for understanding the Christian message has provided a response to liberalism that is parallel and complementary to Barth's. Its understanding of the corporate nature, not only of evil, but also of redemption, has focused attention

---

[20] This is the main criticism of both Barth and Bultmann in Gustaf Wingren's *Theology in Conflict* (Philadelphia: Muhlenberg, 1958).

on the church and has contributed to later ecclesiological discussions. Finally, its rediscovery of forgotten elements in both early Christianity and the Reformation, as well as its close ties with the Church of Sweden—several of its leading figures have become bishops of that church—have been influential in the ecumenical movement.

Dietrich Bonhoeffer (1906–1945) was probably the most influential German theologian of the generation immediately following Barth's. After a brilliant and promising career as a pastor, scholar, teacher, and leader of the Confessing Church, he was executed by the Gestapo a few days before his place of imprisonment was liberated.

Bonhoeffer's early writings soon marked him as both a distinguished theologian and a person of deep insight into the practice of Christian living. In 1937, in *The Cost of Discipleship*, he penned the now famous words about "cheap grace," bemoaning the manner in which Luther's principle of *sola gratia*, which for Luther was the answer to an anguished struggle, has become a doctrine that excuses us from the need to struggle. While it is true that only one who believes is obedient, it is also true that only one who is obedient believes.

> Cheap grace means grace as a doctrine, a principle, a system. It means forgiveness of sins proclaimed as a general truth, the love of God taught as the Christian "conception" of God.[21]

In *Sanctorum Communio*[22] he stressed the communal character of the Christian faith, penning the oft-quoted dictum that "the Church is Christ existing as community." In *Act and Being*[23] he moved beyond his earlier Barthianism by insisting that, while Barth was right in affirming the total sovereignty of God, whose revelation is always "act," one must also remember that by entering into history in Christ and in the church God has been put at our disposal—a theme that would later be carried much further by some of the "death of God" theologians. In *Life Together*,[24] on the basis of the experience of a

---

[21] *The Cost of Discipleship* (New York: Macmillan, 1948), p. 35.
[22] English trans.: *The Communion of Saints: A Dogmatic Inquiry into the Sociology of the Church* (New York: Harper and Row, 1963).
[23] New York: Harper, 1961.
[24] New York: Harper, 1954.

"monastic-like" clandestine school of theology which he had directed, he reflected on the values and practice of such communal life.

His greatest impact, however, was through his emphasis on the value of a "worldly" Christianity. In his notes for an ethics, published posthumously, he had already affirmed that

> In Christ we are offered the possibility of partaking in the reality of God and in the reality of the world, but not in the one without the other. The reality of God discloses itself only by setting me entirely in the reality of the world, and when I encounter the reality of the world it is always already sustained, accepted and reconciled in the reality of God. This is the inner meaning of the revelation of God to man in Jesus Christ.[25]

It was in his *Letters and Papers from Prison*,[26] published after he had sealed with death his life of obedience to the Gospel, that he offered his most tantalizing remarks in this regard—more tantalizing in that they are, as would be the case in any correspondence, fragmentary, exploratory and suggestive rather than systematic and complete. There he spoke of a "world come of age," where the presupposition that human beings are by nature religious would no longer hold. He asked himself, after nineteen centuries in which the "religious a priori" has been the presupposition of all Christian preaching, what will happen when that presupposition no longer holds? His answer, which he found totally in agreement with his own theological outlook, was that there would be need for a "religionless Christianity."

Although Bonhoeffer never had the opportunity to develop fully what he meant by such "religionless Christianity," it is clear that this was much more than an apologetic device in a "world come of age." Much earlier, Barth had insisted on the contrast between religion and Christianity. Bonhoeffer agreed with Barth on this point, but went much further. While Barth spoke of the contrast between religion and Christianity mostly in terms of the contrast between human efforts and divine grace, Bonhoeffer also spoke of "religionless Christianity" in terms of a "secularized" Christianity, a

---

[25] *Ethics* (New York: Macmillan, 1955), p. 61.
[26] London: SCM, 1953 (enlarged edition, 1973).

Christianity which would no longer think and act in terms of a "religious" sphere, or a sphere of "faith" as distinct from the sphere in which all of life takes place. He insisted that the Bible is not a religious book, for religion is concerned with the individual, with inwardness and with the world beyond, while Scripture's concerns are the opposite.

As may be imagined, Bonhoeffer's comments about a "world come of age" and a "religionless Christianity" have been interpreted in various ways, and very different and contrasting schools of thought see in him one of their forerunners.

In any case, Bonhoeffer's positive valuation of the process of secularization cannot be doubted. In this he was both preceded and followed by Gogarten, who several years earlier had begun to explore this theme, but whose most significant work in this regard came after the war.

Further explorations along this line were carried forth by Wolfhart Pannenberg, who in 1961, edited the volume *Revelation as History*,[27] which rejected the common distinction between "world history" and "history of salvation"—*Weltgeschichte* and *Heilsgeschichte*. There is no dimension with which a theologian can work that is beyond history. History itself is the arena of God's revelation, but in such a way that one cannot simply extrapolate some elements and moments of that history and transpose them into a superior "history of salvation." If one is to take history seriously, there must be a unity to it, and all of history must be the concern of the theologian and of the Christian. Likewise, such history, in order to be meaningful, must have an end. This is the significance of the resurrection of Jesus, which is the eschatological event whereby the end can be discerned, so that Christians can affirm that there is meaning and significance to history, and can also claim to have a clue to what that meaning and significance is.

Meanwhile, another field of theological inquiry was developing which would eventually join with the foregoing in order to give shape to much of the theology of the late twentieth century. This was the Marxist-Christian dialogue. A leader in the earlier stages of this dialogue was Josef L. Hromádka, who taught theology in Prague from 1920 until his retirement in 1964—with an interlude between

---

[27] New York: Macmillan, 1968.

1939 and 1947, during which he left Czechoslovakia due to the Nazi occupation, and taught at Princeton Theological Seminary.[28] During the years after his return to Prague, partially through the journal *Communio Viatorum*, which he edited, and partially through his teaching and his books, he explored what it meant for Christians to be obedient in a society controlled by Marxists.

Hromádka's theological outlook was in many ways similar to Barth's. Like Barth, he felt that the major task of the Christian theologian was to critique and correct the proclamation and life of the Church in the light of the Word of God. Like Barth, he was convinced that theology is a task of the Church, and that individual theologians must carry out their work within the context of, and for the benefit of, the Church. Finally, also like Barth, he centered his attention on Christology. While there is no doubt that Barth was an influence on Hromádka—an influence which the latter gratefully acknowledged—these similarities are not to be interpreted exclusively as the result of that influence, for there were also other experiences and currents of thought that led Hromádka's theology in a direction parallel to Barth's. Given the Hussite tradition of Protestant Czechoslovakia, his was always a theology that saw the contrast between the Word of God and the word of society. As an Eastern European, he was more aware than most Western Europeans of the underside of much of Western civilization. He generally agreed with Spengler's thesis that the decline of the West was at hand, and he felt that the Church ought to be aware of this development, and to consider it an opportunity for greater obedience. Thus, when he began reading the works of Barth he was able to recognize a kindred spirit, and to profit from it.

On the basis of the incarnation Hromádka felt that the way to understand what it means to be human is to look at the Word of God in Christ. This does not mean, however, that Christians should be concerned only with the traditionally "religious," for in Christ we are told that God comes to the world. Therefore, to believe in Jesus Christ must immediately involve the believer in the world to which God has come. Furthermore, this is not even a choice, for the Church and Christians exist in the world, and any judgment we may

---

[28] His best known work is *Theology between Yesterday and Tomorrow* (Philadelphia: Westminster, 1957). See also his *Impact of History on Theology: Thoughts of a Czech Pastor* (Notre Dame, Ind.: Fides, 1970), and H. Ruh, *Geschichte und Theologie: Grundlinien der Theologie Hromadkas* (Zurich: EVZ, 1963).

pronounce on the world is *ipso facto* a judgment on ourselves and on the church.

The goal of this world which God has created is the kingdom. Hromádka's writings constantly return to this eschatological expectation, which means both that all human orders can be no more than approximations of God's purpose, and that in every order Christians must work for such approximations. Thus, the task of Christians, be it in the East or in the West, is to work with those forces and individuals in society that are working towards goals of peace and justice. In particular, this means working in favor of those who are oppressed, hungry, or otherwise deprived of their human dignity. It also means working for reconciliation wherever the world or human society is divided. Christ came to reconcile God and humans, but also humans among themselves. Therefore, the mission of the Church must be above all a mission of reconciliation.

This is one of the reasons why Hromádka feels that anticommunism should be rejected by Christians. Anticommunism is an attitude that seeks the victory of some and the defeat of others, rather than reconciliation. Furthermore, it often fosters a self-righteous attitude in which only the evils of communism are decried, and the evils of the society in which the anticommunist lives are ignored or glossed over. While communism stands in need of serious correction, Christians must beware of equating their faith with western liberal democracy.

There is much in communism that Hromádka feels Christians must reject. In particular, Christians must condemn and decry the oppressive and brutal measures that communists have often used to gain power and to retain it. As far as Marxism is concerned, Hromádka criticized it for its shallow understanding of human sinfulness, which leads to the claim that in a classless society a new humanity will be born, and problems of greed and hatred will be solved. Also, classical Marxism dehumanizes the human creature by a view of history that leaves little room for freedom and responsibility.

As to Marxist atheism, Hromádka argues that it must be seen both as a negative and as a positive trait. Negatively, it leads to a view of the world, of humans and of history that is shallow and in the end meaningless. Positively, however, Christians must remember that the god whose existence Marxists deny is not the Christian God. It is rather a god like the idols whom the biblical prophets already attacked. Although it is true that Christian theology and practice has often failed to see this distinction, and thus has fallen prey to idolatry, the destruction of such an idol must be seen as a positive contribution of Marxism.

In situations in which Marxists are working for the betterment of human society, Christians must collaborate with them in seeking to attain that goal. In deciding whom to support in concrete political situations, one cannot simply decide that one will support those who call themselves Christians. Rather, one must support those who with reference to the particular issue at stake are moving towards goals in consonance with the kingdom. Naturally, in different circumstances this will take different concrete forms. But in every circumstance what Christians must do is to work, not for the victory or the defeat of a particular ideology or party, but for the goals of peace and reconciliation.

In any case, what is most important to remember in this entire discussion is that Christian theology is not in competition with Marxism or with any other ideology. The basis for the utterances of Christian theology is the Word of God, which cannot be contained in any ideology, but which comes as judgment and grace on every human endeavor and every human ideology.

The theologies of Barth and Hromádka came even closer in the work of Jan M. Lochman. A former disciple of Hromádka, Lochman taught theology, first at the Comenius Faculty of Theology in Prague —where Hromádka also taught—and then at the University of Basel —where Barth spent most of his teaching career. Like Hromádka, Lochman has continued exploring the encounter between Christianity and Marxism. Like Barth, he has sought to develop a systematic theology based on the Word of God—although giving more attention than Barth to the challenge and opportunities presented by secularization.[29]

Probably the most influential German theologian active at present is Jürgen Moltmann, who has taught theology since 1958, and currently teaches at Tübingen. Not only through his books, but also through frequent visits and lectures, he has been influential in the United States. He has also carried on a lively dialogue with Latin

---

[29] Jan M. Lochman, *The Church in a Marxist Society: A Czechoslovak View* (New York: Harper and Row, 1970); *Encountering Marx: Bonds and Barriers between Christians and Marxists* (Philadelphia: Fortress, 1977); *The Faith We Confess: An Ecumenical Dogmatics* (Philadelphia: Fortress, 1984).

American theologians of liberation. During the Second World War, he was captured by the English, and it was as a prisoner of war that he began his studies in theology. Later, he was influenced by most of the major figures mentioned above—Barth in particular. But it was the reading of the Marxist philosopher Ernst Bloch that sent him in a new theological direction. About Bloch, he says

> I remember very well spending a whole vacation in Tessin with his book *Das Prinzip Hoffnung* (The Principle of Hope)[30] without noticing the beauty of the Swiss mountains. I asked myself: "Why has Christian theology avoided this theme that really ought to be its own theme? What is the place of the primitive Christian spirit of hope within current Christianity?" I then began to work on my *Theology of Hope*.[31]

This momentous book, first published in 1965, sought to recover the centrality of eschatology for Christian faith, and at the same time to show that eschatology was more than "the doctrine of the last things." On the contrary, eschatology includes both that for which the Church hopes and the hope itself by which the Church lives. Therefore, "from first to last, and not merely in epilogue, Christianity is eschatology, is hope."[32] And, after explicating how this hope relates to the resurrection of Jesus Christ, and what it means for the relationship between revelation and history, Moltmann concluded:

> As a result of this hope in God's future, this present world becomes free in believing eyes from all attempts at self-redemption or self-production through labor, and it becomes open for loving, ministering self-expenditure in the interests of a humanizing of conditions and in the interests of the realization of justice in the light of the coming justice of God. This means, however, that the hope of resurrection must bring about a new understanding of the world. This world is not the heaven of self-realization, as it was said to be in Idealism. This world is not the hell of self-estrangement, as it is said to be in romanticist and existentialist writing. The world is not yet finished, but is understood as engaged in a history. It is

---

[30] 3 vols. (Cambridge: M.I.T. Press, 1982).

[31] In T. Cabestrero, *Conversations with Contemporary Theologians* (Maryknoll, N.Y.: Orbis, 1980), p. 123.

[32] *Theology of Hope: On the Grounds and Implications of Christian Eschatology* (New York: Harper and Row, 1967), p. 16.

therefore the world of possibilities, the world in which we can serve the future, promised truth and righteousness and peace. This is an age of diaspora, of sowing in hope, of self-surrender and sacrifice, for it is an age which stands within the horizon of a new future. Thus self-expenditure in the world, day-to-day love in hope, becomes possible and becomes human within the horizon of expectation which transcends this world.[33]

Since at the heart of Christian eschatology stands the hope and promise of the kingdom, an eschatological faith must necessarily be political. To speak of an apolitical Gospel is folly and contradiction. In contrast with all other religions, Christianity "has been political from the beginning. The Christian faith was political because Christ was crucified for political reasons, was crucified as a traitor. The memory of that political death of Christ forces faith to follow Christ in his messianic work of freeing humankind also in the political sense.[34]

What Moltmann is thus proposing is an understanding of the Christian faith which finds God in history—concretely, in those aspects of history which bear the mark of the cross, that is, in the dispossessed, the oppressed and the afflicted. It is also a faith that calls us to join Christ at the cross. This, however, is not the mystical cross of Pietism or of religious sentiment, but the cross of a history in which God is crucified. This is the title of another of Moltmann's most influential books, *The Crucified God*,[35] in which the emphasis is somewhat different from his earlier work, although the theological direction is the same. He has confessed that when he wrote *Theology of Hope* he was overly enthusiastic about the possibilities of immediate political change. The Second Vatican Council was opening new vistas for the Catholic Church. The World Council of Churches, and most of the communions that form part of it, were optimistic about the future possibilities of bridging many of the gaps dividing humanity. Behind the iron curtain, in Czechoslovakia, it appeared that Marxist socialism was beginning to take on a more human face. Then, however, the reaction set in, and in all of these spheres the short-range hope was not as promising as before. Therefore, Moltmann now wrote a second book relating Christian hope, not

---

[33] *Ibid.*, p. 338.
[34] In Cabestrero, *Conversations*, p. 135.
[35] New York: Harper and Row, 1974.

only to the resurrection, but also to the crucifixion. The two, however, are of one piece, and one should not overemphasize the contrast between them. As Moltmann himself has put it, "there's hope for a new future only when you accept the past with all the guilt wrapped up in it and with all the crucifying experiences that it includes. That's why I think that *The Crucified God* has more hope than *Theology of Hope*. The signs of destruction multiply and our hope must stop being childishly optimistic."[36]

Protestant Theology in the United States

As one surveys the course of theology in the United States, and especially the actual life of the churches, one is immediately struck by the degree to which the United States has remained insulated from many of the drastic changes of the twentieth century. While technological changes are nowhere as apparent nor as influential as in the United States, the great political, economic and social upheavals of this century have barely rippled the surface of American life and thought. Thus, for instance, although the United States was a belligerent in both world wars, the immediate aftermath in both cases was a sense of victory and elation, an optimism that contrasted markedly with the mood of Europe—even of those European nations that could count themselves among the "victors." Also, the impact of the breakdown of colonialism was much more subtle in the United States, whose empire in large portions of the Third World was economic rather than overtly political.

For these reasons, Barth and his school did not have in the United States the immediate impact they had in Europe, or even among theologians and church leaders in the Third World. It was only with the sobering effects of the Depression that Barth, whose *The Word of God and the Word of Man* had recently been translated,[37] began to make himself felt in wider American ecclesiastical circles. Besides the direct translation of the works of Barth and Brunner—who in this country gained a wider audience than Barth—the new theology manifested itself in the works of the two Niebuhr brothers, Reinhold (1892–1971) and H. Richard (1894–1962).

Reinhold Niebuhr had been a pastor in Detroit, where his

---

[36] In Cabestrero, *Conversations*, p. 124.
[37] New York: Harper, 1928.

experience was similar to that of Barth at Safenwil. Faced with the suffering of the working classes, and with their dehumanization both by the machine and by social and economic structures, he turned to the Marxist critique of capitalism. While he did not become a Marxist, he was convinced that much of what Marx had said about the inner workings of capitalism was true, and that Christians must reject the facile equation of liberal democratic capitalism with a just economic order. He also became convinced that societies act in ways that contrast with the principles and actions of their individual members. This was the thesis of his book *Moral Man and Immoral Society*,[38] which he later quipped should have been called "immoral man and still more immoral society." What he meant by this was that he had discovered some of the depths of human sin, and how it works, not only in individuals, but also in a compounded fashion in societies. Later, in *The Nature and Destiny of Man*,[39] he developed this theme, and it was through this very influential book that an entire generation of American students of theology came to an understanding of the depths of sin and the significance of grace.

Meanwhile, his brother, H. Richard, had been working on a sociological and theological analysis of American religious life. In *The Social Sources of Denominationalism*, he charged the churches with having capitulated to the gods of class and self-preservation.

> The domination of class and self-preservative church ethics over the ethics of the gospel must be held responsible for much of the moral ineffectiveness of Christianity in the West. Not only or primarily because denominationalism divides and scatters the energies of Christendom, but more because it signalizes the defeat of the Christian ethics of brotherhood by the ethics of caste is it the source of Christendom's moral weakness. The ethical effectiveness of an individual depends on the integration of his character, on the synthesis of his values and desires into a system dominated by his highest good; the ethical effectiveness of a group is no less dependent on its control by a morale in which all subordinate purposes are organized around a leading ideal. And the churches are ineffective because they lack such a common morale.[40]

---

[38] New York: Scribner's, 1932.

[39] First published separately in two volumes (New York: Scribner's, 1941, 1943) and then in a single volume (New York: Scribner's 1949).

[40] 1959 reprint (New York: Meridian), pp. 21-22.

What has happened in denominationalism, Niebuhr argued, is that Christianity has surrendered its leadership, and allowed itself to be molded by "the social forces of national and economic life." When this happens, the Church has very little hope to offer to the world, for it loses its prophetic quality.[41] This indictment he repeated in 1937, in the oft-quoted summary of the bland theology that according to him had gripped much of the nation: "A God without wrath brought men without sin into a kingdom without judgment through the ministrations of a Christ without a cross."[42]

From that point, H. Richard Niebuhr spent the rest of his career as a professor of Christian ethics seeking to destroy the idols of culture and society that prevent Christians and the Church from being fully responsible before God. This was the theme of his more mature work, *Radical Monotheism and Western Culture*, [43] in which he inquired into the meaning of an ethics based on the relativity of all human and cultural authority, under the sovereignty of God.

As Nazism was gaining ground in Germany, Reinhold Niebuhr was instrumental in bringing Paul Tillich (1886–1965) to the United States and to a teaching position at Union Theological Seminary, where he spent most of his career. Tillich had earned the enmity of the Nazi regime, and had to leave Germany. It is likely that Niebuhr hoped that his new colleague at Union, who was noted for his socialist stance in Germany, would provide added support for his critique of American economic and social structures. This, however, would not be the case, for Tillich had always considered himself a "theologian of culture." As such, he was very much interested in modern psychology, as well as in existentialism and eastern religions, and soon these elements overshadowed his interest in economics and the social order.

In contrast to Barth, Tillich felt that the task of theology was above all apologetic, and that in order to do this it must ground itself in philosophy. This is why he argued for the "method of correlation," which consisted essentially in analyzing the existential questions posed by human life, and responding to them in terms of the Gospel.

Systematic theology uses the method of correlation. It has always done so, sometimes more, sometimes less, consciously, and must

---

[41] Ibid., p. 275.
[42] *The Kingdom of God in America* (New York: Harper and Brothers, 1937), p. 193.
[43] New York: Harper and Row, 1960.

do so consciously and outspokenly, especially if the apologetic point of view is to prevail. The method of correlation explains the contents of the Christian faith through existential questions and theological answers in mutual interdependence.[44]

As we analyze our human existence, we discover that it is incomplete, that beyond all our passing attempts at security, at affirming our own being, there is an "ultimate concern." No matter how much modern human beings seek to hide this ultimate concern, or to flee from it, it is always there, for our being cannot stand on itself, but rather on the "ground of all being." This ground is none other than God. God is not a being. God does not exist as beings exist. God is the ground of all being and all existence.

In our brokenness, and in our quest for direction, we may assert our own sufficiency. This is what Tillich calls "autonomy," and it is shallow and self-deceiving, for we are not and cannot be the ground of our own being. The option of "heteronomy," grounding our being on another, and our life on another's authority, does affirm our incompleteness, but then attempts to base our being on a false ground, and thus produces an inauthentic life. The only option is "theonomy," which grounds our being on its proper foundation, and thereby allows us to relate properly—neither "autonomously" nor "heteronomously"—to other beings.

Within this context, the Christian message is the message of the "New Being." This is "essential being under the conditions of existence, conquering the gap between essence and existence."[45] This New Being is Jesus Christ, who bears it in the totality of his being. It is out of the certainty that "the bringer of the new eon cannot finally have succumbed to the powers of the old eon" that faith in the resurrection is born.[46] "It is the certainty of one's own victory over the death of existential estrangement which creates the certainty of the Resurrection of the Christ as event and symbol."[47] Thus, what we have here is a strange reversal in which the resurrection of Jesus is not the seal of his life, but rather it is faith in him and in our own victory that is the guarantee of his resurrection.

---

[44] *Systematic Theology*, vol. 1 (Chicago: University of Chicago Press, 1951), p. 60.
[45] *Systematic Theology*, vol. 3 (Chicago: University of Chicago Press, 1957), pp. 118-19.
[46] *Ibid.*, p. 154.
[47] *Ibid.*, p. 153.

During his lifetime, Tillich's theology was very influential, particularly in the United States. However, in recent years that influence has declined to the point that a British critic appears justified in declaring that "his highly personal work already has a curiously dated quality."[48]

While this judgment may be true, it is also true that no comparable system to take its place has appeared in the theological horizon of the United States. Indeed, American theology in the last twenty years can readily be described as a "shattered spectrum."[49] There have been attempts to develop a theology on the basis of process philosophy, following the earlier lead of Charles Hartshorne. Such is the work of John B. Cobb, who argues that on this basis it is possible to develop a new form of natural theology, and that such natural theology is necessary if faith is to relate actively with contemporary life. The issue of secularization and its positive valorization has been taken up by several theologians, and pursued in different directions. Black and feminist theologies are making a marked contribution to the entire life of the church—these, however, can best be understood if discussed jointly with the emerging Third World theologies.

Finally, it must be noted that probably the most significant theological development in the United States in recent years has been the growing gap, even among evangelicals, between a new evangelical theology that is staunchly anticommunist—sometimes to the point of approaching fascism—and which sees the main task of the church as strengthening the position of the United States among the nations of the world, and another which, in echoes of the Barmen Declaration and very much influenced by the world-wide evangelical community, affirms the absolute authority of Christ over all of life, and seeks to place American life and policies under the judgment of that lordship. Characteristic of this latter form of evangelical theology, which is very much aware of the social and economic injustices in the world, and of American complicity in them, is the movement of "Evangelicals for Social Action," whose basic perspective is clearly expressed in the "Chicago Declaration" of 1973.[50]

---

[48] Heron, A Century, p. 143.

[49] Such is the title of a book by L. D. Kliever, The Shattered Spectrum: A Survey of Contemporary Theology (Atlanta: John Knox, 1981). While Kliever's survey also includes European and Latin American theology, his title appears to apply particularly well to North American theology in recent decades.

[50] R. J. Sider, ed., The Chicago Declaration (Carol Stream, Ill.: Creation House, 1974).

New Directions in Catholic Theology

When we last discussed Roman Catholic theology, in chapter XIV, we saw that during the nineteenth century, faced by the various challenges of the modern world, its general tendency was one of conservative retrenchment—with the qualified exception of Leo XIII's *Rerum novarum*, and the "modernists," who were condemned by ecclesiastical authorities. During the first half of the twentieth century, the papacy followed a similar policy, although trends can now be seen that even at that time were working towards the greater openness of the Second Vatican Council.

The theological conservatism of the popes was seen, as before, in the manner in which they responded to the modern world. Three of the four popes between 1903 and 1958 took the name of Pius, thus indicating their desire to follow the policies of Pius IX: Pius X (1903–1914), Pius XI (1922–1939), and Pius XII (1939–1958). The fourth, Benedict XV (1914–1922) had been made an archbishop by Pius X, and clearly set out to continue the policies of his predecessor. During the early years of the century, one of the main concerns of the Papacy was the temporal power over the city of Rome, to whose loss the popes could not be reconciled. Finally, in 1929, an agreement was reached with Mussolini. The fact that it was Mussolini that was able to settle this matter is significant, for Pius XI, who was then pope, was supportive of Fascism in its early stages. Although eventually he did clash with Mussolini, his successor, Pius XII, was equally ambivalent in his opposition to Fascism, which he appears to have regarded as a lesser evil than communism, particularly as long as it did not openly attack the Church.

On more strictly theological matters, the conservatism of these popes was seen in their efforts to silence the new currents of thought that were emerging within the Catholic Church. Pierre Teilhard de Chardin, probably the most creative Catholic thinker of the century, was ordered not to publish his writings. His works appeared after his death in 1955, and were received enthusiastically by intellectual circles throughout the world. But in 1962, when Jesuit theologian Henri de Lubac published the first volume of a study on Teilhard, he was forbidden to publish a second volume, or to have the volume already published in French translated into other languages. Yves Congar, another leading Catholic theologian, was also silenced by Rome.

On the other hand, there were signs pointing to a new age in Catholic theology.One such sign was precisely that Teilhard, Lubac, Congar, and many others around them, were opening theological avenues that the hierarchy considered too dangerous to be explored. A second sign was the degree to which the Roman Catholic Church was becoming a truly international communion. The conservative popes of the first half of the century did however recognize the growing importance of the Third World. Pius XI consecrated the first native Chinese bishops. Pius XII followed his lead by seeking to place churches under the leadership of native bishops. He also realized that the age of colonialism was over, and that in the future it would be necessary to deal with independent nations throughout the world, and not simply with colonial powers, as before. He therefore strengthened the national churches and, without relinquishing his supremacy, gave them a slight measure of autonomy in addressing their own problems. Finally, a third sign of a new age was the movement of liturgical reformation which, again within very strict limits, the popes encouraged. While much of the felt need for such reformation came from inner theological considerations, part of it did reflect a sense that the Church must take cognizance of the modern world. These promises of change would come to fruition at the Second Vatican Council.

The earlier part of the century was dominated by the Neo-Thomism of philosophical theologians such as Jacques Maritain (1882–1973) and Etienne Gilson (1884–1978), who criticized the earlier forms of Thomism for having interpreted Thomas in "essentialist" rather than "existentialist" terms. The priority of existence over essence as postulated by Thomas was seen by this new generation of Thomists as providing the opportunity for a dialogue with existentialism.

By the 1930's, however, there were other signs of theological disquiet and renewal. The historical and exegetical sciences, that at that time were rapidly developing among Protestants, also found a place among Catholic theologians. In 1942 a new effort was launched at publishing early Christian writings. Under the direction of Henri de Lubac and Jean Daniélou, this series, *Sources chrétiennes*, soon surpassed a hundred volumes. The issues of science and theology were tackled by a number of theologians, foremost among them the Jesuit theologian Pierre Teilhard de Chardin, whose articles dealing with the origin of the human species and with the concept of evolution were widely respected among his colleagues in paleontology.[51] In 1933, Yves Congar published the first of his major works on a theology of the laity.[52]

By 1946, the "new theology" was becoming a subject of controversy. Dominican theologian M. M. Labourdette accused the editors of *Sources chrétiennes* of selecting for publication those texts that appeared to bring into question the validity of scholastic theology, or to agree with various elements of modern thought. R. Garrigou-Lagrange accused the "new theology" of capitulating to the ideas of progress and evolution, taken from the modern world. For a time, the issue appeared as a debate between the Jesuits and the more conservative Dominicans. The result was the silencing of many of the "new theologians," as well as the promulgation of the encyclical *Humani generis*, issued in 1950, which reiterated the earlier condemnation of modernism and warned against innovations in theology. The year 1950 also marked the promulgation by Pope Pius XII of the dogma of the Bodily Assumption of Mary, a dogma which further increased the distance between Catholics and Protestants.

Among the theologians who were silenced during this period, the most creative and original was Pierre Teilhard de Chardin. His theology was apologetic in the broad sense that he attempted to show the validity of Christianity to the scientific world. But it went beyond traditional apologetics in that it also sought a new understanding of Christianity, and felt that modern science had a significant contribution to make to this understanding. At the root of modern thought lies the principle of evolution, declared Teilhard, and he wholeheartedly agreed with this principle. However, he disagreed with the Darwinian understanding of this principle, which sees it as working on the basis of the "survival of the fittest." In contrast, Teilhard proposed that cosmic evolution is guided by the "law of complexity-consciousness." All reality evolves towards greater complexity, which is the same as a higher degree of consciousness. Matter and consciousness are not two different "things," as with Descartes. On the contrary, in the very "stuff of the universe," even in its minutest particle, there is a force calling to consciousness. On the basis of this law, the original "geosphere" evolves into the

---

[51] In his articles, beginning in 1916, in *Annales de paléontologie, Revue de philosophie*, and other journals.
[52] *Jalons pour une théologie du laicat* (Paris: Editions du Cerf, 1953).

"biosphere," in which life appears and develops, and this in turn gives rise to the "noosphere," the realm of intelligent life.

This entire process is not unilinear. There are gropings in which various entities evolve in ways that will not be continued, for they are dead ends. But eventually such gropings produce a higher entity, and this in turn produces new gropings. This is why, taken in parts, the process appears senseless, whereas taken as a whole one can see its movement.

The goal of this movement is the "omega point," which is none other than Jesus Christ. Jesus is the *homo futurus*, the very goal of evolution, for the end is one of communion with God, and in Jesus this communion has reached its highest point. After the image of Jesus, at that point there is both a perfect union with God and a perfect self-identity. Thus, while from one perspective the evolutionary process is a "cosmogenesis"—matter evolving into a universe and towards God—in another sense it is a "Christogenesis"—God coming to matter, the Word made flesh.

This process can also be seen in history. It is possible to study the rise of humankind and its various civilizations as a groping evolution towards the *homo futurus*. In this groping, it was the Mediterranean and Western civilizations that were brought to the point where Jesus could appear and work in them. But now we are in an age of "planetization," groping towards a new civilization that will be a further stage in the evolutionary process. The Church, as the body of Christ, the community ruled by the mind of Christ, is called to play a central role in this process.

The fact that Teilhard's writings were suppressed during his lifetime, and that in the first years after his death he was regarded askance by ecclesiastical authorities, has delayed his impact, so that in a strange sense he became a contemporary and a guiding light for many philosophers and theologians who were beginning to discover him ten years after his death. This impact may be seen in the various contemporary theologies that refuse earlier forms of dualism, as well as in those that insist that the "end" is the best starting point for theology.

While Teilhard de Chardin's wide vision has influenced contemporary theology on these and other points, the great teacher and systematizer of Catholic theology in the twentieth century is Karl Rahner (1904–1984). A former student of Heidegger, Rahner retained some of the emphases of existentialism, but moved beyond its preoccupation with the "moment" and the "encounter," which he felt was too atomistic a view of human existence. While strictly orthodox, he insisted on the need for every generation to understand anew the truth hidden behind the formulas of orthodoxy. Thus, he was able to combine unimpeachable orthodoxy with astounding creativity. There is hardly a traditional theme of theology that he has not examined, discussed, reinterpreted, and revitalized. His voluminous writings, and the many encyclopedic works and periodicals he edited,[53] deal with every heading of Christian doctrine, as well as with a number of themes often neglected by modern theologians. A clear motif that runs throughout his writings is mystery. Mystery makes the theologian stand in awe before the subject matter of theology. But mystery, far from being an excuse for intellectual sloth or for a fideistic obscurantism, is a call both to excitement and to reflection. Thus, in the opening statement to one of his books, he wrote:

> The old theology of faith always knew that for the *rudes* or the uneducated, coming to faith through an adequate reflection upon all of the intellectual grounds of credibility is not possible and is not necessary.
> So I would like to formulate that in today's situation all of us with all of our theological study are and remain unavoidably *rudes* in a certain sense, and that we ought to admit that to ourselves and also to the world frankly and courageously.[54]

Since Rahner's work is too vast to summarize here, it may be well to concentrate on two topics that are of particular significance. The first is Rahner's Christology, and the understandings of anthropology and of grace that flow from it. While agreeing with the Chalcedonian Definition, Rahner feels that too often this has been interpreted in a monophysite or almost docetic way, as if the incarnation somehow diminished or reduced the real humanity of Jesus. In contrast to this, he finds in the New Testament the witness to a truly human Jesus.

---

[53] Including a second edition of the *Lexikon für Theologie und Kirche* and, jointly with E. Schillebeeckx, the very influential journal *Concilium*. His collected essays have been translated into English: *Theological Investigations* (New York: Crossroad, 1961-1983).

[54] *Foundations of Christian Faith: An Introduction to the Idea of Christianity* (New York: Seabury, 1978), p. 9.

This is important to Rahner, since a Christian anthropology must be based on what we see in Jesus to be the true and full humanity. The incarnation is not simply God's response to human sin, but is the very goal of creation, the very reason for human existence. Such existence is possible only because God is willing to be human. This does not mean, however, that we ought to speak or think of ourselves as nothing, for—thanks to the incarnation—this would be to speak or think poorly of God. It does mean that our very existence is an act of grace. There is no such thing as a "natural" human being without grace. Therefore, although the function of the Church and its sacraments as means of grace must not be obscured, it is also true that every good human act, no matter where performed or by whom, is an act of grace.

Another theme of extreme significance in Rahner's theology is his understanding of the catholicity of the Church. While most theologians around him understood such catholicity in terms of uniformity, Rahner understood it in terms of incarnation in the various situations throughout the world. He was also very much aware of the rise of the younger nations and of their insistence on the value of their own culture and traditions. Thus, while others saw in the use of Latin a sign of catholicity, Rahner welcomed the use of the vernacular as a sign of that form of catholicity which is manifested in the Church's being truly present—that is, incarnationally present—in every part of the world. Also, still on the theme of catholicity, while others insisted on the power and centralized authority of the pope as the guarantee of such catholicity, Rahner was developing the theme of the collegiality of all bishops, not as a limit to papal authority, but rather as another sign of the Church's catholicity. As is well known, both of these themes were taken up and supported by the Second Vatican Council, and have had a serious impact in the lives of Catholics throughout the world.

Thus, while the hierarchy of the Church was still seeking to put down practically every effort to relate Christianity in a positive way to the modern world, an entire theological outlook was developing which would eventually serve as the driving force in the most momentous event in Catholic life in the twentieth century, the Second Vatican Council.

When Pope John XXIII was elected in 1958, it was expected that the elderly choice of the conclave would be only a "transitional pope," with little impact on the life of the Church. But Pope John had other ideas, as he clearly manifested when, scarcely three months after his election, he announced his plan to call a general council of the church. The opposition of the curia and of conservative elements in the Church was not slow in coming; but the pope's authority prevailed, and the Second Vatican Council finally began its sessions on October 11, 1962.

From the very beginning, it was clear that what was at stake was the entire direction which the Catholic Church would take for at least the rest of the century, particularly in matters having to do with its relationship to the modern world. The Theological Commission that was preparing the various documents for the Council's consideration was dominated by conservative elements. In a speech a year before the Council met, the secretary of the Commission declared that the purpose of the assembly would be to preserve the deposit of the faith against the threats of modern errors, and to tighten discipline within the ranks of the Church, in response to the "crisis of authority."

The pope's understanding of the Council's goals, however, was different. He had earlier spoken of the need for an *aggiornamento*—an updating. In his opening speech before the assembly, on October 11, 1962, he urged those present to seek two goals: to adapt the deposit of revelation to contemporary needs, while remaining faithful to tradition, and to apply the "medicine of mercy" rather than the arms of authority to those who were not faithful children of the Church.[55]

The composition of the Council was such as to receive the pope's invitation with greater enthusiasm than the rather stale documents presented to it by the preparatory commissions. Thanks to the efforts of earlier popes to internationalize the church, the majority of the bishops at the Council were from the Third World. Also, a number of European bishops felt that the "new theology" had much to contribute to the life of the Church, and as a result the theological experts—"periti"—invited to the Council included Rahner, Congar and de Lubac. Therefore, the early sessions of the Council were marked by a constant struggle between the preparatory commissions and the curia, on the one hand, and the Council itself on the other. At

---

[55] These two speeches are compared by J. Comblin in "La teología católica desde el final del pontificado de Pío XII," in H. Vorgrimler and R. van der Gucht, *La teología en el siglo XX*, vol. 2 (Madrid: BAC, 1973), p. 61.

the repeated insistence of the assembly, new documents were drawn, and the result was a new day for Catholic theology.

The Council issued important documents on liturgical reform—including authorizing the celebration of the mass in the vernacular, and encouraging conferences of bishops from various parts of the world to adapt the liturgy according to the needs of each culture—on religious freedom and tolerance—in which it completely revoked the *Syllabus of errors* of Pius IX—on ecumenism, the Eastern churches, the religious orders, non-Christian religions, and on other matters. However, the document which most clearly expresses the new mood of the church is the "Pastoral Constitution on the Church in the Modern World," also known by its initial words, *Gaudium et spes*. This document, which was not even among the issues initially submitted by the preparatory commissions, dealt with the changes that have taken place in recent generations, and saw in them much that should be supported by Christians, as may be seen in its opening lines and in one of its last paragraphs:

> The joy and hope, the grief and anguish of the men of our time, especially those who are poor or afflicted in any way, are the joy and hope, the grief and anguish of the followers of Christ as well. Nothing that is genuinely human fails to find an echo in their hearts. . . . This is why Christians cherish a feeling of deep solidarity with the human race and its history.[56]
>
> Great numbers of people are acutely conscious of being deprived of the world's goods through injustice and unfair distribution and are vehemently demanding their share in them. Developing nations like the recently independent states are anxious to share in the political and economic benefits of modern civilization and to play their part freely in the world, but they are hampered by their economic dependence on the rapidly expanding richer nations and the ever widening gap between them. The hungry nations cry out to their affluent neighbors: women claim parity with men in fact as well as of rights, where they have not already obtained it; farmers and workers insist not just on the necessities of life but also on the opportunity to develop by their labor their personal talents and to play their due role in organizing economic, social, political, and cultural life. Now for the first time

---

[56] A. P. Flannery, ed., *Documents of Vatican II* (Grand Rapids: Eerdmans, 1975), pp. 903-4.

in history people are not afraid to think that cultural benefits are for all and should be available to everybody.[57]

These words mark much of the theological mood of Catholicism in the latter part of the twentieth century. The spirit of the Council has not always prevailed, and there have been repeated instances in which papal authority has sought to curb those who would carry the consequences of the new openness farther than the popes would like. While the Council was still in session, Paul VI saw fit to add his own cautious interpolations to the decree on ecumenism, even after the assembly had approved it. More recently, during the reign of John Paul II, disciplinary measures have been taken against theologians in Europe, Latin America and the United States. Still, the actions of the Council in opening the Church to the modern world, and in particular to the variety of issues of the Third World, have left their mark on the entire Catholic Church, and have given Catholic theology new freshness and variety, as well as new openness for ecumenical ventures.

Third World Theologies

Perhaps the point at which this new mood in theology is most clearly seen is in the development of Third World theologies. By this is meant theologies—both Catholic and Protestant, and often widely ecumenical—developed by those who, due to their traditional powerlessness, have not usually been at the forefront of the theological dialogue. Therefore, this includes theologies from Third World countries as well as theologies within the "developed" world expressing the experiences, aspirations and perspectives of women and of oppressed minorities.

Such theologies found some of their earlier expressions in the Black Civil Rights Movement in the United States, and particularly in the sermons and writings of Martin Luther King, Jr. While King's gifts as a speaker and a leader, and his courage, have often been highlighted, he should also be seen as a significant theologian.[58] Having received his doctorate from Boston University, he was

---

[57] *Ibid.*, p. 909.
[58] See J. J. Ansbro, *Martin Luther King, Jr.: The Making of a Mind* (Maryknoll, N.Y.: Orbis, 1982); F. Smith, *The Ethics of Martin Luther King, Jr.* (New York: E. Mellen, 1981).

acquainted with the latest developments in white Protestant theology, and at times made use of them. But his own theology was deeply rooted in the tradition of the black church, with its emphasis on the Exodus and its radical eschatological hope. Thus, in King's writings much of what later came to be known as "black theology" can be found.[59]

At about the same time, the feminist movement was gaining new impetus, partially as a result of the Second World War. At first in the North Atlantic, and eventually throughout the world, women insisted on their right to be seen and treated as equal partners and participants in the human adventure. In the field of theology, while some came to the conclusion that Christianity was so male-oriented that it must be rejected,[60] others made significant contributions towards a more inclusive understanding of the Christian faith.[61]

Finally, in the countries that are usually known as the "Third World," new theologies were also developing. In various areas these theologies took different directions. In Asia, while social justice is always an issue, the central theme has been the relationship of Christianity with the cultural traditions of each nation.[62] In black Africa the issue has been similar,[63] while in South Africa theology has developed around the theme of apartheid and a black and "coloured" response to it.[64] In Latin America, the overriding issue

[59] On black theology, see James H. Cone, *A Black Theology of Liberation* (Philadelphia: J. B. Lippincott, 1970); *God of the Oppressed* (New York: Seabury, 1975); *For My People: Black Theology and the Black Church* (Maryknoll, N.Y.: Orbis, 1984); J. Deotis Roberts, *Black Theology Today: Liberation and Contextualization* (New York: E. Mellen, 1983).

[60] Mary Daly, *Beyond God the Father: Toward a Theology of Women's Liberation* (Boston: Beacon Press, 1973).

[61] See, for instance, Letty M. Russell, *Human Liberation in a Feminist Perspective: A Theology* (Philadelphia: Westminster, 1974); *The Future of Partnership* (Philadelphia: Westminster, 1979); *Becoming Human* (Philadelphia: Westminster, 1982); Rosemary R. Ruether, *The Church against Itself: An Inquiry into the Conditions of Historical Existence for the Eschatological Community* (New York: Herder, 1967); *Liberation Theology: Human Hope Confronts Christian History and American Power* (New York: Paulist, 1972); *To Change the World: Christology and Cultural Criticism* (New York: Crossroad, 1981); *Disputed Questions: On Being a Christian* (Nashville: Abingdon, 1982); Elsa Támez, *Bible of the Oppressed* (Maryknoll, N.Y.: Orbis, 1982).

[62] See Kazo Kitamori, *Theology of the Pain of God* (Richmond: John Knox, 1965); Kosuke Koyama, *Waterbuffalo Theology* (Maryknoll, N.Y.: Orbis, 1974); C. S. Song, *Third-eye Theology: Theology in Formation in Asian Settings* (Maryknoll, N.Y.: Orbis, 1979); *Mission in Reconstruction: An Asian Analysis* (Maryknoll, N.Y.: Orbis, 1977); Christian Conference of Asia, *Minjung Theology: People as the Subjects of History* (Maryknoll, N.Y.: Orbis, 1983).

[63] John S. Mbiti, *New Testament Eschatology in an African Background: A Study of the Encounter between New Testament Theology and African Traditional Concepts* (London: Oxford University Press, 1971); G. H. Muzorewa, *The Origins and Development of African Theology* (Maryknoll, N.Y.: Orbis, 1985).

[64] Allan A. Boesak, *Black and Reformed: Apartheid, Liberation, and the Calvinist Tradition* (Maryknoll, N.Y.: Orbis, 1984).

has been social and economic justice, usually employing Marxian analysis to understand the nature of the current oppression.[65]

While these theologies differ widely among themselves, they have some characteristics in common. Most of them reject classical liberalism as the expression of a particular time, cultural, and social situation, and seek to base their utterances on the Word of God. On this point, particularly among Protestants, the influence of Barth may be seen. There is also a strong eschatological element in several Third World theologies—a point on which they have found the work of Teilhard de Chardin and of Moltmann particularly significant. Thirdly, most of these theologies are radically incarnational. This means not only that they see in Jesus Christ the heart of the Christian faith, but also that from the doctrine of the incarnation they seek to draw their understanding of the nature of God's action in the world, of the unity of human history—no dichotomy between "world history" and "history of salvation"—of Christian participation with non-Christians in the political and other arenas, etc. Fourth, there is a strong ecumenical emphasis. Most Third World theologies either seek to overcome or simply set aside a number of the issues that have traditionally divided Western Christianity. Finally, while each of these theologies works specifically on its concrete concerns—social justice, Christianity and culture, women's rights, etc.—they usually go beyond a mere attempt to relate traditional theology to those concerns. Rather, they seek to reconstruct the entirety of theology in such a way that those concerns are reflected at every point. In this they differ from earlier attempts to "apply" theology to various human problems and situations, and see those problems and situations rather as challenges and calls to new departures in theology.

Often criticized for their "parochialism," these theologies point out that so-called traditional theology is just as parochial in that it

---

[65] While the bibliography on Latin American liberation theology is too great to list here, the following are basic: Gustavo Gutiérrez, *A Theology of Liberation* (Maryknoll, N.Y.: Orbis, 1973); Juan Luis Segundo, *Theology for Artisans of a New Humanity*, 5 vols. (Maryknoll, N.Y.: Orbis, 1973-1974); Juan Luis Segundo, *The Liberation of Theology* (Maryknoll, N.Y.: Orbis, 1976). A basic Protestant introduction is José Míguez Bonino, *Doing Theology in a Revolutionary Situation* (Philadelphia: Fortress, 1975). See also Richard Shaull, *Heralds of a New Reformation: The Poor of South and North America* (Maryknoll, N.Y.: Orbis, 1984), for a valuable reflection on the significance of this theology for the First World.

reflects the conditions and perspectives of the North-Atlantic, and that the reason why it does not appear parochial is the traditional dominance of the North-Atlantic. In any case, as this is being written there is increasing dialogue among these various theologies as well as between each of them and North-Atlantic male theologians.

A Final Overview

The twentieth century poses to the historian of Christian thought problems that are very different from those presented by the previous nineteen centuries. The reason for this is not so much the complexity of the theological scene in this century—which is great—as the fact that this particular century has been the vantage point from which every other period in the history of the Christian church has been viewed by the historian. Therefore, when we come to it, our methodology must be entirely different. It is for this reason that the study of contemporary theology is normally undertaken by a discipline other than historical theology. As a hypothetical exercise, let us attempt to fantasize about the manner in which someone standing in the twenty-first century will view our epoch. That this is a purely hypothetical construction, however, must be emphasized, for it is impossible for us to know what will be the issues raised by the twenty-first century, and those issues will determine the perspective from which we shall be seen. Indeed, as our twentieth-century perspective has affected our understanding of the preceding periods, the same will be true of our successors as they look at us.

The first thing that our hypothetical observer will note in our century will probably be that the power basis from which theology speaks has been greatly reduced. The Russian Revolution and its repercussions in Eastern Europe, the Far East, Latin America, and elsewhere, have meant that now, more than ever since the fourth

472

century, theology must be done from a position of political weakness. The same may be said about the development of the secular liberal state, whose origins we have already seen in the nineteenth century. In France, Poland, and Latin America, it is becoming increasingly evident that some of the most creative Roman Catholic theology is being written precisely as a response to this challenge, and on the basis of an acceptance of the new situation. This is also true of Protestants, as may be seen in theological responses to Nazi Germany, socialist Czechoslovakia, and secular North America. No contemporary theologian can be understood apart from these circumstances.

Second, and partially as a result of the foregoing, the scope of theology has also been narrowed because in most cases its audience has been increasingly limited. Theology is no longer "the queen of all sciences," and theologians will be the first to assert that it should never have been. In any case, theologians speak mostly to the church, or to those at its borders who are contemplating the possibility of belief. But their voice in the forum of humanity is often hardly audible. The impact of this new situation may be seen in the refusal of Karl Barth to do apologetic theology, and also in the largely unsuccessful attempts of many others to do such theology. The one point at which theology is most often heard with interest—or at least with curiosity—in the world at large is in its pronouncements on social justice and such related subjects as violence, revolution, etc. The various attempts to relate the Christian gospel to the philosophies of our time will have to be judged by future generations. They may have served to offer some believers a deeper understanding of their faith. But their ability to communicate with the world at large is still very much in question. This is true of the sundry attempts to theologize from the perspectives of existentialism, neo-Thomism, process philosophy, logical positivism, etc.

On the other hand, however, there has been a great expansion in the scope of theology. This expansion has been geographical, confessional and sociological. The geographical expansion in the scope of theology may in the long run prove to be the most significant development of the twentieth century. Theology is no longer a North Atlantic enterprise. The so-called younger churches of Asia, Africa and Latin America are making significant contributions to it. This widened scope of theology will prove to be important for several reasons. It will obviously help to counteract the narrow provincialism and even nationalism that so often has tempted theologians in the past. It will also pose the question of Christianity and culture in a radical way in which it has not been posed since the early centuries of the church. The entire development of Christian thought has taken place within the context of a Greek philosophical background, and therefore the question that the younger churches will be asking, and that will have enormous consequences for Christian theology, will be whether or not there is a need to become a Greek as one becomes a Christian. Cannot other philosophical and cultural perspectives be regarded as a *praeparatio evangelica*, as the early Greek "Fathers" regarded the culture in which they were born? Compared to this, the questions posed by Western theology in the sixteenth and the nineteenth centuries hardly seem radical. And the impact that this may have on the future shape of theology may well be increased by the fact that, numerically speaking, the center of Christianity has moved away from the North Atlantic.

The scope of theology has also expanded confessionally. In general, it has been possible to narrate the development of Christian theology up to this point along confessional lines. Although there were debates, and sometimes even positive influences, between one confession and another, these were minor compared with the cohesiveness that existed in the theology of each of the major traditions of Christianity. This has ceased to be the case in the twentieth century. Our hypothetical historian a hundred years from now will not find it possible to write a chapter on "Reformed Theology in the Twentieth Century," apart from its counterparts in Roman Catholicism, Lutheranism, etc. The dialogue across denominational lines has become too active and significant for that kind of easy division. Theologians are reading the works of their colleagues in other traditions, not simply as a matter of curiosity or even to refute them, but in order to learn from them and enter into dialogue with them. This was already largely true of Protestantism in the nineteenth century, but the twentieth has made it true also of Roman Catholics and Eastern Orthodox. The Second Vatican Council, in clear contrast to the previous one, reflects the new mood within Roman Catholicism—especially when one remembers that Protestant theologians were able to make an input into some of its decrees before they were brought to the floor. Eastern Orthodoxy has also been forced out of its isolationism of the last few centuries by political events as well as by the fact that vast members of its constituency now live in countries where the majority of Christians is either Roman Catholic or Protestant. It is impossible to foretell the impact that this will have on theology as a whole. It is already evident that biblical and patristic studies have profited from the new situation. It is also clear that theologians are being forced to look anew at the confessional standards that mark the distinctiveness of their own denominations, and ask whether or not these can be reinterpreted in a more ecumenical fashion. This can be seen in the manner in which contemporary Roman Catholic theologians are interpreting the councils of Trent and First Vatican, in the shape that the revival of Luther studies among Protestants has taken, and even in some relatively recent conversations between orthodox and so-called monophysite theologians regarding the decisions of the Council of Chalcedon. When all this comes to fruition, the entire history of the Christian church will have to be rewritten.

Finally, what I have here called "sociological expansion" means two things. It means, first of all, an expansion in the subject matter of theology, so as to include the crucial issue of the attitude of Christians in the struggle for social justice. Some of the chapters preceding this one will have shown that this is not an entirely new subject in theological circles. What is new is the greater political, economic, and sociological realism with which this work is now being done, and that this realism has led theologians to the conclusion that the question is no longer what can Christians by themselves do for the transformation of society, but how ought they to view and discover what God is already doing in society. It is within this context that the current dialogue between Christian theologians and various ideologies is to be viewed. This may also be the place to point out that studies in psychology are having a similar effect on theology, and that the final outcome of this process is not yet known.

Second, the sociological expansion of contemporary theology means that entire groups who were previously excluded from the center of the theological enterprise have now come to their own. This is most evident in the United States, where blacks and women are making unique and significant contributions to theology. It is also true of Protestants in Latin America, who are now being heard by Roman Catholics and others. In a way, the contribution of the younger churches, to which we have already referred above, is part of this movement. Again, it is impossible to foretell what our imaginary future historian will see in this new situation. It would seem significant, however, that precisely at a time when, as we have already pointed out, so much of theological reflection has to be done from a position of political weakness, these persons who have traditionally been among the powerless in society are making their voices heard.

If indeed all this is true, it may well be that our future historian will look back upon our age and be able to affirm that in the midst of the almost incredible complexity of our theological scene, which so perplexed us, a unity was developing across traditional lines of confession, class, nationality, race, and sex, and that this growing unity was a sign that once again, as in every preceding generation, God was using the church to proclaim the initial and central message of the Christian faith—that God was in Christ reconciling the world unto himself.

Appendix

Suggestions for Further Reading

I. Luther (chapter II):
  A. *Ninety-five Theses*
    1. H. T. Lehman, ed., *Luther's Works*, vol. 31 (Philadelphia: Muhlenberg, 1957), pp. 25-33
    2. C. J. Barry, ed., *Readings in Church History,* 3 vols. (Westminster, Maryland: Newman Press, 1965), 2:15-20
    3. B. L. Woolf, ed., *Reformation Writings of Martin Luther,* vol. 1 (London: Lutterworth, 1952), pp. 32-43
    4. J. Dillenberger, ed., *Martin Luther: Selections from His Writings* (Garden City, New York: Doubleday, 1961), pp. 490-500
    5. E. G. Rupp and B. Drewery, eds., *Martin Luther* (New York: St. Martin's Press, 1970), pp. 19-25
  B. *The Freedom of a Christian*
    1. *Luther's Works,* 31:343-77
    2. Woolf, pp. 357-79
    3. Dillenberger, pp. 52-85
    4. Rupp and Drewery, pp. 50-54 (selections)
  C. *Heidelberg Disputation*
    1. LCC, 16:276-307
    2. *Luther's Works,* 31:39-70
    3. Rupp and Drewery, pp. 27-29 (selections)

II. Zwingli (chapter III)
    A. *On the Clarity and Certainty of the Word of God,* LCC, 24:59-95
    B. *On the Lord's Supper,* LCC, 24:185-238

III. Anabaptism and the Radical Reformation (chapter IV)
    A. Conrad Grebel, *Letters to Thomas Müntzer,* LCC, 23:73-85
    B. Menno Simons, *On the Ban,* LCC, 23:263-71

IV. Lutheran Theology (chapters V and IX)
    A. *The Augsburg Confession*
      1. T. G. Tappert, ed., *The Book of Concord* (Philadelphia: Muhlenberg, 1959 and other printings), pp. 24-96
      2. Separate printing of same text (Philadelphia: Fortress, 1980), pp. 5-57
      3. H. T. Kerr, ed., *Readings in Christian Thought* (Nashville: Abingdon, 1966), pp. 158-60 (selection)
    B. *The Formula of Concord,* Part I: Tappert, pp. 464-501
    C. Martin Chemnitz, *The Lord's Supper,* chapter 5 (St. Louis: Concordia, 1979), pp. 57-64

V. Calvin (chapter VI)
    A. *Reply to Sadolet*
      1. Calvin, *Tracts and Treatises on the Reformation of the Church,* 3 vols. (Grand Rapids: Eerdmans, 1958), 1:25-68
      2. LCC, 22:221-56
    B. *Institutes,* 1. 1-7
      1. LCC, 20:35-81
      2. H. Beveridge, trans., 2 vols. (London: James Clarke and Co., 1957 and other printings), 1:37-73
      3. H. T. Kerr, ed., *A Compendium of the Institutes of the Christian Religion* (Philadelphia: Presbyterian Board of Christian Education, 1939), pp. 3-29 (good selection summarizing the argument)

VI. Reformation in Great Britain (chapter VII)
    A. Thomas Cranmer, selection, Kerr, pp. 175-77
    B. Richard Hooker, *Laws of Ecclesiastical Polity*
      1. Barry, 2:79-87 (selection)
      2. Kerr, pp. 178-79 (different selection)

VII. The Catholic Reformation (chapter VIII)
    A. Council of Trent, *Decree on Justification*

1. J. H. Leith, ed., *Creeds of the Churches*, 3d ed. (Atlanta: John Knox, 1982), pp. 408-25

2. C. L. Manschreck, ed., *A History of Christianity: Readings in the History of the Church from the Reformation to the Present* (Englewood Cliffs, N.J.: Prentice-Hall, 1964), pp. 133-35 (selections)

B. Ignatius of Loyola, *Autobiography*, chapter 1

1. J. N. Tylenda, *A Pilgrim's Journey: The Autobiography of Ignatius of Loyola* (Wilmington: Michael Glacier, 1985), pp. 7-19

2. There are many other excellent translations of the *Autobiography*. The most recent among these are:

a. W. J. Young (Chicago: Regnery, 1956)

b. J. F. O'Callaghan (New York: Harper, 1974)

c. P. R. Divarkar (Rome: Gregorian University, 1983)

C. St. Teresa, *The Interior Castle* (New York: Paulist Press, 1979), Prologue and "First Dwelling," pp. 33-48

VIII. Reformed Orthodoxy (chapter X)

A. Synod of Dort, Canons, in H. Petersen, ed., *The Canons of Dort: A Study Guide* (Grand Rapids: Baker Book House, 1968), pp. 93-115

B. *Westminster Confession*, Leith, pp. 193-230

IX. The Pietist Tradition (chapter XI)

A. P. J. Spener, *Pia Desideria* (Philadelphia: Fortress, 1964), pp. 87-122

B. J. Wesley, *The Principles of a Methodist*, in *The Works of John Wesley*, vol. 8 (Grand Rapids: Zondervan, reprint of 1872 edition), pp. 359-74

X. New Movements in Philosophy (chapter XII)

A. Descartes, *Arguments Demonstrating the Existence of God*, in E. S. Haldane and G. R. T. Ross, eds., *The Philosophical Works of Descartes*, vol. 2 (New York: Dover Publications, 1955), pp. 52-59

B. Kant, *Religion Within the Limits of Reason Alone*, selections in Kerr, pp. 213-16

XI. Protestant Theology in the Nineteenth Century (chapter XIII)

A. Schleiermacher, *The Christian Faith*, chapter 1, sections I and III

     1. H. R. Mackintosh and J. S. Stewart, trans. (Edinburgh: T. & T. Clark, several printings since 1928), pp. 5-31, 52-76

     2. Kerr, *Readings,* pp. 221-22 (selection)

  B. Hegel, *Lectures on the Philosophy of Religion,* ed. by P. C. Hodgson (Berkeley: University of California Press, 1984), selection on pp. 83-109

  C. Kierkegaard, *Concluding Unscientific Postscript,* Book 2, Part I, Chapter II, Section 4 (Princeton: Princeton University Press, 1941), pp. 97-113

  D. Ritschl, *The Christian Doctrine of Justification and Reconciliation,* selection in Kerr, *Readings,* pp. 232-34

  E. Schweitzer, *The Quest of the Historical Jesus,* selection in Kerr, *Readings,* pp. 288-91

  F. Rauschenbush, selections in Kerr, *Readings,* pp. 266-70

  G. Newman, *An Essay on the Development of Christian Doctrine,* selections in Kerr, pp. 241-44

XII. Roman Catholic Theology (chapter XIV)

  A. *Syllabus or Errors*

     1. Barry, 3:70-74

     2. Manschreck, pp. 372-74

  B. Leo XIII, *Rerum Novarum*

     1. E. Gilson, ed., *The Church Speaks to the Modern World: The Social Teachings of Leo XIII* (Garden City, N.Y.: Doubleday, 1954), pp. 205-40

     2. G. C. Treacy, ed., *Five Great Encyclicals* (New York: Paulist Press, 1939), pp. 1-30

     3. Kerr, pp. 246-49 (selection)

XIII. Eastern Theology (chapter XV): V. Lossky, *In the Image and Likeness of God* (New York: St. Vladimir's Seminary Press, 1974), chapter 8: "Tradition and traditions," pp. 141-68

XIV. Theology in the Twentieth Century (chapter XVI)

  A. Barth, *Church Dogmatics,* selections in Kerr, *Readings,* pp. 293-310

  B. Bultmann, "New Testament and Mythology," selections in Kerr, *Readings,* pp. 330-37

  C. Bonhoeffer, selections in Kerr, *Readings,* pp. 357-66

  D. Tillich, *Systematic Theology,* selections in Kerr, *Readings,* 338-56

E. K. Rahner, *Foundations of Christian Faith* (New York: Seabury, 1978), selection on pp. 39-43

F. Second Vatican Council, *Pastoral Constitution on the Church and the Modern World* (also known as *Gaudium et spes*), 1-32, 63-93

    1. W. M. Abbott, ed., *The Documents of Vatican II* (New York: Herder, 1966), pp. 199-231, 271-308

    2. A. P. Flannery, ed., *Documents of Vatican II* (Grand Rapids: Eerdmans, 1975), pp. 903-32, 968-1001

    3. G. Baum and D. Campion, eds., *Pastoral Constitution on the Church and the Modern World* (New York: Paulist Press, 1967), pp. 81-125, 183-232

G. E. Cardenal, *The Gospel in Solentiname*, vol. 2 (Maryknoll, N.Y.: Orbis, 1978), pp. 147-57

Index of Subjects and Authors

Principal references are in bold type; references to footnotes are in italics; all other references are in roman type.